RED ROCK
CANYON
A CLIMBING GUIDE

RED ROCK CANYON
A CLIMBING GUIDE

ROXANNA BROCK & JARED McMILLEN

THE MOUNTAINEERS BOOKS

THE MOUNTAINEERS BOOKS
*is the nonprofit publishing arm of The Mountaineers Club,
an organization founded in 1906 and dedicated to the exploration,
preservation, and enjoyment of outdoor and wilderness areas.*

1001 SW Klickitat Way, Suite 201, Seattle, WA 98134

First edition: first printing 2005, second printing 2010

Distributed in the United Kingdom by Cordee, www.cordee.co.uk

Manufactured in the United States of America

Acquiring Editor: Christine Hosler
Project Editor: Mary Metz
Copy Editor: Julie Van Pelt
Cover and Book Design: The Mountaineers Books
Layout Artist: Marge Mueller, Gray Mouse Graphics
Cartographers: Ben Pease and Hassan E. Mahmoud
Route Overlays: Ani Rucki
All photos by Jared McMillen unless otherwise noted.

Cover photograph: *Climber on* Straight Shooter *(5.9) overlooking Pine Creek Canyon.* Photo by Jared McMillen
Frontispiece: *Joe Herbst summiting on his turf in Red Rock.* Photo by Larry Hamilton

Library of Congress Cataloging-in-Publication Data
Brock, Roxanna, 1966-
    Red Rock Canyon : a climbing guide / Roxanna Brock, Jared McMillen.—1st ed.
        p. cm.
    Includes bibliographical references and index.
    ISBN 0-89886-486-0
    1. Rock climbing—Nevada—Red Rock Canyon National Conservation Area—Guidebooks. 2. Red Rock Canyon National Conservation Area (Nev.)—Guidebooks. I. McMillen, Jared, 1975– II. Title.
    GV199.42.N32R435 2005
    796.52'23'0979313—dc22
                                        2004031025

ISBN (paperback): 978-0-89886-486-1
ISBN (ebook): 978-1-59485-119-3

CONTENTS

ACKNOWLEDGEMENTS

WE OWE SPECIAL THANKS to all the locals and nonlocals who helped us to produce the best guidebook we could. We could not have done it without their help and contributions. Thank you.

Nick Nordblom
Wendell Broussard
Larry DeAngelo
Jay Smith
Dan McQuade
Danny Meyers
Sal Mamusia
Mark Limage
Larry Hamilton
Pier and Randy Marsh
Bob Conz
Richard Harrison
Michelle Locatelli
Chris Burton
Dan Kruleski
John Long
Jed Botsford
Patrick Putnam
Dave Wonderly
Kevin Daniels
Bryan "Lil' B" O'Keefe
Jason Sellman
Gary Fike
John Heimen
Lynn Hill
Joanne Urioste
Mike Ward
Russ and Leah Ricketts
Paul Crawford
Tom Beck
Ed Boddy
Paul and Steven Van Betten
Karrie and Jamie Anderson
George Urioste
Mike Clifford
Tom Cecil
Mike Moore

Thanks also to the authors of the following guidebooks, which we used as references: *Red Rock Odyssey, Classic Traditional Climbs,* by Larry DeAngelo and Bill Thiry; *Rock Climbing Red Rocks* by Todd Swain; and *The Red Rocks of Southern Nevada* and *Red Rock Canyon, the Red Rock Supplement,* by Joanne Urioste.

And thanks especially to Nate and Harvest (for putting up with our endless work and for having to stay inside way too much).

We apologize if we have forgotten anyone.

A NOTE ABOUT SAFETY

Safety is an important concern in all outdoor activities. No guidebook can alert you to every hazard or anticipate the limitations of every reader. Therefore, the descriptions of roads, trails, routes, and natural features in this book are not representations that a particular place or excursion will be safe for your party. When you follow any of the routes described in this book, you assume responsibility for your own safety. Under normal conditions, such excursions require the usual attention to traffic, road and trail conditions, weather, terrain, the capabilities of your party, and other factors. Keeping informed on current conditions and exercising common sense are the keys to a safe, enjoyable outing.

The Mountaineers Books

Red Rock Canyon lovely signage

INTRODUCTION

LOCATED JUST WEST OF LAS VEGAS in the Mojave Desert, Red Rock Canyon National Conservation Area (RRCNCA) is one of the largest and most popular rock-climbing areas in the United States. In the late 1960s the U.S. Bureau of Land Management (BLM) designated 10,000 acres as Red Rock Canyon Recreation Lands. Then in 1990, Congress expanded protection to 83,100 acres, creating the conservation area. Today the area has grown to 197,000 acres.

Red Rock Canyon attracts all sorts of onlookers, and every year its popularity grows. The Calico Hills and surrounding sandstone canyons are home to breathtaking natural land formations in a fragile desert environment. The beauty of this area is enjoyed by more than a million visitors each year, and rock climbers represent 7 to 9 percent of that number—nearly 100,000 patrons.

Since the early 1970s, rock climbing has been a popular activity in Red Rock. Sport climbing, traditional climbing, and bouldering are in large supply, with more than 1600 routes to choose from. Six-pitch sport routes are in close proximity to up to twenty-pitch traditional climbs, and boulder problems dot the area. The highest concentration of sport climbing is in the Calico Hills area: Calico Basin, the First and Second Pullouts (Calico I and II), and Sandstone Quarry. The majority of traditional climbing is in the canyons located west and south of the Calico Hills. Boulders are located throughout Red Rock, but the highest concentration of developed problems is in Calico Basin.

Our aim is to provide an affordable, comprehensive guide to this popular destination, correctly documenting the character of the routes, their first ascensionists, and the environment in a way that will help you enjoy the routes as much as those who have gone before you and that will promote responsible use of the area.

We ask that you leave Red Rock Canyon in the same or better condition as you found it. It is a delicate setting that sees immense human contact. Defacing, damaging, removing, or digging for any reason is prohibited by law. Also keep a lookout for bighorn sheep, coyotes, ground squirrels, wild burros, and desert tortoises. All are a pleasure to see, but please do not disturb the wildlife. The wild horse and burros are protected under the Wild Horse and Burro Act. Feeding or harassing them is illegal.

RED ROCK CANYON ROCK CHARACTER

The land that comprises the RRCNCA was at the bottom of a deep ocean for much of the past 600 million years. A rich array of marine life populated the sea and left shell and skeleton deposits more than 9000 feet thick, which were compressed into limestone.

Approximately 225 million years ago the seabed began to rise due to movements in the earth's crust. The change in sea level trapped large bodies of water. As they evaporated they left behind layers of sediment. Exposure to the atmosphere as the water receded caused minerals to oxidize, resulting in the red-and-orange-colored rock seen today.

About 180 million years ago the area was an arid desert. Giant sand dunes, measuring as much as a half mile deep, stretched from the Las Vegas area into Colorado. As wind shifted the dunes, it left curving, angled lines in the sand known as "crossbeds." The shifting sands were buried by other sediments and were eventually cemented into sandstone by iron oxide and calcium carbonate. Known as Aztec Sandstone, it forms the cliffs of the Red Rock Canyon escarpment. In some areas the iron in the rock has been altered and concentrated, giving the rock its vibrant red color.

The most significant geologic trait of the area is the Keystone Thrust Fault. Part of a large system of thrust faults extending north into Canada, the Keystone Thrust Fault began to develop around 65 million years ago. A thrust fault is a break in the earth's crust resulting from compression forces that drive one crustal plate over the top of another. The result is that the oldest rocks on the bottom of the upper plate rest directly on top of the youngest rocks of the lower plate. In the RRCNCA, the gray limestone of the ancient ocean has been thrust over the tan and red sandstone in one of the most dramatic and easily identified thrust faults to be found. The Keystone Thrust Fault extends from the Cottonwood Fault along State Route 160 north for 13 miles along the crest of the Red Rock escarpment. It then curves east along the base of La Madre Mountain before it is obscured by very complex faulting north of the Calico Hills. (Information on the area's formation can be found in *Final Environmental Assessment, Oil and Gas Leasing in the Red Rock Canyon Recreation Lands*, U.S. Department of the Interior, Bureau of Land Management, 1980.)

Rock Character

When climbing on the Aztec Sandstone of the RRCNCA, it is important to consider a few things. Due to its unique physical qualities, including high porosity, sandstone is prone to deterioration when moist. After rainfall, it is recommended to wait 24 hours before attempting to climb the rock. In following this recommendation you help maintain the integrity of established routes and decrease the possibility of accidents due to the fracturing of weak or loose rock. There are many limestone crags near Red Rock Canyon to climb when the sandstone is wet. The Gun Club and Lone Mountain are just a few that are easily accessed. (For more information on limestone climbing, check out *Las Vegas Limestone* by Roxanna Brock.)

In general, the sandstone in Red Rock Canyon is fragile. Be aware when climbing. If you see fractures around a hold, keep weight on other extremities to avoid a fall. For this reason, using sparse gear placements and soloing are not recommended.

RED ROCK CLIMBING HISTORY

Climbing in Red Rock all started with **Joe Herbst** back in the early 1970s. Best known for his pioneering routes on the Black Velvet, Rainbow, and Aeolian Walls, Joe also climbed an endless string of shorter routes. Many of his old notes have been lost, so the full extent of his exploration may never be recorded.

Herbst's significance was not merely in his record of first ascents. His approach to climbing stressed the clean, bold ascent, with a premium placed on absorbing the adventurous experience. Many of Herbst's big routes were done with his frequent partners Tom Kaufman and Larry Hamilton, but he also did many climbs with younger climbers who would soon make their own marks in the Red Rock arena. His bold routes and exemplary style have made Herbst a Red Rock icon, and the standard he set was proudly maintained by the next generation of climbers in the years to come. Nearly all his routes feel more difficult than their "old school" rating. Joe Herbst quit climbing after his wife, Betsy, passed away.

John Williamson was one of the few climbers other than Joe Herbst to be pursuing new Red Rock routes in the early 1970s. His first ascent of the east face of Mount Wilson in 1970 was the biggest route of its day. Some of his crag routes, such as *The Fox* and the *Great Red Book,* are still considered classics. Williamson carried the Leave No Trace ethic to such an extreme that it is only due to a chance meeting with Joanne Urioste during a visit in the middle 1970s that his routes have even been recorded

The late **Randal Grandstaff** was a Nevada native and owner of the Sky's the Limit guide service. He began climbing as a young teenager in the early 1970s under the wing of Joe Herbst. Although Grandstaff put up some big routes such as *Emerald City* and *Spectrum*, he is probably best known as Red Rock's biggest promoter. Even before starting his guide service, Grandstaff's old house was the nerve center of Las Vegas climbing. Spurred by Grandstaff's enthusiasm and love for Red Rock, countless visiting climbers stayed in his house as they hatched plans for big routes on the sandstone walls. Grandstaff died in a rappeling accident in 2002.

Geoff Conley was climbing out in Joshua Tree in the early 1970s when he struck up a conversation with a retired Marine. "Do you guys ever do any climbing on those cliffs out near Las Vegas?" asked the Marine. Conley went to check the area out. In the next few years, he and his partners put up a number of big and serious routes, culminating in the famous *Resolution Arête* on Mount Wilson. Conley was probably the first outsider (who was not a friend of Joe Herbst) to make a significant mark in Red Rock.

George and Joanne Urioste put up many of the ultraclassic routes in Red Rock from the mid-1970s to the 1980s. They worked hard to create spectacular lines. Their willingness to employ fixed ropes and a lot of bolts sometimes put them at odds with other climbers of the era, but their efforts have stood the test of time. Routes such as *Crimson Chrysalis*, *Levitation 29*, and *Prince of Darkness* are now some of the area's most popular climbs. In addition to being one of the few women putting up routes then, Joanne wrote the first Red Rock guidebook, *The Red Book*, which is still widely used.

Just as Joe Herbst personified Red Rock climbing in the 1970s, **Richard Harrison** personified it in the 1980s. Harrison was the driving force behind an extensive list of first ascents, many featuring bold leads done in the very purest of styles. Harrison's influence goes beyond his impressive resume of climbs. In his company, the cream of the new generation of Red Rock climbers blossomed and carried forward his standards of difficulty and boldness. Climbers such as Paul Van Betten, Sal Mamusia, and Nick Nordblom all absorbed the Richard Harrison philosophy.

A partner of Harrison's, **Paul Van Betten** learned from the best and became one of the best in the early 1980s and '90s. Van Betten's name is smeared on multitudes of first ascents in Red Rock. His enthusiasm and drive had him and his partners putting up the most difficult routes of their time. His favorite route is the demanding *Desert Gold*, a finger and hand crack to a huge roof. Van Betten's frequent partner, Nick Nordblom, described him as "the most talented climber I have ever known."

Sal Mamusia was another of the hard-core crew. John Long and Richard Harrison were his mentors "thrashing us on long routes." Local Wendell Broussard remembers Mamusia climbing 5.11 in his first week on the rock. His natural talent was beyond good. One of his most proud sends is the *Hidden Wall*, above Icebox Canyon. To anyone's knowledge it has been repeated only once, and Mamusia was in on that ascent as well.

Also part of the Richard Harrison gang was **Nick Nordblom**, who put up numerous routes including the Rainbow Wall's *Desert Solitaire* (V, 5.10, A3+) rope solo. He talks of this route's ascent as an attempt to follow in the footsteps of "the masters," Joe Herbst and Larry Hamilton. He spent an entire winter contemplating the ascent, while riding on the chairlifts of Mount Charleston. Upon completion of this route he rightly felt he was "in their shoes." Nordblom describes Van Betten, Mamusia, and himself as "the team." His partners remember his stoic solidity while drilling bolts off tenuous, featureless stances, and Nordblom is notorious for climbing hard "off the couch."

Jay Smith spent time in Red Rock during the 1980s putting up difficult climbs. Like his hard-core buddies, Paul Van Betten, Sal Mamusia, and Nick Nordblom, Smith was committed to a minimum-bolt ethic. He would visit Red Rock for two to three weeks at a time, climbing every day. His route *Rock Warrior* is one of the prizes on the Black Velvet Wall. He loved the canyons in Red Rock and had a great reason for climbing there: "ninety-five FAs, good friends, and a brave new world." Nick Nordblom recalled, "Nobody had more motivation than Jay. He was the tech master, showing us how to use new gear and teaching us new techniques in climbing."

Coming to Red Rock with Jay Smith during his second year out of high school, Paul Crawford remembered Red Rock having a lot of charm. "The placements were artsy-craftsy, requiring tricky RPs, knotted slings." With no trails through the canyons and few climbers, he remembered a phrase he often said: "when you're lost in Red Rock nobody hears you cry." Crawford recalled that the way they determined if a route had been climbed was whether or not there was a fire ring at the base. They never repeated routes because there were too many first ascents to do.

Wendell Broussard not only was in on the first ascents of too many routes to count in Red Rock, he also was a father figure to the cranking local "kids" (Mamusia and Van Betten). Said Mamusia, "I would have never climbed if it weren't for Wendell." Broussard has been pulling 5.11s for as long as anyone can remember. If you want to know about a good route, or get route beta, Broussard is your walking guidebook. His partners were Richard Harrison, Nick Nordblom, Sal Mamusia, and Paul Van Betten. Said Nordblom of Broussard, "Nobody has more climbing days in Red Rock than The Dean."

Other notable first ascensionists in Red Rock in-

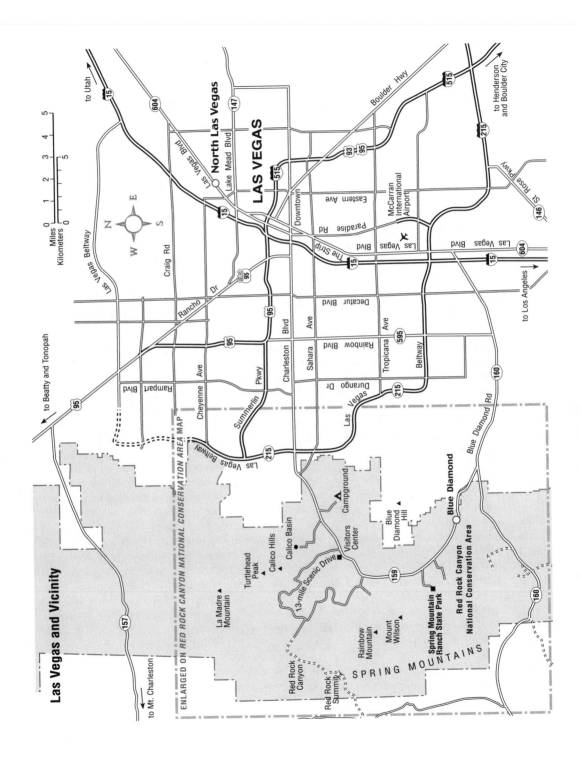

Las Vegas and Vicinity

ENLARGED ON RED ROCK CANYON NATIONAL CONSERVATION AREA MAP

LAS VEGAS

North Las Vegas

Downtown

The Strip

McCarran International Airport

Blue Diamond

SPRING MOUNTAINS

Red Rock Canyon National Conservation Area

Spring Mountain Ranch State Park

Visitors Center

Campground

Calico Basin

13-mile Scenic Drive

Red Rock Canyon

Red Rock Summit

La Madre Mountain ▲

Turtlehead Peak ▲

Calico Hills ▲

Rainbow Mountain ▲

Mount Wilson ▲

Blue Diamond Hill ▲

to Utah

to Beatty and Tonopah

to Mt. Charleston

to Charleston

to Henderson and Boulder City

to Los Angeles

Las Vegas Beltway

Craig Rd

Rancho Dr

Cheyenne Ave

Rampart Blvd

Summerlin Pkwy

Charleston Blvd

Sahara Ave

Rainbow Blvd

Decatur Blvd

Durango Dr

Las Vegas Blvd

Tropicana Ave

Beltway

Las Vegas Blvd

Lake Mead Blvd

Boulder Hwy

Eastern Ave

Paradise Rd

St Rose Pkwy

Blue Diamond Rd

Miles

Kilometers

N E S W

15 604 147 515 93 95 215 146 604 160 159 157 95 BUS 95 595 215

clude "Iron Bob" Finlay, Danny Meyers, Dan McQuade, Shelby Shelton, Bob Conz, Mike Tupper, Greg Mayer, and Mike Ward.

For a more detailed look at early Red Rock climbing history, we strongly recommend *Red Rock Odyssey* by Larry DeAngelo and Bill Thiry. The many photographs and anecdotes convey a good feeling for the spirit of the times.

GETTING THERE

Las Vegas is a tourist town and most of its revenues are derived from that industry. Use it to your advantage and get one of the inexpensive travel packages that are continuously offered by major airlines and casino hotels.

Due to massive city growth, roadways are constantly changing. We apologize in advance for difficulties in reading the enclosed maps due to road changes.

The airport is on the southeast side of town, just off the 215 Beltway (Clark County 215), near the infamous Las Vegas Strip (Las Vegas Boulevard). Red Rock is only 17 miles to the west. To get there from the airport, take the 215 Beltway west. After passing Sahara Avenue take the next exit onto Charleston Boulevard. Turn left (or west) onto Charleston Boulevard, which turns into Nevada State Route 159 and takes you to Red Rock Canyon.

Charleston Boulevard is a major road in Vegas, extending east to west and crossing Interstate 15 and the Strip. If traveling from another part of the city, get on Charleston Boulevard, heading west. Follow above directions from passing over the 215 Beltway at the far western end of Charleston Boulevard.

The Red Rock Canyon Campground is 3.4 miles west of the 215 Beltway, on the left (south) side of the road. The turnoff for Calico Basin is 3.9 miles from the Beltway on the right (north) side of the road, off of Calico Basin Road. The conservation area's 13-mile Scenic Drive is 5.9 miles west of the Beltway on the right (north) side of the road.

Driving times from selected areas:

Salt Lake City, UT .... 6 hours
St. George, UT .... 2 hours
Moab, UT .... 8 hours
Flagstaff, AZ .... 4 hours
Phoenix, AZ .... 6 hours
Bishop, CA .... 4.5 hours
Joshua Tree, CA .... 3 hours
The Valley (Yosemite), CA .... 8 hours
Los Angeles, CA .... 4 hours
San Francisco, CA .... 10 hours
Jackson, WY .... 12 hours
The Gunks, NY .... 36 hours
Ceuse, France .... 36 hours (by plane)

WEATHER

Red Rock averages 300 days of sunshine per year, 4.13 inches of rain, 29 percent humidity, and 66.3 degrees Fahrenheit.

Seasonal Highs and Lows (degrees F)

	Highs	Lows
JANUARY	56	32
FEBRUARY	62	37
MARCH	68	42
APRIL	78	50
MAY	88	59
JUNE	98	68
JULY	104	75
AUGUST	102	73
SEPTEMBER	94	65
OCTOBER	81	53
NOVEMBER	66	40
DECEMBER	57	33

Note: Although the weather seems dreamy, keep in mind that Red Rock Canyon is in a mountainous environment. High winds and sudden showers can come on quickly and alter climbing conditions. Be prepared with windbreakers, noncotton clothing, and plenty of food and water, particularly on longer routes.

HOURS, FEES, AND REGULATIONS

The Red Rock Canyon National Conservation Area is managed by the BLM's Las Vegas Field Office. The 13-mile Scenic Drive is open for day use except with special permits. Hours of operation vary, depending on the season of the year. The road is usually open between 6:00 A.M. and dusk. If you leave your vehicle parked along the Scenic Drive outside of the open hours, your vehicle will be cited and possibly towed at your expense. For late access to the Scenic Drive and the

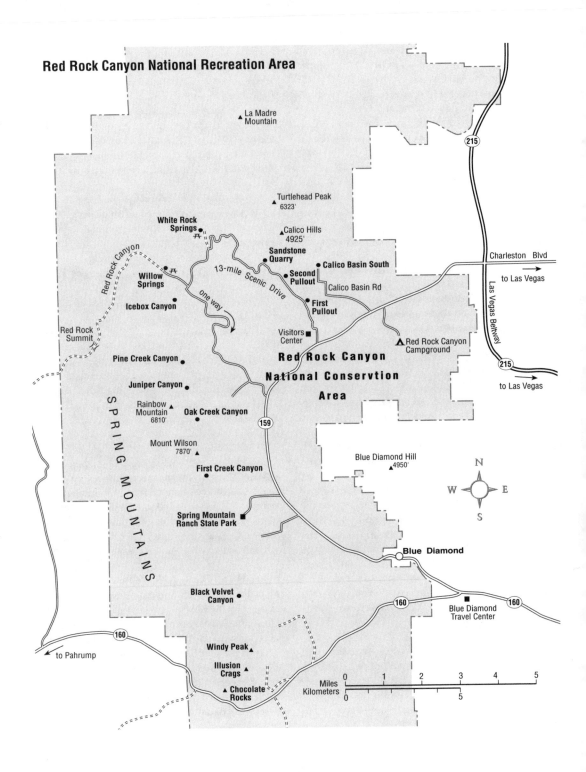

Red Rock Canyon National Recreation Area

La Madre Mountain

Turtlehead Peak
6323'

White Rock Springs

Calico Hills
4925'

Sandstone Quarry

Calico Basin South

Second Pullout

Calico Basin Rd

Willow Springs

13-mile Scenic Drive

one way

Red Rock Canyon

Icebox Canyon

First Pullout

Red Rock Summit

Visitors Center

Red Rock Canyon Campground

Pine Creek Canyon

Red Rock Canyon National Conservtion Area

Juniper Canyon

Rainbow Mountain
6810'

Oak Creek Canyon

Mount Wilson
7870'

First Creek Canyon

S P R I N G   M O U N T A I N S

159

Blue Diamond Hill
4950'

Charleston Blvd
to Las Vegas

Las Vegas Beltway

215

215

to Las Vegas

N
W   E
S

Spring Mountain Ranch State Park

Blue Diamond

Black Velvet Canyon

160

Blue Diamond Travel Center

160

to Pahrump

160

Windy Peak

Illusion Crags

Chocolate Rocks

Miles
Kilometers

0   1   2   3   4   5

0   5

backcountry you must get a permit. See Extended Access Permits, below.

The Scenic Drive is open:
Winter (November 1–February 28/29)
6:00 A.M.–5:00 P.M.
Spring (March 1–March 31)
6:00 A.M.–7:00 P.M.
Summer (April 1–September 30)
6:00 A.M.–8:00 P.M.
Fall (October 1–October 31)
6:00 A.M.–7:00 P.M.

The Visitors Center is open:
Winter (November 1–March 31)
8 A.M.–4:30 P.M.
Summer (April 1–October 31)
8 A.M.–5:30 P.M.

Entrance fees as of this book's printing are $5 per vehicle, $3 for motorcycles, $20 for a yearly pass, and $65 for a Golden Eagle Pass (good for all national parks).

If you have questions about usage hours or fees, ask at the kiosk entrance booth or call the Red Rock Canyon Visitors Center (see Appendix E, Contact Information).

Extended Access Permits
Depending on the climbing route, passes are granted for access to the Scenic Drive after it has closed (see Appendix E, Contact Information for registration). For some routes you can get a 3-hour late pass (Late Access Permit). Overnight passes can be given for grade V routes (Overnight Bivy Permit). This pass allows you overnight parking along the Scenic Drive for a given number of days. If you leave your vehicle parked along the road without a permit, your vehicle will be cited and possibly towed.

Late Access Permit: The late access permit allows you to exit the 13-mile Scenic Drive after it is closed. These permits are for long, multipitch routes only. None are issued for sport climbing or single-pitch routes.

Overnight Bivy Permit: You can get this permit for routes on Mount Wilson, Levitation Wall, Rainbow Wall, Bridge Mountain, Hidden Wall, and the Buffalo Wall. The bivy permit does not allow you to camp in the canyons, but it does allow you to sleep on the wall. The following permits are for on-route and summit bivies only:

Mount Wilson: All routes, 1-night permit
Levitation Wall: All routes, 1-night permit
Rainbow Wall: All routes, 1- or 2-night permit
Buffalo Wall: All routes, 1-, 2-, or 3-night permit
Bridge Mountain: All routes, 1-night permit
Hidden Wall: All routes, 1-night permit

Remember, you cannot camp at the base of any of the routes. And note that if you get an extended access permit you may delay a rescue, should you have an emergency situation.

Parking
Heavy traffic areas already show the challenges of wear and abuse. Please keep this in mind when you climb in the RRCNCA or in other wilderness areas. Parking areas, especially at the First and Second Pullouts (Calico I and II), can become congested. Consider carpooling at the parking lot by the entrance booth. If a parking area for your climb is full, park in a different lot and walk back using the trails that parallel the road, or choose another climb. If you park on the side of the 13-mile Scenic Drive you run the risk of receiving a parking ticket, and you jeopardize climber access in Red Rock Canyon.

Handicap Access
Handicap access is located at the Red Springs Area in Calico Basin, the First Pullout (Calico I), Sandstone Quarry (Third Pullout), and Willow Springs.

Camping
Overnight camping is only allowed in the Red Rock Canyon Campground or on bivies on specified routes (above 5000 feet elevation). Camping along the main escarpment, in any canyons, or along the Scenic Drive is prohibited. The Red Rock Canyon Campground is 2 miles east of the Scenic Drive entrance on State Route 159, on the south side of the road, just off Moenkopi Road. The campground is open Labor Day through Memorial Day. Quiet hours are from 10:00 P.M. to 6:00 A.M., and access may be closed after 10:00 P.M. to those not previously registered. To reserve a group campsite call the Visitors Center. Individual campsites are assigned on a first come, first served basis.

Guiding

Several guide services have permits to guide in the RRCNCA. See Guide Services in Appendix D, Supplies, Lodging, Food, and Resources, or ask the local rock-climbing shops or the Visitors Center. If you use a guide who does not have a permit, you and your guide run the risk of a sizable ticket. In addition, you will not be covered under RRCNCA insurance if there is an accident.

SAFETY

Emergency phones are located at the Sandstone Quarry, White Rock Springs, Icebox Canyon, and Pine Creek Canyon pullouts along the 13-mile Scenic Drive Road. Emergency phone numbers are in Appendix E, Contact Information.

Water. Red Rock Canyon is located in the Mojave Desert, and even if it is not scorching hot, the air is still very dry. You should always bring surplus water to stay hydrated while climbing or hiking. It is suggested you drink four liters of water per day in the summer. Do not drink untreated water as it may be contaminated.

Weather. Winter in the desert can be very cold and snow is not uncommon. In the summer months temperatures can top 110 degrees Fahrenheit. Summer storms can cause very cold conditions on long backcountry routes, and canyons can flash flood without warning.

Avoid drainages after thunderstorms or severe weather because of flash floods. Stay away from high points during thunderstorms; lightning can kill. Check the weather before embarking on your adventure.

Insects/reptiles. There are poisonous species in Red Rock Canyon. Rattlesnakes, black widow spiders, bees, wasps, and velvet ants are all creatures to be aware of and to avoid.

Rock quality. Sandstone is naturally porous and friable rock. The BLM asks that routes be given 24 hours to properly dry. Beware of loose holds.

Cliffs. When hiking, stay on established trails and watch your footing at all times. Steep slopes and cliff edges are dangerous.

Rockfall. Do not roll or throw rocks and other items from high places; other visitors may be below you.

Plan. To reach many of the routes in Red Rock Canyon requires significant walking, hiking, and scrambling. Keep this in mind when planning your climbs, not only as a time constraint but also in terms of food and water.

If you have never climbed at Red Rock Canyon and are unfamiliar with route locations, use climbing guidebooks, which provide extensive route information and are available at the Visitors Center and in Vegas climbing shops. Hired guides are also available.

Theft. Lock your vehicle while climbing and do not leave tempting or valuable items in plain sight. An organized group of thieves is aware that climbers leave their wallets hidden in cars and has stolen cash and credit card numbers from unknowing victims.

Wildlife may appear to be tame, but may attack if threatened. Stay a safe distance away while observing animals and watch children closely; they often do not recognize potential dangers.

The **burros** at Red Rock are not domesticated animals and can be dangerous. It is illegal to feed or pet them. Feeding burros encourages them to congregate on roadways where many have been killed and have killed the drivers who hit them. To observe these animals safely, pick a safe place to stop, pull completely off the roadway, and watch from a distance. Staying in your car is the safest way to photograph and observe the burros.

ACCESS AND CONDUCT

Red Rock Canyon is an extremely popular area. Please respect the natural and cultural resources of this beautiful land, and leave all natural features just as you found them.

Climbing is prohibited on or within 50 feet of Native American archaeological sites including rock faces on which rock art (etched petroglyphs or painted pictographs) is present.

Chipping, scarring, or defacing of the rock in any way is illegal on RRCNCA land.

Do not change, remove, or add bolts to an established route without obtaining BLM permission. As of November 6, 2002, the Wilderness Study Areas of Red Rock Canyon were designated as wilderness areas. At that time, Kraft Mountain and Gateway Canyon were added to existing wilderness areas. No bolting is allowed in wilderness areas. Contact the BLM for permission to add or replace existing bolts.

Respect other climbing parties! Some of the more popular long routes get crowded. If possible, allow faster parties to climb through on multipitch climbs.

Minimize the wear on anchors by top-roping using your own gear. Do not set up a top rope directly through the anchors.

Use drab or camouflaged webbing for rappels and anchors.

Do not change clothes or brush your teeth in parking areas.

Do not litter; pack out whatever you pack in. Practice Leave No Trace and do not leave your toilet paper or cigarette butts behind.

Do not build any ground fires. Cook only with a barbecue grill or camp stove.

Stay on established and maintained trails.

Do not trample vegetation or cut trees for any reason.

Pets must be on a leash. And pick up your pet dookey (particularly near the parking areas).

Respect the area speed limits: the speed limit on State Route 159 is 60 miles per hour; in Calico Basin, 25 miles per hour; and on the 13-mile Scenic Drive, 35 miles per hour. The Scenic Drive is a two-lane, one-way road. Allow faster vehicles to pass on the left.

Respect the rights of other visitors to enjoy Red Rock Canyon.

Leave No Trace Principles

"Take only pictures, leave only footprints." Visit the Leave No Trace website at *www.LNT.org* for LNT's expanded list.

1. Plan ahead and prepare.
2. Travel and camp on durable surfaces.
3. Dispose of waste properly.
4. Leave what you find.
5. Minimize campfire impacts.
6. Respect wildlife.
7. Be considerate of other visitors.

FIRST ASCENT RECOMMENDATIONS

The sandstone of the RRCNCA is extremely soft and brittle rock. It is of utmost importance that correct bolting procedures are followed for your safety and for the safety of those who climb your routes.

Bolting along the main escarpment is illegal. Bolting is legal along the Calico Hills (Calico Basin and

A wild burro amongst Joshua Trees in Red Rock Canyon

the First and Second Pullouts). Consult the BLM before establishing a new route.

Bolting suggestions:

▲ No less than 3/8-inch diameter, 3.5-inch length bolts (Rawl five-piece or glue-in bolts are highly recommended).

▲ For anchors use 1/2-inch diameter, 4-inch length Rawl five-piece or glue-in bolts.

▲ Chain anchors are recommended (five or more links) because cold-shuts spin too easily in the soft sandstone.

▲ When you create an anchor be sure you do not make or create the American death triangle (see *Mountaineering: The Freedom of the Hills*, The Mountaineers Books).

▲ When putting hangers on bolts be sure the washer is between the head of the bolt and the hanger (not against the rock, behind the hanger).

▲ Paint bolt hangers a color similar to the rock you are placing them on. Be sure to do so prior to placing them on the rock.

RATINGS

Routes in the RRCNCA are rated using the Yosemite Decimal System (YDS). All class 5 routes (those involving the use of protection) range in difficulty from 5.0 (easiest) to 5.15 (most difficult). These ratings are based on the skills, abilities, and opinions of the climbers who ascended them. If you are not familiar with this rating system or are unsure of what level you and your abilities fit into, be sure to choose your routes with care. Red Rock Canyon offers more than 1500 established sport and traditional climbs.

Class Designations

Class 1: Extremely easy, such as walking along a horizontal trail.

Class 2: Off-trail hiking or boulder hopping, requiring occasional use of hands for balance. Little exposure or danger.

Class 3: Climbing that requires the constant use of hands. Steep scrambling with exposure. Ropes are needed for inexperienced people. An unroped fall on third-class terrain could be fatal.

Class 4: Steeper scrambling on smaller holds with considerable exposure. Ropes are needed for most people; an experienced climber might climb without intermediate protection, but set a belay anchor to bring other climbers up.

Class 5: Technical rock climbing where the leader places intermediate protection, and in case of a fall, the intermediate protection with the use of a rope would keep the leader from hitting the ground. Further divided by decimals (YDS), currently the grades of difficulty range from 5.0 to 5.15, where the "5" represents the class. Above 5.9 the grades are subdivided again into a, b, c, and d designations. Also referred to as "free" climbing because equipment is not used for upward progress.

Class 6: Artificial or "aid" climbing, where the climber is unable to ascend the rock without using equipment for upward advancement.

Free-Climb Ratings

The YDS was invented by Don Wilson, Royal Robbins, and Chuck Wilts in 1956 and was used to rate free climbs on an initially closed decimal system: 5.0 (easiest) to 5.9 (hardest).

After many difficult climbs accumulated in the 5.9 range, the decimal system was "broken" and the 5.10 rating came into existence. It was followed by 5.11, 5.12, 5.13, 5.14, and now 5.15. These upper grades were further subdivided into four letter grades to further refine the rating: suffixes a, b, c, and d were associated with increasing difficulty (i.e., "easy 5.10" = 5.10a or 5.10b, "hard 5.10" = 5.10c or 5.10d).

In this guide, we generally define class-5 divisions as follows:

5.0–5.9	beginner/novice
5.10a–5.12c	intermediate
5.12d and up	difficult

On routes 5.9 and easier we have used the "+" and "−" designations to indicate routes on the more difficult or lighter ends of these grades.

Aid Ratings

In aid climbing you ascend on your gear, hanging on each piece. A few aid lines in Red Rock use these ratings.

A0: Fixed protection is in place.

A1: Extremely easy, solid gear placements.

A2: Easy gear placements that are relatively straightforward and strong.

A3: May involve many tenuous placements in a row and/or difficult placements. Testing of placements is necessary.

A4: Difficult, many placements are weak and only hold body weight. Potential for long, 60- to 100-foot falls with uncertain landings.

A5: Extremely difficult, very weak placements. No piece is capable of catching a fall for the entire pitch. High potential for long and dangerous falls that could cause serious injury or death.

Grade Ratings

Grade ratings indicate the overall commitment or time needed to complete a route. Grades are subjective, greatly depending on the experience, abilities, and equipment used by the climber. Therefore, we have not included grade ratings unless they are greater than III.

Grade I: Very short climbing requiring 1–2 hours.

Grade II: Short climb taking approximately half a day.

Grade III: A climb requiring most of a day to complete.

Grade IV: A climb requiring a very long day to complete.

Grade V: A long climb that takes 2–3 days to complete.

Grade VI: A long climb taking 4 days or more to complete.

Grade VII: A grade VI in an extremely remote location.

Danger Ratings

The danger rating describes the danger level faced by the leader should the leader fall. These are crude descriptions.

R: Run-out, a fall would likely result in serious injury.

R/X: Very run-out, a fall at the wrong place will likely result in serious injury or death.

X: Extremely run-out, a fall at the wrong place will likely result in death.

GEAR SUGGESTIONS

Each route climbs differently for different people. We cannot always predict the gear you will need for a route. We have not done every route and have had to rely on the advice of others. It is best to scope the route before you climb to determine any gear you might need. That said, we recommend the following.

Traditional rack: A standard rack includes one set of stoppers, 10 24-inch slings with carabiners, and a single of each cam from Friends sized #00 to #3.5. On most routes it is wise to include a set of brass stoppers.

Sport rack: A rack of 10 quickdraws will get you up just about anything.

Rope. A 60-meter rope is recommended on all multipitch routes. A 50-meter rope is acceptable on most sport and single-pitch routes.

HOW TO USE THIS GUIDE

Please note that some route names, first-ascent parties, and grades have been changed from previous guidebooks. This book is a compilation of much research and information from discussions with many locals and first ascensionists. We hope you will find an accurate record.

Areas

This guide is divided into climbing areas within Red Rock, presented counterclockwise from the start to finish of the one-way 13-mile Scenic Drive and be-

yond. Each climbing area is named for the parking area you start from and is then divided into subareas and finally into cliffs.

The climbing areas are characterized as follows:

Calico Basin/Kraft Mountain/Gateway Canyon: small cliffs; short approaches; traditional climbs, sport climbs, and bouldering.

First and Second Pullouts (Calico I and II)/Sandstone Quarry: small cliffs; short approaches; mostly sport climbs.

White Rock Springs: multipitch traditional climbs; short approaches.

Willow Springs: mostly single-pitch traditional climbs; short approaches.

Icebox Canyon: single- and multipitch traditional climbs; moderate to 1-hour approach.

Pine Creek Canyon: multipitch traditional climbs; moderate to multihour approach.

Juniper Canyon: multipitch traditional climbs; moderate to multihour approach.

Oak Creek Canyon: multipitch traditional climbs; moderate to a multihour approach.

Mount Wilson: multipitch traditional climbs; multihour approach.

First Creek Canyon: multipitch traditional climbs; moderate to multihour approach.

Black Velvet Canyon: multipitch traditional climbs; moderate to multihour approach.

Windy Peak: single- and multipitch traditional climbs; short to multihour approach.

Illusion Crags: single pitch; 1-hour approach.

Chocolate Rocks: single pitch; short approach.

Route Descriptions

Route descriptions are grouped on cliffs within the larger areas. A sample follows:

▲ DICKIES CLIFF
N AM Sun   Approach: 15 minutes

This formation is located on the same level as the Ranch Hands Wall, about 300 yards west of the gate remnants, up the road and into the canyon. You arrive at the cliff just before the trail heads uphill into the canyon at a meadow and streambed. Routes start on a large rock ledge and are described from left to right.

Descent: Traverse right (west) down to the Gnat

Man Crag, directly below *Ghouls Just Wanna Have Fun*. Then third-class scramble down into the gully just west of Dickies Cliff.

97. Guys and Ghouls 5.6 ★★★ Traditional. Climbs the obvious crack system in the center of the feature. Bouldery start. Gear: standard rack; #4 Friend helps at the start and a #3 is good for the anchor.
FA: Todd and Donette Swain 1994

Directions to the climb are generally given from the main parking for the climbing area. Each climbing area is named after the area where you park. A general hiking description is given for each subarea. Then a hiking description is given for each cliff within that subarea. All directions are given from the climber's perspective, meaning looking up at the cliff. Descents are given the same way (hiking down from the cliff). In most cases north, south, east, and west directions accompany left/right descriptions.

The **orientation** of climbing areas or routes are indicated with abbreviated compass directions: N indicates that a climbing area or route faces north. S indicates south-facing. E indicates east-facing. And W indicates west-facing. Finer distinctions are achieved with SW, NE, and so on.

All-Day Sun or **No Sun** indicates a crag that spends most of the day in the sun or most of the day in the shade. Remember that the sun and shade information can change with season based on where the sun is in the sky. Further detail is indicated by **AM Sun** (sun in the morning) or **PM Sun** (sun in the afternoon).

Approach times for a cliff or route are subjective. Because everyone hikes at a different pace and weight (we might have longer or shorter legs than you, or your pack might be heavy or light), it is difficult to come up with exact approach times. We measured our time on the hikes and added some time since we know the area and terrain.

Route numbers begin at 1 in each climbing area. Next, the **route name** is given. Class, grade, and danger **ratings** come next, followed by other information.

TR means the route is top roped; no gear exists on the route.

Our **quality ratings** indicate a consensus judg-

ment of the route. (Projects—because they are unfinished routes—are usually unrated.)

★★★★★ The best routes in the RRCNCA
★★★★ Must do, a classic
★★★ Very enjoyable
★★ Worth doing once
★ Mediocre

Routes are said to be **Sport** when bolts comprise all the protection on the route. They have fixed anchors unless the route description says they do not.

Routes are said to be **Traditional** when all the protection on the route, excluding anchors, is natural or traditional gear. No bolts exist on the climbing portion of the route.

Routes are said to be **Mixed** when both sport and traditional gear are found on the route.

Routes are denoted **Aid** when aid techniques are utilized to climb.

The number of bolts is given for sport and mixed routes and does not include anchor bolts. We often list the type of **gear** needed for traditional and mixed routes when it is unusual or in addition to a standard traditional rack. If gear information is not given, assume you will need a standard traditional rack (see Gear Suggestions, above).

Assume sport routes have fixed **anchors** unless indicated otherwise. Anchors on mixed and traditional routes are described. Belay anchors can only be used for belaying, not for rappeling or lowering.

The **height** of a route is given if it is necessary to determine what length of rope to use to climb or descend.

Following the route description we give first-ascent information, abbreviated **FA**. This usually means the first free ascent without falls. When possible, we give the year. When multiple names appear it usually is a route that was put up ground-up (rather than on rappel)—a more difficult and strenuous method. Often after a bolt was placed the person who placed it would come down and allow another member of the party to place a bolt and/or push the line upward. In the case of multipitch climbs, multiple first ascensionists mean the party took turns leading and/or free climbing the pitches. The order of climbers represents their contribution to the climb. Usually the first name listed is the person who led the route first, free. For aid climbs, the first ascent is not the first free ascent; therefore, where needed both the first ascent and first free ascent (**FFA**) parties are listed.

Descent information is given for most routes. All sport routes are rappeled or the leader is lowered off the anchors by their belayer. Similarly, rappel off routes with fixed anchors. If no descent is given—and the climb is not a sport route and has no fixed anchors—look for a standard descent for that area or section at the beginning of the route descriptions.

COMPLAINT DEPARTMENT

Climbing grades are subjective. The grades in this book are a result of combining the opinions of many climbers, most of whom have climbed the routes multiple times. Some grades may be soft and others hard.

Gear suggestions are based on opinions of those who climbed the routes. Always use your best judgment in determining gear needs and bring more if you are unsure.

Hiking times may be more or less depending on your abilities and hiking speed relative to ours. We have tried to lengthen them so they would be more suited to someone who has not hiked in the area. Allow yourself extra time, especially in new areas.

Some routes were not included because we had to keep the book at a manageable length. We apologize if routes you would like to see are not here.

We realize that some route information is incomplete: there are routes, route names, and even some grades missing in this guide. We list all possible information in hopes of keeping the best historical record of Red Rock Canyon route history to date. We hope to improve upon it in the future. If you have changes or information for future editions of this guide, please contact us through our publisher, the Mountaineers Books.

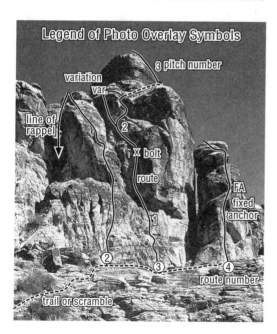

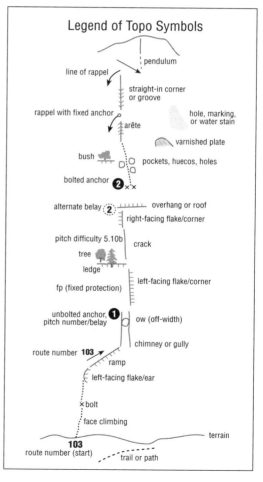

CALICO BASIN SOUTH

RED SPRINGS AREA
Moderate Mecca ▲ Jabba the Hut

CALICO HILLS EAST
Cannibal Boulder ▲ Shit Howdy Boulder ▲ Risk Brothers Roof ▲ Riding Hood Wall
Ranch Hands Wall ▲ The Fox ▲ Dickies Cliff ▲ Gnat Man Crag ▲ Cowlick Crag
Happy Acres ▲ Alternative Rock

FROM LAS VEGAS, take West Charleston Boulevard west, which turns into State Route 159. Drive over the 215 Beltway and zero your odometer. Turn right on Calico Basin Road, 3.9 miles past the 215 and 2 miles before reaching the Red Rock Canyon National Conservation Area 13-mile Scenic Drive. Follow the road 1.1 miles to the entrance to the Red Springs Picnic Area, on your left (south). On the right is a large pullout; park there. You can also park in the Red Springs Picnic Area, but you are restricted by the same policies that govern the Scenic Drive. You must enter and leave the area at the times posted by the BLM. You can park any time in the pullout. In an attempt to rehabilitate Red Springs to its natural state and to eliminate parking problems in the area, the BLM will construct a 125-car parking lot near the entrance to Red Springs (the lot should be completed during 2005).

Access Issues
Access is a delicate issue at Calico Basin. The residents enjoy solitude and are sensitive to the impact of climbers. How you behave can affect everyone's privilege to climb here. It is of utmost importance that climbers are aware and respectful. Some things you can do to reduce tension and difficulties: park your car inside or just outside the Red Springs Picnic Area (as indicated above), be quiet while walking by homes, do not undress in parking lots or within sight of any home, use rest rooms provided in the picnic area, drive the speed limit, and pick up all trash (even if it is not yours).

RED SPRINGS AREA

Access the Red Springs area by walking through the Red Springs Picnic Area.

▲ MODERATE MECCA
S AM Sun   Approach: 15 minutes

Hike through the Red Springs Picnic Area until you reach the end of the parking area (the west end of the picnic area). An old, blocked-off, jeep road heads up a steep hill left, directly to the south and just west of the bathrooms. Hike up this road; you will pass the main Red Springs boulder halfway up the hill on your right. When you are nearly to the top of the hill a trail splits off the road, to the right. Take the trail. After hiking 50 feet downhill the trail splits again. Take the trail heading downhill, veering right to reach the following route, *Side Effects*. This route is located on a prominent red pillar at the base of the hill.

New Trail Alert! As part of the area's rehabilitation, the access to Red Springs will be closed. In that case, from the entrance to Red Springs Picnic Area, follow the road to the first bathroom where there will be a parking lot. From the bathroom follow the trail that heads south, above and left (east) of the rehabilitated Red Springs road. Follow this trail until you run into the blocked-off jeep road that heads up the steep hill. Continue, using the directions given above.

1. Side Effects 5.10b ★★★★ Sport, 5 bolts. The route ascends the southeast corner of the huge freestanding

block. Climb cool-looking huecos up the arête to a chain anchor.
FA: Mike Ward 1991

If you continue on the trail, west, past the *Side Effects* pillar for 200 feet you will find a large red slab that can be top-roped via an anchor on the top. These routes range from 5.3 to 5.7 and are not described here.

To get to the main portion of Moderate Mecca go right (west) where the trail first splits after heading downhill and before reaching *Side Effects*. This trail will take you to a ledge system running east-west along the entire portion of the Moderate Mecca crag. All the routes start off this ledge system. Most are short,

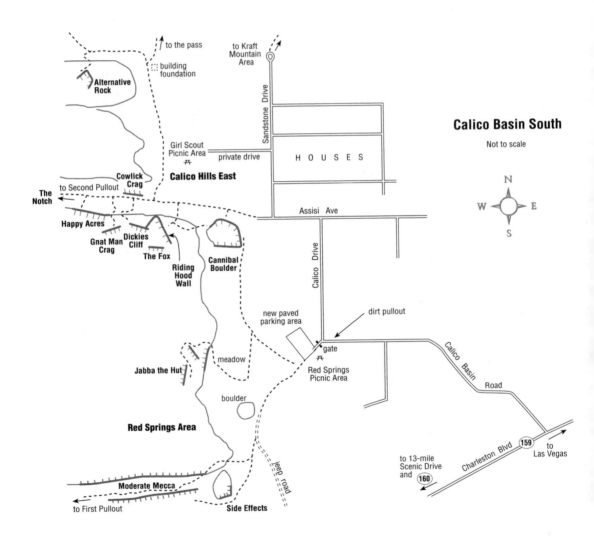

low-angle cracks and corner systems on soft, low-quality rock. Be careful because of the extreme fragility of the rock. Routes are described from right to left, as they are approached.

The following routes are located off the ledge system that sits atop the *Side Effects* pillar.

2. Unknown 5.7 ★ Sport, 3 bolts. This is the first, very short bolted route you come to on the ledge system. Start off of a boulder at the base, 200 feet to the west of the top of *Side Effects*. Gear anchor. Walk off.
FA: Unknown

3. Stew on This 5.10a ★★ Mixed, 2 bolts. Start 240 feet left of the top of *Side Effects* and 40 feet left of the previous route. Clip the first bolt, about 7 feet off the ground. Climb over a little roof to a good stance and get a placement in the horizontal crack about 12 feet up. Continue to another bolt. Bolted anchor left of the arête at the top. Gear: #2–#3 Friends.
FA: Kevin Campbell, Todd Swain 1998

4. Is It Soup Yet 5.10b ★★ Mixed. Start 10 feet left of *Stew on This*. Clip the first funky grey-colored hanger, then follow the thin seam just left of the arête. Shared anchor with *Stew on This*. Gear: small nuts and #1–#3 Friends.
FA: Kevin Campbell, Todd Swain 1998

5. Chicken Gumbo for Your Dumbo 5.6– ★ Traditional. Begin 20 feet left of the previous route. Climb up the obvious corner for about 25 feet. Gear: #1–#3 Friends and larger Rocks. Walk off right, along the upper ledge.
FA: Todd Swain, Patty Gill, Teresa Krolak 1999

6. Soupy Sales 5.7– ★ Traditional. Begin 6 feet left of *Chicken Gumbo for Your Dumbo*. Climb up the crack and corner system, stemming the corner. Gear: selection of Rocks and Friends; solid gear placements. Walk off right, along the upper ledge.
FA: Unknown

7. From Soup to Nuts 5.7– ★ Traditional. Climb

the crack located 20 feet left of the big corner system and 6 feet left of the last route. This crack is wide and has a bunch of loose blocks in it, including a chockstone about 17 feet up. Gear: set of Rocks and bigger Friends to #4. Walk off right, along the upper ledge.
FA: Unknown

8. The Singing Love Pen 5.9– ★ Traditional. Start 40 feet left of the previous route in a shallow dihedral. Climb up to the black-varnished face. Gear: Friends to #3.5. Walk off right, along the upper ledge.
FA: Unknown

9. Valentines Day 5.8+ ★★★ Traditional. Climb up the big left-facing corner 25 feet left of the last route. Gear: Friends to #3 and midsized Rocks. Bolted anchor at the top left.
FA: Randal Grandstaff, Danny Rider 1988

10. Ace of Hearts 5.10d ★★ Traditional. Climb the thin seams 12 feet left of *Valentines Day*. Gear: small wires and brass nuts, small Friends. Shared anchor with *Valentines Day*.
FA: Unknown

11. Immoral 5.10d ★★ Mixed, 4 bolts. Fifteen feet left of *Ace of Hearts* is an area of light-colored rock with a smooth roof, 12 feet off the ground. Begin at the left-facing, chossy corner. Clip a bolt, and continue up to a hand traverse left on smooth rock, clipping 2 bolts (crux). Join *Immoderate* to the shared anchor. Gear: thin wires and quickdraws. 80 feet.
FA: Pier and Randy Marsh

12. Immoderate 5.9, A0 ★★ Mixed. Begin 20 feet left of *Immoral* at the obvious roof. Stick-clip the first or second bolt. "Haul your butt up to the stance" and start climbing. Climb a wobbly flake to its top, pull a bulge, and continue on a low-angled face. Follow seams to the shared anchor with *Immoral* under an overhang. 80 feet.
FA: Pier and Randy Marsh

The next routes are located 150 feet left of *Valentines*

Day, to the right of a huge chossy corner, lighter in color than the surrounding rock and created by falling rock and scree deposited at the base of the wall.

13. Pending Disaster 5.9+ ★ Traditional. This route starts in front of a small tree and boulder. Climb out the little roof using the left-angling crack. Proceed to the anchor at the top. Gear: Friends to #4 and midsized Rocks.
FA: Todd Swain, Kevin Campbell 1998

14. Unknown Aid line. Located 30 feet left of *Pending Disaster*. Equipped with some bolts and button heads. Descent unknown.
FA: Unknown

15. Penny Lane 5.3 ★ Traditional. Start in the loose, very chossy-looking corner and climb to the top. Not recommended due to extreme loose rock and very low quality. Walk off right, along the upper ledge.
FA: Unknown

16. Abbey Road 5.4 ★ Traditional. Climb up just left of *Penny Lane*, using small seams and heading slightly up and left. Gear: smaller Rocks to #3.5 Friend. Walk off right, along the upper ledge.
FA: Unknown

17. Fleet Street 5.8 ★ Mixed, 2 bolts. Climb up the big slabby varnished face 40 feet left of the big chossy corner. Start atop a small ledge system, clip 2 bolts and add gear. Move left to join *Muckraker*. Fixed anchor.
FA: Kevin Campbell, Todd Swain 1998

18. Muckraker 5.8 ★ Traditional. Climb up the big crack/corner system that heads to the right, 10 feet left of the previous route. Gear: set of Rocks and larger Friends to #4. Fixed anchor.
FA: Todd Swain, Paul Ross 1998

19. Scalawag 5.10 ★★ Traditional. Begin 12 feet left of the previous route, on the left side of the roof. Climb out the steep hand crack to a low-angled face above. Gear: Rocks and Friends to #3.5.

Fixed anchor.
FA: Todd Swain, Paul Ross 1998

20. Boodler 5.8 ★ Traditional. Start around the
corner left of *Scalawag*. Climb the left-angling crack/
corner system. Gear: an assortment, including
smaller Rocks and Friends to #3. Walk off.
FA: Unknown

21. Carpetbagger 5.6+ ★ Traditional. Start 20 feet
left of *Boodler*. Join *Boodler* at about 50 feet. Gear:
Friends to #3. Walk off.
FA: Unknown

The next routes are located farther west on the same
ledge system. Some scary fourth class movement is
required to get there so you might want to hike down
a few steps and move around and back up. The hike
will take you just to the left of the following routes.
   Descent: Walk off right, along the upper ledge,
to the trail you hiked in on.

22. The Haj 5.9 ★ Traditional. Start 40 feet left of
the big chossy corner system, in front of two very
large barrel cacti. Fixed anchor.
FA: Jake Burkey, Todd Swain, Winston Farrar 1999

23. Sir Climbalot 5.7 ★★ Traditional. Start in the
same spot as the previous route, traverse slightly
left, and climb the left-angling crack system. Gear:
smaller Rocks and midsized Friends. Shared anchor
with *The Haj*.
FA: Winston Farrar, Jake Burkey, Todd Swain 1999

24. The Route to Mecca 5.7 ★ Traditional. Start
just left of the two previous routes and slightly right
of the big barrel cacti. Gear: midsized Rocks and
Friends to #3. Shared anchor with *The Haj*.
FA: Unknown

25. Treacherous Journey 5.9 ★ Traditional. Climb
corner just left of the previous route. Join *The Route
to Mecca* near the top. Gear: large Rocks and Friends
to #3.5. Shared anchor with *The Haj*.
FA: Todd Swain, Jake Burkey 1999

▲ JABBA THE HUT
NE AM Sun   Approach: 10–15 Minutes

Jabba the Hut is made up of the Lower and Upper
Tiers. Many cracks are located on the lower section
of this cliff. From the gate, hike until you reach the
first bathroom/parking area (the proposed 125-car
parking lot will be near this bathroom). Go right,
heading southwest toward the rock on a prominent
trail. Follow the trail alongside a wooden fence to a
meadow. (As part of the Red Springs rehab, a boardwalk will be built that begins near the bathroom and
climbs the hill and across the meadow. Use the boardwalk whenever possible to protect the meadow.) Cross
the meadow (heading northwest) and take a gully left
and behind a highly huecoed tuft of rock. Angle up
and right. The cliffs are on the left. Routes are described from left to right.

LOWER TIER
The Lower Tier is characterized by three rounded features with cracks through their middle, below and left
of *The Classic Corner of Calico* feature—the obvious
left-angling crack left of a prominent arête and prow,
high on the skyline.

The following routes are on the Lower Tier's leftmost
feature.
   Descent: Hike down the second gully left (south)
of the Lower Tier's leftmost edge.

26. Hans Soloing 5.4 ★★★ TR. Begin 20 feet left of
the obvious crack up the middle of this leftmost
face. Climb a low-angled ramp to the top of the feature. Begin on the face between this and the next
route for variations between 5.8 and 5.10. Gear:
Friends to #4 for the anchor. 70 feet.
FA: Unknown

27. Aliens Have Landed 5.10a ★★ Traditional.
Climb the finger crack up the leftmost side of this
feature, beginning under a small left-facing roof.
Gear: small Rocks, brass nuts, and Friends to #1.
Friends to #3.5 for the anchor. 80 feet.
FA: Unknown

28. Carrie Fissure 5.9 ★ Traditional. Begin 10 feet right of the previous route at a short, right-facing corner under a small overhang. Proceed up the face after the crack and head right to an ear at the top. Gear: to #2 Friend. 80 feet.
FA: Unknown

The following routes are on the middle Lower Tier, which is a taller section of rock up and 100 feet to the right of routes 26–28.

    Descent: Hike down the second gully left (south) of the Lower Tier's leftmost edge.

29. Obie-One Keone 5.8 X ★★ Traditional. Start at the obvious crack that splits this section of rock. Climb the ramp to the left, 20 feet up to a ledge. Climb off the ledge at a small left-facing, varnished

flake. Move to a varnished, shallow, left-facing scoop. Move right out of the scoop to the top of the crack. Bad rock and gear placements. Gear: small Rocks and Friends. 80 feet.
FA: Chris Gill, Keone Kim 1998

30. Shallow Fried Cracken 5.9 ★★ Traditional. Climb crack up the middle of this face (an obvious hueco is just right of the crack, 10 feet up). Gear: brass nuts, Rocks, and small Friends. 80 feet.
FA: Larry Ferber, Lesley Tarleton 1991

31. Gold Bikini and Cinnamon Bun Hairdo 5.10a ★ Mixed, 1 bolt. Begin 20 feet right of the previous route on a left-diagonaling crack, left of "Janet Loves Todd" graffiti. Climb to a bolt with a bad, sharp, unrated hanger. Move left to double

cracks, then climb up a left-facing groove. Gear: Rocks and Friends to #3. 60 feet.
FA: Todd Swain, Patty Gill 1998

COCO CRAG (RIGHT LOWER TIER)

The following routes are on the right Lower Tier, also called Coco Crag. Hike right of *Gold Bikini and Cinnamon Bun Hairdo* past a lower-angled section (for scrambling to the Upper Tier) for 50 yards to a black, varnished wall, right of a big, dirty chimney.

Descent: Traverse right 50 feet and hike down a rocky gully with bushes at the base unless otherwise noted.

32. Hidden Meaning 5.8 ★ TR. Climb the face inside the chimney. 80 feet.
FA: Randal Grandstaff, Danny Rider

33. Cocopuss 5.10b ★★★★ Sport, 8 bolts. Climb the varnished face right of the chimney. It is steeper than it looks. Fixed anchors on slab above. 80 feet.
FA: Pier and Randy Marsh 1996

34. Stupid Cat 5.10d ★★ Sport, 7 bolts. Climb the thin, varnished face, 5 feet right of *Cocopuss*, up the middle of the wall. Anchors are around to the right. 70 feet.
FA: Pier and Randy Marsh 1996

35. Fontanar de Rojo 5.8 ★ Traditional. Begin 15 feet right of the previous route at a right-facing flake. Ascend the flake to the top of a pillar. Then move left into a chimney and then to a varnished hand crack. At the ledge at the top of this crack, at a bush, move right behind the bush and up a left-angling, wide flare. Gear: medium and large Friends and Rocks. 100 feet.
FA: Unknown

36. Ruta de Roja 5.7 ★★ Traditional. Begin the same as the previous route. Upon reaching the top of the pillar, angle up and right on big holds on a varnished face to a finger crack. Climb to the top of the cliff. Move left and finish on *Fontanar de Rojo*. Gear: all sizes needed. 100 feet.
FA: Unknown

37. Variations on the previous routes 5.7, 5.8
★★ Mixed, 2 bolts. Climb either of the two previous routes. Upon reaching the sloping ledge 80 feet up, traverse left to the black, varnished face. Climb the face past 2 bolts to a fixed anchor. 100 feet. Rappel.
FA: Pier and Randy Marsh 1996

UPPER TIER

To reach the Upper Tier, follow directions to the Lower Tier. Then either take the second gully left (south) of *Hans Soloing* on the leftmost edge of the Lower Tier, or climb fourth class between the middle and right features of the Lower Tier (where the rock breaks down, directly below *The Classic Corner of Calico* and just left of a pink tower). Routes are described from left to right as if you hiked from the Lower Tier's left side.

Where the trail coming from the Lower Tier's left side meets the Upper Tier, there is an unmistakable prow with a varnished slab at the base of the wall, to its right. If you look directly south you will see a black, varnished wall with a dogleg seam on its left side, facing north. This is where the following two routes are located. Scramble onto a small ledge (on the left side of the prow) and head left (south) for 300 feet along the cliff base. *Red Vines* begins on the first buttress 20 feet right of the dogleg seam, at a prominent crack behind a scrub oak tree.

Descent: Rappel off the oak tree on top of the ledge for the following two routes.

38. Red Vines 5.8 ★★ Traditional. Begin just left of a low ceiling. Climb the obvious crack. Gear: medium to large Rocks and Friends. 60 feet.
FA: Paul and Marea Ross, Todd and Donette Swain 1998

39. Black Licorice 5.9 ★★ Mixed, 3 bolts. Begin 10 feet right of *Red Vines*, just right of a low ceiling. Climb to a low bolt. Continue up a right-facing crack to another bolt. Move up a varnished face to a bulge. Continue past another bolt to reach the top. Gear: Rocks and small Friends. 60 feet.
FA: Todd and Donette Swain, Paul and Marea Ross 1998

Boulder Dash is located about 100 feet downhill of

the previous routes, or 50 feet around the corner left of the prominent prow at the top of the trail.

40. Boulder Dash 5.10d ★★★ Sport, 7 bolts. This route is located 50 feet left of the obvious prow, on a lower-angled, varnished face with a seam up its middle. Climb the lower-angled face past 3 bolts to the seam. Descend off anchor. 60 feet.
FA: David Parker, Raquel Spears 1994

The next two routes start in a corner 100 feet right of *Boulder Dash*, between it and the prow. Easy fifth-class scrambling takes you to the base.
Descent: Traverse right and descend right of the prow (the same descent as for *The Classic Corner of Calico*).

41. Haberdasher 5.10 ★★ Traditional. Climb the steep, varnished crack 5 feet left of *Habeas Corpus*. Gear: medium to large Friends. 40 feet.
FA: Unknown

42. Habeas Corpus 5.10 ★★ Traditional. Climb the off-width crack where the prow meets the varnished rock feature to its left. Gear: large Friends. 40 feet.
FA: Unknown

The next four routes are located right (north) of the prominent prow. Scramble through boulders to just below a sharp arête. A thin, pink, slightly steep left-facing corner begins these routes. They all start around right, under the steep, black-varnished north face of the prow.
Descent: Same as the previous two routes.

43. Contempt of Court 5.12a ★★ Mixed, 9 bolts. Climb the overhanging arête left of the off-width, left of a huge flake. Move onto the face and climb to the anchors. Gear: #1.5 Friend. 100 feet.
FA: Mike Tupper 1986

44. Allied Forces 5.11a ★★ Traditional. Climb the off-width right of the previous route to the left-facing huge flake system. Shared anchors with *Love on the Rocks*, located below the top

of the flake. Gear: leaver slings for the anchor. 60 feet.
FA: Bob Finlay, Paul Van Betten 1986

45. Love on the Rocks 5.12d ★★ Mixed, 5 bolts. Climb the black, varnished steep face just right of the previous route. Gear: #1.5 Friend. 50 feet.
FA: Mike Tupper 1986

46. Rocky Road 5.10 ★★ Traditional. Climb the off-width crack right of the previous route, splitting the prow and the feature to its right. 50 feet.
FA: Unknown

The following routes are probably the best routes on the Upper Tier. Hike right (north) from the approach gully (the second gully, left of the Lower Tier) for 150 feet until you come to another ship's prow feature with a crack up its left side. This is where the fourth-class approach from the Lower Tier takes you. You cannot go any farther right without descending to the Lower Tier.
Descent: Move left to the backside of *The Classic Corner of Calico* feature. Hike left down a bushy gully.

47. Badger's Buttress 5.6 ★★★★ Mixed, 2 bolts. This route is on the blunt arête 20 feet left of *The Classic Corner of Calico*. Begin around the corner, in a gully sheltered by an overhanging boulder. Traverse right onto the arête and climb up the arête. Gear: #2–#2.5 Friend. 110 feet.
FA: Todd and Donette Swain, Paul and Marea Ross 1998

48. The Classic Corner of Calico 5.7 ★★★★ Traditional. This route is located 20 feet right of the previous route. Follow the obvious left-facing and leaning, varnished crack left of the ship's prow arête. Head to the top of feature. Gear: an assortment to #4 Friend. 110 feet.
FA: Unknown

49. Flying Pumpkin 5.9 R ★ Start in a bushy corner 15 feet right of *The Classic Corner of Calico*. Take the crack angling up and left to the cliff top. Gear: assortment. 80 feet.
FA: Randal Grandstaff, Danny Rider

50. Welcome to N.I.M.B.Y. (Not in My Back Yard) Town 5.8 ★★★ Sport, 4 bolts. Begin on the south-facing feature, right of the previous route. Climb up and right to the chain anchors.
FA: Mark Limage, Dave Melchoir 1998

51. Attack Dogs 5.10d ★★★ Sport, 5 bolts. Climb the varnished face right of the previous route. Move past the lieback at the second bolt and through a small roof to the anchors.
FA: Dave Melchoir 1998

CALICO HILLS EAST

Hike the road past the suggested parking area, where the road makes a 90-degree turn and becomes Calico Drive. Take the first left onto Assisi Avenue and walk for 300 feet. When the road makes a sharp 90-degree turn to the right, go straight, passing through a small pullout/parking area (not recommended). Hike the dirt road heading west that is blocked by a line of boulders.

▲ CANNIBAL BOULDER
Approach: 5 minutes

Take the first left fork from the old dirt road, following a trail to the obvious boulder 300 yards up the hill. Cannibal Boulder routes are divided into sections based on compass directions (south, east, north) and are described from left to right.

Anchors: At different times there are bolts on top of the boulder that you can use for anchors. You may want very long slings or another rope to set up anchors and top ropes.

Descent: Descend the boulder off its south side. Third-class scrambling through a thin corridor allows you to exit either to the east or west. The first ascents

of most of these routes took the line to the top of the boulder from the last bolt. Since then, anchors have been added to several of the routes.

CANNIBAL BOULDER SOUTH
S AM Sun

Although this part of Cannibal Boulder is south-facing, it stays shaded for most of the day.

52. Man-Eater 5.12a ★★★ Sport, 4 bolts. Climb the leftmost bolted route on the boulder's south face.
FA: Dan McQuade 1992
TR FA: Pier and Randy Marsh 1989

53. Wonderstuff 5.12d ★★★ Sport, 6 bolts. Begin on the arête right of *Maneater*. You may want to stick-clip the first bolt.
FA: Paul Van Betten, Richard Harrison, Sal Mamusia 1991

54. New Wave Hookers 5.12c ★★★★ Sport, 6 bolts, black bolt hangers. Climb up the beehive features to the chain anchor.
FA: Paul Van Betten, Richard Harrison, Sal Mamusia 1991

55. Fuck this Sport 5.12b ★★ Sport, 5 bolts. Begin right of the last route. Angle up and right to the anchors.
FA: Paul Van Betten, Richard Harrison, Sal Mamusia 1991

CANNIBAL BOULDER EAST
SE AM Sun

Most of these routes are vertical in nature.

56. Caliban 5.8+ ★ Sport, 4 bolts. *Caliban* meanders away from the bolt line during the meat of the route at the second bolt—like the satellite of Uranus that is sixteenth in distance from Earth, called Caliban.
FA: Sal Mamusia, Paul Van Betten 1993

57. You Are What You Eat 5.4 ★★★ Traditional. Start in the leftmost and wider of two cracks in the middle of the boulder. Climb up and then link with the crack angling left and to the top. Continue to the top of the boulder. Alternate finish: traverse left to the anchors of *Caliban*.
FA: Unknown

58. Unknown 5.9 ★★ Traditional. Climb the crack just right of *You Are What You Eat*. Traverse left into a large left-diagonaling crack and finish on *You Are What You Eat*.
FA: Unknown

59. Suck upon My Baseboy 5.10d ★★ Sport, 4 bolts. Begin on the previous route. Move right onto the face and up 4 bolts.
FA: Paul Van Betten, Richard Harrison, Sal Mamusia 1991
      Variation: 5.11b Sport, 6 bolts. Begin 5 feet right of the start and climb a line of 4 bolts linking with the finish of *Baseboy*.
FA: Pier and Randy Marsh 1997

60. Save the Heart to Eat Later 5.12a ★ Sport, 5 bolts. Climb the middle of the face.
FA: Sal Mamusia, Paul Van Betten, Richard Harrison, Shelby Shelton 1991

61. Pickled Cock 5.11c ★★ Sport, 5 bolts. Start right of *Save the Heart to Eat Later*. Finish up and left of the next route.
FA: Paul Van Betten, Sal Mamusia, Richard Harrison 1991

62. Unknown 5.11a ★★ Sport, 5 bolts. Begin the same as the previous route. Finish up and right at separate anchors.
FA: Unknown

63. Caustic Cock 5.11b ★★★★ Sport, 4 bolts. It is best to stick-clip the first bolt. Climb the stunning, steep arête on the north corner. Traverse left to the shared anchors with *Pickled Cock* or belay at the top of the boulder (as first ascensionists intended). Stay right at the bottom of the route due to rock art.
FA: Paul Van Betten, Dan Kruleski, Shelby Shelton, Richard Harrison, Sal Mamusia 1991

CANNIBAL BOULDER NORTH
NW PM Sun

64. Have a Beer with Fear 5.11a ★ Sport, 4 bolts. This route climbs the north face's left arête and is reachy past the first bolt. You can move right after the last bolt to clip the anchors of *Fear This* (with some rope drag). Gear anchor.
FA: Richard Harrison, Paul Van Betten 1992

65. Fear This 5.11c ★★ Sport, 3 bolts. Begin right of the previous route. Cold-shut anchor.
FA: Sal Mamusia, Paul Van Betten 1992

66. Elbows of Mac and Ronnie 5.11a ★ Sport, 4 bolts. Climb the face right of *Fear This*. Cold-shut anchor.
FA: Todd Swain 1992

67. What's Eating You? 5.10a ★★ Sport, 3 bolts.

Climb the face right of *Elbows of Mac and Ronnie*. Gear anchor.
FA: Todd Swain 1992

68. A Man in Every Pot 5.8+ ★★★ Sport, 3 bolts. Begin on the left edge of a large white flake/boulder leaning against the wall. Finish on a slab. Gear anchor.
FA: Debbie Brenchley, Todd Swain 1992

69. Mac and Ronnie in Cheese 5.10a ★★ Sport, 4 bolts. Start to the right of the flake leaning against the wall. Gear anchor.
FA: Todd Swain, Debbie Brenchley 1992

70. Ma and Pa in Kettle 5.7– R ★★★ Mixed, 3 bolts. Begin on the left-facing crescent on a varnished face at the right edge of the wall. Stick-clipping the first bolt is recommended. Gear anchor and 1 bolt.
FA: Todd Swain 1992

▲ SHIT HOWDY BOULDER
N PM Sun   Approach: 15 minutes

After passing the turnoff for Cannibal Boulder, continue to the remnants of a gate. Turn left off the road and head up toward the rocks on a prominent trail. When you look to the south you will see a large boulder at about ten o'clock, near the skyline. *Shit Howdy* is a crack that starts near the boulder's left end and splits it diagonally, finishing on the right side. Begin hiking up on polka-dotted rock, moving left through low places to reach the boulder. Remember to scramble with care.

Descent: The crack ends on the ground up and right of the start. Scramble down to the start of the crack.

71. Shit Howdy 5.10d ★★★ Traditional. The crack starts in the middle of the boulder and traverses right to the upper edge. At the top, step down and you are on the ground.
FA: Paul Van Betten, Nick Nordblom 1986

▲ RISK BROTHERS ROOF
NE AM Sun   Approach: 20 minutes

Follow directions to the Shit Howdy Boulder (above) until you reach the polka-dotted rock. When you look south you will see a large boulder leaning on another boulder to its right, on the skyline. The left boulder has an obvious crack in it that moves up and left over a roof. Take the small gully left of the feature to reach it (a few fourth-class moves).

72. Risk Brothers Roof 5.11a ★★★ Traditional. The obvious crack starts off a ledge in the center of the northeast face and moves up and left to a short roof. Pull the roof and continue moving up and left (under the next roof). Face-climb to the fixed, bolted anchors. Gear: to #2 Friend.
FA: Paul Van Betten, Sal Mamusia, Richard Harrison 1986

73. Zona Rosa 5.9 ★★ Traditional. Around the corner from this route is a finger crack expanding to an off-width at the top. Gear: to #5 Friend. Scramble off the backside of the formation and hike around

the left (south) side of the boulder.
FA: Bob Finlay, free solo 1986

▲ RIDING HOOD WALL
NE AM Sun   Approach: 20 minutes

After passing remnants of a gate, turn left off the road and head up toward the rocks on a prominent trail. An inconspicuous trail begins at some polka-dotted rock and scrambles up to the far left of the Riding Hood Wall and then traverses right to the Riding Hood Wall. Look for the dark, wide crack, *Riding Hood*, at the top of the hill. Scramble with care. Routes are described from left to right.

Descent: From the top of the climbing, angle up and left, alongside a bulge and below the true summit. Upon reaching a flat area, head left until you can go no farther. Scramble down a short slab between a boulder and the wall. Continue down and south for 50 feet. Scramble and hike down the gully, heading east and veering slightly left. It will take you to just south of the start of the routes. Scramble with care (leaving climbing shoes on is best).

74. Riding Hood 5.8 ★★ Traditional. This is a black, varnished, right-facing open-book corner 20 feet up and left of *Physical Graffiti*. Begin left of two scrub oak trees. Climb up and left. Gear: to #4 Friend.
FA: John Williamson, Bob Logerquist 1970

75. Unknown 5.9 R ★★ Traditional. Begin just right of *Riding Hood* on an incipient seam angling right, between two scrub oak trees. Take big varnished plates and seams to the top of the cliff. Gear: small Rocks and Friends, including brass nuts. 150 feet.
FA: Unknown

76. Physical Graffiti 5.7 ★★★★★ One of the ultra classics of the area. Start at the left side of the front side of the wall in a steep, varnished corner.

Pitch 1: 5.5 Climb the crack up through a roof. Continue up the crack, finishing on a small foot ledge, right of the crack at a bolted anchor. 150 feet.

Pitch 2: 5.7 Traverse slightly right and take the crack that heads up the wall. Move beyond where the

A young Paul Van Betten on Risk Brothers Roof *5.11a. Photo by Sal Mamusia*

crack peters out, topping out on the slab. Find a crack for building a natural anchor. 200 feet.

FA: Jon Martinet, Randal Grandstaff, Scott Gordon 1973

77. Unknown 5.8 R/X ★★ Mixed.

Pitch 1: *Physical Graffiti* pitch 1.

Pitch 2: Climb up left on a sandy, poorly protected slab to a headwall 100 feet up. Veer left and climb a crack that ends up on another slab with 1 bolt. Belay on the slab or atop *Physical Graffiti* (with a 200-foot rope). 175 feet.

FA: Unknown

78. Over the Hill to Grandmother's House 5.10a ★★★ Traditional. This route climbs cracks just right of *Physical Graffiti*. Gear: to #3 Friend.

Variation 1: Begin at the first crack right of *Physical Graffiti*. Climb the right-angling crack over a roof to easier ground. Continue up the left face with no gear, or inch your way up the crack to finish on the first-pitch anchors of *Physical Graffiti*. Rappel with 2 ropes or continue up *Physical Graffiti* for two pitches.

Variation 2: Begin at the second crack right of *Physical Graffiti*, 15 feet right of variation 1, under a large roof. Climb the crack through the roof. Continue up the left face with no gear or inch your way up the crack to finish on the first-pitch anchors of *Physical Graffiti*. Rappel with 2 ropes or continue up *Physical Graffiti*.

FA: Bob Logerquist, John Williamson 1970

79. Lil' Red 5.9 ★ Traditional. Start 25 feet right of the previous climb, at a right-leaning crack. Begin on the crack right below a large hueco on a varnished wall. Climb up 15 feet and then move left into the main, left-angling crack. Follow the crack up and right until it ends in the backside gully. Gear: to #3.5 Friend. 60 feet. Descend via gully.

FA: Unknown

▲ RANCH HANDS WALL
Approach: 10 minutes

Ranch Hands Wall lies below the Riding Hood Wall at trail level. The wall's eastern exposure gets morning sun and its northwestern exposure gets afternoon sun.

RANCH HANDS EAST
E AM Sun

None of these routes have anchors. Use Rocks and/or small Friends to protect to the top sections. This portion of the wall faces southeast, getting morning sun only. The routes are characterized by thin, slippery climbing and gear anchors. Routes are described from left to right.

Descent: Hike directly west, avoiding the first gully on the right (dangerous), moving slightly around left and down into the gully west of the feature. There are several possible slabby 10- to 20-foot scrambles down into the gully.

80. Payless Cashways 5.11a ★★ Mixed, 5 bolts. The first bolt is an old angle iron located just right of a large hueco on the left side of the vertical wall.

FA: Richard Harrison, Sal Mamusia, Paul Van Betten, Shelby Shelton 1991

81. Spanky 5.11a ★★ Mixed, 4 bolts. A small pocket is located 2 feet below the first bolt. Climb the bolted face and then traverse right to a seam.

FA: Richard Harrison, Paul Van Betten, Shelby Shelton 1991

82. Mexican Secret Agent Man 5.11b ★★★ Mixed, 4 bolts. Climb small pockets to reach a right-facing flake and continue up the face.

FA: Paul Van Betten, Richard Harrison 1991

83. Swilderness Experience 5.11c ★ Mixed, 5 bolts. Climb off the rightmost side of a large boulder. Tend right.

FA: Paul Van Betten, Richard Harrison, Shelby Shelton 1991

84. Swilderness Permit 5.12c ★★ Mixed, 7 bolts. Begin on a light-brown, steep section of rock, down and right of the previous route. Start with a long move to a hueco, right of the first bolt. Climb pockets to fourth bolt and then move right at a flake. Run-out in spots.

FA: Sal Mamusia, Paul Van Betten, Richard Harrison 1991

85. Roman Meal 5.11b ★★ TR. Climb the huecoed

face 50 feet right of *Swilderness Permit* to crumbly rock.
FA: Todd Swain 1994

RANCH HANDS WEST
NW PM Sun

Obtain this wall by walking around right of Ranch Hands East. Routes are on the wall's first and second tiers. There are 3 bolts on top of the cliff for the belays.

Roman Hands is the approach route to the wall's second tier.

86. Roman Hands 5.4R ★ Traditional. Begin below the ship's-prow–like feature, located 50 feet off the ground. Climb a somewhat loose face to a ledge. Traverse left to a crack and finish on the huge ledge below the large, overhanging orange wall. Continue on a second-tier route or walk off to the right.
FA: Richard Harrison, Paul Van Betten, Sal Mamusia 1990

The next three routes are on the wall's second tier.
    Descent: Rappel off the anchors of *Ranch Hands* (same descent as for Ranch Hands East).

87. Jack Officers 5.12c ★★ Mixed, 3 bolts. Begin in the center of the wall. Angle up and left on the steep wall. Traverse right to the rappel station of *Ranch Hands*.
FA: Paul Van Betten, Sal Mamusia, Richard Harrison 1991

88. Ranch Hands 5.12b ★★★ Sport, 4 bolts. Begin right of the previous route and angle up and slightly right. Bolted anchor.
FA: Richard Harrison, Paul Van Betten, Sal Mamusia, Bob Conz 1991

89. Blood Stains 5.10d R/X ★★ Mixed, 1 bolt. Begin on the right edge of the wall. Traverse right to a loose dirty crack system. Climb up to an obvious loose block (a reddish block on a black, varnished wall). Pull over this steep section and navigate some horizontals to a bolt. Continue up the steep, varnished arête to the top. Rappel off the anchors of *Ranch Hands*. Warning: the loose block

may be ready to go!
FA: Richard Harrison, Paul Van Betten, Sal Mamusia 1990

 ## THE FOX
Early AM Sun   Approach: 10 minutes

Stay on the old road, passing remnants of a gate. After 200 yards, *The Fox* is visible as a large right-facing corner high above the trail. There is no trail to it; you will have to scramble up the rock gully below and slightly east of the formation. Scramble with care. Routes are described from left to right.

90. Unknown 5.11b ★★ Sport, 6 bolts. This route is located on the wall left of *The Fox*.

91. The Fox 5.10d (aka The Eighth Wave) ★★★★★ Traditional. This one will bring back Indian Creek memories. Climb the obvious right-facing corner/crack system right of the previous route. Gear: #0.5–#5 Friends. Hike off left, down the gully left of the route.
FA: John Williamson, Bob Logerquist 1970

To reach the following routes, hike *The Fox* ledge right and up 70 feet, traveling through some thick scrub oak to a gully heading left and uphill (south). Hike up the gully for 35 feet and then move right, traversing a bushy ledge. Routes are described from left to right.

92. Unknown 5.6 ★★ Traditional. Five feet along the bushy ledge is a low-angle left-facing crack. 40 feet. Walk off left, down the gully.
FA: Unknown

93. Unknown 5.11c ★★★ Sport, 5 bolts. This steep, classic-looking line is located 15 feet right of the previous route. Run-out to chain anchors.
FA: Unknown

94. Unknown 5.12a ★★★ Sport, 5 bolts. Located 5 feet right of the route. Chain anchor.
FA: Unknown

▲ DICKIES CLIFF
N AM Sun　Approach: 15 minutes

This formation is located on the same level as the Ranch Hands Wall, about 300 yards west of the gate remnants, up the road and into the canyon. You arrive at the cliff just before the trail heads uphill into the canyon at a small meadow and streambed. Routes start on a large rock ledge and are described from left to right.

Descent: Traverse right (west) down to the Gnat Man Crag. Directly below *Ghouls Just Wanna Have Fun*, third-class scramble down into the gully just west of Dickies Cliff.

95. Seams like a Butt 5.7 ★ TR. Climb the slabby, whitish face left of *Gigantor*. Bolted anchor.
FA: Mark Limage

96. Gigantor 5.10b ★★ Mixed, 3 bolts. Clip the first bolt off the boulder on the wall's left edge. Clip the second bolt and then traverse right using an obvious line of pockets to reach the arête. Clip the third bolt and head up the varnished face to the top.
FA: Richard Harrison, Paul Van Betten, Wendell Broussard, Mike Forash 1991

97. Guys and Ghouls 5.6 ★★★ Traditional. Climbs the obvious crack system in the center of the feature. Bouldery start. Gear: standard rack; #4 Friend helps at the start and a #3 is good for the anchor.
FA: Todd and Donette Swain 1994

98. Booby Trap 5.12c ★★ Sport, 5 bolts. Climb the thin, varnished face just right of *Guys and Ghouls*, to the left of the obvious roof. Lower off the last bolt or hike off per the shared descent. Gear anchor.

FA: Sal Mamusia, Paul Van Betten 1991

99. Stukas over Disneyland 5.12a ★★ Mixed, 2 bolts. Begin under a roof in middle of this section of wall. You may want to stick-clip the first bolt. After clipping the second bolt, move over the roof and take discontinuous cracks up a varnished face. Gear: small to medium Rocks and Friends.
FA: Paul Van Betten, Richard Harrison 1991

100. Lancaster Levels Luxor 5.9+ ★ Traditional. This route is located just right of the last route. Move over a bulge to reach an obvious crack system to the top. Gear: small to medium Rocks and Friends.
FA: George Reid, Donette and Todd Swain 1994

101. Monster Island 5.11a ★★ Mixed, 3 bolts. This is a thin seam 3 feet right of *Lancaster Levels Luxor.* Gear: small to medium-sized Rocks and Friends.
FA: Paul Van Betten, Sal Mamusia 1991

▲ GNAT MAN CRAG
NE AM Sun   Approach: 15 minutes

Gnat Man Crag is located just right of Dickies Cliff. Hike up the gully to the right of Dickies Cliff and scramble up third-class to reach the base of route, *Ghouls Just Wanna Have Fun.* Routes are described from left to right.

Descent: Hike off right and down the farthest gully to the north (running down east). Scramble across a choppy ledge, heading south, to the base of the routes.

102. Unnamed 5.9+ ★★ Traditional. Begin in gully on the wall's left edge. Climb the crack that angles right through two roofs. Gear anchor. 80 feet.
FA: Mark Limage, Andy Carson, Andrew Fulton 1997

103. P-Coat Junction 5.9 ★★ Traditional. Climb the crack left of *P-Coat Sleeve.* Follow it as it joins *P-Coat*

Sleeve and finishes atop *Ghouls Just Wanna Have Fun*. Gear: small to medium Rocks and Friends. 110 feet. *FA: Todd and Donette Swain 1994*

104. P-Coat Sleeve 5.10a ★★ Traditional. This route climbs a finger crack just left of *Ghouls Just Wanna Have Fun* and joins it at the top. Gear: small to medium Rocks and Friends. 110 feet. *FA: Paul Van Betten, Sal Mamusia 1991*

105. Ghouls Just Wanna Have Fun 5.7 ★★★★ Traditional. This is an obvious right-facing dihedral in the center of the wall. Gear: small to medium Rocks and Friends; you can use a few large pieces (#3–#4 Friends). 110 feet. *FA: Donette Swain, Catriona Reid 1994*

106. Gnat Man on Ranch Hands 5.11c ★★ Mixed, 5 bolts. Begin in a pod-hueco feature just right of the previous route. Gear anchor. 110 feet. *FA: Paul Van Betten, Sal Mamusia 1991*

107. Knock the Bottom Out of It 5.10a ★★ Mixed, 4 bolts. Climb the varnished face right of the previous route. Varnished jugs take you to the top. Gear anchor. 120 feet. *FA: Paul Van Betten, Sal Mamusia 1991*

108. Bottoms Up 5.7 ★ Traditional. Climb the left-facing corner right of the previous route. Go left at the top of this corner to a right-facing corner. Difficult start. Gear: small to medium Rocks and Friends. 120 feet. *FA: Bob Conz, free solo 1991*

▲ COWLICK CRAG
S AM Sun   Approach: 15 minutes

Across the trail from the Gnat Man Crag is the Cowlick Crag, which is characterized by two red dome-ish features that are separated by a small gully. These routes are located on the rightmost (eastern) larger feature. The rock on this wall is very soft and fragile. Handle with care. Routes are described from left to right. The following routes are located in the small corridor left of the main face.

109. Unnamed 5.6 ★ TR. Top-rope off the 2-bolt anchor located on the left side (west-facing) face of this wall. *FA: Mark Limage*

110. Unnamed 5.5 ★ TR. Top-rope off the 2-bolt anchor right of the previous anchor. Climb a crack feature to a thin face. *FA: Mark Limage*

The remaining routes climb the main south face.

111. Cowlick Co. Crag 5.7 ★★ Sport, 4 bolts. Start in the middle of the main face, just below the start of a prominent left-leaning overlap. Continue over the overlap and right onto the face. *FA: Todd Swain*

112. Flying Chuckwalla 5.7 R ★ Sport, 3 bolts. Climb the pocketed face with the X-looking feature on it, just right of the previous route. *FA: Mark Limage and Dave Melchoir 2000*

113. Unnamed 5.7 ★ TR. A 2-bolt anchor is located down and right of the anchors of the previous route, left of a notch in the top of the rock. *FA: Mark Limage*

▲ HAPPY ACRES
NE AM Sun   Approach: 20 minutes

Happy Acres is located about 300 yards past Gnat Man Crag and faces northeast. It is a huge, black, varnished wall located high in the canyon; it sits 100 yards down and left of the saddle that is at the head of the canyon, 100 feet before reaching the obvious notch or saddle at the head of the canyon (over which is the Second Pullout). Take the trail past the Gnat Man and Cowlick Crags up the canyon. When you reach two pine trees right next to each other, hike up and left to the obvious tall varnished north-facing wall. Several large pine trees grow at the base of the right wall. The wall is broken up into two parts, separated by a big right-facing corner. Routes are described from left to right.

Descent: Descend by traversing right (west) 100

yards along the ridge to a large, bushy gully, heading right and downhill.

114. One Hand Clapping 5.9+ ★★ Mixed, 3 bolts. Begins on the black wall down and left of *Life Chuckle*. Traverse (fourth-class) onto a terrace below the wall. Climb straight up the center of the wall. Long pitch.
FA: Nick Nordblom, solo 1995

115. The Life Chuckle 5.8 R/X ★ Mixed. This route is located 75 feet left of *Spontaneous Enjoyment*. Start in a shallow right-facing corner. Climb up the corner and onto the black, varnished face above. Gear: a set of Rocks and a hefty selection of midsized Friends.
FA: Nick Nordblom, Paul Van Betten 1984

116. Greek Tragedy 5.8 R ★ Traditional. Begin 30 feet left of *Spontaneous Enjoyment*, up and left on a short flake/ramp. Where the ramp ends, go straight up the face. Gear: practice your slip hitches and take a few Rocks. Bolted anchor on the ledge. 60 feet.
FA: Chris Burton, Michael Burton (no relation) 2002

117. Spontaneous Enjoyment 5.8+ ★ Mixed. Start 40 feet left of the big left-facing corner. Climb the low-angled slab past 2 bolts to a midway anchor. Continue past the first anchor, heading right to a flake. Continue up and then right to the top of a pillar. Gear: Rocks and a wide range of Friends. A rappel anchor is on the left side of the large corner, atop the pillar.
FA: Paul Van Betten, Nick Nordblom 1984

The next route is located just right of a fifth-class gully on the left face of the big right-facing corner system that splits the Happy Acres Wall.

118. Unnamed 5.7 ★★ Mixed. Begin around the corner right of the previous route, just left of a short orange left-facing corner. Gear: standard rack to #3 Friend.
    Pitch 1: 5.5, 2 bolts. Somewhat loose rock. Bolted anchors. 50 feet.
    Pitch 2: 5.7 Continue up, veering right up several cracks to a spacious ledge on the right side of the wall. Bolted anchors. 60 feet.

Descend in two rappels.
FA: Mark Limage and Gary Sanders 1998

The next routes are located 50 feet right of the previous route (80 feet right of the big corner). Hike the base of the crag to an obvious ramp heading up and left.

119. Guys from Josh are so Cool 5.10c ★★★ Sport, 7 bolts. This route starts about 50 feet up and left on the ramp. There is an ice-cream scoop feature at the start. Chain anchor.
FA: Randy and Pier Marsh 1998

120. Todd's a God 5.10a ★★★ Sport, 8 bolts. Start off the ramp, 12 feet down and right of the previous route. Climb the black, varnished face to the chain anchor.
FA: Randy and Pier Marsh 1998

121. Cram It 5.9– ★★★ Mixed, 1 bolt. Start 6 feet right of *Todd's a God*. Clip the first bolt and head up and into the left-facing corner system. Gear: to midsized Rocks and up to #3.5 Friend. The FA was a scary lead without the first bolt.
FA: Randal Grandstaff, Danny Rider 1988

For the next route, hike another 100 yards upcanyon and right of *Cram It*. A pillar rests against the wall, with a small arch at its base in the first 30 feet.

122. Mother's Day 5.10b ★★ Traditional. Climb the right side of the pillar. This route offers a little of everything, from fingers to fist to face and wider.
FA: Randal Grandstaff, Danny Rider 1988

The next route begins about 100 yards upcanyon from *Mother's Day*, 100 feet before reaching the obvious notch or saddle at the head of the canyon (over which is the Second Pullout). The route is on the right (northeast) side of the wall, facing southwest. It is directly across the canyon from the descent gully for the other Happy Acres routes.

123. November Daze 5.7 ★★ Mixed, 4 bolts. Begin this south-facing route at a thin seam 5 feet left

of the wall's right edge and a large hueco. Climb varnished edges on a dark orange face. Fixed anchors. 50 feet. Rappel the route.
FA: Mark Limage and Gary Sanders 2000

The next routes are located on a steep east-facing wall that is around the corner from and 15 feet right of *November Daze*.

124. Unknown Project Mixed, 1 bolt. One white-painted hanger marks the first and only bolt. Chain anchors.

125. Unknown Project Mixed, 1 bolt. Begin 5 feet right of the previous route. Shared anchor.

▲ ALTERNATIVE ROCK
NE AM Sun   Approach: 45 minutes

Follow the roadbed approximately 300 yards past the gate remnants toward the canyon. Before entering the canyon (before the Cowlick Crag), take a split to the right, skirting the base of the rock. The trail passes a building foundation and then curves into the next canyon north, heading northwest. Alternative Rock is 15 minutes up this canyon from the foundation. As you walk in, look up and left for a natural bridge. It is about halfway up the hillside and hard to miss. Just before the trail dips into a drainage, head up and left toward the bridge. Walk over it and head straight up the hillside, veering left. The main portion of the cliff faces north, and there is a large pine tree at the base. *Stone Age* (V5) is a traversing boulder problem on the left edge of the crag and is a good warm-up.

Note: A flake at the top of *Nirvana* has broken and so Route 129, (unknown 5.12c) and *Nirvana* may be more difficult than indicated here.

126. It's All Rock 5.12b ★★★ Sport, 10 bolts. This is the leftmost bolted route on the wall. Shares a first bolt with *The Prophet*.
FA: Leo Henson

127. Stage Dive 5.12c/d ★★ Sport, 10 bolts. Shares bolts with *The Prophet*. After clipping the fifth bolt, climb left to a right-facing corner and 5 more bolts to the anchor.
FA: Leo Henson

128. The Prophet 5.12b ★★★ Sport, 9 bolts. Climb *Stage Dive* to its fifth bolt, then go straight up 4 more bolts.
FA: John Heimen

129. Unknown 5.12c ★★★★ Sport, 10 bolts. Climb *The Prophet* to its fifth bolt and then go right, finishing on the anchors of *Nirvana*.
FA: John Heimen

130. Unknown 5.12d ★★ Sport, 9 bolts. Start on *Nirvana*. Three-quarters of the way up, move left and finish on *The Prophet*.
FA: John Heimen

131. Nirvana 5.13 a ★★★ Sport, 10 bolts. Start in the middle of the north face. Traverse left and then back right to the anchor. Hard for the grade; holds have broken.
FA: John Heimen

132. Hot Line 5.12a ★★★ Sport, 7 bolts. Climb the arête on the northwest corner.
FA: John Heimen

133. Flying Rats 5.11d ★★★ Sport, 6 bolts. This is the first route on the left side of the north face.
FA: John Heimen

134. Paralyzed 5.11b ★ Sport, 5 bolts. Climb the first 3 bolts of *Flying Rats* and then traverse into the top of *Psychic Eye*.
FA: John Heimen

135. Psychic Eye 5.12b ★ Sport, 4 bolts. Climb the middle of the north face. Boulder problem to easy climbing.
FA: John Heimen

136. Alternative Nation 5.12b/c ★ Sport, 5 bolts. Climb the right side of the north face.
FA: John Heimen

Alternative Rock

126. It's All Rock 5.12b
127. Stage Dive 5.12c/d
128. The Prophet 5.12b
129. Unknown 5.12c

130. Unknown 5.12d
131. Nirvana 5.13a
132. Hot Line 5.12a
133. Flying Rats 5.11d

134. Paralyzed 5.11b
135. Psychic Eye 5.12b
136. Alternative Nation 5.12b/c

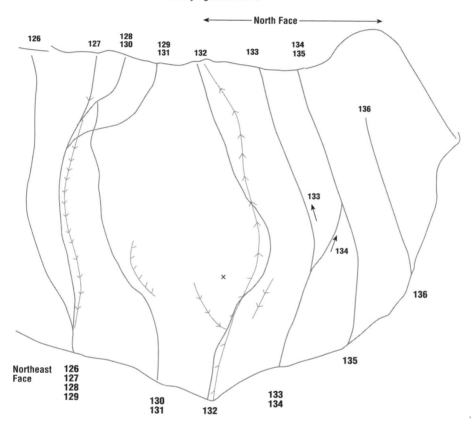

The next two routes are located on the just-over-vertical wall below and right of Alternative Rock. They also face northeast (you walk past them to get to Alternative Rock).

137. Grunge 5.11d ★ Sport, 8 bolts. Climb the thin face and varnished edges.
FA: Leo Henson

138. Grunge Dyno 5.12b ★★★ Sport, 12 bolts. Begin 20 feet right of the previous route, left of huge huecos. Climb a thin face with white-painted hangers.
FA: Leo Henson

KRAFT MOUNTAIN
AND GATEWAY CANYON

KRAFT MOUNTAIN
Kraft Rocks ▲ The Mall ▲ Conundrum Crag ▲ Family Crag ▲ Caligula Crag

GATEWAY CANYON
The Garbled Mass ▲ The Cop Crag ▲ Cannabis Crag

GATEWAY CANYON NORTHWEST
Winter Heat Wall ▲ Sunny and Steep Wall ▲ Golden Nugget Boulder
Judgment Day Crag ▲ Chunder Bolt Wall ▲ Atman Crag ▲ Meyers Cracks

KRAFT MOUNTAIN and Gateway Canyon are geographically located within Calico Basin, on its east side. Many of these eastside areas and features are named for Ozzie Kraft, one of the first landowners in the basin.

For both Kraft Mountain and Gateway Canyon, park in the areas suggested for Calico Basin. From Las Vegas, take West Charleston Boulevard westward, which turns into State Route 159. Drive over the 215 Beltway and zero your odometer. Turn right on Calico Basin Road, 3.9 miles past the 215 and 2 miles before reaching the Red Rock Canyon National Conservation Area 13-mile Scenic Drive. Follow the road 1.1 miles to the entrance to the Red Springs Picnic Area, on your left (south). On the right is a large pullout suggested for Calico Basin parking.

Though it may seem like a long hike, remember that you do not want to disturb the residents of this small community. They are very aware of the climbers in this area. It is of utmost importance that we present a good image to keep our climbing rights here and to avoid further access problems.

Hike the road past the suggested parking area as it makes a 90-degree turn and becomes Calico Drive. Take the first left onto Assisi Avenue and walk 300 feet. Follow the road when it makes another 90-degree turn to the right, turning into Sandstone Drive. Continue on the road until it ends between two fences: on the right is a fenced-in house with a bunch of barking dogs, and on the left is a large empty lot.

Walk between the two fences on the trail, taking the trail down and back up through two small washes. Hike directly north until you run into an east-west trail, located about 400 feet to the south of the boulders on the hillside. To the left (west) is Turtlehead Peak. Kraft Mountain and Gateway Canyon are located to the right (east).

Note that as of November 2002, the Wilderness Study Areas of Red Rock Canyon were designated as wilderness areas. At that time, Kraft Mountain and Gateway Canyon were added to the wilderness area, so bolting is not allowed.

KRAFT MOUNTAIN

▲ KRAFT ROCKS
S AM Sun   Approach: 15 minutes

Head right (east) on the east-west trail and you will soon be in the heart of the Kraft Boulders. You will see a large, split boulder 200 feet north of the trail and

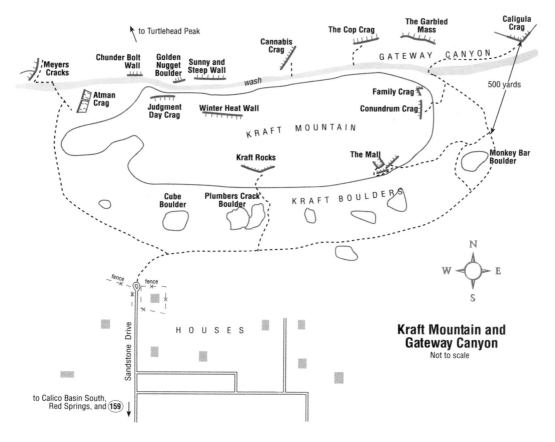

**Kraft Mountain and
Gateway Canyon**
Not to scale

on the hillside. This is the Plumbers Crack Boulder, the largest boulder on the hillside; the split creates a large off-width/chimney boulder problem. From the backside of this boulder, hike directly up the hillside to the north until you run into Kraft Mountain. Most of the routes in this area consist of very soft, fragile rock and difficult descents. Routes are described from left to right.

LOWER TIER

This wall is pink in color and has a huge right-facing dihedral and roof on its left side.

Descent: Traverse the cliff top for about 150 yards and descend a fourth-class gully. Difficult.

1. California Reverse 5.11b ★★ Mixed, 1 bolt. Begin up and left of *High Roller*. The route looks like the state of California reversed (thus the name) and faces southeast. Climb past 1 bolt to get into the crack.
FA: Paul Van Betten, Randal Grandstaff 1986

2. High Roller 5.11d R ★ Traditional. Begin 15 feet left of the huge right-facing dihedral and roof, behind a large boulder.

Pitch 1: 5.11d R Climb the right-facing dihedral. Move over a roof and step left onto a sloping ledge at the base of an off-width. 70 feet.

Pitch 2: 5.10d Climb the off-width to the top of the cliff. 70 feet.
FA: Paul Van Betten, Jay Smith 1986

3. Shark Vegas 5.11a ★★ Mixed, 1 bolt. Begin 50 feet right of *High Roller* (30 feet right of the big overhang), behind the rightmost of two large, side-by-side

boulders. Climb up thin cracks to a varnished slab with a bolt. Finish on a left-facing flake and lieback.
FA: Paul Van Betten, Nick Nordblom 1986

4. Viva Las Vegas 5.11a ★ Traditional. Begin 12 feet right of *Shark Vegas* behind a barrel cactus. Climb a left-leaning seam to right-angling flake. Move left to obtain a ledge and take the broken corner system straight up. Gear: thin Rocks to protect the start.
FA: Paul Van Betten, Robert Findlay, Mike Ward, Randal Grandstaff 1986

5. Vegas Girls 5.11b/c R ★ Mixed, 3 bolts. Begin 5 feet right of *Viva Las Vegas* on a pocketed face. Take the face to a roof. Follow big huecos to a thin seam past bolts and right onto the arête. Follow the arête and right face to the top. 125 feet.
FA: Paul Crawford, Paul Van Betten, Nick Nordblom 1986

UPPER TIER
The following routes are located 150 yards right of the Lower Tier. Reach these routes on easy fifth-class terrain, up and right on a ramp, or climb *Porch Pirate*.

6. Weasel Yeast 5.10b/c ★ Climb a left-leaning hand crack that starts above *Porch Pirate*. Rappel.
FA: Paul Van Betten, Nick Nordblom 1986

7. Weasel Cheese 5.11a ★ TR. Top-rope from the top of the previous route. After going partway up the *Weasel Yeast* hand crack, move right over a roof. Rappel.
FA: Nick Nordblom, Paul Van Betten 1986

Porch Pirate is located 150 yards right and slightly uphill from the Lower Tier and begins off a ledge about 20 feet up. Scramble up a second-class ramp for 40 feet to reach the base of a large, varnished black flake against the wall.

8. Porch Pirate 5.11b/c R ★★ Mixed, 2 bolts. Climb off the ledge where there is a Hot Wheels car wedged in the crack. Follow thin cracks up and left to a shallow dihedral. Climb the dihedral and finish on a run-out face above. Descend the gully to the left, with some fifth-class moves.
FA: Paul Van Betten, Paul Crawford, Sal Mamusia 1991

The next two routes are located 75 feet to the right of the right edge of the ramp that leads to *Porch Pirate*.
   Descent: Hike off right 50 yards.

9. Unknown 5.10 ★★★ Traditional. Begin 80 feet left of *The Classic Crack of Calico*. Gear: standard rack to #4 Friend.
   Pitch 1: 5.10a Climb the deep, short crack (boulder problem; hands to #4 Friend size). End on a ledge.
   Pitch 2: 5.10 Move up a chimney and exit right underneath a roof. Traverse underneath (crux) and turn the roof to climb the face. Gain the arête (5.9), finishing up the wall.
FA: Unknown

10. The Classic Crack of Calico 5.9+ ★★★★ Begin on a lighter-colored rib on a left-facing dihedral with a roof high up.
   Pitch 1: 5.7 Climb the dihedral to the roof. Move left, up the chimney, and belay on a ledge with a large tree.
   Pitch 2: 5.9+ Climb a varnished crack straight up, moving left at the top.
FA: Unknown

11. Unnamed 5.10b ★★★ Traditional. This route is 200 feet right of *The Classic Crack of Calico* and climbs splitter cracks for 100-plus feet, with a tips crack at the top.
   Descend by moving right and protect the downclimb for both partners through a chimney.
FA: Unknown

▲ THE MALL
SSE AM Sun   Approach: 15 minutes

The Mall is located at the right (east) end of Kraft Mountain and faces south southeast. Head right (east)

on the east-west trail, skirting the edge of the Kraft Boulders and then following the trail as it goes left and around Kraft Mountain. Once the trail starts to head directly north, you will see a large boulder in front of you, the Monkey Bar Boulder. It has a steep northeast face and is littered with chalk-filled huecos.
   The Mall climbs are located on three separate tiers. All are left (west) of the Monkey Bar Boulder. From the boulder, head west along the base of Kraft Mountain (toward the way you entered, but along the cliffside) for 150 yards. At this point you can look up and see a nice-looking hand crack about 75 yards up, on a boulder leaning against a steep face. This is where the Lower Tier routes begin.

LOWER TIER
The Lower Tier is about 150 yards northwest of the Monkey Bar Boulder and 75 yards above the trail. It is a cliff with an obvious hand crack at the base on somewhat of a boulder. Routes are listed from left to right.

12. Show Burro 5.11a ★★★ Mixed, 3 bolts. Climb the low-angled hand crack to its top and then go up and left along an easy crack until it ends. Climb the steep face above, past 3 bolts to a chain anchor on the bulge. Gear: to #3 Friend.
FA: Shelby Shelton, Danny Rider 1993

13. Lick It 5.11b ★★★★ Mixed, 4 bolts. Climb the previous route and hand crack to its top and then move right around a nose to a bolt. Continue past 3 more bolts to a chain anchor. Gear: to #3 Friend. Walk off.
FA: Danny Rider, Luis Saca 1993

MIDDLE TIER
From the left side of the Lower Tier, move uphill 75 feet to the base of the Middle Tier. Routes are listed from left to right.
   Descent: For routes 14–19, walk off left, to the gully that leads to the Upper Tier from the Middle Tier.

14. Practice Crack 5.8 ★ Traditional. This route climbs a crack on the leftmost part of the Middle Tier. Gear: to #4 Friend.
FA: Unknown

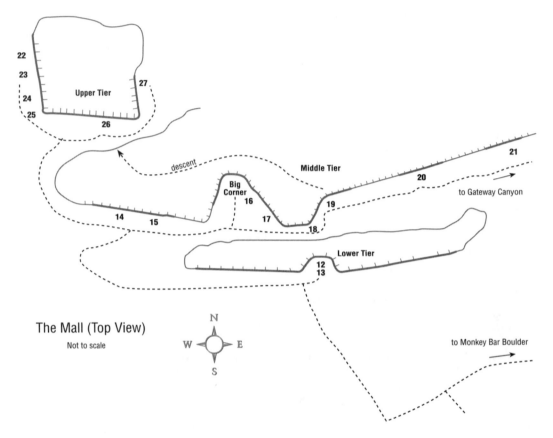

The Mall (Top View)

Not to scale

15. Electric Orange Peeler 5.9 ★★ Traditional. Climb the obvious left-angling crack 25 feet to the right of the previous route. Gear: to #5 Friend.
FA: Todd Swain, Mary Hinson 1995

16. Gold-Plated Garlic Press 5.11d ★★★ Mixed, 4 bolts. The route is located just right of the previous route, right of a big corner. Climb past 4 bolts and then head slightly left and into a crack/corner system. Gear: you may need Rocks and small Friends for the upper section. Open cold-shut anchor.
FA: Paul Van Betten, Shelby Shelton 1993

17. Dirty Little Girl 5.10d ★★ Sport, 6 bolts. Start right of the previous route at an arête with huecoed rock. Climb along and left of the arête on big holds and then up the face past 6 bolts to the shared an-

chor with *Messie Nessie*.
FA: Danny Rider, Luis Saca 1994

18. Messie Nessie 5.11c ★★★★ Sport, 7 bolts. Begin 7 feet right of the previous route. Climb up the pink section of rock. This climb faces east. Cold-shut anchor.
FA: Danny Rider, Luis Saca 1994

19. Repo Man 5.11a ★★★ Mixed, 5 bolts. Begin directly above the two routes on the Lower Tier at the base of a chimney. Move left and up past 2 bolts (dicey), then up the steeper face past 3 bolts to open cold-shut anchor.
FA: Danny Rider, Dave Kruleski 1995

Descent: For routes 20 and 21, walk north and

east along the top of the wall, heading north until you join the base of the Middle Tier.

20. Unknown 5.10d ★ Traditional. Climb the fist crack 75 feet right of the previous route. Gear: to #5 Friend.
FA: Unknown

21. The Figurine 5.10a ★★ Traditional. Climb the dogleg crack 200 feet right of the top of the Lower Tier. Gear: to #5 Friend.
FA: Dave Kruleski, Danny Rider 1995 '

UPPER TIER

High and left of the Middle Tier is a large boulder and face overlooking Kraft Basin. Routes are listed from left to right.

22. City Slickers 5.11a ★★ Mixed, 1 bolt. Begin in the chimney at the left edge of the face. Move out right, under a roof, to a vertical crack. Follow the crack up, past 1 bolt to a chain anchor. Gear: to #4 Friend.
FA: Randy Marsh, Donny Burroughs, Wendell Broussard 1990

23. Country Bumpkin 5.11a ★★★★ Sport, 4 bolts. Climb the center of the face on the boulder's southwest side. Start on the varnished section and continue up to lighter rock. Chain anchor.
FA: Danny Rider, Dan Kruleski 1994
TR FA: Pier and Randy Marsh 1989

24. Unknown Project 1 bolt. There is 1 bolt located on the far left corner of the wall below the arête that separates the southwest and southeast faces.

25. Crime and Punishment 5.12a ★★ Sport, 5 bolts. This route is located about 5 feet left of the arête. Move up and left past 3 bolts, then move up right past 2 more bolts to chain anchors.
FA: Richard Harrison, Michelle Locatelli 1994

26. Headmaster Ritual 5.11c ★★ Sport, 4 bolts. Begin 10 feet right of the previous route, behind a large boulder at the base of the wall. Climb up the center of the wall to chain anchors.
FA: Paul Van Betten, Luis Saca 1994

27. Powder Puff 5.9+ ★ Traditional. Begin 20 feet right of the previous route. Climb a wide, dogleg

crack up to varnished edges. Continue up the arête taking you to the summit. Walk off.
FA: Unknown

▲ CONUNDRUM CRAG
SE and S AM Sun   Approach: 20 minutes

This area is located at the east end of Kraft Mountain, about 75 yards right or north of The Mall. Conundrum Crag is made up of several boulder features. The leftmost small boulder feature faces southeast and the northern boulder faces south; both get morning sun. Continue north past the Monkey Bar Boulder on the good trail. Just before the trail drops down into the wash and Gateway Canyon, head left (west) and up the hill 250 feet to Conundrum Crag. Routes are described from left to right.

28. Arrowhead Arête 5.11d ★★★★ Sport, 4 bolts. This route is on the southeast-facing cliff that is the smallest boulder feature on the left (southernmost) side of Conundrum Crag. Begin on a pillar facing southeast. Chain anchor.
FA: Leo Henson 1994

29. Unknown 5.10a ★★ Sport, 4 bolts. Begin 20 feet around the corner and right of the previous route, on the north side of the boulder. Climb up the steep, tan, pocketed face to lower-angle, black, varnished rock. Black bolt hangers. You may want to stick-clip the first bolt. Long moves. Gear anchor. Walk off left, down and around the left edge of the formation.
FA: Unknown

30. Satan in a Can 5.12c ★★★★ Mixed, 3 bolts. This is the leftmost route on the south face of the next boulder, about 50 feet right (north). An easy scramble up some slabs takes you to the base of the route. The climb is short, steep, and bouldery. Gear: smaller Rocks and Friends will be useful in spots, especially at

the start; or use a stick clip. Fixed anchors.
FA: Jonathan Knight 1992

31. Drilling Miss Daisy 5.11a ★★ Sport, 4 bolts. This route is located 20 feet right of the previous route. Steep climbing on big jugs. Gear: smaller Rocks and Friends might make you feel better at the start, or use a stick clip. Chain anchor.
FA: Steve Bullock 1992

▲ FAMILY CRAG
S AM Sun   Approach: 20 minutes

Family Crag is located upcanyon about 60 yards from Conundrum Crag on the largest boulder feature of this section of cliff. Routes are described from left to right.

32. Unknown 5.8 ★★ Traditional. From the start of the next route, climb the crack to the left to reach a ledge. Move left and around a flakelike feature to reach a crack. Take it to the top of the boulder. Gear: to #5 Friend. Walk off left.
FA: Unknown

33. Wayward Son 5.9 ★ Sport, 6 bolts. Climb up the leftmost bolted route to an open cold-shut anchor. This climb is just right of the corner where the wall begins.
FA: Danny Rider 1998

34. Family Circus 5.9 ★ Sport, 7 bolts. Climb the face 10 feet right of the previous route. Open cold-shut anchor.
FA: Danny Rider 1998

35. Family Affairs 5.8 ★★ Sport, 7 bolts. Begin right of *Family Circus*, on the prow of this boulder. Fixed anchor.
FA: Danny Rider 1998

▲ CALIGULA CRAG
SW PM Sun   Approach: 25 minutes

After passing the Monkey Bar Boulder, the trail enters Gateway Canyon, initially paralleling an old roadbed

and a wash. Caligula Crag is across the roadbed and wash, about 500 yards northeast of the Monkey Bar Boulder. Routes are described from left to right.

36. Ms. October 1995 5.9 ★ Traditional. Begin on the left edge of the wall, left of an acacia bush and barrel cactus. Climb vertical cracks to a stance below a steep bulge. Pull the bulge to gain left-slanting cracks. Finish in a chimney. Gear: to #4 Friend. Walk off the backside of the formation; head down and around the right side.
FA: Todd Swain, Mary Hinson 1995

37. Penthouse Pet 5.11a ★ Mixed, 1 bolt. Begin just right of the previous route. Climb the thin corner on the left edge of the wall. Toward the top, head left and clip a bolt. Finish on the fixed anchor of *Disguise the Limit*.
FA: Paul Van Betten, Richard Harrison 1990

38. Disguise the Limit 5.11d ★★★ Mixed, 3 bolts. Climbs the arête and up and over the roof (#3 Friend under roof). Finish on fixed anchor.
FA: Paul Van Betten 1990

39. Caligula 5.12a ★★★ Traditional. Climb up a crack to a roof, and move over roof. Finish on a crack to a ledge with rappel anchors.
FA: Paul Van Betten, Richard Harrison 1990

40. Guccione 5.11c ★★★ Mixed, 5 bolts. This route is located just left of an obvious chimney. Gear: #3 Friend for the roof. Walk off the backside of the formation; head down and around the right side.
FA: Richard Harrison, Paul Van Betten 1990

GATEWAY CANYON

▲ THE GARBLED MASS
SW PM Sun   Approach: 20 minutes

Continue north past the Monkey Bar Boulder on the good trail. The trail drops down into the wash and into

Gateway Canyon. Follow the wash up the canyon for 5 minutes to a striking, varnished, south-facing wall, near the canyon's mouth on the right (north) side of the wash. The feature is 100 feet or so in height.

41. Old School 5.11b ★★★ Traditional. This route starts on the right side of the cliff. Climb the crack system that ascends a roof near the top. Good rock, protects well. Two pitches.
FA: Paul Van Betten, Dan Rider 1998

▲ THE COP CRAG
S All-day sun Approach: 25 minutes

The Cop Crag is so named because locals believed the routes were put up by metro cops. About 3 minutes past the main portion of the Garbled Mass is a light-red boulder on the skyline, right of the wash and south-facing. This cliff is also about 100 yards east of the Cannabis Crag. Approach the Cop Crag from directly below and slightly left (west). Reach the base by ascending a large, pink, third-class ledge system from the left. Routes are described from left to right.

42. Saltwater Taffy 5.10d ★★ Sport, 6 bolts. Start just right of a crack on a face.
FA: Unknown

43. Turkish Taffy 5.11b ★★★★ Sport, 6 bolts. Begin left of a low roof. Step off a boulder to the right and under the roof to clip the first bolt. Shares anchors with the previous route.
FA: Unknown

44. Chocolate Swirl 5.11a/b ★★★ Sport, 6 bolts. Start on a low-angle section of rock, right of the low roof and left of a large scoop. After clipping the second bolt, move right and up to anchors.
FA: Unknown

THE COP CRAG

to wash and
Gateway Canyon

45. Unknown 5.10b/c ★★★★ Sport, 6 bolts. Begin right of the large scoop. Finish on chain anchors.
FA: Unknown

▲ CANNABIS CRAG
S AM Sun   Approach: 30 minutes

Cannabis Crag is on the right, approximately 100 yards past the Cop Crag where the canyon begins to narrow. The wall is very large and characterized by a bright orange color and large, black water streaks. The crag extends to the left and chokes into the wash. Routes are described from left to right.

46. The Felon 5.11c ★ Sport, 4 bolts, black bolt hangers. This route is the leftmost one on the wall. It begins just right of a large varnished streak and left of two prominent water streaks (the next two

routes). Run-out to the anchor (open cold-shuts).
FA: Dan McQuade, Jim Greg 1993

47. Cavity Search 5.12c ★★ Sport, 7 bolts, black bolt hangers. Climb the leftmost of two large, black water streaks. Climb thin face and pockets to lower-angle rock and then to anchors.
FA: Dan McQuade 1993

48. The Fiend 5.12c ★ Sport, 7 bolts. Climb the rightmost black water streak.
FA: Dan McQuade, Jim Greg 1993

49. Synapse Collapse 5.11d ★★ Sport, 5 bolts, black bolt hangers. Begin at a left-angling crack and move straight up on a series of horizontal jugs over a small roof. Open cold-shut anchors.
FA: Dan McQuade, Jim Greg 1993

50. Cannabis 5.12a ★★★★ Sport, 5 bolts, black bolt hangers. Begin right of *Synapse Collapse* and left of another large, black water streak. The route pulls a small bulge going to the fourth bolt. Cold-shut anchors.
FA: Dan McQuade, Jim Greg 1993

51. KGB 5.12a ★★ Sport, 7 bolts. Climb to a ledge; clip the first bolt just below the ledge. Angle left for 2 bolts and then move up to finish.
FA: Dan McQuade, Jim Greg 1993

52. Freak Brothers 5.12c ★★★★ Sport, 8 bolts.

Start as for *KGB* sharing the first bolt, then climb straight up the wall.
FA: Paul Van Betten, Shelby Shelton 1994

53. One Man's Kokopelli is Another Man's Side Show Bob 5.12c ★★★ Sport, 6 bolts. Climb up a seam using 3 bolts to the right, and then head straight up the slopey face.
FA: Paul Van Betten, Richard Harrison, Michelle Locatelli 1993

54. Smokin' 5.12b ★ Sport, 4 bolts. This route is located up a large ramp that begins at the base of

Cannabis Crag

46. The Felon 5.11c
47. Cavity Search 5.12c
48. The Fiend 5.12c
49. Synapse Collapse 5.11d
50. Cannabis 5.12a

51. KGB 5.12a
52. Freak Brothers 5.12c
53. One Man's Kokopelli is Another
    Man's Side Show Bob 5.12c

54. Smokin' 5.12b
55. Good Friday 5.11b

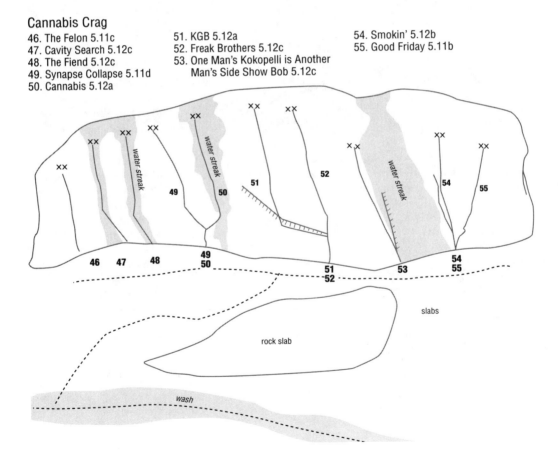

One Man's Kokopelli is Another Man's Side Show Bob. Ascend scary fifth class to get to the base, with a potential fall into a cat's claw bush. Yow! A stick clip is recommended for the first bolt. A large pink rock scar is located just up and right of the last bolt, where a huge rock fell and threatened the first-ascent party. Open cold-shut anchors.
FA: Unknown 1993

55. Good Friday 5.11b ★★★ Sport, 4 bolts. This route starts off the far right side of the cliff. It takes a separate line of bolts, but shares the first couple moves with *Smokin'*.
FA: Mike Moore 2003

The following routes are located on another crag, across the wash from the Cannabis Crag and about 75 yards up the south side of the wash, on the same level as the Winter Heat Wall. Look for a corner with a big, clean roof—this is *Horizontal Departure*.

56. Harshwidth 5.9 ★★ Traditional. Start left of *Horizontal Departure*. Somewhat difficult third-class scrambling is required to reach the base. Climb the clean off-width. Gear: to #4 Friend. Walk off.
FA: Paul Van Betten 1983/84

57. Horizontal Departure 5.10b ★★ Traditional. Climb the left-facing 25-foot corner that leads to a clean, horizontal roof. Walk off.
FA: Randy Marsh, Wendell Broussard, Pete Absolon 1984

GATEWAY CANYON NORTHWEST

Gateway Canyon narrows again as you head west past the Cannabis Crag. Hike through a canopy of scrub oak into an area where huge pink boulders block the wash. Hike up and right on the boulders and then through the wash on slippery rock. The wash continues to narrow and eventually some large boulders will block your way. Scramble up and over the boulders. Obtain a limestone boulder and continue through the narrow drainage. Pass several large red boulders lying in the white rock of the wash. When the wash opens back up, you will see a very large, black, varnished wall in the distance on the left (south). This is the Winter Heat Wall, which is north-facing. Slightly up the wash, on the right, is the south-facing Sunny and Steep Wall.

▲ WINTER HEAT WALL
N No Sun   Approach: 40 minutes

Winter Heat Wall is located up and left (south) about 100 feet out of the wash. The wall is a large, black-varnished face on the left (south) side of the canyon, facing north. This wall has a large, ramping chimney on the left edge and a distinct right-leaning hand crack on the right. Just below this crag is a short 10-foot outcropping of pink polka-dotted rock. Routes are described from left to right.

Descent: Rappel off one of the two sets of rappel anchors using a single rope, or descend the unnamed chimney.

58. Under the Reign of Swain 5.10d ★★★ Sport. Start 50 feet left of the obvious chimney. Climb the black, varnished face.
FA: Pier and Randy Marsh 1993

59. Judy's Route 5.10c/d ★★★ Sport. Start just right of *Under the Reign of Swain. Judy's Route* is named in the memory of Judy Nightingale. This was her hardest on-sight.
FA: Pier and Randy Marsh 1993

60. Unnamed 5.0 ★★ Traditional. This is the short chimney angling up and left, on the left side of the wall. Traditionally, this was the descent off the wall rather than a climb. Natural belay; rappel from a small tree at the top.
FA: Unknown

61. Mo Hotta, Mo Betta 5.8 R ★★★ Traditional. Begin at the start of the chimney. Follow a left-leaning ramp up, and move left to a face. Climb huecos and pockets to the top. Finish in a thin, vertical seam.
FA: Todd and Donette Swain 1994

62. Nuttin' Could be Finer 5.7 R ★★ Traditional. Begin the same as *Mo Hotta, Mo Betta*. After reaching the top of the ramp, go straight up the huecoed face to finish in the leftmost of two cracks on the face above.
FA: Bobby Knight, Todd and Donette Swain 1994

63. Couldn't be Schmooter 5.9 ★★★★ Traditional. Climb the obvious, nice-looking thin crack in the center of the wall, angling somewhat left at the start. At the top, take the rightmost crack of the two on the upper face. Gear: to #3.5 Friend.
FA: "The Dean" Wendell Broussard, Richard Harrison, Paul Crawford 1983

64. Autumnal Frost 5.11d ★★ Mixed, 1 bolt. Begin below a single bolt and a line of large pockets. Climb the technical face to a thin seam at the top of the cliff. This route is extremely reachy!
FA: Todd Swain (taller than 6 feet 3 inches) 1994

65. Winter Heat 5.11c ★★★ Traditional. Climb the obvious crack, angling somewhat left and up. When it reaches a large scoop feature, step right to an overhang. Discontinuous seams lead to the top of the cliff. Traverse up the ramp and right to cold-shut anchors.
FA: Paul Crawford, Jay Smith, Richard Harrison, Paul Van Betten 1983

TR variation: Vernal Thaw 5.11b Begin on *Winter Heat* and then traverse into *Seasonal Controversies*.
FA: Bobby Knight, Todd Swain 1994

66. Seasonal Controversies 5.11d R ★★★ Mixed, 3 bolts. Start at 2 bolts, 20 feet right of *Winter Heat*. Climb to the shared *Winter Heat* anchors. Gear: standard rack to #2.5 Friend.
FA: Bob Conz, Tony Yinger 2002

67. High Class Ho 5.10a ★★★★ Traditional.

Climb the obvious finger crack on the far right side of the wall. Upon reaching a ledge, traverse up and right along a scoop-shaped corner, angling up and left. Traverse either right or left to sets of cold-shut anchors.
FA: Richard Harrison, Paul Van Betten, Wendell Broussard 1983

68. Pimpin' da 5.11d ★★★ TR. Using the cold-shut anchors on the far right of the upper ramp; climb the bottom portion of *High Class Ho*. At the ledge, go straight up the face using thin seams.
FA: Pier and Randy Marsh 1993

69. Strip Tease 5.12a ★★★ Mixed, 4 bolts. Start as for *High Class Ho*, but go straight up and right at the overhang. Finish at a bolted anchor. Heady. Gear: standard rack to #3.5 Friend and brass wires.
FA: Bob Conz, Tony Yinger, Danny Rider 2002

70. Hole in My Pants 5.7 ★ Traditional. Climb lower-angled rock right of the Winter Heat Wall. Poor rock.
FA: Gary Savage

▲ SUNNY AND STEEP WALL
S All-Day Sun   Approach: 45 minutes

Continue heading up the wash (west), past the Winter Heat Wall. Sunny and Steep Wall is located just beyond it, 200 feet on the right and visible on the right side of the wash. Below the cliff, head to the left and walk up the slabs. Most of the anchors on this wall are large, glue-in eye bolts. Because Jeremy Wetter flashed all the routes in his La Sportiva Boulders we permitted him to downrate them. Routes are described from left to right.

71. Claim Jumper's Special 5.10a ★★★ Sport, 5 bolts. This is the wall's leftmost route. It climbs over a bulge into a small dihedral.
FA: Chris and Ward Smith 1994

72. Black Happy 5.11d ★ Sport, 5 bolts. Start 5 feet right of the previous route. Crimpy moves on in-cut edges.
FA: Chris and Ward Smith 1994

73. Blackened 5.11d ★ Sport, 5 bolts. Start right of *Black Happy*. Long crimpy moves on in-cut edges.
FA: Ward Smith 1994

74. Scorpions 5.11a ★★★ Sport, 5 bolts. Climb huecos up the chossy-looking overhang along the left crack to a crimpy crux.
FA: Chris and Ward Smith 1994

75. Turtle Wax 5.11b ★★★ Sport, 5 bolts. Climb huecos right of a crack and bolt line. Move right at the top to the anchors of *Sunny and Steep*.
FA: Dave Quinn 1994

76. Sunny and Steep 5.11d ★★★★ Sport, 6 bolts. The wall's namesake climbs steep rock to a roof and then continues up a steep face. Shared anchors with *Turtle Wax*.
FA: Ward Smith, Dave Quinn 1994

77. Tour de Pump 5.12b ★★★ Sport, 6 bolts. This is the first route left of the obvious chimney in the center of the wall. Reach moves take you over two roofs low on the route. Steep face-climbing takes you to the top.
FA: Ward Smith 1994

78. The Sport Chimney 5.8 ★★★★ Sport, 5 bolts. Squirm, wiggle, and giggle your way up the bolted chimney. Have any big bros?
FA: Steve Wood, Chris and Ward Smith 1994

79. Gimme Back My Bullets 5.12a ★★★ Sport, 6 bolts. This is the first route right of the chimney. When you lower off the anchors beware of the cactus at the base.
FA: Ward Smith 1994

80. Steep Thrills 5.12a ★★★ Sport, 6 bolts. Begin by pulling a low roof, then move up to another roof and take the steep face to the top.
FA: Ward Smith 1994

81. Turbo Dog 5.12d ★ Sport, 7 bolts. Begin below a low roof. Pull the roof and continue to the steep, stiff, fingery crux. Then face-climb to the top. Holds have broken on this route making it a bit harder since the FA.
FA: Ward Smith 1994

82. Peak Performance 5.11d ★ Sport, 7 bolts. Begin behind boulders. Climb the steep face right of the previous route, the one with a large hueco at its start. Pulling the lip of the hueco is scary because the boulder behind the route is very close and you do not want to hit it if you fall. Shares anchor with *Turbo Dog*.
FA: Dave Quinn, Chris and Ward Smith 1994

83. Solar Flare 5.11d ★ Sport, 6 bolts. Follow a left-leaning seam. Somewhat chossy and difficult.

FA: Chris and Ward Smith, Dave Quinn 1994

84. Mr. Choad's Wild Ride 5.11b ★★★★ Sport, 10 bolts. Begin on a shallow left-facing corner. Head up, then left, then back right to the shared anchor with *Cirque du Soleil*. A 60-meter rope is needed to lower off, or use the midway anchor.
FA: Ward Smith, Steve Wood 1994

85. Cirque du Soleil 5.11b ★★★★ Sport, 10 bolts. Begin stemming in the chimney and then move out on the face. Climb up a sort of ramp and end on a technical face. A 60-meter rope is needed to lower off, or use the midway anchor.
FA: Paula King, Steve Wood, Ward Smith 1994

86. Working for Peanuts 5.9 ★★ Sport, 5 bolts. Climb the arête just right of the large chimney that

separates this feature from the main wall. Difficult start.
FA: Ward Smith, Chris Smith, Dave Quinn 1994

▲ GOLDEN NUGGET BOULDER
SW All-Day Sun and SE AM Sun
Approach: 45 minutes

The Golden Nugget Boulder is the next major feature up the wash, located about 75 yards west of Sunny and Steep Wall. A free-standing yellow-colored boulder, sitting by itself, it is located on the right (north) side of the wash. (It is not the bright-yellow, self-standing plate far behind Sunny and Steep Wall.)

87. Edward Silverhands 5.10a ★ Sport, 3 bolts. This is the chossy route located on the southwest side of the boulder, on the right. Move up a short, left-leaning ramp. Climb a thin seam until it ends and then traverse right to another seam. At the top of the boulder step left to clip the cold-shut anchor.
FA: Todd and Donette Swain 1994

88. Golden Nugget 5.11d ★★ Sport, 4 bolts. This route is located on the southeast side of the boulder, on the far left side. Climb just right of the arête on the steep face. Glue-in bolts and anchors.
FA: Chris and Ward Smith 1994

▲ JUDGMENT DAY CRAG
N No Sun   Approach: 45 minutes

Reach this crag by hiking west, up the wash, 75 yards past the Sunny and Steep Wall. It is located directly across from the Golden Nugget Boulder. Take the gully left (south), up to an overhanging, rounded, ship's-prow arête. To the right (west) of this feature is a long varnished face with several cracks; a similar face with cracks is on the level below the upper face. Access the crag through the obvious gully/drainage left of the walls and directly below the ship's-prow feature.

89. Judgment Day 5.12a ★★★ Sport, 4 bolts, chain anchor. Climb the left arête of the ship's prow, located left of the crack that splits the feature. Devious sequence with sucker holds. Crimpy,

pumpy, and fairly run-out.
FA: Lynn Lee 1996

90. Play with Fire 5.11d ★★★ Sport, 4 bolts. Climb the right arête of the ship's prow. Finish on the face right of the arête. Tricky. Two-bolt rappel anchor with webbing.
FA: Lynn Lee 1996

The following two routes are located on the black, varnished faces right of the ship's-prow feature.

91. Unknown 5.10 ★ Mixed, 1 bolt. This route is located on the upper tier, on the face right of the ship's prow. Climb the varnished face below a bush and up a short, right-leaning ramp at the top of the cliff, right of a crack (incipient at its base). Walk off right.
FA: Unknown

92. Unknown 5.10d ★ Mixed, 1 bolt. This route is on the lower tier, directly below the previous route. Climb the crack on the varnished face. Walk off left or continue to the top of the previous route.
FA: Unknown

▲ CHUNDER BOLT WALL
S All-Day Sun   Approach: 50 minutes

This cliff is the next yellow, south-facing formation west of the Golden Nugget Boulder. It is located on the right (north), just as the wash opens up again and the rock begins to break down and recede upcanyon into gold sandstone.

93. Chunder Bolt 5.12a ★★★ Sport, 9 bolts. Follow a steep seam and huecoed face on the right side of the wall. The rock is not so good but the climbing is. Chain anchor.
FA: Shelby Shelton, Paul Van Betten, Danny Rider, Michelle Locatelli, Richard Harrison 1994

▲ ATMAN CRAG
Approach: 45–60 minutes

There are two ways to reach the Atman Crag:
   Approach option 1 : Rather than hiking via the

trail to Monkey Bar Boulder, go left (west) to skirt the left side of Kraft Mountain. Parallel the mountain and tend uphill to reach a pass that goes along the west end of Kraft Mountain to Gateway Canyon. Head up right (north) on a steep prominent trail to reach a saddle. Then head downhill toward Gateway Canyon and the wash. Atman Crag is located on the right, approximately 300 yards from the saddle. It is the last sizable formation, with four to five west-facing cracks on it.

Approach option 2 : Or you can continue west up the Gateway Canyon wash, after passing the Chunder Bolt Wall. A trail to the pass meets up with the wash on its south side, approximately 200 yards past the Chunder Bolt Wall, and heads up and left (southeast). Alternately, you can scramble third-class directly across from Chunder Bolt, heading southwest through a boulder field to reach the upper portion of the pass. Atman Crag is the large boulder on the left.

It is the first sizable formation out of the wash, with four to five west-facing cracks on it.

Routes are described from left to right.

Descent: Easy walk off on the boulder's south side.

EAST SIDE
E AM sun

94. Ying Yang Crack 5.11c ★★★★ Traditional. This is the obvious crack on the left side of the wall. Move up, traverse right for a distance, and then angle up and left to the top of the boulder. Gear: Friends to hand-sized.
FA: Unknown

95. Unnamed 5.3 ★★★ Traditional. Climb a chimney that splits the wall. Gear: bring a selection.
FA: Unknown

96. Atman 5.10a ★★★★ Traditional. This gorgeous hand crack (and fist, depending on your hand size) splits the right wall. Start off a large boulder, right of the chimney. Gear: #2–#3.5 Friends.
FA: Unknown

WEST SIDE
W PM sun

97. Unknown 5.7 ★★ Traditional. The hand crack on the left side of this face begins at a small roof.
FA: Unknown

98. Sport Wanker Extraordinaire 5.11d ★★★ Traditional. The obvious wide crack splits the middle of this face. Begin in a small alcove below boulders at the base. Hand-jam to an off-width roof. Loose at the top. Gear: wide; hand-sized to #6 Friend.
FA: Roxanna Brock 2000

The next two routes climb in a small, varnished alcove behind boulders, 10 feet right of the previous route.

99. Unknown 5.10c ★★ Traditional. Climb a short finger crack in a right-facing corner on the left of the alcove. Gear: small Friends and a #4 Friend for the top.
FA: Unknown

100. Unknown 5.9 ★ Traditional. This route is in the same alcove as the previous route. Climb the short, wide left-facing corner on the right of the alcove. Gear: big, to #5 Friend.
FA: Unknown

▲ MEYERS CRACKS
E AM Sun   Approach: 1 hour

Reach Meyers Cracks via the Monkey Bar Boulder or via the pass, as described for the Atman Crag. The area is at the far west end of Gateway Canyon, 500 yards west of Chunder Bolt Wall. Look for an east-facing crag on the north side of the canyon, with two prominent crack systems.
   Descent: Walk off.

101. Meyers Crack 5.10a ★★★ Traditional. Climb the crack on the left. Gear: to #3.5 Friend.
FA: Danny Meyers 1992

102. Conz Crack 5.10d ★★★ Traditional. Climb the right-hand crack with an off-width in the middle. Gear: to #5 Friend.
FA: Bob Conz 1992

THE FIRST PULLOUT (CALICO I)

FIRST PULLOUT EAST
Climb Bandits Area ▲ The Black Hole Wall ▲ Velvet Elvis Crag ▲ Climb Bomb Cliff
Universal City ▲ Cactus Massacre Wall ▲ Meat Puppets Wall ▲ The Bowling Ball Wall
Mark's Beginners Crag

FIRST PULLOUT NORTH
Circus Wall ▲ Dog Wall ▲ Fixx Cliff ▲ Tuna and Chips Wall ▲ The Oasis

FIRST PULLOUT WEST
Tiger Stripe Wall ▲ Panty Wall ▲ The Panty Prow ▲ The Great Red Roof Wall
Ultraman Wall ▲ Mark and Jake's Area ▲ New Castle Crag

TO REACH THE FIRST PULLOUT from Las Vegas, take West Charleston Boulevard west, which turns into State Route 159. Drive over the 215 Beltway and zero your odometer. Turn right into the Red Rock Canyon National Conservation Area, 5.9 miles past the 215 (2 miles past Calico Basin Road). Enter the 13-mile Scenic Drive through the kiosk entrance booth.

The First Pullout, as its name implies, is the first parking area on the Scenic Drive, located 1 mile from the entrance kiosk. There is a large paved parking lot.

FIRST PULLOUT EAST

To reach the areas on the east side of the First Pullout, follow the trail out of the parking lot that heads straight for the cliffs (north) and goes downhill. It angles slightly to the right (east) and dips into a wash. The yellowish wall on the left, emerging from the wash, is the Circus Wall. From the base of the trail, at the Circus Wall, hike up out of the wash, heading right (northeast) on a rock ramp. Shortly, the trail will dip into a saddle with large scrub oak. Move out of there, scrambling in the northeast direction. The first major wall on the left, approximately 50 yards from the saddle, is the Cactus Massacre Wall.

▲ CLIMB BANDITS AREA
SW All-Day Sun   Approach Time: 25 minutes

Continue past the Cactus Massacre Wall, heading east. Hike into and out of a gully. Upon reaching the second gully, go up it, heading left (northeast) about 100 yards (some scrambling required). The spot where the gully forks at a large boulder is where the following routes are located. Routes are described from left to right.

Descent: Descend a gully south of the wall.

1. Climb Bandits 5.10b ★★ Traditional. An obvious crack is located on the southwest side of the wall that splits the gully. The crack angles right, then traverses left at a bulge to climb seams and horizontals. Gear: small Rocks and Friends. Gear anchor. 40 feet.
FA: Paul Van Betten, Sal Mamusia 1989

Karrie Anderson climbing the tiger stripes on A Fraction of the Action *5.10a at the Tiger Stripe Wall*

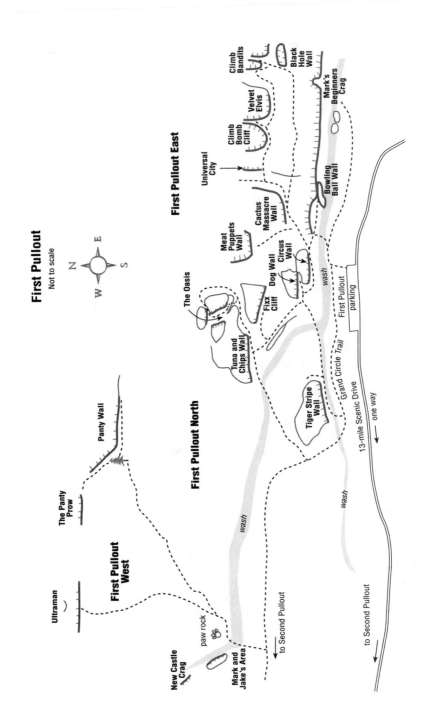

First Pullout

Not to scale

First Pullout East

First Pullout North

First Pullout West

Climb Bandits

Black Hole Wall

Velvet Elvis

Mark's Beginners Crag

Climb Bomb Cliff

Universal City

Bowling Ball Wall

Cactus Massacre Wall

Meat Puppets Wall

Circus Wall

Dog Wall

Fixx Cliff

The Oasis

wash

First Pullout parking

Tuna and Chips Wall

Grand Circle Trail

Tiger Stripe Wall

13-mile Scenic Drive

one way

Panty Wall

The Panty Prow

Ultraman

paw rock

New Castle Crag

Mark and Jake's Area

to Second Pullout

wash

wash

to Second Pullout

The large south-facing feature downgully and right (southeast) of the Climb Bandits Area is characterized by a large varnished face. The south face is characterized by a chossy pillar on the far-right side of a ramp on the south side.

2. Claw Hammer 5.9 ★★ Mixed, 1 bolt. Begin slightly left of the prow. Climb up and right to the prow, and clip the bolt (the bolt was hand-drilled using a claw hammer, giving the climb its name). Continue angling up and right on a steep face. 60 feet.
FA: Jim Lybarger 1989

3. Unknown 5.10 ★ Traditional. Begin just right of the prow. Climb varnished jugs to a right-leaning crack. 60 feet.
FA: Unknown

▲ THE BLACK HOLE WALL
S All-Day Sun   Approach: 20 minutes

Continue past the Cactus Massacre Wall, heading east. Hike into and out of a gully. Upon reaching the second gully, go straight east. The Black Hole Wall is on the left, a large, black, varnished wall. Getting to the base requires a bit of scrambling through a thin fin. Routes are described from left to right.

Descent: Walk off the backside of the wall. Take a gully behind it that leads you to a north-south gully. Hike south to reach the start of the routes.

4. Unknown 5.10 ★ Traditional. Climb the seam heading up and left to a large ledge on the left side of the wall. Traverse right on the ledge and over a bulge to reach the anchors of the next route, or climb to the top of the feature. 60 feet.
FA: Unknown

5. Unknown 5.10a ★★★ Sport, 8 bolts. Climb the varnished face just right of the seam.
FA: Unknown

6. Unknown 5.10 ★★ Mixed, 5 bolts. Climb the dark face 8 feet right of the previous route. There is a long distance between the fourth and fifth bolts where the angle eases. A crack begins the traditional section above the last bolt. Gear anchors. 60 feet.
FA: Unknown

The next route is on an upper tier to the right (southeast) of the previous route. From atop the boulder south of the previous routes, scramble easy fifth class to reach an even higher boulder where the next route starts (or, climb the chimney right of the rightmost route).

7. Unknown 5.10 ★★ Sport, 4 bolts. Climb the face to the top of the cliff. Gear anchors.
FA: Unknown.

▲ VELVET ELVIS CRAG
Approach: 25 minutes

Continue past the Cactus Massacre Wall, heading east. Hike into and out of a gully. Upon reaching the second gully head north, hiking uphill directly to the crag. The varnished west face is located in a thin corridor and orange sandstone makes up the right or south face. (This area is just west of Climb Bandits, across the gully). Routes are described from left to right.

WEST FACE
W No Sun

8. Black Tongue 5.11a ★★★★ Mixed, 2 bolts. Begin on the varnished face just right of a right-facing corner in some scrub oak bushes. Climb the face past 1 bolt into a shallow crack. Clip a bolt going through a bulge and continue to the top of the cliff. Gear anchor. Walk off left.
FA: Paul Van Betten, Sal Mamusia 1989

9. Unknown 5.11 ★ Sport, 5 bolts. Start about 10 feet right of the previous route. Climb past 2 bolts on a bulge and finish on the steep face up to the bolted anchors.
FA: Unknown

10. Isis 5.11a ★★ Mixed, 3 bolts, gear anchor. Begin just left of the arête and move right as it angles up to the top of the cliff. A hueco is just up and right of the first bolt. Climb thin seams and edges on a varnished face. The first-ascent party intended this route to go to the top of the cliff (where you can walk off left), but you can escape

to the chains of the route on the right.
FA: Sal Mamusia, Paul Van Betten 1989

SOUTH FACE
S All-Day Sun

This south face is orange and smoother than the west face.

Descent: Walk to the back of the formation and down the gully housing the west side routes.

11. Unknown 5.12 ★ Sport, 6 bolts. Climb the arête or prow on orange, slopey huecos.
FA: Unknown

12. Velvet Elvis 5.12a ★★ Mixed, 3 bolts. Climb the rightmost of two cracks on the face up to horizontal edges and bolts to the top. Chain anchor added since the first ascent.
FA: Paul Van Betten, Don Welsh 1988

▲ CLIMB BOMB CLIFF
S All-Day Sun   Approach: 25 minutes

Continue past the Cactus Massacre Wall, heading east. Hike into and out of a gully. Upon reaching the second gully, head north, hiking uphill directly toward the Velvet Elvis Crag. The first corridor south of the Velvet Elvis Crag takes you around the corner 30 feet to the Climb Bomb Cliff, located just left (west) of Velvet Elvis. The wall appears as a pedestal with a huge boulder sitting on top of it. Routes are described from left to right.

Descent: Walk to the back of the boulder and then west (emerging from the left side of the cliff).

13. Climb Machine 5.9 ★★ Traditional. Climb the crescent-shaped thin crack on the left side of this wall. Gear: small Rocks and Friends.
FA: Unknown

14. Climb Traveler 5.5 ★ Traditional. Climb the arête right of the previous route. Gear: small Friends, Rocks, and slings for the varnished plates.
FA: Todd Swain 1992

15. Climb Warp 5.11a ★★ Mixed, 1 bolt. Begin on

a right-facing crack above some large boulders. Climb to a break at the top of the pedestal. Pull over onto the crack and finish using 1 bolt to the top of the cliff. Bolted anchor.
FA: Paul Van Betten, Bob Finlay 1988

16. Climb Bomb 5.11d ★★★ Mixed, 2 bolts. Begin in a hand crack on the right side of the pedestal. Climb to a break. Clip a bolt, down and just left of a prominent hueco. Pull the roof, clip a bolt, and continue on a left-angling seam to the top. Bolted anchor.
FA: Paul Van Betten, Bob Finlay 1988

▲ UNIVERSAL CITY
W PM Sun   Approach: 20 minutes

Continue past the Cactus Massacre Wall, heading east. Hike into a gully, heading north, moving up through several scrub oak bushes. When the boulders in the gully get large, scramble out and right (east). Universal City is the bright orange, tall, steep cliff on your right, located about 100 yards upgully from the Cactus Massacre Wall. (Universal City is also just northwest of Climb Bomb.) The right side of the wall is smooth, black, and varnished. Routes are described from left to right.

17. Ed MacMayonnaise 5.8 ★ Traditional. Climb the obvious left-facing corner on the far left (north) side of the feature. It gets wide at the top. Bring larger Friends for the anchor and walk off left—or step right near the top and use the anchors of *Quiet on the Set*.
FA: Todd Swain 1992

18. Quiet on the Set 5.10c ★★ Sport, 5 bolts, black bolt hangers. This route climbs the smooth, pink, dimpled face just right of the corner.
FA: Louie Anderson, Bart Groendyke 1991

19. Star Search 5.11c ★★★ Sport, 6 bolts. Climb the thin seam 10 feet right of the previous route.
FA: Randy Faulk, Doug Henze 2001

20. Celebrity Roast 5.12b ★★ Sport, 7 bolts.

Climb the thin face right of *Star Search* crack.
FA: Leo Henson, Randy Faulk, Dan McQuade 1991

21. Cameo Appearance 5.11c ★★ Sport, 6 bolts. Begin above a scrub oak and to the right of the previous route.
FA: Randy Faulk 1991

22. Prime Ticket 5.11b ★★ Sport, 7 bolts. Begin just left of a wide crack. Climb over a bulge to a seam on steep terrain.
FA: Randy Faulk 1991

▲ CACTUS MASSACRE WALL
S PM Sun   Approach: 15 minutes

Follow the general directions for the First Pullout East area. Routes are described from left to right.

Descent: Exit off the east side of the wall and hike down the gully to the east of the main wall.

23. Cactus Massacre 5.11d ★★★ Mixed, 4 bolts. Climb the face up the middle of the wall through seams, edges, and slopers. Gear anchor.
FA: Paul Van Betten, Sal Mamusia, Mike Ward 1987

24. Cactus Root 5.11d ★ Mixed, 3 bolts. About 10 feet right of the previous route, climb the left-facing, left-diagonaling corner to a seam. At the top of the first seam, traverse right to reach another seam and follow it to the top of the cliff. Gear anchor.
FA: Paul Van Betten, Sal Mamusia, Jim Olson 1987

25. Cactus Head 5.9 ★★ Traditional. Climb a left-facing corner to a roof. Traverse right under the roof to a right-leaning crack, taking you up to the top of the right side of the cliff. Gear: everything from #3.5 to #5 Friend.
FA: Paul Van Betten, Don Welsh 1989

The following route is on the east face, around the corner from the right side of the wall, in a gully with many scrub oak; it may see early-morning sun.

26. Unknown 5.8 ★ Traditional. Climb an obvious crack heading up and right, beginning on the far

left (south) end of the wall. Gear: to #4 Friend.
FA: Unknown

▲ MEAT PUPPETS WALL
S All-Day Sun   Approach: 25 minutes

This is one of the most obvious features on this side
of the First Pullout, as its wide, varnished face rises
above many of the other features here. Hike left of the
Cactus Massacre Wall, heading northwest. Hike up the
gully, moving up through several scrub oak bushes.
When the boulders in the gully get large, scramble out
and left (west). Hike up and left until reaching the left
(west) side of a large varnished wall (100 yards west
of Cactus Massacre). All gear anchors. Routes are described from left to right.
  Descent: Reach the highest point of the formation. Walk down the slabs on the back west side.

27. Blanc Czech 5.11c ★★ Sport, 4 bolts. Begin on
the left (west) side of the wall, on the prow. Move
right and up after clipping the first bolt. Climb thin
edges and seams near the top.
FA: Nick Nordblom, Paul Van Betten 1989

28. Hodad 5.12a ★★ Mixed, 3 bolts. Begin on a
small ledge and move left to clip the first bolt.
Traverse right to clip the second. Finish on a seam
going to the top of the cliff.
FA: Paul Van Betten 1989

29. Crawdad 5.11d ★★★ Mixed, 3 bolts. Climb
the varnished face to a seam to the top.
FA: Paul Van Betten 1989

30. Yellow Dog 5.11a ★ Mixed, 1 bolt. Climb up
the face to a thin crack to finish. Gear: small, including brass wires.
FA: Paul Van Betten 1989

The next several routes start on a level a bit higher
than the previous few. Scramble on top of the large
boulder at the base of the crag.

31. Ranger Danger 5.10a ★★★ Traditional. This
route was named after the first ascensionists were
shot at by a car full of banditos, while exiting the loop
road. When the BLM rangers caught up, they drew
guns on all involved. The climbers were released,

while the others were shipped south of the border. The route is a very short crack, just right of the previous. Gear: takes good Rocks. 20 feet.
FA: Bob Conz, Mike Ward, Tom Ray 1989

32. Meat Puppet 5.11a ★★ Traditional. This is a thinner crack. Gear: small to medium Rocks. 30 feet.
FA: Paul Van Betten, Mike Ward, Sal Mamusia 1989

33. Gay Nazis for Christ 5.12a ★ Mixed, 2 bolts. Climbs thin seam using two bolts on the left side of the seam.
FA: Paul Van Betten 1989

34. Green Eagle 5.12a ★★ Mixed, 1 bolt. Climb another thin crack right of the previous route.
FA: Paul Van Betten 1989

35. The Max Flex 5.11c ★★★ Sport, 5 ring bolts. Climb the face just right of the previous route, on the far right side of the wall.
FA: Craig Reason 1989

▲ THE BOWLING BALL WALL
N No Sun   Approach: 10 minutes

From where you can see Circus Wall, hike downstream (east) in the wash about 50 yards. The Bowling Ball Wall faces north and is in a corridor where the wash pinches off. The black rock rises out of the wash here.

36. Take the Skinheads Bowling 5.12 ★ Mixed, 4 bolts. This thin crack climbs the middle of the north side of the boulder. Gear anchor. Walk off.
FA: Paul Van Betten 1988

▲ MARK'S BEGINNERS CRAG
S All-Day Sun   Approach: 10 minutes

Just before the main trail from the parking lot dips into the wash, take a trail branching right (east) that parallels the front cliffs. Hike downhill for about 100 yards. You will come to two very large boulders in the wash. Routes are described from left to right.
   Descent: Move left, across the ledge above the routes. Third class down and left on slabs and end up on the far left (west) side of the wall.

37. Unknown Boulder Route 5.9 ★ Mixed, 1 bolt. This route climbs the east face of the leftmost (west) boulder. One bolt is located near the top, just over a small bulge or roof. Gear anchors.
FA: Unknown

North of the boulders and slightly right (east) is a short 40-foot wall.

38. Unnamed Corner 5.6 ★★ Traditional. Climb the obvious left-facing corner on the far left (west) side of the wall. At the top of the corner, traverse left under the roof and build an anchor using small Friends in the roof, backed up with a #3 Friend in the corner to the left.
FA: Mark Limage

39. Unnamed 5.8 ★ TR. Climb a corner to a bolt, then traverse up and slightly right to the anchors below a bush.
   Variation: Climb the face directly below the anchors.
FA: Mark Limage

40. Unnamed 5.6 ★ TR. Climb the crack and face directly below the anchors in the middle of the wall. Several variations exist.
FA: Mark Limage

41. Unknown Chimney 5.6 ★★ TR. On the far-right side of this wall, and around the corner, is a thin chimney facing east.
FA: Unknown

FIRST PULLOUT NORTH

To reach the north section of the First Pullout, follow the trail out of the parking lot that heads straight north and goes downhill. After the trail dips into a wash the yellowish wall on the left, emerging from the wash, is the Circus Wall.

▲ CIRCUS WALL
S PM Sun   Approach Time: 10 minutes

Circus Wall is located on the same level as the wash and has a huge arch in its center. Routes are described from left to right.

Descent: There are gullies on both sides of the cliff. Walk down on the east or west, whichever is the closest to where you topped out.

42. Human Cannonball 5.9 ★ Mixed, 1 bolt. Start on the far left side of the wall. This route is right of a left-leaning ramp and just right of graffiti reading "Black Panthers Local." Climb over a bulge to a downward-sloping stance. Climb the face past 1 bolt and continue to the top of the ledge. Gear anchor.
FA: Kurt Maurer 1982

43. High Wire 5.9 ★★ Traditional. Climb the fin-ger crack 8 feet right of the previous route. It angles up and slightly right, ending just left of a short boulder/pillar-like feature.
FA: Unknown

44. Unknown 5.9+ ★★ Mixed, 2 bolts. Climb up 10 feet left of the water streak and directly in front of a small tree hugging the base of the cliff. Gear anchor.
FA: Unknown

45. Careful of Clowns 5.10 R ★★ Mixed, 2 bolts. This route climbs just left of a grey-and-white water streak in the center of the wall. Gear anchor.
FA: Unknown

46. Lion Tamer 5.11c R ★★★ Traditional. Begin in right-facing corner comprising the left edge of the arch. Climb up to where the crack breaks up and

NORTH SECTION OF FIRST PULLOUT FROM PARKING LOT

the rock of the arch melts into the rock under the arch. Climb over the arch feature to a vertical seam to the top.
FA: Unknown

47. Unknown 5.11c R ★ Traditional. Climb a face up to the point where the rock of the arch melts into the rock under the arch. Move slightly right and over the arch onto the face. Take a thin seam to the top. This route has 2 bolts, just above the arch, whose hangers have been removed (the reason for the R rating).
FA: Unknown

48. Circus Boy 5.11c ★★ Mixed, 2 bolts. Climb the face 5 feet right of the previous route, to the left edge of the highest point of the arch feature. Climb over the roof using 2 bolts and finish on the face above. This route was the first with bolts placed with a hammer drill in Red Rock Canyon. Gear anchor.
FA: Paul Van Betten, Sal Mamusia 1987

49. Main Attraction 5.12b ★★★ Mixed, 1 bolt. Climb the face below the center of the arch. Move over the arch, climbing slots to the top and the chain anchor. Gear: a large slot over the roof takes a #4 Friend.
FA: Paul Van Betten, Sal Mamusia 1987

50. Midway 5.12a ★★ Mixed, 3 bolts. Climb the seam left of the arch's right edge. Move out over the arch, clipping a bolt. Continue up onto the face, clipping two more bolts. Follow a seam to a 2-bolt rappel anchor.
FA: Paul Van Betten, Nick Nordblom 1987

51. Crowd Pleaser 5.12a ★★★ Mixed, 3 bolts. Begin just right of the base of the large arch. Climb a left-leaning crack to a large edge and a bolt. Take the crack as it angles up passing two more bolts. Continue, finishing just below a large boulder.
FA: Paul Van Betten, Sal Mamusia 1987

52. Elephant Man 5.11a ★★★ Mixed, 1 bolt. Begin just right of *Crowd Pleaser*, but angle up and right. Continue up the face, clipping a bolt. Finish at the top of *Crowd Pleaser*.
FA: Jay Smith, Paul Van Betten, Sal Mamusia 1987

53. Big Top 5.10c ★ Mixed, 1 bolt. Begin just right of the center of the small arch's roof. Climb the crack past 1 bolt to the face. Angle left at the top and finish the same as *Crowd Pleaser*.
FA: Jay Smith, Sal Mamusia 1987

54. Unknown 5.10a ★ Traditional. Climb the right-facing flake system 5 feet right of the previous route. Upon reaching the roof, move over it onto the face. Finish the same as the previous routes.
FA: Unknown

▲ DOG WALL
S All-Day Sun   Approach: 15 minutes

Follow the trail out of the parking lot north towards the cliffs and into the wash. Hike left (west) up the wash past the Circus Wall. Once reaching the left (west) edge of the Circus Wall, head right (north) up the canyon, up the rightmost gully. Dog Wall is the next distinct wall on the right (east), above the Circus Wall. Hike up and right, out of the drainage, at a large scrub oak tree. Routes are described from left to right.

Descent: Hike to the west end of the wall and take ledges downgully to the base.

55. Doggy Style 5.8 ★★★ Traditional. Climb the first shallow corner left of *Wok the Dog*. Follow the flake and ramp up to a shallow left-facing dihedral to the top. Walk off left.
FA: Scott Brainard, Kevin Frank, Chris Dabrowski 1998

56. Wok the Dog 5.7 ★★ Traditional. Climb the right-leaning ramp just right of *Doggy Style*.
FA: Todd Swain 1992

57. Cat Walk 5.10a ★★ Sport, 4 bolts. Begin on a right-leaning ramp and follow bolts to a chain anchor. High first bolt.
FA: Don Burroughs, Alan Busby 1992

58. It's a Bitch 5.10b ★★★ Sport, 4 bolts. Climb up a right-leaning ramp and start on the face about 5 feet right of *Cat Walk*. Climb up the face 4 bolts to chain anchors.
FA: Alan Busby, Don Burroughs 1992

59. Man's Best Friend 5.10c R ★ Traditional. Climb the right-leaning ramp, passing the starts of *Cat Walk* and *It's a Bitch*. Continue up the ramp and onto the run-out face to finish. Use anchors of *Here Kitty Kitty* or walk off left at the top.
FA: Todd Swain 1992

60. Here Kitty Kitty 5.11c ★★ Sport, 5 bolts. Start off a small rock fin, right of the ramp mentioned in *Man's Best Friend*. The fourth bolt is slightly off to the right.
FA: Geoff Weigand 1987

61. K-9 5.12b ★ Sport, 5 bolts. Begin off the right side of a small rock fin, 15 feet right of *Here Kitty Kitty*. Climb the face to the open cold-shut anchor.
FA: Geoff Weigand 1987

62. Cujo 5.11d ★★★ Sport, 5 bolts. Start 10 feet right of *K-9*, just left of another right-leaning ramp. Five bolts climb just right of a small seam.
FA: Geoff Weigand 1987

63. Poodle Chainsaw Massacre 5.11c ★★ Sport, 3 bolts. Begin directly right of *Cujo* on a seam above a right-leaning ramp.
FA: Randy Faulk, Karin Olson 1991

 FIXX CLIFF
S All-Day Sun   Approach: 20 minutes

Follow the trail out of the parking lot toward the cliffs, down into the wash. Hike left (west) up the wash, past the Circus Wall. Once you reach the left edge of the Circus Wall, go right (north) up the gully, staying in the rightmost branch. You will have to do some second- and third-class moves. Continue up the gully, past the Dog Wall (the distinct vertical wall above the Circus Wall), to where the wash opens up onto a ledge. The Fixx Cliff is the wall up and to the right (above or north of the Dog Wall). Many large boulders are scattered in a gully to the left of this wall. This area is characterized by tricky gear placements and run-outs. Gear: bring brass wires on all routes. Gear anchors for all. Routes are described from left to right.

Descent: Hike left (west) along the top of the cliff and then down the gully/drainage.

64. The Whiff 5.10a ★★ Traditional. Climb a thin seam to a hand and finger crack on the left edge of the cliff. Difficult to protect.
FA: Jay Smith, Mike Ward 1987

65. Snow Blind 5.11c R ★ Mixed, 1 bolt. Begin just left of a right-facing flake, below a small roof. Climb up and left using a series of huecos to a left leaning seam. Move up to a right facing, left angling scoop with big holds.
FA: Paul Crawford, Jay Smith, Nick Nordblom 1987

66. Stand or Fall 5.11a ★ Mixed, 1 bolt. Begin on a right-facing flake. Climb up huecos to a seam and clip a bolt. Move up a varnished crack and edges to a right-facing crack. Continue to the top.
FA: Paul Van Betten, Jim Lybarger 1987

67. Crack 5.11b ★★★ Traditional. Climb a varnished, thin, flared crack to a left-facing crack to the top.
FA: Paul Crawford, Jay Smith 1987

68. Free Base 5.12a ★★ Mixed, 3 bolts. Begin about 10 feet right of *Crack*, above a scrub oak bush. Climb a seam and ledges angling up and left. There is no hanger on the third bolt; overall, the bolts are not in the best condition. Gear: 3 #00, 1 #0, 1 #4 Friends, #5 and #6 Rocks.
FA: Paul Crawford, Paul Van Betten, Nick Nordblom, Jay Smith 1987

69. Saved by Zero 5.11b ★★★★ Traditional. This was the first route put up in the entire First Pullout area, before there was a pullout. Locals previously

Fixx Cliff

64. The Whiff 5.10a
65. Snow Blind 5.11c R
66. Stand or Fall 5.11a
67. Crack 5.11b
68. Free Base 5.12a
69. Saved by Zero 5.11b
70. Red Skies 5.11d

71. The Geezer 5.11c R
72. Cocaine Hotline 5.11b
73. Reach the Beach 5.11b
74. Eight Ball 5.11a

75. One Thing Leads to Another 5.11a
76. The Skag 5.11b
77. Running 5.11a
78. Outside the Envelope 5.11

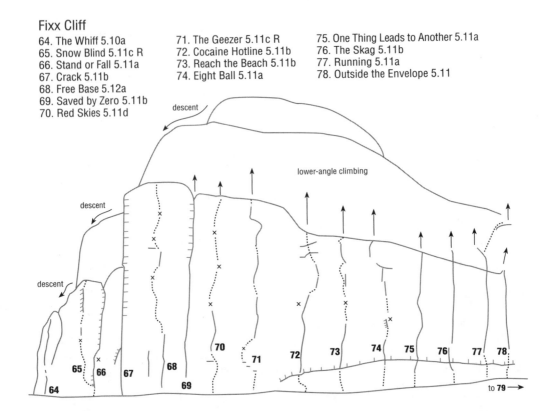

considered the area to be small and insignificant, thinking the rock was "dirt." Danny Meyers took Nick Nordblom to look at a crack he had spotted, not even bothering to take gear. After looking at it, they raced back to their vehicle and back again to send the route. Begin 10 feet right of *Free Base*. Climb the steep, varnished crack to the top. The classic on the wall.
FA: Nick Nordblom, Danny Meyers 1986

70. Red Skies 5.11d ★★★ Mixed, 3 bolts. Climb about 20 feet to the first piece of protection. Climb a thin seam to 3 bolts on a face. Gear: small Rocks and Friends.
FA: Paul Van Betten, Paul Crawford 1987

71. The Geezer 5.11c R ★ Traditional. Climb the smooth face to a drilled piton and continue up a thin seam. Gear: 2 each of #4, #5, and #6 RPs.
FA: Jay Smith, Paul Crawford 1987

72. Cocaine Hotline 5.11b ★★ Mixed, 1 bolt. Begin about 10 feet right of *The Geezer*, above a cat's claw bush. Climb the pink-striped face to a seam and then to a bolt. Move right to another seam. Climb lower-angled rock and varnished edges to the top.
FA: Paul Crawford, John Rosholt, Jay Smith 1987

73. Reach the Beach 5.11b ★★ Mixed, 1 bolt. Start on the face and seam left of a small varnished dish, 10 feet right of the previous route. Climb a seam to a bolt. Traverse slightly left to another seam and continue to a horizontal. Move right to a crack on lower-angle, varnished rock.

FA: Nick Nordblom, Jay Smith, Paul Crawford, Jenni Stone 1987

74. Eight Ball 5.11a ★★★ Mixed, 1 bolt. Climb the face to a thin seam, then to a shallow right-facing dihedral with a bolt. Move left and follow a seam to the varnished face to the top. Gear: 2 sets of brass wires; #0 and #1.5 Friend.
FA: Paul Crawford, Jay Smith 1987

75. One Thing Leads to Another 5.11a ★★
Traditional. Begin 10 feet right of *Eight Ball*. Climb the face to a thin varnished seam and continue to lower-angle rock near the top.
FA: Nick Nordblom, Jay Smith, Paul Crawford, Jenni Stone 1987

76. The Skag 5.11b ★ Traditional. Begins 15 feet right of the previous route. Climb a short, thin seam that widens as the angle lessens toward the top. 30 feet.
FA: Mike Ward, Paul Van Betten, Jay Smith, Paul Crawford 1987

77. Running 5.11a ★★ Traditional. Begin left of a varnished bulge. Climb a seam to a crack. 30 feet.
FA: Nick Nordblom, Jay Smith 1987

78. Outside the Envelope 5.11 ★ Traditional. Move up a short seam and edges to the top. 20 feet.
FA: Nick Nordblom, free solo 1987

79. The Bindle 5.11 ★ Traditional. This is a very short seam, with jugs where the angle changes.
FA: Jay Smith and gang, late 1980s

▲ TUNA AND CHIPS WALL
S All-Day Sun   Approach: 20 minutes

Tuna and Chips Wall is left (west) of the Fixx Cliff. You can follow directions to the Fixx Cliff, and then hike up and left (west and slightly north). Or, for an easier approach, hike down the main trail from the parking lot. Take the first trail left (west) off the main trail and follow it down a hill into a wash. As it comes out of this first wash and starts heading back uphill, a big pink slab will be on your right. This is the Tiger Stripe Wall. Take the trail around this wall and back uphill. At the top of the hill, leave the trail and head down and right (northeast) on slabs into the wash behind the Tiger Stripe Wall. Hug the south-facing wall on the left side of the wash for 100 yards. The Tuna and Chips Wall will be the obvious 150-foot wall on the left. Routes are described from left to right.

Descent: Hike and scramble right (east) until you drop down into the canyon (the Oasis area). Walk down, south and out of the canyon, veering right until the Tuna and Chips Wall appears on your right.

80. Unknown 5.8 ★★★ TR. Hike up the ramp on the left side of the wall to reach the top of a small pillar with a black-patina face. Set up anchors on the 2 bolts on top of the pillar. Use slings through the bolt hangers, as carabiners will hang on the cliff edge.
FA: Unknown

81. Dolphin Safe 5.7 R ★★★ Mixed, 5 bolts. Climb the face right of the pillar, just right of a right-facing corner. Gear: medium-sized cams to reach the first bolt. 100 feet.
FA: Mark Limage, Dave Melchoir, Derek Reinig 2000

82. Tuna and Chips 5.7 R ★★ Mixed, 3 bolts.
   Pitch 1: 5.7 R, sport, 3 bolts. Climb the face between *Dolphin Safe* and *Albacore Man*, past 3 bolts. Gear anchor 100 feet.
   Pitch 2: 5.3 Continue to the top of the cliff, climbing the obvious crack up the center.
FA: Bob Conz, Jim Lybarger 1987

83. Albacore Man 5.7 R ★★★★ Sport, 4 bolts. Start on the large boulder at the base of *Chips and Salsa*. Climb the face left of a small pillar to the first bolt. Continue up the face.
FA: Mark Limage, Gary Sanders 1999

84. Unnamed 5.7 ★★ TR. Start on *Albacore Man*. Climb straight up to the anchors right of the third bolt on *Albacore Man*. You can reach the anchors via

Albacore Man or Chips and Salsa.
FA: Mark Limage 2001

85. Chips and Salsa 5.3 ★★★★ Traditional.

Pitch 1: 5.3 Start in the chimney at the base of a large boulder. Follow a crack as it angles up and right into an alcove with 2 bolts and a drilled piton. Rappel from here or continue with pitch 2.

Pitch 1 variation: 5.5 Start on Albacore Man and climb to the top of a small pillar left of the Chips and Salsa chimney. Traverse right and finish on the pitch anchor of Chips and Salsa.

Pitch 2: 5.2 Continue up the crack to the top of the cliff.
FA: Unknown

86. Water Streak 5.8 R ★★★ Sport, 3 bolts. Climb the water streak up and left to the alcove and shared anchors of Chips and Salsa. There is a long run-out between the second and third bolts.
FA: Jim Kessler 1987

Variation: 5.10a Climb the water streak the entire way, never moving to the right or left on bigger holds.

87. Unnamed 5.7 ★★★ TR. Climb the face right of Water Streak to bolt anchors. You can reach the anchors via Chips and Salsa or Water Streak.
FA: Mark Limage 2001

88. Tuna Cookies 5.7 R ★★★ Mixed, 2 bolts. Begin right in a cluster of scrub oak trees.

Pitch 1: 5.7 R, 2 bolts. Move left on a sort-of ramp system to above the scrub oaks. The first bolt is about 40 feet off the ground, just above a varnished section. Continue on the face using small protection to one more bolt. Move up the crack, past the second bolt to the left edge of a large roof and build an anchor.

Pitch 2: 5.2 Climb the varnished face to the top.
FA: NOLS 1987

89. Chips Ahoy II, 5.9 R ★★★ Mixed. Begin just

left of a cluster of scrub oak bushes and some left-leaning cracks low on the wall.

Pitch 1: 5.8 R, 1 bolt. Use small obscure gear on the face to reach the first bolt. Bolted anchor. 100 feet.

Pitch 2: 5.9 Continue up the face to the roof. Climb through the roof, past 1 bolt, where the varnish meets the red-colored rock on a right-facing flake. Climb to the top of the cliff.

FA: Mike Ward, Paul Van Betten 1986

90. Unknown 5.5 ★ Traditional. Begin in a scrub oak cluster about 10 feet right of *Chips Ahoy*, above a Y in a scrub oak branch. Climb the most prominent left-angling crack on the left side of a low-angle trough on the rock face. Start moving left toward the top to the anchors on the first pitch of *Chips Ahoy*. 100 feet.

FA: Unknown

91. Unknown 5.3 ★ Traditional. Climb the sort-of trough a few feet right of the previous route. Climb it up to the Oasis ledge. Descend by hiking through the Oasis corridor and head right at your first opportunity. Continue per the *Tuna and Chips* descent.

FA: Unknown

▲ THE OASIS
Approach: 30 minutes

Three walls make up the Oasis, facing east, south, and west. Usually one of these is in the sun. This is a nice place to get away from the crowds. The routes are short, steep, and mostly good quality. Hike down the main trail from the parking lot. Take the first obvious trail heading left (west) off the main trail. Follow this trail down a hill into a wash. As it comes out of this first wash and starts heading back uphill, a big pink slab will be on the right. This is the Tiger Stripe Wall. Take the trail around this wall and back uphill. At the top of the hill, leave the trail and head down and right (east) on slabs into the wash behind the Tiger Stripe Wall. Hug the south-facing wall, following a trail. When the wash opens up, continue past the Tuna and Chips Wall on the left. Move into the drainage up and left (north/northeast), through some large boulders and scrub oak. From here, either veer left to where the drainage is closed off or veer

right and continue up the gully. The left variation requires a single, easy boulder move out of the drainage and then easy fourth- or fifth-class scrambling up and left on a slab to the Oasis platform. If this is too scary, continue up the gully, veering slightly left. Upon reaching an east-west ledge, take it west until it drops into the Oasis corridor. Routes are described from left to right.

ARUBA WALL
E AM Sun

92. Crack Bar 5.8 ★ Traditional. Climb the obvious right-leaning crack on the far-left edge of the wall. Rappel.

FA: Unknown

93. Casino 5.12a ★★★ Sport, 5 bolts. Climb the steep, varnished face.

FA: Brian McCray 1998

94. Mai Tai II, 5.12a ★★★ Sport, 5 bolts. Climb the steep, varnished face right of the previous route.

FA: Brian McCray 1998

95. Snack Crack 5.11d ★★★★ Sport, 4 bolts. Climb an overhanging crack to a steep face.

FA: Brian McCray 1998

96. The Warming 5.10d ★★★ Sport, 3 bolts. Climb a steep, huecoed start to an overhanging face.

FA: Brian McCray 1998

JAMAICA WALL
S All-Day Sun

Jamaica Wall is on a platform above the Aruba and Bermuda Walls.

97. Money 5.10d ★★★★ Sport, 3 bolts. Climb a very steep, southeast-facing wall on large slopers and jugs. 30 feet.

FA: Mike "Lunch Box Jackson" Lewis 1998

98. Insecure Delusions 5.12b ★★ Sport, 4 bolts. This is steeper than *Money*.

FA: Mike Lewis 1998

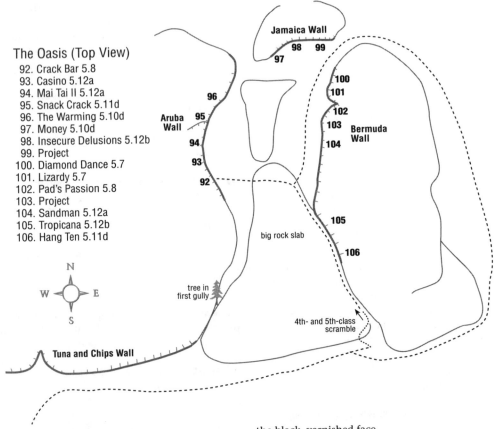

The Oasis (Top View)
92. Crack Bar 5.8
93. Casino 5.12a
94. Mai Tai II 5.12a
95. Snack Crack 5.11d
96. The Warming 5.10d
97. Money 5.10d
98. Insecure Delusions 5.12b
99. Project
100. Diamond Dance 5.7
101. Lizardy 5.7
102. Pad's Passion 5.8
103. Project
104. Sandman 5.12a
105. Tropicana 5.12b
106. Hang Ten 5.11d

99. Project One bolt is located 8 feet off the ground and right of the previous route.

BERMUDA WALL
W PM Sun

100. Diamond Dance 5.7 ★★★ Traditional. Climb a short hand crack angling up and then right. Finish on chain anchors left of the crack.
FA: Chris Lowry 1998

101. Lizardy 5.7 ★★ TR. Climb the face to the right of *Diamond Dance*.
FA: Elizabeth Craig 1998

102. Pad's Passion 5.8 ★★ Sport, 4 bolts. Climb

the black, varnished face.
FA: Tim Henkles 1998

103. Project Short route right of *Pad's Passion*.

104. Sandman 5.12a ★ Sport, 8 bolts. Climb steep, sandy rock to cold-shut anchors.
FA: Brian McCray 1998

105. Tropicana 5.12b ★★ Sport, 8 bolts. Climb steep rock to cold-shut anchors.
FA: Brian McCray 1998

106. Hang Ten 5.11d ★★★ Sport, 5 bolts. Climb a thin seam to a right-facing dihedral, then to cold-shut anchors.
FA: Brian McCray 1998

FIRST PULLOUT WEST

To reach the areas on the west side of the First Pull-out, follow the trail out of the parking lot that heads north, downhill and toward the cliffs. Take the first trail splitting off left (west)—this is the Grand Circle Trail (Second Pullout/Calico II) to the Second Pullout. It follows along the top of some short cliffs and then dips into a wash. The Tiger Stripe Wall is the first feature on your right after exiting the wash.

▲ TIGER STRIPE WALL
S PM Sun   Approach: 10 minutes

This big pink slab is the first feature you see on the west side of the First Pullout when looking north from the parking area. It is a lighter color, whitish or pinkish with stripes, than the rest of the rock. Routes are described from left to right.

107. White Tigers 5.10b ★★ Mixed, 4 bolts. Climb the dotted face 40 feet left of a distinct seam splitting the center of the wall. Cold-shut anchors. *FA: Dan McQuade, S. Fischbacher, R. Horn 1990*

108. Action by the Fraction 5.10b R ★★★ Mixed, 2 bolts. Climb the obvious seam splitting the center of the wall, 40 feet right of the previous route. Begin slightly left of the seam, left of a large scrub oak. Climb up to a bolt. Traverse right into the seam. Finish at the shared anchor with *A Fraction of the Action*, or top out and walk off left. Gear: small Friends, small and brass nuts. *FA: Danny Meyers, Jenni Stone 1984*

109. A Fraction of the Action 5.10a ★★★★ Sport, 8 bolts. Begin 25 feet right of the previous route. Climb 15 feet to the first bolt, above a right-leaning seam. Climb the face up and slightly left to

a ramp. Move over the ramp to steeper rock and the chain anchors. You may want to supplement the bolts with small gear.
FA: Paul Van Betten, Don Welsh 1988

110. Bengal 5.9+ ★★ Traditional. Climb the thin seam 10 feet right of the previous route, up to the beginning of a left-leaning ramp. Move straight up into a wide crack to the top of the formation. Walk off left.
FA: Paul Van Betten, Sal Mamusia 1988

111. Unknown 5.9 ★★ Mixed, 1 bolt. This short but fun little arête is located around the east corner of the south face. Gear anchor. 30 feet. Walk off.
FA: Unknown

▲ PANTY WALL
W and S PM Sun   Approach: 30 minutes

Panty Wall is a black, varnished wall on bright red sandstone that sits high on the horizon, west of and above the Tuna and Chips Wall. A large pine tree can be seen at the base. Take the trail around the Tiger Stripe Wall and back uphill along its west side. The trail curves to the left and then starts downhill again, paralleling the cliffs, heading west. Just before it goes uphill again there is a trail that splits off the main trail, heading right and down into the wash. If you look at the boulders just above and across the wash there is one slightly upstream with a black pawlike feature on it. Head down into the wash toward the paw (northwest). Take a right at the paw, hiking below it and northeast (right). Continue uphill on a huge red sandstone ramp until reaching the area below the Panty Wall. Scramble up to the base. Sometimes cairns mark the way. The left side of the Panty Wall is west-facing and begins in a gully left of the main south-facing wall. Routes are described from left to right.

WEST-FACING WALL

112. Totally Clips 5.11a ★★★ Sport, 6 bolts. The route is located on the far-left side of the Panty Wall, where the gully narrows. Begin off a left-leaning

ramp. Climb a left-facing flake to varnished edges to a chain anchor.
FA: Steve Bullock, Scott Carson 1990

113. Wedgie 5.12a ★★ Sport, 6 bolts, camouflaged hangers. Start off the right edge of a left-leaning ramp. Follow stair-stepping seams through horizontals to a bolted anchor. The angle lessens after the second bolt.
FA: Leo Henson, Albert Newman 1996

114. Viagra Falls 5.12a ★★ Sport, 6 bolts. Climb the bolted, blunt arête right of the previous route. You may want to supplement the bolts with Rocks in the 20 feet between the fifth and sixth bolts.
FA: Leo Henson, Albert Newman 1998

SOUTH-FACING WALL

Top rope set-up and descent: There is an easy fifth-class ramp between *Scanty Panty* and *Cover My Buttress*. Use it to reach the top of the cliff and set up top ropes. Use it to walk off the south face routes if desired.

115. Edible Panties 5.9 R/X ★★★ Traditional or TR. Begin 15 feet right of the previous route at a right-leaning crack. Follow the crack up and right. When the crack peters out, continue straight up the face to the top of the wall. Difficult transition from the crack to the face. Gear: smaller Rocks and Friends. Closely spaced bolts make up the anchor on the wall above the ledge, at the top of the route.
FA: Todd and Donette Swain 1994

116. Panty Raid 5.9+ ★★★★★ Traditional. Begin directly behind the pine tree. Climb the most obvious crack system up the center of the main Panty Wall, through the varnished face. A 2-bolt belay anchor exists about 15 feet back from the top of the route on the ledge, but it is difficult to use.

The *Edible Panties* anchor is better. Gear: small Rocks and Friends, one large Rock.
FA: Paul Van Betten, Nick Nordblom 1987

117. Panty Line 5.10a R ★★★ Traditional. Climb discontinuous crack systems up the right edge of the varnished face, about 5 feet right of *Panty Raid*. Use the *Panty Raid* anchors. Gear: standard rack plus extra-large stoppers.
FA: Nick Nordblom, Paul Van Betten 1987

118. Brief Encounter 5.8 ★★★★ Sport, 6 bolts. Just right of the previous route, start where the varnish meets red-colored rock. Climb up a series of discontinuous seams.
FA: Leo Henson, Albert Newman 1998

119. Sacred Undergarment Squeeze Job 5.8 ★★★ Sport, 6 bolts. Climb the bolted line right of the previous route.
FA: Mark Limage 2004

120. Boxer Rebellion 5.8 ★★★★ Sport, 7 bolts. Begin 20 feet right of the previous route on the varnished face. Climb to the red face.
FA: Leo Henson, Albert Newman 1996

121. Unknown 5.7+ ★★★ Sport, 6 bolts. Climb the face right of *Boxer Rebellion*.
FA: Unknown

122. Silk Panties 5.7 ★★ Sport, 5 bolts, black homemade bolt hangers. Begin 40 feet right of the previous route, on the face left of a scrub oak bush. Climb up to a seam and move right on loose blocks to three cold-shut anchors. You can also move left to the anchors of the previous route.
FA: Todd and Donette Swain 1994

123. Panty Loon 5.8 R/X ★ Traditional. Climb the face and seams just right of *Silk Panties*. Gear: small Rocks and Friends. Use the *Silk Panties* anchors.
FA: B. Binder, Em Holland 2001

124. Scanty Panty 5.5 X ★★ Traditional or TR from *Silk Panties* anchor. Start 5 feet right of *Silk*

Panties and just left of a scrub oak. Climb the face to a seam, then to the *Silk Panties* anchor.
FA: Todd and Donette Swain 1994

RIGHT SIDE
There is a break in the cliff after *Scanty Panty*.

Top rope set-up and descent: Right of *Thong* the cliff breaks down. You can reach the top of the previous four routes via this breakdown. Also use it to descend: walk off right.

125. Cover My Buttress 5.4 ★★ Traditional. Climb the left-facing open corner after the cliff break. Gear: large Friends toward the top. Two-bolt anchor.
FA: Todd Swain 1994

126. Butt Floss 5.10a ★ TR. Traditional. Begin 5 feet right of the previous route. Climb over a small roof to a seam to the top. Two-bolt belay anchor.
FA: Unknown

127. Thong 5.7 ★ Traditional. Begin 10 feet right of *Butt Floss* and climb the short crack. Two-bolt anchor.
FA: Todd Swain, Marion Parker 1994

128. Unknown 5.5 ★ Traditional. Climb the right-leaning ramp 10 feet right of *Thong* up to a left-leaning ramp and then to the *Cover My Buttress* anchors. Gear: nuts only.
FA: Unknown

▲ THE PANTY PROW
S PM Sun   Approach: 35 minutes

To reach the Panty Prow hike to the Panty Wall. Once you reach the Panty Wall, hike up the gully to its left, where the west-facing routes exist. You will pass a large 15-foot yucca bush on the left. The Panty Prow is the south-facing wall about 500 feet above the main Panty Wall ledge. All the routes on this wall share the bolted anchor at the top of the wall. Routes are described from left to right.

129. Panty Shield 5.10d R ★ Mixed, 4 bolts. Begin on the right-angling, right-facing, varnished crack

and seam on the left side of the wall. Long distance to the first bolt. Bring large Friends for the belay or traverse right to the bolted anchors at the top of the cliff. Descend by rappeling off bolted anchor or by walking left and down the gully on the left (west) side of the wall.
FA: Nick Nordblom 1987

130. Panty Mime 5.10c ★★★ Sport, 6 bolts, homemade bolt hangers. Climb the thin left-facing flake to the first bolt in orange rock. Just over a varnished bulge is the second bolt. Continue up the face, angling slightly right to the bolted anchor at the top of the wall. Difficult to see all the bolts from the ground.
FA: Todd and Donette Swain 1994

131. Victoria's Secret 5.10d ★★ TR. Top-rope the face between *Panty Mime* and *Panty Prow* off the bolted anchor at the top of the cliff. Several variations exist.
FA: Unknown

132. Panty Prow 5.6 ★★★ Sport, 5 bolts, homemade bolt hangers. Climb the stair-stepped arête up the right edge of the wall.
FA: Todd and Donette Swain 1994

133. Project 1 bolt. About 20 feet right of the Panty Prow wall, across the drainage, is a route with a single bolt. Left-facing shallow dihedral to discontinuous seams.

▲ THE GREAT RED ROOF WALL
SW PM Sun   Approach: 40 minutes

This cliff lies above the Panty Prow, at the top of the Panty Wall drainage. Hike to the Panty Prow, then continue up the difficult fifth-class drainage to its right (east). Or hike up the drainage to the left (west) and then hike over the top of the Panty Prow to the base of the large red roof.

134. The Great Red Roof A1 ★★ Climb the obvious crack going through the large, red roof, using aid-climbing techniques. Clean aid only needed. Fin-

ish out the face above the roof to a 2-bolt anchor.
FA: Paul Van Betten, Sal Mamusia, Nick Nordblom 1987

▲ ULTRAMAN WALL
S All-Day Sun   Approach: 20 minutes

Ultraman Wall is a very long orange slab with a smile-shaped ledge in its center with bushes on it. It sits high on the horizon, between the First and Second Pullouts. Take the trail around the Tiger Stripe Wall and back uphill along its west side. The trail curves to the left and then starts downhill again, paralleling the cliffs, heading west. Just before it goes uphill there is a trail that splits off the main trail, heading right and down into the wash. If you look at the boulders just above and across the wash there is one, located slightly upstream, with a black pawlike feature on it. Head down into the wash toward the paw (northwest). Take a right at the paw, hiking below it and then head straight north, moving uphill. Hike toward the left (west) side of the wall, taking the easiest route. (Note: You can reach the Panty Prow area from the Ultraman Wall. Traverse the bench east [right] past the dead tree right of *Teletubby Scandal*.)

Most of these routes are more than 100 feet in length. Routes are described from left to right.

135. Scent of an Ultraman 5.7 ★★ Sport, 7 bolts. Climb the face on the far-left edge of the wall, about 40 feet right of a blocky right-facing corner. The route climbs to a ledge with an overhang. A bolted anchor is located on the right side of the overhang. 110 feet. Walk off left or rappel and downclimb.
FA: Mark Limage, Hal Edwards 1999

136. Unknown 5.7 ★ TR. Top-rope by way of *Scent of an Ultraman*. Begin 10 feet right of the previous route on a right-angling seam and crack. Climb to a left-angling, slightly steep, left-facing crack.
FA: Mark Limage 1999

137. Clutch Cargo 5.7 ★★★ Sport, 7 bolts. Begin 40 feet right of the previous route at a short overhang and left-facing corner, above a rounded boulder.

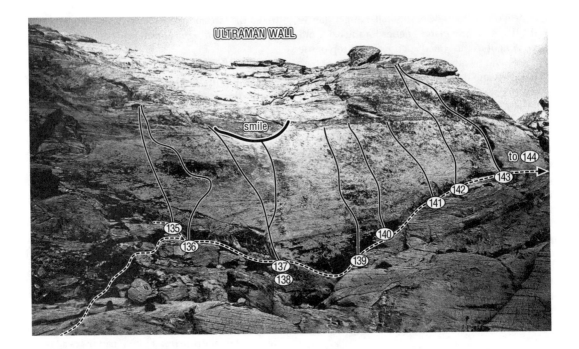

Climb up, angling left to the left edge of the crescent-shaped ledge to anchors.
FA: Dan McQuade, Pier Marsh 1996

138. Ultraman 5.8+ ★★★★ Sport, 7 bolts. Begin the same as the previous route. After clipping the first bolt (shared), angle up and right to the center of the crescent-shaped ledge atop the cliff.
FA: Scott Gordon, Jon Martinet 1977

139. Speed Racer 5.8+ ★★★★ Mixed, 8 bolts. From *Ultraman*, head downhill, scrambling over some boulders and across a very small ravine. Move up on a ledge about 10 feet right of the ravine. Begin at a small seam leading to a left-facing flake. Continue up the face to a bolted anchor. 150 feet.
FA: Ed Prochaska 1990

140. Godzilla 5.7 ★★ Mixed, 7 bolts. Begin on a seam 40 feet right of the previous route, just left of a small scrub oak bush, on a varnished face. The first bolt is about 10 feet off the ground.

Bolted anchor. 150 feet.
FA: Ed Prochaska 1990

141. Rodan 5.7+ X ★★ Traditional. About 50 feet right of the previous route is a slabby face leading up to a small roof. Under the roof, on varnished rock, is a bolted anchor. 100 feet.
FA: Unknown

142. Science Patrol 5.8 ★★★ Sport, 9 bolts. Located about 100 feet right of the previous route on the upper tier, this route is midway between *Ultraman* and the next route. Reach it by scrambling up some boulders, right of the previous routes. Begin just left of a boulder ledge and the beginning of a somewhat horizontal seam moving left, across the wall. Climb the face using homemade, angle-iron hangers to a 2-bolt anchor at the top of the cliff. You may want to supplement the bolts with small gear. This route has been retroed since the first ascent party did it with only 2–3 bolts. 160 feet.
FA: Jon Martinet, Nick Nordblom 1978

143. Unnamed 5.7 ★★★ Traditional. This large left-facing crack begins on the far-right side of the wall and about 100 feet right of the previous route, just above a large pine tree. Climb the crack to the top. Rappel off the anchors of *Science Patrol*. 160 feet.
FA: Nick Nordblom, Jon Martinet 1978

The next route is located on a large boulder about 150 feet right of the pine tree at the base of the Ultraman Wall and about 150 feet left of a dead tree.

144. Telletubby Scandal 5.11 ★★★ Sport, 4 bolts. The route climbs a smooth face on the boulder's right side, right of a big varnished bowl. Gear anchor. Walk off.
FA: J. Fallwell 1999

▲ MARK AND JAKE'S AREA
NE AM Sun   Approach: 15 minutes

This wall is located in the wash below and west of the Ultraman Wall. Take the trail around the Tiger Stripe Wall and back uphill along its west side. The trail curves to the left and then starts downhill again, paralleling the cliffs, heading west. Just before it goes uphill there is a trail that splits off the main trail, heading right and down into the wash. If you look at the boulders just above and across the wash there is one, located slightly upstream, with a black paw-like feature on it. Head into the wash and hike upstream (northwest). Pass the paw (on your right) and head into the narrow, dark canyon. Mark and Jake's Area will be on your left and faces northeast. Routes are listed from left to right.

145. Unnamed 5.9 ★ TR. Begin on the far-left side of the wall and climb up ledges to a bolted anchor on top of a ledge.
FA: Jake Burkey, Mark Limage 1999

146. Unnamed 5.9 ★ TR. Climb the obvious left-facing crack in the center of the wall to a bolted anchor painted black.
FA: Jake Burkey, Mark Limage 1999

147. Unnamed 5.9 ★ TR. Climb the seamy crack and face right of the previous route.
FA: Jake Burkey, Mark Limage 1999

▲ NEW CASTLE CRAG
NE AM Sun   Approach: 15 minutes

New Castle Crag is located farther up the canyon, 200 feet past Mark and Jake's Area, on the same side. This crag is essentially behind the Tsunami Wall (in the Second Pullout area). All routes have black-painted bolt hangers and chain anchors. Routes are listed from left to right.

148. Brown Ale 5.11c/d ★★★ Sport, 6 bolts. The leftmost route on the wall.
FA: Jay Foley, Kurt Arend 2001

149. Pale Ale 5.11b ★★★ Sport, 6 bolts. Climb the route right of *Brown Ale*.
FA: Jay Foley, Kurt Arend 2001

150. Guinness 5.11a ★★★ Sport, 6 bolts. Climb the route right of *Pale Ale*.
FA: Jay Foley, Kurt Arend 2001

151. Full Sail 5.10+ ★★★ Sport, 6 bolts. The rightmost route on the wall.
FA: Jay Foley, Kurt Arend 2001

THE SECOND PULLOUT (CALICO II)

SECOND PULLOUT EAST: RIGHT
Tsunami Wall ▲ California 5.12 ▲ Trundle Wall ▲ Iron Man Wall
Jane's Wall ▲ Truancy Cliff

SECOND PULLOUT EAST: LEFT
Rescue Wall ▲ The Arena

MIDDLE SECOND PULLOUT
Meister's Edge Area ▲ The Magic Bus

MIDDLE NORTH SECOND PULLOUT: EAST FORK
Kitty Crag ▲ The Sandbox ▲ Sun City ▲ Ethics Wall

MIDDLE NORTH SECOND PULLOUT: WEST FORK
The Black Corridor ▲ Hunter S. Thompson Dome ▲ Poser Crag
The Great Red Book Area ▲ Sweet Pain Wall ▲ Stone Wall

SECOND PULLOUT WEST
The Observatory ▲ The Gallery ▲ The Wall of Confusion
Resin Rose Area ▲ The B and W Wall

TO REACH THE SECOND PULLOUT from Las Vegas, take West Charleston Boulevard west, which turns into State Route 159. Drive over the 215 Beltway and zero your odometer. Turn right into the Red Rock Canyon National Conservation Area, 5.9 miles past the 215 (2 miles past Calico Basin Road). Enter the 13-mile Scenic Drive through the kiosk entrance booth.

The Second Pullout is the second parking area on the 13-mile Scenic Drive, located 1.6 miles from the entrance kiosk. There is a large paved parking lot there, with restrooms.

SECOND PULLOUT EAST: RIGHT

Take the trail downhill out of the parking lot. At the first fork, head right, taking the Calico I Trail and going farther downhill, toward the wash. At the next fork, stay right. Upon reaching the wash, head east, paralleling the wash on the right side. After about 100 yards the trail heads uphill. At the top of the hill, notice the huge, steep, blocky, south-facing Tsunami Wall (directly to the north). Hike down and right off

Bryan O'Keefe making it look easy on S.O.S. 5.13a, Tsunami Wall

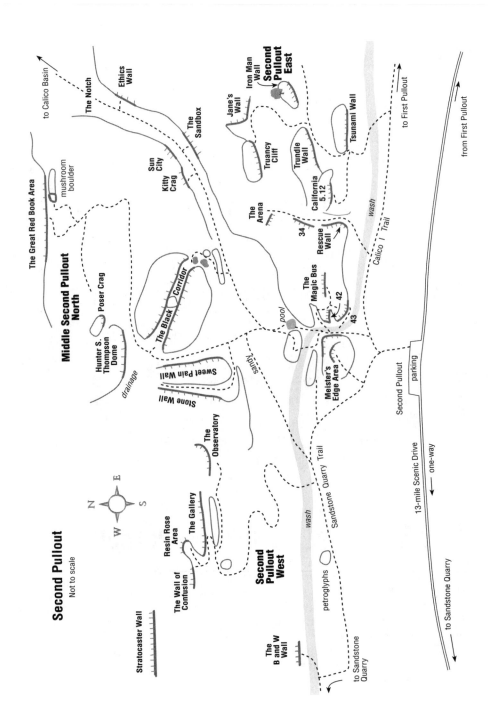

Second Pullout
Not to scale

Stratocaster Wall

The Wall of Confusion

Resin Rose Area

The Gallery

The Observatory

Sweet Pain Wall

Stone Wall

Second Pullout West

The B and W Wall

petroglyphs

wash

Sandstone Quarry Trail

to Sandstone Quarry

to Sandstone Quarry

Meister's Edge Area

pool

sandy

Middle Second Pullout North

Hunter S. Thompson Dome

Poser Crag

drainage

The Black Corridor

The Great Red Book Area

mushroom boulder

Kitty Crag

Sun City

The Sandbox

The Notch

Ethics Wall

to Calico Basin

The Arena

The Magic Bus

34

42

43

Rescue Wall

California 5.12

Truancy Cliff

Trundle Wall

Jane's Wall

Iron Man Wall

Second Pullout East

Tsunami Wall

to First Pullout

Calico I Trail

wash

Second Pullout parking

13-mile Scenic Drive

one-way

from First Pullout

N
E   W
S

the hill (if you are looking at the Tsunami Wall), onto slabs and into a wash. Hike upstream (west) 75 feet to the other side of the wash, obtaining slabs.

The routes on the east end of the Second Pullout can also be reached via the First Pullout. This includes Iron Man Wall, Jane's Wall, Truancy Cliff, Trundle Wall, and Tsunami Wall. To reach these areas from the First Pullout, follow the trail out of the parking lot that heads straight for the cliffs and downhill (north). Take the first trail splitting off to the left or west (Grand Circle Trail to the Second Pullout/Calico II). Follow this trail as it parallels the cliffs and eventually heads downhill at some red outcroppings. A trail splits off right here and goes into a wash (to Panty Wall, Ultraman Wall, and New Castle Crag). Do not take this trail. Follow the Grand Circle Trail as it goes uphill. Take the next trail that splits off to the right (north), heading down into a wash. Follow the Second Pullout directions from there.

▲ TSUNAMI WALL
S PM Sun   Approach: 15 minutes

Follow the directions for Second Pullout East. Hike right on the slabs to the base of the large, red, blocky-looking feature with a sharp, varnished south face. Tsunami Wall looks like a huge ocean wave, as the name suggests. Routes are described from left to right.

1. Poseidon Adventure 5.12b ★ Sport, 4 bolts. Climb the very steep, detached boulder, separated from the main wall and to its left.
FA: Chris Knuth, Leo Henson 1993

2. The Big Gulp 5.10d/11a ★ Traditional. Climb the crack located on the far-left side of the cliff. An overhanging hands, fist and slightly off-width gave even "The Bird" a run for his money. Short. Walk off left.

FA: Jim "The Bird" Bridwell, Jay Smith, Paul Crawford 1988

The following seven routes begin under a low roof and most of their first bolts are clipped under the roof.

3. Barracuda 5.13b ★★★★★ Sport, 5 bolts. Climb the seam that goes through a low roof and onto the steep face to chain anchors with carabiners.
FA: Chris Knuth 1993

The next three routes share the same start.

4. Land Shark 5.12b ★★ Sport, 6 bolts. Start under a low roof and move left after the second bolt to the anchor.
FA: Leo Henson 1992

5. Angler 5.12c ★★★ Sport, 5 bolts. Start as for *Land Shark*. Head straight up the wall after clipping

the third bolt to the anchors.
FA: Leo Henson 1992

6. Threadfin 5.12c ★★★★ Sport, 5 bolts. Start as for *Land Shark*, but head up and right to the anchor of *SOS*.
FA: Leo Henson 1992

7. SOS 5.13a ★★★ Sport, 5 bolts. Start 10 feet right of the previous route. Climb over the roof, move left to a horn, and then up a seam.
FA: Leo Henson 1992

8. Man Overboard 5.12d ★★★ Sport, 5 bolts. Begin 5 feet right of the previous route. Climb the steep face.
FA: Leo Henson 1992

9. Aftershock 5.12b ★★★ Sport, 5 bolts. Begin 5 feet right of the previous route. Climb the steep face.
FA: Leo Henson, Randy Faulk 1992

10. Abandon Ship 5.12a ★★★ Sport, 5 bolts. Begin 10 feet right of the previous route. Climb up and angle left to anchors.
FA: Leo Henson, Randy Faulk 1992

11. Women and Children First 5.6+ ★★ Traditional. Climb the dihedral right of the previous climb. Descend by walking right or east and heading down a ledge right of the next two routes.
FA: Todd and Donette Swain 1993

The following two routes are on the wall right of the main wall and face southwest.

12. Tremor 5.10b ★★★ Sport, 4 bolts. Begin 30 feet right of the main, steep Tsunami Wall. Climb the black, varnished plates.
FA: Leo and Karin Henson 1992

13. Low Tide 5.10b ★★ Sport, 4 bolts. Climb the varnished seam 20 feet right of the previous route.
FA: Leo and Karin Henson 1992

▲ CALIFORNIA 5.12
SW PM Sun   Approach: 20 minutes

California 5.12 is located about 100 yards northwest of the Tsunami Wall. Follow the Second Pullout East directions. From the left (west) edge of the Tsunami Wall, walk west up the wash. After a short distance, head north up a slab. Hike across the slab and back around west to the base of the cave. This route climbs out the center of a large cave near the back of this drainage.

14. California 5.12 5.12c ★★★★★ Sport, 6 bolts. Climb the crack and jugs out of a steep cave to anchors left of the crack.
FA: Unknown

▲ TRUNDLE WALL
S All-Day Sun   Approach: 25 minutes

Follow the Second Pullout East directions. Pass the left (west) edge of the Tsunami Wall. Hike and scramble another 100 yards north to the next cliff, arriving at its left (west) edge. Routes are described from left to right.

15. Before It's Time 5.12a ★★ Sport, 8 bolts, white-painted bolt hangers. Begin 10 feet right of a large, rotten, right-facing corner/chimney. Pull the roof after clipping the second bolt and head up the face to the anchor.
FA: Leo Henson 1994

16. Standing in the Shadows 5.12a ★★ Sport, 6 bolts, yellow-painted homemade bolt hangers. Begin 10 feet right of the previous route. Turn the roof after clipping the first bolt and head up to a right-facing corner. Climb edges to the top.
FA: Greg Mayer 1990

17. Master Beta 5.12d ★★★ Sport, 5 bolts, homemade bolt hangers. Located 5 feet right of the previous route. This route is characterized by a right-facing flake just above the first bolt.
FA: Scotty Gratton 1994

18. Pocket Rocket 5.11d ★★★★ Sport, 6 bolts. Begin 20 feet right of the previous route. Start at huecos. Climb right of an obvious groove up and into a hole above the groove, and out of the hole to anchors. The first two bolt hangers are homemade and painted yellow.
FA: Mike Tupper 1990

19. Life Out of Balance 5.11c ★★ Sport, 4 bolts. Begin just left of a large right-facing corner. Start by traversing left along a handrail and then up huecos and edges to the anchor left of a large hole.
FA: Greg Mayer, Mike Tupper 1990

20. Bone Machine 5.11c ★★★ Sport, 5 bolts. Begin 20 feet right of a large right-facing corner. Climb to fixed anchors.
FA: Danny Meyers, Scotty Gratton 1994

▲ IRON MAN WALL
S All-Day Sun   Approach: 25 minutes

The next rock climbing route is on the Iron Man Wall, the cliff lying directly east of the Trundle Wall. Hike over a small saddle and head downhill to the base of the wall.

21. Iron Man 5.10d ★ Mixed, 1 bolt. Climb the right-facing corner arch feature angling up and right, above a huecoed face. The crack separates red rock above from white rock below. Climb about two-thirds of the way to a roof. Clip the bolt over the roof and continue up, angling right to the top. Traverse back left to reach the top and a small pine tree. Bolted anchor. Hike off the backside.
FA: Jay Smith, Paul Van Betten 1983

▲ **JANE'S WALL**
S All-Day Sun   Approach: 25 minutes

Jane's Wall is the cliff above the Trundle Wall. Follow the Second Pullout East directions. Hike past the left edge of the Tsunami Wall, heading north. Hike and scramble another 100 yards north to the next cliff, the Trundle Wall. Hike right (east) toward a saddle. Before passing over the saddle move up a gully north (left). Do a short scramble and then hike left (west) at a large

scrub-oak outcropping. The large, black, varnished, rounded feature is Jane's Wall. The left side of the wall is steep, huecoed, and capped by a large overhang. Routes are described from left to right.

22. Every Mother's Nightmare 5.12b ★★★ Sport, 6 bolts. Begin at the mouth of a small corridor between the Truancy Cliff and Jane's Wall. Climb a low-angled, right-leaning ramp to a crack diagonaling left. Climb steep, dished overhangs up the left side of a blunt arête feature, right of the crack. Keep moving left through a series of roofs to a face and anchors.
FA: Greg Mayer 1990

23. Stealin' 5.12b ★★★ Sport, 5 bolts. Same start as the previous route. After reaching the fourth bolt, move right to clip the last bolt. Face-climb to the bolted anchors.
FA: Don Welsh 1991

24. Naked and Disfigured 5.12b ★★★★ Sport, 4 bolts. Start as for the previous routes. Upon reaching the blunt arête move right 5 feet. Climb through a scoop right of the arête. Move up and right, climbing steep rock on vertical edges. Runout to anchors.
FA: Don Welsh 1990

25. Pigs in Zen 5.12b ★★ Sport, 6 bolts. Begin 10 feet right of the previous route. Move up a left-leaning crack to clip the first bolt under a roof. Climb slopey huecos to a vertical, thin face to bolted anchors.
FA: Don Welsh 1990

26. Idiots Rule 5.11b ★★★ Sport, 6 bolts. Begin the same as *Pigs in Zen*. Move up low-angled rock and step right to some large huecos. Then move straight up to 1 cold-shut and a chain anchor.
FA: Don Welsh 1990

27. See Dick Fly 5.10d ★★★ Sport, 5 bolts, homemade bolt hangers. This route is about 25 feet to the right of *Idiots Rule*. Begin on a boulder at the wall's right edge, just left of an eyebrow-shaped roof two-thirds of the way up the wall. Climb low-angled rock to a vertical face. Bolted anchor.
FA: Greg Mayer 1991

▲ TRUANCY CLIFF
S All-Day Sun   Approach: 25 minutes

Follow the directions to Jane's Wall. The short crag left (west) of Jane's Wall is the Truancy Cliff. Routes are described from left to right.

28. Doctor's Orders 5.10b ★ Sport, 3 bolts. Start on the face right of a low, right-facing flake. Climb up 3 bolts and then move up and right to clip chain anchors.
FA: Greg Mayer 1990

29. Playing Hooky 5.10a ★ Sport, 3 bolts. Begin about 10 feet right of *Doctor's Orders*. Climb a right-facing, large scoop/shallow dihedral. Traverse left to clip the third bolt with a homemade hanger and

then climb up to the shared chain anchor with *Doctor's Orders*.
FA: Greg Mayer 1990

30. Ditch Day 5.7 ★ Traditional. Climb a short, varnished, huecoed, chossy face about 10 feet right of the previous route. Descend by walking to the back of the feature and then down the drainage between the Truancy Cliff and Jane's Wall.
FA: Unknown

SECOND PULLOUT EAST: LEFT

Take the trail downhill out of the parking lot. At the first fork, head right, taking the Calico I Trail and going farther downhill, toward the wash. At the next fork, go right (northeast), heading down into the wash. At the wash, head right (downstream and east) for about 100 yards to where the rock breaks down. Take the first narrow drainage heading left (north)—difficult to see from the main wash. Follow a faint trail.

▲ RESCUE WALL
E No Sun   Approach: 15 minutes

The Rescue Wall climbs out of the narrow drainage on the left (west) side. It is characterized by a sort-of mushroom-shaped section of rock on its top. The top of this feature is visible from the main wash. Routes are listed from left to right.

31. Airlift 5.11c ★★ Sport, 8 bolts. Begin on the left side of the wall, just as you walk into the thin corridor. Start off blocks above a cat's claw bush and just below a small scrub-oak grove. The first bolt is on a face below and left of a left-facing flake system. Move up and right onto the main face. Climb the left side of the face through various horizontal seams. Pull the overhang at the top and move right to clip one cold-shut anchor (there is also a bolt stud at the anchor point).
FA: Randy Faulk, Bart Groendyke 1992

32. Jaws of Life 5.12a ★★★ Sport, 7 bolts. Start 20 feet right of *Airlift*, below a small roof. Pull the roof and climb the face through a series of horizontal seams. Climb through the overhang at the top and clip the shared *Airlift* anchor.
FA: Leo Henson 1998

33. 911 5.11d ★★ Sport, 6 bolts. Climb the right-facing flake on the right side of the wall, just left of a small drainage. Continue up the face through horizontal seams, over the overhang, to anchors.
FA: Randy Faulk, Bart Groendyke 1992

This wall is located 100 yards up the drainage from the Rescue Wall. It is a steep, chossy-looking wall on the left (west). It faces east and gets morning sun.

34. Unknown ★★ Sport, 6 bolts, brown-painted bolt hangers. Begin on the far left side of this wall (south end). The first bolt is located about 20 feet up. Climb large huecos up the steep overhang to the black chain anchors at the top of the cliff.
FA: Unknown

▲ THE ARENA
NE AM Sun   Approach: 25 minutes

Follow the directions to the Rescue Wall. The Arena is up the drainage from the previous route another 100 yards. A very large boulder is located at the top of the drainage, on the left. Hike up the drainage until you reach some large boulders. Traverse slightly right (east) and then back left (west) to a corner under a huge roof. Continue up another 100 feet to reach the following routes on a steep, huecoed, dark red face. Routes are described from left to right.

35. Shadow Warrior 5.12d ★★ Sport, 6 bolts. Begin on the left side of the wall. Start on large huecos, left of a right-facing edge. Move up slopey huecos to the third bolt. Traverse right to a big edge and continue up a very thin face to the anchor.
FA: Leo Henson 1994

36. Gladiator 5.12c ★ Sport, 5 bolts. Begin about 10 feet right of the previous route, at a shallow, left-facing

dihedral. Climb the thin face up three bolts to where the route links in and finishes on *Shadow Warrior*.
FA: Leo Henson 1994

MIDDLE SECOND PULLOUT

Take the trail downhill out of the parking lot. At the first fork, head right, taking the Calico I Trail and going farther downhill, toward a wash. At the next fork take a left, heading northwest into a canyon on a red-dirt trail, parallel to the wash, on its left side. You will pass several large, red, huecoed boulders and walls on your left (west). Just past these is a section of deep red sand that skirts several boulders.

▲ MEISTER'S EDGE AREA
Approach: 5 minutes

After passing the sandy section, skirting several boulders, you will be able to see *Meister's Edge*, the prominent arête on the left behind a huge boulder. Most of the rest of the routes in this area are located right of *Meister's Edge* on the north face of this wall. Routes are described from left to right.

   Top-rope set-up and descent: Access the top of the *Meister's Edge* formation via its far-west edge. To descend, traverse west on the formation's upper tier. Prepare to do a little scrambling. Make sure you hike all the way to the far-west edge before going down.

37. Meister's Edge 5.11a ★★★ Sport, 3 bolts. Climb the striking arête that points northeast (gets morning sun). Finally there's an anchor!
FA: Eric Charlton 1988 (originally top-roped by Paul Van Betten, Sal Mamusia, Richard Harrison 1986)

38. Sandman 5.11c ★ TR. Top-rope from the top of *Meister's Edge*. *Sandman* is the obvious, steep, huecoed face 40 feet right of *Meister's Edge*. It faces north and gets no sun.
FA: Paul Van Betten 1987

39. Johnny Rotten 5.11a ★★ Traditional. This route climbs the obvious crack up the center of the

north-facing section of the *Meister's Edge* wall, emerging directly out of the east-west wash. Follow the flaring, wide crack with a thin seam in the back as it moves up and angles right into a large scoop halfway up the wall. Gear: to #3.5 Friend.
FA: Paul Van Betten, Sal Mamusia 1986

40. Jonny Jamcrack 5.8 ★ Traditional. Walk right of *Johnny Rotten* about 75 feet to where the formation starts to break down. Follow the left-leaning hand crack, located just left of a chimney, up to a ledge. Take a left-leaning seam to a low-angled face that leads to the top. Gear: to #5 Friend.
FA: Sal Mamusia, Paul Van Betten, free solo 1986

41. Yucca 5.11d ★ TR. This route is located just above and about 20 feet right of the top of *Jonny Jamcrack*. Set up the top rope from the top of the formation, just off the trail heading to the Gallery. Not-so-good rock; climb large huecos to the top of the cliff.
FA: Paul Van Betten 1987

The next two routes are located across the main (north-south) wash from the *Meister's Edge* formation. Before reaching the *Meister's Edge* arête, head right (east) and down into the wash.

Descent: Traverse left from the top of the formation to the gully after *Malice Alice*. Descend this second gully back west to the main wash. (This descent gully is also the hike up to the Magic Bus area.)

42. Shut Up and Dance 5.10c ★★★ Mixed, 2 bolts. This route climbs directly out of the wash on a slabby, west-facing wall. It gets afternoon sun. Clip the first bolt just over a small roof, 20 feet up. Clip the second bolt on the face about 20 feet above the first. Move up to an undercling. Climb thin seams to a crack up and left to the top. Bolted anchor.
FA: Danny Meyers 1985

43. Malice Alice 5.9 ★★ Traditional. This route is just past *Shut Up and Dance* (heading north), in the first east-west corridor/gully. Hike up the corridor

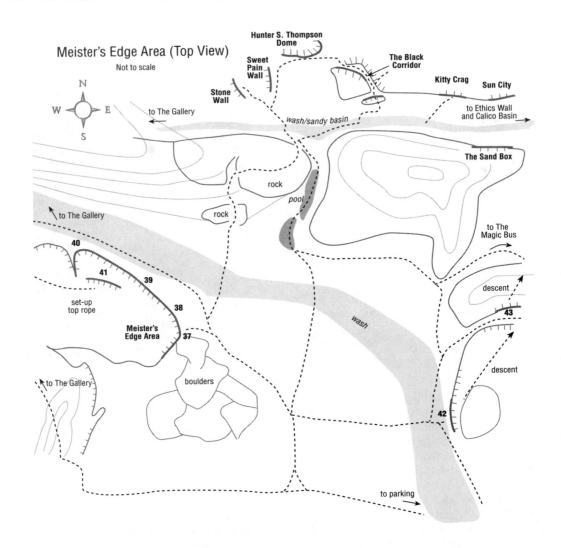

100 feet. The route climbs the north face, just right of a dead tree. Climb up and over two small roofs. Gear: small to midsized Rocks, #00–#1 Friend.
FA: Sean Ward, Chuck Carlson 1996

▲ THE MAGIC BUS
S All-Day Sun   Approach: 20 minutes

This feature is an enormous red boulder visible north of the parking lot at about the one o'clock position.

Follow the Middle Second Pullout directions. After passing the sandy section, skirt several boulders and dip into the wash. Hike up the second and larger gully on the right (the descent gully for *Shut Up and Dance* and *Malice Alice*), below a prominent arête with three large huecos on its right side (the arête is at the top of the gully). Go right at the base of the arête along a thin trail between scrub oak and rock. Take a red-dirt trail, meandering up into a small east-west corridor. Hike up the rock ramp in the corridor to a ledge. Cross over a gap between the ledge and a rock ledge below. Head east, crossing some boulders to a large flat rock section, then head northeast. Approach the Magic Bus from the right side. Routes are described from left to right.

44. Electric Kool-Aid 5.10a ★★ Sport, 5 bolts. Begin on the far-left side of the wall. Climb the bolted face, angling up and right to the anchors of *Blonde Dwarf*.
FA: Unknown

45. Blonde Dwarf 5.10a ★★ Mixed, 2 bolts. Climb the crack beginning 5 feet right of the previous route. Move up and right to a varnished dish. Climb left out of dish, clipping 2 bolts, to anchors. There were originally no bolts on this route.
FA: Nick Nordblom, Paul Van Betten 1988

46. Neon Sunset 5.8 ★★★★★ Sport, 9 bolts. Begin 15 feet right of the start of *Blonde Dwarf*. Climb up the face in the center of the wall.

FA: Kevin Pogue, Craig Dodson 1993

47. Zipperhead 5.8 ★ Mixed, 2 bolts. Begin in a varnished, thin, vertical crack 10 feet right of the previous route. Climb the crack and then move right to climb a thin seam up to a varnished face and a bolt. Move up and left to clip the last bolt and anchors of *Neon Sunset*. There were originally no bolts on this route. Gear: no large gear needed.
FA: Paul Van Betten, Nick Nordblom 1988

48. Technicolor Sunrise 5.8 ★ Sport, 5 bolts. Begin 5 feet right of the previous route on a varnished face just left of a right-facing corner. Angle up and right to bolted anchors.
FA: Todd and Donette Swain 1993

49. Ken Queasy 5.8 R ★ Mixed, 3 bolts. Climb through a steep, varnished crack beginning 15 feet right of the previous route and just left of the wall's right edge. Clip the first bolt at the top of the crack,

20 feet up. Continue up the varnished face, angling left to another bolt and anchors.

FA: Todd and Donette Swain 1993

MIDDLE NORTH SECOND PULLOUT: EAST FORK

Take the trail downhill out of the parking lot. At the first fork, head right, taking the Calico I Trail and going farther downhill, toward a wash. At the next fork take a left, heading northwest into a canyon on a red-dirt trail, parallel to the wash, on its left side. You will pass several large, red, huecoed walls on your left (west). After passing a sandy section, skirting several boulders, you will be able to see *Meister's Edge*, the prominent arête on the left behind a huge boulder. Pass the arête and continue, crossing an east-west wash onto another rock formation. Move up left (northwest), passing scrub oak and hiking alongside an overhang. Upon reaching an upper tier, go right (east) hugging a short buttress. Angle around left to face north and a big, sandy, flat, east-west basin. Hike down into the large, sandy wash.

The east fork of the wash holds the Kitty Crag, Sun City, the Sandbox, and the Ethics Wall. Hike right (northeast) up the drainage. After about 50 feet of hiking the boulders get large. Move up and right onto a ledge system paralleling the wash. Shortly, drop back down into the wash through scrub oak and more boulders. The trail heads back to the left side of the wash and drops down to a sandy low point.

▲ KITTY CRAG
SW PM Sun   Approach: 15 minutes

Kitty Crag is located on the left side of the wash at the low, sandy point, just past an etching of an angel on a boulder along the trail. The crag has a smooth, black-streaked face that creates a large, right-facing flake system, comprising the leftmost route on the wall. All the routes begin off a pillar on the left side of the wall. Routes are described from left to right.

50. Suffering Cats 5.11c ★★★ Sport, 6 bolts. On

the left side of the wall, climb the crack that angles up and left. After the third bolt, do some thin moves right and then continue straight up the edgy face to bolted anchors.

FA: Pier and Randy Marsh 1992

51. Titty Litter 5.10d ★★★★ Sport, 5 bolts. Climb the right-facing flake just right of the previous route.

FA: Pier and Randy Marsh 1992

52. Nine Lives 5.11d ★★★ Sport, 5 bolts. Climb the right-facing, discontinuous flake system just right of the previous route. Move right to the crack and then angle up and left on varnished edges to the anchors of *Titty Litter*.

FA: Leo and Karin Henson 1994

53. Gatito Tieso 5.12a ★★★ Sport, 5 bolts. Start 15 feet right of the previous route, just below some underclings. Move up using tiny edges. Richard Harrison and his daughter Lisa equipped the route.

FA: Jason Butts 2004

▲ THE SANDBOX
N No Sun   Approach: 25 minutes

Follow directions to the Middle North Second Pullout areas. Across the wash from Kitty Crag, and up about 100 yards, where the trail crosses back to the right side of the gully, is the north-facing and very steep Sandbox. This wall is dubbed the Sandbox for good reason: beware of loose rock and sandy holds. The climbing is bouldery. Routes are described from left to right.

54. Project This is the leftmost unfinished bolted line.

55. Public Enemy 5.13a ★★ Sport, 7 bolts. Begin at the huge, oblong hueco located on the far-left end of the crag. Finish up the black streak on the headwall.

FA: Mike Moore 2003

56. Flavor Flav (project) ★★ Sport, 7 bolts. This is the third bolted route from the left end of the crag. This route shares the same first couple moves with *Public Enemy*. Bouldery climbing up the steep wall leads to a difficult throw. Finish up the thin vertical face.

57. Rubber Biscuit 5.13a ★★ Sport, 7 bolts. Begin at a large knob on light-colored, steep rock. Move up steep huecos. Difficult moves to get over a steep section onto a vertical, thin face.
FA: Leo Henson 1997

58. Mr. Yuck 5.12c ★ Sport, 7 bolts. Start in the black bulge with huecos. Climb up slightly left, through chossy rock to a good headwall.
FA: Mike Moore 2003

59. Crimson Crimp 5.12b ★★★ Sport, 6 bolts. Begin a few feet right of the previous route. Climb huecos to thin face moves.
FA: Leo Henson 1997

60. Samadhi 5.11d ★★★ Sport, 6 bolts. Climb up 100 feet right of the previous route at a big hole. The anchor is left of a huge hole at the top of the wall.
FA: Jaret Hunter 2003

61. Sand Boxing 5.12c ★★ Sport, 6 bolts. Begin about 60 feet right of the previous route, past a large hole at the top of the cliff, at a bulge. You may want to stick-clip the first bolt. Move up a steep varnished face on overhanging jugs. Try to avoid the large, loose pancake flake left of the second bolt. Continue up and left to a thin face and finish on the slab to anchors. Long moves.
FA: Leo Henson 1997

62. Sandblaster 5.12b ★★★ Sport, 7 bolts. Begin 5 feet right of the previous route, just right of a scrub-oak bush in a black, huecoed groove. Move up and left on steep rock to a right-leaning, right-facing crack. Climb this feature and finish on the face.
FA: Leo Henson 1997

63. Sand Rail 5.12b ★ Sport, 6 bolts. Begin on a steep section where the first bolt is close to the ground. Move up large huecos to a sloping ledge.

The Sand Box

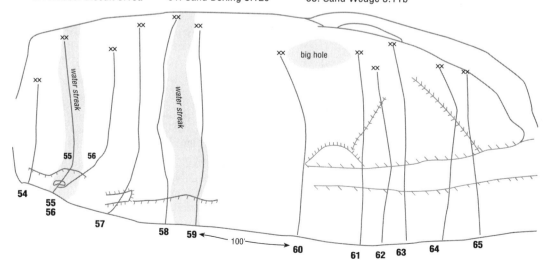

Move left, up a right-facing, left-leaning corner. Finish on the slab.
FA: Leo Henson 1997

64. Sand Buckets 5.11b ★★★ Sport, 6 bolts. Begin 10 feet right of the previous route, above a low overhang. Move up the varnished face past 2 bolts to a large horizontal. Continue up a seam, to the steepening, huecoed face. Link up with a left-leaning seam and then step right to clip the anchors.
FA: Leo and Karin Henson 1997

65. Sand Wedge 5.11b ★★ Sport, 5 bolts. Start on black streaks at the right edge of the wall above a small scrub-oak bush. Stick-clipping the first bolt is recommended. Climb up the face and horizontals to a left-leaning crack. Move up right of the crack on huecos to chain anchors.
FA: Leo and Karin Henson 1997

▲ SUN CITY
S All-Day Sun   Approach: 25 minutes

Follow directions to the Middle North Second Pullout areas. This route is on the 300-foot, south-facing slab directly across the wash from the middle portion of the Sandbox.

66. Retirement Plan 5.7 ★★ Mixed. So named because one of the first ascensionists was over sixty! Start behind a stack of boulders, 50 feet right of a right-facing corner and large water streak. Gear: standard rack to #2.5 Friend. Two ropes needed to rappel the route.
  Pitch 1: 5.7, 4 bolts. Head up and left to a left-facing flake. Move up to a small crescent feature and then straight up the wall to belay at a horizontal. 160 feet.
  Pitch 2: 5.7, 2 bolts. Continue up the face passing 2 bolts, finishing on a right-facing crack. 125 feet.
FA: Gary Sanders, Mark Limage 1998/99

▲ ETHICS WALL
N No Sun   Approach: 35 minutes

Follow directions to the Middle North Second Pull-

out areas. At the top of the wash is the north-facing Ethics Wall, at a saddle between this area and Calico Basin ("the Notch"). The routes are on the right, just before you hike over the saddle. Routes are described from left to right.

67. Rafter Man 5.12a ★★★ Sport, 8 bolts. Start right of a right-facing, left-leaning flake system on varnished rock. Move up and right to a right-facing flake under a roof. Pull the roof and continue up huecos to the anchor.
FA: Unknown

68. The Laying on of Hands 5.11d ★★ Sport, 7 bolts. Begin 20 feet right of the previous route. Climb huecos and flakes, up and right. Continue up the face to anchors.
FA: Unknown

69. Mine Field 5.11c ★ Sport, 7 bolts. Begin 30 feet right of the previous route. Climb the steep face to lower-angle rock as you approach the top of the wall. Long distance to the first and third bolts. Slings and rappel rings for anchors; slings may need to be replaced.
FA: Unknown

70. Ethical Behavior 5.11c ★★★ Sport, 5 bolts. Climb the varnish streak on the wall's right side, 20 feet right of the previous route, to a thin seam. Move up the seam to a huecoed groove. Finish on varnished edges. Long distance between the second and third bolts; you may want to supplement with gear.
FA: Unknown

MIDDLE NORTH SECOND PULLOUT: WEST FORK

Follow directions for the Middle North Second Pullout's east fork and hike down into the large sandy basin. The west fork of the wash gives access to the Black Corridor, Hunter S. Thompson Dome, Poser Crag, the Great Red Book Area, Sweet Pain Wall, and Stone Wall.

▲ THE BLACK CORRIDOR
NE/SW No Sun   Approach: 15 minutes

Once in the sandy basin, head straight northeast toward a rock ledge running east-west. Hike over this ledge and then carefully traverse it, moving right (east). Enter the corridor on the right through some boulders and trees. This area usually gets sun only in the middle of the day and for a very short time. Routes are on the left and right walls of the corridor, on lower and upper tiers. Routes are described from left to right, beginning at the lower left (northeast-facing) wall.

LEFT WALL: LOWER TIER

71. Bonaire 5.9 ★★★ Sport, 6 bolts. Start off the middle of a rock ledge at the base of the corridor. Climb the low-angle face right of a large hueco at the top of the cliff. Pull over a steep section to a slab.
FA: Jim Steagall, Kevin Sandefur, Chris Werner, Dave Sobocan 1990

72. Bon Ez 5.9+ ★★★ Sport, 6 bolts. Begin right of the previous route. Climb the low-angled face to a left-leaning ramp, which leads to a right-facing flake. Pull onto a slab to clip the last bolt and anchors.
FA: Jim Steagall, Kevin Sandefur, Chris Werner, Dave Sobocan 1990

73. Crude Boys 5.10d ★ Sport, 5 bolts. Begin 10 feet right of the previous route. Start behind a small tree at a left-leaning ramp. Move up the vertical wall and a steep section to the fifth bolt. Angle up and slightly right to the anchor.
FA: Jim Steagall, Kevin Sandefur, Chris Werner, Dave Sobocan 1990

74. Black Corridor Route 4 Left 5.11a ★★★
Sport, 5 bolts. Begin 10 feet right of the previous route at another left-leaning ramp and pocketed face. Move up pockets 20 feet to the first bolt. Climb sloped, varnished huecos past the second bolt to a horizontal crack. Traverse left to finish on *Crude Boys.*
FA: Jim Steagall, Kevin Sandefur, Chris Werner, Dave Sobocan 1990

75. Black Corridor Route 5 Left 5.10d ★★★
Mixed, 1 bolt. Begin 15 feet right of the previous route at a seam above a scoop and pocketed face. Clip the bolt and then climb the seam to a lower-angled crack to the top of the cliff. Gear anchor. Hike off right.
FA: Jim Steagall, Kevin Sandefur, Chris Werner, Dave Sobocan 1990

76. Vega Bonds 5.10a ★★★★★ Sport, 9 bolts. The best route in the corridor! Climb the perfect varnished face 5 feet right of the previous route.
FA: Jim Steagall, Kevin Sandefur, Chris Werner, Dave Sobocan 1990

77. Crude Control 5.12a ★ Sport, 7 bolts. Begin 5 feet right of the previous route, just left of boulders that block the corridor and separate the lower and upper tiers. Climb tiny pockets on the varnished face, then angle up and right to anchors. Stick-clipping the first bolt is recommended.
FA: Jim Steagall, Kevin Sandefur, Chris Werner, Dave Sobocan 1990

LEFT WALL: UPPER TIER
Reach routes on the upper tier by scrambling up on the left (west) side of the boulders blocking the center of the corridor.

78. Thermal Breakdown 5.9+ ★★ Sport, 6 bolts. This is the first route right of the climb-up from the lower tier. Climb the ledgey, varnished face that steepens as you move up to anchors.
FA: Jim Steagall, Kevin Sandefur, Chris Werner, Dave Sobocan 1990

79. Crude Street Blues 5.9+ ★★ Sport, 5 bolts. Begin 5 feet right of the previous route. Climb above the right-leaning ledge up the ledgey, steepening face.
FA: Jim Steagall, Kevin Sandefur, Chris Werner, Dave Sobocan 1990

80. Crude Behavior 5.9+ ★★ Sport, 4 bolts. Begin 5 feet right of the previous route. The first bolt is 20 feet up; clip it from a large ledge. Climb large scoops and the huecoed face.

FA: Jim Steagall, Kevin Sandefur, Chris Werner, Dave Sobocan 1990

81. Dancin' with a God 5.10a ★★★ Sport, 6 bolts. Begin 5 feet right of the previous route. Start on the

face left of a seam and left-facing flake that are up on a ledge above the first bolt.

FA: Jim Steagall, Kevin Sandefur, Chris Werner, Dave Sobocan 1990

82. Live Fast, Die Young 5.10d ★ Sport, 5 bolts. Begin 5 feet right of the previous route. Start on a small left-facing flake. Stick-clipping the first bolt is recommended. Pull the mantel then move up face to anchor.

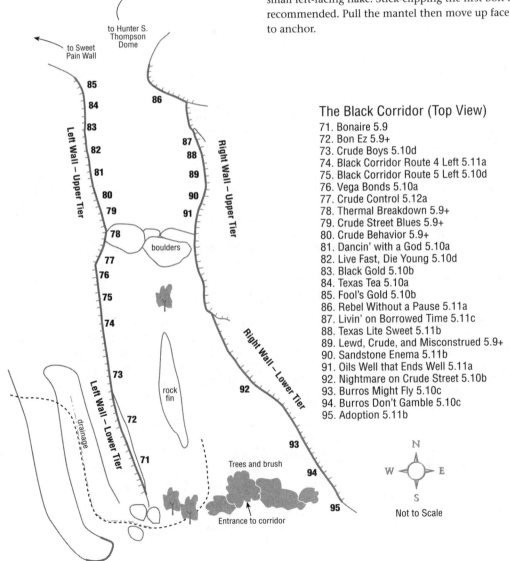

The Black Corridor (Top View)

71. Bonaire 5.9
72. Bon Ez 5.9+
73. Crude Boys 5.10d
74. Black Corridor Route 4 Left 5.11a
75. Black Corridor Route 5 Left 5.10d
76. Vega Bonds 5.10a
77. Crude Control 5.12a
78. Thermal Breakdown 5.9+
79. Crude Street Blues 5.9+
80. Crude Behavior 5.9+
81. Dancin' with a God 5.10a
82. Live Fast, Die Young 5.10d
83. Black Gold 5.10b
84. Texas Tea 5.10a
85. Fool's Gold 5.10b
86. Rebel Without a Pause 5.11a
87. Livin' on Borrowed Time 5.11c
88. Texas Lite Sweet 5.11b
89. Lewd, Crude, and Misconstrued 5.9+
90. Sandstone Enema 5.11b
91. Oils Well that Ends Well 5.11a
92. Nightmare on Crude Street 5.10b
93. Burros Might Fly 5.10c
94. Burros Don't Gamble 5.10c
95. Adoption 5.11b

FA: *Jim Steagall, Kevin Sandefur, Chris Werner, Dave Sobocan 1990*

83. Black Gold 5.10b ★ Sport, 5 bolts. Begin on a right-facing flake. Stick-clipping the first bolt is recommended. It's a long distance between the first and second bolts; it may be difficult for a short person to put the draws on the bolts.
FA: *Jim Steagall, Kevin Sandefur, Chris Werner, Dave Sobocan 1990*

84. Texas Tea 5.10a ★★★ Sport, 5 bolts. Begin on *Fool's Gold* and climb up and left, avoiding the roof (5.10d if you climb up under roof). Stick-clipping the first bolt is recommended.
FA: *Jim Steagall, Kevin Sandefur, Chris Werner, Dave Sobocan 1990*

85. Fool's Gold 5.10b ★★★★ Sport, 5 bolts. Start up a ramp at the bottom of a left-facing flake and crack. Move onto the face to clip the first bolt. Continue up huecos and pull a bulge at the top.
FA: *Jim Steagall, Kevin Sandefur, Chris Werner, Dave Sobocan 1990*

RIGHT WALL: UPPER TIER

Reach routes on the upper tier by climbing up on the left (south) side of the boulders blocking the center of the corridor. These routes are on the right (east) side of the Upper Tier.

86. Rebel Without a Pause 5.11a ★★★★ Sport, 4 bolts. Start on a ledge on the far-left (west) end of the corridor. Climb steep huecos up the orange, overhanging face.
FA: *Jim Steagall, Kevin Sandefur, Chris Werner, Dave Sobocan 1990*

87. Livin' on Borrowed Time 5.11c ★★ Sport, 4 bolts. Climb the thin, varnished face right of a large, right-facing flake.
FA: *Jim Steagall, Kevin Sandefur, Chris Werner, Dave Sobocan 1990*

88. Texas Lite Sweet 5.11b ★ Sport, 3 bolts. Climb the thin, varnished face 5 feet right of the

previous route. Ends below a large boulder.
FA: *Jim Steagall, Kevin Sandefur, Chris Werner, Dave Sobocan 1990*

89. Lewd, Crude, and Misconstrued 5.9+ ★★★ Sport, 6 bolts. Begin at a left-facing corner, 10 feet right of the previous route. Climb the corner and arête, moving under a large boulder roof. Finish on a vertical face above. Stick-clipping the first bolt is recommended. A 60-meter rope is needed to get to the ground.
FA: *Jim Steagall, Kevin Sandefur, Chris Werner, Dave Sobocan 1990*

90. Sandstone Enema 5.11b ★★★ Sport, 7 bolts. Start 10 feet right of the previous route at a seam. Move up the thin face to a wavy bulge between lower-angle and steeper top sections. Finish on anchors of *Lewd, Crude, and Misconstrued*. A 60-meter rope is needed.
FA: *Jim Steagall, Kevin Sandefur, Chris Werner, Dave Sobocan 1990*

91. Oils Well that Ends Well 5.11a ★★ Sport, 5 bolts. Climb the face 5 feet left of a left-facing corner. Climb the varnished face and seam to anchors.
FA: *Jim Steagall, Kevin Sandefur, Chris Werner, Dave Sobocan 1990*

RIGHT WALL: LOWER TIER

The following routes begin on the right (east) side of the lower tier.

92. Nightmare on Crude Street 5.10b ★★★★ Sport, 6 bolts. Begin opposite *Bonaire*. Climb the right side of a large scoop. Move left after the third bolt to climb the big, huecoed groove. Finish in a seam.
FA: *Jim Steagall, Kevin Sandefur, Chris Werner, Dave Sobocan 1990*

93. Burros Might Fly 5.10c ★★ Sport, 7 bolts. Begin 80 feet right of the previous route. Climb up edges to a right-facing flake and a small roof. Continue up the face to anchors.
FA: *Harrison Shull, Todd Hewitt 1994*

94. Burros Don't Gamble 5.10c ★★★ Sport, 7 bolts. Begin on a right-facing flake 10 feet right of the previous route, behind a large scrub-oak tree. Climb huecos up to a small roof, move right around the roof, and continue up to anchors. Most people traverse into the first bolt from a right-facing flake below *Burros Might Fly*.
FA: Harrison Shull, Todd Hewitt 1994

95. Adoption 5.11b ★ Sport, 6 bolts. Climb the thin face above the obvious pocket and right of a thin seam, 10 feet right of the previous route.
FA: Leo and Karin Henson 1991

▲ HUNTER S. THOMPSON DOME
S All-Day Sun   Approach: 20 minutes

Follow directions to the Middle North Second Pullout areas. Once in the sandy basin, head slightly left (northwest) toward a canyon running north-south. Climb through the narrow corridor to reach the Sweet Pain Wall and continue past it. The far-left edge of the Hunter S. Thompson Dome is located at the top of the Sweet Pain corridor. It is a large, south-facing feature, also above the upper tier of the Black Corridor. Gear: traditional gear should be used to supplement the bolts on all of these routes; bring brass wires, Rocks, and small Friends to #2.5. Slings may need to be replaced

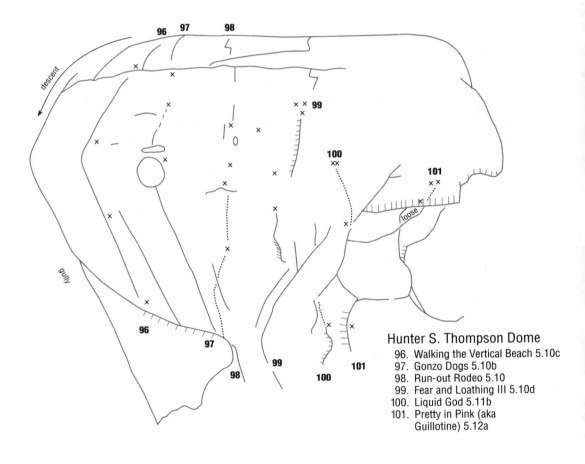

Hunter S. Thompson Dome
96. Walking the Vertical Beach 5.10c
97. Gonzo Dogs 5.10b
98. Run-out Rodeo 5.10
99. Fear and Loathing III 5.10d
100. Liquid God 5.11b
101. Pretty in Pink (aka Guillotine) 5.12a

for rappeling. Routes are described from left to right.

Descent: Hike down and to the back west side of the top of the feature. Come down the gully on the left (west) side of the wall.

96. Walking the Vertical Beach 5.10c ★★ Mixed, 4 bolts.

Climb the leftmost left-leaning seam starting off the left-leaning ramp on the wall's left side. Clip the first bolt and move left into another seam. Move up to the top of the seam with good gear and then head to a right-angling seam. Move right to another seam, angling up and right to a horizontal. Clip the bolt just over the horizontal and take a varnished crack to the top of the cliff.
FA: Don and Karen Wilson, Jack Marshall 1988

97. Gonzo Dogs 5.10b ★★ Mixed, 3 bolts.

Climb a seamy ramp leaning left, up to a large hueco. Clip a bolt right of the hueco. Move up a seam and varnished edges to the second bolt above varnish. Move back into a seam, hitting a horizontal and the third bolt. Move over the bulge to a crack and continue to the top of the cliff.
FA: Jack Marshall, Dave Wonderly 1987

98. Run-out Rodeo 5.10 ★ Mixed, 4 bolts.

Begin as for the previous route. Climb a thin, seamy ramp up and then traverse right to another nut seam. Continue up and right on the face to the first bolt (it's a long distance to this bolt). Climb up varnished edges for three more bolts, reaching the varnished horizontal near the top. Pull past the horizontal to a thin crack and continue to the top of the cliff.
FA: Paul Van Betten, Don Burroughs 1990

Note that there is a single bolt located between *Run-out Rodeo* and *Fear and Loathing III.*

99. Fear and Loathing III, 5.10d ★ Mixed, 3 bolts.

Move up a right-leaning seam and then up right-facing, varnished edges and seam to the first bolt (50 feet up). Continue up, clipping the second bolt. Move right into a right-facing seam. Clip the third bolt just below the anchors.
FA: Dave Wonderly, Jack Marshall, Warren Egbert 1987

100. Liquid God 5.11b ★ Mixed, 2 bolts.

Begin about 40 feet right of the previous route. Begin at a right-facing corner with the first bolt at its top, under a roof. Follow a crack up and right. Clip the second bolt and then face-climb left to a 2-bolt anchor.
FA: Jack Marshall, Dave Wonderly, Warren Egbert 1987

101. Pretty in Pink (aka Guillotine) 5.12a ★

Mixed, 3 bolts. Begin 15 feet right of the previous route, at a right-facing flake. Move up and left to a right-leaning seam. Climb the seam right to a bolt under the roof. Pull over a loose block (the Guillotine) to another bolt. Pull the overhang onto the face and the anchor.
FA: Paul Van Betten, Don Burroughs 1991

▲ POSER CRAG
SE All-Day Sun Approach: 25 minutes

Follow directions to the Middle North Second Pullout areas. Once you reach the sandy basin, head slightly left (northwest) toward a canyon running north-south. Climb through the narrow corridor to reach the Sweet Pain Wall and continue past it. The far-left edge of the Hunter S. Thompson Dome is located at the top of the Sweet Pain corridor. It is a large, south-facing feature, also above the upper tier of the Black Corridor. Take the ledge below the Dome to the east (traversing from left to right). Pass the east edge of the Dome; the two Poser Crag routes can be seen up on a varnished vertical wall. Hike east past the Dome for 100 yards. Do a small scramble to reach a boulder field on the left (north). Follow a faint trail heading uphill (north) through the boulders. Head for a large pine tree up and left (west) and a corridor running east-west. Upon reaching many scrub oak, look left and down (southeast) to find a tiny corridor or chimney to hike through to reach a ramp, moving down and west to the base of the routes.

102. Special Guest Posers 5.11a ★★ Sport, 4 bolts.

Start 15 feet right of a left-facing flake system. Climb the left-facing flake up to a seam. Climb edges into a scoop to the anchors.
FA: Pier and Randy Marsh 1990

103. Tin Horn Posers 5.11d ★★★ Sport, 5 bolts. Begin 10 feet right of the previous route. Climb the seamy, edgy face left of a dark varnish patch on the wall's right side. Move up and right to anchors under a small roof at the top of the cliff.
FA: Pier and Randy Marsh 1990

▲ THE GREAT RED BOOK AREA
S All-Day Sun   Approach: 35 minutes

Follow directions to the Middle North Second Pullout areas. Once you reach the sandy basin, head slightly left (northwest) toward a canyon running north-south. Climb through the narrow corridor to reach the Sweet Pain Wall and continue past it. The far-left edge of the Hunter S. Thompson Dome is located at the top of the Sweet Pain corridor. It is a large, south-facing feature, also above the upper tier of the Black Corridor. Take the ledge below the Dome

to the east (traversing from left to right) for 100 yards. Do a small scramble to reach a boulder field on the left (north). Follow a faint trail uphill (north) through the boulders to the Great Red Book Area. The most obvious feature on this wall is *The Great Red Book*—the huge, left-facing, open-book corner in the center of the wall. Anchor slings may need to be replaced for rappeling. Routes are described from left to right.

Descent: Hike to the top of *The Great Red Book*. Descend the gully behind (north of) the top-out and move down the drainage left (west) of the Great Red Book Area. After reaching the base of the wall, traverse east. Or rappel *Ground-Up Vocabulary* using a 60-meter rope.

104. Unknown 5.8 ★★ Traditional. This route is on the far-left side of the wall, about 100 yards left of *The Great Red Book*. Start at a crack, 5 feet right of a huge hole 4 feet above ground level. Climb a steep

seam up to a left-angling crack. Gear: to #3 Friend. 50 feet. Hike off left.
FA: Unknown

A wide, right-facing flake and corner angles up and left, between routes 104 and 105.

105. Unknown 5.6 ★★ Traditional. This is the right-curving crack located 10 feet right of the previous route. Gear: to #4 Friend. 100 feet. Rappel from the anchors of *G-Dog*.
FA: Unknown

106. G-Dog 5.6 R ★★ Sport, 3 bolts. Climb the run-out face just right of the previous route. Rappel.
FA: Unknown

107. The Great Red Book 5.8 ★★★★ Mixed, 3 bolts. This is the obvious, left-facing, open-book corner in the center of the wall. Gear: to #4 Friend.

Pitch 1: 5.6 Begin on the ledge below and left of the corner at a scrub-oak bush. Climb a crack to where it widens. Slab left onto the face, moving up a thin right-facing flake to an anchor. 130 feet.

Pitch 2: 5.8, 3 bolts. Move up the face, clipping 2 bolts. Move right into the crack. Take the crack to a chimney. Chimney or face-climb to the top. One bolt anchor and Friends to #3. 120 feet.

Walk off left.
FA: John Williamson, Bob Logerquist 1971

108. Animal Boy 5.11d ★★ Mixed. Climb the arête that makes up the corner of *The Great Red Book*.

Pitch 1: 5.11d, 1 bolt. Move up the right side of the arête to a left-angling seam and bolt. Move over a bulge to varnished plates. 100 feet.

Pitch 2: 5.10 Climb the face on the arête's right side. 60 feet.

Pitch 3: 5.10a, 2 bolts. Continue up the arête, moving past 2 bolts and over the top of *The Great Red Book*. Airy. 80 feet.
FA: Don Wilson, Jack Marshall 1988

The remainder of the Great Red Book Area routes are located on the slab right of *The Great Red Book* and climb off a large ledge. These can also be reached by hiking up and right from where the trail emerges from the boulder field. Hike up to the slab on its far-left (west) side, right of *The Great Red Book*, just left of a mushroom-shaped boulder.

109. Tomato Amnesia 5.9 R ★ Mixed, 3 bolts. Begin above large boulders at the top of the slab hike-up, just left of a mushroom-shaped boulder. Start on a left-facing, rounded flake. Gear: small wired and brass nuts, #00–#1 Friends.

Pitch 1: 5.9, 3 bolts. Three well-spread bolts lead up and left to a varnished seam and anchor. 100 feet.

Pitch 2: 5.9 Take another seam up and right to the top. 110 feet.
FA: Don and Karen Wilson, Jack Marshall 1988

110. Abandoned Line 5.10a R ★★ Mixed, 2 bolts. Begin right of *Tomato Amnesia*, taking an obvious ramp and seam that diagonals right across and up the wall. Gear: small wired and brass nuts, #00–#1 Friends.

Pitch 1: 5.10a R Take the ramp up and right to a diagonal seam. Gear belay anchor below a horizontal bulge/seam. Long pitch.

Pitch 2: 5.10a, 2 bolts. Follow the seam through a bulge to the top of the cliff. 75 feet.
FA: Nick Nordblom, Jenni Stone 1986

111. See Spot Run 5.6 R ★★ Mixed, 3 bolts. Begin right of a large, mushroom-shaped boulder on the highest section of rock on the wall, left of a large scrub-oak bush. Climb the slabby, run-out face to anchors. Gear: small and brass nuts and the smallest Friends. 60 feet.
FA: Mark Limage 1998

112. Chips Ahoy I, 5.9 R ★★ Mixed, 2 bolts. Begin the same as *See Spot Run*. Gear: Small and brass nuts, #Z3 to #1 Friends.

Pitch 1: 5.9 R, 2 bolts. Climb the direct line to the higher anchor on a slabby run-out face. 70 feet. This pitch was originally climbed without bolts.

Pitch 1 variation: 5.9 R Begin 5 feet right of the normal start, directly above a scrub-oak bush.

Pitch 2: 5.8 Shorter pitch, starting at a seam, to the

second set of anchors.
FA: Nick Nordblom, Jenni Stone 1986

113. Elementary Primer 5.7+ R ★★ Mixed, 3 bolts. Begin 15 feet right of the previous route. Start at a left-facing flake above a small scrub-oak bush. Sketchy gear, except at the top where it's easy. 70 feet.
FA: Mark Limage 1998

114. Stone Hammer I, 5.8 R ★★★ Mixed, 4 bolts. So named because the first-ascent party had to bash the first bolt in with a rock. Begin 10 feet right of the previous route. Climb a right-angling seam for 25 feet, then move onto the face left of the seam for 3 bolts, connecting with discontinuous seams to the top of the cliff. Gear: includes small and brass nuts, #00–#2 Friends; need a #0 Friend for the start.
FA: Alan Bartlett, Eliza Moran 1984

115. Seams Novel 5.7+ ★★★ Mixed, 2 bolts. Begin the same as the previous route, climbing the right-angling seam and clipping 1 bolt. When the seam thins out, continue up the bulging face past another bolt to anchors in a scooplike feature. Gear: need a #0 Friend for the start.
FA: Mark Limage 1998

The remainder of the routes begin out of a gully behind the upper ledge system.

116. Chips Away 5.10d ★★★ Mixed, 3 bolts. Begin 5 feet right of the previous route. Climb the face right of a right-angling seam, behind a small pine tree. Gear: small and brass nuts, Friends between #Z3 and #1.
　　Pitch 1: 5.10d R, 2 bolts. Move up and right, clipping bolts. Climb through steeper, varnished edges to a bolted anchor. 100 feet.
　　Pitch 2: 5.9 R, 1 bolt. Continue up the face to the top of the cliff. 100 feet.
FA: Unknown

117. Ground-Up Vocabulary 5.9 R/X ★★ Mixed, 5 bolts, black-painted bolt hangers. Climb the thin face 8 feet right of the previous route, just right of the small pine. This route was the unfortunate site

of a broken leg when a climber attempted to ascend the fragile, run-out start shortly after it had rained.
　　Pitch 1: 5.9, 5 bolts. Step across a gap to gain the wall (from a small pine). Move up varnished edges and seams to a bolted anchor. Sketchy getting to the first bolt above a loose, undercling flake. 90 feet.
　　Pitch 2: 5.6, 1 bolt. Continue up the face past 1 bolt to the anchor in a small hueco/cave at the top of the cliff. 90 feet.
FA: Mark Limage 1998

118. Dangling Participles 5.8 ★★★ Sport, 8 bolts. Begin at the plumb line below the anchors of *Ground-Up Vocabulary*.
FA: Mark Limage

　119. A Question of Balance 5.8 R ★★ Mixed, 2 bolts. Begin off a high boulder on the right side of the upper ledge, directly above a scrub-oak bush. Two bolts spaced far apart take you to a seam. Continue up and right to the shoulder of the formation. Gear: small and brass nuts, #00–#1 Friends.
FA: Nick Nordblom, Jon Martinet 1978

120. Subject-Verb Agreement 5.8 ★★★ Sport, 7 bolts. Named in honor of the ever-literate President George W. Begin 15 feet right of the previous route. The first bolt is above a big varnished section and big edges. Climb the varnished edges to anchors in a recession below a steep bulge.
FA: Mark Limage, Gary Sanders 2000

121. Sandstone Cowboy 5.10b X ★ Mixed, 2 bolts, gold-colored, quarter-inch bolts. This is a serious route up discontinuous cracks. Start 15 feet right of the previous route on the right edge of the ledge. Gear: small and brass nuts, #00–#1 Friends.
　　Pitch 1: 5.10b, 1 bolt. Climb up and right of a varnished section at the base to the first bolt. Protect the pitch by lassoing a horn halfway up. Take a seam up and left to a bolt and drilled piton anchor.
　　Pitch 2: 5.9, 1 bolt. Wander up and left on the face, passing another bolt, to the top of the cliff.
FA: Jack Marshall, Dave Wonderly 1987

122. Unknown ★★ Mixed, 2 bolts. Bushwhack down and right to another ledge with a varnished base and pockets at a scrub-oak tree. Gear: small and brass nuts, #00–#1 Friends.

Pitch 1: Climb varnished edges and a thin seam to directly above a horizontal white-colored streak on the wall. 100 feet. Rappel or continue on pitch 2.

Pitch 2: Climb to the top of the wall. 150 feet.

FA: Unknown

▲ SWEET PAIN WALL
E AM Sun   Approach: 15 minutes

Follow directions to the Middle North Second Pull-out areas. Once you reach the sandy basin, head slightly left (northwest) toward a canyon running north-south. Climb through the narrow corridor to reach the base of the Sweet Pain Wall. Routes are described from left to right.

123. Sweet Pain 5.11d ★★★★ Sport, 5 bolts. Begin on the left side of the cliff. Clip the first bolt above 2 large huecos. Traverse left across a handrail, and move through overhanging jugs. This route has been led on gear! This route was stolen from the people who bolted the route, Pier and Randy Marsh, who let a new climber to town top-rope it the day before he redpointed it. They planned to name it "The Boy with the Baggy, Shiny Lycra," in his memory.

FA: Leo Henson, Randy Faulk 1991

124. Glitter Gulch 5.11b ★★★★ Sport, 6 bolts. Start in the center of the wall, off the left edge of a ledge 15 feet above the base of the wall. Move up and slightly left on edges and horizontals to anchors. There were short, questionable bolts on the lower section as of this guide's publication.

FA: People from Colorado

125. Slave to the Grind 5.11b ★★★★ Sport, 7 bolts. Start 5 feet right of the previous route on a large handrail edge. Angle up and right to anchors. There were short, questionable bolts on the lower section as of this guide's publication.

FA: People from Colorado

126. Sister of Pain 5.11c ★★★ Sport, 7 bolts. Begin 15 feet right of the previous route at a low, left-facing flake. Climb pockets and a slick face to huecos and a steep face.

FA: Leo and Karin Henson 1992

127. Lee Press-On 5.12b ★★ Sport, 7 bolts. Begin 20 feet to the right of *Sister of Pain*, right of a water streak. Climb a thin face to a sloping ledge. Move up and left to a right-leaning ramp. Finish on open cold-shut anchors to the right of a left-leaning crack.

FA: Leo and Karin Henson 1992

128. Pain in the Neck 5.10a ★★★ Sport, 5 bolts. Climb a varnished face just left of a prominent right-leaning crack and large scoop.

FA: Unknown

129. A-Cute Pain 5.8 ★★ Mixed, 4 bolts, home-made hangers. Begin 10 feet right of the previous route, just right of a right-leaning crack at some letter-box slots. Climb up and left to link in with the crack. Traverse left out of the crack to the second bolt. Finish up and left on the face and a seam.

FA: Todd and Donette Swain 1993

▲ STONE WALL
E AM Sun   Approach: 15 minutes

Follow directions to the Middle North Second Pull-out areas. Once you reach the sandy basin, head slightly left (northwest) toward a canyon running north-south where the Sweet Pain Wall is located. Before heading into the Sweet Pain canyon, you will see a narrow east-west drainage to the left (west). Hike into this corridor. Shortly, it makes a 90-degree bend and heads into a north-south corridor, taking you over numerous boulders to the base of Stone Wall. Routes are described from left to right.

130. Purple Haze I, 5.10d ★★★ Sport, 6 bolts. Begin on the left side of the cliff, 50 feet right of a left-facing corner. Climb steep rock to a thin face and

large hueco under the anchors.
FA: Don Burroughs, Alan Busby 1993

131. Haunted Hooks 5.10d ★★★ Sport, 9 bolts.
Start 15 feet right of the previous route at a small
left-facing flake. Climb a series of huecos heading
up to a lower-angled face and rappel bolts.
FA: Don Burroughs, Alan Busby 1993

132. Roto Hammer 5.10c ★★★★ Sport, 7 bolts,
brown-painted bolt hangers. Start 5 feet right of the
previous route at the larger of two left-leaning flakes
at the base.
FA: Daryl Ellis 1992

133. Nirvana 5.11a ★★★★ Sport, 7 bolts. Start 15
feet right of the previous route and begin at a left-
facing flake leading to a right-facing flake. Take
edges and seams to the bolted anchor.
FA: Don Burroughs, Alan Busby 1993

134. Stonehenge 5.11b ★★★★ Sport, 8 bolts.
Start 10 feet right of the previous route, just above a
scrub-oak bush, in a deep hueco. Climb varnished
scoops to a thin face and anchors.
FA: Don Burroughs, Mike Ward, Alan Busby, 1993

135. Stone Hammer II, 5.10d ★ Mixed, 4 bolts. So
named because the first ascensionists forgot their
hammer and had to use a rock to drill the holes and
bash the bolts in. Climbs a thin crack system behind a large scrub-oak tree, 25 feet right of the previous route. Finish up and right on the face to anchors. Gear: small nuts, #00–#2.5 Friend.
FA: Mike Ward, Mike Clifford 1986

136. Birthstone 5.10d ★★ Sport, 6 bolts. Start off
a boulder and right-facing flake below a varnished
face. Climb the thin face to the *Stone Hammer II*
anchors.
FA: Leo and Karin Henson 1993

137. April Fools 5.10b ★★★ Sport, 6 bolts. Climb
just right of a left-facing hole. Move up the thin
face through varnished scoops to a steep face.
FA: Don Burroughs, Alan Busby 1993

SECOND PULLOUT WEST

Follow the trail downhill out of the parking lot. At the
first fork, head left, staying on the higher Sandstone
Quarry trail. Continue as the trail moves up onto a red-
rock pedestal and then goes back downhill, paralleling
the wash. After the trail starts going downhill, take the
third trail heading right (north) at a large, black,
dead tree. Cross the wash and begin hiking north into
the red rock. When you dead-end into a large ravine,
hike left (west) along a series of ledges. At the top of
the ledge system, move around a large boulder leaning over the ravine, passing a scrub-oak tree. Move
onto a slab ledge system on the north side of the ravine. To the northeast will be the steep walls of the
Gallery. The Wall of Confusion is northwest and behind the Gallery, and the Observatory is approximately
100 yards to the right (east) of the Gallery.

▲ THE OBSERVATORY
S All-Day Sun   Approach: 25 minutes

Follow the Second Pullout West directions. Once on
the slab ledge system, take the ledgey, lower portion
of this slab about 100 yards right (east) to reach the
first Observatory route, located about 50 feet below
and 20 feet right of the rightmost (easternmost) route
of the Gallery. The slings on these routes may need
to be replaced for rappeling. Routes are described from
left to right.

138. Witches' Honor 5.8 R ★ Mixed, 3 bolts. This
route starts at a left-leaning crack leading to a large
hueco (big enough to stand in), with several loose
boulders down and right of it.
   Pitch 1: Scramble up the perfect right-leaning crack
leading up and right out of the large hueco. Climb 50
feet to a large, loose pillar, left of the crack.
   Pitch 2: Move up the crack just right of a loose
pillar and then onto the face. Angle right to under a
small overhang. Continue up and right to a seam.
Move up to a face, passing a bolt to the anchor.
   Walk off left.
FA: Danny Meyers 1988

The following routes are located right of the base of

Joel Kruatstrunt being a Slave to the Grind *5.11b at the Sweet Pain Wall*

Witches Honor. Move up about 100 feet to an overhang on the far-right side of this wall. The routes start just left of the overhang on a ledgelike feature at the same level as the top of the overhang.

Descent: Rappel using two ropes from the anchors of *Bewitched*.

139. Which Hunters 5.10a R ★ Mixed, 4 bolts. Begin 40 feet left of the left edge of the overhang. Move straight up the face, clipping bolts to reach a small overhang. Move up and far right to the anchors of *Bewitched*.
FA: Unknown

140. Warlock 5.9 R ★ Traditional. Begin 20 feet right of the previous route and 20 feet left of the overhang's left edge. Climb the face, past a low-angle bulge to a vertical crack, angling up and slightly right. Move up between two huge huecos/caves. After reaching the horizontal crack, traverse right in the crack to link up with *Bewitched*; or

climb past the horizontal and angle right to the arête, finishing on *Bewitched*.
FA: Todd and Donette Swain 1994

141. Bewitched 5.3 ★★★ Mixed, 6 bolts. This route starts on the left edge of the overhang. Climb up and right, aiming for the hueco/cave above the start and left of the arête. Clip 2 bolts before getting into the large hueco. Move right, out of the cave, clipping 1 bolt, to reach the arête. Continue up the arête clipping 3 more bolts to anchors.
FA: Unknown

▲ THE GALLERY
S All-Day Sun   Approach: 20 minutes

Follow the Second Pullout West directions. From where you pass around the large boulder, continue up and right on slabs about 100 yards to the base of the large overhanging wall. There is a large rock ledge just south of the Gallery; you can either hike up its ramping left

(west) edge onto the top of it, or, you can hike past it and come up around its right (east) edge where the most difficult routes are located. Most of the routes on this wall top out on a slab and often the last bolt and anchors are fairly distant from each other, making for a wild finish. Routes are described from left to right.

142. Range of Motion (aka The Cracked Hanger Route) 5.10d ★ Sport, 4 bolts, homemade bolt hangers. Begin 150 feet right of the Gallery wall's left edge, left of a right-leaning crack. Climb small edges to the top. Bouldery crux. At least one bolt hanger is cracked on this route. These homemade, cracked hangers have been used all over Red Rock Canyon, placed by one of the first ascensionists, who even admitted some were cracked when the routes were put up.
FA: Todd Swain, Dick Peterson, Peggy Buckeye 1990

143. Sport Climbing is Neither 5.8 ★★ Sport, 3 bolts. Most people who adhere to this slogan are not very good sport climbers. Begin 100 feet right of the previous route at a short, right-curving crack. Move over the crack to steep edges.
FA: Unknown 1991

144. Bucks Muscle World 5.9 ★★ Sport, 3 bolts, homemade bolt hangers. Begin right of a scoop feature at head height. Climb steep edges.
FA: Greg Mayer 1990

145. Gelatin Pooch 5.10a ★★ Sport, 4 bolts, homemade bolt hangers. Begin 10 feet right of the previous route on steep, varnished rock, right of a prominent seam.
FA: Greg Mayer 1990

146. Pump First, Pay Later 5.10b ★★ Sport, 4 bolts. Move up the steep face and edges, 10 feet right of the previous route.
FA: Greg Mayer 1990

147. Running Amuck 5.10c ★★★★ Sport, 4 bolts. Begin 10 feet right of the previous route, at the bottom of a left-facing, shallow dihedral. Move up a ramp and then angle left and up. Shared anchors

with routes 148 and 149.
FA: Greg Mayer 1990

148. Unknown 5.11a ★★★ Sport, 5 bolts. Begin 5 feet right of the previous route, at a large horizontal edge, earlike feature. Move straight up and slightly right to link in with *Gridlock* at the third bolt. Shared anchors with routes 147 and 149.
FA: Unknown

149. Gridlock 5.11c ★★ Sport, 5 bolts. Begin in a left-leaning crack on the left edge of a large, varnished scoop. Climb left. Follow seams and edges to a crack. Pull out of the crack, left and up to shared anchors with routes 147 and 148. Beware of the loose undercling below the fifth bolt.
FA: Greg Mayer 1990

150. Social Disorder 5.11d ★★ Sport, 5 bolts. Start as for *Gridlock*, but move right after the first bolt. Climb edges, continuing up and right to the anchors of *A Day in the Life*.
FA: Steve Bullock, Jonathan Knight 1991

151. A Day in the Life 5.11b ★★★ Sport, 5 bolts. Begin on the right edge of the large, varnished scoop, 5 feet right of the previous route, behind a cat's claw bush. Move up and right out of the scoop and then straight up the edgy face to the anchors.
FA: Bill Boyle 1990

152. Minstrel in the Gallery 5.12b ★★★★ Sport, 5 bolts. Begin 5 feet right of *A Day in the Life*, between two seams and two trees at the base. Stick-clip the first bolt from the ledge behind the route. Climb thin edges up and right to chain anchors.
FA: Mike Tupper 1990

153. Yak Crack 5.11c ★★★★ Sport, 6 bolts. Begin 5 feet right of the previous route, at a left-leaning crack. Climb the face and crack up and left to anchors right of the crack.
FA: Bill Boyle 1990

154. The Gift 5.12d ★★★★ Sport, 6 bolts. *The Gift* shares the first bolt with *Yak Crack*. Move right after

the first bolt to the second and third bolts and then continue straight up.
FA: Boone Speed 1990

155. The Sissy Traverse 5.13b ★★★★ Sport, 8 bolts. This is the variation that most people prefer. Start the same as for *Yak Crack*. Clip the first three bolts of *The Gift*, and then continue heading up and right, finishing on *Nothing Shocking*. The traverse was originally done by starting on *Minstrel in the Gallery*.
FA: Don Welsh 1991

156. Where the Down Boys Go 5.12d ★★★★ Sport, 5 bolts. Start at the base of a right-leaning crack, 5 feet right of *The Gift*. Climb up and veer left for 4 bolts. Move right and up to anchors.
FA: Mike Tupper 1990

157. Who Made Who 5.12c ★★ Sport, 5 bolts. Begin as for *Where the Down Boys Go*. Clip 2 bolts, moving up and right along the crack. Then climb straight up 3 bolts to anchors.
FA: Mike Tupper 1990

158. Nothing Shocking 5.13a ★★★★ Sport, 6 bolts. Begin the same as for *Who Made Who*. Climb right, along the crack for 3 bolts, then climb straight up 3 more bolts to anchors (use the second set of anchors, higher up).
FA: Don Welsh 1990

159. The Glitch 5.12c ★★★ Sport, 6 bolts. Begin the same as the previous two routes. Climb the right-leaning crack up and right, finishing on huecos and slopers. A long crux move.
FA: Mike Tupper 1990

▲ THE WALL OF CONFUSION
S All-Day Sun   Approach: 20 minutes

Follow directions to the Gallery. Hike up on its left edge. Continue left (west) from the base of the Gallery. Pass through a narrow drainage and then move slightly right into a sandy area at the base of the following routes. Routes are described from left to right.

160. The Runaway 5.10b ★★ Sport, 4 bolts, homemade bolt hangers. Begin at the left edge of the wall behind a scrub oak. Climb up and angle slightly right on the vertical face.
FA: Greg Mayer 1989

161. American Sportsman 5.10c R ★★ Sport, 4 bolts. Begin 5 feet right of the previous route and climb edges up a vertical face. Stick-clipping the first bolt is recommended. Several belayers have been injured when the leaders fell on them at the start of this route. After the last bolt, move right to the anchors.
FA: Boone Speed, Bill Doyle 1988

162. Desert Pickle 5.11c ★★★ Sport, 4 bolts. Begin 10 feet right of the previous route at a short right-leaning crack. Stick-clipping the first bolt is recommended. Run-out to anchors.
FA: Boone Speed, Bill Doyle 1988

163. Sudden Impact 5.11d ★★ Sport, 5 bolts. Climb edges up the vertical face, 5 feet right of the previous route. Stick-clipping the first bolt is recommended.
FA: Bill Doyle, Boone Speed 1988

164. Big Damage 5.12b ★★★ Sport, 7 bolts. Begin on right-facing flake, 10 feet right of the previous route. Move up and slightly left to the anchors.
FA: Boone Speed 1988

165. Promises in the Dark 5.12b ★★★★ Sport, 7 bolts. Begin right of the previous route, at a dihedral capped by a roof. Move up and right on steep rock into a varnished pod. Run-out to anchors.
FA: Mike Tupper 1988

John Bachar soloing Fear and Loathing *5.11d on the* Wall of Confusion. *Photo by Dan McQuade*

166. Fear and Loathing III, 5.11d ★★★★ Sport, 8 bolts. Climb the very steep, overhanging wall, 10 feet right of the previous route.
FA: Bill Doyle, Boone Speed 1988

167. Body English 5.12c ★ Sport, 4 bolts. Begin left of a large hueco at the base, 15 feet right of *Fear and Loathing III*. Climb the left-curving crack, moving right onto the steep face to the anchors.
FA: Mike Tupper 1988

▲ RESIN ROSE AREA
S All-Day Sun   Approach: 20 minutes

Follow directions to the Wall of Confusion. The Resin Rose Area is 50 feet up the low-angle slab that is below *Fear and Loathing III*. These routes all climb out of a large pod with brown-colored rock.

168. Unknown ★★ Sport, 8 bolts. Climb up the left side of the pod. Pass the right-leaning crack to reach the second bolt. Move straight up the steep face to anchors.
FA: Unknown

169. Unknown ★★★ Sport, 7 bolts. Climb the previous route to the fifth bolt. Then move up and right past two more bolts to an anchor below a seam, or continue right to anchors. Run-out to anchors.
FA: Unknown

170. Resin Rose 5.11d ★★★ Traditional. Start 15 feet right of the previous route and climb the large crack that splits the pod in half. Take the wide crack up, angling right after hitting the roof. Gear: #0.5– #4 Friends.
FA: Paul Van Betten, Jay Smith, Paul Crawford 1987

171. Unknown ★ Sport, 5 bolts. Begin just right of the crack. Climb the steep face, and move right into the crack at the third bolt. Climb up two more bolts on a steeper face to anchors.
FA: Unknown

172. Unknown ★ Sport, 5 bolts, red-painted bolt

hangers. Begin 5 feet right of the previous route, just left of the orange/brown rock border on the right side of the pod. Climb straight up. Move right at the top to the lower-angle face.
FA: Unknown

▲ THE B AND W WALL
S PM Sun   Approach: 25 minutes

Follow the trail downhill out of the parking lot. At the first fork, head left, staying on the higher, Sandstone Quarry trail. Continue as the trail moves up onto a red-rock pedestal and then goes back downhill, paralleling the wash. Take the trail downhill, skip the Gallery turnoff, and continue, paralleling the Calico Hills. Pass around a huge boulder with Native American petroglyphs. The trail heads back downhill and meets up with huecoed boulders on both sides. If you look up you will see the B and W Wall, with an unmistakable, black-water streak down its center. Head down and right into the wash. Scramble up the rock on the right side of a thin water gully below and right of the water streak. Routes are described from left to right.

Alternate approach: From the *Stratocaster* and *One-Eyed Jack* hike south to the southernmost ledge system. Follow descent directions.

Alternate Sandstone Quarry approach: Take the Calico II Trail from Sandstone Quarry and follow directions from where the huecoed walls are.

Descent: Hike left (west) on the large ledge system to a 10-foot downclimb on big varnished edges. Continue down the ramp to reach the cliff base and traverse left (east).

173. Unknown ★★ Traditional. Climb the right-diagonaling crack and then straight up the face to rappel anchors next to the anchors of *The Negative*. Gear: to #2 Friend.
FA: Nick Nordblom

174. The Negative 5.10b R ★ Traditional. Begin 15 feet right of the previous route, in a left-facing crack. Climb up and angle left onto the face to the fixed anchors.
FA: Jack Marshall, Dave Wonderly 1988

175. Black Streak 5.9 ★★★ Sport, 5 bolts. Begin 5 feet right of the previous route and follow bolts up the obvious black water streak to an alcove below the top of the cliff. Gear: #00–#1 Friends to supplement bolts. This FA was done with one piece of gear, no bolts—essentially a solo. Good job Wendell!
FA: Wendell Broussard, "Little Rick" 1982

176. Five Card Stud 5.10a R ★ Mixed, 3 bolts. Begin 10 feet right of the previous route at the start of a right-diagonaling crack/seam.

Pitch 1: 5.10a, 3 bolts. Climb the face past 3 bolts to a natural anchor.

Pitch 2: 5.9 Continue to the top of the face.
FA: Don and Karen Wilson, Jack Marshall 1988

177. The Don't Come Line 5.10a R ★★★ Mixed, 5 bolts. Begin off the boulder right of the previous route, in the approach gully. The start is the obvious crack between two tall features on the right and left. Gear: #00–#2 Friends, brass and aluminum nuts.

Pitch 1: 5.10a R, 3 bolts. Climb the obvious dihedral for 80 feet and then move slightly right and up over a bulge to a fixed belay. 80 feet.

Pitch 2: 5.8 R/X, 2 bolts. Follow an arching finger crack. When the crack thins out, head straight up. Belay in a chasm at the top. 130 feet.
FA: Don and Karen Wilson, Jack Marshall 1988

178. High Stakes Roulette 5.10b ★ Mixed. Follow steep, dark rock 60 feet right of *The Don't Come Line*. Run-out.
FA: Unknown

SANDSTONE QUARRY (THIRD PULLOUT)

SANDSTONE QUARRY EAST
Boschton Marathon Block ▲ Running Man Wall ▲ Red Heat Gully Area
Stratocaster Wall ▲ Sub-Americrag ▲ Americrag
The Pier ▲ California Crags

SANDSTONE QUARRY PARKING AREA
Front Corridor ▲ Front Slab ▲ Sandy Corridor ▲ Requiem Wall

SANDSTONE QUARRY WEST
The Asylum ▲ Sonic Youth Lower Wall ▲ Sonic Youth Upper Wall
Boast and Toast Wall ▲ Numbers Crag
Common Time Wall ▲ Wake Up Wall

SANDSTONE QUARRY NORTH
The Twinkie ▲ The Marshmallow ▲ Bull Market ▲ Satellite Wall
Avian Wall ▲ The Trophy ▲ Secret 13

SANDSTONE QUARRY BACKSIDE
The Beach ▲ Blister in the Sun Wall ▲ Mass Production Wall
The Scoop ▲ Hall of Fame ▲ Holiday Wall ▲ Next Wall
James Brown Wall ▲ The Sweet Spot

TO REACH SANDSTONE QUARRY from Las Vegas, take West Charleston Boulevard west, which turns into State Route 159. Drive over the 215 Beltway and zero your odometer. Turn right into the Red Rock Canyon National Conservation Area, 5.9 miles past the 215 (2 miles past Calico Basin Road). Enter the 13-mile Scenic Drive through the kiosk entrance booth.

Sandstone Quarry is the third parking area on the Scenic Drive, located 2.6 miles from the entrance kiosk. There is a large, paved parking lot with pit toilets. It is actually the former location of a quarry and some of the sandstone blocks are still lying around in places.

SANDSTONE QUARRY EAST

From the parking lot, follow a trail exiting from the southeast corner, paralleling the rock and heading east (right). Parallel the cliffs for 5 minutes (approximately

Tincho Garcia getting evil on Pablo Diablo 5.12d, Stratocaster Wall. Photo by Roxanna Brock

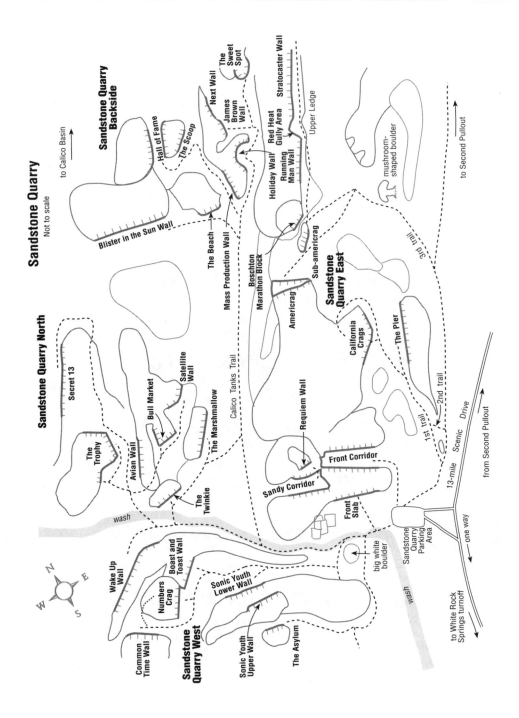

Sandstone Quarry

Not to scale

to Calico Basin

Sandstone Quarry Backside

Hall of Fame

The Scoop

Next Wall

James Brown Wall

The Sweet Spot

Holiday Wall/ Red Heat Gully Area

Stratocaster Wall

Running Man Wall

Upper Ledge

Blister in the Sun Wall

The Beach

Mass Production Wall

Boschton Marathon Block

Sub-americrag

mushroom-shaped boulder

to Second Pullout

3rd trail

Sandstone Quarry North

Secret 13

Satellite Wall

Bull Market

The Marshmallow

The Trophy

Avian Wall

The Twinkie

Americrag

Sandstone Quarry East

California Crags

The Pier

Calico Tanks Trail

Requiem Wall

Front Corridor

Sandy Corridor

Front Slab

wash

2nd trail

1st trail

13-mile Scenic Drive

from Second Pullout

Sandstone Quarry Parking Area

one way

Wake Up Wall

Boast and Toast Wall

Numbers Crag

Sonic Youth Lower Wall

big white boulder

Common Time Wall

Sandstone Quarry West

Sonic Youth Upper Wall

The Asylum

wash

to White Rock Springs turnoff

N
W E
S

300 yards). Take the third trail heading left (north), down into a gully toward a mushroom-shaped boulder. Follow the trail past the mushroom boulder and into the wash and then hike right (east) down the wash.

▲ BOSCHTON MARATHON BLOCK
S All-Day Sun   Approach: 15 minutes

Follow the Sandstone Quarry East directions. In the wash, pass a wall on your right with two natural threads about 4 feet off the ground. After seeing the threads, move left and scramble up red slabs to the north. At the top of the slabs is the Boschton Marathon Block, a large southwest-facing boulder with a black-colored face. Routes are described from left to right.

The first route is 200 yards west and then northeast of the Boschton boulder. Hike around left (west) of the Boschton boulder for about 100 yards. Then hike northeast another 100 yards to a huge, right-facing (and southwest-facing) dihedral.

1. Brain Damage 5.11c R/X ★★★★ Traditional. Climb the striking, thin open-book dihedral located above a downward-sloping ledge. You may wish to use 2 ropes; one for getting to the ledge and one for climbing the crack. Gear: to #1 Friend. Walk off.
FA: Robert Findlay, Paul Van Betten, Mike Ward 1987

The following routes climb the Block.

2. Boschton Marathon 5.12b ★★ Sport, 6 bolts. Located at the top of the hike-up. Approach from the left or right. Climb the thin face straight up the center of the Boschton Marathon Block. Downclimb carefully off the back right (east) side.
FA: Geoff Weigand 1987

3. Frictiony Face, Panty Waist 5.8+ ★★★ Sport, 8 bolts. Begin on the large red slab right of the Boschton boulder, behind a big dead tree. Take the obvious thin seam angling up and left, and then slab up to the fixed anchors. Sporty slab climbing. 100 feet.

FA: Danny Meyers, Brad Stewart 1989

▲ RUNNING MAN WALL
S All-Day Sun   Approach: 15 minutes

Follow the Sandstone Quarry East directions. In the wash, pass a wall on your right with two natural threads about 4 feet off the ground. After seeing the threads, move left and scramble up red slabs to the north. At the top of the slabs, head right (east) for 50 feet. The Running Man Wall is the tall wall on the left with a low roof on its lower left (west) side. The base of the wall is littered with boulders. Routes are described from left to right.

Descent: Nearly all these routes need 2 ropes or a 70-meter rope to descend.

4. True Lies 5.9 ★★ Mixed, 2 bolts. On the wall's far-left side is a smooth right-facing flake above a large yucca. Climb to the roof and then move up and left to reach a water streak that leads to fixed anchors. Gear: Rocks and Friends to #4.

FA: Unknown

5. Calico Terror 5.11c ★★ Mixed, 3 bolts. Begin 20 feet right of *True Lies*. Move up and right past 3 bolts with white hangers to a thin seam heading straight right. When the seam merges with a vertical crack, take the crack to fixed anchors on a left-facing, varnished face above a ledge. Gear: to #1 Friend, brass wires.

FA: Mike Ward, Paul Van Betten 1987

6. There Goes the Neighborhood 5.11d ★★★ Mixed, 11 bolts, homemade bolt hangers. Begin 100 feet right of *Calico Terror*, 30 feet right of the right

edge of the low roof, at a stack of cheater stones. Varnished, edgy face. Gear: #1.5 Friend.
FA: Greg Mayer 1989

7. Second Fiddle to a Dead Man 5.11d ★★★
Sport, 10 bolts, white-painted, homemade bolt hangers. Begin 5 feet right of the previous route.
FA: Greg Mayer 1993

8. New Traditionalists 5.11d ★★ Sport, 11 bolts,
SMC bolt hangers. Begin 15 feet right of *Second Fiddle* on a thin, varnished face. The bolt up and left of the third one is for the next route. You may want to supplement bolts with small Friends. Sporty.
FA: Mike Tupper 1989

9. The Predator 5.10d R ★★ Mixed, 3 bolts. Start
5 feet left of *Running Man* and climb the crack angling up and left across the wall. Clip a bolt on the *New Traditionalists*, then clip another bolt, and then a bolt on *Second Fiddle*, and then continue up and left to 2-bolt belay. Gear: Rocks and mostly smaller Friends to #2.
FA: Nick Nordblom, Paul Van Betten 1988

10. Running Man 5.11d ★★★★★ Mixed, 11 bolts.
This is no *Yak Crack*. Get ready to do some rock climbing on this area mega classic! Gear: bring a small Rock or Friend for the start and other gear if you're worried about the run-out.
FA: Paul Van Betten, Sal Mamusia, Mike Ward 1987

11. Graveyard Waltz (aka The Parasite) 5.11d
★★ Mixed, 9 bolts, homemade bolt hangers. Start right of *Running Man*, heading to the right up very thin edges. Gear: small Rock or Friend for the start.
FA: Mike Tupper 1989

12. Commando 5.12b ★★★ Sport, 9 bolts. Begin 5
feet right of *Graveyard* , on the left side of a small, low roof. Head up and right to anchors in a big scoop.
FA: Louie Anderson, Bart Groendycke 1992

13. Project 2 bolts. Begin 15 feet right of *Commando*. Anchors are next to the *Commando* anchors.

14. Galloping Gal 5.11a ★★★ Sport, 10 bolts. Start
on a ledge 10 feet up, 25 feet right of *Commando*, at the far right edge of the wall. Reachy.
FA: Unknown 1990

15. Vile Pile 5.10b ★★ Mixed, 6 bolts. Begin 5 feet
right of *Galloping Gal*, climbing the red slab on the next formation right. Gear: bring #0–#2 Friends to supplement the bolts.
FA: Bob Conz, Mike Ward, Danny Meyers, Jessie Baxter 1989

▲ RED HEAT GULLY AREA
S All-Day Sun   Approach: 20 minutes

Follow the Sandstone Quarry East directions and head to the Running Man Wall. In the wash, pass a wall on your right with two natural threads about 4 feet off the ground. After seeing the threads, move left and scramble up red slabs to the north. At the top of the slabs, head right (east) for 50 feet. The Running Man Wall is the tall wall on the left with a low roof on its lower left (west) side. The following routes are located in the gully 60 feet right of the Running Man Wall's right edge. Routes are described from left to right.

16. Funk Flex 5.11d ★★ Sport, 9 bolts. Begin on
the left side of the large, south-facing wall at the top of the gully, 10 feet right of the far-left edge. Climb the thin face up and right to the anchor of *Red Heat*.
FA: Mike Ward 1999

17. Red Heat 5.10c ★★★ Sport, 9 bolts. Climb the
varnished, right-facing ramp and corner, 25 feet right of *Funk Flex*. Finish moving up and left on thin edges. Heady.
FA: Nick Nordblom, Mike Ward, Danny Meyers 1989

The following two routes are located down and right of *Red Heat*, on the west-facing wall (right side of the gully) and climb out of a steep, varnished scoop.

18. Synthetic Society 5.11a ★★★ Sport, 8 bolts.
Climb out the left side of the steep, varnished scoop

through the roof. Move right at the top to share the last bolt and anchor of *Plastic People*. 90 feet.
FA: Mike Ward, Louie Anderson, Bart Groendycke 1990

19. Plastic People 5.10b ★★★ Sport, 8 bolts. Climb out the right side of the scoop. Anchors are located above a bulge. 90 feet.
FA: Louie Anderson, Bart Groendycke 1990

The next few routes climb the orange slab on the right of the entrance to the Red Heat Gully.

20. Unknown 5.10d ★★★ Sport, 11 bolts. Climb the gorgeous-looking seam system beginning on the left. Run-out to the first bolt and then there's no fear—lots o' bolts. 100 feet.
FA: Unknown

21. Fibonacci Wall 5.11d ★★ Sport, 8 bolts. Begin 10 feet right of the previous route, on the nose on the left edge of the orange slab. After pulling the

bulge, move up discontinuous seams to the top of the cliff and a bolted anchor.
FA: Paul Van Betten, Don Welsh 1987

22. Northern Lights 5.11d ★★ Sport, 9 bolts. Begin 30 feet right of *Fibonacci*. It is recommended to stick-clip the first bolt. Climb the middle of the face, left of an obvious crack.
FA: Unknown 1991

23. Falstaff 5.10a R ★★ Mixed, 2 bolts, homemade bolt hangers. Begin 15 feet right of *Northern Lights*, right of the obvious crack that splits the wall. Climb the face past 2 bolts, then move left to the crack, taking it to the top. Gear: to #3.5 Friend. 150 feet. Descend the Red Heat Gully to the left (west).
FA: Nick Nordblom, Paul Van Betten 1985

24. Yodritch 5.11d R ★★ Mixed, 5 bolts, homemade bolt hangers. Begin the same as for *Falstaff*. Gear: to #2 Friend.

Pitch 1: 5.11d R Climb past 2 bolts as for *Falstaff*. Continue up and right on the slab to the third bolt. Move right to a varnished crack, then up the steep face past a bolt to anchors. 100 feet.

Pitch 2: 5.7 Take the highly featured, varnished edges to the top using 1 bolt. 60 feet.

Descend the Red Heat Gully to the left (west).
FA: Paul Van Betten, Mike Ward 1987

The following route is located 45 feet right of *Yodritch*, right of a pine tree and left of a large, round boulder.

25. Split Crack 5.7 ★ Traditional. Climb the large crack on the right, beginning just left of the boulder against the wall. Gear: to #5 Friend. 160 feet. Descend the Red Heat Gully to the left (west).
FA: John Williamson, John Taylor 1973

The next routes are located 5 feet right of *Split Crack* and begin on top of the large, round boulder. Slab up the right side of the boulder on somewhat loose big blocks.

26. Split Ends 5.10a ★★★ Sport, 8 bolts. Climb the leftmost seam.
FA: Unknown

27. Split Infinitive 5.9 ★★★ Sport, 7 bolts. Begin the same as the previous route, sharing the first 2 bolts, then split off right, climbing another seam.
FA: Unknown

28. Unknown 5.10 ★★ Mixed, 4 bolts, homemade bolt hangers. Climb the seam on the right side of the wall (just left of the wall's right corner). After the fourth bolt, move right to the next seam and up to anchors. Gear: small and brass wires, to #1 Friend.
FA: Unknown

29. Nevada Book 5.8 ★★ Traditional. Begin 5 feet right of the previous route, on the wall's leftmost, left-facing corner. Gear: to #4 Friend.

Pitch 1: 5.5 Scramble up and right on a ramp to the fixed anchor in the crack. 60 feet.

Pitch 2: 5.8 Climb the left-facing, varnished corner to the top. Lots of pods, wide and awkward. 160 feet.

Descend the Red Heat Gully to the left (west).
FA: John Taylor, John Williamson 1973

The following route begins at the base of the wall, right of the boulder.

30. Super Nova 5.10d R ★★ Mixed, 3 bolts. Begin 12 feet right of *Nevada Book*, on the face right of the large, round boulder. Gear: brass wires, small Rocks, and small Friends.

Pitch 1: 5.9+ R Climb a short, right-facing, varnished corner. Move right onto a slab and up, passing 2 bolts and climbing between seams and varnished edges. Anchors are just below a horizontal break. 120 feet.
FA: Paul Van Betten, Jay Smith 1988

Pitch 2: 5.10+ R Climb over a bulge above the belay, and take a seam to a bolt to the top. Belay at huecos with fixed slings. 80 feet.

Rappel using 2 ropes.
FA: Nick Nordblom, Jay Smith 1988

31. Spikes and Twine 5.9 ★★ Mixed, 1 bolt. Begin 25 feet right of *Super Nova*. Gear: to #3 Friend, mostly small stuff.

Pitch 1: 5.9 Climb the obvious crack that splits the face, then move left to another crack system. Belay at a horizontal break below an overhang. 100 feet.

Pitch 2: 5.9 Move right and through the steep section, clipping a bolt. Then go left to a seam, heading up and right through a groove. 75 feet.

Descend via the Red Heat Gully or by rappeling the previous route.
FA: Nick Nordblom, Jenni Stone 1988

32. Swedish Erotica 5.10a ★ Mixed, 2 bolts. Begin 10 feet right of *Spikes and Twine*. Gear: to #3 Friend.

Pitch 1: 5.10a Climb the face past 2 bolts to a thin seam. Take the seam up and angle around left to the horizontal break below an overhang. 100 feet.

Pitch 2: 5.9 Connect with the second pitch of *Spikes and Twine*.

Pitch 2 variation: Traverse 20 feet up and right on a ramp and rappel with 2 ropes off the anchors of *Flame Ranger*.
FA: Paul Van Betten, Katja Tjornman 1988

33. Flame Ranger 5.11d/5.12a ★★ Mixed, 7 bolts. Begin 25 feet right of the previous route, at the next seam on varnished rock. Climb the seam to a right-leaning ramp and flake. Move right, up a flake, and then break up the face 7 bolts to the fixed anchor. Gear: to #1 Friend, mostly smaller stuff. Rappel with two ropes.
FA: Bob Conz, Paul Van Betten, Sal Mamusia, Shelby Shelton 1991

34. Rock Nazi 5.12a ★★★ Mixed, 7 bolts. Climb *Flame Ranger*, but continue right on the ramping flake for 15 feet. Take bolts, moving up and alongside a seam to fixed anchors. Run-out finish. Gear: small.
FA: Paul Van Betten, Bob Conz, Shelby Shelton, Sal Mamusia 1991

35. Titan Rocket 5.12a ★★ Sport, 8 bolts. Begin 30 feet right of the previous route, left of a chimney.
FA: Paul Van Betten, Bob Conz, Shelby Shelton, Sal Mamusia 1991

▲ STRATOCASTER WALL
S All-Day Sun   Approach: 25 minutes

Follow the Sandstone Quarry East directions. In the wash, pass a wall on your right with two natural threads about four feet off the ground. After seeing the threads, move left and scramble up red slabs (north). At the top of the slabs, head right (east) for 10 minutes, following the cliff base. You will know you are at the Stratocaster Wall when you see the obvious chalked, bolted arête in the middle of a cave (*Pablo Diablo*). Routes are described from left to right.

36. Project Two bolts on the bulge on the far-left side of this wall are located 10 feet right of a thin gully.

37. Break Loose 5.11a ★★ Traditional. Begin 10 feet right of the project. Climb a crack that goes through the left side of a giant roof. Gear: to #4 Friend. 120 feet. Descend the thin gully on the left side of the wall.
FA: Jay Smith, Jo Bentley 1988

38. Diablo 5.10, A1 ★ Traditional/aid. Begins 20 feet right of the previous route. Originally aided without pins or bolts, this route climbs the left-facing corner 3 feet left of the *Pablo Diablo* arête. At the roof, move out to a large hueco. Descend the thin gully on the left side of the wall.
FA: Paul Van Betten, Sal Mamusia 1988

39. Pablo Diablo 5.12d ★★★★★ Sport, 5 bolts. Climb the arête in the middle of the cave. Classic!
FA: Paul Van Betten, Sal Mamusia 1993

40. Pablo Diablo Extension 5.12d ★★ Sport, 9 bolts. From the anchor of *Pablo Diablo* continue climbing out the roof past 3 more bolts. Watch the rope running over the sharp roof. Rappel.
FA: Unknown

41. Cut Loose 5.11a ★★★★ Mixed, 2 bolts. Five feet right of *Pablo Diablo*, climb a crack and huecos to a roof, move right, clipping 2 bolts, to the anchors. Gear: small and medium Friends.
FA: Jay Smith, Nick Nordblom 1988

42. One-Eyed Jack 5.11b ★★★ Sport, 5 bolts. This route is referred to by some as *Blind Jack* because the eye feature at the start has broken. About 30 feet right of *Pablo Diablo*, this route begins on some steep huecos. Finish at the anchors or continue to the *Footloose* anchors for more climbing at the same grade.
FA: Donny Burroughs, Alan Busby 1993

43. Footloose 5.11b ★★★★ Sport, 7 bolts. Climb the face left of a small gully and 5 feet right of *One-Eyed Jack*. Loose rock at start.
FA: Craig Reason 1991

To reach the next two routes, scramble up the gully right of *Footloose* to the next ledge (15 feet). Both routes climb the tall, southwest face, right of a scrub oak.

44. Flying V 5.11b ★★ Sport, 7 bolts. Begin out of the gully behind the scrub oak. It is about 20 feet to

first bolt. Take the face up and left through a bulge at the top to reach the anchors. Scary with loose holds.
FA: Kelly Rich, Mark Swank 1993

45. Party Line 5.10d R ★ Mixed, 1 bolt. Begin 15 feet right of *Flying V*, right of a thin seam. Climb the lightning-bolt crack and seam obtained by scrambling up behind a small bush. The route was a novelty climb to reach the top of the tier and a huge "party hueco." Gear: small and brass nuts, small Friends.

Pitch 1: 5.10d, 1 bolt. Diagonal up and right to the belay. 120 feet.

Pitch 2: 5.10a Climb up the right side of the big hueco and bushy ledge. One-bolt anchor. 30 feet. Rappel and hike down the gully to the west.
FA: Nick Nordblom, Jay Smith, Jo Bentley, Jenni Stone 1988

The following routes are located on the next feature right of *Footloose* and below the previous two routes.

46. Party Down 5.12b ★ Sport, 2 bolts. This route is a short one, located 30 feet right of *Footloose*.
FA: Dan McQuade 1995

47. Choad Hard 5.12c ★ Sport, 12 bolts. Five feet right of *Party Down*, climb past 6 bolts to an anchor. Continue up 5 more bolts, moving through a steep bulge, to a second anchor. You may want to stick-clip the first bolt.
FA: Tim Roberts 1995

48. Choad Warrior 5.12c ★★★★ Sport, 12 bolts. Climb to a big ledge/hole you can sit in (first anchor) and continue climbing out the steep bulge at the top. Rappel.
FA: Dan McQuade 1992

Dan de Lang at the top of Stratocaster Direct *5.12b.*
Photo by Dan McQuade

49. Choad Warrior Variation 5.12a ★★★ Sport,
5 bolts. Climb to the first anchor of *Choad Warrior*.
FA: Dan McQuade 1992

50. When the Shit Hits the Fan 5.11d R ★ Tradi-
tional. Climb suspect rock up the crack system 5

feet right of *Choad Warrior*. Go right at a roof and
continue up the crack using gear to #5 Friend. Finish on a thin seam angling up and left. This route
was rappelled when one of the first ascensionists
was injured in a fall. Unfinished.
FA: Jay Smith, Paul Crawford 1987

51. Unknown 5.11c ★★★ Sport, 9 bolts. Right of
the previous route, jump to jug at head height and
continue up the steep, huecoed wall to fixed anchors. You may want to stick-clip the first bolt.
Rappel using a 60-meter rope.
FA: Unknown

52. Marshall Amp 5.11b ★★★★ Sport, 10 bolts.
Climb the bolted line 5 feet right of the previous
route. Climb the right-angling crack and move left
to below a roof. Continue up huge jugs and huecos.
It is best to stick-clip the first bolt. A 70-meter rope
rappel.
  Alternate finish: Climb to the eighth bolt and
move left to the anchors of the previous route. From
here you can rappel using a 60-meter rope.
*FA: Bob Conz, Shelby Shelton, Jay Smith, Paul Van
Betten 1991*

53. Stratocaster Direct 5.12b ★★★★★ Sport, 8
bolts. Start in a cave right of the previous route.
Climb out of the steepest part of the cave on its right
side. If you get through the bottom of this route, you
better go to the top. A 70-meter rope is needed for
rappeling, or use midway anchors to rappel.
  Variation: 5 bolts. Climb the steepest part of the
route to the first set of anchors.
FA: Dan McQuade 1992

54. Stratocaster 5.11c ★★★★★ Mixed, 7 bolts.
Begin at the chimney right of *Stratocaster Direct*, at
the black water streak.
  Pitch 1: 5.10b R, 3 bolts. Climb the chimney/crack
to a pod. Move left, clipping 3 bolts to bolted anchors
40 feet above the first set of anchors on *Stratocaster
Direct*. 90 feet.
  Pitch 2: 5.11c, 4 bolts. Move up the face just left
of the arête. 100 feet. A 70-meter rope is easiest for

getting down or use the midway anchors.
FA: Jay Smith, Nick Nordblom 1988

55. Beyond Reason 5.13b ★★★ Sport, 7 bolts. A slam on the person who put the bolts in the wall. Start on the prominent face, just right of *Strato-caster*. Powerful climbing with a hard clip. Best to stick-clip the first 2 bolts.
FA: Dan McQuade 1995

56. Purple Haze II, 5.12c ★★★ Sport, 8 bolts. Start off a big block. Climb a blunt arête and then move up and left onto a steep, rounded prow. Finish on the steep face. Rappel.
FA: Dan McQuade 1995

57. The Bristler 5.12a ★ Mixed, 3 bolts. Named after Richard Harrison's term for a bolt. Begin as for *Purple Haze*, passing the first 3 bolts, and then move straight up, through the notch. 30 feet. Descend by traversing right and down.
FA: Sal Mamusia, Paul Van Betten 1987

58. Telecaster 5.11c ★ Traditional. Climb the overhanging crack 5 feet right of *The Bristler* up and left. Join *The Bristler* at the notch and descend as for *The Bristler*. 40 feet.
FA: Jay Smith, Paul Crawford 1988

The next route is located about 200 yards right (east) of the *Telecaster* on the far edge of the ledge system, directly above the Observatory (described in the Second Pullout chapter). A scramble takes you to the base.

59. Cowboy Café 5.12b ★★★★ Sport, 6 bolts. Climb the steepest, rightmost section of this dark-colored wall. Take huecos to a thin face.
FA: Don Welsh 1990

▲ SUB-AMERICRAG
S Midday Sun   Approach: 10 minutes

Follow the Sandstone Quarry East directions, taking the trail past the mushroom-shaped boulder into the wash. Go all the way down into the wash, cross it, and take the gully moving up and left (northwest) on rock slabs. Sub-Americrag is a short, 40-foot face with varnished edges, up 100 feet on the right. Routes are described from left to right.

60. Unknown 5.7 ★★★ Sport, 3 bolts. Climb the varnished edges up the middle of the wall to a bolted anchor over the top of the cliff.
FA: Mark Limage, Chris Burton, Gary Sanders

61. Stuck on You 5.8 ★★ Sport, 3 bolts. Start right of the previous route. Begin at the start of the rock rib and climb a red slab with varnished plates.
FA: Unknown

▲ AMERICRAG
NE AM Sun   Approach: 25 minutes

Follow the Sandstone Quarry East directions and head for Sub-Americrag, taking the trail past the mushroom-shaped boulder into the wash. Go all the way down into the wash, cross it, and take the gully moving up and left (northwest) on rock slabs. Sub-Americrag is a short, 40-foot face with varnished edges, up 100 feet on the right. Hike past it and then move down a rock rib into the wash south of the Sub-Americrag cliff. Scramble up red rock ribs (a few third-class moves) until you cannot go any farther and have to move left into the gully. Routes are described from left to right.

62. That Wedged Feeling 5.10d ★★ Traditional. Climb the crack system on the left wall, midway up the gully to Americrag. It is down and left 50 feet from where the approach hike forces you into the gully. Take a left-facing corner into a pod, then move over an overhang and take a crack to the top. Gear: Rocks, double set of Friends to #4. Walk off to the right.
FA: Jay Smith, Lee Erickson 1990

The remaining routes are located 200 yards up the approach gully on the large, dark-brown, over-hanging wall. Approach the routes from the left side or from the white rock rib northwest of (in front of) the face. Gear: small #00–0.5 Friends, Rocks, and brass nuts. Routes are described from left to right.

Descent: Rappel slings may need to be replaced on the fixed anchors.

63. Toxic Playboy 5.12b ★★ Mixed, 10 bolts. Begin 50 feet up from the white boulder field.

Pitch 1: 5.12a Mixed, 4 bolts. Climb the face and seam to the fixed anchor. 60 feet.

Pitch 2: 5.12b Mixed, 6 bolts. Continue to the fixed anchor. 60 feet.

FA: Paul Van Betten, Richard Harrison, Sal Mamusia, Bob Conz 1990

64. Mr. Moto 5.11c ★★ Mixed, 4 bolts. Begin 10 feet right of the previous route. Climb the right-angling crack and then move left under the overhang to clip the first bolt. Take discontinuous seams up and gently left to the first anchors of *Toxic Playboy.*

FA: Paul Van Betten, Richard Harrison, Shelby Shelton 1990

65. Jimmy Nap 5.11c ★★★ Sport, 5 bolts. Start on *Mr. Moto.* Move over the right edge of the ceiling. Take the face and seams to a fixed anchor in the center of the wall.

FA: Paul Van Betten, Richard Harrison, Shelby Shelton 1990

66. Americragger 5.12a ★★ Sport, 4 bolts. Begin 10 feet right of *Jimmy Nap.* Get ready for some excitement—dynamic climbing to the fixed anchor.

FA: Paul Van Betten, Richard Harrison 1990

67. Rebel Yell 5.11d ★★★ Mixed, 7 bolts. Begin 25 feet right of the previous route. Take a crack and flake up and left to a varnished plate. Move left to a seam. Follow discontinuous seams to the fixed anchor.

FA: Paul Van Betten, Danny Meyers, Jenni Stone 1990

▲ THE PIER
NW No Sun   Approach: 5 minutes

The approach is short and the Pier is easy to find. From the parking lot, follow the trail exiting from the southeast corner, paralleling the rock and heading east

(right). Take the first trail that cuts off the main trail left, at the far edge of the white rock outcroppings. Take the trail into the gully (heading northeast). The Pier is the steep, northwest-facing cliff on the right side of the gully. Routes are described from left to right.

68. Long Walk On A Short Pier 5.9 ★★★ Sport, 7 bolts. Climb up the leftmost bolted route at the crag, around the east corner and about 15 feet down the slab.

FA: Leo and Karin Henson 1996

69. Basement 5.11b ★★★★ Sport, 6 bolts. Start atop the left side of the rock pillar/boulder at some big huecos. Move up and left.

FA: Leo Henson 1996

70. Destiny 5.12c ★★ Sport, 6 bolts. Start atop the rock pillar/boulder, and climb the seam straight up to the anchor.

FA: Leo Henson 1996

71. Poco Owes Me a Concert 5.12c ★ Sport, 8 bolts. Start just right of the rock pillar. Climb past 5 bolts to a crack and move left up the face for 3 more bolts.

FA: Leo Henson 1996

72. Almost, But Not Quite 5.12c ★ Sport, 9 bolts. Start in a big hueco. Climb up the right side of a seam. Move left after the third bolt and then up to the anchor.

FA: Leo Henson 1996

73. Pier Pressure 5.12b ★★★ Sport, 8 bolts. Start as for the previous route. Move up, staying slightly left of the seam after the third bolt.

FA: Leo and Karin Henson 1996

74. Under the Boardwalk 5.10b ★★★★ Sport, 6 bolts. Climb the very huecoed face 6 feet right of *Pier Pressure.* Climb straight up all the holds.

FA: Leo and Karin Henson 1996

75. Cling Free 5.12b ★★ Sport, 6 bolts. Climb the featured face between two seams. Reachy.

FA: Leo and Karin Henson 1996

76. Thirsty Quail 5.12b ★★★ Sport, 5 bolts. Climb out and over a small roof, 8 feet off the ground, up a thin seam.
FA: Leo and Karin Henson 1996

77. Drug-Sniffing Pot-Bellied Pig 5.12d ★★ Sport, 5 bolts. This is another thin seam, 5 feet right of *Thirsty Quail*. Begin at a left-facing flake.
FA: Leo Henson 1996

78. Geometric Progression 5.12a ★★★★ Sport, 5 bolts. Begin 5 feet right of the previous route. Climb the left side of the crack that marks the middle of the crag. There is a cool hueco at midheight. Bouldery, reachy.
FA: Leo and Karin Henson 1996

79. False Alarm 5.12c ★ Sport, 5 bolts. Start in front of the yucca plant, 3 feet right of the previous route. Very bouldery start, using a tiny undercling.

FA: Leo and Karin Henson 1996

80. How Do You Like Them Pineapples? 5.13b ★★ Sport, 5 bolts. Start in front of a bush, and climb up the two scoops. Bouldery right off the deck.
FA: Leo Henson 1996

81. Desert Oasis 5.12c ★ Sport, 4 bolts. Climb up the dark-colored rock and the small seam.
FA: Leo and Karin Henson 1996

82. This Is the City 5.12a ★★ Sport, 4 bolts. Start in front of the bush 5 feet right of the previous route, and climb the thin seam. Loose toward the top.
FA: Leo and Karin Henson 1996

83. Seventh Hour 5.11a ★★ Sport, 5 bolts. Start 10 feet right of the previous route, right of a bush at a small overhang. Climb up using the sidepulls.
FA: Leo and Karin Henson 1996

Jason Sellman Under the Boardwalk *5.10b at the Pier*

84. Scantily Clad Bimbo 5.11b ★★ Sport, 4 bolts. Climb the rightmost bolted route on the wall.
FA: Leo and Karin Henson 1996

▲ CALIFORNIA CRAGS
S All-Day Sun   Approach: 10 minutes

From the parking lot, follow the trail exiting from the southeast corner, paralleling the rock and heading east (right). Take the first trail that cuts left off the main trail, at the far edge of the white rock outcroppings. Take the trail into the gully (heading northeast) and then turn left (north). Cross the drainage and head for a dark-colored, pointed boulder on the huge red slab to the north. Take the rocky breakdown left of the boulder to reach a ledge below a dark, huecoed overhang. Routes are described from left to right.

Reach the following routes by moving left (west) at the overhang and around to a ledge above the drainage. Traverse the ledge all the way to its left edge.

85. Cal West 5.10c ★★★ Sport, 7 bolts. Begin 10 feet left of the blunt arête. Move up the seam to the face and connect with the *Hurricane* anchors.
FA: Albert Newman, Leo Henson 1998

86. Hurricane 5.11b ★★★ Sport, 8 bolts. Climb the right side of the blunt arête, left of a tiny gully. Move left and up the face to shared anchors with the previous route.
FA: Leo Henson, Albert Newman 1998

87. Quicksand 5.11d ★ Sport, 5 bolts. Begin 60 feet right of the previous route and 10 feet left of a left-facing corner. Move up and around the left side of a roof, up to anchors below a big ledge.
FA: Louie Anderson 1996

88. Far Cry From Josh 5.10c ★★ Sport, 4 bolts. Begin in the deepest part of a recession, across from *Quicksand* at a large, right-facing flake. Take the steep face up to the top of the cliff.
FA: Louie Anderson 1996

89. Just in from L.A. 5.11a ★★ Sport, 4 bolts. Begin 5 feet right of the previous route at a smaller, right-facing flake. Take the overhanging face to a 2-bolt anchor. Gear: optional small Friend between the second and third bolts.
FA: Louie Anderson 1996

90. The Staircase 5.3 ★★★ Traditional. Begins 100 feet right of *Just in from L.A.* on the right side of the dark overhanging section at the top of the approach hike (below an enormous boulder with a crack splitting it). Begin on the red arête on the far-right side of the cave. Move up a slab and then take huge huecos left across darker rock (above the overhang and beneath the boulder) to the top of the feature (the Second Tier).
FA: Unknown

SECOND TIER

The remainder of the routes are on the Second Tier. Approach via *The Staircase* or by going around the bushy gully right, to behind the feature, and hike up to a notch between routes 91–93 and 94–95.

91. Nevadatude 5.12b ★★ Sport, 5 bolts. Climb a vertical seam on the face above *Quicksand*.
FA: Leo Henson 1998

92. Serious Leisure 5.12a ★★★★ Sport, 6 bolts. Begin 20 feet right of the previous route, across from the *Escalator*. Take a crack up and left to the anchor.
FA: Louie Anderson 1996

93. Orange County 5.11b ★★ Sport, 6 bolts. Begin 10 feet up and right of the previous route.
FA: Leo Henson 1998

The following routes are located on the huge boulder east and across from the previous Second Tier routes.

94. People Mover 5.8 ★ Traditional. Climb the right-facing flake in the huge left-facing corner on the large boulder. Gear: to #4 Friend. Rappel off fixed gear in the roof (bring replacement slings).
FA: Unknown 1995

95. The Escalator 5.10 ★★ Mixed, 2 bolts. Climb the varnished slab right of *People Mover*. Gear: Rocks and smaller Friends. Descend off the back of the boulder.
FA: Unknown 1995

SANDSTONE QUARRY PARKING AREA

▲ FRONT CORRIDOR
E/W PM/AM Sun   Approach: 2 minutes

The Front Corridor is the first corridor directly east of the parking area. Walk up some smaller-sized boulders until you can see the entrance to the corridor, and head north into the narrow corridor. Routes are described from left to right, starting on the left (west) side of the corridor.

WEST FACE

96. Unknown 5.10 ★ Sport, 5 bolts. This is the leftmost bolted route on the west wall.
FA: Unknown

97. Churning in the Dirt 5.12c ★ Mixed, 3 bolts. Begin 30 feet right of the previous route, on the black-plated face with a crack going through it. Shared anchor with *Sound of Power*. Low quality, high choss factor.
FA: Mike Tupper, Craig Reason 1988

98. Sound of Power 5.12b ★★★ Sport, 4 bolts. Begin 5 feet right of the previous route. Run-out. The flakes keep breaking and the route keeps getting harder.
FA: Mike Tupper, Craig Reason 1988

Top View of Front Corridor, Front Slab and Sandy Corridor

96. Unknown 5.10
97. Churning in the Dirt 5.12c
98. Sound of Power 5.12b
99. Sun Splash 5.13b
100. Monster Skank 5.13b
101. Gun Control 5.11b
102. To Bolt or Toupee 5.10c
103. Hair Today, Gone Tomorrow 5.11a
104. High Noon 5.11b R

105. A Thousand New Routes 5.11b R
106. Crumbling Community 5.10c
107. Affliction for Friction 5.11a R
108. Friction Addiction 5.10c
109. Prescription Gription 5.10c R
110. Sicktion 5.9
111. The Only Way 5.8 R
112. Fender Bender 5.5
113. Unknown Seam 5.8 R
114. Unknown Face 5.8 R/X

115. White Slab 5.8 R
116. Unknown 5.6 R
117. Unknown 5.7
118. The Ring Leader 5.8
119. Bolt Route 5.9+ R/X
120. John's Wall 5.10b R/X
121. Belay Delay 5.10a R/X
122. Seams to Me 5.10b
123. Inn Zone 5.9
124. Chicken Boy 5.11a
125. Forbidden Zone 5.11d
126. Bark at the Moon 5.11b
127. Octopussy 5.10c
128. You Only Live Twice 5.10c
129. Chrysler Crack 5.10a
130. Unknown 5.12d
131. Knarls 5.11d/5.12a
132. Shibu Discipline 5.11b R
133. Centurion 5.10d R
134. Rat Boy 5.9
135. Monk Watch 5.9+
136. Forced Feltch 5.10a
137. Integrity of Desire 5.12a
138. Flying Cowboys 5.12d
139. Plastic Pistol 5.12b

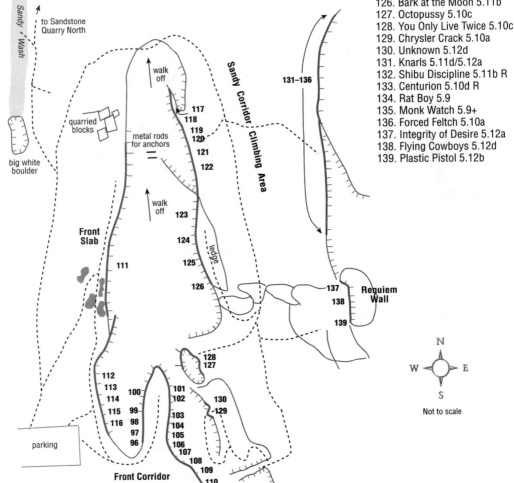

99. Sun Splash 5.13b ★★★★ Sport, 8 bolts. Climb the pockets and seams right of *Sound of Power*. The grade has settled in at solid 5.13b. Red Rock test piece.
FA: Dan McQuade 1995

100. Monster Skank 5.13b ★★★★ Sport, 8 bolts. This is the area classic, just right of *Sun Splash*. Easy climbing up jugs leads to the second bolt, and then the pumping pain begins.
FA: Dan McQuade 1993

EAST FACE
All of these routes are run-out to the first bolts.
   Descent: Walk off the slab down and right.

101. Gun Control 5.11b ★★★★ Sport, 8 bolts. Begin 10 feet right of the end of the corridor on a black, varnished face. Climb past bolts and through a crack in the scoop, then exit left to the anchor. 120 feet.
FA: Bob Conz, Shelby Shelton, Nick Nordblom 1988

102. To Bolt or Toupee 5.10c ★★★★ Sport, 7 bolts. Climb up 5 feet right of *Gun Control*. Climb the right-facing corner and then up the right side of a scoop to the anchors. 120 feet.
FA: Mike Ward, Paul Van Betten 1988

103. Hair Today, Gone Tomorrow 5.11a ★★★ Mixed, 7 bolts. Climb a seam, moving up 25 feet right of the previous route. 120 feet.
FA: Nick Nordblom, Paul Van Betten 1988

104. High Noon 5.11b R ★★ Mixed, 6 bolts. Begin 15 feet right of the previous route at a varnished, right-facing corner. Gear: to #3.5 Friend. 120 feet.
FA: Nick Nordblom, Jenni Stone 1988

105. A Thousand New Routes 5.11b R ★★ Mixed, 3 bolts, homemade bolt hangers. Climb a crack angling up and left out of a sort of alcove, 35 feet right of *High Noon*. Move up and right to finish at a bolted belay. 130 feet.
FA: Paul Van Betten, Nick Nordblom 1986

Bill McLemore getting ugly on Monster Skank *5.13b in the Front Corridor*

106. Crumbling Community 5.10c ★★★ Mixed, 3 bolts. Begin 25 feet right of the previous route at a gray water streak. Continue up a crack, angling up and left. Gear: to #3 Friend. 100 feet.
FA: Paul Van Betten, Danny Meyers 1989

107. Affliction for Friction 5.11a R ★ Mixed, 5 bolts. Begin 15 feet right of the previous route, with a hard mantel. After the second bolt, move left to a seam to the top. Gear: larger Friends for the belay. 90 feet.
FA: Mike Ward, Danny Meyers 1989

108. Friction Addiction 5.10c ★★ Mixed, 5 bolts. Begin right of a scrub-oak tree, 5 feet right of the previous route. Climb to a seam up and left. Gear: larger Friends for the belay. 80 feet.
FA: Bob Conz, Shelby Shelton 1988

109. Prescription Gription 5.10c R ★ Mixed, 4 bolts. Start 10 feet right of the previous route. Climb a bolted slab to a left-leaning seam and then to a vertical crack. Gear: larger Friends for the belay. 80 feet.
FA: Nick Nordblom, Jenni Stone 1988

110. Sicktion 5.9 ★★★ Mixed, 3 bolts. Begin 12 feet right of the previous route. Climb the vertical seam beginning below a flake. No anchor. Gear: larger Friends and a small one for the anchor. 80 feet.
FA: Nick Nordblom, Randy Marsh 1988

▲ FRONT SLAB
W PM Sun   Approach: 1 minute

This big white slab is the first section of rock you see once you have parked at the Sandstone Quarry parking lot. The cliff is directly northeast of the parking lot and faces west. There are no rappel or lower-off anchors on these routes. Routes are described from left to right.
   Descent: Walk east to the top of the formation and then head down and north on colorful slabs. Upon reaching the ground, hike left around the front of the formation (south).

111. The Only Way 5.8 R ★ Traditional. Climb the red face 100 feet left of *Fender Bender*, below a roof and obvious notch in the top of the cliff. Gear: to #2 Friend.
FA: Scott Gordon, Jon Martinet, Randal Grandstaff

112. Fender Bender 5.5 ★★ Traditional. Climb the obvious right-facing flake on the main Front Slab wall. One bolt for an anchor; or use the bolt for a directional and build the anchor up and right at a more pleasant stance.
FA: Matt McMackin, Jim Whitesell 1973

113. Unknown Seam 5.8 R ★★★ Traditional. Climb the seamy slab 10 feet right of the previous route. Gear: small, to #1 Friend. One-bolt anchor.
FA: Unknown

114. Unknown Face 5.8 R/X ★★★ Traditional. Climb the face right of the previous route. Best to top-rope.
FA: Unknown

115. White Slab 5.8 R ★★★ Sport, 4 bolts. Begin 5 feet right of the previous route. Climb up the center of the wall. Sporty. Gear: good to supplement bolts with small Friends. Fixed anchor.
FA: Unknown

116. Unknown 5.6 R ★ Traditional or TR. Begin 100 feet right of the previous route in a scrub-oak patch. Climb up and right to a small tree above. Short. Gear: to #2.5 Friend.
FA: Unknown

▲ SANDY CORRIDOR
N/E/W   No Sun   Approach: 8 minutes

From the Sandstone Quarry parking lot, follow the main trail north to the quarried blocks. Continue hiking north along the base of the west-facing cliff (the wall will be on the right). After about 140 yards, the rock begins to break down and the colors sharply contrast between red and white. Pass this section, continuing right along the cliff base and into the Sandy Corridor. Walk into the corridor, heading right (southeast).

SANDY CORRIDOR WEST FACE
The following routes are on the east-facing wall (on the right) as you enter the corridor. Gear: bring a large

selection of gear up to a #4 Friend, and smaller Rocks including brass nuts. Sections are described from right to left.

Descent: Walk off north down the red and white slabs directly to the north toward Turtlehead Peak (same descent as Front Slab).

117. Unknown 5.7 ★★★ Traditional. Climb up the 25-foot, big off-width. Belly-roll over the rounded lip to the north. This route will be hard to protect due to its massive size.
FA: Unknown

The following three routes begin 8 feet left of the previous route and end at a large break where metal spikes are driven into the rock. Use the spikes for anchors. Routes are described from right to left.

118. The Ring Leader 5.8 ★★ Mixed, 2 bolts. Start up the slabby face 8 feet left of the big off-width. Climb to a bolt 15 feet up. Continue up, passing another bolt with no hanger (sling a nut). Follow up the main crack to the top of the wall.
FA: Unknown

119. Bolt Route 5.9+ R/X ★ Mixed, 1 bolt. Start on the slabby face 20 feet left of the big off-width. Climb to the first bolt, 40 feet up. Continue to the crack system, 60 feet up, and take it to the top of the wall.
FA: Unknown

120. John's Wall 5.10b R/X ★ Traditional. Start 50 feet left of the off-width. Climb up the slabby face to the varnished face 20 feet off the ground. Continue, using the thin seam to a bolt with no hanger (sling a nut). Follow the thin crack and join the previous route toward the top.
FA: Paul Van Betten, rope solo 1986

121. Belay Delay 5.10a R/X ★ Mixed, 1 bolt. Begin 60 feet left of the off-width. Climb the varnished face to a half-moon feature, 10 feet off the ground. Follow thin seams to a bolt with no hanger (sling a nut). Take the main crack to a ledge. Pass

the ledge to a steeper face with a bolt. Then follow a crack leading to the top.
FA: Paul Van Betten, Robert Tyler 1988

122. Seams to Me 5.10b ★★ Mixed, 1 bolt. Climb up 15 feet left of the previous route. Move up the slab directly in front of a tree. Follow underclings and a crack system to the same ledge as the previous route. Traverse right and finish the same as *Belay Delay*.
FA: Paul Crawford, Paul Van Betten 1986

The next four routes start atop a large ledge system located about 50 yards up the corridor on the east (right) face. These are serious mixed routes on round, dirty, downsloping rock, which may or may not have anchors (they keep getting removed because they are located over the top where they are easily snagged by thieves). Mike Tupper said you need a "catcher's mitt and a dust buster" to climb them. Routes are described from right to left.

123. Inn Zone 5.9 ★ Traditional. Climb the crack located on the far-right end of the wall.
FA: Nick Nordblom, Paul Van Betten 1986

124. Chicken Boy 5.11a ★★★ Mixed, 1 bolt. Begin left of *Inn Zone*. Climb up past a horizontal seam. Clip the first bolt and angle left into the main crack. Continue to the top of the wall and red-colored rock.
FA: Paul Van Betten, Paul Crawford 1986

125. Forbidden Zone 5.11d ★★ Mixed, 1 bolt. Start just left of the bush at the base of the wall. Climb up a tiny seam to the first bolt, about 9 feet up. Continue, finishing on the crack that heads to the top of the wall.
FA: Paul Van Betten, Nick Nordblom 1986

126. Bark at the Moon 5.11b ★★★ Mixed, 3 bolts. Begin on the left side of the ledge. Climb black-pocketed rock to a bolt, 10 feet off the deck. Continue to a second bolt, below a horizontal seam. Follow a vertical seam, passing yet another bolt, to the top.
FA: Paul Crawford, Paul Van Betten, Mike Tupper 1986

Approach the next two routes by scrambling 200 feet up the hillside to the right after passing through the first set of boulders in the gully. Continue uphill to the base of an east-facing, red pillar formation. Routes are described from left to right.

127. Octopussy 5.10c ★ Sport. This is the leftmost bolted route on the freestanding block 200 feet southwest of the previous route. There was a lot of

controversy surrounding this route, as it was rap-bolted when that practice was not acceptable in Red Rock Canyon. The bolts were chopped on the route and later replaced.
FA: Larry Moore

128. You Only Live Twice 5.10c ★★ Sport. Climb the face/corner 5 feet right of the previous route.
FA: Unknown

For the next two routes, hike farther southeast to the top of the gully (some bushwhacking). Look for a narrow, slot corridor on the right (west) and scramble up to it. At the mouth, hike and scramble right (north) and west up the white slabs. At the top of the slabs, hike 40 feet right to *Chrysler Crack*. It is the huge, open-book off-width up the black, varnished center of the wall. Routes are described from left to right (as approached).

129. Chrysler Crack 5.10a ★★★★ Traditional. Run-out. A #6 Friend and a couple of very small Friends or TCUs will get you through the bottom section. Two small nuts are all you can hope for in the center. It gets easier toward the top. Exit right. 100 feet. Walk and downclimb off to the left (south).
FA: Randal Grandstaff, Jon Martinet

130. Unknown 5.12d ★ Sport. Climb up the obvious east-facing bolted arête right of *Chrysler Crack*.
FA: Jeff Weigand 1990s

SANDY CORRIDOR EAST FACE
Routes 131–139 are on the west-facing wall (on the left) and are described from left to right as you enter the corridor. Routes 131–136 require the following gear: #2–#3.5 Friends needed for anchors.

Descent: Walk off directly north and down the big slab system located at the mouth of the corridor.

131. Knarls 5.11d/5.12a ★ TR. This is a white-colored seam located on the west-facing wall as you enter Sandy Corridor. Climb the white seam to chain anchors.
FA: Paul Van Betten, Sal Mamusia

Roxanna Brock worming up Chrysler Crack, *old school 5.9, in the Sandy Corridor*

132. Shibu Discipline 5.11b R ★ Mixed, 1 bolt. Begin on the north edge of the west-facing wall, right of *Knarls* and directly in front of a large group of trees. Follow a thin vertical seam to a bolt, 15 feet off the ground. Continue angling right to another seam, leading to a horizontal crack three-quarters of the way up. Gear: bring a #2 Friend for the horizontal seam at the top.
FA: Paul Van Betten, Sal Mamusia 1989

133. Centurion 5.10d R ★ Traditional. Start at the base of a big, right-angling crack that runs up and across the wall. Follow this crack for 10 feet and then head straight up using a small seam to the top. Gear: set of smaller Rocks.
FA: Paul Van Betten, Sal Mamusia, Kevin Biernacki 1989

134. Rat Boy 5.9 ★★★ Traditional. Climb the right-angling arch/crack system that heads up and right. Gear: bring a wide selection, up to a #3 Friend.
FA: Paul Van Betten, Shelby Shelton 1989

135. Monk Watch 5.9+ ★★ Traditional. Begin 30 feet right of the big crack system marking the start of the previous route, in front of a large tree. Follow the crack and join *Rat Boy* three-quarters of the way up. Gear: a set of Rocks and Friends to #4.
FA: Sal Mamusia, Paul Van Betten 1989

136. Forced Feltch 5.10a ★ Traditional. Begin 25 feet right of the big tree and the previous route. Climb up the seam/crack that runs up the wall at the blue spray paint. Gear: a set of Friends to #3.5 and Rocks.
FA: Sal Mamusia, Paul Van Betten 1989

◣ REQUIEM WALL
W PM sun   Approach: 15 minutes

This wall is tucked away in the back end of the Sandy Corridor. From the Sandstone Quarry parking lot, follow the main trail north to the quarried blocks. Continue hiking north along the base of the west-facing cliff (the wall will be on the right). After about 140 yards, the rock begins to break down and the colors sharply contrast between red and white. Pass this section, continuing right along the cliff base and into the Sandy Corridor. From the entrance of the Sandy Corridor, hike southeast, moving deeper into the corridor. Upon reaching a point requiring some scrambling, the Requiem Wall is up and left, past the large pine trees in the center of the gully. The wall sits 50 yards down and left of the top of the main gully system, almost directly across from *Chrysler Crack*. Routes are described from left to right.

137. Integrity of Desire 5.12a ★★★ Sport, 6 bolts. Climb and stem the leftmost bolted route on the wall. Begin just right of the crack/corner system and finish at the chain anchor.
FA: Mike Tupper 1991

138. Flying Cowboys 5.12d ★★★ Sport, 6 bolts. Climb up just right of the big rounded corner and 20 feet right of the previous route.
FA: Don Welsh 1991

139. Plastic Pistol 5.12b ★★★ Sport, 5 bolts. Climb the rightmost route on the wall, starting 20 feet left of the cliff's right edge.
FA: Don Welsh 1991

SANDSTONE QUARRY WEST

◣ THE ASYLUM
NE Sun AM   Approach: 15 minutes

This little boulder formation is located at the top of the Sonic Youth Wall. From the parking area, follow the main northerly trail into the wash. Just before the big white boulder, on the left in the wash (with boulder problems on it), turn left (west). Follow the trail for about 200 feet and continue as it moves uphill. At the crest of the hill, at the first white rock formation, go right (north), staying on the right (east) side of the white formation. Walk past this formation for about 100 feet, moving up white slabs of rock. The

Asylum is the huge boulder that sits atop this big formation. Upon reaching the boulder at the top, go right and around the corner. The routes will be on your left and are described from left to right.

Descent: Walk off the backside of the Asylum, heading down and right (north).

140. Lounge Tomato 5.12b ★ Mixed, 4 bolts, black-painted bolt hangers. Climb up using a thin seam and crimpers.
FA: Chris Burton, Jeremy Taylor 1998

141. Comforts of Madness 5.11b ★ Mixed, 5 bolts. Climb up using grey-painted bolt hangers; the fourth is black. Power up lighter-colored rock using small pockets and huecos.
FA: Daniel Hudgins, Jeremy Smith 1997

142. Flip the Switch 5.10d ★★ Mixed, 5 bolts. Climb the shallow seam on the right side of the formation, clipping closed cold-shut bolt hangers painted white.
FA: Chris Burton, Jeremy Taylor, Jeremy Smith 1997

▲ SONIC YOUTH WALL
NE AM Sun   Approach: 15 minutes

From the parking area, follow the main northerly trail into the wash. Pass a big white boulder in the wash on the left (with boulder problems on it—a fun place to warm up). On the north side of the boulder is a low, white, rock formation that is long and flat on the top. At the end of this formation is a faint trail that heads left (west). Follow this trail up the hill. After the trail leads to level ground, take a right and hike about 100 yards north. The Sonic Youth Wall is the steep wall on the left with two big black streaks running down it. Routes are described from left to right.

SONIC YOUTH LOWER WALL

143. Project ★ Mixed, 3 bolts. Start 8 feet left of the big bush at the base of the wall. Climb up passing 3 bolts. After the third bolt, enter a crack system. Toward the top of the route, traverse a handrail to finish at the *Hooligans* anchor.
Equipped by: Paul Van Betten, Gary Savage

144. Hooligans 5.11c ★★ Sport, 7 bolts. Start 5 feet left of the big bush at the base of the wall. Follow a thin seam and continue to the anchor.
FA: Greg Meyer 1992

145. GBH 5.11c ★★★ Sport, 9 bolts. Climb up at the left edge of the bush at the base of the wall. Start at the huecos. Climb to a slopey ledge and then follow a seam to the anchor.
FA: Paul Van Betten, Richard Harrison, Kevin Biernacki 1989

146. Black Flag 5.11c ★★ Sport, 7 bolts. Start on the right side of the bush located at the base of the wall. Follow the seam located left of the large black streak in the middle of the wall.
FA: Paul Van Betten, Bob Conz 1989

147. Loki 5.12a ★★★ Sport. Start 10 feet right of the bush. Climb up the right side of the big black streak located in the middle of the wall.
FA: Don Welsh 1991

148. Agent Orange 5.12b ★★★ Sport, 9 bolts. Start atop the ramp/ledge system located on the right side of the crag. Climb the orange rock.
FA: Paul Van Betten, Bob Conz 1989

149. Sonic Youth 5.11c ★★★★★ Sport, 5 bolts. Begin just left of the water streak on the right edge of the cliff. Climb lighter-colored rock to an anchor located on the upper bulge.
FA: Paul Van Betten, Sal Mamusia, Bob Conz 1989

150. Everybody's Slave 5.11c ★★ Sport, 6 bolts. Start in the middle of the black streak on the right side of the wall and just right of *Sonic Youth*. Climb up the black pocketed face to the anchor at the bulge.
FA: Don Welsh 1991

SONIC YOUTH UPPER WALL

The following four routes start off the ledge system that is about three-quarters of the way up the Sonic Youth Wall. To reach the ledge, either climb up on one of the lower wall routes or take a scary scramble around the right (north) side of the cliff.

Descent: Walk off directly to the south from atop of the formation, passing the Asylum on the right. Continue down the white slabs toward the parking lot to a good trail. Take the trail back around the south corner of the Sonic Youth Wall.

151. Hip-Hoppin' with the Hutterites 5.8 ★
Traditional. Start on the left end of the upper wall. Climb up 40 feet left of a big, right-facing corner. Follow a seam to a horizontal break in the wall. Take a good crack past the break to the top. Gear: #0–#2.5 Friends, mid- to smaller-sized Rocks.
FA: Todd and Donette Swain 1994

152. Seka's Soiled Panties 5.11b ★★ Mixed, 1 bolt. Climb up 20 feet right of the big, right-facing corner system and 15 feet left of a big water streak. Climb thin seams to a bolt in the roof. Clip the bolt and follow cracks to the top. Gear: #00–#0 Friends, smaller Rocks.
FA: Richard Harrison, Paul Van Betten 1989

153. Crankenstein 5.10c ★★★ Mixed, 3 bolts. Climb the big black streak in the middle of the wall. Gear: bring a #00 Friend for the start and some larger Friends for the upper huecos and anchor.
FA: Danny Meyers 1988

154. Slam Dancin' with the Amish 5.9 ★★ Mixed, 3 bolts. Start in the little, right-facing corner system. Follow this up to a bolt located just right of the seam. Climb past 2 more bolts to a good crack that leads to the top of the wall. Gear: mid-sized Rocks for the start and a #3 Friend for the top and anchor.
FA: Paul and Pauline Van Betten 1989

▲ BOAST AND TOAST WALL
SW PM Sun   Approach: 18 minutes

The Boast and Toast Wall is the big, southwest-facing cliff just past the Sonic Youth Wall on the right. From the parking area, follow the main northerly trail into the wash. Pass a big white boulder in the wash on the left (with boulder problems on it—a fun place to warm up). On the north side of the boulder is a low, white, rock formation that is long and flat on the top. At the end of this formation is a faint trail that heads left (west) to the Sonic Youth Wall. Continue heading north past the Sonic Youth Wall, walking up light tan–colored slabs and the main gully system to the north. The Boast and Toast Wall is the first wall on the right. Routes are described from left to right.

Descent: Walk off to the northwest, down the slabs. Head toward the Common Time Wall and back to the base of the wall.

155. C.H.U.D. 5.11c ★★★ Sport, 6 bolts. Scramble up two ledge systems at the far-left side of the main formation. Climb up the light-colored face using sidepull flakes.
FA: Paul Van Betten, Sal Mamusia, Richard Harrison, Bob Conz, Shelby Shelton 1989

156. Girls Skool 5.12a ★★ Sport, 7 bolts. This new addition to the cliff is the second bolted route from the left, with bomber Fixe anchors.
FA: Michelle Locatelli 2004

157. Desert Sportman 5.11a ★★ Sport, 8 bolts. Scramble up the ledges as for Girls Skool and start 20 feet right of Girls Skool. Climb to the second bolt and then head slightly left. Three-quarters of the way up, take a crack leading to the anchor.
FA: Paul Van Betten, Sal Mamusia 1988

158. Roasted Ramen 5.9 ★ Traditional. Begin on the left side of the cave formation at the base of the wall. Climb up the face heading to the A-shaped roof. Continue heading up and left following two separate seam and crack systems to the top. Gear: smaller Friends and small Rocks.
FA: Paul Van Betten, Don Burroughs, Sal Mamusia 1988

159. Calico Jack 5.11a ★★★ Mixed, 3 bolts. Start as for the previous route. Climb the face heading to the A-shaped small roof. Follow a crack out the roof. Ten feet past the roof, head right to steeper climbing, passing 3 bolts to the top.

FA: Richard Harrison, Paul Van Betten, Don Burroughs 1989

160. Rap Bolters Need to be Famous 5.11c ★★
Mixed, 5 bolts. Begin at the right edge of the cave formation at the base of the wall, just left of a big, smooth, dark-brown section of rock. Climb thin seams past 5 bolts. The route gets steeper the higher you go.
FA: Richard Harrison, Paul Van Betten 1989

161. Burnt Toast 5.10c ★★★ Mixed, 3 bolts. Start at the right edge of the cliff, atop a boulder at the base, just below a small roof system. Follow the crack just under the roof, staying left. At 20 feet up, follow a curving crack to steeper rock, clipping 3 bolts to the top. Gear: a set of small to mid-sized Rocks.
FA: Paul Van Betten, Sal Mamusia, Bob Conz, Jim Lybarger 1988

162. Fairy Toast 5.10c ★★ Mixed, 4 bolts. Start the same as the previous route. At the peak of the roof, head slightly right, up the series of slanting seams leading to a good crack that runs to the top of the wall. Gear: a set of Rocks and Friends to #3.
FA: Richard Harrison, Paul Van Betten, Wendell Broussard 1989

▲ NUMBERS CRAG
SW PM Sun Approach: 20 minutes

The Numbers Crag is located just past the Boast and Toast Wall on the right. From the parking area, follow the main northerly trail into the wash. Pass a big white boulder in the wash on the left (with boulder problems on it—a fun place to warm up). On the north side of the boulder is a low, white, rock formation that is long and flat on the top. At the end of this formation is a faint trail that heads left (west) to the Sonic Youth Wall. Continue heading north past the

Sonic Youth Wall, walking up light tan–colored slabs and the main gully system to the north. The Boast and Toast Wall is the first wall on the right. Continue past it to the shorter Numbers Crag, on the right side of the gully. Routes are described from left to right.

Descent: Walk off the slabs east toward the Boast and Toast Wall. You will end up in the drainage between the Numbers Crag and Boast and Toast Wall.

163. Number 0 5.10 ★ Mixed, 2 bolts. Start 20 feet in from the left (west) end of the formation. Climb through scoop features. Join a seam 15 feet up and follow it to the top. No anchor.
FA: Paul Van Betten, Sal Mamusia, Richard Harrison 1992

164. Number 0.5 5.12c ★★ Mixed, 3 bolts. Start 20 feet right of the previous route. Climb to the crack and small roof filled with chockstones. Follow a seam, heading left to the top. No anchor.
FA: Sal Mamusia, Paul Van Betten 1992

165. Number 1 5.11d ★★★ Sport, 6 bolts. Begin up 4 feet on a small ledge. Move up to the double hueco feature. At the second bolt, take a seam to the top.
FA: Sal Mamusia, Paul Van Betten, Richard Harrison 1992

166. Number 2 5.11c ★★★ Sport, 5 bolts. This route climbs the middle section of the main wall. The first bolt is located 10 feet off the deck.
FA: Richard Harrison, Shelby Shelton, Sal Mamusia, Paul Van Betten, 1992

167. Number 3 5.11d ★★ Sport, 5 bolts. Climb to the first bolt, 15 feet up. Continue to easier climbing and a pumpy finish.
FA: Shelby Shelton, Richard Harrison, Paul Van Betten 1992

168. Number 4 5.12a ★★★ Sport, 5 bolts. Climb up 10 feet left of the big hueco. Follow a thin seam to steeper climbing toward the anchor.
FA: Paul Van Betten, Sal Mamusia, Richard Harrison 1992

169. Number 5 5.12b ★★★★ Sport, 5 bolts. Start at the left side of the huge hueco at the base of the wall's right side. Climb a technical seam just past the first bolt. The climbing steepens as you move up.
FA: Paul Van Betten, Sal Mamusia, Richard Harrison, Bob Conz 1992

170. Project 1 bolt is located on the left side of a big hueco.

171. Number 6 5.11d ★★★★ Sport, 4 bolts. Start in the huge hueco on the right side of the wall. Climb up a dark tan face using good edges. The route steepens after the last bolt.
FA: Paul Van Betten, Sal Mamusia, Richard Harrison 1992

▲ COMMON TIME WALL
E/N AM Sun   Approach: 20 minutes

From the parking area, follow the main northerly trail into the wash, heading north. Pass a large white boulder in the wash on the left (with boulder problems on it—a fun place to warm up). On the north side of the boulder is a low, white, rock formation that is long and flat on the top. At the end of this formation is a faint trail that heads left (west). Follow this trail up the hill. After the trail leads to level ground, hike about 100 yards north to reach the Sonic Youth Wall, the steep wall to the left with two big black streaks running down it. Walk past the Sonic Youth Wall, heading up the main gully. Pass a big vertical wall on the right, the Boast and Toast Wall, and continue to the Numbers Crag. At the left (west) end of the Numbers Crag there is a white rock gully that heads north. Walk up this gully 200 feet. The Common Time Wall will be on the left. Routes are described from left to right.

172. Time Off 5.11a ★ Sport, 4 bolts. This is the leftmost bolted route on the east-facing wall. Start right of a crack.
FA: Leo and Karin Henson, Albert Newman 1998

173. Paradiddle Riddle 5.11b ★★ Sport, 4 bolts. Start 7 feet right of *Time Off.* Climb up the fragile

flake with brown-painted bolt hangers.
FA: Phil Bowden 1992

174. Myxolidian 5.11b ★★★ Sport, 4 bolts. This is
the rightmost bolted line. Begin 25 feet right of the
previous route. Climb up the short face on the
whitish colored rock.
FA: Greg Mayer 1992

The next route is located on the east side of the tiny
canyon directly across from the previous routes.

175. One Move Number 5.12a ★★ Sport, 3 bolts.
Climbs the middle of the north-facing boulder.
Short.
FA: Leo and Karin Henson, Albert Newman 1998

▲ WAKE UP WALL
N No Sun   Approach: 20 minutes

From the parking area, follow the main northerly trail
into the wash. Pass a big white boulder in the wash
on the left. Continue north on the main trail until
reaching a sign for Turtlehead Peak on the left. Take a
left on this trail. After about 240 yards, head up a
mound of dirt. From atop the mound, white rocks will
be visible on the left. Just before the trail drops back
down into the wash, turn left and cross white slabs,
and head toward the north-facing Wake Up Wall.
Routes are described from left to right.
   Descent: Walk off to the left (east) from the top
of the wall.

176. Monkey Rhythm 5.10c ★★★ Traditional.
This route is located on the wall's far-left side.
Climb the crack in the dihedral and finish at the
chain anchor.
FA: Paul Van Betten, Robert Finlay 1983

177. First Born 5.10b ★★ Mixed, 3 bolts. Start 10
feet right of the previous route, down in a pit between a slab of rock and the wall. Climb to the first
bolt, and continue to a good #4 Friend placement
in the roof. Follow the crack to the anchor. Gear: a
selection of larger Rocks to supplement the bolts.
FA: Ed Prochaska 1990

178. Shut Up and Climb 5.11b ★★★★ Sport, 5
bolts. There's some good advice! Begin just right of
First Born. Climb the right side of the big hole/
hueco.
FA: Randy Faulk, Rick Denison 1991

179. Pound Cake 5.8 ★ Sport, 3 bolts. This is a
short climb. It is easy to top-rope from the line just
to the right (*Crack of Noon*), off the same anchor.
FA: Gail and Jay Mueller 1997

180. Crack of Noon 5.8 ★ Traditional. This is the
thin crack right of *Pound Cake* and shares its anchor.
Gear: #00–#1.5 Friends.
FA: Gail and Jay Mueller 1997

181. Shape of Things to Come 5.11a ★★ Sport, 3
bolts. Start just right of the big ramp, on the ledge 6
feet up. Short. Long distance to first bolt.
FA: Greg Mayer 1990

182. The Healer 5.11d ★★ Sport, 4 bolts. Start just
right of *Shape of Things to Come.* Shared anchor with
Rise and Wine.
FA: Greg Mayer 1989

183. Rise and Wine 5.12a ★★★ Sport, 4 bolts.
Start just right of the previous route. Shared anchor
with *The Healer.*
FA: Mike Tupper 1990

184. Pain Check 5.12a ★★ Sport, 5 bolts. Begin
right of *Rise and Wine.*
FA: Bill Boyle 1990

185. Good Morning 5.11b ★★★ Sport, 5 bolts.
Start 10 feet right of *Pain Check*, left of a small seam.
FA: Bill Boyle 1990

186. Native Son 5.11c ★★ Sport, 5 bolts. Begin in
the hueco right of *Good Morning.*
FA: Mike Tupper 1990

187. Where Egos Dare 5.12a ★★ Sport, 4 bolts.
Start as for *Native Son,* but climb up and right.
FA: Greg Mayer 1991

Wake Up Wall

177. First Born 5.10b
178. Shut Up and Climb 5.11b
179. Pound Cake 5.8
180. Crack of Noon 5.8
181. Shape of Things to Come 5.11a
182. The Healer 5.11d
183. Rise and Wine 5.12a

184. Pain Check 5.12a
185. Good Morning 5.11b
186. Native Son 5.11c
187. Where Egos Dare 5.12a
188. XTZ 5.8
189. Onsight Fight 5.12b
190. Stand and Deliver 5.12b

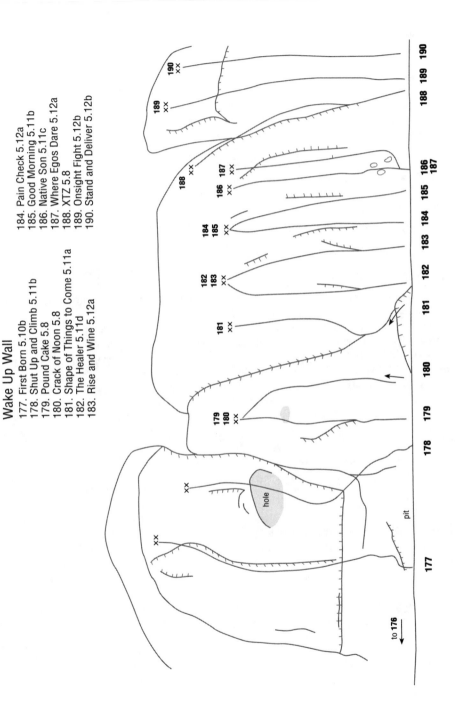

188. XTZ 5.8 ★ Traditional. Climb the ugly-looking off-width to the bolted anchor. Gear: a selection of large gear for the start and #3 and #4 Friends for the top.
FA: Greg Mayer 1990

189. Onsight Fight 5.12b ★★★ Sport, 5 bolts. Start just right of the left-leaning ramp. Climb the technical face to the anchor over the bulge. Run-out after the last bolt.
FA: Don Welsh 1990

190. Stand and Deliver 5.12b ★★ Sport, 4 bolts. This is the rightmost bolted route on the wall. Start 15 feet right of the previous route. Climb the vertical face to the anchor over the bulge.
FA: Mike Tupper 1990

SANDSTONE QUARRY NORTH

▲ THE TWINKIE
SW PM Sun   Approach: 15 minutes

From the parking area, follow the main northerly trail into the wash. Pass a big white boulder in the wash on the left. Continue north on the main trail until reaching a sign for Turtlehead Peak. Take a left on this trail and hike in a wash for about 450 yards. The Twinkie is the lowest formation in the wash on the right (just before the approach to the Trophy). Gear: all routes take brass nuts and #00–#1 Friends. Routes are described from left to right.

   Descent: Walk off the backside, heading north. This will drop you into the approach area to the Trophy, Bull Market, and so on. Walk around the north end of the Twinkie and then east, back down into the main-trail wash.

191. Short But Sweet 5.10 R/X ★ Mixed, 2 bolts. Start in between two separate sets of bushes/small trees at the base of the wall, toward its left end.

Climb the crack that angles right. Reach a scary stance on a small ledge and clip the first bolt. Continue climbing up the black streak to the top. Gear: a #0 Friend is needed at the start.
FA: John and Ralph Day, Tony Williams 1988

192. Flake Eyes 5.10c ★ Mixed, 3 bolts. Start directly in front of the bushy tree. Climb to a horizontal crack (#2 Friend), then head up past 3 bolts to the top.
FA: Tony Williams, John and Ralph Day 1988

193. Like Mom Used to Make 5.11c ★★ Mixed, 4 bolts. Climb the smooth face to the first bolt. Continue climbing up a crack, clipping 2 more bolts to the top.
FA: Tony Williams, John and Ralph Day 1988

▲ THE MARSHMALLOW
S PM Sun   Approach: 17 minutes

The Marshmallow is the formation to the east of the Twinkie. From the Twinkie, walk east in the wash for about 75 yards. The Marshmallow is located directly north of the wash. The routes start up on a ledge system that runs across the base of the cliff band. Scramble up to the second ledge system via the right side of the base of the entire wall. The routes begin on the left side of the wall and are described from left to right.

   Descent: Walk off to the northwest (back and left) toward the Twinkie. This will drop you down near the Twinkie. Scramble down into the uppermost gully on the west side of the Marshmallow. Follow the gully around to the start of the routes.

194. Mojave Green 5.8+ ★ Mixed, 3 bolts. Named after the most poisonous rattler found in the Mojave Desert, this route might be spicy. Climb the thin, slabby, technical face, passing 3 bolts. Gear: smaller Rocks can be used to supplement the bolts; 1 bolt anchor, supplement with a #3.5 and a #5 Friend.
FA: Jim Lybarger, Bob Conz 1989

195. Dime Edging 5.10 R ★★★ Mixed, 3 bolts.

Start 75 feet to the right of the previous route. Climb a smooth, slabby face, passing 2 bolts. Move over the small roof to another bolt and follow a seam to the top. Gear: Rocks to supplement the bolts; save a small Friend for the anchor.
FA: Bob Conz, Mike Ward 1989

▲ BULL MARKET
W PM Sun   Approach: 20 minutes

From the parking area, follow the main northerly trail into the wash. Pass a big white boulder in the wash on the left. Continue north on the main trail until reaching a sign for Turtlehead Peak. Take a left on this trail and walk up the wash about 450 yards. Pass the Twinkie, the lowest formation on the right side of the wash, and take the next drainage right through an open section of desert. After you make the right into the drainage, on the left (north), is a large, dark brown, smooth and wavy, east-facing rock formation that looks similar to the Tsunami Wall in the Second Pullout. Directly south of this formation is Bull Market, split by two gully systems on either side of the main wall. Walk up the white rock steps to the base of the wall. Routes are described from left to right.

196. Twentieth Century Ultra 5.11c ★★ Sport, 7 bolts. Start in the chimney at the far-left side of the formation, and work your way up onto the face.
FA: Mike Tupper 1992

197. Scudder Global 5.11b ★★ Sport, 5 bolts. Climb the slab to the right of *Twentieth Century Ultra* and move back left to a ledge. Move up the face to the anchor.
FA: Mike Tupper 1992

198. Fidelity Select 5.12a ★★★ Sport, 6 bolts. Climb the slab to the smooth vertical face. Finish on the arête and face.
FA: Mike Tupper 1992

199. Liar's Poker 5.11a ★★ Sport, 6 bolts. This is the leftmost route on the west face, located on the northwest corner.
FA: Mike Tupper 1992

200. Leveraged Buyout 5.11a ★★ Sport, 6 bolts. Start on *Liar's Poker*, sharing the first bolt. Climb the right line of bolts and then move back to the shared anchor with *Liar's Poker*.
FA: Mike Tupper 1992

201. Hostile Takeover 5.11b ★ Sport, 4 bolts. Begin 12 feet right of the previous route, right of a bush at the base of the wall.
FA: Mike Tupper 1992

202. Pinkies for the Dean 5.11c ★★★ Sport, 3 bolts. This is the rightmost bolted route on the wall.

Start the same as the previous route, sharing the first bolt and anchor.
FA: Mike Tupper 1992

▲ SATELLITE WALL
W PM Sun   Approach: 23 minutes

The Satellite Wall is located up and right of, southeast and behind, Bull Market. From the parking area, follow the main northerly trail into the wash. Pass a big white boulder in the wash on the left. Continue north on the main trail until reaching a sign for Turtlehead Peak. Take a left on this trail and walk up the wash about 450 yards. Pass the Twinkie, the lowest formation on the right side of the wash, and take the next drainage right through an open section of desert. On the left (north), visible from the main wash, is a large, dark brown, smooth and wavy, east-facing rock formation that looks similar to the Tsunami Wall in the Second Pullout. Directly south of this formation is Bull Market, split by two gully systems on either side of the main wall. Take the gully on the right side of Bull Market to the base of the Satellite Wall. This wall gets a lot of afternoon sun. Routes are described from left to right.

203. Stargazer 5.12b ★★★ Sport, 7 bolts. Climb the leftmost bolted route on the wall. Start in a small seam and head up cool hueco features to the anchor. A one-move wonder to 5.10a climbing.
FA: Leo and Karin Henson 1993

204. Sputnik 5.12a ★★★ Sport, 6 bolts. Climb up 5 feet right of the previous route. Head to a basketball-sized hole, about 15 feet up, and continue up loose, chossy, rotten sidepull flakes leading to the anchor.
FA: Leo and Karin Henson 1993

205. Supernova II, 5.12c ★★★ Sport, 8 bolts. Start just left of the tree. After the third bolt, continue climbing straight up the wall, finishing up the white pumpy rock.
FA: Jim Tobish, Randy Faulk, Tony Becchio 1991

206. Cosmos 5.12b ★ Sport, 8 bolts. Start as for the previous route, but at the third bolt head out right and up steeper terrain.
FA: Leo and Karin Henson 1993

▲ AVIAN WALL
N No Sun   Approach: 20 minutes

From the parking area, follow the main northerly trail into the wash. Pass a big white boulder in the wash on the left. Continue north on the main trail until reaching a sign for Turtlehead Peak. Take a left on this trail and walk up the wash about 450 yards. Pass the Twinkie, the lowest formation on the right side of the wash, and take the next drainage right through an open section of desert. On the left (north), visible from the main wash, is a large, dark brown, smooth and wavy, south-facing rock formation that looks similar to the Tsunami Wall in the Second Pullout. Pass the

base and hike east into a narrowing drainage/canyon for about 100 yards. The Avian Wall is the low-angle, white with varnished edges, south-facing, vertical wall on the right. The Trophy is located directly across the wash drainage from it. Routes are described from left to right.

In December 2003 a large boulder broke off the ledge of the Trophy and hit the Avian Wall at *Coyote Moon*. Now *Coyote Moon* is 1 bolt shorter. Also, the ground has risen beneath *Thunderbird*, making a ground fall likely between the second and third bolts.

207. Spotted Eagle 5.10a ★★★ Sport, 4 bolts. This is the leftmost bolted route, left of the fallen boulder that rests against the base of the wall.
FA: Don Burroughs, Alan Busby 1992

208. Coyote Moon 5.9+ ★★★ Sport, 3 bolts. Start atop the fallen boulder that sits in the middle of the gully.
FA: Don Burroughs, Alan Busby 1992

209. Thunderbird 5.11b R ★★★ Sport, 5 bolts. Begin down and right of the fallen boulder. Since the rockfall, this route is more dangerous because the ground has risen. Be careful going to the third bolt.
FA: Don Burroughs, Alan Busby 1992

210. Spotted Owl 5.11a ★★★ Sport, 5 bolts. This is the rightmost route on the wall, 50 feet right of the previous route. Climb the smooth face out of the wash. Heady.
FA: Don Burroughs, Alan Busby 1992

▲ THE TROPHY
SE AM Sun   Approach: 20 minutes

From the parking area, follow the main northerly trail into the wash. Pass a big white boulder in the wash on the left. Continue north on the main trail until reaching a sign for Turtlehead Peak. Take a left on this trail and walk up the wash about 450 yards. Pass the Twinkie, the lowest formation on the right side of the wash, and take the next drainage right through an open section of desert. On the left (north), visible from

the main wash, is a large, dark brown, smooth and wavy, south-facing rock formation that looks similar to the Tsunami Wall in the Second Pullout. Pass the base and hike east into a narrowing drainage/canyon for about 100 yards. The Avian Wall is the low-angle, white with varnished edges, north-facing, vertical wall on the right. The Trophy is located directly across the wash drainage from it. Routes are described from left to right.

211. Fifi Hula 5.11a ★★ Sport, 6 bolts. This route is just around the corner on the left side of the Trophy proper, on the big south-facing wall. But it is better accessed from the Trophy approach drainage (filled with scrub oak and manzanita): walk up the slabs between the dark, wavy wall and the Avian Wall, heading north to reach the base. Hiking from the Trophy proper is fourth-class and

scary. Climb up using grey-painted hangers, left of a crack and water streak.
FA: Don Burroughs, Alan Busby 1992

The following routes are on the Trophy proper.

212. Unknown 5.10a ★ Mixed. Begin on the left side of the cave, left of *Shark Walk*. Climb up to a ledge and then finish in the crack system, angling up and right to the anchor.
FA: Unknown

213. Shark Walk 5.13a ★★★ Sport, 6 bolts. This is the Trophy's leftmost bolted route. Get ready for a big move on this pumpy one-move wonder.
FA: Mike Tupper 1992

214. Indian Giver 5.12d ★★ Sport, 5 bolts. Climb

Shelley Dunbar showing off her double-jointed knees on Pet Shop Boys *5.12d at The Trophy.* Photo by Roxanna Brock

the bolted line 5 feet right of a crack/corner system right of *Shark Walk*.
FA: Mike Tupper 1992

215. Mystery Remover 5.12c ★ Sport, 7 bolts. Start just right of the left-facing corner system. Head up right, working your way through the bulge.
FA: Greg Meyer 1994

216. Pot Lickers Project ★★ This is the direct start to *Midnight Cowboy*. The bolts are there, but the hangers are missing. Sure to be in the mid-5.13 range.

217. Midnight Cowboy 5.13a ★★★ Sport, 8 bolts. Climb out the roof using the flake system. Continue up and left and join a crack system about halfway up the wall.
FA: Mike Tupper 1992

218. Twilight of a Champion 5.13a ★★★★ Sport, 10 bolts. Start as for the previous route, but head straight up after the third bolt.
FA: Mike Tupper 1992

219. Pet Shop Boys 5.12d ★★★★ Sport, 5 bolts. Just right of the two previous routes, climb up the center of the main portion of the cliff. Mega classic.
FA: Mike Tupper 1992

220. Keep Your Powder Dry 5.12b ★★★★ Sport, 10 bolts. Climb up left out the steepest part of the cave and move straight up the pumpy face.
FA: Mike Tupper 1992

221. The Trophy 5.12c ★★★★ Sport, 11 bolts. Start right of the previous route. Head right, out the steep crack and then up the steep face.
FA: Mike Tupper 1992

222. Caught in the Crosshairs 5.12a ★ Sport, 7 bolts. Start just right of *The Trophy*, where the angle of the wall becomes more vertical. Be careful at the first and second bolts: you could hit the deck if you fall.
FA: Greg Meyer 1993

223. Dodging a Bullet 5.12a ★★★ Sport, 5 bolts. Start just right of *Caught in the Cross Hairs*. Climb the technical vertical face.
FA: Greg Meyer 1991

224. Meatlocker 5.13a ★ Sport, 3 bolts. Climb out the roof at the far right side of the cliff.
FA: Unknown late 1990s

▲ SECRET 13
N No Sun   Approach: 25 minutes

This cliff is tucked away at the back end of the sand-stone rock of Sandstone Quarry. From the parking area, follow the main northerly trail into the wash. Pass a big white boulder in the wash on the left. Continue north on the main trail until reaching a sign for Turtle-head Peak. Take a left on this trail and walk up the wash about 450 yards. Pass the Twinkie, the lowest forma-tion on the right side of the wash, and take the next drainage right through an open section of desert. On the left (north), visible from the main wash, is a large, dark brown, smooth and wavy, south-facing rock for-mation that looks similar to the Tsunami Wall in the Second Pullout. Pass the base and hike east into a nar-rowing drainage/canyon for about 100 yards. The Avian Wall is the low-angle, white with varnished edges, north-facing, vertical wall on the right. The Trophy is located directly across the wash drainage from it. From the base of the Trophy, walk across the white slabs right, heading directly east for 500 feet. A small east-west running gully is located down and right (south) of the top of the white slab and Secret 13 (at the end of the white slabs). This is the first, small, bush-filled gully, below the white slabs. Scramble down the gully, head-ing east. At the bottom, where it opens up, head left (north) and around the corner for 3 minutes to the base of the wall. It is the obvious, large, orange, north-facing cliff with big black water streaks running down its face. Routes are described from left to right.

225. GM Dihedral 5.11b ★★★★ Sport, 5 bolts. This is the leftmost bolted route on the wall. Start in the left-facing corner just left of an arête. Climb up and over the roof at midheight and finish up us-ing the edges and a thin seam.
FA: Mike Tupper

226. GM Arête 5.11d ★★ Sport, 6 bolts. Start 5 feet right and down from the previous route. Climb the face, working left to the right edge of the arête. Use the arête and finish up the face, to the anchor.
FA: Mike Tupper

227. GM Black Streak 5.12a ★★★ Sport, 7 bolts.

Don Welsh on You Are What You Is *5.13b, Secret 13*

Climb the black streak next to a green patch of lichen. Move up using thin seams and sidepulls—it gets easier the higher you go.
FA: Mike Tupper

228. GM Crack 5.11d ★★★ Sport, 5 bolts. Climb the shallow crack and seam, moving up the middle of the black water streak. A little slippery. Gear: a #1 Friend might ease your mind between the second and third bolts.
FA: Greg Meyer

229. Project Sport, 6 bolts. Begin just right of the previous route, behind some trees at a thin seam. Finishes under a roof on a foot ledge.

230. Project ★★★ Sport. Climb up 20 feet right of *GM Crack*. Work up the face using the small crisscrossing seams.

231. Project Sport, 8 bolts. Climb the S-curving, discontinuous seams leading to a main seam running up the wall.

232. You Are What You Is (aka The Don Welsh Memorial Bolted Sport-Climbing Route) 5.13b ★★★★ Sport, 8 bolts. Start in the large, rightmost hueco. Move up, undercling the hueco, and head up left to the first bolt, a glue-in. Continue heading left and up, using pumpy edges and sidepulls to the anchor.
FA: Don Welsh 2004

233. Project Sport, 7 bolts. Climb up and past the first two red bolt hangers, 12 feet right of the previous route. Follow the seam to midheight and continue up the black streak and bulge to the top.

234. Project Sport, 7 bolts. Start down and left of a basketball-sized hueco. Climb to the hueco and continue to a horizontal rail. Advance up the wall and at midheight angle left. Head back right to the anchor.

235. GM Pimp 5.11c ★★ Sport, 7 bolts. This is the rightmost bolted line on the wall. Begin 4 feet right

of a crack running up and right across the wall. Climb a series of bulges to the top.
FA: Mike Tupper

SANDSTONE QUARRY BACKSIDE

▲ THE BEACH
W PM Sun   Approach: 15 minutes

From the parking area head north, passing a big white boulder in the wash. Upon reaching a sign for Calico Tanks, about 100 yards past the big white boulder, turn right (east). This trail goes between two rock formations, on the north and south sides of the trail. Continue east on this good trail for 300 yards, where the ground is comprised of red sand. Look up and left, while hiking, for the red cliffs of the Beach. The Blister in the Sun Wall is a huge, white, west-facing cliff high up and left. The Beach is west-facing and is located down and right of this wall, 75 yards left (northeast) of the main trail, where the trail starts veering south. Routes are described from left to right.

These routes are located 100 feet to the left of the Beach proper.

236. RF Gain 5.10c ★ Mixed, 2 bolts. This route climbs the black, varnished corner system behind the big boulder that sits at the base of the wall. Mantel up a series of ledges, passing 2 bolts. Gear: a #2 Friend is good after the second bolt.
FA: Nick Nordblom 1987

237. Squelch 5.10a ★★ Traditional. Climb the black, smooth, varnished face using the crack and seam feature. Gear: small Friends and a selection of midsized Rocks.
FA: Kurt Mauer 1987

238. Static 5.6 ★ Traditional. Climb the crack 13 feet to the left of *Wizard of Odds*. Move up the wide crack that sits at the left edge of the Beach

proper. Gear: to #5 Friend.
FA: Unknown

The following routes are on the Beach proper, about 100 feet right of the previous routes.

Descent: From the top of the cliff, head directly left (north) to the first gully leading west, just past the main cliff.

239. Wizard of Odds 5.12a ★ Sport, 7 bolts. Begin just right of a big, red arête.
FA: Greg Meyer 1992

240. Southern Cross 5.12b ★★★ Sport, 7 bolts. Start just right of the big arête on the main wall. Climb the face to the anchor.
FA: Leo Henson 1994

241. Southern Comfort 5.12d ★★★★ Sport, 8 bolts. Climb the cool-looking arête leading to a

face, just left of the far edge of the Beach proper.
FA: John Heimen 1997

▲ BLISTER IN THE SUN WALL
W PM Sun   Approach Time: 20 minutes

From the parking area head north, passing a big white boulder in the wash. Upon reaching a sign for Calico Tanks, about 100 yards past the big white boulder, turn right (east). This trail goes between two rock formations, on the north and south sides of the trail. Continue east on this good trail for 300 yards, where the ground is comprised of red sand. Look up and left, while hiking, for the red cliffs of the Beach. The Blister in the Sun Wall is a huge, white, west-facing cliff high up and left, the uppermost wall to the northeast. Hike up past the Beach, heading north toward the big limestone peak (Turtlehead Peak) for about 100 yards. Scramble up one of the several gully systems (running east) that bring you to the base of the wall. The wall is easily recognized by the crack system that runs up and across it. Routes are described from left to right.

Descent: Hike off right (southeast) and down the gully that runs between the Beach and the Blister in the Sun Wall.

242. Teenage Mutant Ninja Turtles 5.11b ★

Mixed, 3 bolts. Climb the leftmost bolted section of the cliff. Start 15 feet right of a big rock formation that is resting against the base of the wall. Climb the slabby white face into a crack about 50 feet up. Follow these crack systems to the top of the wall. Gear: bring a set of Rocks and small to midsized Friends; save a #3.5 and a #4 Friend for the belay anchor.
FA: Bob Conz, Jim Lybarger 1989

243. Blister in the Sun 5.11b ★★★ Mixed, 2

bolts. Start as for *High Scalin'*. Once in the crack system that heads up and right, move up the wall and slightly left, following the main crack system that runs up the center of the wall. Head for a bolt atop the first crack, then head slightly right into another crack capped by another bolt. Move back left to finish in the crack that leads to the top of the wall. Gear: a good selection of Rocks and small to midsized Friends; save a #3.5 and a #4 Friend for the anchor.
FA: Bob Conz, Shelby Shelton 1988

244. Tortugas Mutant 5.11d ★ Mixed, 7 bolts.

Start the same as *High Scalin'*. At the crack system, head up and right. Continue climbing straight up the face, passing 7 bolts to the top. Gear: a set of Rocks and #00–#1 Friends for the start; Friends to #3 to supplement the bolts; save a #3.5 and a #4 Friend for the belay.
FA: Richard Harrison, Jimmy Dunn 1989

245. High Scalin' 5.7 ★★ Traditional. This route

climbs the main crack system that runs up and to the right across the cliff face. Start directly in front of a dead tree stump, 8 feet up on a small ledge. Gear: good selection of Rocks; mid- to larger-sized Friends to #5; save larger Friends for the belay anchor.

Pitch 1: Climb thin seams for about 40 feet until reaching the main crack heading up and right.

Pitch 2: Finish up the main crack system, angling up and right.
FA: Nick Nordblom, Paul Van Betten, "team solo" 1987

▲ MASS PRODUCTION WALL
N No Sun   Approach: 20 minutes

This cliff sits just off of the Calico Tanks Trail. From the parking area head north, passing a big white boulder in the wash. Upon reaching a sign for Calico Tanks, about 100 yards past the big white boulder, turn right (east). This trail goes between two rock formations, on the north and south sides of the trail. Continue east on this good trail for 300 yards, where the ground is comprised of red sand. Look up and left, while hiking, for the red cliffs of the Beach. The Blister in the Sun Wall is a huge, white, west-facing cliff high up and left. The Beach is down and right of this wall. When the trail starts veering south, the Beach will be 75 yards to the left and is west-facing. Continue a couple minutes past the Beach, taking rock steps toward Calico Tanks (southeast). The Mass Production Wall will come into view on the left. It faces northwest. Routes are described from right to left.

246. Some Assembly Required 5.10c ★★ Sport, 6

bolts. Start in front of the big pine tree. Climb the rightmost bolted route on the wall. The fourth bolt is missing, but a #1 Friend works nicely instead.
FA: Greg Mayer 1991

247. Kokopelli 5.10c ★★★ Sport, 4 bolts. Climb to

the cavelike feature and out the steep right corner.
FA: Don Burroughs, Alan Busby 1992

248. Parts is Parts 5.8 ★★ Sport, 3 bolts. Climb

up 50 feet left of *Kokopelli*. Begin on the level surface in front of two small trees.
FA: Todd Swain, Jeff Rickerl 1992

249. Battery Power 5.9 ★ Sport, 6 bolts. Climb

the smooth face just left of *Parts is Parts*.
FA: Greg Mayer 1991

Mass Production Wall

246. Some Assembly Required 5.10c
247. Kokopelli 5.10c

248. Parts is Parts 5.8
249. Battery Power 5.9
250. Foreman Ferris 5.11b
251. Trigger Happy 5.10a
252. Hit and Run 5.9
253. Unknown 5.10a

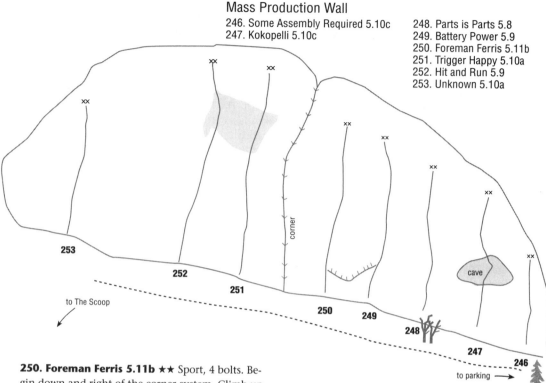

250. Foreman Ferris 5.11b ★★ Sport, 4 bolts. Begin down and right of the corner system. Climb up the face.
FA: Leo Henson 1994

251. Trigger Happy 5.10a ★★★ Sport, 6 bolts. Start 50 feet left of *Foreman Ferris*. Climb the right side of the big, dark-brown chunk of rock located halfway up the cliff.
FA: Greg Mayer 1991

252. Hit and Run 5.9 ★★ Sport, 5 bolts. Climb the left side of the big brown section of rock located halfway up the cliff.
FA: Greg Mayer 1991

253. Unknown 5.10a ★ Sport, 7 bolts. Start 15 feet left of the big brown section of rock. This is the leftmost bolted route on the wall.
FA: Unknown

▲ THE SCOOP
S PM Sun   Approach: 25 minutes

This cliff is properly named for it looks as if someone had a giant ice-cream scoop and cleaned out the rock to form the cliff. The best and easiest way to approach this cliff is via the Mass Production Wall. From the parking area head north, passing a big white boulder in the wash. Upon reaching a sign for Calico Tanks, about 100 yards past the big white boulder, turn right (east). This trail goes between two rock formations, on the north and south sides of the trail. Continue east on this good trail for 300 yards, where the ground is comprised of red sand. Look up and left, while hiking, for the red cliffs of the Beach. The Blister in the Sun Wall is a huge, white, west-facing cliff high up and left. The Beach is down and right of this wall. When the trail starts veering south, the Beach will be

75 yards to the left and is west-facing. Continue a couple minutes past the Beach, taking rock steps toward Calico Tanks (southeast). The Mass Production Wall will come into view on the left. From the top east end of the Mass Production Wall, walk straight north for about 75 yards. The Scoop is located on the right (east). Hike up the first major gully running to the east. The cliff faces directly south, and it looks as if mud has been baked on the wall. With some rain and traffic, this could be a good wall. Routes are described from left to right.

254. Turbulence 5.12a ★ Sport, 5 bolts. Climb the short, leftmost bolted route on the wall. Climb the steep arête heading left to the anchor.
FA: Unknown

255. Artificial Intelligence 5.12a ★★ Sport, 6 bolts. Start 20 feet right of the previous route, in a tiny seam. Move up and right to the top.
FA: Unknown

256. Unknown 5.12b ★★ Sport, 7 bolts. Climb the light tan scoop at the base of the wall. Follow this to a dark-brown water streak and join a seam to the anchor.
FA: Unknown

257. Project 1 bolt. Located right of the previous route.

258. Unknown 5.11c ★ Sport, 5 bolts. Start atop some broken boulders. Climb the crack that angles up and right. Finish on the face above.
FA: Unknown

259. First Impression 5.11d ★ Sport, 4 bolts. Climb up 25 feet right of the previous route, at a small, left-facing corner system. Follow homemade hangers, angling left to the anchor.
FA: Unknown

▲ HALL OF FAME
N PM Sun   Approach: 30 minutes

The best and easiest way to approach this cliff is via the Mass Production Wall. From the parking area head

north, passing a big white boulder in the wash. Upon reaching a sign for Calico Tanks, about 100 yards past the big white boulder, turn right (east). This trail goes between two rock formations, on the north and south sides of the trail. Continue east on this good trail for 300 yards, where the ground is comprised of red sand. Look up and left, while hiking, for the red cliffs of the Beach. The Blister in the Sun Wall is a huge, white, west-facing cliff high up and left. The Beach is down and right of this wall. When the trail starts veering south, the Beach will be 75 yards to the left and is west-facing. Continue a couple minutes past the Beach, taking rock steps toward Calico Tanks (southeast). The Mass Production Wall will come into view on the left. From the top east end of Mass Production hike straight north for about 100 yards. You will run into a wall that runs east-west. Walk around to the left (west) corner of this wall, between a group of smaller broken boulders. Hike through the boulders and around the northwest side. Head straight north along the base of the wall for about 100 feet. There will be a gully on the right, and from this gully the Hall of Fame corridor will come into view. The wall faces north and runs east-west. Walk 200 feet east, up this gully straight to the base of the Hall of Fame. Routes are described from right to left as you enter the Hall of Fame corridor.

260. Yearnin' and Learnin' 5.11a ★★ Sport, 5 bolts. This is the first route in the corridor on the north-facing wall.
FA: Don Burroughs, Alan Busby 1992

261. Repeat Offender 5.10d ★★ Sport, 5 bolts. Start as for the previous route but head left at the second bolt.
FA: Greg Mayer 1991

262. Armed and Dangerous 5.10d ★★★ Sport, 6 bolts. Climb to the hole, 12 feet up, then continue up the face to the anchor.
FA: Phil Bowden 1991

263. Bad Reputation 5.11b ★★★ Sport, 5 bolts. Start left of *Armed and Dangerous*.
FA: Phil Bowden, Guy Pinjuv 1991

264. Innocent Bystander 5.10a ★ Sport, 5 bolts. Start left of the previous route. Climb up, clipping funky homemade hangers.
FA: Greg Mayer 1991

265. Paid Training 5.9 ★ TR. Begin 7 feet left of *Innocent Bystander*. Climb to the bolted belay anchor.
FA: Chris Burton 2000

266. Ms. Adventure 5.7 ★ Sport, 3 bolts. Start three-quarters of the way up the corridor from the west entrance. This is a short little climb up the smooth face.
FA: Chuck Mayer 1991

▲ HOLIDAY WALL
W PM Sun   Approach: 25 minutes

Approach the Holiday Wall via the Mass Production Wall. From the parking area head north, passing a big white boulder in the wash. Upon reaching a sign for Calico Tanks, about 100 yards past the big white boulder, turn right (east). This trail goes between two rock formations, on the north and south sides of the trail. Continue east on this good trail for 300 yards, where the ground is comprised of red sand. Look up and left, while hiking, for the red cliffs of the Beach. The Blister in the Sun Wall is a huge, white, west-facing cliff high up and left. The Beach is down and right of this wall. When the trail starts veering south, the Beach will be 75 yards to the left and is west-facing. Continue a couple minutes past the Beach, taking rock steps toward Calico Tanks (southeast). The Mass Production Wall will come into view on the left. Continue heading south toward Calico Tanks. The Holiday Wall is about 200 yards past the Mass Production Wall and sits just off the trail on the left side. Routes are described from left to right.

267. Presents of Mind 5.12a ★★ Sport, 4 bolts. This is the leftmost route on the wall. Climb the west face and corner of the formation.
FA: Unknown

Holiday Wall
267. Presents of Mind 5.12a
268. The Grinch 5.12b
269. Death Before Decaf 5.12b
270. Gift Wrapped 5.11b
271. Red Sky Mining 5.11a
272. Red Sky Rising 5.11a
273. When the Cat's Away 5.11b
274. Saddam's Mom 5.11c
275. Moments to Memories 5.11a
276. Moving Train 5.11a

268. The Grinch 5.12b ★★★ Sport, 4 bolts. Start just right and around the corner from the previous route. The first bolt is missing.
FA: Mike Tupper 1990

269. Death Before Decaf 5.12b ★★★ Sport, 6 bolts. Climb the line of bolts 10 feet right of *The Grinch*. This route has weird-shaped, homemade hangers.
FA: Don Welsh 1991

270. Gift Wrapped 5.11b ★★ Sport, 6 bolts. Start in front of a small pine tree and climb the curving crack.
FA: Karen Peil 1990

271. Red Sky Mining 5.11a ★★ Sport, 7 bolts. Start 5 feet right of *Gift Wrapped*. Climb the face using the small crack system on the wall.
FA: Karen Peil 1990

272. Red Sky Rising 5.11a ★★★ Sport, 5 bolts. Climb up just left of the corner system that makes up the left portion of the wall. Follow the seams and edges to the anchor.
FA: Karen Peil 1990

273. When the Cat's Away 5.11b ★★★★★ Sport, 5 bolts. Begin at the right side of the roof located at the bottom of the route. Climb flakes in the middle of the formation.
FA: Greg Mayer 1990

274. Saddam's Mom 5.11c ★★ Sport, 6 bolts. Start just right of *When the Cat's Away* and climb the arête and face.
FA: Karen Peil 1990

275. Moments to Memories 5.11a ★ Sport, 4 bolts. Climb the arête on the next formation to the right, 35 feet right of the previous routes.
FA: Greg Mayer 1990

276. Moving Train 5.11a ★★★ Sport, 4 bolts. Start just right and around the arête from *Moments to Memories*. Climb the striking arête, working your way back and forth.
FA: Greg Mayer 1990

▲ NEXT WALL
SW PM Sun   Approach: 28 minutes

Approach the Next Wall via the Holiday Wall. From the parking area head north, passing a big white boulder in the wash. Upon reaching a sign for Calico Tanks, about 100 yards past the big white boulder, turn right (east). This trail goes between two rock formations, on the north and south sides of the trail. Continue east on this good trail for 300 yards, where the ground is comprised of red sand. Look up and left, while hiking, for the red cliffs of the Beach. The Blister in the Sun Wall is a huge, white, west-facing cliff high up and left. The Beach is down and right of this wall. When the trail starts veering south, the Beach will be 75 yards to the left and is west-facing. Continue a couple minutes past the Beach, taking rock steps toward Calico Tanks (southeast). The Mass Production Wall will come into view on the left. Continue heading south toward Calico Tanks. The Holiday Wall is about 200 yards past the Mass Production Wall and sits just off the trail on the left side. Continue hiking south past the Holiday Wall for about 150 yards, staying on the left side of the main wash. Angle slightly left out of the wash and onto red slabs leading you up to the base of the Next and James Brown Walls. Routes are described from left to right.

277. Nexus 5.12c ★★★★ Sport, 10 bolts. Start off the ledge on the left side of the crag. Climb out a steep section of rock and join a seam, which will lead into a crack. Finish up the crack to the anchor.
FA: Greg Mayer 1995

278. Connect the Dots 5.12b ★★★★★ Sport, 11 bolts. Begin 40 feet right of the previous route. Climb cool hueco and scoop features.
FA: Greg Mayer 1995

279. They Just Don't Make Outlaws Like They Used To 5.12a ★★★ Sport, 11 bolts. Start at the

base of the main portion of the cliff, just down and right of the previous two routes. Start just right of the cave at the base of the wall. Climb the scoop and join the crack after the third bolt.
FA: Greg Mayer 1993

280. The Heteroclite 5.11c ★★ Sport, 9 bolts. Climb up 10 feet right of the previous route. Follow the crack that angles up and to the right.
FA: Greg Mayer 1993

281. Mirage II, 5.10c ★ Sport, 10 bolts. Climb the rightmost bolted route. Start atop a small boulder and climb the light tan–colored face. It keeps getting steeper!
FA: Greg Mayer 1996

▲ JAMES BROWN WALL
SW PM Sun   Approach: 28 minutes

Approach the James Brown Wall via the Next Wall. From the parking area head north, passing a big white boulder in the wash. Upon reaching a sign for Calico Tanks, about 100 yards past the big white boulder, turn right (east). This trail goes between two rock formations, on the north and south sides of the trail. Continue east on this good trail for 300 yards, where the ground is comprised of red sand. Look up and left, while hiking, for the red cliffs of the Beach. The Blister in the Sun Wall is a huge, white, west-facing cliff high up and left. The Beach is down and right of this wall. When the trail starts veering south, the Beach will be 75 yards to the left and is west-facing. Continue a couple minutes past the Beach, taking rock steps toward Calico Tanks (southeast). The Mass Production Wall will come into view on the left. Continue heading south toward Calico Tanks. The Holiday Wall is about 200 yards past the Mass Production Wall and sits just off the trail on the left side. Continue hiking south past the Holiday Wall for about 150 yards, staying on the left side of the main wash. Angle slightly left out of the wash and onto red slabs leading you up to the base of the Next and James Brown Walls. The James Brown Wall is located about 75 feet up and around the left (west) corner of the Next Wall. From the Next Wall, hike up the left side of the crag and head northeast to the base of the James Brown Wall. Routes are described from left to right.

282. James Brown 5.11b ★★★★ Sport, 7 bolts. Climb the thin and technical brown streak on the southwest portion of the wall.
FA: Randy and Pier Marsh 1991

283. Brand New Bag 5.10d ★★★ Sport, 4 bolts. Climb up just right of the previous route. Head up the darker brown, broken but solid-looking rock.
FA: Randy and Pier Marsh 1991

284. Soul Power 5.11d ★★ Sport, 8 bolts. Climb the south face just right of *Brand New Bag*, passing bolts to the anchor.
FA: Randy and Pier Marsh 1991

▲ THE SWEET SPOT
NE No Sun   Approach: 30 minutes

Approach via the Holiday Wall. From the parking area head north, passing a big white boulder in the wash. Upon reaching a sign for Calico Tanks, about 100 yards past the big white boulder, turn right (east). This trail goes between two rock formations, on the north and south sides of the trail. Continue east on this good trail for 300 yards, where the ground is comprised of red sand. Look up and left, while hiking, for the red

cliffs of the Beach. The Blister in the Sun Wall is a huge, white, west-facing cliff high up and left. The Beach is down and right of this wall. When the trail starts veering south, the Beach will be 75 yards to the left and is west-facing. Continue a couple minutes past the Beach, taking rock steps toward Calico Tanks (southeast). The Mass Production Wall will come into view on the left. Continue heading south toward Calico Tanks. The Holiday Wall is about 200 yards past the Mass Production Wall and sits just off the trail on the left side. Hike up the main wash found at the base of Holiday Wall, directly south. Follow the wash for 150 yards until it becomes bush-filled. Continue south on slabs of red rock, passing the Next and James Brown Walls, up and to the left. Keep walking south on the slabs, heading for the second rock formation to the south of the Next Wall. Walk up the bush-filled gully to the base of the Sweet Spot. The routes are located on the shady, steep portion of rock, facing north, and are described from left to right.

285. Absolute Zero 5.12a ★★★ Sport, 7 Bolts. Climb the steeper of the two routes—this is the leftmost bolted route. Follow dark-colored rock to the chain anchor.
FA: Greg Mayer 1993

286. Disposable Blues 5.11c ★★★★ Sport, 5 Bolts. Climb up 10 feet right of the previous route. Time to get your pump on.
FA: Greg Mayer 1993

WHITE ROCK SPRINGS

Sheep Skull Crags ▲ The Ledger Crags ▲ Angel Food Wall

TO REACH WHITE ROCK SPRINGS from Las Vegas, take West Charleston Boulevard west, which turns into State Route 159. Drive over the 215 Beltway and zero your odometer. Turn right into the Red Rock Canyon National Conservation Area, 5.9 miles past the 215 (2 miles past Calico Basin Road). Enter the 13-mile Scenic Drive through the kiosk entrance booth.

White Rock Springs is 5.8 miles from the entrance kiosk on the Scenic Drive. Turn right on a gravel road (pass a parking area). Drive 0.5 mile down the gravel/washboard road until it dead-ends in a fenced-in parking area where there is a pit toilet.

▲ SHEEP SKULL CRAGS
NE AM Sun   Approach: 30 minutes

The Sheep Skull Crags are located in the southern portion of White Rock Springs and can easily be seen from the parking area. Look for a big, light tan,

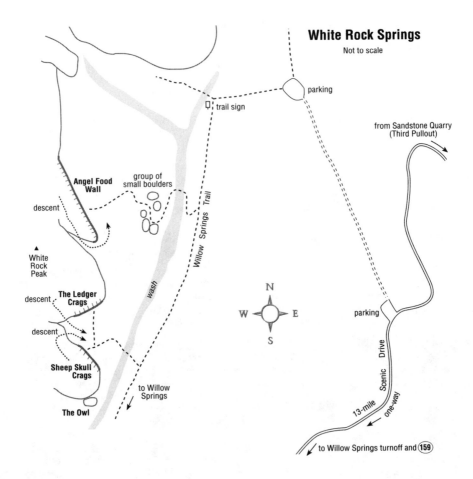

White Rock Springs

Not to scale

fingerlike formation on the left edge of the cliff, 300 yards left of the taller Angel Food Wall. Follow signs to the Willow Springs Trail out of the west end of the parking area. Hike the trail for about 75 yards. At the trail sign, head left (south) on the Willow Springs Trail, following the old road/trail for about 20 minutes. Look for a gully running north up the hillside. The Sheep Skull Crags are just left of this gully. Take a faint trail, branching off the main trail, heading into the wash and up the gully, north. When even with the base of the Sheep Skull Crags on the left, hike up and out of the gully left (west) to the base of the wall. Routes are described from right to left as they are approached.

Descent: Walk off. Traverse the top of the cliff and drop down into the gully that heads down and back to the base and the southeast edge of the wall.

1. It's a Love Thing 5.9 ★ Traditional. Begin 100 yards left of the large, tan, fingerlike formation (*Intestinal Flu*), in a right-facing dihedral with a pine tree in front of it.

Pitch 1: 5.8 Climb the corner to a large ledge.

Pitch 2: 5.9 Climb an overhanging face with a crack in the center. Above this is white rock and thin protection. 100 feet.

Walk off right. Do one short rappel leading to an

easy walk off, down and around to the base of the wall.
FA: T. Sloane 1992

2. Dust to Dust 5.9 ★★★ Traditional. Climb the crack on the left side of the big, light tan, fingerlike formation *(Intestinal Flu)*.
FA: Joe and Betsy Herbst 1974

3. Intestinal Flu 5.8 ★★★ Traditional. Climb the chimney on the right side of the light tan, finger-like formation. There is a rather large block wedged in the chimney about 40 feet off the deck. Climb up and around the left side of the block.
FA: Joe Herbst, Randal Grandstaff 1974

4. Black Glass 5.9 ★★ Traditional. Climb black-colored rock right of the previous route, which makes up the corner system. About halfway up, the route begins angling left toward a black face with a good crack running to the top. Gear: to a #6 Friend.
FA: Joe and Betsy Herbst 1974

5. Pneumonia 5.9 ★★ Traditional. Climb the chimney and large crack system 20 feet right of the previous route. A quarter of the way up, head left into the crack system leading to the top.
FA: Joe Herbst, Matt McMackin 1974

6. Pencil Lead 5.10a ★ Traditional. Begin 30 feet right of *Pneumonia*, or four crack systems right. Climb the right-facing corner using a tiny crack in the back of the corner.
FA: Joe Herbst 1974

▲ THE LEDGER CRAGS
SE All-Day Sun   Approach: 30 minutes

The Ledger Crags are on the opposite side of the gully (east) of the Sheep Skull Crags. Follow signs to the Willow Springs Trail out of the west end of the parking area. Hike the trail for about 75 yards. At the trail sign, head left (south) on the Willow Springs Trail, following the old road/trail for about 20 minutes. Look for a gully running north up the hillside. The Ledger Crags are on the right side of this gully. Take a faint trail branching off the main trail heading into

the wash and up the gully. Pass the Sheep Skull Crags on the left and continue up the main gully for about 5 minutes. Hike slightly to the right (east), to the base of the Ledger Crags. Routes are described from left to right.

Descent: Walk off to the southwest, down the gully between some small cliffs and the Sheep Skull Crags.

7. The Ledger 5.7 ★★ Traditional. Start at the leftmost dihedral capped by an overhang.
   Pitch 1: Climb the corner system to a bush-filled ledge.
   Pitch 2: Continue up to another obvious, large ledge system.
   Pitch 3: Follow a left-leaning crack off the belay ledge up and left.
FA: Joe and Betsy Herbst, Tom Kaufman, Phil Jones, Steve Jones 1974

8. Holed Up 5.10 ★ Traditional. Start just right of *The Ledger*. Follow a crack leading to a black hole and continue up the face. Gear: bring a large selection and 2 #5 Friends.
   Pitch 1: Climb loose, rotten rock, heading right toward a large scrub-oak bush. Belay just beneath the main crack on the headwall.
   Pitch 2: Follow the main crack up and belay at a large black hole.
   Pitch 3: Climb up, heading slightly right and over the roof. Continue up the face.
FA: Steve Allen, Joe Herbst, Tom Kaufman 1974

▲ ANGEL FOOD WALL
NE AM Sun   Approach: 20 minutes

From the parking area at White Rock Springs, hike to the west on the Willow Springs Trail. This trail runs south around the base of White Rock Springs. Follow the trail out of the west end of the White Springs parking area for 75 yards. At the trail sign, head left (south) on the Willow Springs Trail. Follow this old road/trail for about 10 minutes. When it starts to get close to the wash/ravine on your right, look for a narrow trail heading down into the wash. Follow this trail into and back out of the wash, crossing it. The trail then heads

northwest and into a gully. Do some easy scrambling over a group of small boulders toward the wall. Once you have scrambled up the trail, the dirt changes to a bright red color. Follow a red-dirt trail up to the base of the Angel Food Wall. Traverse the base of the wall right to reach the routes. Routes are described from left to right.

Descent: From the top of the Angel Food Wall, descend left into the large south-southeast running gully that separates the Angel Food Wall from White Rock Peak. The entrance to the gully is gained by a short rappel or by downclimbing. Continue down the gully until it is split by a large rock formation in the center. The left side requires a short rappel; the right side can be quickly downclimbed (third to fourth class) for 15 feet. The descent trends left after this until almost at the bottom, then goes back toward the center/right side. Reach the southeast corner of the cliff and go straight to the parking lot unless you cut up to the cliff. 1 hour.

9. Psychomania 5.10d ★★ Traditional. This three-pitch route is located on the far-left side of the Angel Food Wall, 200 feet left of *Sandy Hole*. Scramble up a large boulder to a nice ledge to begin the climb.

Pitch 1: 5.5 Climb a face, heading toward a roof. Belay just under the roof.

Pitch 2: 5.10d Climb around the roof and follow a hand crack on the right. When the crack thins out to 1-inch size, pass a large hole on the right. Continue to a ledge.

Pitch 3: 5.7 Finish up the face with funky protection. Continue to the descent gully.
FA: Danny Meyers, Sam Hokit 1986

10. Sandy Hole 5.6 ★★ Traditional. Climb the huge, most obvious, right-facing flake and corner system on the wall. At the roof continue up, following a chimney directly behind the large flake. When the flake closes down, head out onto the face. Eventually move back left on the face and head to the top.

Pitch 1: 5.6 Follow the right-facing corner system to a large flake with a chimney behind it. Squirm through the chimney and belay on the face just above the chimney.

Pitch 2: 5.6 Continue climbing straight up the easy face until nearly even with a hollow flake feature on the right (the tunnel on *Tunnel Vision*). Start heading left across the face and belay from a good crack below the tunnel exit on *Tunnel Vision*. Bolts have been added to a variation of *Tunnel Vision*; you will be able to clip a couple of them.

Pitch 3: 5.5 Continue traversing up and left, following a crack system leading toward the descent gully.
FA: Betsy Herbst, Joanne and George Urioste 1977

11. Eigerwand 5.9 ★★ Traditional. Begin on *Sandy Hole* and then tend up and left, left of the *Sandy Hole* flake. At the top of the flake, continue straight up the wall. At the headwall, tend left toward the descent gully.

Pitch 1: 5.8 Begin on *Sandy Hole* and then take the left-slanting crack. Belay at the base of the large, flared portion of rock.

Pitch 2: 5.9 Continue up the crack until it ends. Move out right across the face (poor protection), and belay before a large hole (the "Sandy Hole").

Pitch 3: 5.4 Climb into the hole and continue straight up the crack and face, climbing a crack. Belay just before a straight-in crack.

Pitch 4: 5.7 Climb the crack located directly above the belay until it starts to flare and get large. Head left onto the face, toward a groove in the rock. Belay from the top part of the groove.

Pitch 5: 5.6 Climb up slabs, heading left for the descent gully.
FA: John Long, Randal Grandstaff, Randy Marsh 1981

12. Tunnel Vision 5.7 ★★★★ Traditional. Begin 20 feet right of *Sandy Hole*, under a small roof and be-

hind some bushes and the trail. Gear: a full set of nuts and Friends to #4, doubles of #3 and #4 Friends.

Pitch 1: 5.6+ Climb to under the roof crack and then step right to a vertical crack. Pull through a steep section with some loose blocks to the base of a large right-facing corner, that creates an alcove. Climb the

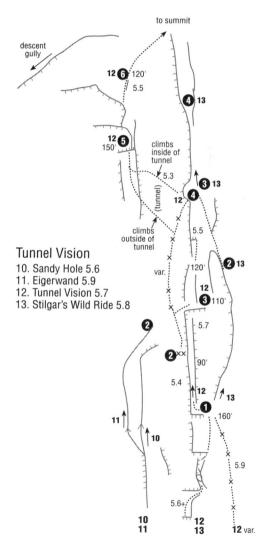

Tunnel Vision
10. Sandy Hole 5.6
11. Eigerwand 5.9
12. Tunnel Vision 5.7
13. Stilgar's Wild Ride 5.8

wide right-facing corner to the next rounded ledge system. Watch for rope drag. 160 feet.

Pitch 1 variation: 5.9 Take the bolted line that starts right of the traditional start.

Pitch 2: 5.4 Climb the chimney directly above the anchor. Belay midway using large gear in an awkward, wider section or connect with the next pitch. 90 feet.

Pitch 3: 5.7 Continue up the chimney to a ledge below an arching, thin, right-facing corner. 110 feet.

Pitch 3 variation: From the second belay you can step out left and climb the bolted face. Either rejoin *Tunnel Vision* at the third-pitch belay (one pitch). Or continue climbing up and left clipping the bolts and adding gear as needed, rejoining *Tunnel Vision* either before or after the tunnel (two pitches).

Pitch 4: 5.5 Climb up, using the straight-in crack, passing over the roof. Climb right facing corner to the mouth, right of the tunnel. 120 feet.

Pitch 5: 5.3 Move left, into the tunnel, as deep as possible. Chimney up using big holds. Continue up the wall, just left of the tunnel in a thin crack. Belay under a small roof up and left. 150 feet.

Pitch 6: 5.5 Move up and right, taking one of two side-by-side cracks to a large ledge. Take discontinuous cracks to the top of a sort-of pillar or escape left on the ledge. 120 feet.

FA: Joe Herbst, Randal Grandstaff 1974

13. Stilgar's Wild Ride 5.8 ★★★ Traditional. This

route starts the same as *Tunnel Vision*, but heads out right after the first pitch. It rejoins *Tunnel Vision* at the fourth-pitch belay but heads straight up through an overhang instead of climbing through the tunnel. Gear: standard rack to #5 Friend.

Pitch 1: 5.6+ Climb to under the roof crack and then step right to a vertical crack. Pull through a steep section with some loose blocks to the base of a large right-facing corner, that creates an alcove. Climb the wide right-facing corner to the next rounded ledge system. Watch for rope drag. 160 feet.

Pitch 2: Climb off the right edge of the ledge and then take crack systems straight up the wall.

Pitch 3: Traverse the face left to belay at the top of *Tunnel Vision* pitch 4.

Pitch 4: 5.8 Traverse slightly right and follow a crack to belay in chimney.

Pitch 5: Follow the crack and chimney to the top of the wall.

FA: Bob Healy, Joe Herbst 1974

14. Rude Rocks 5.10a ★★★ Traditional. This route

is located 50 feet left of *Group Therapy*.

Pitch 1: 5.5 Climb a left-facing corner to a bushy belay ledge.

Pitch 2: 5.10a Take a crack running up off the right side of the ledge. Follow it, staying right of a block to a small ledge. Pass the ledge, staying in the crack leading to fixed nuts. 165 feet.

Rappel to the first belay ledge, then rappel off a tree to the ground. Or climb pitch 3.

Pitch 3: 5.7 Face-climb to the top and hike off.

FA: Danny Meyers, Moore, Brad Stewart 1986

15. Group Therapy 5.7+ ★★ Traditional. This

climb is located on the right side of the Angel Food Wall. From the start of *Tunnel Vision* traverse the base of the wall right (north). Upon reaching a point where you have to scramble up boulders a bit, head for a large platform about 15 feet up left off the main trail. Once up you will see a large deep narrow corridor on the left. *Group Therapy* begins just outside the corridor on the left side.

Pitch 1: Start at the base of a 10-inch crack and small pocket, which opens up the higher you get and turns into a squeeze chimney. Belay just above the low-angled face atop the ledge. 130 feet.

Pitch 2: 5.6 Climb the seam and head left at a small left-facing crack. Work your way left into the next crack system and follow this to a ledge and belay. 90 feet.

Pitch 3: 5.6 Follow the seam and crack up and belay at the bush/tree. 90 feet.

Pitch 4: 5.7+ Work your way up the crack and climb into the off-width. Belay at the top of the off-width where it opens up. 90 feet.

Pitch 5: 5.8 There are two options on this pitch. Continue heading up the off-width to a small roof and onto a belay ledge. Or, 5.7+ head out left to easier climbing and scrambling, which will lead you around the roof and back to the belay ledge. 130 feet.

Pitch 6: Traverse left to reach the summit.

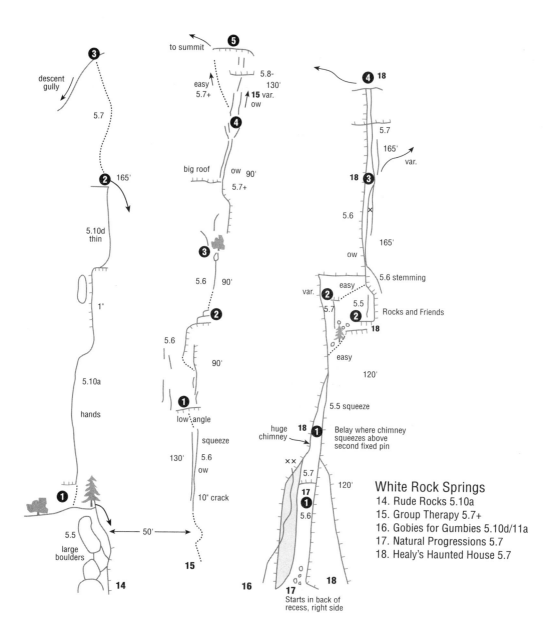

White Rock Springs
14. Rude Rocks 5.10a
15. Group Therapy 5.7+
16. Gobies for Gumbies 5.10d/11a
17. Natural Progressions 5.7
18. Healy's Haunted House 5.7

FA: Joe and Betsy Herbst, Randal Grandstaff, Matt McMackin 1974

16. Gobies for Gumbies 5.10d/11a ★★★ Traditional. This thin hand crack starts just to the right of *Group Therapy*. Climb the crack and continue, angling right. Pull over the bulge at the top. Climb the hand crack, which opens up into a large chimney toward the top—you might be able to stem across to the right-hand wall if you are tall enough. Gear: standard rack, 4 #2 Friends, 3 each #2.5 and #3 Friends. Rappel with 2 ropes from the fixed anchor. 140 feet.
FA: Paul Van Betten, Nick Nordblom, Randal Grandstaff 1985

17. Natural Progressions 5.7 ★ Traditional. This route begins in the same notch as *Gobies for Gumbies*. Climb the left-facing corner/open book, located on the right side of the wall. Climb to the roof, turn a corner, and protect the seam before dropping to the ramp. Belay from just under the roof.
FA: Donny Boardhead, Gerard Delany

18. Healy's Haunted House 5.7 ★★ Traditional. Start 50 feet right of *Gobies for Gumbies* and back in the deepest part of the narrow corridor described in *Group Therapy*.

Pitch 1: 5.7 Climb the face inside of the chimney feature. Set up a belay where the chimney narrows. 120 feet.

Pitch 2: 5.5 Finish the chimney section and then head out right. Take a face littered with pockets up and right to a ledge with a small tree at the base of a left-facing corner. Belay there. 120 feet.

Pitch 2 variation: 5.7 Stay in the crack heading straight up. Belay below a little roof and then climb back right to the original route.

Pitch 3: 5.6 Head up and right, moving over a roof. Continue up the crack system to a stance. 165 feet.

Pitch 4: Continue up the crack located in the middle portion of the headwall. Follow the crack to the top. 165 feet.

Pitch 4 variation: Instead of climbing the headwall and crack, traverse 40 feet right, climbing around the main headwall portion of the rock forma-

tion. After the traverse, head straight up the wall, climbing on the white rock and passing several small trees and shrubs to the top.
FA: Bob Healy, Joe Herbst 1974

19. Echolalia 5.9 ★ Traditional. Start on the rightmost portion of the Angel Food Wall. Look for a large white slab and a crack system with a large off-width crack forming a boundary between the main wall and white slabs, 40 feet right of a large

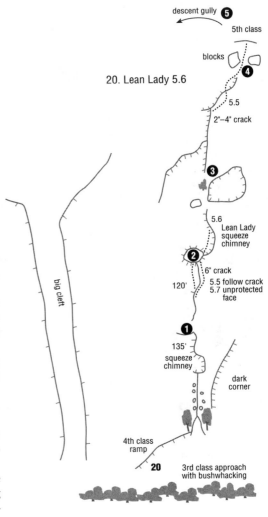

corridor feature. The route follows the crack system left of the off-width. Long pitches, bring 200 foot rope. This route can be done in four long pitches instead of five: after the second pitch, follow the main crack to the top of the cliff.

Pitch 1: Begin up a fourth-class chimney system. Pull a bulge above a block with stems and finger locks.

Pitch 2: Climb the overhanging black dihedral to its top. Head right and climb the face to a small belay stance in a recess.

Pitch 3: Continue up the obvious crack system.

Pitch 4: Continue climbing up, staying in the main crack.

Pitch 5: Finish up the prominent crack that leads to the top of the wall.

FA: Joe Herbst, Jim Rosser 1974

20. Lean Lady 5.6 ★★★ Traditional. Climb up the leftmost major crack system on the slabby white rock just right of *Echolalia. Lean Lady* can be done in four pitches with long ropes. Gear: standard rack to #4 Friend.

Pitch 1: Scramble up the fourth-class ramp and start climbing at a tree. Follow a seam with small pockets, located just left of a large, dark corner. Climb up past a small squeeze chimney to a belay ledge. 135 feet.

Pitch 2: 5.5 Follow a crack that widens to about 6 inches. It is possible to climb out on the face (5.7), but the protection is very poor. Belay from the eye-like feature. 120 feet.

Pitch 3: 5.6 Climb up and right, working your way into a squeeze chimney (Lean Lady Chimney). Belay just left of the big blocklike feature.

Pitch 4: 5.5 Continue climbing the crack system as it widens from 2 to 4 inches. Belay just below the blocks.

Pitch 5: Scramble fifth-class to the top.

FA: Barbara Euser, Jineen Griffith 1978

WILLOW SPRINGS

WILLOW SPRINGS EAST
Outhouse Wall ▲ The Dark Thumb ▲ The Owl

WILLOW SPRINGS SOUTHWEST
Nadia's Niche ▲ N'Plus Ultra ▲ Pillar Talk

LOST CREEK AND HIDDEN CANYON
Bigfoot Wall ▲ Upper Tier ▲ Lower Tier

WILLOW SPRINGS NORTHWEST
Ragged Edges Cliff ▲ Graduate Cliff ▲ The Case Face ▲ The Egg
Mossy Ledges Area ▲ Children's Crag and Sumo Greatness

FROM LAS VEGAS, take West Charleston Boulevard west, which turns into State Route 159. Drive over the 215 Beltway and zero your odometer. Turn right into the Red Rock Canyon National Conservation Area, 5.9 miles past the 215 (2 miles past Calico Basin Road). Enter the 13-mile Scenic Drive through the kiosk entrance booth.

Willow Springs is located in the middle of the 13-mile Scenic Drive, at the deepest point in the RRCNRA. Drive 7.3 miles from the entrance kiosk and turn right on the paved road.

WILLOW SPRINGS EAST

These cliffs are located on the right (east) side of the road that leads into the Willow Springs area. They face west and southwest and get midday and afternoon sun.

▲ OUTHOUSE WALL
W PM Sun   Approach: 3 minutes

Park where the paved road ends, in a dirt parking area. A pit toilet and picnic area are located on the right (east) just before the pavement ends. Outhouse Wall is a short cliff located left (north) of the outhouse/pit toilet behind some large trees; the cliff has upper and lower sections. Routes are described from left to right.

UPPER OUTHOUSE
The following routes are located 150 yards north of the outhouse on the right side of the road.

1. Karate Crack 5.9 ★★★ Traditional. This is a classic straight-in crack angling up and left. Descend by hiking left and rappeling off a tree.
FA: Paul Van Betten, Brad Stuart 1984

2. Decepta Roof 5.11d/12a ★★★ Traditional. This is a roof crack 5 yards right of *Karate Crack*. Walk off left.
FA: Paul Van Betten, Mike Ward 1984

Jam Session is 100 yards left (north) of the outhouse and 100 feet up on a ledge. Approach from the far north end of the parking lot (at the fence). Cross the dirt road to reach a trail heading up and left for 200 feet, to the left side of a long ledge. Traverse the ledge right until it dead-ends at the north-facing

Wendell "The Dean" Broussard on Sheep Trail 5.10a, Ragged Edges Wall

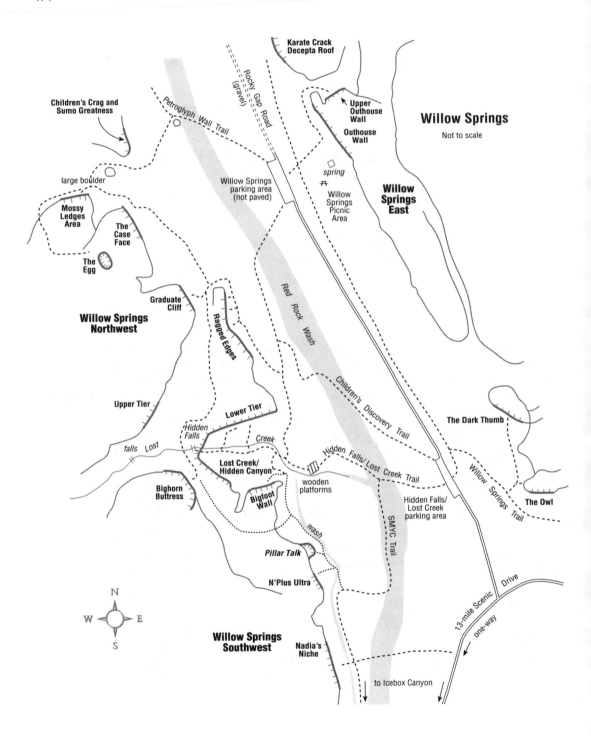

Karate Crack
Decepta Roof

Upper
Outhouse
Wall

Outhouse
Wall

Willow Springs

Not to scale

Rocky Gap Road
(gravel)

Petroglyph Wall Trail

Children's Crag and
Sumo Greatness

large boulder

Mossy
Ledges
Area

The
Case
Face

The
Egg

Willow Springs
parking area
(not paved)

spring

Willow
Springs
Picnic
Area

**Willow
Springs
East**

Graduate
Cliff

**Willow Springs
Northwest**

Ragged Edges

Red Rock Wash

Upper Tier

Lower Tier

Hidden
Falls

falls   Lost   Creek

Lost Creek/
Hidden Canyon

Bighorn
Buttress

Bigfoot
Wall

Children's Discovery Trail

Hidden Falls/ Lost Creek Trail

wooden
platforms

Hidden Falls/
Lost Creek
parking area

The Dark Thumb

Willow Springs Trail

The Owl

Pillar Talk

N'Plus Ultra

Wash

SMYC Trail

N
W   E
S

**Willow Springs
Southwest**

Nadia's
Niche

to Icebox Canyon

13-mile Scenic Drive

one-way

crack. You should be standing directly in front of the crack.

3. Jam Session 5.11b ★ Traditional. Climb the short hand and fist crack, angling up and left. Gear: to #4 Friend. Descend the chimney to the right (5.2 R) or traverse the upper ledge heading north (left) and down.
FA: Paul Van Betten, Sal Mamusia 1984

LOWER OUTHOUSE
The following routes are located below and left of *Jam Session*, 40 yards behind and left (north) of the outhouse/pit toilet on a steep, smooth, huecoed, and small cliff.

Descent: Hike to the right side of the cliff top and then scramble down.

4. Sin City 5.11b X ★ Traditional. Start on the left edge of the face, directly behind a grill and 50 feet left of the wooden fence surrounding the spring. Begin on a 2-foot-high rock platform at a black streak. Climb up to two pockets, 15 feet above the ground, and then move up and right to a big hold. Continue up and right to a thin seam. Finish left on the vertical face. Gear: standard rack with extras of small Rocks. 50 feet.
FA: Paul Van Betten, Sal Mamusia 1983

5. Jethro Bodine 5.9+ ★★ Traditional. Climb the left-facing corner right of *Sin City*.
FA: Paul Van Betten, Sal Mamusia 1982

6. Ellie Mae 5.9+ ★★ Traditional. Climb the right-facing corner right of *Jethro*.
FA: Paul Van Betten, Sal Mamusia 1982

7. Rasting Affair 5.10a ★ Traditional. Climb up the huecoed face, 50 feet right and around the buttress from *Sin City*. Climb the plated, varnished face at the top. Scary. Gear: some fixed gear; standard rack to #3 Friend. 50 feet.
FA: Wendell Broussard, Richard Harrison 1983

8. Spiderline 5.7 ★ Traditional. Start 2 feet right of *Rasting Affair*, in the corner behind the last picnic table in Willow Springs. Climb a wide crack to a ledge. Move left to reach a varnished flake. Continue up and right to the top of the cliff. Gear: standard rack to #4 Friend. 50 feet.
FA: Unknown

9. Tricks are for Kids 5.10a ★ Traditional. Begin right of *Spiderline* at a flake. Climb the flake to a ledge, and then move up a left-angling crack. Finish right at the dogleg.
FA: Paul Van Betten 1982

▲ THE DARK THUMB
SW All-Day Sun Approach: 20 minutes

Park at the Hidden Falls and Lost Creek parking area, the first parking area on the left after turning onto the road into Willow Springs. The Dark Thumb is a sunny crag located northeast of the parking area. It is a small, dark-brown feature located 200 yards up and left (northwest) of the Owl. A crack is visible, ascending left of the center of the wall. From the north end of the parking area, hike across the road to the trail on the opposite side of the road. This trail joins the Willow Springs Trail, which runs northwest to southeast. Take the trail southeast, heading

uphill for about 200 feet to where the red dirt ends and the rock dotting the left side of the trail ends. Branch off the main trail and hike directly left (north) and uphill. Hike around a gully and on top of a red band of rock toward the base of the Owl. Continue left (north), uphill for about 200 yards, to reach the Dark Thumb. Properly named, the cliff looks like a big thumb sticking up. Routes are described from left to right.

10. Land of the Free 5.11c ★★★ Sport, 6 bolts. Climb the crack feature using the left line of bolts to the shared anchor with *Home of the Brave*.
FA: Greg Mayer 1986

11. Home of the Brave 5.12b ★★★ Sport, 5 bolts. Climb the black face right of the previous route. You may want to bring a #1 Friend to get you to the first bolt, or use a stick clip.
FA: Mike Tupper 1986

Mike Ward on Sin City *5.11b X.* Photo by Sal Mamusia

▲ THE OWL
SW All-Day Sun   Approach: 15 minutes

The Owl is the freestanding rock outcropping/pillar located at the southernmost portion of White Rock Springs. The routes climb the southwest face. Start as if heading for the Dark Thumb. Take a right on the Willow Springs Trail, heading uphill for about 200 feet to where the red dirt ends and the rock dotting the left side of the trail ends. Branch off the main trail and hike directly left (north) and uphill. Hike around a gully,

on top of a red band of rock, curving around to the base of the Owl. Routes are described from left to right.

12. The Owl 5.8 ★★ Traditional. Climb the obvious slot/crack system located on the south face. Follow the feature up, heading right toward the top to a ledge and belay. Scramble up the fourth-class chimney on the north side of the formation to the top. Rappel and scramble off the backside.
FA: Joe Herbst, Matt McMackin, Nanouk Borche

13. Unknown 5.10d ★★ Traditional. Climb the undercling roof on the southeast section of the feature. Run-out at the top. Rappel and scramble off the backside.
FA: Neil Cannon and friends 1980s

WILLOW SPRINGS SOUTHWEST

Park at the Hidden Falls and Lost Creek parking area, the first parking area on the left after turning onto the road that leads into Willow Springs.

▲ NADIA'S NICHE
E AM Sun   Approach: 20 minutes

This east-facing cliff is about two-thirds of the way to Icebox Canyon from Lost Creek, on a low section of cliff. Take the Hidden Falls/Lost Creek Trail, exiting from the center of the parking lot and heading west toward the canyon about 50 yards. Take the first trail cutting left, the SMYC Trail. Hike through three washes, which takes you left (east) of N'Plus Ultra. Take the SMYC Trail uphill and left along the base of the cliff. Continue hiking until a small mound is on your left, between you and the 13-mile Scenic Drive. A low wash will be between you and the cliffs on the right. This is about a 0.75-mile hike.

Alternate approach from Icebox Canyon: Take the Icebox Canyon Trail from the Icebox Canyon parking area, heading toward the canyon. Reach a split in the trail after about 5 minutes (after walking through a wash and moving up to higher ground).

Here, take the SMYC Trail, cutting off the main trail to the right (north). Hike for about 0.25 mile to the low wash between you and the cliffs.

Walk across the wash and head toward a small cave where the cliff juts out just before recessing as you hike along the trail. Bushwhack up the hillside. People can identify the start of *Nadia's Nine* by walking through a small cave. The back entrance of the cave is just to the right of *Nadia's Nine*.

Routes are described from left to right.

14. Bean and Water 5.10a ★★ Traditional. Climb the obvious corner to a roof left of Nadia's Nine. The first-ascent party thought they were doing *Nadia's Nine* the day they put up this route. Walk off.
FA: Wendell Broussard, Sal Mamusia, Paul Van Betten, Richard Harrison

15. Nadia's Nine 5.9+ ★★★ Traditional. Old-school rating. Begin just left of the back entrance to the cave. Climb the right-facing open-book crack. Gear: standard rack to #5 Friend.

Pitch 1: 5.9++ This is a typical Joe Herbst wide pitch (5.10b).

Pitch 2: 5.9 Continue up the crack as it widens to 4.5 inches.

Walk off.
FA: Joe Herbst, Mark Moore 1977

16. Fun and Games 5.9 ★★ Traditional. Start right of *Nadia's Nine*.
FA: Joe Herbst 1977

The next few routes are located on a higher level on a black, varnished face with a wide crack and roof on the right side. Hike up a lower-angled break in a low, pink, rock band, left of the wall, to reach the base.

17. Dark Star 5.11d ★★★ Mixed. Start 200 feet right of *Nadia's Nine*. A bouldery start leads to a thin flake and then steeper climbing up big black plates takes you to the top.
FA: Paul Van Betten, Bob Conz 1980

18. Wheat Thick 5.11b ★★★ Mixed. So named for similarities to Yosemite's *Wheat Thin*—but thicker. Begin right of *Dark Star*. Climb a large, right-facing flake to the fixed anchor.
FA: Paul Van Betten, Sal Mamusia 1988

▲ N'PLUS ULTRA
E AM Sun   Approach: 20 minutes

The main feature of N'Plus Ultra is visible from the Hidden Falls and Lost Creek parking area. It is a big white pillar with varnish at its base and black, varnished walls on either side. From the parking area, hike

the prominent Hidden Falls/Lost Creek Trail that leaves from the middle of the lot and heads straight west. Stay on the trail for about 0.25 mile, walking across the wooden platforms and continuing west toward a cavelike rock feature (the falls). Just before reaching the falls, after crossing the creek bed and coming up a stone stairway, you will come to a faint trail branching off left. Take this trail and then take the second branch to the right. Before reaching the dark-brown, varnished, north-facing Bigfoot Wall, take a left and hike alongside the base of the northeast-facing cliff. Follow a very faint trail down into a wash (some bushwhacking). Continue down the wash, looking up and right for the huge white pillar. Continue to a red dirt trail heading up and right to the base of the huge roof crack to reach *The Abdominizer* and *N'Plus Ultra*. Or, take the trail below and left of the pillar, moving up and right to its base to obtain *Pillar Talk* and the remaining routes of this area.

Alternate approach: Take the Hidden Falls/Lost Creek Trail west for about 50 yards to the SMYC Trail, the first trail cutting left. Hike through three washes, taking you left or east of N'Plus Ultra. Hike right (northwest) up the third wash until you reach a small, red-dirt trail heading up and right, toward the right side of a low red band of rock. Take the trail up the hill until you are beneath a large ledge with a pine tree and bushes. Above the ledge is *N'Plus Ultra*—a wide crack leading to the left side of a large roof with a crack passing through it. Hike 100 yards right of *N'Plus Ultra* to reach the trail up to the pillar for *Pillar Talk*.

Routes are described from left to right.

19. The Abdominizer 5.11 ★★★ Mixed, 2 bolts. Begin on the wide, right-facing crack of *N'Plus Ultra*. Climb to the roof and then traverse right to the crack. Go left of the crack, taking flakes past 2 bolts in the roof. Pull the roof and finish on a thin crack to the top of the pillar. Gear: large selection, including several #3–#4 Friends for the wide section at the start; small Rocks and Friends for the top. 120 feet. Descend the gully right of the base of the roof.
FA: Paul Van Betten, Richard Harrison, Shelby Shelton 1990

20. N'Plus Ultra 5.10b ★★★★ Traditional. Begin the same as *The Abdominizer*, at a large, wide, right-facing crack. Climb to the roof and then traverse right to the roof crack. Take the fist crack out the roof. Pull over the roof and continue up the crack to the top of the pillar. Gear: large selection, including several #4 and #5 Friends. 120 feet. Descend the gully right of the base of the roof.
FA: Randal Grandstaff 1976

21. Pillar Talk 5.7 R ★★★ Traditional. Begin 100 yards right of the previous routes. Climb the right side of the huge, white pillar. Gear: to #4 Friend.

Pitch 1: 5.7 Climb the obvious off-width crack on the right side of the pillar. Upon reaching the roof, traverse left to the arête. Move up the face to a belay in several crack systems.

Pitch 1 variation: 5.10a (5.10b/c by modern standards) At the roof, continue up the crack, climbing through the roof, and then rejoin the regular route. Gear: must have large cams to #5 Friend. 100 feet.

Pitch 2. 5.4 R Climb the white face to the pillar top. 50 feet.

Hike right and descend off the pine tree right of the pillar using 2 ropes.
FA: John Landaker, Jim Whitesell, Mark Moore, Joe Herbst 1973

22. Big Iron 5.11c ★★★ Mixed, 7 bolts. Climb the steep, varnished face right of *Pillar Talk*, on the pillar. Begin off a gray ledge right of the pillar. Step left onto the varnished face and climb straight up. 110 feet. Rappel *Sleeper* or hike right and descend off the pine tree right of the pillar using 2 ropes.
FA: Paul Van Betten, Bob Conz 1990

23. Sleeper 5.9 ★ Traditional. Begin 15 feet right of *Big Iron*. Climb the finger crack to a pine tree 20 feet up. Climb flakes to a bulge to a thin crack leading to another pine. Gear: to #4 Friend. 140 feet. Rappel from the pine tree with 2 ropes.
FA: Wendell Broussard 1981

24. The Book Itself 5.4 ★ Traditional. This is the second large, right-facing corner, 50 yards right of *Pillar Talk*. Scramble through bushes to the base of the route. Take somewhat loose, yellow rock up 30 feet to a bushy ledge with an open-book crack above it. Climb a wide crack to a small roof. Continue up the crack, climbing through the roof. Continue up a face to the top of the feature. 100 feet. Descend by walking right to the fifth-class gully as described in the shorter/more difficult approach to the upper tier of the Lost Creek/Hidden Canyon area.
FA: Mark Moore 1974

LOST CREEK AND HIDDEN CANYON

The next group of routes is located about 300 yards right of the previous routes in the areas surrounding Hidden Falls. Park at the Hidden Falls and the Lost Creek parking area, the first parking area on the left after turning onto the road that leads into Willow Springs.

▲ BIGFOOT WALL
N No Sun   Approach: 10 minutes

From the parking area, hike the prominent Hidden Falls/Lost Creek Trail that leaves from the middle of the lot and heads straight west. Stay on the trail for about 0.25 mile, walking across the wooden platforms and continuing west toward a cavelike rock feature (the falls). Just before reaching the falls, after crossing the creek bed and coming up a stone stairway, you will come to a faint trail branching off left. Take this trail and then take the second branch to the right. Continue to the Bigfoot Wall—the dark-brown, varnished, north-facing wall. Routes are described from left to right.

25. Unknown 5.7 ★ Sport, 4 bolts. Begin in the middle of the short face on the far-left side of the cliff. Climb to chain anchors. Hopefully someone will have yanked the repulsive, shiny, illegally placed bolts on this 30-foot wonder before you have to lay eyes on them.
FA: Unknown. An out-of-town couple put this up and

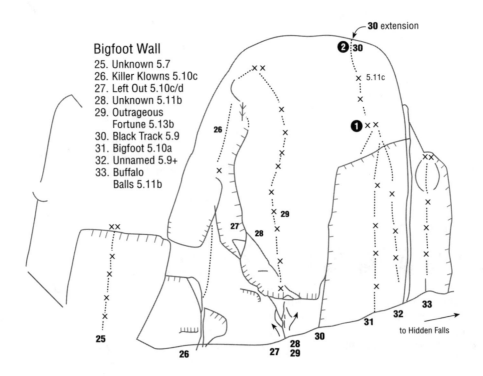

Bigfoot Wall
25. Unknown 5.7
26. Killer Klowns 5.10c
27. Left Out 5.10c/d
28. Unknown 5.11b
29. Outrageous
    Fortune 5.13b
30. Black Track 5.9
31. Bigfoot 5.10a
32. Unnamed 5.9+
33. Buffalo
    Balls 5.11b

left a tag with their names attached to the first bolt. *Lucky for them, when the BLM went to check it out the tag was gone.*

26. Killer Klowns 5.10c ★★ Mixed, 1 bolt. Begin in a recess 10 feet right of the previous route. Climb a crack between two short pieces of rock up to a loose flare beneath a roof. Pull the roof and take a flake up to a face. Take the varnished face to the *Left Out* anchors. Gear: standard rack with Friends to #3.5, including #00–#0.5, and small Rocks. 80 feet. Rappel.
FA: Paul Van Betten, Sal Mamusia, Richard Harrison, Kevin Biernacki 1989

27. Left Out 5.10c/d ★★★★★ Traditional. Begin 5 feet right of the previous route, directly below the bolts on *Outrageous Fortune.* Climb the smooth face to a wide, left-angling crack. Continue up and left to the left edge of the varnished face. Climb across the arête to a crack, angling up and left. Take the

crack to a thin face and veer right and up to clip bolted anchors. A classic and test piece for the area. Gear: Rocks and Friends to #3.5.
FA: Joe Herbst, TR 1975 (first lead unknown)

28. Unknown 5.11b ★★★ Mixed. Start on *Outrageous Fortune.* After clipping a couple of bolts, continue left along a left-angling crack. Join *Left Out* and finish on it. Gear: small Rocks for the traverse and Friends to #3.5. Rappel from the *Left Out* anchors.
FA: Bobby Rotert, John Long 1984 (done without bolts)

29. Outrageous Fortune 5.13b ★★★★ Sport, 9 bolts. Begin directly below the first bolt and move up a face and cracks to the thin, varnished face. At the top, continue up the face and then traverse left over the top of the bulge to the *Left Out* anchors. 90 feet.
FA: Jared McMillen 2004. Bolts were added by an unknown person years ago and the route had been attempted by numerous locals. McMillen sent it his first day on it.

Kris Dockstader not Left Out 5.10d, Bigfoot Wall

30. Black Track 5.9 ★★★★★ Traditional. Climb the obvious crack that splits the face. O-mazing! Move right on a ledge to clip bolted anchors. Gear: to #4 Friend. Rappel or climb the extension.
FA: Joe Herbst 1973
Extension: 5.11c, 2 bolts. Climb the thin face above the anchors. 30 feet. Descend the fifth-class gully as described in the shorter/more difficult approach to the upper tier of the Lost Creek/Hidden Canyon area.
FA: Brad Stuart

A route was removed between *Black Track* and *Bigfoot* because it was a squeeze job and not so good.

31. Bigfoot 5.10a ★★★ Sport, 4 bolts. Climb the middle of the face right of *Black Track* and finish on the *Black Track* anchors. 50 feet.
FA: Unknown

32. Unnamed 5.9+ ★ Sport, 3 bolts. Climb the bolted route 5 feet right of the previous route. Rappel from the *Black Track* anchors.
FA: Nick Nordblom (done without bolts)

33. Buffalo Balls 5.11b ★★ Sport, 3 bolts. Climb the steep, bolted face right of the *Black Track* face on yellow rock.
FA: Don Burroughs, Alan Busby 1992

▲ UPPER TIER AND BIGHORN BUTTRESS
E AM Sun   Approach: 30 minutes

There are two ways to obtain the Upper Tier:

Shorter/more difficult approach: Start as if you are heading for N'Plus Ultra. Just before reaching the falls, after crossing the creek bed and coming up a stone stairway, you will come to a faint trail branching off left. Take this trail and then take the second branch to the right. Before reaching the dark-brown, varnished, north-facing Bigfoot Wall, take a left and hike up a rocky, bushy gully, veering right. The gully is just past a large white flake leaning against the wall (10 yards left of the Bigfoot Wall). Scramble fourth-class up the rocky, bushy gully. Traverse right at a right-facing flake and continue up until you reach the big ledge from where the routes begin. Hike right (north) on the ledge to reach the gully where the first routes start. 25 minutes. (You can also scramble fourth-class up from the right side of Bigfoot Wall, but it is a bit more difficult.)

Longer/safer approach: From the Hidden Falls and Lost Creek parking area, hike the Children's Discovery Trail leaving the far-north end of the lot. Follow the trail as it heads uphill. Where a trail branches right, take it, following signs to Willow Springs and passing through narrow boulders. The trail curves around in front of the obvious, large, varnished wall with a crack through its center (Ragged Edges). When you are even with the right (north) edge of Ragged Edges, take a trail heading up to the right edge. Hike to the top of Ragged Edges and hike left (south) for 200 yards on the big ledge system. Stay high on the ledges. Pass through the creek or waterfall area and curve back around, hiking up on higher ledges above the Hidden Falls and Bigfoot Wall. Bighorn Buttress will be on your right. 40 minutes.

Routes are described from left to right.

The next two routes are located 50 yards left of *Bighorn Buttress*, in a corridor on the face left of a large dead tree.

34. Possum Logic 5.9 ★★★ Mixed, 4 bolts. Begin on a pyramid-shaped face. Take a ramp on the left side of the pyramid and angle up and right to a face. Take the face to fixed anchors. A heads-up route. Gear: small and brass nuts and Friends to #1.
FA: Nick Nordblom, Shelby Shelton 1988

35. The Pocket Philosopher 5.10b ★★★ Mixed, 2 bolts. Climb the face 50 feet right of *Possum Logic*. Fixed anchors.
FA: Nick Nordblom, Danny Rider 1988

This route is located 20 feet right of a large white block/flake leaning against the wall, 50 yards left of the waterfall (or streambed).

36. No Wave 5.10b ★★★ Traditional. Begin 50 yards right of the previous route. Begin right of the large, white flake at a right-facing flake below a low roof. This route was put up before *Bighorn Buttress* and shares the original first pitch. Gear: standard rack.

Pitch 1: 5.10b, 1 bolt. Start in a V notch left of the right-facing flake. Climb right to reach a right-facing corner. Climb the corner and then traverse right on a varnished face to a scoop. Move right out of the scoop, through an unprotected face to a thin crack. Take the crack up to a ledge with a tree. Climb the face above and just left of the tree to a bulge and a bolt. (The first ascensionists debated for nearly two months about placing this bolt, which

Upper Tier and Bighorn Buttress

36. No Wave 5.10b
37. Bighorn Buttress 5.11a
38. Beau Geste 5.9+

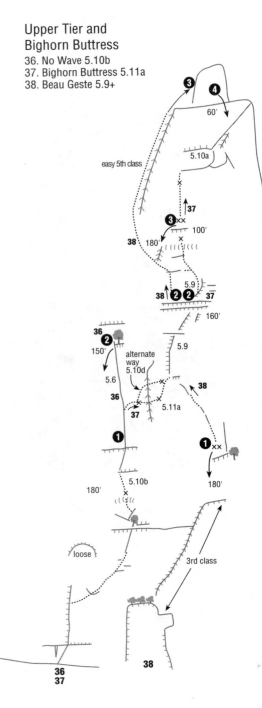

they drilled on aid, on hooks. This reflects the natural evolution of traditional climbing: the first-ascent party thought that deviating from traditional climbing practices was cheating.) Move up to a roof. Pull the roof and take a crack to a ledge. Build an anchor in the vertical crack. 180 feet.

Pitch 2: 5.6 Take the crack straight up to a tree. 150 feet.

Rappel using 2 ropes.

FA: Nick Nordblom, Paul Van Betten 1980s

37. Bighorn Buttress 5.11a ★★★★ Traditional.
Start as for *No Wave*, 50 yards right of the previous route and 50 yards left of the top of the waterfall. Begin right of a large, white flake, at a right-facing flake below a low roof. Gear: standard rack to a #3.5 Friend, small and medium Rocks.

Pitch 1: 5.10b, 1 bolt. Start in a V notch left of the right-facing flake. Climb right to reach a right-facing corner. Climb the corner and then traverse right on a varnished face to a scoop. Move right out of the scoop, through an unprotected face to a thin crack. Take the crack up to a ledge with a tree. Climb the face above and just left of the tree to a bulge and a bolt. Move up to a roof. Pull the roof and take a crack to a ledge. Build an anchor in the vertical crack. 180 feet.

Pitch 2: 5.11a, 3 bolts. Climb the vertical crack off the ledge for 20 feet. Traverse right on varnished edges to a bolt. Continue traversing straight right to a bolt around the arête. Climb up and right to another bolt and enter a right-facing corner. Take it to a big ledge and belay left of the crack. Beware of rope drag at the horizontal traverse. 160 feet.

Pitch 2 variation: 5.10d Once reaching the arête, climb it 8 feet or so and then traverse right to a bolt and then straight up into the corner.

Pitch 3: 5.9, 1 bolt. Climb the face right of the belay. Move up, angling left through ledges. Clip the bolt and continue to bolted anchors. Run-out. 100 feet.

Pitch 4: 5.10a, 1 bolt. Climb the face straight up from the anchors to a bolt. Traverse up and right to a stance left of an arête. Take a crack angling up and right to the top of the cliff. 60 feet.

Rappel using 2 ropes.

FA: Nick Nordblom, Jenni Stone 1987

38. Beau Geste 5.9+ ★ Traditional. This route
begins in broken ground right of *Bighorn Buttress*. Gear: standard rack to #3.5 Friend.

Pitch 1: Scramble third-class up 180 feet to a ledge and fixed anchors above a grungy corner and a small roof (or climb the small roof 5.7/8). This is below and to the right of the arête on *Bighorn Buttress's* Pitch 2.

Pitch 2: 5.9+ From the ledge, diagonal up and left into pitch 2 of *Bighorn Buttress* in the corner above the crux. Continue to the third-pitch anchor of *Bighorn Buttress*. 150 feet.

Pitch 3: 5.9 Step off the belay and climb the steep first 30 feet of pitch 4 of *Bighorn Buttress*. Diagonal up and left around the arête onto the north side of buttress. Continue to the top of *Bighorn Buttress*, climbing fourth or easy fifth class.

Descend by downclimbing the gully to the east as the first-ascent party did or rappel *Bighorn Buttress* using 2 ropes.

FA: Nick Nordblom, Jon Martinet 1979

39. Gray Matter 5.7 R ★ Traditional. This route is
about 40 yards right of *Beau Geste*, above the waterfall. Climb the run-out grey face. It wanders a bit and is grungy. End below a roof.

FA: Kevin Bunderson

40. Crack of Infernity 5.8+ ★ Traditional. Not so
nice. A five-pitch route right of *Gray Matter* and left of the upper waterfall. Gear: to #5 Friend.

Pitch 1: Climb the black dihedral to where you can traverse left to a tree and bolt.

Pitch 2: Continue left to a crack and squeeze chimney. Climb up to a small tree.

Pitch 3: Continue on easier ground to a large chimney.

Pitches 4–5: Unusual climbing to the summit.

Rappel.

FA: Joe Herbst

41. Fiddler Crack 5.9+ ★★★ Traditional. Climb
the finger and hand crack directly above the Lower Tier and *Mind Bomb*. Rappel.

FA: Paul Van Betten, Sal Mamusia 1983

▲ LOWER TIER
S AM Sun Approach: 10 minutes

From the Hidden Falls and Lost Creek parking area, hike the prominent Hidden Falls/Lost Creek Trail that leaves from the middle of the lot and heads straight west. Stay on the trail for about 0.25 mile, walking across the wooden platforms and continuing west toward a cavelike rock feature (the falls). Take the trail all the way back to Hidden Falls (usually dry), where the trail ends. Routes are described from left to right.

Descent: Hike north along the top of the Ragged Edges Cliff. Hike to the north end of the cliff and take a faint trail down the north side where the cliff breaks down. Then follow a prominent trail around the front of the Ragged Edges Cliff. Continue until you pass through some narrow boulders. At a T in the trail, go right, continuing along the cliff base. Curve around until you are at the base of the routes.

The following three routes climb an arête 100 feet left of the waterfall and 50 feet left of a huge roof.

This feature is just left of a smooth slab, highly huecoed and pocketed.

42. Brave Like Flash 5.10b ★★ Mixed, 3 bolts. Climb the face left of the arête. Continue up the steep, pocketed face. Gear: standard rack. Hike off the Upper Tier following the Upper Tier's longer/safer approach, or use the Lower Tier's shared descent.
FA: Paul Van Betten, Richard Harrison, Sal Mamusia, Kevin Biernacki

43. Unknown 5.11 ★ Mixed, 3 bolts. Begin right of the arête on a dark-colored face. Move right after the first bolt and up to the second bolt. Continue up the steep pocketed face. Gear: standard rack. Hike off the Upper Tier following the Upper Tier's longer/safer approach, or use the Lower Tier's shared descent.
FA: Unknown

44. Unknown 5.12c ★★ Sport, 8 bolts, 1 fixed

piece. Begin on the far-left end of the huge roof, 75 feet left of the waterfall. Climb the steep, white rock up to a fixed nut. Clip the nut and then move right onto the orange, pocketed stone. Continue up to the fixed anchor.
FA: Unknown

The rest of the Lower Tier routes begin just right of the waterfall.

45. The Threat 5.10d ★★★ Mixed, 1 bolt. This route climbs up just right of the falls, behind a big scrub oak. The bolt at the start is rusty. Gear: standard rack including a #5 Friend. Rappel from the fixed anchor.
FA: Joe Herbst, Randal Grandstaff 1973

46. Flight Line 5.12d ★★★ Mixed, 2 bolts. Begin 10 feet right of *The Threat* at a large, smooth, left-facing flake. A big move past double bolts takes you up a smooth face.
FA: Paul Van Betten, Richard Harrison 1990

47. Mind Bomb 5.11d ★★★ Mixed, 3 bolts. Follow directions from the waterfall or cut off on a trail that heads up and right about 20 feet before reaching the falls, taking you right to it. Climb the huge arête 30 feet right of *Flight Line*. Start off a large boulder, clipping 2 bolts just off the ground. Gear: small Rocks and Friends to #1.
FA: Paul Van Betten, Richard Harrison 1990

48. Tholean Web 5.10b ★ Traditional. This route name comes from *Star Trek*. Begin 30 feet right of *Mind Bomb*, where the trail heads back into the trees. Look for a thin seam that leans left. When the crack peters out, you obtain easy face climbing. 50 feet.
FA: Jon Martinet, solo 1970s

49. Bowling Balls and BB Brains 5.10c ★★★ Climb the thin, slightly left-diagonaling crack 10 feet right of *Tholean Web* up through a small alcove, to the top of the cliff. The second guy to lead this route broke his leg; this was before small cams had been invented. Gear: brass wires and plenty of small Friends. 50 feet.

Mind blown, Roxanna Brock gets the ascent of Mind Bomb *5.11d, Hidden Falls.*

FA: Wendell Broussard

50. Little Big Horn 5.9+ ★★★★ Traditional. Begin right of *Bowling Balls and BB Brains*. Look for a left-facing corner up high on red-colored rock. Take the rightmost of several cracks at the base. Move up and right and then slightly left to reach the steep left-facing corner. Take it to its top and then move right and over onto the face. Continue to the top of the cliff. Gear: standard rack. 60 feet.
FA: Jay Smith, Randy Marsh 1981

51. Grippitty Gravity 5.10c ★★ Traditional. Begin 50 feet right of *Little Big Horn*, at the base of a low roof where the trail comes close to the base of the wall. Climb the crack that splits the right side of the roof, pull the roof, and move up a low-angle corner on varnished rock. Gear: to #2.5 Friend. 40 feet.
FA: Jon Martinet, Randal Grandstaff 1976

52. Sportin' a Woody 5.11c ★★ Mixed, 3 bolts. Begin 15 feet to the right of the previous route, on a black, varnished face with a left-facing dihedral shaped like a half moon. Climb a crack to the half-moon dihedral, and then move right onto a steep face. Slab to the top. A heads-up route. Gear: small and brass nuts and a Friend or two to #3.5 for the bottom crack. 60 feet.
FA: Paul Van Betten, Sal Mamusia, Bob Conz 1990

To reach the base of the following routes, hike 15 feet right of *Sportin' a Woody,* to where the trail goes downhill. Follow along the cliff base, bushwhacking to the right side of a large white ledge. Scramble onto the ledge and traverse left to the base of the routes.

53. Captain Hook 5.11d ★★★★ Mixed, 2 bolts. Begin 15 feet right of the previous route at a big white boulder, just before the trail takes you downhill. Clip the first bolt on the brown face just right of a cone of rock. Climb a right-facing flake to the second bolt, then continue up the flake until obtaining a second right-facing flake. Climb the face with a seam up and left to the top. Gear: small and brass wires and Friends to #1.5. 100 feet.
FA: Paul Van Betten, Jay Smith 1988

54. Captain Curmudgeon 5.11a R ★ Traditional. Begin 25 feet right of *Captain Hook*. Climb through the middle of the roof. Move up to a loose, right-facing flake. Climb varnished flakes and edges to the top of the cliff. Gear: small and brass wires. 100 feet.
FA: Nick Nordblom, Paul Van Betten, Jenni Stone 1986

55. Captain Crunch 5.10a X ★ Mixed, 1 bolt. Begin 5 feet right of *Captain Curmudgeon*. Pull the right side of the roof to flakes. Move up and left to

larger flakes and a bolt. Climb up and right on varnished edges to the top. Gear: small and brass wires. 100 feet.
FA: Nick Nordblom, Paul Van Betten, Jenni Stone 1988

56. Cochise 5.7 ★ Traditional. Stem up the flaring corner 20 feet right of *Captain Crunch*, on the far-right side of the buttress. Gear: big. 70 feet.
FA: Jim Whitesell, Mark Moore, Debra Devies 1973

57. Tuckered Sparfish 5.10c ★ Mixed, 4 bolts. Begin 25 feet right of the previous route, on the next buttress right of a large, flaring corner. Begin in a thin crack and climb the face past bolts to the top. Gear: wires and Friends to #2 if you want to protect the crack at the start. 100 feet.
FA: Paul Van Betten, Don Burroughs 1992

58. Rock Rastler 5.12b/c R ★ Traditional. Continue right 30 feet from *Tuckered Sparfish* on the trail, uphill to below a large roof (the next feature right of *Tuckered Sparfish*). Climb the groove down and left of the roof crack, or scramble up the groove right of the roof (use 2 ropes). Climb the crack through the roof to a flared chimney to the top of the cliff. Scary because it is short and you cannot get gear in the last section. 30 feet.
FA: Paul Van Betten 1985

59. Heatwave 5.10a R ★★ Mixed, 3 bolts. From the previous route, continue along the cliff base for 50 feet, doing one third-class move across some boulders to reach a varnished slab. Climb a thin seam up the middle of the slab. Gear: small and brass wires to supplement the bolts.
FA: Paul and Pauline Van Betten 1988

60. Hot Climb 5.10d R ★ Traditional. This route climbs the center of a plated, varnished boulder located up and right of the *Heatwave* wall. Hike past *Heatwave*. When the trail heads downhill, go up and left to a large chimney/crevice. Worm your way up onto a ledge and to the base of the boulder. Crimp up the center of boulder. Gear: small and brass nuts and Friends to #1.5. 20 feet.
FA: Nick Nordblom, Wendell Broussard 1989

WILLOW SPRINGS NORTHWEST

For Ragged Edges and Graduate Cliff, park at the Hidden Falls and Lost Creek parking area, the first parking area on the left after turning onto the road that leads into Willow Springs. For the Case Face, Mossy Ledges, and Children's Crag and Sumo Greatness, park where the paved road ends, in a dirt parking area. A pit toilet and picnic area are on the right (east) just before the pavement ends. Hike back to the pavement and look for a trail heading into the wash to the right (west).

▲ RAGGED EDGES CLIFF

E AM Sun   Approach: 10 minutes

From the Hidden Falls and Lost Creek parking area, hike the Children's Discovery Trail that leaves from the far-north end of the lot. Follow the trail as it heads uphill. Where a trail branches right, take it, following signs to the Willow Spring Trail and passing through narrow boulders. After 100 feet, you will reach the first split off the trail, heading up and left

toward the wall. This will take you to the far-left edge of the wall with a little bushwhacking.

To reach the center of the wall (beneath Ragged Edges), continue along the trail, rounding a curve and heading uphill. You will reach a small boulder in front of you next to a trail that heads west, back into the wooded area toward the cliff base. Take that trail directly to the base of Ragged Edges, the obvious splitter crack up the center of the black, varnished wall.

For the routes farther up (right, north), there are several faint trails heading into the bushes to the base of the cliff.

Routes are described from left to right.

Descent: Traverse the top of the Ragged Edges Wall right (north) until it breaks down. Scramble down a faint trail on the far-right side of the wall. Take the trail down and curve around to the base of the cliff. If you cut off toward the base too soon, you will have to do some bushwhacking to get to the base. 5 minutes.

61. Crooked Crack 5.6 ★★★ Traditional. Climb the splitter crack behind a tree, 100 yards left of *Kemosabe* and 5 feet right of a short (5-foot) pillar. Climb the crack to where it opens to a chimney. Continue

up to a tree and belay. 50 feet. Rappel from the tree.
FA: Joe Herbst 1970s

62. Diplomatic Immunity 5.5 ★★★ Traditional. This was one of the first technical rock climbs in Red Rock Canyon. Climb the left side and crack of the pillar formation just left of the tree at the base of the wall. Follow the crack all the way to the top. Gear: standard rack. 130 feet.
FA: Joe Herbst 1970s

63. Revoked 5.5 ★★ Traditional. Climb the right side and crack of the pillar formation just right of the tree at the base of the wall. Begin 10 feet right of the previous route at a right-facing corner. Climb the corner to a face and through a steep splitter crack. Build an anchor in the crack or keep going to the tree on top (the tree needs to be backed up). Gear: standard rack. 130 feet.
FA: Joe Herbst 1970s

64. Lethal Weapon II, 5.8 ★ Traditional. Climb the thin, shallow, right-facing corner system with little to no gear. Follow the seam up to the same ledge as *Midheight*. Gear: smaller Rocks and Friends to #3.5. Rappel off the tree on the ledge.
FA: Joe Herbst 1970s

65. Midheight 5.8 R/X ★ Traditional. Start just left of the white boulder at the base of the wall. Climb the black-streaked face using small gear. Gear: brass wires.
FA: Joe Herbst 1970s

66. Go Ahead and Jump 5.7 ★★★ Traditional. Climb the obvious splitter crack located on the black face, behind a tree, 25 yards left of *Kemosabe* and 5 feet right of a short (5-foot) pillar. Climb the crack to where it opens to a chimney. Continue up to a tree and belay. Rappel off the tree (50 feet), or continue up a wide crack, finishing on the ledge at the top next to a tree. Gear: Friends to #4.
FA: Joe Herbst 1970s

67. Dense Dunce 5.8+ ★★★ Climb the black, varnished face right of *Go Ahead and Jump*. Rappel

Go Ahead and Jump.
FA: Wendell Broussard, solo 1984

68. Ok Ok Ok! 5.6 ★★ Traditional. Begin 10 feet right of the previous route on big huecos, just right of an overhang. Climb up in recess or indentation in the wall (little gear). Move up to obtain a right-facing corner. Take the corner up to a tree. Gear: standard rack to #3 Friend. 50 feet. Rappel *Go Ahead and Jump.*
FA: Joe Herbst 1970s

69. Kemosabe 5.9/10a ★★★ Mixed, 1 bolt. Begin at the enormous, white, right-facing flake. Climb the crack on the outside of the flake/arch. When the crack ends, traverse left onto the thin face. Continue up to a bolt. Climb left of the bolt for the 5.9 variation or right of the bolt for the 5.10a variation. Continue up to a tree with rappel slings. Gear: brass and small wires and a standard rack to #2.5 Friend. 110 feet. Rappel off the tree using a 60-meter rope.
FA: Sal Mamusia, Paul Van Betten, Nick Nordblom, Richard Harrison, Bob Conz, Pauline Schroeder, Wendell Broussard 1983

70. Tonto 5.5 ★★★★ Traditional. Begin 10 feet right of *Kemosabe* and climb the crack splitting the face. Climb the seam as it widens to a hand and then fist crack. At a stance below the roof, cut right onto a face and head up to a left-facing corner. Take it to the top. Step over a gap to a tree begging to be your anchor. Gear: standard rack to #3 Friend. 110 feet. Rappel *Kemosabe* (from the tree left of the top) using a 60-meter rope (it just makes it), or walk off the Ragged Edges descent.
FA: Joe and Betsy Herbst 1972

71. Theme Book 5.9 ★★★ Traditional. Climb the wide, left-facing corner system located to the right of the previous route. Gear: to #5 Friend. 120 feet. Rappel *Kemosabe* using a 60-meter rope, or walk off the Ragged Edges descent.
FA: Joe Herbst 1973

72. Vision Quest 5.12d ★★ Mixed, 3 bolts. Begin on *Theme Book* in the wide crack left of the steep

face. Move right onto the face to clip the first bolt (this is actually the third bolt up on the face). Rappel from a 2-bolt anchor at 50 feet. (Originally this route was done in two pitches, the first pitch moving past the fixed anchor onto a ledge. The second pitch, 5.10a, continues up an overhanging corner off the ledge to the top of the cliff.)
FA: Paul Van Betten, Sal Mamusia 1988

73. Project Many years ago Craig Reason added 2 suspect ring bolts directly below the bolts of *Vision Quest*. He never completed this direct start to *Vision Quest*.

74. Bodacious 5.11b R ★★ Mixed, 4 bolts. This route was originally rated 5.9/10a, but has been upgraded due to holds breaking and local consensus. Begin 5 feet around the corner and right of *Vision Quest*, on the far-left edge of the main Ragged Edges Cliff. Climb past 2 bolts to a thin seam. Then head straight left 15 feet and then up to a bolt on a ramp. Continue to the top of the cliff. This can also be done in two pitches by building an anchor after traversing left onto the wall left of the main Ragged Edges Cliff. Gear: small and brass wires and cams to #2 Friend. 200 feet. Walk off the Ragged Edges descent.
FA: Richard Harrison, Wendell Broussard, Randy Marsh 1984

75. Bodiddly 5.10c R ★★ Mixed, 4 bolts. Begin the same as *Bodacious*. Gear: small and brass wires and Friends to #3.

Pitch 1: 5.10c After clipping the second bolt, diagonal up and left for 30 feet. Build an anchor in a seam. 100 feet.

Pitch 2: 5.10a Take thin seams to the top of the cliff. 80 feet.

Walk off the Ragged Edges descent.
FA: Bob Finlay, Richard Harrison 1985

76. Plan F 5.10a (or 5.11a/b R) ★★★★★ Traditional. Start 15 feet right of *Bodiddly* and just left of *Ragged Edges* (the obvious large crack splitting the cliff) at a right-angling crack. Gear: small and brass wires and Friends to #3.

Pitch 1: 5.10a Immediately move left to a small,

Mike Meoli leading Plan F *5.11a/b, Ragged Edges Cliff*

right-facing corner. Hand-jam up with a lot of face holds as the crack thins. At the top, fingertip through the crack, angling right to the shared anchor with the first pitch of *Ragged Edges*. 60 feet. Rappel from here or climb pitch 2.

Pitch 2: 5.11a/b R, 2 bolts. The crux is height dependent (easier if you are tall). Continue up the face, heading left past 2 bolts on the thin, varnished, face. Run-out. 90 feet.

Walk off the Ragged Edges descent.
FA: Sal Mamusia, Richard Harrison, Paul Van Betten, Nick Nordblom 1983

77. Ragged Edges 5.8 ★★★★★ Traditional. This route climbs the obvious crack that splits the main Ragged Edges Wall, located just right of *Plan F*. Gear: standard rack, #5–#6 Friends for the second pitch (doubles if this grade is the limit of your ability).

Pitch 1: 5.7 Begin on the splitter crack leading to an overhang. Pull the overhang right of the crack and ascend the crack, with plenty of face holds up to another overhang. Put on your hand- and fist-jamming gloves for this one. Pull the overhang and jam to the bolted anchors. 60 feet. Rappel from here or continue on pitch 2.

Pitch 2: 5.8 Move up the widening crack to the right of the anchors (watch your belayer). Above the off-width, climb the steep face to the right. Pull another steep section to reach a ledge. Move up and right to another ledge, hike back to a large pine tree, and belay. Difficult to hear the belayer. 100 feet.

Walk off the Ragged Edges descent.

FA: Joe Herbst, Jeff Lansing 1970

78. Ragged Chicken 5.10a R ★★ Traditional. There used to be a bolt here where a route existed between *Ragged Edges* and *Chicken Eruptus*. It was pulled because the locals gave the first ascensionist flack for placing the bolt. He pulled it and then led the pitch without the bolt. (Other locals claim they gave the first ascensionist flack because it was a squeeze job.) Obviously done before the eruption of sport climbing. Gear: small Rocks and Friends to #3.

FA: Paul Van Betten 1983

79. Chicken Eruptus 5.10b ★★★★★ Mixed, 2 bolts, 1 pin. The quintessential Red Rock Canyon route! Wendell Broussard named it after the unfortunate aftermath of a romantic chicken dinner at a casino the evening before. And he still put up the first ascent—amazing! A heady lead, but well worth it. Begin 10 feet right of *Ragged Edges* on a rock ledge behind a tree. Move up a right-diagonaling rail and crack system. Climb the varnished face on thin holds, clipping 2 bolts and a fixed pin. Continue up, angling slightly left to a left-facing crack. 150 feet. Gear: small Rocks and Friends to #3. Walk off the Ragged Edges descent.

FA: Richard Harrison, Wendell Broussard, Paul Van Betten, Sal Mamusia 1983

80. Aikido Gun Boy 5.11c ★★★ Mixed, 4 bolts. Climb the steep yellow face 15 feet right of *Chicken Eruptus*. Clip the first bolt and move up and right on small flakes and edges to obtain large, varnished ledges. Move through the middle of the ledges to reach the varnished face. Climb straight up the face to a small dish below a petite overhang and clip a bolt. Pull the overhang on tiny edges. Take the face to the ledge and belay out right (descend by traversing the ledge right; do one fourth-class scramble up and then hike down the rest of the Ragged Edges descent on the right side of the cliff). Or take the last 40-foot crack up *Chicken Eruptus*. Gear: small and brass wires, Friends to #1. 150 feet.

FA: Paul Van Betten, Richard Harrison, Danny Meyers, Sal Mamusia 1991

81. Sheep Trail 5.10a ★★★★ Traditional. Heads-up on this one. When John Bachar did the FA he rated it 5.8. Begin 5 feet right of the previous route on a pink rail. Traverse the rail right to a hole. Climb left out of the small hole up onto a varnished face. Move up and right to a blunt arête. Take the arête to a ledge, 40 feet below the top of the cliff. Gear: to #3.5 Friend, many small Rocks. Traverse the ledge right, do one fourth-class scramble up, and then hike down the trail on the right side of the cliff (the Ragged Edges descent).

FA: John Bachar, Mike Lechlinski, Richard Harrison 1983

82. Dense Pack 5.10b ★★★★ Traditional. Begin 10 feet right of *Sheep Trail*, off the left side of a large ledge, 7 feet above ground level. Climb the right-facing corner and head up and left at the top of the crack, before the arch. Gear: brass wires and standard rack to #3 Friend. Descend as for *Sheep Trail*.

FA: Nick Nordblom, Bob Finlay 1984

83. Twelve Pack 5.10d ★★★★ Mixed, 1 bolt. Begin on *Dense Pack*. At the arch, head right and up to a bolt and then to the top of the cliff. Gear: standard rack to #3 Friend. Descend as for *Sheep Trail*.

FA: Paul Van Betten, Luis Saca 1988

84. Why Left 5.11b ★★★ Sport, 4 bolts. Begin 20 feet right of *Twelve Pack*, on the left edge of a black water streak. Climb up 2 bolts and then cut left and up the steep face. Bolted anchors.
FA: Sal Mamusia, Paul Van Betten, Luis Saca 1992

85. Why Right 5.11b ★★★ Sport, 4 bolts. Start the same as *Why Left*. After clipping the second bolt, head straight up, clipping 2 more bolts. Bolted anchors.
FA: Paul Van Betten, Sal Mamusia, Luis Saca 1992

86. Sheep Dip 5.11a R/X ★★★ Traditional. Climb the thin cracks up the black water streak to the ledge on the right side of the wall. Descend as for *Sheep Trail*.
FA: Richard Harrison, Bob Finlay 1986

The following two routes can be top-roped off the trees located on the ledge halfway up the wall on the very right side of the Ragged Edges Cliff.

87. Top Rope 5.11a ★ TR. Anchor off the tree on the ledge.

88. Top Rope 5.11a ★ TR. Begin 10 feet right of the previous route. Anchor off the same tree.

▲ GRADUATE CLIFF
E AM Sun   Approach: 15 minutes

The cliff is directly above the Ragged Edges Cliff. Follow directions to Ragged Edges Cliff, then walk up the rightmost side of it (north side), heading directly west. Once you have reached the top of the cliff, head left (slightly south) to midway along the top of the Ragged Edges Cliff. From there, follow the trail west and uphill for about 70 yards to the base of the Graduate Cliff. Routes are described from left to right.

89. Walk to School 5.7 ★ Traditional. Start atop the large white rock ledge to the right of the shallow corridor entrance. Climb up, heading right on a ledge to share the fixed anchor with *The Graduate*. Gear: standard rack.
FA: Jon Martinet, Randal Grandstaff, Scott Gordon 1975

90. The Graduate 5.10b ★ Traditional. Climb up the large, right-facing corner on the left edge of the wall. Climb up and over the roof to the fixed anchor. For a **5.9 variation**, exit before the roof, climbing left and out onto the face. Gear: standard rack to a couple of #4 Friends.
FA: Randal Grandstaff, Jon Martinet, Scott Gordon 1975

91. Acid Jacks 5.11c ★★★ Mixed, 4 bolts. Climb a slab to a steeper face, clipping bolts and adding gear where needed. Finish at a 2-bolt anchor. Gear: a set of brass wires, a couple of #00–#0.5 Friends, and a #2 Friend for under the roof.
FA: Richard Harrison, Kevin Biernacki 1989

92. Circle Jerks 5.11d ★★★ Sport, 6 bolts. Climb up the rightmost bolted route on the steep wall.
FA: Paul Van Betten, Richard Harrison, Kevin Biernacki 1989

▲ THE CASE FACE
E AM Sun   Approach: 15 minutes

The Case Face is northwest of Ragged Edges Cliff. You can approach Ragged Edges Cliff from the Hidden Falls and Lost Creek parking area, or park where the paved road ends, in a dirt parking area. Then hike back to the pavement and look for a trail that heads into the wash to the right (west). Turn right at the first trail junction, heading up and left toward Ragged Edges Cliff. This will take you to the far-left edge of the wall with a little bushwhacking. Proceed along the base of the wall and from its right edge, and walk up the hillside directly west. Once you have reached the base of another wall, head right (north) for 400 feet to the base of the Case Face. From the parking area at the road end, note the crack in the middle portion of the wall, running up and left. The bottom half of the wall is light tan in color and the top half is dark brown. Routes are described from left to right.

93. Territorial Imperative 5.10b R/X ★★ Mixed, 2 bolts. This route is 100 feet left of the Case Face proper. It climbs the center of the black water streak on a wall sitting back in an alcove. Gear: brass wires, a set of Rocks, and Friends to supplement the bolts.

Walk off down the gully on the left side of the route.
FA: Randal Grandstaff, Augie Klein, Randy Marsh 1979

94. Just in Case 5.5 ★ Mixed, 1 bolt. Climb the left
side of the face, passing 1 low bolt. Continue up the
easier face above. Belay atop a flake. Walk off to the
left, down the gully on the left edge of the crag.
*FA: Todd and Donette Swain, George and Catriona Reid
1994*

95. Space Case 5.7 ★★ Mixed, 1 bolt. Climb to a
bolt just right of the previous route, and then move
onto the low-angled face that has a crack in it.
Angle up and right to the shared fixed anchor with
Head Case.
FA: Unknown

96. Head Case 5.8 ★★ Mixed, 4 bolts. Climb the
middle of the face and sling a horn at midheight
between the second and third bolts. Finish up at the
fixed anchor.
*FA: Donette and Todd Swain, George and Catriona Reid
1994*

97. Hard Case 5.10a ★★★★ Traditional. Climb the
left-angling crack through a weird, low roof to the
shared fixed anchor with *Head Case*. Gear: Friends
to #4.
FA: Joe Herbst, Matt MacMackin 1975

▲ THE EGG
S All-Day Sun   Approach: 20 minutes

A free-standing egg-shaped boulder/gendarme can be
seen from the Willow Springs picnic area as you look
southwest (it is above the Case Face). To approach,
follow directions to the Case Face. Climb an old route
(probably put up by Joe Herbst) right of *Sterling Moss*.
It wanders around broken rock up to the summit ridge
at easy fourth and fifth class (5.2–5.4) for five to six
pitches. The last pitch, below the Egg, is a cool, easy
left-facing corner, the only really good pitch (5.4). This
approach is a mountaineering/canyoneering-type
route.

98. The Egg 5.7 ★ Traditional. Climb the unprotected face on south side of the egg-shaped boulder.

This was Nick Nordblom's first first ascent. He had to tie-off flakes on the top to rappel. 35 feet.
FA: Nick Nordblom, Bruce Kackline 1976

▲ MOSSY LEDGES AREA
N No Sun   Approach: 15 minutes

These two routes are to the right and around the corner from the Case Face. Park where the paved road ends, in a dirt parking area. Hike up the canyon between the Ragged Edges Wall and Sumo Greatness, hiking directly west on the Petroglyph Wall Trail. After 220 yards you will reach a large boulder in the middle of the canyon/wash, on the left. Hike 100 feet past the boulder and then head left and up the hillside 75 yards toward two large pine trees at the base of the wall. Continue past the first large pine tree, scrambling up to the second and a nice, flat belay area. You will pass a sign on your hike up, noting that the canyons of Red Rock are designated wilderness areas.

Descent: Downclimb and scramble down the tiny gully to the left (east) of the top of the routes. The descent is directly between the Case Face and these routes.

99. Soylent Green Jeans 5.10a ★★★★★ Traditional. Climb the large, open-book corner 12 feet right of the upper pine tree. Move up, angling right past the big black water streaks and passing a small tree. Climb up and over the tan, triangular-shaped roof. Finish up a hand crack, angling up and right and then back left. Belay at the top of the dihedral. Gear: Friends between #Z3 and #1, small and brass nuts, sliders; a #4 Friend for the belay. 160 feet.
FA: Paul and Pauline Van Betten 1985

100. Sterling Moss 5.10b R ★★★★★ Mixed. Climb the face 35 feet right of the uppermost large pine tree. The best way to climb this route is to climb the easy slab to the corner below *Soylent Green Jeans* and belay. Then do a second pitch going down and right and then up to a bolt. Enter a flake system, which leads up the right side of the tan, triangular-shaped roof. Climb up and over the right side of the roof and join *Soylent Green Jeans* in the right-angling hand crack. Set up a belay, the same as for *Soylent Green*

Jeans. Gear: small Friends, small and brass nuts, sliders; a #4 Friend for the belay. 160 feet.
FA: Richard Harrison, Wendell Broussard, Nick Nordblom, Sal Mamusia, Paul Van Betten 1982

▲ CHILDREN'S CRAG AND SUMO GREATNESS
E AM Sun   Approach: 10 minutes

Children's Crag and Sumo Greatness is a cliff located directly to the northwest of the second parking area and is the lowest cliff on the hillside. Head out of the parking area from the northwest corner and follow the trail marked Petroglyph Wall Trail. After about a minute on the trail you will enter a large wash. Continue walking west across the wash and follow the trail directly toward the wall that has a large black streak down its center. The center portion of this wall is closed to climbing due to the petroglyphs and pictographs. There are four routes in this section (between *Book 'Em Rudo* and *Tarzan's Arm*) that you cannot climb. Remember: climbing is not allowed within 50 feet of Native American rock art. Routes are described from left to right.

Descent: Walk off to the right (north) from the top of the cliff until it shortens. Walk down and around its northernmost side and around the corner to the base.

101. Unknown 5.10a ★ Traditional. Start just to the right of the two big, black, water streaks at the base of the wall. Follow the vertical crack that leads to the top of the wall. Gear: standard rack to #4 Friend.
FA: Unknown

102. Buckety Goodness 5.11b R ★★★★ Traditional. Start 4 feet left of *Peaches*. Climb the crack and flake on the left edge of a large, left-facing corner. Climb to the large, 5-gallon-bucket-sized hueco. Toward the top, angle left up to the ledge. Chain anchors added after first ascent. Gear: #0.5–#4 Friends.
FA: Paul Van Betten 1987

103. Peaches 5.5 ★★★ Traditional. Climb the center of the large, left-facing corner. Toward the top,

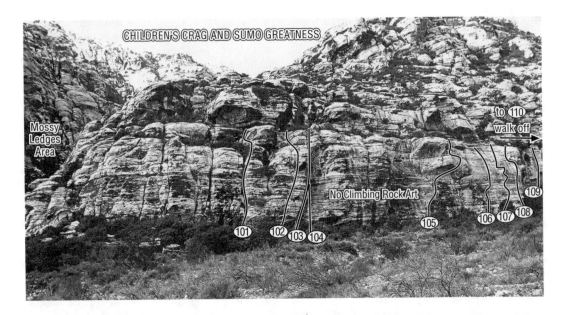

stay right. Gear: a mixture, and don't forget some smaller Rocks.

FA: Joe Herbst

104. Book 'Em Rudo 5.8 ★★★ Traditional. Start 10 feet right of *Peaches*. Climb up and over the small roof located 8 feet off the ground. Above the roof, follow the main seam, joining *Peaches* toward the top. Gear: a hefty selection of smaller gear.

FA: Paul Van Betten, Sal Mamusia, Richard Harrison, Wendell Broussard 1980s

The presence of petroglyphs means you cannot climb these routes between *Book 'Em Rudo* and *Tarzan's Arm*: *Merry Pranksters* (5.11, mixed, 2 bolts), *Paradox* (5.9, traditional), *Lower Butler* (5.6, traditional), *Upper Butler* (5.6, traditional).

105. Tarzan's Arm 5.8 ★★ Traditional. Start 15 feet left of *Sumo Greatness* and the pine tree at the base of the wall. Climb the crack system that angles right toward the top. Angle left into another crack, which will lead to the top. Gear: a set of Rocks along with some midsized Friends.

FA: Probably Joe Herbst

106. Sumo Greatness 5.10a R ★★ Mixed, 2 bolts. Begin in front and a little left of the big pine tree at the base of the wall. Climb a crack, angling up and right. On the left side of the crack is a black face and on the right is a smooth, light-colored face. Climb the crack until it ends. Angle left and up the smooth face, clipping 2 bolts. Gear: a set of Rocks and smaller Friends.

FA: Richard Harrison, Sal Mamusia, Paul Van Betten, Nick Nordblom 1982

107. Ice Climb 5.10a R ★ Mixed. Start 10 feet right of the pine tree at the base of the wall, in a small alcove. Climb the right-angling crack with a chockstone about 20 feet above the ground. Climb past a bush on a ledge, following a seam to a black bolt hanger. Continue up to the next thin seam with a fixed pin, about 7 feet up. Right of the pin is a good #3.5 Friend placement, which will make you feel better on the finishing slab moves.

FA: John Long, Lynn Hill, Doug Robinson, Randal Grandstaff 1981

108. Dean's List 5.10d/11a ★★★ Mixed, 3 bolts. Begin 45 feet right of *Sumo Greatness*, atop a group

of boulders at the base of the wall. Climb to a ledge just below a low roof. Traverse the ledge left and up onto the face above. Climb the face, angling to the right past 3 bolts.
FA: Wendell Broussard, Paul Van Betten, Richard Harrison, Druce Finlay 1990

109. Stemming Dihedral 5.6 ★ Traditional. Climb ugly cracks 50 feet right of *Dean's List*. Start at the green painted graffiti. Climb two separate cracks, stemming between them. Gear: smaller to midsized Rocks and Friends.
FA: Unknown

110. Kilimanjaro 5.11b ★★★ Traditional. Climb the left-facing dihedral right of the previous route.
FA: Pete Absolon

The following two routes are located 75 yards north and up the hill from the *Sumo Greatness* crag. A little scrambling will get you to the base.

111. Cocaine Pizza 5.11a ★★★ Traditional. Climb the roof crack.
FA: Paul Van Betten, Richard Harrison 1982

112. Salmonella Salad 5.11a ★★ Traditional. Climb the roof right of *Cocaine Pizza*.
FA: Paul Van Betten, Sal Mamusia 1982

Up and north of *Salmonella Salad* is a 65-foot hidden corner.

113. Mini-Master Corner 5.12a ★★★ Traditional. Thin tips, stout corner. Led using slider nuts.
FA: Paul Crawford, Paul Obenheim 1985

ICEBOX CANYON

ICEBOX NORTH
Sunnyside Crag ▲ Hot Time Area

ICEBOX WEST
Buffalo Wall ▲ Hidden Wall

ICEBOX SOUTH
South Wall ▲ Refrigerator Wall ▲ Smears for Fears Area ▲ Upper Bridge Mountain
Frigid Air Buttress ▲ The Necromancer ▲ Tango Towers

FROM LAS VEGAS, take West Charleston Boulevard west, which turns into State Route 159. Drive over the 215 Beltway and zero your odometer. Turn right into the Red Rock Canyon National Conservation Area, 5.9 miles past the 215 (2 miles past Calico Basin Road). Enter the 13-mile Scenic Drive through the kiosk entrance booth.

Icebox Canyon is located at the next parking area past the Willow Springs turnoff on the Scenic Drive. Drive 7.9 miles from the entrance kiosk and park on either side of the paved road. There is also a pit toilet here, on the left (east) side of the road.

The trail into Icebox Canyon is 2.5 miles long, taking you to the farthest point you can hike in the canyon. Beware of water during rain, as several waterfalls and washes are in this narrow canyon. You will pass a sign on your hike up, noting that the canyons of Red Rock are designated wilderness areas.

ICEBOX NORTH

▲ SUNNYSIDE CRAG
SW PM Sun   Approach: 20 minutes

These cliffs are on the right (north) side of the trail as you hike into Icebox Canyon. From the parking lot, hike the Icebox Canyon Trail for about 10 minutes,

heading southwest into the canyon and passing the spot where the SMYC and Dale Trails split off. After 20 minutes, the trail approaches the rising walls on the right. Look for a very large boulder. Just left or west of the boulder there is a large pine tree under a roof. Routes are described from right to left.

1. Whipper 5.10b ★★★ Traditional. Begin 150 feet left of the big boulder at a bulge that creates a low roof in an alcove. Pull the bulge through the roof and climb a varnished crack up and slightly right to the fixed anchor. Gear: mostly Rocks, Friends to #2.5. 50 feet. Rappel from the fixed anchor just above a wide section.
FA: Jay Smith, Paul Crawford, Jim Bridwell 1988

2. Backlash 5.11c ★★★ Traditional. Begin 40 feet left of *Whipper*. Climb the crack/flake through a roof up and right. Bolted anchors on the left face. Gear: to #2.5 Friend. 40 feet. Rappel.
FA: Paul Van Betten, Jay Smith 1987

3. Whiplash 5.12a ★★★ Traditional. Start on *Backlash*. Gear: many Rocks, Friends to #2.5.
  Pitch 1: 5.12a Begin the same as *Backlash*. Climb the crack to where it splits under the roof, then head left around the corner. Take a left-angling crack. Belay in a small pod at the top of the crack. 50 feet.
FA: Paul Van Betten, Jay Smith 1987
  Pitch 2: 5.10d Move up and right to the arête,

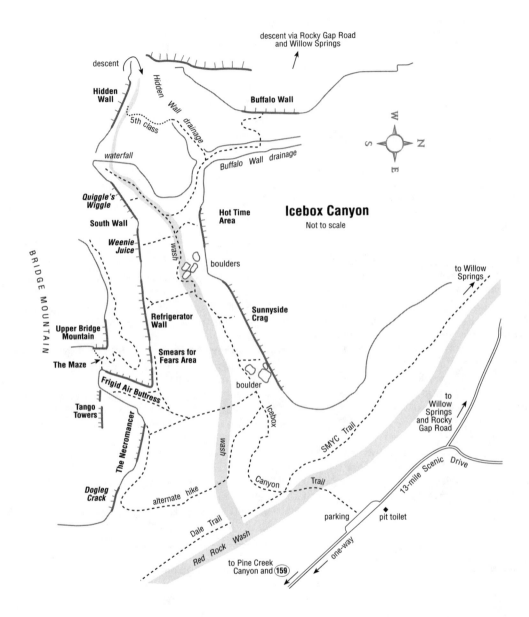

descent via Rocky Gap Road
and Willow Springs

descent

Hidden
Wall

Hidden Wall drainage

5th class

Buffalo Wall

waterfall

Buffalo Wall drainage

W N S E

Quiggle's
Wiggle

South Wall

Hot Time
Area

Icebox Canyon

Not to scale

Weenie
Juice

wash

boulders

BRIDGE MOUNTAIN

Refrigerator
Wall

Sunnyside
Crag

to Willow
Springs

Upper Bridge
Mountain

Smears for
Fears Area

The Maze

boulder

Frigid Air Buttress

to
Willow
Springs
and Rocky
Gap Road

Tango
Towers

SMYC Trail

The Necromancer

13-mile Scenic Drive

Dogleg
Crack

Canyon Trail

alternate hike

Dale Trail

parking

pit toilet

one-way

Red Rock Wash

to Pine Creek
Canyon and (159)

climbing thin cracks. Continue to the anchor below a roof. 60 feet.

FA: Paul Van Betten, Paul Crawford 1987

Rappel using 2 ropes.

4. Meteor 5.11c ★★ Traditional. Begin in a cave 25 feet left of *Whiplash*, on a ledge. Gear: mostly thin Rocks and Friends to #1.5, one #3.5 Friend in the roof.

Pitch 1: 5.11c Climb a left-angling crack, moving through the roof and out of the cave. Take a crack up and left to a fixed anchor in a thin, left-facing corner. 45 feet.

FA: Unknown. Pin scars were found on the FFA: Les Hutchinson, Paul Van Betten 1988

Pitch 2: 5.10d Climb up and right on thin edges to a seam heading up to a large roof. Traverse 10 feet right under the roof and pull it, just left of the anchor

on *Whiplash*. Reach the fixed anchor, just before topping out on the cliff. 70 feet.

Rappel using 2 ropes.

FA: Jay Smith, Paul Crawford 1988

5. Cold September Corner 5.8 ★★★★ Traditional. Begin 10 feet left of *Meteor* at a large, obvious, right-facing dihedral. Gear: to #4 Friend, mostly Rocks and smaller units.

Pitch 1: 5.8 Begin in a wide section and climb to a thin corner to the fixed anchor under the roof on the varnished right face. 70 feet. Rappel or do pitch 2.

Pitch 2: 5.7 Pull over the roof and take the corner to the top of the cliff. 50 feet. (This pitch is probably not worth the descent. The first pitch is where the fun is.)

Descend by moving up and left on the cliff top. Head down to a large boulder with a fixed rappel sling

(may need to be replaced). Rappel to a tree. Rappel down and left to another tree. Rappel to the ground.
FA: Joe Herbst, Stephanie Petrilak, Bill Bradley 1978

6. Mr. Freeze's Face 5.10 ★ Mixed, 1 bolt. Begin 50 feet left and around the corner from *Cold September Corner* on a black, varnished face with thin seams moving up it. Climb up the center of the face using cracks to a bolt 45 feet up. Continue up to a horizontal. Traverse left 10 feet to a fixed anchor. Gear: Rocks and Friends to #2.5. 100 feet. Rappel with a 60-meter rope. 100 feet.
FA: Unknown 1990s

7. Shady Ladies 5.7 ★★★★ Traditional. Begin 5 feet left of *Mr. Freeze's Face* at a varnished corner. Climb the corner for 90 feet to a horizontal. Traverse left 7 feet to the shared fixed anchor with *Mr. Freeze's Face*. A good beginner trad lead. Gear: to

#4 Friend. 90 feet. Rappel with a 60-meter rope, or continue to the top of the cliff and descend as for *Cold September Corner.*
FA: Jineen Griffith, Barbara Euser 1978

8. Magellanic Cloud 5.9+ ★★ Traditional. Begin the same as *Shady Ladies*. Climb the left-leaning crack up and left to an arête and then move up to a small alcove and roof about 40 feet up. Move straight right out of the alcove to a prominent, left-facing flake. Take the flake to the horizontal and the shared fixed anchor of the previous two routes. Gear: to #3 Friend, mostly smaller pieces. 90 feet. Rappel with a 60-meter rope.
FA: Unknown 1980s

9. Van Allen Belt 5.7 ★★★★ Traditional. Begin in the black, varnished corner/alcove 15 feet left of the previous route. Climb to the alcove on *Magellanic*

Cloud, 40 feet up. Move left under a roof and take a crack heading up to a horizontal. Traverse right and rappel with a 60-meter rope from the shared anchors of the previous three routes. Gear: to #5 Friend, mostly Rocks and Friends to #1; also bring long slings. 100 feet.

FA: Unknown 1980s

10. Bad Day at Black Rocks 5.10b ★★★ Mixed, 2 bolts. Begin 60 feet left of *Van Allen Belt*, 15 feet left and around the corner from a small, low cave. Gear: small and brass nuts, Friends to #2.5.

Pitch 1: 5.10 Begin below a low bolt on a varnished, pocketed face at a noselike feature. Take horizontals, pockets, and a pristine, varnished face to a chain anchor. 90 feet. Rappel with a 60-meter rope or climb pitch 2.

Pitch 2: 5.8 Continue up the face using thin seams and horizontals to the top of the cliff. 80 feet.

To descend, continue to the top of the cliff and descend as for *Cold September Corner*. The real climbing is on the first pitch.

FA: Randy Marsh, Greg Child 1989

11. Tie Me Tightly 5.10a ★★★ Traditional. Begin 20 feet left of the previous route, on the varnished, pocketed face and a left-facing flake beneath a bolt. After 15 feet, traverse right to a left-facing flake. Climb up and right to the anchors of *Bad Day at Black Rocks*. Gear: to #3.5 Friend. 90 feet.

FA: Nick Nordblom, Jenni Stone 1988

12. Mercedes 5.11a ★★★ Mixed, 4 bolts. Begin the same as *Tie Me Tightly*, but climb straight up the steep face to the first bolt. Move left to a left-facing, loose flake. Clip the second bolt and move up and right around a bulge, onto a varnished face and the fixed anchor (up and left of previous routes' anchor). 100 feet. Rappel with a 60-meter rope.

FA: Jay Smith 1988

13. Water Dog 5.11c ★ Traditional. Begin 10 feet left of *Mercedes*, at two thin cracks leading to a bulge. Take the crack up the right side of the bulge to a roof. Pull the roof to fixed anchors. Gear: to

#3.5 Friend. 65 feet.

FA: Paul Van Betten, Jay Smith, Paul Crawford 1987

14. Pit Bull 5.10b ★ Traditional. Begin the same as *Water Dog*. Climb the crack on the left side of the bulge and move up to the left side of the roof. Finish on the anchors of *Water Dog*. Gear: to #3 Friend, mostly Rocks and smaller units.

FA: Paul Van Betten, Jay Smith, Paul Crawford 1987

15. Hot Dog 5.11b ★ TR. Climb the right side of thin detached flake, 2 feet left of *Pit Bull*. Top-rope from the *Water Dog* anchors. 65 feet.

FA: Paul Van Betten, Jay Smith, Paul Crawford 1987

16. Water Logged 5.8 ★ Traditional. Climb the left-facing corner and the left side of the thin detached flake, 5 feet left of *Hot Dog*. When you reach the roof described in the previous routes, traverse right on the flake and pull the roof to the *Water Dog* anchors. 65 feet.

FA: Unknown 1987

17. Mister Masters 5.9+ ★★★★ Traditional. Begin 5 feet left of *Water Logged*. Climb a steep crack up and right. At the roof, head up and left to a long horizontal. Clip the fixed anchors of *Spring Break* above the horizontal. Gear: to #3.5 Friend. 100 feet.

FA: Paul Van Betten, Danny Meyers 1987

18. Gotham City 5.12a ★★★★ Traditional. Begin 5 feet left of the previous route, behind a tree at some pockets on a steep face. Climb thin, steep, discontinuous cracks. Upon reaching the lower-angled face, move up and left to the anchors of *Spring Break*. You want a belayer you can trust on this one. Gear: brass wires, Rocks, Friends to #2. 90 feet.

FA: Paul Van Betten, Robert Finlay 1987

19. Spring Break 5.11c ★★★★★ Traditional. Climb the steep varnished crack up the middle of the face, 5 feet left of *Gotham City*. Climb the vertical crack and horizontals to the fixed anchor. One of the best cracks of its grade in Red Rock. Gear: to

#3 Friend. 90 feet.
FA: Paul Van Betten, Sal Mamusia 1986

20. Tarantula 5.12a ★★★ Traditional. Named for the spider discovered on the first ascent. Begin on the previous route. Traverse left at the first horizontal, 12 feet up to the striking arête. Take thin seams up the arête. Traverse right to the anchors of *Spring Break*. Gear: brass wires, Rocks, and Friends to #2.5. 90 feet.
FA: Paul Van Betten, Sal Mamusia 1986

21. Hideous Taco 5.12a ★★ Mixed, 3 bolts. Named after the famed Japanese climber, Hidetaka Suzuki. Begin 25 feet left of *Tarantula*. Climb a face left of a shallow, left-facing dihedral. Clip the first bolt and move right to a right-facing flake. Clip the second bolt and climb a vertical crack to under a roof. Clip the third bolt and lower or rappel. Gear: to #3.5 Friend. 80 feet.
FA: Paul Van Betten, Sal Mamusia

22. Crossfire 5.11b ★★★★ Mixed, 1 bolt. Begin 8 feet left of *Hideous Taco*. Take a left-diagonaling crack to a very small roof 40 feet up. Pull the roof to a tiny, right-angling seam and bolt. Traverse right into a left-facing corner and take it to a ledge and fixed anchors above. Gear: to #2.5 Friend, mostly Rocks and small units. 100 feet.
FA: Jay Smith, Nick Nordblom 1989

▲ HOT TIME AREA
SW PM Sun   Approach: 30 minutes

From the parking lot, hike the Icebox Canyon Trail for about 10 minutes, heading southwest into the canyon and passing the spot where the SMYC and Dale Trails split off. Continue up the main wash left (west) of *Crossfire* for 500 feet until you come to where the wash is blocked by several large boulders. Look for a large index finger–like feature pointing east, high on the skyline above the crag on the right (north) side of the wash. There is also a huge, right-facing corner, capped by a large roof, 100 feet right of the Hot Time Area routes. Scramble up and around the boulders to the left to reach the left side of a ledge beneath the rock on the north side of the wash. The

routes climb either side of a low, downward-sloping, black, varnished roof. Routes are described from left to right.

23. Broussard Buttress 5.6 ★★ Traditional. Climb the large, black, polished face left of *Hot Time*, through crack systems and seams. Gear: standard rack and brass wires. Rappel down and right off small trees. Not recommended for the less-experienced climber. Difficult descent.
FA: Sal Mamusia, Paul Van Betten 1983

24. Hot Time 5.9+ ★★ Traditional. Start below the downward-slanting roof and climb up the left side of the low roof. Gear: to #3.5 Friend.

Pitch 1: 5.8 Climb the thin corner leading to the left side of the downward-slanting roof. Take the flake and crack up over another small roof to a ledge below another, larger roof. 80 feet.

Pitch 2: 5.9+ Move out the right side of the roof, continuing up the face and traversing right to a ledge to belay. 150 feet.

From around the corner, on the right edge of the ledge (just right of the large, right-facing corner capped by the large roof described in the approach), rappel to the gully below using fixed slings.
FA: Joe Herbst, Tom Kaufman 1977

25. Gourmet Miel 5.11c ★★ Traditional. Variation for pitch 1 of *Hot Time*. Climb the right side of the low roof. Belay at the top of the first pitch. 80 feet. Continue up and descend per *Hot Time*.
FA: Joe Herbst, George Miel 1977

ICEBOX WEST

▲ BUFFALO WALL
E AM Sun   Approach: 3 hours

This wall is so named because it looks like a buffalo with a dark patch in its center. From the parking lot, hike the Icebox Canyon Trail for about 10 minutes, heading southwest into the canyon and passing the spot where the SMYC and Dale Trails split off. Follow the trail through the canyon, passing alongside the Sunnyside Crag and continuing into the wash. Once in the wash, continue upstream for 200 yards. Just before reaching the waterfall that blocks the end of the canyon, bushwhack up and right (northwest) in a gully leading deeper into the canyon to walls up higher. Head straight back to the wall above you, the Buffalo Wall. Routes are described from left to right.

The first time this wall was approached, by Richard Harrison and Nick Nordblom, they reached the base, looked at the wall and turned around and went home (and they had carried a haul bag to the base!). Later they came back and put up a couple of pitches on the left side of the wall. Now there are three routes on the wall.

Descent: From the top of the wall, hike north until you run into the Rocky Gap Road. Follow the road north and then back east. You will end up in Willow Springs.

26. Buffalo Wall V, 5.11, A3 ★★★ Traditional/aid. This steep line climbs the guts of the Buffalo Wall—it is long and hard. It follows a series of arches and corners up the center of the wall to a nice ledge at the halfway point and then continues up. All pitches are around 165 feet in length. Gear: Hooks, pitons, cams to #6 Friend.

Pitch 1: 5.10, A1 Start up a loose face toward a large, left-arching roof (5.10). Continue up the arch left to its high point and belay (A1).

Pitch 2: 5.10 Climb out over the roof to the next left-arching roof. Follow the arch heading left and up to its high point and belay.

Pitch 3: 5.11, A2 Once again, exit up and over the roof to gain access to the next left-arching feature, a wide crack (up to 9 inches) 5.11. Follow the arch up to the steep featureless wall and bust out a series of A2 moves.

Pitch 4: A2 Continue aiding up the smooth black face, heading left, toward a nice party ledge.

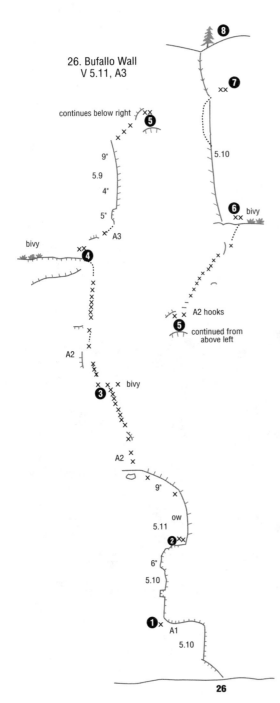

26. Bufallo Wall
V 5.11, A3

Pitch 5: 5.9, A3 From the ledge, climb to the left-facing corner system, passing a bolt. Continue up the corner (5.9). The corner gets very thin toward the top. A3 moves required to reach the belay.

Pitch 6: A2 This pitch is the aid crux and a lot of hooking is required. Head up the right side of a large white section of rock. Use bolts between hook moves leading to a belay ledge.

Pitch 7: 5.10 From the ledge, climb a series of cracks leading to a belay out right.

Pitch 8: Continue up the face, heading right up a crack to the top of the wall.

FA: Paul Van Betten, Richard Harrison, Sal Mamusia 1991

27. Tatanka V, 5.10, A3 ★★★ Traditional/aid. Another long challenging route, this is the best of the three on the wall. Similar to *Buffalo Wall*, it climbs the face using a series of arching cracks and then continues up, staying right of a large white portion of rock. Gear: brass wires, standard rack plus hooks and pitons.

Pitch 1: 5.7 Climb and scramble up a ramp that runs up and right. Belay at the top of the ramp below the start of the first left-arching crack.

Pitch 2: A2 Follow the left-arching crack to its top and belay from an anchor just above the roof.

Pitch 3: A3 From the belay, head right, to a ledge and then a left-facing corner. Finish up a bolted face to the belay on a ledge.

Pitch 4: A3 Continue up the wall, taking a left-facing corner and face (A1). Head toward a large white section of rock while staying on the right side of it (A3 hooking). Belay above the white rock on a black face.

Pitch 5: 5.10 Climb the smooth black face, passing a couple of bolts to reach a nice ledge—the Pabst Blue Ribbon Ledge.

Pitch 6: A2 From the PBR Ledge, continue up the face (A2), which leads to a belay ledge.

Pitch 7: 5.10, A3 From the belay ledge, head up the wall alongside a right-facing crack system. The climbing gets really thin (5.10) near the top of the crack. Continue to a ledge with a tree. Finish the pitch with another series of A3 hook moves.

Pitch 8: 5.10 Finish the route by climbing up the

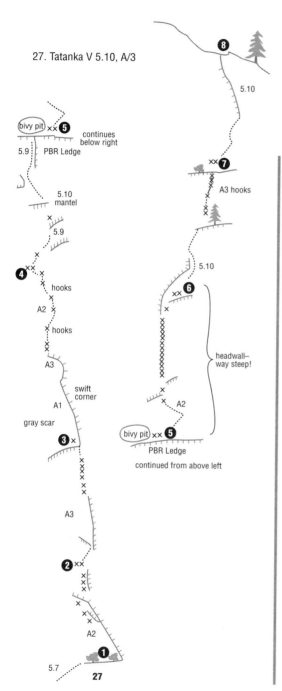

27. Tatanka V 5.10, A/3

face, right, to a right-facing crack. Finish up the crack, pulling onto a ledge near a large pine tree.

FA: Richard Harrison, Paul Van Betten, Sal Mamusia 1993

28. Buffalo Soldiers, 5.11, A2 ★★★ Traditional/ aid. Climb the right side of the wall, per the Buffalo Wall overlay. See the climbers topo for detail.

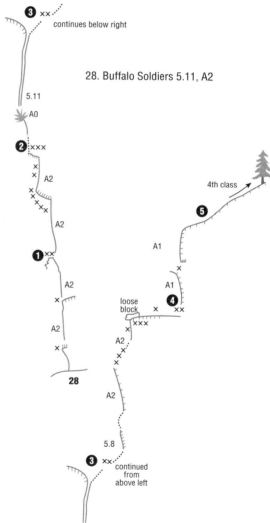

28. Buffalo Soldiers 5.11, A2

Gear: 5 knifeblades, 3 Lost Arrows, Rocks, and Friends to #5.
FA: Paul Van Betten, Sal Mamusia 1998

▲ HIDDEN WALL
E AM Sun   Approach: 3 hours

From the parking lot, hike the Icebox Canyon Trail for about 10 minutes, heading southwest into the canyon and passing the spot where the SMYC and Dale Trails split off. Follow the trail through the canyon, passing alongside the Sunnyside Crag and continuing into the wash. Once in the wash, continue upstream for 200 yards. Just before reaching the waterfall that blocks the end of the canyon, bushwhack up and right (northwest) in a gully leading deeper into the canyon to walls up higher. Upon reaching the approach gully for the Buffalo Wall, head left, deeper into the canyon. This is a long approach with loose

rock. There is a cruxy, loose traverse off a bushy ledge, about midway up the Hidden Wall drainage, that heads left before obtaining the wall. Though the *Blitzkrieg* first-ascent party soloed it, you may want to rope up for the ensuing crack system leading to a large bird's nest. Watch for loose rock. Continue through a bulge and then make a scary traverse to the right with a sling threaded through a hole to protect it. Scramble off and right, continuing up the gully to the base of the Hidden Wall.

29. Blitzkrieg V, 5.10d R ★★★ Traditional. Climb the prominent water streak up the center of the wall. See the climbers topo for detail. No bolts on the route! As far as the locals know, this route has only seen two ascents (the second involving the first-ascent party). Gear: standard rack including a good selection of small wires and Friends to #4. To descend, hike north until you can rejoin the fork of

Icebox Canyon that you hiked in on and follow the canyon out. You can also continue north to Rocky Gap Road and hike out as per Buffalo Wall—down Rocky Gap to Willow Springs.
FA: Richard Harrison, Sal Mamusia 1982

ICEBOX SOUTH

▲ SOUTH WALL
N No Sun   Approach: 40 minutes

South Wall is directly across from the Hot Time Area. From the parking lot, hike the Icebox Canyon Trail for about 10 minutes, heading southwest into the canyon and passing the spot where the SMYC and Dale Trails split off. Follow the trail through the canyon, passing alongside the Sunnyside Crag and continuing into the wash. Once in the wash continue upstream for 75 yards. On the left-hand, north-facing wall is a prominent right-facing arch. Bushwhack up the hill from downstream of the arch, for 100 feet to obtain a platform below *Weenie Juice*. Scramble 50 feet up to a bushy ledge. Routes are described from left to right.

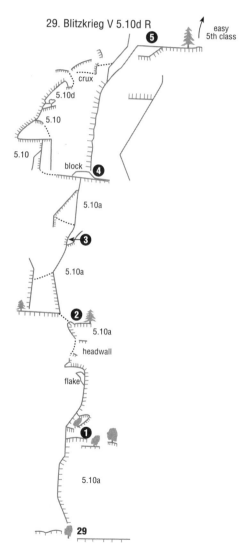

29. Blitzkrieg V 5.10d R
⑤ easy 5th class
crux
5.10d
5.10
5.10
block ④
5.10a
⑧
5.10a
❷
5.10a
headwall
flake
❶
5.10a
29

30. Weenie Juice 5.9+ ★★★ Traditional. Climb a crack and flake to a single-bolt belay. 120 feet. Gear: standard rack plus 4 #5 Friends. Rappel with 2 ropes.
FA: Richard Harrison, Paul Van Betten, Wendell Broussard, Sal Mamusia, Lynn Cronin 1983

From the wash beneath *Weenie Juice*, continue upstream for 200 yards to the waterfall that blocks access to the upper canyon.

31. Quiggle's Wiggle 5.9 R ★ Traditional. Begin left of the waterfall at a breakdown in the cliff, before it gets steep and just before the slab to the base of the waterfall. Gear: brass wires, Rocks, and Friends to #3.5.

Pitch 1: 5.8 R Climb an unprotected, low-angle face to a short, right-facing corner to a ledge. Move straight left and belay. 70 feet.

Pitch 2: Third-class left for 80 feet to the base of a right-leaning corner.

Pitch 3: 5.9 R Climb a crack to a ledge with a tree and a large block to its right. Step off the block onto the face right of the crack. Take the face up and right, past pockets, right of the crack. Belay after climbing through jugs. 150 feet.

Sal Mamusia on the first ascent of Weenie Juice *5.9+ on the South Wall in Icebox Canyon.* Photo by Paul Van Betten

Pitch 4: 5.8 Traverse back left into the crack and take it to the summit. 150 feet.

Descend a gully left (east), marked with cairns, taking you below the waterfall area.

FA: Dave Gloudemans, Jason Quiggle 1996

▲ REFRIGERATOR WALL
N No Sun   Approach: 30 minutes

This area is named the Refrigerator Wall for good reason: bring your jacket. From the parking lot, hike the Icebox Canyon Trail for about 10 minutes, heading southwest into the canyon and passing the spot where the SMYC and Dale Trails split off. Follow the trail through the canyon for about 25 minutes, passing alongside the Sunnyside Crag and continuing into the wash. Cross the wash, heading upstream about 30 feet until you are directly across from the apron/ledge sys-

tem separating the left and right sides of the Refrigerator Wall. Hike up a faint, dense trail to the south side of the canyon and an enormous black, varnished wall. Three large pine trees, one of which is dying, mark the left side of the wall. Routes are described from left to right.

The following routes begin on the left side of the apron, left of the three pine trees. Hike the bowl-like base to the far left of the pine trees, about 50 feet.

32. Greased Lightning 5.10a ★★★★ Traditional. Begin at a small, left-facing flake. Climb a thin, lightning bolt–shaped crack at the left end of a ramp. Climb up and right to a fixed anchor on a ledge. Gear: small and brass nuts, cams to #2 Friend. 120 feet. Rappel with 2 ropes.

FA: Nick Nordblom, Randy Marsh 1989

33. Swing Shift 5.10b R ★★ Traditional. Begin at the top of a right-angling ramp, left of a large recess and 20 feet right of *Greased Lightning.* Gear: standard rack with a good selection of small brass and wire nuts, cams to #3.5 Friend.

Pitch 1: 5.6 Begin in a left-facing corner below the top of a right-angling ramp. Climb to a ledge with some trees below a thin vertical crack system. Climb the leftmost of two vertical cracks. 60 feet.

Pitch 2: 5.9 Start on the left side of the ledge, move up a thin crack and belay in a recess on a ledge. 100 feet.

Pitch 3: 5.8 R, 1 bolt. Move left over loose rock to a rotten, chossy corner system. Climb the corner for about 15 feet and then hand-traverse left, past a protruding flake. Continue through a steep section, clipping 1 bolt. Climb up and left to a ledge with a single-bolt belay below converging vertical cracks. 50 feet.

Pitch 4: 5.10a R Climb an unprotected face up and right for 15 feet to a varnished, flared crack. Take the crack to lower-angle rock to the left side of a pillar feature. Move up a corner to a white belay ledge. 70 feet.

Pitch 5: 5.10b R Climb the tiny corner and crack up and right using small gear. Belay beneath a chimney. 80 feet.

Pitch 6: 5.10b R Climb the chimney for 80 feet to a ledge. Traverse 40 feet left and up to reach the anchor. 160 feet.

Pitch 7: Scramble straight up past two trees. Move right to a corner and then up to a blocky ledge. 150 feet.

Two rappels take you to a tree in a steep corner. Rappel from the tree to the belay anchors above pitch 5. Rappel down and right to another tree. Rappel to the belay ledge above pitch 1. Rappel to the ground.
FA: Mark Moore, Joe Herbst 1977

34. Grape Nuts 5.10c ★★★ Mixed, 6 bolts. Begin 30 feet right of *Swing Shift* or 15 feet left of the leftmost pine tree. Climb a fourth-class bulge to a ledge and clip the first bolt on a slab right of a water streak. Take the water streak up to the right side of a roof. Move right of the roof and head to the left-facing flake of *Amazing Grace*. Finish on *Amazing Grace*. Gear: small and brass nuts and Friends to #4. Rappel using 2 ropes.
FA: Rick Dennison, Randy Faulk, Alex Malfatto 1991

35. Amazing Grace 5.9 ★★ Mixed, 3 bolts. Begin about 5 feet right of *Grape Nuts*. Climb the fourth-class bulge up to another ledge with a bolt. Continue up the thin, varnished face, passing 2 more bolts. Move right to a left-facing flake, following it to the fixed anchor. Sustained climbing. Gear: to #5 Friend and long slings. Rappel with 2 ropes.
FA: Danny Meyers, rope solo 1985

36. Kisses Don't Lie 5.12a ★★ Mixed, 12 bolts. This route was attempted some time ago and was later completed by Greg Mayer. Begin 20 feet right of *Amazing Grace*, on a face behind the rightmost pine tree. Gear: large Rocks, small Friends to #2.

Pitch 1: 5.12a, 10 bolts. Climb the thin, varnished face past 10 bolts to a fixed anchor above and right of a ledge, below a small roof. Fixed long slings are located on bolts that are dangerous to clip otherwise. 180 feet.

Pitch 2: 5.11d. Climb up and left to the face. Take the face to a right-angling crack. Climb the crack up and right. Pull the roof above the crack and climb to a fixed anchor on a varnished face. 110 feet.

Rappel with 2 ropes.
FA: Greg Mayer 1994

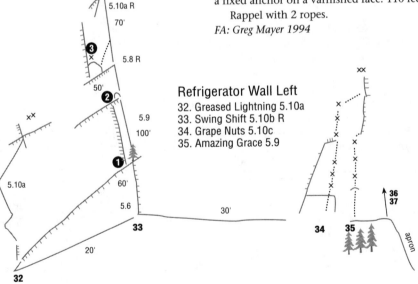

Refrigerator Wall Left
32. Greased Lightning 5.10a
33. Swing Shift 5.10b R
34. Grape Nuts 5.10c
35. Amazing Grace 5.9

37. Earth Juice 5.10d ★★★ Mixed, 5 bolts. Begin 10 feet up and right of *Kisses Don't Lie*, right of the rightmost pine tree and below a large, left-facing corner. If this is your difficulty limit, beware! Brilliant route.

Pitch 1: 5.10d, 4 bolts. Begin on the ledge system up and right of *Kisses Don't Lie*. Climb the varnished face up and left to a shallow, left-facing dihedral right of the fixed anchor. 100 feet.

Pitch 2: 5.10d, 1 bolt. Climb up and right to a right-angling flake. Continue up to a right-facing, thin corner. Clip a bolt under a small roof and then downclimb and move up and left past a flake to the first-pitch belay anchors of *Kisses Don't Lie*. 100 feet.

Rappel using 2 ropes.

FA: Kurt Reider, Chris Robbins, Augie Klein 1979

The following routes begin on the right side of the apron, about 100 feet right of the three pine trees. Take the rocky trail (also a small streambed) along the base of the apron to reach these routes.

38. Breakaway 5.10d ★★★ Mixed. Begin on the left side of a white pillar at a dirty recess or cave feature, 100 feet right of *Earth Juice* on the black water streak. You will destroy the route if you climb it when it is even the slightest bit wet. And do not bother tapping on the holds; they all sound very "breakable." Gear: Friends to #2.5 and 15 quickdraws.

Pitch 1: 5.8, 4 bolts. Climb cracks up the pillar and then move up the varnished face, passing 4 bolts. Belay in cracks directly below the water streak and 10 feet left of 2 bolts (the first-pitch anchors of *Strawberry Shubert*), using medium-sized Friends. 150 feet.

Pitch 2: 5.10d, 12 bolts. Climb up and left to the first bolt and then continue up the face past 11 bolts. 140 feet.

Rappel using 2 ropes.

FA: Danny Meyers, Mike Ward 1991

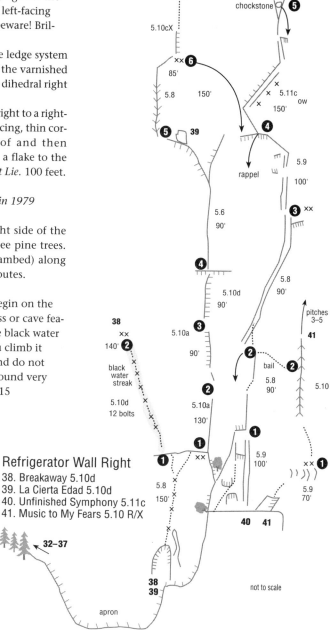

Refrigerator Wall Right
38. Breakaway 5.10d
39. La Cierta Edad 5.10d
40. Unfinished Symphony 5.11c
41. Music to My Fears 5.10 R/X

39. La Cierta Edad 5.10d ★★★ Mixed. This Spanish phrase refers to the age when a person is not likely to be persuaded by public opinion. The name was chosen as a celebration of bolts placed to create a beautiful route, when bolting was not accepted by the local community. Begin as for *Breakaway,* follow a continuous crack system.

Pitch 1: 5.8, 4 bolts. Start as for *Breakaway* and then move right into a large chimney and belay. 150 feet.

Pitch 2: 5.9+, 1 bolt. Climb the chimney and move up the crack system to a bolted belay. 130 feet.

Pitch 3: 5.10a Keep on up the crack to a bolted, hanging belay. 90 feet.

Pitch 4: 5.10d Stay in the crack and belay on a large ledge. 90 feet.

Pitch 5: 5.6 Continue up the crack, moving left at a split. Climb over a detached block/ledge. Belay at the base of a varnished corner.

Pitch 6: 5.8 Climb the corner and then step right to a fixed anchor. 85 feet. Rappel 150 feet to a ledge. Walk right on the ledge to the fixed anchor at the top of the fourth pitch of *Unfinished Symphony.*

Traverse ledge right, easy fifth class, and rappel *Unfinished Symphony* using 2 ropes.

FA: George and Joanne Urioste 1981

Pitch 7: 5.10c X Continue up.

Rappel using 2 ropes or continue up *Unfinished Symphony.*

FA: Bob Conz and Nick Nordblom, last pitch late 1980s ("Bob was having a good day that day!" says Nordblom.)

40. Unfinished Symphony 5.11c ★★★★ Traditional. Begin 30 feet right of *La Cierta Edad* at the top of a rocky trail. Climb the crack in the large, black, varnished open book, just right of a large black water streak. A great route for all levels. If you do not climb 5.11, just enjoy the first four pitches. Ultraclassic off-width heaven! Gear: to #5 Friend, mostly cams.

Pitch 1: 5.9 Climb the boulders and blocks in a sort of gully to a ledge below a corner. 100 feet.

Pitch 2: 5.8 Move up and right into the crack, pull a bulge, and then continue on easier ground to a sloping ledge. 90 feet.

Pitch 3: 5.8 Climb a chimney to a cavity (40 feet up), and then move up the killer overhanging off-width to a stance on the right. Belay in the crack. 90 feet.

Pitch 4: 5.9 Follow the crack up to a stance at the base of a sickle-like roof. 100 feet.

Pitch 5: 5.11c Climb a thin crack to a right-facing corner (5- to 6-inch off-width). Use downward pointing bolts that stick out 2 inches from the wall or bring a couple of #5 Friends. Killer pitch. Awkward and chossy belay. 150 feet.

Rappel with 2 ropes.

FA: Ross Hardwick, Joe Herbst, Andre Langenbacher 1978

41. Music to My Fears 5.10 R/X ★ Traditional. Start 5 feet right of *Unfinished Symphony* at a huge, varnished, right-facing flake and block, leaning against the wall. Several local hardmen have bailed off the top pitches of this crumbly wonder. Gear: minimal.

Pitch 1: 5.9 Climb the varnished flake to a thin crack up to another blocky section. Move up to a right-facing, loose corner. Head up and right on a face to a 2-bolt anchor. 70 feet.

Pitch 2: 5.10 Head left on thin seams and the face to the blunt arête. Continue up arête. From here most people choose to traverse left to the second-pitch anchors of *Unfinished Symphony,* rappeling with 2 ropes.

Pitches 3–5: Climb the loose arête directly above the belay, continuing to the top of the cliff.

FA: Robert Finlay, Brad Ball 1984

▲ SMEARS FOR FEARS AREA
N No Sun   Approach: 25 minutes

From the parking lot, hike the Icebox Canyon Trail for about 10 minutes, heading southwest into the canyon and passing the spot where the SMYC and Dale Trails split off. Follow the trail through the canyon. At the point where the canyon narrows and the Sunnyside Crag is on the right, head left down into the wash. Cross the wash and scramble up the hillside to the far-left edge of a north-facing, smooth, black, varnished wall. Hike right (west) to the base of the wall and follow the base until you reach the ledge where *Lebanese JoJo* begins. Routes are described from left to right.

42. Lebanese JoJo 5.9+ ★★ Traditional. Begin on the far-left side of the wall. Climb onto a ledge, about 10 feet off the ground. Move up the right-facing corner just below the left edge of the roof. Gear: standard rack including some small Rocks for the upper face.

Pitch 1: 5.9 Climb to a large pine tree and then traverse right on the nice black face, staying above the roof. Belay at a thin crack. 40 feet.

Pitch 2: 5.9+ Climb the most obvious crack up the face. 90 feet.

Pitch 2 variations 1 and 2: Climb up one of the other crack systems on the face at the same grade.

Rappel off the fixed anchor using 2 ropes.

FA: Sal Mamusia, Bob Conz, "Frodo" Lybarger, Mike Ward, Paul Van Betten 1990

43. Smears for Fears 5.11c ★★★★ Mixed, 5 bolts. Begin 100 feet right of the previous route, 10 feet up on a ledge and just right of a large right-facing corner. Climb a thin, right-facing dihedral for 20 feet to a slabby face. Move above a small roof and continue on a thin face and slab to the fixed anchor. Scary. One of the original holds broke off, making for a difficult clip and a harder grade (up from original 5.11b). Gear: small and brass nuts to supplement the bolts. 100 feet. Rappel using 2 ropes.

FA: Sal Mamusia, Mike Ward, Robert Findlay, Paul Van Betten 1989

44. Rojo 5.11d ★★ Mixed, 3 bolts. Begin 15 feet right of *Smears for Fears* on a large ledge below the varnished face. Climb the right-angling crack and water streak. Move up a face to a shallow right-facing corner. Climb the corner and face to the bolted anchor. The bolt at the crux was added after the first ascent, where the leader took a huge fall and reclimbed the route a couple of times before being able to get the next bolt in. Gear: wide selection including some small nuts. 100 feet. Rappel with 2 ropes.

FA: Paul Van Betten, Sal Mamusia 1989

45. Romeo Charlie 5.9 ★ Traditional. This route is about 140 feet right of *Smears for Fears*. Begin on a small ledge and climb up the right-leaning crack,

right of a mossy portion of the crag. Follow the crack and face up, staying just left of the small roof. Move up and right to a moss-covered slab to clip the fixed anchor. Rappel with 2 ropes. Moss covered.

FA: Sal Mamusia, Robert Findlay, Jimmy Olsen 1989

46. Project ★ Mixed, 3 bolts. This route is 5 feet right of *Romeo Charlie* and 20 feet left of two white boulders resting at the base of the wall. Climb the black face between two patches of moss. Follow the face up to the third bolt and lower or rappel. A contrived line that weaves left and right though the bottom section offers nice movement.

▲ UPPER BRIDGE MOUNTAIN
NE AM Sun   Approach: 2–3 hours

Bridge Mountain is the peak that separates Icebox and Pine Creek Canyons. Approach upper Bridge Mountain via an Icebox Canyon climb, for instance, one on the Frigid Air Buttress; or approach from the Bridge Mountain Trail. Reach this trail via the road into Willow Springs, 7.3 miles along the Scenic Drive from the entrance kiosk. Drive the Willow Springs road until you reach the four-wheel-drive Rocky Gap Road, which ascends behind Bridge Mountain. Drive 5 miles up this road to a parking lot and then hike toward the summit of Bridge Mountain on the established Bridge Mountain Trail. Traverse around the north side of Bridge Mountain, reaching the Maze, a wash and gully system that meanders along the base of Bridge Mountain's north side. Hike through the Maze to obtain Bridge Mountain's Northeast Arête (Rainbow Bridge). The easiest line through the Maze takes 2–3 hours and requires you to stay high and west. The easiest way around the cliff band below the northeast arête is to the east. (See page 208 for a route overlay photo of Bridge Mountain.)

47. Rainbow Bridge (aka The Northeast Arête)
IV, 5.7 ★★★ Traditional. This route climbs a crack system up the northeast arête of Bridge Mountain.

Pitch 1: 5.6 Head up the arête, climbing the obvious crack. Move over a small roof and continue up the crack until it ends at a large ledge. 130 feet.

Pitch 2: 5.6 Climb the crack off the right side of the ledge up to a small ledge below a chimney. 140 feet.

Pitch 3: 5.5 Climb the chimney to a ledge. Move right to another chimney and belay on a large ledge. 160 feet.

Pitch 4: 5.3 Climb the crack in the low-angled face. Belay at the large ledge under the roof. 160 feet.

Pitch 5: Fourth-class around the roof left, and then scramble third-class to the summit.

To descend, from the west side of the summit find a ramp sloping down and southwest. Marked with cairns, the ramp will lead you to the south side of a wooded area called the Hidden Forest. Hike out to Rocky Gap Road and down to the north end of the Willow Springs area.

FA: Sal Mamusia, Richard Harrison, solo 1982

Continue around the east face of Bridge Mountain to reach the southeast side of the wall. Or, hike up the north fork of Pine Creek Canyon (from the Pine Creek Canyon parking area). Traverse under the south face of Lower Bridge Mountain, the Pisces Wall, to a gully and then head up the ridge to the west.

48. The Southeast Arête IV, 5.5 X ★★★ Traditional. Climb a 60-foot exposed face to a chimney. From the top of the chimney, the route rounds out to the summit. There may be gear on the route. *FA: Unknown*

▲ FRIGID AIR BUTTRESS
NE AM Sun   Approach: 25 minutes

From the parking lot, hike the Icebox Canyon Trail for about 10 minutes, heading southwest into the canyon and passing the spot where the SMYC and Dale Trails split off. Follow the trail directly west, toward the mouth of the canyon. At the point where the

canyon narrows and the Sunnyside Crag is on the right, head down into the wash (south). Cross the wash, and start heading for the large rock amphitheater located to the southwest in the deepest part of this sort-of canyon. Boulder-hop and scramble up the boulders that lead to a huge corner system on the east-facing wall. *Burlesque* starts off a ledge system, 50 feet right of the huge corner system that houses a spring-time waterfall. Routes are described from left to right.

49. Burlesque 5.9 ★★ Mixed. This route is on the right side of an obvious waterfall amphitheater at a large flake that leans against the wall. The left side of this flake forms a dihedral and off-width crack. Scramble up a mossy slab, easy chimney, and gully to reach the starting ledge 150 feet up (third class). Gear: standard rack to #6 Friend.

    Pitch 1: 5.7 Climb up and right to a ledge with a tree. 80 feet.

    Pitch 2: 5.8+ Climb straight up to a left-facing corner/crack to a ledge. Follow the ledge left to belay beneath a flake. 160 feet.

    Pitch 3: 5.9, 1 bolt. Climb the flake to a chimney and belay on a ledge atop the chimney section. 160 feet.

    Pitch 4: Climb the loose third-class rock to a belay tree at the top. (Not really worth doing.)

    Rappel with 2 ropes.

FA: Joe Herbst, Tom Caufman 1979

50. Come Again 5.10a ★★ Traditional. Begin at a smooth, 50-foot, gray chimney 120 feet right of *Burlesque*. Gear: a heavy rack up to #4 Friend.

    Pitch 1: Take the chimney to its end and then move left to a large belay ledge.

    Pitch 2: Climb the left-facing corner with a crack off the right edge of the belay ledge.

    Pitch 3: Climb up and left to a chimney. Climb the chimney and traverse right over a chunk of rock to a left-facing corner and belay.

    Pitch 4: Move up the left-facing corner, angling left onto a large, vegetated belay ledge.

    Pitch 5: Climb up the face, angling left to the chimney formed by a large detached slab. Take the chimney to the top. To descend, head left (east) behind the last-pitch chimney. Scramble down to a large ledge above *Burlesque*.

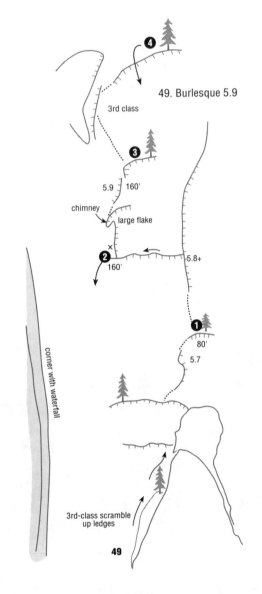

49. Burlesque 5.9

Rappel *Burlesque* using 2 ropes.
FA: Tom Caufman, Joe Herbst 1979

The next two routes are located right of *Come Again* and immediately left of *Frigid Air Buttress* on a separate tombstone feature.

51. Chill Out 5.10b/c ★★ Traditional. Begin *Chill Out* left of *Hot Point*. See climbers topo for details. Gear: doubles of Friends #Z3–#1, a #1.5 Friend, a #2 Friend, and brass wires (HBs and RPs). Rappel.
FA: Jay Smith, Nick Nordblom 1988

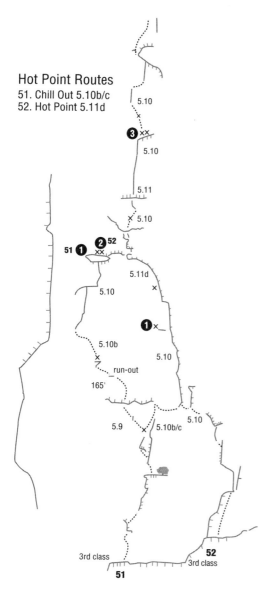

Hot Point Routes
51. Chill Out 5.10b/c
52. Hot Point 5.11d

52. Hot Point 5.11d ★★ Traditional. Climb the face up the center of the feature. Third-class up to a ledge at the base and climb two pitches to shared anchors with *Chill Out*. Continue through the aborted pitch 4—the route stops in the middle of this pitch, where the rock began to get bad. See the climbers topo for details. Gear: a #3.5 Friend, 2–3 each of #00–#2.5 Friends and brass wires (HBs and RPs). Rappel.
FA: Jay Smith, Nick Nordblom 1988

53. Frigid Air Buttress IV, 5.9+ ★★★★ Traditional. *Frigid Air Buttress* is on the pillarlike buttress right of *Hot Point* and just left of the buttress's right edge. Follow directions to *Smears for Fears*, exiting out of the drainage to the right. Bushwhack to the base of the prow making up the division between the *Burlesque* area and Smears for Fears Area. This route can be used to access Bridge Mountain for a nice, *long* day. Begin on small black flake ascending an enormous block. Gear: standard rack with cams to #5 Friend.

Pitch 1: 5.7 Start on the right side of a short, narrow flake. After 75 feet, take a small crack to a belay on the left.

Pitch 2: 5.8 Step off the ledge right, climb to the next ledge. Take a left-facing corner to yet another ledge. 160 feet.

Pitch 3: 5.2 Step off left and scramble up the face left to the next large ledge. 100 feet.

Pitch 4: 5.2 Climb the easy chimney to another ledge. 80 feet.

Pitch 5: 5.9- Climb the hand crack to a chimney and belay at a ledge.

Pitch 6: 5.8 Move up another chimney, then traverse left to another chimney to a ledge. 120 feet.

Pitch 7: 5.4 Climb the obvious crack and continue up the face right to below the varnished headwall. 165 feet.

Pitch 8: 5.9+ Climb the splitter crack up the center of the varnished wall.

Pitch 9: Fourth class. Traverse the ledge to the right and then head up and left.

To descend, from the top go down and left (south) to a short rappel, leading down into a south-facing enclosure. Hike up and then follow the south shoulder down and then left to a pine tree at the edge of the buttress. Rappel this tree to a flat ledge (1 rope). From the ledge do an airy rappel down and right to join *Burlesque* (2 ropes). Rappel *Burlesque* in three rappels. Follow the wash down and to the base of the buttress.

FA: Larry Hamilton, Joe Herbst 1976

54. Blue Bunny 5.7+ ★★★ Mixed, 5 bolts. Experience counts for a lot on this one. Climb the dark-brown bolted face just right of *Frigid Air Buttress*, placing gear wherever possible. Run-out. 140 feet. Gear: up to #2 Friend. Rappel with 2 150-foot ropes.

FA: Tom Beck

55. Linda's Route 5.9+ ★★★ Traditional. This route is 75 feet to the right of *Frigid Air Buttress* (the route) and climbs the center portion of the Frigid Air Buttress feature. Begin at an obvious hand crack, located directly in front of a pine tree at the base of the wall.

Pitch 1: 5.9 Climb a somewhat vegetated hand crack up to a ledge. 100 feet.

Pitch 2: 5.7 Move right into some bushes and then up and left to a chimney. 100 feet.

Pitch 3: 5.8 Climb the chimney to midway. 200 feet.

Pitch 4: Second to third class. Traverse right.

Pitch 5: 5.7 Climb the huecoed wall to a ledge.

Pitch 6: 5.7 Traverse to the right of the ledge and then move up north-facing cracks to a ledge.

Pitch 7: 5.9+ Climb a black, varnished headwall until you join pitch 9 of *Frigid Air Buttress* (the route) and fourth-class to the top of the buttress.

Follow the descent for *Frigid Air Buttress*.

FA: Linda Marks, Joe Herbst, Nanouk Borche, Matt McMackin 1978

▲ THE NECROMANCER
NE AM Sun   Approach: 20 minutes

From the parking lot, hike the Icebox Canyon Trail for about 10 minutes, passing the spot where the SMYC and Dale Trails split off. The Necromancer is a large, obvious, black, varnished face across the wash, left (south) of the trail. Stay on the Icebox Canyon Trail until you are across from the far-right corner of the wall. Then head downhill on a rocky trail toward the wash. Go through the wash and uphill to the base and the right edge of the Necromancer

Frigid Air Buttress
53. Frigid Air Buttress IV 5.9+
54. Blue Bunny 5.7+

53 continues below right

6 — 120'

5.8

5

5.9-

4 — 80'

5.2 chimney

big corner ramp
loose rock

3 — 100'

5.2

2

5.8 — 160'

1

5.7

53 9

4th class

8

5.9+

7 — 165'

5.4

53 6

continued from above left

smooth black face

flake

54

53

← to 49   to 55 →

proper (some bushwhacking). Routes are described from left to right.

Descent: Rappel the gully just left of the Necromancer wall and right of *Atras*. You may want "leaver" slings for the rappel.

56. Dogleg Crack 5.8 ★★★ Traditional. Bushwhack left (east) along the base of the main wall. The *Dogleg Crack* begins behind a pine tree, on the far-left edge of the northeast-facing wall, just right of a varnished, free-standing pillar and 200 yards left (east) of the Necromancer proper. Gear: to #5 Friend.

Pitch 1: 5.8 Climb a flared, right-facing chimney/off-width slot left of large huecos up high. Follow the crack as it thins to the top of the pillar right, under an overhang. 80 feet.

Pitch 2: Continue to the top of the feature. 60 feet.

Pitch 2 variation: Step left to obtain a crack heading up and then move left to a ledge. Continue to the top of the pillar.

Descend the gully left and behind the freestanding pillar.

FA: Bill Bradley, Joe Herbst 1979

57. Atras 5.8 ★★ Climb the obvious, varnished, right-facing dihedral just left of the descent gully, located 50 feet left of the Necromancer proper and 195 yards right of *Dogleg Crack*. Scramble up 120 feet from the ground to reach the black base. Gear: to #6 Friend.

Pitch 1: 5.8 Climb the wide corner up to a bushy section and loose rock and belay below a roof. 100 feet.

Pitch 2: Angle right under and around the roof through a chimney. Continue up right of the roof. To avoid rope drag you might want to divide this into two pitches. 75 feet. Rappel the descent gully.

FA: Joe Herbst, Bill Bradley 1979

The following routes are located on the Necromancer proper, the dark, black, varnished wall at the top of the described approach, 50 feet right of *Atras*.

58. Hop Route Direct 5.8 ★★★ Traditional. Climb the right-facing corner on the left side of the varnished wall to the top of the cliff. Gear: to #4.5 Friend.

Pitch 1: 5.8 Climb through loose chockstones up to a stance. 100 feet.

Pitch 2: 5.7+ Climb pitch 2 of the *Hop Route*.

Rappel the descent gully.

FA: Unknown

59. Hop Route 5.7+ ★★★ Traditional. Begin at the left edge of the Necromancer proper, 15 feet right of a large, right-facing corner. Gear: standard rack to #4.5 Friend.

Pitch 1: 5.7 Climb the straight-in hand crack right of the large, right-facing corner. At the top of the crack, move left into the corner and up to fixed anchors. 100 feet. Rappel with a 60-meter rope or climb pitch 2.

Pitch 2: 5.7+ Continue up the crack to where it ends at a horizontal. Move around left and take another crack to the top of the cliff. 120 feet.

Rappel the descent gully.

FA: Dave Hop, Joe and Betsy Herbst 1975

60. Black Magic Panties 5.10a ★★★ Mixed, 2 bolts, 1 piton. Begin 12 feet right of the *Hop Route*, below large undercling flake. Take the crack up to a left-angling ramp and up onto the face. Follow discontinuous seams, cracks, and features past bolts and a piton to a roof. Climb the crack splitting the roof. Gear: to #3.5 Friend. Traverse down and right to a belay and rappel *Sensuous Mortician*; or move left to finish on the *Hop Route* and then rappel the descent gully.

FA: Nick Nordblom, Jenni Stone, Danny Rider 1988

61. Sensuous Mortician 5.9 ★★★★★ Traditional. Begin 10 feet right of *Black Magic Panties* at a large, detached white block creating a roof 15 feet up. Begin in the crack on right side of block and climb up

a right-facing flake. Veer right into a black water streak. Take the water streak to a small roof and then move left and up to the bolted anchor ("the worst anchor in Red Rock"). Gear: small and brass nuts and Friends to #3. 150 feet. Rappel with 2 ropes or continue to the top of the cliff and rappel the descent gully.

FA: Nick Nordblom, John Martinet 1979

62. Fold Out 5.8+ ★★★★★ Traditional. Begin 20 feet right of the previous route behind a pine tree. Take the wide slot through huecos to a finger crack on a varnished face. Gear: standard rack to #4 Friend. Rappel with 2 ropes off the bolted anchor 120 feet up or continue to the top of cliff and rappel the descent gully.

FA: Tom Kaufman, Joe Herbst 1976

▲ TANGO TOWERS
NE AM Sun   Approach: 1 hour

The following routes are located on the wall above the Necromancer. Tango Towers proper is the tower feature on the far right of this upper tier, past the skirt that comes up from the right of Necromancer. It takes an "expedition" type adventure to obtain these routes, up dangerous third- and some fifth-class sections. You may need to haul packs as well. Follow the directions to the Necromancer and take the gully right of the Necromancer wall. There is no terrace at the base of these routes, and each route requires a somewhat different approach through bushes and gullies. Routes are described from left to right.

63. Crawford's Corner 5.10c R ★★★ Traditional. Climb the white corner directly above *Sensuous Mortician* to a hanging ledge. Much better than it looks. Follow the gorgeous white, obvious corner to a crow's nest belay—a sort of pocket. (Possibly a technical 5.7/5.8 pitch to obtain the corner.) Rappel.

FA: Paul Crawford, Jay Smith 1987

64. Rojo Tower 5.10d/11a R ★★ Traditional. This is the next route right of *Crawford's Corner*. It ends

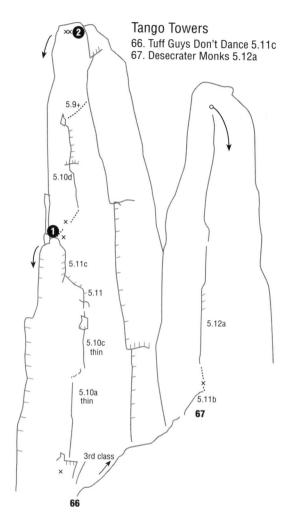

Tango Towers
66. Tuff Guys Don't Dance 5.11c
67. Desecrater Monks 5.12a

5.9+

5.10d

5.11c

5.11

5.10c
thin

5.10a
thin

3rd class

66

5.12a

5.11b

67

atop an obvious red minispire. Rappel off the top.
FA: Jay Smith, Sal Mamusia, Mike Ward 1988

65. Unknown 5.10 ★★ Mixed. Begin right of the
previous route. Climb the black, varnished, low-
angle face in between two corners. Unfinished.

On the far-right of this upper tier, past the skirt that
comes up from the right of the Necromancer, is a
tower feature. This is Tango Towers proper.

66. Tuff Guys Don't Dance 5.11c ★★★ Mixed.
Third-class to the route's base. Climb thin cracks to
a belay, then pass a bolt to a crack and corners to
the top. See climbers topo for detail. May need an
anchor. Gear: standard rack to #2.5 Friend and brass
wires. Rappel.
FA: Jay Smith, Sal Mamusia, Mike Ward 1988

67. Desecrater Monks 5.12a ★★ Mixed, 1 bolt.
Start right of *Tuff Guys Don't Dance* (third-class to
base) and climb cracks to the top. See climbers topo
for some detail. Rappel.
FA: Paul Van Betten, Robert Finlay 1984

PINE CREEK CANYON

LOWER BRIDGE MOUNTAIN EAST SIDE
Bridge Mountain Plateau ▲ The Abutment ▲ Upper East Side
Gemstone Gully Area ▲ Flight Path Area

LOWER BRIDGE MOUNTAIN SOUTH SIDE
Stick Gully ▲ Straight Shooter Wall ▲ Beer and Ice Gully ▲ The Brass Wall

NORTH FORK PINE CREEK CANYON
Out of Control Area ▲ Northeast Pine Creek ▲ Pisces Wall
Dark Shadows Wall ▲ Mescalito East Face

SOUTH FORK PINE CREEK CANYON
Mescalito South Face ▲ Challenger Wall ▲ Jet Stream Wall
Crabby Appleton Area ▲ Community Pillar/Magic Triangle ▲ The Pink Corner

To REACH PINE CREEK CANYON from Las Vegas, take West Charleston Boulevard west, which turns into State Route 159. Drive over the 215 Beltway and zero your odometer. Turn right into the Red Rock Canyon National Conservation Area, 5.9 miles past the 215 (2 miles past Calico Basin Road). Enter the 13-mile Scenic Drive through the kiosk entrance booth.

Pine Creek Canyon is 10.5 miles from the entrance kiosk. Park in a paved, looped parking area. There are two pit toilets.

LOWER BRIDGE MOUNTAIN EAST SIDE

Bridge Mountain is the peak that separates Pine Creek and Icebox Canyons. Most of the routes on the east side, up to the Stick Gully, are one or two pitches long and require a long hike.

▲ **BRIDGE MOUNTAIN PLATEAU**
E AM Sun   Approach: 1 hour

From the Pine Creek Canyon parking area, hike back (north) on the 13-mile Scenic Drive to the center of the big, swooping curve just before the parking lot (before mile marker 10). There should be a slight pull-off (do not park here). Hike directly west (left) toward the buttress, moving down a hill, through a wash, and into the desert. Hike up the talus field and then head right to reach the base of the wall. Routes are described from left to right.

1. Waterfall Wall 5.10a ★★★ Mixed. Climb the obvious white crack left of a large water streak.
Gear: standard rack including brass wires.
    Pitch 1: 5.10a Ascend the white crack.
FA: Bob Conz, Sal Mamusia 1987
    Pitch 2: 5.10 Continue up and onto the face.
    Pitch 3: 5.10 Finish up the face.
    Rappel.
FA: Unknown (pitches 2–3)

Eric CaMello and Jean Paul Finne on Cat in the Hat *5.6+ in the South Fork Pine Creek Canyon.*
Photo by Dan McQuade

2. Where Eagles Dare 5.10b R ★★★ Mixed. Climb the crack and face right of the previous route. On pitch 3 there is a white-to-red color change in the rock. Gear: standard rack including brass wires.

Pitch 1: 5.10b Begin in a big chimney leading to a cave, right of *Waterfall Wall*.

Pitch 2: 5.10a Pull onto the face and follow bolts up the wall to a bolted belay.

Pitch 3: 5.10a Climb the bolted face. Wander up and left on the face looking for a 2-bolt rappel station.

Rappel *Waterfall Wall*.
FA: Bob Conz, Sal Mamusia 1987

▲ THE ABUTMENT
E AM Sun   Approach: 40 minutes

To reach the Abutment, take the trail out of the parking lot heading into Pine Creek Canyon. Hike for 10 minutes and take the first right turn at the Dale Trail

sign. Follow the trail for about 30 minutes: Walk through the first wash. Pass by Skull Rock, a huge brown boulder with a park bench, on the left. After Skull Rock the trail starts curving toward the cliff. Cross a larger, deeper wash to a dark red dirt trail on the other side. At a large yellow boulder, just before a tiny drainage and some large flat red rocks, head straight or directly uphill to the Abutment.(You have gone too far down the Dale Trail if you reach a sign with an arrow.) Bushwhack uphill for 10 minutes, toward a huge boulder. Continue around the boulder to the base of the cliff. Routes are described from left to right.

Descent: Hike off right and scramble down smaller boulders right of *Robin Trowel* and the pine tree.

3. Pier-less 5.10b ★ Traditional. On the wall left of the main varnished wall, just left of a dihedral splitting the two walls, are two cracks. The cracks split the left wall into three sections. This route climbs the

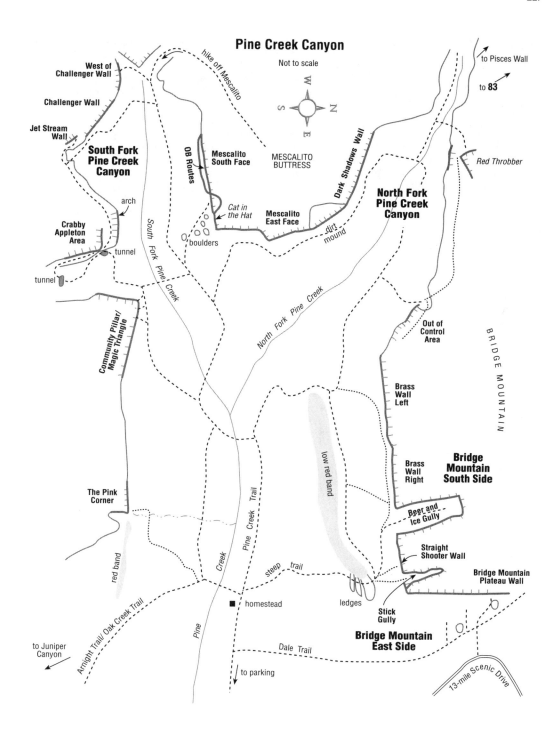

Pine Creek Canyon

Not to scale

West of Challenger Wall

Challenger Wall

Jet Stream Wall

South Fork Pine Creek Canyon

arch

Crabby Appleton Area

tunnel

tunnel

hike off Mescalito

OB Routes

Mescalito South Face

Cat in the Hat

boulders

Mescalito East Face

MESCALITO BUTTRESS

dirt mound

Dark Shadows Wall

to Pisces Wall

to **83**

Red Throbber

North Fork Pine Creek Canyon

South Fork Pine Creek

North Fork Pine Creek

Community Pillar/ Magic Triangle

Out of Control Area

B R I D G E   M O U N T A I N

Brass Wall Left

Brass Wall Right

Bridge Mountain South Side

The Pink Corner

low red band

Pine Creek Trail

Beer and Ice Gully

Straight Shooter Wall

Bridge Mountain Plateau Wall

red band

steep trail

homestead

ledges

Stick Gully

Bridge Mountain East Side

Arnight Trail/ Oak Creek Trail

to Juniper Canyon

Pine Creek

Dale Trail

to parking

13-mile Scenic Drive

left crack. Gear: standard rack to #4.5 Friend. 20 feet.
FA: Unknown

4. Crazy Girls 5.10a ★★ Mixed, 3 bolts. Begin 20 feet right of the dihedral that splits the walls. Climb the left side of the varnished face using small edges. Gear: small and brass nuts to supplement the bolts. 45 feet.
FA: Dave Wonderly, Warren Egbert 1988

5. Coffee Generation 5.11a ★★ Mixed, 1 ¼" bolt. Start in the middle of the varnished face, 20 feet right of *Crazy Girls* at a small, left-facing dihedral. Climb to a chossy ledge under a roof. Pull the roof to a varnished horizontal above a seam. Continue up, angling right to a bolt 30 feet up (with a black bolt hanger). Continue to the top of the cliff. Route not recommended due to bad rock at the base and sketchy gear. Paul Crawford nearly fell 40 feet when a hold broke on the cold winter day when he did

this first ascent. Gear: many small Rocks, brass nuts, and big kahunas. 45 feet.
FA: Paul Crawford, Richard Harrison, Wendell Broussard 1984

6. Bridge of Sighs 5.9 ★★ Traditional. Begin left of a pine tree and 20 feet right of the previous route. Climb a chimney with many chockstones/ blocks in the base to a right-facing flake. Enter a thin crack as it widens to the top. Gear: to #5 Friend. 40 feet.
FA: Unknown

7. Robin Trowel 5.7 ★ Traditional. Start 10 feet right of the previous route, behind a pine tree. Begin in a flared wide section. Climb the left-facing dihedral and flake system that curves up and right, on a white feature separate from the main face. Gear: #2–#4.5 Friend. 25 feet.
FA: Unknown 1980s

8. Tri-Burro Bridge 5.9+ ★ Traditional. Begin left of *Robin Trowel*, on the far-left side of the triangular-shaped rock feature, about 50 feet left of a white pillar leaning against the wall. Gear: standard rack to #4.5 Friend.

Pitch 1: 5.6 Ascend the right-facing crack, right of a huecoed face to a large pine tree. 130 feet.

Pitch 1 variation: 5.10a Ascend the center of the huecoed face left of the crack to bolted anchors. 100 feet.

Pitch 2: Third class. Scramble up and left 100 feet to the bolted anchor atop a large block at the base of a chimney. 100 feet.

Pitch 3: 5.8, 1 bolt. Climb a corner to a roof. Move left around the roof to a left-facing crack, which leads to a belay ledge. 80 feet.

Pitch 4: 5.8 Climb the arching, left-facing corner up to a widening vertical crack. Finish on the thin crack leading to a bolted anchor. 90 feet.

Pitch 5: 5.9+, 3 bolts. Climb up, heading left to a bolt. Pass the bolt, entering into a right-facing crack. Belay toward the top of the crack from fixed gear. 130 feet.

Rappel the route.

FA: Todd Swain, Jake Burkey, Reina Downing 1999

▲ UPPER EAST SIDE
E AM Sun   Approach: 1.25 hours

The following routes are located above the Gemstone Gully Area. To get there, take the trail out of the parking lot heading into Pine Creek Canyon. Hike for 10 minutes and take the first right turn at the Dale Trail sign. Follow the trail for about 30 minutes: Walk through the first wash. Pass by Skull Rock, a huge brown boulder with a park bench, on the left. After Skull Rock the trail starts curving toward the cliff. Cross a larger, deeper wash to a dark red dirt trail on the other side. Pass the Abutment on the Dale Trail and pass a trail sign with an arrow. Take the next gully heading above and right of the Abutment. Bushwhack up the gully for 20 minutes to reach the base of a bushy gully heading up and left, behind a large triangular shaped rock. Take the bushy gully to a saddle. Routes are described from left to right.

9. Fear and Loathing I, 5.10c R ★★★ Traditional.

This route is on the black, varnished ridge above the rest of the Upper East Side routes, atop the smile feature above the Gemstone Gully. From the saddle, scramble up to the dark red rock. Climb the corner right of a crack that begins partway up the wall, with big loose blocks and left of a huge chimney. A heads-up route. Gear anchors. Gear: standard rack and #4 Friend.

Pitch 1: 5.10c R Climb a face to a right-facing corner and belay.

Pitch 2: 5.9 Climb the obvious right-facing corner.

Pitch 3: 5.10a Move up the corner and belay on a block. 75 feet. A difficult descent involves some downclimbing and at least two rappels on natural and/or fixed gear.

FA: Richard Harrison, Nick Nordblom 1982. Prior to this ascent, people claimed that the route to the left of Fear and Loathing *had been climbed along with* Fear and Loathing *(and that the two were called* Fear . . . *and* Loathing). *When Harrison and Nordblom reached the base of the route, they found that the left crack did not even reach the ground and was full of enormous loose blocks. The pair climbed the right crack and called it the real first ascent.*

10. Gemstone 5.10a ★★★★ Traditional. From the saddle, descend to below the dark red rock of *Fear and Loathing*. Begin on the obvious brown face with a left-arching crack.

Pitch 1: 5.10a Climb a hand crack to a fixed nut belay. 140 feet.

Pitch 2: 5.9 Move through a wide crack and then up in a left-curving crack. Follow it to a white, right-facing flake. Pass the flake, and move up the face and belay. 140 feet.

Rappel down the gully right of the route in two short rappels.

FA: Nick Nordblom, Jenni Stone 1985

▲ GEMSTONE GULLY AREA
E AM Sun   Approach: 35 minutes

To reach the Gemstone Gully Area, take the trail out of the parking lot heading into Pine Creek Canyon. Hike for 10 minutes and take the first right split at the Dale Trail, marked by a sign. Follow the Dale Trail for

20 minutes and at the first wash, hike up the wash to the cliff. Or you can continue to Skull Rock, a huge brown boulder on the left with a park bench next to it. From Skull Rock, bushwhack uphill for 15 minutes, toward a smile-shaped rock feature midway up the wall. Hike to the base of the black, varnished wall directly below the Upper East Side. These routes are 200 yards left of the Abutment and just right of Gemstone Gully. Routes are described from left to right.

11. Human Chockstones 5.6 ★ Traditional. Climb the Gemstone Gully water groove around the corner, through some bushes, 30 feet left of the main wall. Gear: to a #3.5 Friend. Rappel using 1 rope. *FA: Unknown 1970s*

12. Spanning the Gap 5.9 ★ Mixed, 2 bolts. Begin in the center of the varnished face, 50 feet right of the previous route. Move up very chossy, pink-colored rock to a varnished, left-facing corner. Take the corner to a small, left-facing flake, clipping a bolt at the top of the flake. Move left to clip another bolt in the pinkish colored rock. Move into the black varnish. Climb straight up, angling right toward a small roof. Move over the roof to a left-facing flake. Continue up to a bulge. Pull the bulge and belay on a ledge or continue up and left to a fixed anchor. Gear: standard rack to #3.5 Friend. 130 feet. Rappel with 2 ropes. *FA: Todd and Donette Swain 1999*

13. Cantilever Corner 5.8+ ★★ Traditional. Begin 30 feet right of the previous route, behind a large flake of rock (right of a large, white flake). Hand-over-hand up a rope to the top of the 15-foot block. Climb the thin, varnished, left-facing corner, past a tiny roof and up, angling left to a fixed anchor. Gear: standard rack to #3.5 Friend. 60 feet. *FA: Unknown 1998*

▲ FLIGHT PATH AREA
E AM Sun   Approach: 30 minutes

To reach the Flight Path Area, take the trail out of the parking lot heading into Pine Creek Canyon. Hike for 10 minutes and take the first right split at the Dale

Trail, marked by a sign. Follow the trail for 20 minutes. At the first wash, hike up the wash toward the cliff or continue to Skull Rock, a huge brown boulder with a park bench next to it, on the left. Bushwhack uphill for 10 minutes, to the left side of the low red rock band. Hike through boulders and then up and right to reach the base of the routes. You will pass a sign on your hike up, noting that the canyons of Red Rock are designated wilderness areas.

Routes 14–16 are 200 feet left of Gemstone Gully on a free-standing pinnacle. These routes are just left of a big rectangular block, perched above and right of routes 17–26. The block is easily spotted from the parking area. Routes 17–26 are 100 feet left of the Flight Path Area. Routes are described from left to right.

Note that another guidebook describes a route left of *Flight Path*, called *Clyde Crashcup*. Luckily no one has attempted this right-facing chimney with numerous loose, death chockstones.

14. Project Begin on *Flight Path*, doing the entrance moves. Then step left to a bolt. Climb the arête, past a sustained bulge and finish on the main Flight Path wall.

15. Flight Path 5.10b ★★ Mixed. Climb the varnished face just right of the low-quality chimney. Start in a dihedral, move left, and then dogleg up into a patch of black varnish. Gear: standard rack to #3.5 Friend.
   Pitch 1: 5.8+, 3 bolts. Lieback up the hand and fist crack. Then move right and up. 120 feet.
   Pitch 2: 5.7+ Continue, climbing through "angel food" rock. 85 feet.
   Pitch 3: 5.10b Move right from the belay and undercling up. Climb incipient cracks over to the headwall bulge. Finish up the headwall. 150 feet.
   Rappel with 2 150-foot ropes.
FA: Tom Beck, Steve Haase 1999

16. Pattizabzent 5.10a or 5.10b ★★ Mixed. To the right of *Flight Path* is a large, clean dihedral with three or four oak trees growing out of its middle. Gear: 2 to 3 #00–#1 Friends and doubles of #2–#3.5 Friends.
   Pitch 1: 5.9 R A serious pitch requiring white-rock

technique (travel lightly!) on the upper section. Little protection.

Pitch 2, right variation, *Mother's Lament*: 5.10b Take the 5.9 splitter crack up to a triangular-shaped scoop in the face. Continue to a bulging, steep corner. Stem, lieback, and fist- jam to the fixed anchor. Continuous. A #4 Friend is helpful. 85 feet.

Pitch 2, left variation: 5.9+ Climb straight up using a series of cracks that eventually peter out. Traverse straight left on thin holds to the anchors of *Mother's Lament*. 85 feet.

Pitch 3: 5.10a Climb straight up a dihedral to the anchors. 100 feet.

Rappel using 2 150-foot ropes.

FA: Tom Beck, Clarissa Hageman, Mark Rosenthal 2000

The following routes are located 100 feet to the left of *Pattizabzent*.

17. Commuted Sentence 5.9+ ★ Traditional. Climb a huge, right-facing corner to a dead pine tree on a ledge. Gear: to #4.5 Friend. 80 feet. Rappel.

FA: Todd Swain, Jake Burkey 1999

18. Doin' the Good Drive 5.9 ★ Traditional. Begin 30 feet right of *Commuted Sentence*. Climb a prominent finger crack to a roof and then move up a varnished crack to a ledge.

Variation: You can avoid the finger crack by climbing the face to the right. Traverse right to an anchor on a ledge. Gear: standard rack to #3.5 Friend. Rappel using 1 rope.

FA: Tom Beck, Steve Haase 1998

19. Car Talk 5.9 ★ Traditional. Begin on *Doin' the Good Drive*. After the finger crack, move right at a roof and climb a dihedral. Move up a varnished face to the shared anchor with *Doin' the Good Drive*. Gear: standard rack and #3–4.5 Friends. Rappel using 1 rope.

FA: Todd Swain, Jake Burkey 1999

20. A Simple Expediency 5.9– ★ Traditional. Begin at the same spot as the previous two routes. Climb up and right, on the right side of the face, to

a crack. Take the crack up to a low-angle, varnished face. Follow a thin crack up the face to the shared anchor with *Doin' the Good Drive* and *Car Talk*. Gear: nuts and Friends to #4. Rappel using 1 rope.

FA: Tom Beck, Steve Haase 1998

The following routes are located 50 feet to the right of *A Simple Expediency* and begin off a ledge approached from the far right of the wall. The wall is 30 feet tall.

21. They Call the Wind #!&% 5.8 ★ Mixed, 5 bolts. Climb the obvious arête on the left edge of a very large, right-facing corner. Take the arête up and left onto the face of the feature. Gear: standard rack to #2.5 Friend. Rappel with 2 ropes.

FA: Todd Swain, Teresa Krolak 1999

22. Sex in the Scrub Oak 5.7 ★ Traditional. Climb the enormous right-facing corner for 20 feet. At the top, traverse right to *Ignore the Man Behind the Screen*. Gear: to #3 Friend. Rappel from the shared anchor on the ledge.

FA: Unknown 1970s

23. Ignore the Man Behind the Screen 5.6 ★★★★ Traditional. Begin just right of the previous route. Climb the vertical crack to the ledge. Gear: mostly small Friends to #3.5. Rappel.

FA: Unknown 1970s

24. Belief in Proportion to the Evidence 5.10a ★★★ Mixed, 5 bolts. Begin 5 feet right of the previous route. Climb the face to the shared belay anchor with the previous two routes. Gear: may need a small Friend or Rock between the fourth and fifth bolts. Rappel.

FA: Tom Beck, Teresa Krolak, Jules George 1999

25. Common Bond of Circumstance 5.9+ ★★★ Sport, 7 bolts. Begin 5 feet right of the previous route. Climb the face up and left to the shared anchor with the previous routes. Rappel.

FA: Steve Haase, Tom Beck 1999

26. Radio Free Kansas 5.7+ ★★★ Mixed, 3 bolts. Begin 10 feet right of the previous route, below and

right of large boulders. Climb the left-angling crack and then jump onto the face past 3 bolts to the shared anchor with the previous routes. Gear: standard rack with Friends to #2.5. Rappel.
FA: Teresa Krolak, Tom Beck 1999

LOWER BRIDGE MOUNTAIN SOUTH SIDE

▲ STICK GULLY
SE AM Sun   Approach: 90 minutes

To reach Stick Gully, take the trail out of the parking lot heading into Pine Creek Canyon. Just before a low red band of rock appears on the right side of the trail, look for a large white boulder with smaller boulders leaning against it. Take the trail heading uphill and right just past this boulder. Skirt the ridge to the rightmost side of the red band. When on top of the red band, head right (east), following cairns toward some large, flat rock ledges. Once on top of the rock ledges, take a trail to the first gully up and right (northeast).

The routes begin 200 vigorous yards up the gully through big boulders. There is no prominent trail. Hike in along the left (south) side of the gully. After reaching the top of a hill, where a big white flake leans against the south wall, start hiking right, into the gully. Scramble up huge boulders through the gully until you reach a large, white, 100-foot pillar leaning against the left wall, right of many varnished cracks on a white wall. This is *The Elephant Penis*. You will pass a sign on your hike up, noting that the canyons of Red Rock are designated wilderness areas. Routes are described from left to right, beginning on the left side of the gully.

27. The Elephant Penis 5.10a ★★ Traditional. Begin behind a large pine at a huge white pillar leaning against the wall. Gear: double set of gear to #4 Friend.

Pitch 1: 5.10a Climb to the top of the "member" using the chimney on the left. 100 feet.

Pitch 2: Traverse left into the varnished cracks on the white face. Climb up and left to a tree. 100 feet.

Pitch 3: Take the left crack up to another alcove/ledge. 80 feet.

Pitch 4: Finish the crack to the top of the cliff. 110 feet.

Rappel off the north side of the "member," off a fixed nut.
FA: Richard Harrison, Paul Van Betten, Sal Mamusia, Nick Nordblom 1983

28. Nature is Fun 5.9+ ★★ Traditional. The name is a "Sal-ism." Begin 100 feet right of *The Elephant Penis*, on the level above it (up big boulders), directly across from the Stick routes. Tunnel through the boulders to get to the base. Gear: to #4 Friend.

Pitch 1: Begin in a varnished hand crack in white rock. Move around a flake and into a slot. Belay above the alcove. 120 feet.

Pitch 2: Traverse left on face holds into another hand crack. Take it up, angling right to some huecos and belay. 100 feet.

Pitch 3: Take a flare up to a bulge and varnished rock. Move right into a large crack. Take the crack to the top of the cliff. 150 feet.

Walk off to the south.
FA: Sal Mamusia, Richard Harrison, Paul Van Betten, Nick Nordblom 1983

The following routes are on the right (north) side of the gully, directly across from *Nature is Fun*. The Stick cracks climb either side of a steep, blank, brown face.

29. Stick Left 5.10c ★★★★★ Traditional. Climb a right-facing corner and hand crack straight up; it gets wide at the top. Fixed anchor. Gear: 3 #3.5 Friends and Friends to #4.5. 100 feet.
FA: Richard Harrison, Paul Van Betten, Sal Mamusia, Nick Nordblom 1982

30. Stick Right 5.9 ★★ Traditional. Begin 15 feet right of *Stick Left*, at a left-facing corner. Watch for a loose block above the start. Climb through loose, blocky rock to where the crack becomes right-facing. Gear: standard rack with Friends to #5. 100 feet. Rappel from a shared fixed anchor with *Stickball*.

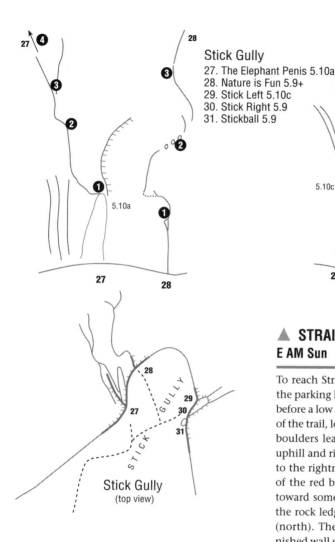

Stick Gully
27. The Elephant Penis 5.10a
28. Nature is Fun 5.9+
29. Stick Left 5.10c
30. Stick Right 5.9
31. Stickball 5.9

Stick Gully
(top view)

*FA: Richard Harrison, Paul Van Betten, Sal Mamusia,
Nick Nordblom 1982*

31. Stickball 5.9 ★ Traditional. Begin 8 feet right
of the previous route, on an arête that begins off a
small, white boulder. Climb the arête, crossing *Stick
Right* to the shared fixed anchor. Gear: to #3 Friend.
100 feet.
FA: Todd and Donette Swain 1999

▲ STRAIGHT SHOOTER WALL
E AM Sun   Approach: 25 minutes

To reach Straight Shooter Wall, take the trail out of
the parking lot heading into Pine Creek Canyon. Just
before a low red band of rock appears on the right side
of the trail, look for a large white boulder with smaller
boulders leaning against it. Take the trail heading
uphill and right just past this boulder. Skirt the ridge
to the rightmost side of the red band. When on top
of the red band, head right (east), following cairns
toward some large, flat rock ledges. Once on top of
the rock ledges, take a trail straight toward the rock
(north). The Straight Shooter Wall is the first varnished wall up the red dirt trail. When the trail splits,
take the fork heading straight uphill through cacti.
You will pass a sign on your hike up, noting that the
canyons of Red Rock are designated wilderness areas.
Routes are described from left to right.

32. Forget Me Knot 5.11 ★★ Mixed, 2 bolts. Begin 20 feet left of the obvious *Straight Shooter* crack.
Climb a very thin crack until it ends. Traverse
slightly right to a bolt and a left-facing flake. Take
the flake to a ledge. Take a right-leaning crack past

Roxanna Brock loading up for Straight Shooter 5.9, *Straight Shooter Wall*

another bolt up and right. Follow the crack up and left to a fixed anchor on a downward-sloping ledge. Gear: small and brass nuts and Friends to #2. 80 feet. Rappel.
FA: Mike Tupper 1985

33. Slabba Dabba Do 5.11b ★★ Mixed, 3 bolts. Begin 5 feet right of *Forget Me Knot*, on a smooth, var-

nished face below several bolts. At the top, traverse 15 feet right to rappel using the shared anchor with *Straight Shooter*. Gear: supplement the bolts with small and brass nuts. Rappel with 1 rope.
FA: Mike Tupper 1985

34. Straight Shooter 5.9+ ★★★★ Traditional. Begin 10 feet right of the previous route. Climb the perfect finger crack that splits the wall. Bolted anchor. Gear: small Rocks and Friends to #2.5. 60 feet. Rappel with 1 rope.
FA: The finder of perfect splitters, Joe Herbst 1975

Pitch 2, **Bird Crack 5.10d** ★★★ Traditional. From the top of *Straight Shooter*, traverse left about 20 feet to the base of a vertical finger- and hand-crack. Climb to a fixed anchor. 80 feet. The pitch is so named because, midpitch, a pigeon squeezed out of the crack between the leader's two tight hand jams, hit him in the chest, and flew off.
FA: Paul Van Betten, Sal Mamusia 1984

35. Sidewinder 5.11a ★★ Mixed, 5 bolts. This is the right-angling crack just right of *Straight Shooter*. Take the crack to right-facing flakes. Gear: small and brass nuts. Rappel from the shared *Straight Shooter* anchor.
FA: Rick Dennison, Daryl Ellis 1991

36. The Lazy Fireman 5.11a ★★★ Mixed, 4 bolts. Climb the right-facing corner/flake beginning 20 feet right of the previous route on the right edge of the wall. Gear: Rocks and a #3 Friend. 60 feet.
FA: Cameron Robbins, Randy Marsh 1991

▲ BEER AND ICE GULLY
SE AM Sun   Approach: 45–90 minutes

This gully is just west of Straight Shooter Wall. To get there, take the trail out of the parking lot heading into Pine Creek Canyon. Just before a low red band of rock appears on the right side of the trail, look for a large white boulder with smaller boulders leaning against it. Take the trail heading uphill and right just past this boulder. Skirt the ridge to the rightmost side of the red band. When on top of the red band, head right (east), following cairns, toward some large, flat rock

ledges. Once on top of the rock ledges, take a trail straight toward the rock (north). When the trail splits, take the left fork. Hike up and left for about 200 feet to the gully left of Straight Shooter Wall. Continue up the rocky, bushy gully. You will pass a sign on your hike up, noting that the canyons of Red Rock are designated wilderness areas. Routes are described from right to left as you enter the gully, beginning on the right (east) side of the gully.

37. Maybell 5.9 ★★ Traditional. Begin 100 feet left of Straight Shooter Wall, about 70 feet right of Beer and Ice Gully, on a black, varnished face and left-leaning chimney and off-width. Bushwhack up and right to the base: scramble up third-class ledges with a few fifth-class moves for about 200 feet to the base of a corner that climbs left across the wall. Gear: to #5 Friend.

Pitch 1: Use large face holds to climb the corner to its middle.

Pitch 2: Finish climbing the corner in a chimney.

Pitch 3: Move right onto a face, over to an obvious crack. Take the crack up to a large ledge.

Pitch 4: Take the thin crack located up and left of the ledge to a small pedestal.

Pitch 5: Move right, beneath a bad bolt into a crack. Jam the crack to a small stance.

Pitch 6: A short pitch leads to the top.

Rappel the route.

FA: Mark Moore, Joe Herbst 1977

38. Orange Clonus 5.10d ★★ Mixed. This route starts at the mouth of Beer and Ice Gully at a very large, varnished dihedral with 3 visible bolts, 70 feet left of *Maybell*. Gear: standard rack plus 3 each of Friends #1.5 to #4.

Pitch 1: Mixed, 5.10d, 4 bolts. Head straight up the large dihedral to a stance. 30 feet.

Pitch 1 variation: 5.9+ Begin 12 feet left of the 5.10d variation at a small, varnished, left-facing corner.

Move up to a ledge and then traverse right into the large corner. Belay.

Pitch 2: 5.5 X Climb the face left of the crack to a ledge beneath a chimney. 30 feet.

Pitch 3: Fourth class. Move up and right, climbing chimneys and wide cracks.

Pitch 4: Third class. Scramble up and right to a large bushy ledge. Belay at a left-facing, white corner.

Pitch 5: 5.8+ Climb the corner and belay beneath a finger crack on a broken ledge.

Pitch 6: 5.10d Climb the finger crack past a ledge with a fixed piton. Move into steep hand and finger crack to a belay 10 feet below a roof. Great pitch!

Pitch 7: 5.10a Head right around the ceiling to a

right-facing corner and then up to a large ledge. Descend by hiking left on the ledge above the gully. Three 80-foot rappels and some downclimbing take you to the base.

FA: Tom Kaufman, Joe Herbst 1977

Scramble up the gully for about 200 feet. You will notice a large, huecoed, varnished wall on your right. This wall ends in a recess or cave where the rock turns black and these routes start.

39. Twenty-nine Posers 5.11d ★★★ Mixed, 2 bolts. Begin in the cave at a large right-facing flake. Climb up to a steep, huecoed face to a large tree. Gear: #0.75–#1.5 Friends. Rappel with 1 rope.

FA: Paul Van Betten, Bob Yoho 1987

Variation 1, Posby: 5.12b ★★ Top-rope the line 5 feet right of *Twenty-nine Posers.*

Variation 2, Too Pumped to Pose: 5.12b ★★ Top-rope the line of pockets 15 feet right of *Posby.*

FA: Paul Van Betten 1987 (both variations)

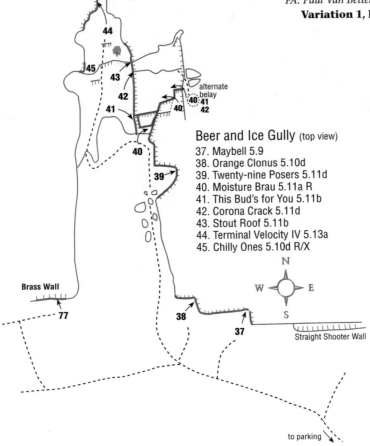

Beer and Ice Gully (top view)

37. Maybell 5.9
38. Orange Clonus 5.10d
39. Twenty-nine Posers 5.11d
40. Moisture Brau 5.11a R
41. This Bud's for You 5.11b
42. Corona Crack 5.11d
43. Stout Roof 5.11b
44. Terminal Velocity IV 5.13a
45. Chilly Ones 5.10d R/X

Scramble up fourth- and fifth-class ledges to the base of a large, obvious, black dihedral, located 50 yards up the gully left of *Twenty-nine Posers.*

40. Moisture Brau 5.11a R ★★ Traditional. Climb the hand crack that begins on a ledge 10 feet right of the dihedral. Climb the crack up and left to a vertical crack system. Take it up to a low-angled face. Rappel from fixed nuts or head straight up a left-facing crack system and traverse left and up to the anchors of *This Bud's for You.* Gear: small Rocks to #5 Friend. 150 feet. Rappel with 2 ropes.

FA: Paul Van Betten, Bob Conz 1988

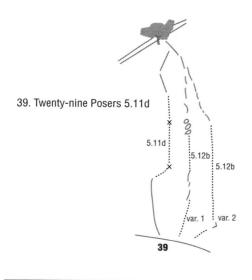

39. Twenty-nine Posers 5.11d

41. This Bud's for You 5.11b ★★★★ Traditional. Climb the obvious left-facing dihedral with a finger crack moving up it. Finish on fixed nut anchors above a ledge. Gear: small and brass nuts, up to #4 Friend. 110 feet. Rappel with 2 ropes.
FA: Paul Van Betten, Bob Conz 1990

42. Corona Crack 5.11d ★★★ Traditional. Begin 20 feet left of *This Bud's for You* at a vertical finger crack 15 feet above the drainage floor. Climb the curving crack system. Traverse right at the top, under big blocks, to the shared anchor with *This Bud's for You*. Gear: small Rocks, brass nuts, doubles of #Z3–#2.5 Friends, #3.5 Friend. 120 feet.
FA: Paul Van Betten, Sal Mamusia, Bob Conz 1988

43. Stout Roof 5.11b ★★★ Traditional. Begin 15 feet left of *Corona Crack*. Climb a crack through a roof and belay on a ledge. Gear: to #3.5 Friend.
FA: Mike Ward, Paul Van Betten, Bob Yoho 1987

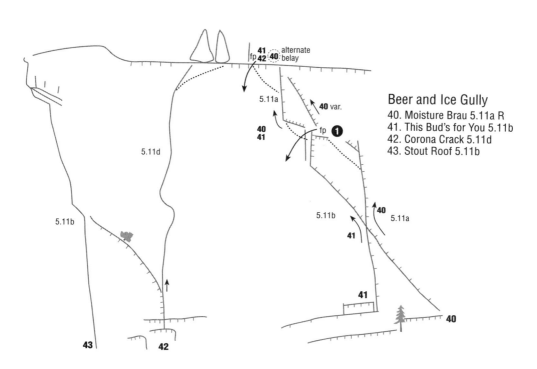

Beer and Ice Gully
40. Moisture Brau 5.11a R
41. This Bud's for You 5.11b
42. Corona Crack 5.11d
43. Stout Roof 5.11b

44. Terminal Velocity IV, 5.13a ★★★ Traditional. Scramble up the Beer and Ice Gully until it dead-ends. After passing *Twenty-nine Posers,* continue up easy fourth- and fifth-class ledges. Hand-over-hand up a fixed rope (test it first) or do a short 5.8 pitch (up a varnished, left-facing corner) to reach a veg-etated ledge. 90-minute approach. Gear: standard rack with Friends to #3.5, brass wires, and Sliders or Lowe Balls.

Pitch 1: 5.9 Climb up the dirty, chossy chimney/gully at the back of the main gully for 30 feet. At a large block leaning against the left wall, begin face climbing up the left face. Continue up, passing loose blocks to reach the crack up and left. Take the crack up to a small alcove and belay at a single-bolt anchor. 160 feet.

Pitch 2: 5.11d, 7 bolts. Move straight right from the belay to obtain a right-facing flake. Follow bolts up the flake and then traverse left and up. Climb a blank face to a small ledge and belay at a fixed bolted anchor. 60 feet.

Pitch 3: 5.11d, 5 bolts. Traverse right over a roof for 15 feet to gain a right-facing dihedral. Follow it up and right, toward the arête, and then traverse back left across a varnished face and clip another bolt. Continue up to a 2-bolt belay at a ledge. 70 feet.

Pitch 4: 5.13a, 1 bolt. Climb a thin dihedral for 30 feet and then move left to obtain a thin finger crack.

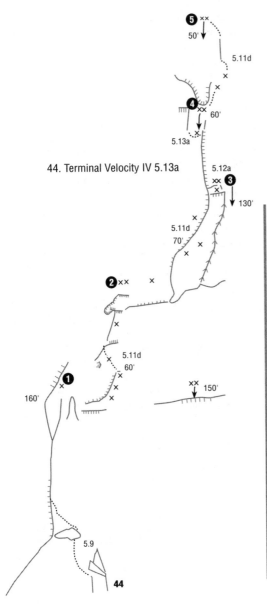

44. Terminal Velocity IV 5.13a

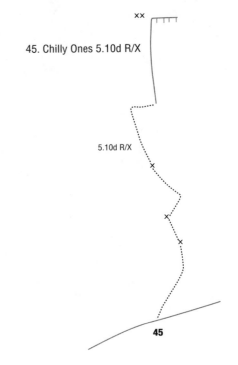

45. Chilly Ones 5.10d R/X

Take the crack to another bolted belay.

Pitch 5: 5.11d, 2 bolts. Stem up a corner to a finger crack for 50 feet. Move left, across a slab, to the bolted belay. 50 feet.

Descend using 2 ropes. Rappel to the top of pitch 3. Rappel pitch 3 to a ledge with bolts. Rappel from there to the ground.

FA: Mike Tupper, Greg Mayer 1989

45. Chilly Ones 5.10d R/X ★★ Mixed, 3 bolts. Begin across the gully from *Stout Roof*, from where you have to climb to obtain the deeper portion of the gully. Climb up the white face with varnished pockets to a hand and fist crack. Belay from a ledge. Rappel using 2 ropes.

FA: Paul Van Betten, Sal Mamusia 1988

▲ THE BRASS WALL
SE AM Sun   Approach: 35 minutes

The Brass Wall is a very dark, varnished wall on the southeast side of Bridge Mountain. You can approach from its left side or its right side.

BRASS WALL LEFT

To reach the left side of the Brass Wall, take the trail out of the parking lot heading into Pine Creek Canyon. The trail takes you alongside a low band of red rock below the Brass Wall. Continue on the trail until it splits at the far-west end of the red band (at the north fork of Pine Creek), after about 20 minutes. Take the north fork trail on the right. The trail takes you up a stair-step of red rock comprising the left edge of the red band. Once on top of the red band, take a trail heading up and right (northeast) toward the black rock of the Brass Wall. Take the first trail cutting to the left, toward the west portion of the wall, below the tallest yellow face on the wall. You will pass a sign on your hike up, noting that the canyons of Red Rock are designated wilderness areas. Routes are described from left to right.

46. The Big Horn 5.8 ★★★ Traditional. Climb the black face below and right of a large right-facing corner at midheight on the cliff. Same start as *Birdland*.

Pitch 1: 5.6 Climb the leftmost of three cracks on a black, varnished face to a huge ledge with scrub-oak trees and a bolted anchor. 110 feet.

Pitch 2: 5.7 Climb straight up the chimney left of the anchor. At the top of the chimney, take the crack on the right. Continue up the crack to a large ledge with loose rubble and a bolted anchor. 90 feet.

Pitch 3: 5.3 Scramble up and left to the base of a large, right-facing, varnished corner. 50 feet.

Pitch 4: 5.8 Climb the crack through the center of the black, varnished left face of the right-facing corner. 90 feet.

Pitch 5: 5.8 Finish up the crack. 90 feet.

Pitch 6: 5.7 R Traverse left onto the low-angled face and head up the cliff. 90 feet.

Pitch 7: 5.7 R Finish up the face to the top of the cliff. 100 feet.

Scramble up and right to the Beer and Ice Gully and rappel. Or rappel *Spectrum*.

FA: Joe and Betsy Herbst, Matt McMackin, Randal Grandstaff

47. Birdland 5.7+ ★★★ Traditional. Begin below a single scrub oak on a ledge, 100 feet above a black, varnished wall with a distinct crack through its middle. Same start as *The Big Horn*. Gear: standard rack to #3 Friends, Rocks and plenty of long slings.

Pitch 1: Climb pitch 1 of *The Big Horn*.

Pitch 2: 5.7 Begin on the face above the anchors and right of the chimney. Climb to a left-facing corner. At the top of the chimney, stay right. Move right up out of an alcove and then step left into the crack. Follow the crack to the ledge and anchor atop *The Big Horn*'s Pitch 2.

Pitch 3: 5.7+, 1 bolt. Head up and right for 10 feet, then take a rampy left-leaning (right-facing) corner to its end and a protection bolt. Traverse left slightly and then head straight up a small, right-facing corner and thru overlaps. Continue up and right to a nice ledge and bolted anchor. 85 feet.

Pitch 4: 5.6 Head up and tend right on the face, using discontinuous crack systems for protection. Fixed anchor. 90 feet.

Pitch 5: 5.7+ Climb up and right to a right-facing corner, coming off a ledge and just below a roof. Climb the crack straight up, over a bulge to the anchor. The crux is getting stood up on the triangular-shaped belay ledge. 105 feet.

Pitch 6: 5.7 R Head straight up through small bulges, just right of the roof. Weird gear, a little scary. The anchor is up and slightly right in a small, right-facing corner. Be careful, loose rock. 80 feet.

Rappel the route with a 70-meter rope.

FA: Mark Limage, Chris Burton 2001

48. Psycho Date 5.10d ★★★ Traditional. Start left of *Spectrum*.

Pitch 1: Climb up the crack system that leads to a ledge.

Pitch 2: 5.10d, 3 bolts. Climb up the corner and work out right onto the face, passing bolts on the way to a fixed anchor.

FA: Danny Meyers, Brad Stuart 1986

49. Spectrum IV, 5.11a R ★ Traditional. Begin 75 feet right of *Birdland*, at the most obvious large, right-facing, arching corner and roof on the Brass Wall's left side. Take the corner up and right to the

next right-facing corner and arch to the top of the cliff. A loose route without a lot of gear placements. Gear: standard rack with doubles of Friends #2– #4.

Pitch 1: 5.9 Climb the chimney to a chockstone three-quarters of the way up. Belay off the chockstone. Best pitch on the route. 95 feet.

Pitch 2: 5.10c Finish up the chimney and traverse right under the roof, stepping down to a fixed anchor. 70 feet.

Pitch 3: 5.7 R Keep traversing right to a right-facing corner splitting a roof. Climb up and left to reach a ledge beneath another right-facing corner. Belay. 100 feet.

Pitch 4: 5.9 Take the black, varnished, right-facing corner to its top. 130 feet.

Pitch 5: 5.7 R Climb up and right. Belay under the roof. 90 feet.

Pitch 6: 5.11a Climb the crack heading out the right side of the roof and follow a varnished thin crack up to a belay. 120 feet.

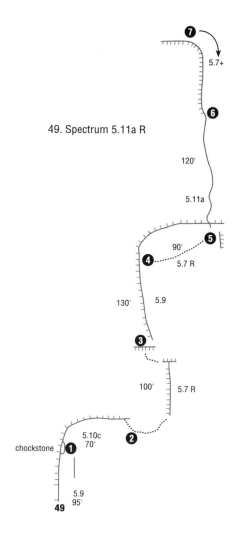

49. Spectrum 5.11a R

bon that indicates the project (on the project's first bolt). A bit loose. Gear: standard rack to #5 Friend. Be sure your rope is at least 200 feet for the rappel!

Pitch 1: 5.10d, 1 bolt. Scramble up to a ledge on the left side of a large, detached pillar, which looks like a thumb. Climb over the roof (crux), above a right-facing corner, protected by a bolt. Easier climbing (5.5) leads to the bolted belay at the base of a chimney. 80 feet.

Pitch 2: 5.9 Climb the chimney with minimal but adequate protection using the outside edge (easier than the inside). Top out and climb to a big, right-facing corner to a precarious-looking overhang. Traverse right, using the overhang, to the bolted anchor next to a small cave. 100 feet.

Pitch 3: 5.7+ Take the corner directly up from the anchors. Move right under an overhang to a bolted station. 80 feet.

Pitch 3 variation: There is a large ledge 15 feet below the top of the second pitch. Traverse the ledge 20 feet to the right of the anchors and set up a natural belay for the 5.10 hand/fist crack that goes right up the middle of the slab directly to the third-pitch anchors. 80 feet.

Pitch 4: 5.9 Take the corner to the left (awkward). Use the parallel crack for protection. A thin section leads to a short, easy chimney and a bolted anchor next to a tree. 80 feet.

Pitch 5: 5.9 Awkward. Ooze up the off-width. Place a cam on either side of a wiggly flake wedged in the crack. A crack in the roof sucks up everything from a #3.5 to #5 Friend. Fun and safe. Pull the roof and continue up the crack.

Rappel using a 60-meter rope (any shorter will not make it).
FA: Donny Burroughs, Gary Fike 1998

Pitch 7: 5.7+ Continue to the top of the cliff. Rappel.
FA: Jay Smith, Randal Grandstaff 1980

These routes are located just left of Brass Wall's right side. You can approach these routes from the Brass Wall's left or right side. A project is located left of *Brass Balls* (see red ribbon tied on a single bolt).

50. Brass Balls 5.10d ★★ Traditional. Begin 100 yards right of the previous route, 200 feet left of *Sea of Holds*. Begin under a small roof, right of the rib-

51. Free Fall (aka Ripcord) 5.12a R ★★ Mixed. Start right of *Brass Balls* on the right side of the arête separating the *Sea of Holes* wall from the walls left. The first ascensionists stopped the climbing when the rock got bad. The first pitch is the best pitch on the route.

Pitch 1: 5.12a, 2 bolts. Difficult climbing up on the arête. 80 feet.

Pitch 2: 5.10d R Climb up and left using varnished edges.

Brass Wall

50. Brass Balls 5.10d
51. Free Fall (AKA Ripcord) 5.12a R
52. Unknown 5.11
53. Cut Away 5.10d
54. The Black Hole 5.10c
55. Sea of Holes 5.10c R
56. Drop Zone 5.10c/d R
57. FRAP 5.10d R
58. Sky Dive 5.11b/c
59. Arachnoworld 5.4
60. Zen and the Art
    of Web Spinning 5.4
61. Snivler 5.7 R
62. Raptor 5.10b R
63. Heavy Spider Karma 5.6
64. Topless Twins 5.9

65. Mushroom People 5.10d
66. Bush Pilots 5.10a R
67. Fungus Folks 5.11a
68. Varnishing Point 5.9
69. No Laughing Matter 5.10a
70. Serious Business 5.10d
71. One Stop in Tonopah 5.11a R/X
72. Unknown 5.10
73. Unknown 5.9
74. Unknown 5.9
75. Go Greyhound 5.9+
76. Simpatico 5.10c
77. The Bus Stops Here 5.8

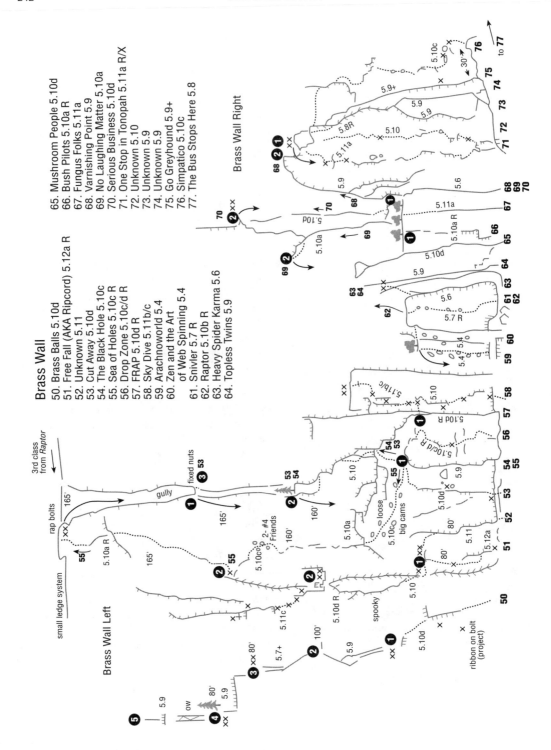

Brass Wall Right

Brass Wall Left

small ledge system

3rd class
from *Raptor*

rap bolts

Pitch 3: 5.11c, 7 bolts. Unfinished. Climb up and left from the pitch 2 anchors.

Rappel.

FA: Nick Nordblom, Jay Smith 1989

52. Unknown 5.11 ★★ Traditional. Begin right of *Free Fall*. Traverse left at the top to the first pitch anchors of *Free Fall*. 80 feet. Rappel.

FA: Randal Grandstaff

53. Cut Away 5.10d ★★ Mixed, 1 bolt. Begin 30 feet right of *Free Fall*. Gear: standard rack, brass wires, and #4 Friend.

Pitch 1: 5.10d Climb through varnished seams to a bolt and right-facing flakes. Finish up and right at the fixed anchors of *The Black Hole*, atop a large, black, varnished flake/pillar feature under the roof. 110 feet.

FA: Jay Smith, Mark Hesse 1989

Pitch 2: 5.10 Climb through the roof right of the anchors, on its right side.

Pitch 3: Continue up the chimney.

Rappel using 2 ropes.

FA: Jay Smith, Nick Nordblom 1989

54. The Black Hole 5.10 ★★★★ Traditional. Begin 10 feet right of the previous route. Gear: to #4 Friend.

Pitch 1: 5.9 Climb the very black, varnished, left-facing flake and corner below the center of a roof. Halfway up the pitch is a large black hole. Climb a large chimney to a narrow crack to a bolted anchor. 110 feet.

FA: Jay Smith, Dougald McDonald 1980

Pitch 2: 5.10 Climb straight up through the wide flare in the roof. 50 feet.

Rappel using 2 ropes.

FA: Jay Smith, Nick Nordblom 1980

55. Sea of Holes 5.10c R ★★ Traditional. Local, Russ Ricketts, describes it as "more hole than rock." Begin on pitch 1 of *The Black Hole* and then head left and up. Gear: to #3.5 Friend, 2 #4 Friends, and brass nuts.

Pitch 1: 5.9 Climb *The Black Hole* pitch 1.

Pitch 2: 5.10c Traverse left on the face, underneath the roof and through huecos. Climb the crack through

the left side of the roof to a single belay bolt on a blunt arête. Two #4 Friends needed for this pitch. 160 feet.

Pitch 3: 5.10a R Move up the varnished face. Pull over a small roof to belay on a shoulder. 165 feet.

Rappel into the gully right of the route from 2 bolts below the top of the route and the shoulder. Do two more rappels (three total), 165 feet each.

FA: Nick Nordblom, Jay Smith 1988

56. Drop Zone 5.10c/d R ★ Mixed, 1 bolt (added after the FA). Begin 5 feet right of *The Black Hole* on the right-hand, black, varnished face of the *Black Hole* flake. Sketchy start. Climb above the pink, loose rock and roof to a thin, technical face. Finish on the fixed anchors of *The Black Hole* (the first ascensionists finished on *Cut Away*). Gear: small wires needed. 110 feet. Rappel.

FA: Jay Smith, Jo Bentley, Mark Hesse 1989

57. FRAP 5.10d R ★ Traditional. Climb the huge, left-facing, varnished corner to a fixed anchor. Gear: standard rack and brass nuts. 40 feet. Rappel.

FA: Jay Smith, Nick Nordblom 1989

58. Sky Dive 5.11b/c ★ Mixed, 6 bolts. Begin 15 feet right of *FRAP*'s large, left-facing corner, on a black, varnished face 20 feet left of *Arachnoworld*. Climb the thin corner up and left to a bolt. Move up and left to a thin corner and another bolt. Head to a right-facing flake and take a thin seam up and right to the fixed anchor.

FA: Jay Smith, Jo Bentley 1989

BRASS WALL RIGHT

Brass Wall Right is located on the black, varnished face left of the Beer and Ice Gully. Take the trail out of the parking lot, heading into Pine Creek Canyon. Just before a low red band of rock appears on the right side of the trail, look for a large white boulder with smaller boulders leaning against it. Take the trail heading uphill and right just past this boulder. You will move uphill, skirting the ridge to the rightmost side of the red band. When on top of the red band, head right (east), following cairns toward some large flat rock ledges. Once on top of the rock ledges, take the red dirt trail straight towards the rock (north). When the trail forks, take the left fork, hiking parallel to the cliff in a westerly direction. Stay close to the base, on the easiest trail. Pass Beer and Ice Gully. The next varnished wall is the Brass Wall Right. Routes are described from left to right.

59. Arachnoworld 5.4 ★★ Traditional. Begin on the far-left side of the wall at a pink-colored band of rotten rock, left of a roof. This is 20 feet right of *Sky Dive*. Climb a ledge from atop a large boulder on the wall's right side. Traverse the ledge to its left edge and climb varnished huecos to the top and a bushy ledge. Tread softly on the ledge; there may be a huge white owl living there. Gear: to #3 Friend. 30 feet. Rappel.
FA: Unknown 1980

60. Zen and the Art of Web Spinning 5.4 ★★★ Traditional. Begin the same as the previous route. Once on the ledge, traverse it to a featured crack. Take the crack to the top and the same bushy ledge as the previous route. Gear: to #3 Friend. 30 feet. Rappel.
FA: Unknown 1980

61. Snivler 5.7 R ★ Traditional. Begin 10 feet right of the previous routes, on the left end of the lowest part of the roof, off a large boulder. Climb huecos up a varnished face. Traverse right on the ledge. Gear: Friends to #3.5. Belay and rappel off the bolted anchors of *Heavy Spider Karma*. 100 feet.
FA: Unknown 1980s

62. Raptor 5.10b R ★★ Traditional. This is the multipitch continuation of *Snivler*. Dirty and scary. Gear: to #3 Friend, doubles of #1 Friend and brass nuts; must have 2 #1 TCUs for pitch 2.
　　Pitch 1: 5.7 R Climb *Snivler* and belay on top of the large ledge (not on *Heavy Spider Karma*). 60 feet.
　　Pitch 2: 5.10a R, 1 bolt. Climb up a face, moving up and right to a ramp. Take the ramp to a left-facing corner. Take the corner to a stance and belay. 80 feet.
　　Pitch 3: 5.10a, 1 bolt. Move up, pulling a bulge and clipping a bolt to a belay at a right-facing corner. 70 feet.

Pitch 4: 5.9 Take the right-facing corner up to a face. Climb the face to another right-facing corner. Belay.
　　Pitch 5: 5.10b Take the corner up to a face.
　　Descend by hiking left (west), third and fourth class, into the gully right of *Sea of Holes*. Do three rappels using 2 ropes.
FA: Nick Nordblom, Randy Marsh 1990

63. Heavy Spider Karma 5.6 ★★★ Traditional. Begin 10 feet right of *Snivler*, on the right side of a low roof. Take the straight-up crack until it widens. Move right onto the face and up to the anchors of *Topless Twins*. Gear: to #4 Friend. 100 feet. Rappel.
FA: Mass assault team of Nick Nordblom, Paul Van Betten, Sal Mamusia, Randal Grandstaff, Randy Marsh, Wendell Broussard, and more 1980s

64. Topless Twins 5.9 ★★★★ Traditional. Begin 5 feet right of *Heavy Spider Karma* in a corner between two scrub-oak trees. Follow two cracks up to where they split. Take the left crack up and left to the shared anchors with *Heavy Spider Karma*. Gear: Rocks and Friends to #3. 100 feet. Rappel.
FA: Randal Grandstaff, Wendell Broussard 1980

65. Mushroom People 5.10d ★★★★ Traditional. Begin 30 feet right of *Topless Twins*, at a left-angling, thin seam up a smooth, black, varnished face. Gear: small Rocks and Friends to #1. 100 feet. Rappel from the anchor below the large hueco.
FA: Dave Diegelman, Randal Grandstaff, Greg Child 1979

66. Bush Pilots 5.10a R ★★★ Traditional. Begin 15 feet right of *Mushroom People* at a low, right-facing corner. Take the corner to a low roof. Traverse right under the roof to another right-facing corner. Move up the corner and then back left onto a face and some discontinuous cracks to the bushy ledge at the top. Gear: small and medium Rocks and Friends to #2. 50 feet. Belay and rappel off trees on top.
FA: Randy Marsh, Paul Van Betten 1984

67. Fungus Folks 5.11a ★ Traditional. Begin 20 feet right of *Bush Pilots* beneath a thin seam. Climb

the seam to where it ends, move right, and then take another seam to the same bushy ledge as *Bush Pilots*. Gear: small and brass wires, Friends to #1. 50 feet. Rappel.
FA: Randal Grandstaff 1982

68. Varnishing Point 5.9 ★★★★ Traditional. Begin 20 feet right of *Fungus Folks* beneath the far-right side of the bushy ledge marking the top of *Fungus Folks*. Gear: plenty of gear to #4 Friend; bring doubles if this is the limit of your ability.

Pitch 1: 5.6 Climb a crack leading through ledges and huecos to a roof. Traverse left under the roof and move up to obtain a ledge. Belay on the ledge below and left of a left-facing pillar with a crack in it. 50 feet.

Pitch 2: 5.9 Ascend the crack up the left side of the pillar. Climb through a thin, steep section to a wide section. Mount the top of the pillar and traverse right. Scramble down to fixed bolted anchors. It is difficult to hear the second from the belay. 150 feet.

Rappel using 2 ropes.
FA: Joe Herbst, Larry Hamilton 1976

69. No Laughing Matter 5.10a ★★ Traditional. Climb the first pitch of *Varnishing Point*. Move left 20 feet on the large bushy ledge (the top of *Bush Pilots* and *Fungus Folks*). Climb a left-angling crack to a roof. Face-climb left around the roof to an anchor. Rappel using 2 ropes.
FA: Greg Child, Randal Grandstaff 1979

70. Serious Business 5.10d ★ Traditional. Climb the first pitch of *Varnishing Point*. Move left 10 feet on the large bushy ledge, to just right of *No Laughing Matter*. Take a varnished face to a seam, moving straight up to a crack system. Face-climb to a flare and continue to the top. Rappel with 2 ropes.
FA: Paul Van Betten, Randy Marsh 1982

71. One Stop in Tonopah 5.11a R/X ★ Mixed, 2 bolts. This route, along with *Go Greyhound* and *The Bus Stops Here*, was named for a guy who was really bugging Paul Crawford. Crawford gave him a bus ticket and told him to take a ride. Begin 15 feet right of *Varnishing Point*, on the left side of a large, yellow

flake. Climb the flake and then step left to a right-facing, thin flake. Move up another right-facing flake. Take the face past 2 bolts and then move right, passing a tree to an arête. Take the arête to a ledge and the shared anchors with *Varnishing Point*.

Variation: Instead of escaping to the arête, move straight up to the anchors. Gear: thin wires and brass nuts, #00–#1 Friends. Rappel using 2 ropes.
FA: Paul Crawford, free solo 1980

72. Unknown 5.10 ★★ Mixed, 1 bolt. Begin 5 feet right of the previous route. Climb the right side of the yellow flake up to a bolt. Continue up the face, passing two ledges, and then move up and right to the varnished face. Take the face to the ledge and shared anchors with *Varnishing Point*. Gear: small and brass nuts, Friends to #2. Rappel using 2 ropes.
FA: Paul Crawford 1980

73. Unknown 5.9 ★ Traditional. Begin right of the previous route, at a right-angling crack. Take it up and then traverse up and left on cracks to a right-facing corner. Climb the corner to an arête. Climb the arête and then traverse left onto the face. Climb the face (5.8 R) to the top of the feature. Rappel using 2 ropes off the *Varnishing Point* anchors.
FA: Unknown

74. Unknown 5.9 ★ Begin just right of the previous route, on a crack making a small dogleg left to a straight-up crack. Take it up to the arête and to the anchors of *Varnishing Point*. Rappel using 2 ropes.
FA: Unknown

75. Go Greyhound 5.9+ ★ Mixed, 1 bolt. Climb the prominent right-facing corner right of the previous route and continue up to link with that route. Rappel with 2 ropes from the *Varnishing Point* anchors.
FA: Paul Crawford, free solo 1980

76. Simpatico 5.10c ★★ Mixed, 2 bolts. Begin 30 feet right of the previous route in a bushy gully. Scramble up 5 feet onto a ledge. Climb a face to a right-facing flake/corner and then face-climb left to

the fixed *Varnishing Point* anchors. Rappel with 2 ropes.
FA: Jay Smith, Jo Bently, Jenni Stone 1980

77. The Bus Stops Here 5.8 ★★ Traditional. Begin 10 feet right of the previous route, on the far-right edge of the wall. Ascend the right side of the large, varnished, right-facing flake. Climb the widening crack to the *Varnishing Point* anchors. Gear: to #4 Friend. 110 feet. Rappel using 2 ropes.
FA: Paul Crawford 1980

NORTH FORK
PINE CREEK CANYON

▲ OUT OF CONTROL AREA
S All-Day Sun   Approach: 40 minutes

The Out of Control Area sits on a ledge up and left of the Brass Wall. Take the trail out of the parking lot heading into Pine Creek Canyon. The trail takes you alongside a low band of red rock below the Brass Wall. Continue on the trail until it splits at the far-west end of the red band (at the north fork of Pine Creek), after about 20 minutes. Take the north fork trail on the right. Once you reach the top of the red band, take a trail heading left (west) toward the inside of the canyon. Keep your eyes right. At the first cliff break, scramble up and right to a ledge system. Traverse the ledge right about 120 yards. You will pass a sign on your hike up, noting that the canyons of Red Rock are designated wilderness areas. Routes are described from left to right.

78. American Ninja 5.11b ★★★ Traditional. Climb the thin crack up a huge dihedral on a boulder in the center of this large ledge. Gear: thin, including brass wires. 30 feet. Rappel from fixed anchors.
FA: Paul Van Betten, Robert Finlay 1986

79. Control Freak 5.10 ★★★ Traditional. Begin 20 feet left of *Out of Control*. Climb the finger crack that heads up and left into the main crack. Finish on a

Russ Ricketts showing control on Out of Control *5.10d*

big ledge. Traverse left (west) to a bolted station.
FA: Unknown

80. Out of Control 5.10d ★★★★★ Traditional. An ultraclassic! Begin on a crack in varnish, left of a left-facing corner at the far-right edge of the ledge, about 60 feet right of *American Ninja*. This is the route where local Wendell Broussard believes Paul Van Betten got *bold*. Prior to climbing this route, Van Betten got scared like the rest of us. On *Out of Control*, he climbed past where the fixed anchor is today (and where climbers back then normally cut right to rappel from the anchors of *Remote Control*). He continued up, placing a knot in the crack, ran it out, and then created a belay from many so-so RPs. He said if he got out of that predicament alive he would never climb again. From then on Van Betten was a leader in the climbing community, "becoming brilliant and calm in his climbing ability. He became a pioneer overnight." Gear: doubles of #1, #1.5, #2 Friends, other sizes through #4.

Pitch 1: 5.10c Climb to a white bulge, then pull to a hand crack, continuing to a roof. Pull the roof to clip fixed anchors. 160 feet. Rappel with 2 ropes or climb pitch 2.

FA: Randal Grandstaff, Dave Anderson 1978

Pitch 2: 5.10d Continue up the crack, heading up and slightly left to the top of the cliff.

Descend down and left.

FA: Paul Van Betten, Richard Harrison, Sal Mamusia 1984

81. Remote Control 5.9 ★★★ Begin 15 feet right of *Out of Control* on the left-facing corner with white flakes sticking out like teeth. Take the corner to a fixed anchor. Gear: to #4 Friend. 140 feet. Rappel with 2 ropes.

FA: Dave Anderson, Randal Grandstaff 1978

▲ NORTHEAST PINE CREEK
S All-Day Sun

To reach Northeast Pine Creek, take the trail out of the parking lot heading into Pine Creek Canyon. The trail takes you alongside a low band of red rock below the Brass Wall. Continue on the trail until it splits at the far-west end of the red band (at the north fork of Pine Creek), after about 20 minutes. Take the north fork trail on the right and, once you reach the top of the red rock band, take a trail heading left (west) toward the inside of the canyon, as you would for the Out of Control Area. Routes 82 and 83 are located 40

minutes apart and are approached differently. You will pass a sign on your hike up, noting that the canyons of Red Rock are designated wilderness areas.

82. Red Throbber Spire IV, 5.9+ ★★ Traditional. Approach: 2 hours. This route climbs an obvious red arête, often stared at from the Dark Shadows Wall belays, directly across the canyon. To reach *Red Throbber Spire*, continue heading toward the Out of Control Area, but instead of scrambling up and right onto the ledge at the first cliff break, head up and left, up a third-class gully. This is a long hike up and down.

Pitch 1: 5.9+ R Climb a corner to a belay ledge. 160 feet.

Pitch 2: 5.8 Move off the belay near a boulder on the ledge. 50 feet.

Pitch 3: 5.8 R, 1 bolt. Move up the face to a notch. 140 feet.

Pitch 4: 5.7 Take the arête to the summit. 120 feet.

Rappel to a notch and then rappel again into a bowl. Hike down the gully west of the spire.

FA: Bryan Kay, Dave Polari 1993

83. A Rope, a Rubber Chicken, and a Vibrator IV, 5.10a ★★ Traditional. Approach: 2.5 hours. Once you have turned onto the north fork trail, hike 2.5 miles up the north fork, passing the Dark Shadows Wall. This route is on the right (north) wall.

Pitch 1: 5.6 Climb a huecoed face to the right of a right-facing corner.

Pitch 2: 5.10a Head up a right-facing corner, through a roof to a belay ledge.

Pitch 3: 5.6 Take a crack to the summit. 60 feet.

Pitch 3 variation: 5.7 Climb left of the crack.

Descent unknown.

FA: George Watson, Norman Boles 1990

▲ PISCES WALL
S All-Day Sun   Approach: 2.5 hours

To reach the Pisces Wall, take the trail out of the parking lot heading into Pine Creek Canyon. The trail takes you alongside a low band of red rock below the Brass Wall. Continue on the trail until it splits at the far-west end of the red band (at the north fork of Pine Creek), after about 20 minutes. Take a right onto the north fork trail and hike up the north fork of Pine Creek Canyon to the base of Lower Bridge Mountain's south face. This wall is sometimes called the Peeing Fish Wall (you will know why when you see it).

84. The Pisces Wall V, 5.9, A2 ★★ Climb the
1000-foot water streak up the south face of Bridge Mountain. Andrew Fulton took a 75-plus-foot fall on the first ascent. This route is heady and likely sandbagged.

Pitch 1: 5.8, A0 Begin in the left water streak.

Pitch 2: A1 Ascend an overhang.

Pitch 3: 5.9, A1 Climb the huge huecoed wall. There is a bolt about 15 feet up. Continue through huecos to an arching thin crack taking you to a big ledge.

Pitch 4: 5.9, A1 Head up and right. Climb the face on very polished rock. Some hook moves mixed in with free climbing.

Pitch 5: A2 Two hundred feet of bat hooking. Bring your bat.

To descend, either hike west to Rocky Gap Road and descend it to Willow Springs, or rappel. You can also downclimb the southeast face of Bridge Mountain (5.5 X). See Icebox Canyon, Upper Bridge Mountain, *The Southeast Arête.*

FA: Andrew Fulton, Dan Briley 1998

▲ DARK SHADOWS WALL
N No Sun   Approach: 35 minutes

The Dark Shadows Wall is the large, black, varnished wall on North Fork Pine Creek Canyon's south side. Take the trail out of the parking lot heading into Pine Creek Canyon. The trail takes you alongside a low band of red rock below the Brass Wall. Continue on the trail until it splits at the far-west end of the red band (at the north fork of Pine Creek), after about 20 minutes. Take a right onto the north fork trail and once you reach the top of the red band, take the trail that heads left (west) toward the inside of the canyon. Follow the trail until it drops you into the creek bed. Hike across the creek bed to a pool and the north-facing wall. This is one of the more spectacular fea-

tures in Red Rock Canyon. You will pass a sign on your hike up, noting the canyons of Red Rock are designated wilderness areas. Routes are described from left to right.

Descent: Descend the south side of Mescalito Buttress (the opposite of the side you climbed). Upon reaching the red band at the summit of Mescalito, head southwest on a huge ledge system. As the ledge system breaks down, look for a place to descend (there eventually is a chimney you can downclimb for 30 feet). Do a 200-foot rappel off fixed Rocks (they were new when placed) and then third- and fourth-class down a gully into South Fork Pine Creek Canyon. It is also possible and possibly more dangerous to descend the north side of Mescalito.

85. Negro Blanco IV, 5.11a ★★ Traditional. Lo-
cated on the far left of the wall, this route climbs the enormous right-facing flake that seems to extend to the top of the wall. Climb the flake system separating the white wall left of the Dark Shadows Wall from the black, varnished Dark Shadows Wall. A very bold lead, especially on the upper pitches. No bolts were drilled on the first ascent. Fixed ropes were left while the first-ascent party worked on the route. After they were stolen, Lynn Hill had to relead the first pitch and she took an enormous whipper when a hold broke, landing her on a #3 RP. Gear: brass wires and gear to #5 Friend.

Pitch 1: 5.10d Begin in a right-facing dihedral. After the flared portion, traverse left across a face to belay beneath a flaring crack.

Pitch 2: 5.8 Climb the crack to the top of a flake with 1 bolt for the belay.

Pitch 3: Climb the flake. Move right 15 feet to a belay stance.

Pitch 4: 5.8 Traverse back left into a corner. Climb to a face and continue up until you reach the belay ledge.

Pitch 5: 5.9 Climb a face to an obvious crack. Belay midway up the crack.

Pitch 6: 5.11a Continue up the crack. When it merges into a ramp, follow the ramp up and right. At the top of the ramp, this pitch joins the top of pitch 8 of *Heart of Darkness.* Take *Heart of Darkness* to the top.

FA: Lynn Hill, John Long, Richard Harrison 1981

86. Lethal Weapon 5.12a ★★★ Traditional. Start just right of *Negro Blanco*. Gear: wide selection, from small Rocks to a couple of #3 Friends.

Pitch 1: 5.10c, 1 bolt. Climb the shallow, left-angling dihedral/corner system. Face-climb up under the small roof and traverse right under the roof, clipping 1 bolt.

Take the right-facing corner to the belay. 85 feet.

Pitch 2: 5.12a Climb out left to the large, right-angling flake that runs up and right. Continue following the wandering crack to the final fixed anchor. 100 feet.

Rappel with 2 ropes.

FA: Mike Tupper, Greg Mayer 1989

Dark Shadows Wall

85. Negro Blanco IV 5.11a
86. Lethal Weapon 5.12a
87. Parental Guidance 5.12a
88. Short Circuit 5.11c
89. Risky Business 5.10c
90. Excellent Adventure 5.11a R
91. Sandstone Sandwich 5.10c

92. Dark Shadows IV 5.8
93. Heart of Darkness IV 5.10d
94. Chasing Shadows 5.10a

95. Edge Dressing 5.10c
96. Unknown 5.8+
97. Slot Machine 5.10c

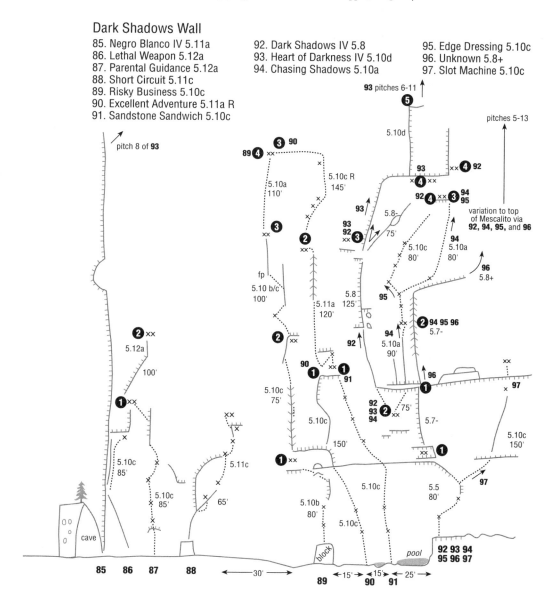

87. Parental Guidance 5.12a ★★★★★ Traditional. Begin 8 feet right of *Lethal Weapon* where a block leans against the wall. One of the best pitches in Red Rock, according to local aficionado, Wendell Broussard. Gear: wide selection, from small Rocks to a couple of #3 Friends.

Pitch 1: 5.10c, 4 bolts. Climb the bolted face. Clip the fourth bolt and then angle up and left to a right-facing flake. Take the flake up and then traverse left to the pitch 1 belay on *Lethal Weapon*. 85 feet.

Pitch 2: 5.12a Continue on pitch 2 of *Lethal Weapon* to the final fixed anchor. 100 feet.

Rappel with 2 ropes.

FA: Mike Tupper, Greg Mayer 1988

88. Short Circuit 5.11c ★★★★ Mixed, 4 bolts. Start atop a block resting against the wall and in front of a pine tree at the base of the wall. Climb up right of the shallow, left-facing corner. Follow a line of bolts to the fixed anchors. Gear: small Friends, large Rocks, and slings. 65 feet. Rappel.

FA: Mike Ward, Nick Nordblom 1992

89. Risky Business 5.10c ★★★★ Traditional. Start 30 feet right of the previous route, atop a block that leans against the wall and some trees. There is a reason for the name.

Pitch 1: 5.10b Climb up and right to a left-facing flake. Obtain the face, moving past 2 bolts. Head right to a right-facing flake, then move up and left under a roof to fixed anchors. 80 feet.

Pitch 2: 5.10c, 1 bolt. Climb up and left through the roof to a dihedral. Continue up to a face and crack to the anchor under a roof. 75 feet.

Pitch 3: 5.10b/c, 1 bolt. Move left and up to clip a bolt, then move back right to obtain a crack. Climb the crack and then veer left, clipping a fixed pin to reach a straight-in crack. Jam to the anchor. 100 feet.

Pitch 4: 5.10a Climb the varnished face to the anchors. 110 feet.

Rappel using 2 ropes.

FA: Mike Tupper, Greg Mayer 1985

90. Excellent Adventure 5.11a R ★★★★★ Traditional. Begin 15 feet right of *Risky Business* on a water-polished slab, above a whitish boulder.

Pitch 1: 5.10c, 2 bolts. Climb up the water-polished slab past 2 bolts to the right side of the arching roof at the top of the first pitch of *Risky Business*. Take the roof left 15 feet and then pull it. Head up and right to a belay ledge with fixed anchors. 150 feet.

Pitch 2: 5.11a, 1 bolt. Climb up and clip a bolt then move down and left. Climb up past the left side of a roof. Move up the right side of a blunt arête to the anchor on its left. 120 feet.

Pitch 3: 5.10c R. Take bolts out the lip of the huge roof and then head straight up. Traverse left to the pitch 4 anchors on *Risky Business*. Heads-up on this one. 145 feet.

Rappel using 2 ropes.

FA: Mike Tupper, Greg Mayer 1989

91. Sandstone Sandwich 5.10c ★★★★★ Mixed, 8 bolts. A better start to *Excellent Adventure*. Begin in the (usually) dry spot between the pool below the waterfall and the pool below that, 15 feet right of *Excellent Adventure*. Either climb the water-polished slab or start right at *Dark Shadows*, and hand-traverse left on a big horizontal ledge. Continue up the center of the wall (20 feet to first bolt). Head left of the second-pitch belay on *Dark Shadows*. Continue up and left, clipping bolts to the first-pitch anchor of *Excellent Adventure*. Gear: #1 and #1.5 Friends to supplement the bolts. Rappel using 2 ropes or finish on *Excellent Adventure*.

FA: Bob Conz, George Smith, Jim Lybarger 1990

92. Dark Shadows IV, 5.8 ★★★★★ Traditional. You don't get cracks much better than this one. The route goes straight to the top of the cliff, but most people rappel after pitch 4. Most anchors above pitch 4 have 1 old and 1 newer bolt. All can be backed up with natural protection. Gear: standard rack to #3 Friend.

Pitch 1: 5.5, 2 bolts. Begin 25 feet right of the previous route on the ledge above the waterfall. Climb huecos to edges. After clipping the second bolt move left into the crack and up a leftward-slanting ramp. Bolted belay. 80 feet.

Pitch 2: 5.7- Climb to a right-facing, varnished corner. At its top, under a small roof, hand-traverse left 15 feet. Step down onto a big ledge and a bolted anchor. (Often combined with pitch 1.) 75 feet.

Pitch 3: 5.8 Climb a steep crack directly above the anchor. Continue, moving right onto a huecoed, varnished face. Use the right-facing crack and the face to make your way up and slightly left to the bolted anchor on a small ledge. 125 feet.

Pitch 4: 5.8- Move right to obtain a thin crack that enlarges as you ascend. After pulling through the wide section, move right and up. 75 feet. Belay at any of these bolted anchors: (1) up underneath a small roof (right of the massive roof of *Heart of Darkness*); (2) straight right once you hit the downward-sloping ledge (10 feet below and right of the small roof)—this one is best for rappeling the route; or (3) continue up and right around a blunt arête right of the roof—do this if you intend to continue to the top of Mescalito Buttress. Rappel from the top of pitch 4 with 2 ropes in two rappels (the first rappel takes you to the top of pitch 2).

Pitch 5: 5.9 After climbing around the corner from the *Heart of Darkness* roof, obtain a left-leaning finger crack leading to a big ledge. 100 feet.

Pitch 6: 5.8, 1 bolt. Move left off the ledge, across a gap to reach a seam. Climb the seam for 40 feet, clip a bolt, and continue up another 30 feet. Traverse left 30 feet and then head straight up to a bolted belay. 150 feet. (Avoid the dirty chimney where you cross the gash.)

Pitches 7–13: Climb the crack and face systems leading to the top. The route has been done in 11 and 13 pitches. There are stations along these last pitches. *FA: Joe Herbst early 1970s (Jon Martinet and Nick Nordblom went up the route in 1979 and found an old steel Cassin leaver biner belonging to Herbst)*

93. Heart of Darkness IV, 5.10d ★★★ Traditional. Begin on *Dark Shadows*. Gear: standard rack to a #4 Friend.

Pitch 1–4: Climb *Dark Shadows* to the fourth pitch middle anchor, underneath the roof.

Pitch 5: 5.10d, 1 bolt. Hand-traverse left under the roof, clipping 1 bolt and 1 fixed pin. Pull over the roof at its center and climb the crack above it. Belay on a large ledge (the top of pitch 6 of *Dark Shadows*).

Pitch 6: 5.8 Traverse left for 25 feet to a crack in the varnished face. Take the crack and the subsequent

Karrie Anderson in the dark on the third pitch of Dark Shadows *5.8*

face up and slightly left to a bolted belay.

Pitch 7: 5.9 Pull a bulge and take discontinuous cracks up to a long roof. Traverse right to the rightmost of two cracks and belay at a bulge.

Pitch 8: 5.8 Pull the roof and move up a 2-inch crack to a large ledge.

Pitch 9: 5.7 Take a crack up and right.

Pitch 10: 5.9 Head straight up the wall, pulling a bulge and then face-climbing to the belay.

Pitch 11: Climb the crack systems leading to the top. 200 feet. Scramble to the top of the feature.
FA: John Long, Lynn Hill, Richard Harrison 1981

94. Chasing Shadows 5.10a ★★ Traditional. Begin on *Dark Shadows*. Gear: standard rack to a #4.5 Friend.

Pitch 1: 5.7- Climb *Dark Shadows* to the top of pitch 2. 145 feet.

Pitch 2: 5.10a Move up and right to the rightmost of two vertical cracks. Take the crack up somewhat loose rock to a black face and small stance at a bolted anchor. 90 feet.

Pitch 3: 5.10a Move up, clip 1 bolt, and then move right, staying just left of the arête formed by a large roof. Continue right to another bolt and then straight up the wall to the *Dark Shadows* option 2 anchor on the slab at the edge of the steep wall. Little protection on this pitch. 80 feet. Rappel *Dark Shadows* with 2 ropes.
FA: Randy Marsh, Pier Locatelli 1990

95. Edge Dressing 5.10c ★★★★ Sport, 6 bolts. This is a variation of *Chasing Shadows'* pitch 3. From the top of pitch 2 on *Chasing Shadows* move up and left to climb straight up the center of the wall, clipping bolts. Move right after the last bolt to clip the anchor at the top of *Dark Shadows* pitch 4. Gear: a #3 Friend to supplement bolts (or just run it out). 80 feet. Rappel *Dark Shadows* with 2 ropes.
FA: Randy Marsh, Pier Locatelli, Brett Fishman 1993

96. Unknown 5.8+ ★★ Mixed, 5 bolts. Begin on *Dark Shadows*. Gear: standard rack to #3 Friend.

Pitch 1: 5.7-, 2 bolts. Climb pitch 1 of *Dark Shadows*. Start out on *Dark Shadows* pitch 2, but build an anchor before the hand traverse, at the top of the right-facing corner. 145 feet.

Pitch 2: 5.7- Move right into a large right-facing corner with a couple of cracks moving up through it. Somewhat loose. Climb up underneath the large roof and traverse left to the second-pitch anchors of *Chasing Shadows*. 60 feet.

Pitch 3: 5.8+, 3 bolts. Climb past the first 2 bolts of *Edge Dressing*, and then head right above the huge roof. Clip 1 bolt and then move straight up the wall to connect with the anchor atop pitch 4 of *Dark Shadows*.

Rappel *Dark Shadows* from here or continue up to the top of Mescalito via *Dark Shadows*.
FA: Unknown

97. Slot Machine 5.10c ★★★★★ Mixed, 3 bolts. Start on *Dark Shadows*. After clipping the second bolt, move up and right to underneath an overhang. Move over steep rock to a thin seam and face past 1 bolt to fixed anchors. Gear: small nuts and brass wires and Friends to #3. 150 feet. Rappel with 2 ropes.
FA: Bob Conz, Sal Mamusia 1990

The next route is located 150 feet right (up the creek) from *Slot Machine*. Other routes have been done on this wall but are not listed in this guide.

98. Peyote Power 5.9+ ★★ Traditional. Ascend a slab to reach a large, wide ledge. Begin right of a scrub oak on the far-right edge of the ledge. Gear: doubles to #3.5 Friend, many long slings.

Pitch 1: 5.6 Traverse left on the ledge and take a thin crack above a horizontal up and left to the right of a roof. Pull around right of the roof. Move up and left to reach a varnished crack. Take it to bolted anchors on a slab under a roof. 180 feet.

Pitch 2: 5.7 Slab out right, moving up onto a sloping ledge. Move up and right, taking a white flakey corner up and right to a small ledge on its left and belay at the bolted anchor. 210 feet.

Pitch 3: 5.9+ Climb up 10 feet to a downward-sloping ledge. Move up and left onto a steep varnished section, left of a large chimney. Take jugs up to a slopey face to bolted anchors. 190 feet.

Pitch 4: 5.7, 1 bolt. Continue up the face to a V slot that creates a chimney on a ledge. Fixed anchors. 170 feet.

Pitch 5: 5.7, 1 bolt. Face-climb up and left to a bolt. Take a varnished trough/crack up, over a roof. Face-climb a white slab up and left to bolted anchors.

Pitch 6: 5.9 R, 3 bolts. Face-climb up and left into a white corner. Move up and right up the steep white corner. Finish at a bolted anchor on a big ledge right of trees.

Pitch 7: Fourth and easy fifth class. Scramble 30 minutes to the summit! Head west on the ledge until you reach the main west ridge of Mescalito Buttress. Continue up and left to the summit.

Rappel using 2 ropes.

FA: Unknown

▲ MESCALITO EAST FACE
E AM Sun   Approach: 30 minutes

The east face of Mescalito Buttress is just left of Dark Shadows Wall. To get there, walk the trail into Pine Creek Canyon for 20 minutes. The trail takes you alongside a low band of red rock below the Brass Wall. Continue until the trail forks at the far-left (west) end of the red band. Take the left fork, moving into a wash and hiking into the south fork of Pine Creek. Follow a trail out of the wash, up the steep right (west) edge of the wash toward Mescalito Buttress. Approach on the left side about 100 feet right of the formation's southeasternmost point. Hike up a faint trail directly to the base of Mescalito. Some bushwhacking may be required. You will pass a sign on your hike up, noting that the canyons of Red Rock are designated wilderness areas. Routes are described from left to right.

LEFT SIDE

The first routes begin on the far-left side of the wall, 100 feet left of a ledge system, at the southeast corner of the buttress.

99. WASP 5.10a ★★ Traditional. Climb the crack system up the prow on the southeast corner of the buttress. This

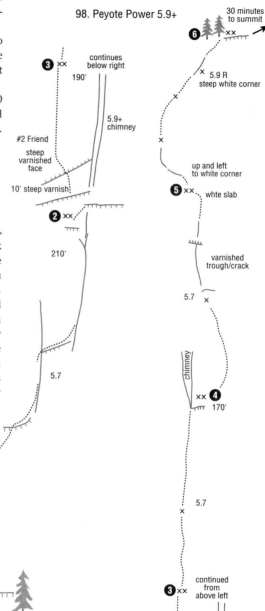

98. Peyote Power 5.9+

MESCALITO EAST FACE: LEFT SIDE

route joins *Cat in the Hat*'s third pitch. Gear: standard rack including brass nuts.

Pitch 1: 5.10a Climb the first corner on the east face of Mescalito. Follow it up, staying to the right. Belay atop a large, white, rounded ledge.

Pitch 2: Head slightly left and climb up the southeast corner of Mescalito Buttress. Follow the buttress up until it is possible to traverse left and join with the top of pitch 3 of *Cat in the Hat*.

From there you can either continue up *Cat in the Hat* or rappel *Cat in the Hat* using 2 ropes.
FA: Joe Herbst, Randal Grandstaff 1976

100. Black Widow Hollow 5.9 ★★★ Traditional. Climb the right-facing corner 50 feet right of *WASP*. Climb the corner to its high point and then join *Cat in the Hat*, on the south face of Mescalito. Gear: standard rack with larger cams, including a couple of extra #4 Friends.

Pitch 1: 5.9 Follow the large obvious corner straight up the wall. 100 feet.

Pitch 2: 5.8 Continue climbing up the large, right-facing corner until you reach the southeast buttress of Mescalito and belay. Traverse slightly left to finish atop the third pitch of *Cat in the Hat*. 110 feet.

Rappel *Cat in the Hat* or continue up it.
FA: Joe Herbst, Mark Moore 1976

101. Pauline's Pentacle 5.10a R ★★★ Traditional. Climb the black, varnished, huecoed face left of a huge, deep recess and chimney, on the ledge right and above the start of *Black Widow Hollow*. Finish on the ledge down and right of pitch 4 of *Cat in the Hat*. Look for the star hidden on the route, the reason for the name. Old-school trad route.

Pitch 1: 5.10a R Begin on the right side of the face, amidst large huecos. Climb to bolted anchors. Not-so-good rock. 115 feet.

Pitch 2: 5.9 Continue up the face to bolted anchors just below the ledge down and right of *Cat in the Hat*. 115 feet.

Rappel with 2 ropes or 1 70-meter rope (two rappels).
FA: Randal Grandstaff, Randy Marsh, Pauline Schroeder 1982

102. The Cookie Monster 5.7 ★★★ Traditional. Climb the large corner just right of *Pauline's Pentacle*, through a deep black chimney recessed into the wall. Follow the chimney feature to its top and join *Cat in the Hat*, on the ridge.

Pitch 1: 5.6 Climb the crack in the corner. 140 feet.

Pitch 2: 5.7 Continue up the crack to an alcove. 120 feet.

Pitch 3: 5.7 Climb the crack up and right to the shoulder. 80 feet.

Join *Cat in the Hat* by descending 40 feet to the west to the top of its third pitch. Finish on the final pitch of *Cat in the Hat* or rappel that route.
FA: Joe and Betsy Herbst 1970s

103. The Walker Spur 5.10c ★★★ Traditional. Start 15 feet right of *The Cookie Monster* atop a large ledge, 75 feet below a large roof. Climb up the arête, past the left side of the roof. Continue up the arête to its top and the corner of the southeast buttress. Suspect gear. Join *Cat in the Hat*. Gear: good selection up to a #3 Friend.

Pitch 1: 5.10c, 1 bolt. Climb the thin cracks past bolts and sloping ledges to the prow. Continue up the prow, staying to the left of the small roof. 80 feet.

Pitch 2: 5.9, 1 bolt. Climb past a bolt and continue to climb up the prow, to the belay just right of the prow. 150 feet.

Pitch 3: 5.9 Continue up, angling right onto a face. Belay on a ledge below and right of the last pitch of *Cat in the Hat*. 150 feet. Climb up and left to the huge tower feature with slings wrapped around it at the top of *Cat in the Hat*'s pitch 4.

Rappel *Cat in the Hat*.
FA: John Long, Lynn Hill, Richard Harrison 1981

104. Pine Nuts 5.10b R ★ Traditional. Begin just right of *The Walker Spur*, off the same ledge and below the large roof, left of a striking crack. Gear: standard rack to a #3.5 Friend.

Pitch 1: 5.10b, 2 bolts. Climb up the huecoed center section of the face, past 2 bolts. Pull the roof to reach fixed anchors on a varnished face. 100 feet.

Pitch 2: 5.8 Continue up the black, varnished face, veering slightly left to a set of bolted anchors. 130 feet.

Rappel the route using 2 ropes.
FA: Chris Gill, Paul Ross, Todd Swain 1998

105. When a Stranger Calls 5.8 ★★★ Traditional. Begin 12 feet right of the previous route, beneath a striking crack that goes straight up the wall. Gear: #1–#5 Friends.

Pitch 1: 5.8 Climb the crack through the right edge of the roof and continue up to belay in an alcove. 170 feet.

Pitch 2: Continue up the crack for another 150 feet.

Pitch 3: Exit out left of the crack and onto the face. Climb up to the southeast corner of Mescalito to a huge tower feature with slings wrapped around it at the top of *Cat in the Hat's* pitch 4. 100 feet.

Continue up *Cat in the Hat*, or rappel *Cat in the Hat*.
FA: Randal Grandstaff, Steve Anderson 1981

106. Unknown 5.8 R ★ Traditional. Start right of *When a Stranger Calls* and left of the huge white pillar leaning against the middle of Mescalito's east face. Climb the center of the black, varnished face. Very loose. Finish on a bushy ledge with an anchor. Gear: standard rack with many midsized Rocks. 160 feet. Rappel with 2 ropes.
FA: Unknown

107. $C_{11}H_{17}NO_3$ 5.5 ★★★ Traditional. The chemical formula for mescaline (peyote), this route is sure to get you high. Start 20 feet right of the previous route, on the left side of a huge pillar that leans against the middle of Mescalito's east face. Climb the nicest looking chimney system on the face. Gear: standard rack with a few big Friends to #4.

Pitch 1: 5.5 Climb up the obvious right-leaning crack, 15 feet left of the large white rock pillar. Follow the crack to just left of a small pillarlike formation and set up a belay. 75 feet.

Pitch 2: Traverse slightly right across the face to another vertical crack running up the wall—this crack heads up and left. Follow the cracks until you come to a large, rounded, right-sloping ledge. Belay.

Pitch 3: Finish by traversing up and left to join the southeast corner of Mescalito Buttress. Climb up and left to the huge tower feature with slings wrapped around it at the top of *Cat in the Hat's* pitch 4.

Continue up or rappel *Cat in the Hat* using 2 ropes.
FA: Bob Logerquist, John Williamson 1971

108. Mescalito Regular Route 5.5 ★★ Traditional. Start right of $C_{11}H_{17}NO_3$ on the left side of a huge pillar that leans against the middle of Mescalito's east face. Gear: standard rack with Friends to #4.

Pitch 1: 5.5 Climb the obvious crack just left of the white pillar. Follow the crack to its top and belay.

Pitch 2: Traverse/scramble right from the belay to a large right-facing flake. Climb the left edge of the flake to its top and belay.

Pitch 3: Finish up a large right-facing corner, leading to the corner of the southeast buttress of Mescalito. Traverse left to a huge tower feature with slings wrapped around it at the top of *Cat in the Hat's* pitch 4.

Continue up or rappel *Cat in the Hat* using 2 ropes.
FA: Jeff Lansing, Peter Wist 1968

109. This Ain't No Disco 5.10a ★★★ Mixed, 6 bolts. Climb the dark brown face just right of the large white pillar that leans against the middle of Mescalito's east face. Finish on anchors three-quarters of the way up the wall. This route was originally done without any of the bolts—somebody added them later. Gear: to #1 Friend.
FA: Randal Grandstaff, Randy Marsh 1982

110. Welcome to the Red Rocks 5.12a ★★★★★ Traditional. Begin around the right corner of the large white rock pillar that leans up against the middle of Mescalito's east face, 10 feet left of *Pauligk Pillar*. Gear: brass and small wires and Friends to #2.5.

Pitch 1: 5.7 Climb a left-leaning ramp up and left to a ledge just below a very thin, clean, right-facing corner, halfway up the ramp. Step right and belay. 50 feet.

Pitch 2: 5.12a, 1 bolt. Climb the thin corner past a bolt. When the corner ends, climb the black, varnished face to the top of *Pauligk Pillar*. 150 feet.

Pitch 2 variation: 5.11a Avoid the crux by taking a horizontal crack, moving up the face right and then traversing back left to the crack. 150 feet.

MESCALITO EAST FACE: RIGHT SIDE

Perception Tower

Rappel *Pauligk Pillar*.
FA: Sal Mamusia, Paul Van Betten 1986

111. Pauligk Pillar 5.7+ ★ Traditional. The Australian who invented the RP probably used some on his first ascents. Climb the right-facing corner 10 feet right of the previous route. A large pine tree sits on the ledge at the top of this large pillar. Gear: standard rack to #3.5 Friend and RPs (see, we told you).

Pitch 1: 5.7 Climb the corner to its midpoint and a fixed anchor. 180 feet.

Pitch 2: 5.7+ Continue up the corner to white flakes, up and left to a varnished face. Continue to the top of the pillar. 160 feet.

Rappel using 2 ropes.
FA: Mrs. and Mr. Roland Pauligk ("RP"), Randal Grandstaff 1981

112. Y2K 5.10a ★★★ Mixed, 10 bolts. Start 5 feet right of the previous route at a pink right-facing corner topped by a roof. Begin atop a boulder. Beware of loose rock. Gear: standard rack with cams to #3 Friend and brass nuts, extras of small nuts.

Pitch 1: 5.10a, 6 bolts. Climb thin seams up and right past several bolts to the right edge of the roof. Pull the roof to a varnished crack. Face-climb to a bolted anchor. 155 feet.
FA: Unknown 1997

Pitch 2: 5.8+, 3 bolts. Continue up the face to a ledge with a fixed anchor. 155 feet.

Pitch 3: 5.5, 1 bolt. Move up to a ledge. Traverse straight right to a corner and belay. 60 feet.

Pitch 4: 5.9 Climb the varnished corner to a ledge. Move left and climb up to the bolted belay at another ledge. 130 feet.

Do three rappels using 2 ropes: (1) pitch 4 anchor to pitch 2 anchor; (2) pitch 2 anchor to pitch 1 anchor; (3) pitch 1 anchor to the ground.
FA: Todd Swain, Paul Ross 1998 (pitches 2–4)

113. The Next Century 5.10c/d ★★★★★ Traditional. Begin 50 feet right of *Y2K* at the base of a large dirt mound on the right. Gear: standard rack with Friends to #3 and brass nuts.

Pitch 1: 5.7 Climb the right-facing corner, right of a low roof, to a ledge. Move up a varnished crack left

to a fixed anchor. 90 feet.
FA: Unknown

Pitch 2: 5.10d, 4 bolts. Move right to climb the varnished arête up to a thin seam. Continue up to a horizontal below a roof. Traverse right to the bolted anchors. 100 feet.

Rappel with 2 ropes.
FA: Todd Swain, Paul Ross 1998

114. Ride the Tiger 5.9 ★ Traditional. Begin down and left of *Bloodline*. Ascend the left side of the apron of the *Deep Space* buttress.

Pitch 1: 5.7 Climb a *Wheat Thin*–looking flake (like the Yosemite route).

Pitch 2: 5.9 Traverse the flake left to around an arête. Climb the steepening face around the corner left.
FA: Nick Nordblom, Randal Grandstaff 1982

Pitch 3: 5.9 Traverse left into the top of the second pitch of *Y2K*.

Rappel *Y2K*.
FA: Paul Van Betten 1982

115. Bloodline 5.11a ★★★★ Traditional. Climb the first pitch of *Ride the Tiger* or ascend the right side of the apron up the *Deep Space* buttress. Start right of a black water streak, 5 feet left of the wide crack of *Deep Space*. Difficult approach.

Pitch 1: Climb the pocketed face and crack up and left to join a straight-in crack system on the face. Continue to a ledge and belay.

Pitch 2: 5.11a Continue up and right in the finger crack, through a steep section to a bolted anchor on a ledge. 25 feet.

Rappel using 2 ropes.
FA: Unknown

RIGHT SIDE

Climb the black northeast face of the right side of the *Deep Space* apron, 50 feet left of *Negro Blanco*, to reach the start of routes 116–119.

Descent: Use the Dark Shadows Wall descent: Descend the south side of Mescalito Buttress. Upon reaching the red band at the summit of Mescalito, head southwest on a huge ledge system. As the ledge system breaks, look down for a place to descend (there eventually is a chimney you can downclimb for 30

Joe Herbst rappeling the first ascent of **Deep Space** *in 105-degree heat, 1975.* Photo by Larry Hamilton

feet). Do a 200-foot rappel off fixed Rocks (they were new when placed) and then third- and fourth-class down a gully into South Fork Pine Creek Canyon. It is also possible and possibly more dangerous to descend the north side of Mescalito.

116. Deep Space 5.9 ★★ Traditional. This route is the chimney located at the top of the apron 100 feet left of the sharp dihedral marking the left edge of Dark Shadows Wall (*Negro Blanco*). (Ascend the two-pitch apron by way of the first two short pitches described below.) Gear: medium to large nuts and Friends to #5.

Pitch 1: Third class. Begin at a right-facing flake. Climb the swallowing chimney to halfway up and belay.

Pitch 2: Third class. Finish up the easy chimney and belay below another chimney.

Pitch 3: 5.9 Stem the big chimney to a crack on the right wall. Take the crack over a small ceiling and belay.

Pitch 4: 5.9 Face-climb to the left side of a shelf, belaying below another wide crack.

Pitch 5: Climb the off-width.

Pitches 6–8: Continue up, eventually moving left into a hand crack. Follow it as it widens, to the top. *FA: Larry Hamilton, Joe Herbst 1975*

117. Centerfold 5.10a R ★ Traditional. Approach per the first two pitches of *Deep Space* and then climb off the apron 100 feet down and right of the start of *Deep Space*. Climb the cracks that summit the left side of Perception Tower, a huge tower with a white top attached to the Mescalito east face. Continue to the summit after obtaining the top of Perception Tower. Beware of poor rock on the crux pitch (pitch 3). The climbing gets easier after that and eases considerably toward the top, but involves bushwhacking and crumbly rock. If the pitch 5 bolt anchor has not been replaced yet, it definitely should be. Gear: standard rack.

Pitch 1: 5.8 Climb the face leading to an obvious ledge at the base of the main crack system.

Pitch 2: 5.9 Climb the rightmost of two chimneys to an overhang. Traverse down around a corner and left. Difficult climbing up a thin crack leads to another fine belay.

Pitch 3: 5.8 Take a vertical gully, moving right at the top to a comfy ledge. Beware of loose rock, flexing flakes, and questionable protection. Crux pitch.

Pitch 4: 5.7 Climb a couple of feet and make an obvious, long traverse right to a narrow ledge.

Pitch 5: 5.8 Move up through a varnished section and then angle left and up to a thin, exposed ledge with a bolt anchor. Check the bolt; it may be suspect.

Pitch 6: 5.10a Downclimb from the left side of the belay ledge. Traverse left to regain the main crack system. Continue over a bulge and belay.

Pitch 7: Easy fifth class. Long, rope-length pitch to a dirty belay.

Pitch 8: 5.7 Climb the strenuous chimney and crack.

Pitch 9: Fourth class. Take the unprotected, left-hand chimney to ledges marking the end of the *Centerfold* crack. Hike and scramble west on ledges until it is feasible to walk to the summit.
FA: Scott Woodruff, Joe Herbst, Larry Hamilton 1977

118. Flakes of Wrath 5.10d R/X ★ Traditional. Begin 15 feet left of the obvious flake that goes up the entire length of the wall (*Negro Blanco*), at the huecoed face left of a big chimney/cave feature. Gear: plenty of brass wires and many small Friends to #1.5.

Pitch 1: 5.8 R Climb the varnished, huecoed face up to a ledge. Move up the ledge/ramp 10 feet and climb the varnished face to a fixed anchor (pin and nut). 100 feet.

Pitch 2: 5.8+ Continue up the face to a big, black, varnished plate at a bolted anchor, just before the crack doglegs left. 75 feet.

Pitch 3: 5.10 R Climb left and up through cracks connecting varnished plates. Move back right to a pin and bolt anchor. 150 feet.

Pitch 4: 5.10d R/X Step left to a crack. Move over a small roof and follow a crack to a pin and bolt belay on the shoulder.

Descend in four 2-rope rappels. Sketchy!
FA: Nick Nordblom, Kevin Lowell 1990

119. Unknown 5.10d R/X ★ Gear has been seen on this route. Begin the same as *Flakes of Wrath*. Climb the headwall up and right, between *Flakes of Wrath* and *Negro Blanco*. Sketchy! Gear: plenty of brass wires and many small Friends to #1.5.

Pitch 1: 5.8 R Climb the first pitch of *Flakes of Wrath*. Climb the varnished, huecoed face up to a ledge. Move up the ledge/ramp 10 feet and climb the varnished face to a fixed anchor (pin and nut). 100 feet.

Pitch 2: 5.8+ Continue up the face to a crack. Take a small crack in white rock up and right. Belay at a fixed anchor at the top of the crack at a tiny roof, before the crack doglegs left. One piton. 75 feet.

Pitch 3: 5.10 R Traverse up and left using flakes to a slab. Climb back right on the white slab to the base of a tiny, varnished, left-facing corner and belay. 150 feet.

Pitch 4: 5.10d R/X Climb the corner up and left to a face. Move up the face to a fixed anchor.

Descend in four 2-rope rappels.
FA: Unknown

SOUTH FORK PINE CREEK CANYON

▲ MESCALITO SOUTH FACE
S AM Sun   Approach: 40 minutes

The south face of Mescalito Buttress is around the feature left (southwest) of Mescalito's east face. To get there, walk the trail into Pine Creek Canyon for 20 minutes. The trail takes you alongside a low band of red rock below the Brass Wall. Continue until the trail forks at the far-left (west) end of the red band. Take the left fork, moving into a wash and hiking into the south fork of Pine Creek. Follow a trail out of the wash, up the steep right (west) edge of the wash toward Mescalito Buttress. Follow alongside the buttress, paralleling it, through scrub oak and manzanita bushes, heading farther into the south fork of Pine Creek. Upon approaching the mouth of a gully, go right (northwest), scrambling up some boulders. You will pass a sign on your hike up, noting that the canyons of Red Rock are designated wilderness areas. Routes are described from left to right.

120. Unknown 5.9 ★★ Traditional. Climb the off-width 40 feet right of *Cat in the Hat*, up and then

left on ledges to the first-pitch anchor of *Cat in the Hat*. Gear: to #5 Friend. Rappel with 2 ropes.
FA: Unknown

121. Cat in the Hat IV, 5.6+ ★★★★★ Traditional.
This route climbs the center of the right wall, visible as you come up the boulders, and is 40 feet left of a wide crack on the right side of the wall.

Pitch 1: 5.6 Take the obvious crack that splits the face up and angle left. Pass the first ledge and anchors. Continue up past another small, downward-sloping ledge, and climb up and left in the crack. Obtain a very large ledge. Traverse right and belay at bolted anchors on a large boulder. 165 feet.

Pitch 2: 5.5 Do one fifth-class move to get on top of the boulder above the anchors (come from the right side of the boulder). Move up and right to reach a tree in a crack. Here you will be below a steep section with cracks heading up the wall. 70 feet.

Pitch 3: 5.6 Pull the overhang and move up the crack, taking it to a scrub-oak tree with slings and rappel rings. 100 feet.

Pitch 4: 5.6 Take the crack left of the tree up under a roof. Do some face moves left to pull the roof and reach a straight-in crack on varnished rock. Take the crack all the way up to a good ledge. Continue up to a tower feature with slings wrapped around it. 125 feet.

Pitch 5: 5.6+ Step down and right, below the anchor and a bolted arête above the belay. Traverse the ledge right 50 feet to a perfect crack in varnished rock. Climb the crack as it thins out. At the top, clip a bolt and slab up to the bolted anchors. 160 feet.

Pitch 5 variation: 5.10b/c, 4 bolts. Climb the arête above the belay to the anchors.

Rappel over the bolted arête to the pitch 4 anchor. Difficult rope drag and pull on the first rappel. Continue rappeling using 2 ropes for all rappels.
FA: Bruce Eisener, Joanne Urioste 1976

Hike 200 yards past *Cat in the Hat*, deeper into the south fork, alongside Mescalito Buttress. Approach the following routes by ascending an easy fifth-class chimney/gully system that angles up and right to a ledge. Once on the bushy ledge, climb one of either splitter cracks on the yellow face, left of a left-facing

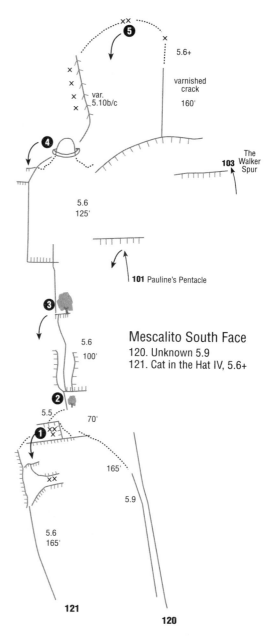

Mescalito South Face
120. Unknown 5.9
121. Cat in the Hat IV, 5.6+

corner. The routes climb the cracks through a roof.
Descent: Shaky anchors for rappeling.

122. OB Button 5.10a ★★ Traditional. This is the leftmost of the two routes.
Pitch 1: 5.10a Climb a varnished face to a roof. Climb the most obvious crack going through the roof.
Pitch 2: Continue up.
FA: Paul Obenheim 1982

123. OB Fist 5.10a ★★★ Traditional. Climb a varnished face to a roof. At the roof, move right to a varnished wide crack heading through the roof. Continue up. One pitch. Gear: to #4 Friend.
FA: Nick Nordblom, Paul Obenheim 1982

The next two routes are located on the face across the wash from the OB routes. They climb the large, obvious arch reached just after passing the large gully system that leads to the Crabby Appleton Area. From *Cat in the Hat*, hike 200 yards upstream (west) and then take a left (south) and bushwhack up to the base of the arch.

124. Yurawanka Arch 5.10a ★★ Traditional. Climb the lower, left arch. Rappel from fixed nuts.
FA: Jay Smith, Paul Van Betten 1986

125. Unknown A3 ★★★Climb the higher arch and rappel from sketchy fixed anchors.
FA: Unknown

▲ CHALLENGER WALL
NE AM Sun   Approach: 2 hours

The Challenger Wall is located in the back of the south fork of Pine Creek Canyon. To get there, walk the trail into Pine Creek Canyon for 20 minutes. The trail takes you alongside a low band of red rock below the Brass Wall. Continue until the trail forks at the far-left (west) end of the red band. Take the left fork, moving into a wash and hiking into the south fork of Pine Creek. Follow a trail out of the wash, up the steep right (west) edge of the wash toward Mescalito Buttress. Hike alongside the southeast cor-

ner of Mescalito, heading into the canyon through scrub-oak bushes and manzanita. Continue hiking alongside the south fork of the wash, between the wash and Mescalito Buttress, for about 15 minutes or 600 yards, passing *Cat in the Hat* on your right. Once in the wash, start looking up and left and the Challenger Wall will come into view. It is a dark, black, varnished wall with patches of green lichen high on the horizon at about 11 o'clock. Hike up the wash, passing a boulder on the left with a bunch of spider-webbed huecos at about head height. Continue past this for another 5 minutes to a point where it is necessary to scramble up. Look for an obvious short, white, cliff band on the left. Hike past the lowest cliff band, scramble up out of the wash, and traverse the top of the white cliff band back left (toward the east). Scramble up slabs and a bushy gully for another 10 minutes to the base of Challenger Wall. You will pass a sign on your hike up, noting that the canyons of Red Rock are designated wilderness areas.

The routes on this wall are much more difficult than routes of the same grade elsewhere in Red Rock. Climbers should have a good handle on unusual gear placements, small gear, and practice at "running it out" before climbing here. Some of the bolts and anchors on this wall have been retrobolted. Routes are described from left to right, first on the Challenger Wall proper and then to the right (west) of the Challenger Wall.

Descent: Rappel the routes using 2 ropes. Bring leaver nuts and slings just in case; not all anchors are properly equipped.

CHALLENGER WALL PROPER

126. Explorer 5.10d ★ Traditional. This is the leftmost route on the wall.
Pitch 1: 5.10d Climb the face to a small right-facing corner. Continue to a roof. Traverse left under the roof, moving up and left. Climb back right to the bolted anchor.
Pitch 2: 5.9 Continue up to another small roof. Traverse left and finish up the crack to the anchor.
FA: Paul Van Betten, Jay Smith 1986

Challenger Wall

126. Explorer 5.10d
127. Right Stuff 5.11b
128. Mission Control 5.11c
129. Space Cowboy 5.10b
130. Sheer Terror 5.10c
131. Challenger 5.10d
132. Jupiter II 5.11b
133. Astral Winds 5.11b
134. Steep Space 5.10c
135. Starfighter 5.11a
136. Invasion of Privacy 5.10c
137. Voyager 5.11b
138. Enterprise 5.11a
139. Unknown 5.10c
140. X-15 5.10d

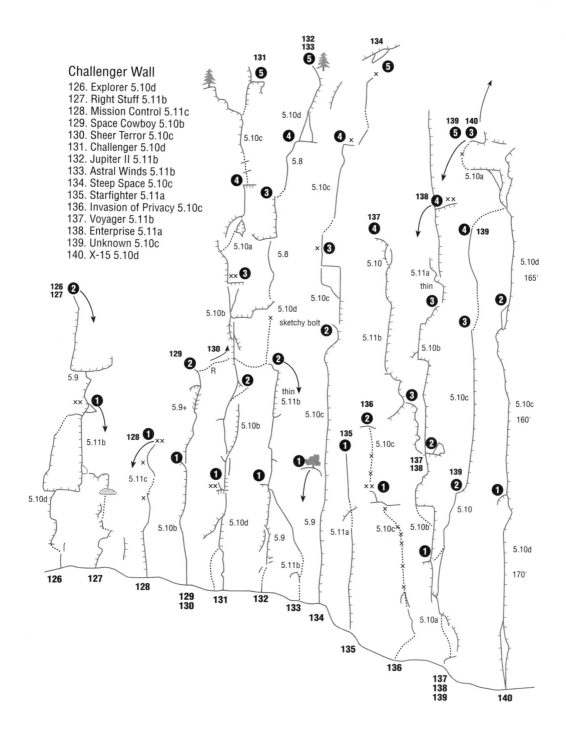

127. Right Stuff 5.11b ★★★★ Traditional. This route starts 12 feet right of *Explorer* and it shares the second pitch with *Explorer*. Stiff.

Pitch 1: 5.11b Climb the face, working between sets of cracks. Just below the anchor, traverse left to gain the right side of a roof and the right-facing crack system. Take the crack to the shared anchor with *Explorer*.

Pitch 2: 5.9 Climb the second pitch of *Explorer*.
FA: Jay Smith, Paul Van Betten 1986

128. Mission Control 5.11c ★ Mixed, 2 bolts. Climb a shallow right-facing corner to a bolt, located about halfway up the route. Continue up a thin seam, passing another bolt (crux) to the bolted anchor. Gear: brass wires and gear to #3 Friend.
FA: Mike Tupper, Paul Van Betten, Paul Crawford 1986

129. Space Cowboy 5.10b ★★★★ Traditional. This route starts just right of *Mission Control* and climbs up an obvious vertical crack system.

Pitch 1: 5.10b Climb the crack to about midheight, where the crack turns into a right-facing corner. Take the corner to a fixed anchor.

Pitch 2: 5.9+ Continue up the crack system to a small ledge and anchor.

Rappel with 2 ropes or continue on *Sheer Terror*.
FA: Paul Van Betten, Ron Olevsky 1986

130. Sheer Terror 5.10c ★★★★ Traditional. Climb *Space Cowboy* and then traverse right into *Challenger*.

Pitches 1–2: Climb *Space Cowboy*.

Pitch 3: 5.10b From the top of the second pitch, traverse right, across the run-out face to join pitch 3 of *Challenger*.

Pitches 4–5: Finish on *Challenger*.
FA: Paul Van Betten, Ron Olevsky 1986

131. Challenger 5.10d ★★★★ Traditional. Start right of *Space Cowboy*. Really good, sustained climbing on this one.

Pitch 1: 5.10d Climb up, just left of the left-facing crack near the center of the wall. Continue up to a roof. Pull the roof and continue up and left in the

crack to a small sloping belay ledge.

Pitch 2: 5.10b Continue up the crack which turns into a right-facing crack. Take it to its end and traverse right to fixed anchors.

Pitch 3: 5.10b Traverse right to another vertical crack. Take it up to a roof. Move left under the roof to an arête. Climb to the belay ledge.

Pitch 4: 5.10a Head up discontinuous cracks. After reaching the face, traverse right to the top of a pillarlike feature and bolted anchors.

Pitch 5: 5.10c Climb up a thin, technical face to a left-running ramp with a tree on it. Do not climb the ramp; pass it and head slightly back and right to the final belay ledge.
FA: Jay Smith, Randal Grandstaff 1986

132. Jupiter II 5.11b ★★★★★ Traditional. Begin on a face 20 feet right of the previous route. A good adventure.

Pitch 1: 5.9 Climb the smooth dark face to a short left-leaning crack, which turns into a small chimney. Continue up, following a right-facing crack to a tiny belay ledge.

Pitch 2: 5.11b Follow a thin seam straight up the wall, leading to a left-facing corner. Belay above the corner on a tiny ledge. This pitch is the meat of the route; some say it is one of the best pitches in Red Rock.
FA: Paul Van Betten, Sal Mamusia 1986 (pitches 1, 2)

Pitch 3: 5.10d From the belay, head slightly left and up the face to a sketchy bolt just below a small roof. Climb past the right edge of the roof and continue up to under another small roof. Head right and up a right-facing corner. Belay atop the corner.

Pitch 4: 5.8 Move out right to gain a crack running up and right to a belay ledge.

Pitch 5: 5.10d Follow the left edge of a flake up and finish on a left-facing corner, leading to a tree.
FA: Paul Van Betten, Paul Crawford, Nick Nordblom 1986 (pitches 3, 4, 5)

133. Astral Winds 5.11b ★★ Traditional. This route starts right of *Jupiter II* and joins *Jupiter II* at the second pitch.

Pitch 1: 5.11b Climb the face to an obvious crack,

running up and left to the first belay of *Jupiter II*.

Pitches 2–5: Climb *Jupiter II*.

FA: Paul Van Betten, Sal Mamusia 1986

134. Steep Space 5.10c ★★★ Traditional. This route climbs up a prominent left-facing corner capped by a roof above the second pitch (crux), and then takes crack systems to the top of the route.

Pitch 1: 5.9 Work your way up the corner to a bushy belay ledge.

Pitch 2: 5.10c Continue up the corner, finishing at a roof. Head left and up to another belay ledge.

Pitch 3: 5.10c Climb the face using the crack systems to a small, 1-bolt belay ledge.

Pitch 4: 5.10c Climb up, heading slightly right to the crack. Continue to another 1-bolt belay anchor.

Pitch 5: Continue to the pitch 5 belay, below a roof.

FA: Paul Van Betten, Paul Crawford, Paul Obenheim 1986

135. Starfighter 5.11a ★ Traditional. Climb the next major crack right of *Steep Space*. Follow the left-facing crack until it ends. Continue up a face to a small roof. Finish up the small crack, which leads to a rappel anchor.

FA: Robert Finlay, Paul Van Betten 1986

136. Invasion of Privacy 5.10c ★★★★ Mixed, 8 bolts. This route climbs the short crack that is capped with a bolted, thin face.

Pitch 1: 5.10c, 6 bolts. Start up the crack, placing gear. Once the crack ends, continue up the lichen-covered, thin face, clipping bolts that lead up to a bolted belay/rappel anchor.

Pitch 2: 5.10c, 2 bolts. From the anchor continue up the face, passing 2 more bolts to a small ledge.

FA: Unknown

137. Voyager 5.11b ★★★ Traditional. Start right of *Invasion of Privacy*. Routes 137–139 share the first pitch.

Pitch 1: 5.10a Start up a small, short ramp below and left of a high right-facing corner. Climb up just left of the corner to a belay ledge below a straight-in crack.

Pitch 2: 5.10b Climb the left-facing corner above

the belay ledge and skirt the roof, heading left on the face below the roof. Finish up the crack to the belay ledge.

Pitch 3: Traverse the face left to gain a large flake system. Climb this to its top and belay.

Pitch 4: 5.11b Head left from the belay to gain a left-facing corner. Climb it to a small ledge. Angle left again to the belay above a tiny rock formation.

FA: Jay Smith, Paul Van Betten 1986

138. Enterprise 5.11a ★★ Traditional. Climb the first two pitches of *Voyager* and then head straight up the left-facing crack system.

Pitches 1–2: Climb the first two pitches of *Voyager*.

Pitch 3: 5.10b Climb straight up the obvious left-facing crack, which opens up after about 40 feet. Set up a belay near the top.

Pitch 4: 5.11a Finish up using two crack systems, climbing right after the first crack to obtain another left-facing corner that leads to a bolted belay anchor.

FA: Jay Smith, Randal Grandstaff 1986

139. Unknown 5.10c ★ Traditional. Climb the first pitch of *Voyager* and then traverse right to another—you guessed it!—crack.

Pitch 1: 5.10a Climb the first pitch of *Voyager*.

Pitch 2: 5.10 Head right across the face to gain another crack system, which runs straight up the wall. Follow this up to just below a left-facing corner and set up a belay.

Pitch 3: 5.10c Climb the left-facing corner to its top.

Pitch 4: Sketch your way up the face until you gain a crack that runs up the wall. Belay from atop the crack, beneath a face.

Pitch 5: 5.10a Traverse right on the face and link in with pitch 3 of *X-15*.

Pitches 6–9: 5.7–5.9 Climb three more short pitches to the top of the cliff.

Rappel.

FA: Unknown

140. X-15 5.10d ★★★★ Traditional. This route ascends a big, obvious, left-facing, wide corner on the right edge of the wall. Bring some wide gear.

Pitch 1: 5.10d Climb the wide crack heading toward the big band of red rock. Belay on a good ledge. 170 feet.

Pitch 2: 5.10c Continue climbing up the corner, through the band of red rock. 160 feet.

Pitch 3: 5.10d Like the previous pitch, continue up the corner, following the feature as it starts to head left. Traverse left and up under the roof, clip a bolt, and belay on a tiny ledge. 165 feet.

Pitches 4–7: This route has been topped out, but is not recommended because of loose and extremely dirty rock.

FA: Jay Smith, Paul Van Betten 1986

WEST OF CHALLENGER WALL

The following route is located right of the Challenger Wall, around the corner from it. It begins at a much lower elevation, but higher than the wash.

141. Adventure Punks 5.10c ★★ Traditional. Climb left-facing corners for five pitches. See the climbers topo for detail. Very poor belay on the final anchor. Another heads-up climb put up by the adventure punks themselves. Gear: Friends to #6. Rappel the route.

FA: Richard Harrison, Nick Nordblom, Paul Van Betten 1983

The next three routes are right of the large, dark brown wall you reach before the Challenger Wall on the hike up, just five minutes west of Challenger Wall proper.

142. The Rooster Ranch 5.10c ★★ Mixed. This route consists mostly of bolts, but may require some gear.

Pitch 1: Climb the leftmost bolted line on the large, dark brown face around the corner, right, from the Challenger Wall. Belay from the bolted anchor.

Pitch 2: Continue climbing the line of bolts, adding gear where needed.

Rappel from the upper bolted anchor using 2 ropes.

FA: Paul Obenheim 1986

143. Cocaine Tiger 5.11d ★★ Mixed. Climb the hand crack right of *The Rooster Ranch*, located

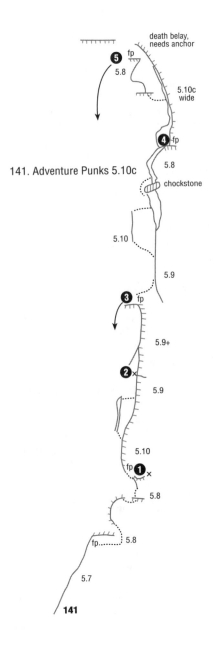

141. Adventure Punks 5.10c

slightly up a small gully. Climb the crack to a roof. Pull the roof on the left side, pass a couple of bolts, and rappel or lower off the bolted anchor. Gear: standard rack to #3 Friend and brass wires.
FA: Paul Crawford, Paul Van Betten, Richard Harrison, Charles Cole, Rusty Reno 1986

144. Unknown 5.10a ★ Mixed. This is the rightmost bolted route in this sector. Climb up, clipping bolts to the bolted belay.
FA: Unknown

▲ JET STREAM WALL
NE AM Sun   Approach: 1.3 hours

Jet Stream Wall is up and left of Challenger Wall. Walk the trail into Pine Creek Canyon for 20 minutes. The trail takes you alongside a low band of red rock below the Brass Wall. Continue until the trail forks at the far-left (west) end of the red band. Take the left fork, moving into a wash and hiking into the south fork of Pine Creek. Follow a trail out of the wash, up the steep right (west) edge of the wash toward Mescalito Buttress. Hike alongside the southeast corner of Mescalito, heading south into the canyon through scrub-oak bushes and manzanita. Continue hiking alongside the south fork of the wash, between the wash and Mescalito Buttress, for about 15 minutes or 600 yards, passing *Cat in the Hat* on your right. Once in the wash, start looking up and left and the Challenger Wall will come into view. It is a dark, black, varnished wall with patches of green lichen high on the horizon at about 11 o'clock. Hike up the wash, passing a boulder on the left with a bunch of spider-webbed huecos at about head height. Continue past this for another 5 minutes to a point where it is necessary to scramble up. Look for an obvious short, white, cliff band on the left. Hike past the lowest cliff band, scramble up out of the wash, and traverse the top of the white cliff band back left (toward the east). Scramble up slabs and a bushy gully for another 10 minutes to the base of Challenger Wall and continue east past it. Jet Stream Wall is so named because when a gust of wind blows through the area, the wall snaps and cracks like a giant flag snapping in the wind.

145. Sidewinder Select 5.10a ★★★ Traditional. Climb an obvious corner on the wall in three pitches.
FA: Paul Van Betten, Bob Finlay 1986

▲ CRABBY APPLETON AREA
E AM Sun   Approach: 1 hour

To reach the Crabby Appleton Area, take the trail out of the parking lot, heading into Pine Creek Canyon. The trail takes you alongside a low band of red rock below the Brass Wall. Continue until the trail forks at the far-left (west) end of the red rock band (at the north fork of Pine Creek). Take the left fork, moving into a wash, hiking into the south fork of Pine Creek. Follow a trail out of the wash, up the steep right (west) edge of the wash toward Mescalito Buttress. Follow alongside Mescalito, paralleling it and heading farther into the south fork of Pine Creek through scrub-oak and manzanita bushes. Upon approaching the mouth of a gully on the right, go left, hiking down into the wash. Bushwhack up the hill on the other side of the wash (southeast) toward a gully on the opposite (south) side of the wash. Upon reaching the entrance to the gully, fourth- and fifth-class up it, staying on the right side. You will first enter a small tunnel. Continue up the gully to a small cave; crawl through a hole/tunnel in the top of the cave and continue hiking to a big ledge on the right. Fifth-class scrambling leads to the ledge. You will pass a sign on your hike up, noting that the canyons of Red Rock are designated wilderness areas. Routes are described from left to right.

Descent: Hike right (northwest) along the top of the feature. Take a ramp heading down and east, toward the beginning of the routes. Take the ramp to the base.

146. Crabby Appleton 5.9+ ★★★ Traditional. Hike around left and up to another large ledge where the route begins. Start at the top of a left-facing ramp above the ledge. Run-out and described as loose by some.

Pitch 1: 5.3 Traverse along a ledge to reach a vertical crack. Climb the crack to a ledge. 100 feet.

Pitch 2: 5.7 Climb a crack up, traversing right into

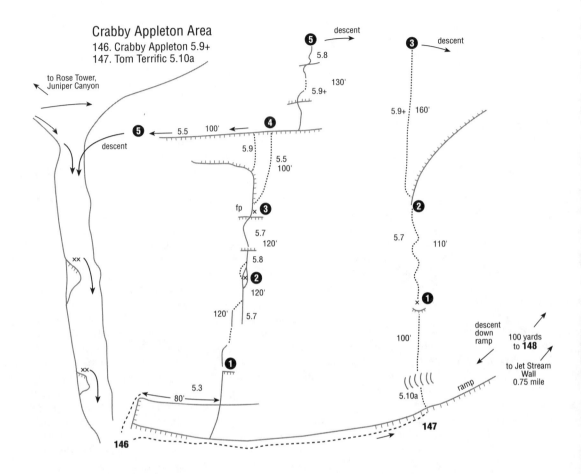

Crabby Appleton Area
146. Crabby Appleton 5.9+
147. Tom Terrific 5.10a

another crack. Take the second crack to a hueco and belay. 120 feet.

Pitch 3: 5.8 Move left out of the hueco and connect with a crack, pull a roof, and continue up to a ledge with a bolt and pin anchor. 120 feet.

Pitch 4 variation 1: 5.5 Ascend the left-facing arch for 20 feet. Move right and up onto a black, varnished face leading to a ledge below a headwall. 100 feet.

Pitch 4 variation 2: 5.9 Continue up the arch, heading straight up the wall where the arch starts to curve left. Finish on the large ledge above. 100 feet.

Pitch 5 variation 1: 5.9+ Move right on the ledge for 20 feet to a vertical crack. Climb up and over

a roof, onto the headwall to the top of the cliff. Belay in a crack. 130 feet.

Pitch 5 variation 2: 5.5 Traverse left along the large ledge. 100 feet.
FA: Richard Harrison, Wendell Broussard, Paul Van Betten 1982

147. Tom Terrific 5.10a ★★ Traditional. Begin right of *Crabby Appleton* on the descent ramp. Gear: standard rack to a #4 Friend.

Pitch 1: 5.10a Pull a bulge and then climb the face to a scoop with a bolt. 100 feet.

Pitch 2: 5.7 Continue up the face to the bottom

left edge of a huge right-facing arch. Large Friends for the anchor. 110 feet.

Pitch 3: 5.9+ Move left of the arch and up the face to the top of the cliff. 160 feet.

FA: Richard Harrison, Wendell Broussard 1985

148. Creepshow 5.10d ★★ Mixed, 4 bolts. Climb through black water streaks on the face 100 yards right and up the ramp from *Tom Terrific*. The first ascent was done without any of the bolts (R/X), which were later added by another party who thought they were doing a first ascent.

Pitch 1: Climb a crack to a hueco to a bolted anchor.

Pitch 2: 5.10d, 4 bolts. Climb the face through bulges to the top of the cliff.

FA: Robert Finlay, Richard Harrison 1985

▲ COMMUNITY PILLAR/MAGIC TRIANGLE
NW PM Sun   Approach: 45 minutes

Take the trail out of the parking lot, heading into Pine Creek Canyon. The trail takes you alongside a low band of red rock below the Brass Wall. Continue until the trail forks at the far-left (west) end of the red

rock band (at the north fork of Pine Creek). Take the left fork, moving into the wash.

These routes are located left (east) of the mouth of the *Crabby Appleton* gully. Most of the routes are between the *Crabby Appleton* gully and the first gully to its left (the *Cartwright Corner/Chocolate Flakes* gully).

Approach option 1: Continue up the wash into the south fork. Follow a trail out of the wash, up the steep right (west) edge of the wash toward Mescalito Buttress. Follow alongside Mescalito, paralleling it, heading father south into the south fork of Pine Creek through scrub oak and manzanita bushes. Upon approaching the mouth of the gully leading to *Cat in the Hat* on the right, go left, hiking down into the wash. Bushwhack up the hill on the other side of the wash (southeast) toward the gully. The rightmost routes in this area (*Edge of the Sun* and *Lunar Escape*) begin on the wall at the bottom left side of the mouth of the gully (east side of the gully).

Approach option 2: Hike across the wash and obtain a trail on the other side that parallels the northwest-facing cliffs above. Follow the trail, which dips in and out of the wash, until you can take a trail uphill to the base of the routes. This is a less distinct trail and is more difficult than option 1, but requires

less bushwhacking.

Bushwhack along the base to reach the routes. Routes are described from left to right.

149. Community Pillar 5.9 ★★★ Traditional. Located just 70 feet left (east) of the *Cartwright Corner/Chocolate Flakes* gully, this route begins in an enormous chimney that is about 10 feet wide. Gear: to #6 Friend.

Pitch 1: 5.9 Climb the chimney to the enormous chockstone. Move left around the chockstone to a ledge or squeeze through a hole between the chockstone and the wall. Belay on the ledge above. 140 feet.

Pitch 2: Fourth class. Move up the crack for about 100 feet to the top of a short pillar.

Pitch 3: 5.6 Move up the chimney right and then squeeze through another hole created by a giant chockstone against the wall. 80 feet.

Pitch 4: 5.8 Climb a wide crack on the right to a ledge under a roof. 130 feet.

Pitch 4 variation: 5.9 Climb the crack left of the off-width to the belay ledge under the roof.

Pitch 5: 5.8 Climb the crack left of the roof and belay in the slot. 100 feet.

Pitch 6: 5.8 Move up the chimney to a ledge to its left. 120 feet.

Pitch 6 variation: Climb the crack outside the chimney. 120 feet.

Pitch 7: Fourth-class up a crack, angling up and right to a ledge.

Pitch 8: 5.6 Climb and scramble 200 feet to the top of the buttress.

Descend by rappeling from a pine tree into the *Cartwright Corner/Chocolate Flakes* gully. There is a lot of loose rock, so tread lightly. Bushwhack down the gully. An alternate descent involves hiking up the buttress to the Crabby Appleton Area and taking that descent or the gully east of *Crabby Appleton*. *FA: Joe Herbst, Tom Kaufman 1976*

Hike right to the first gully you come to. Enter it to find the next two routes.

150. Cartwright Corner 5.10b ★★★★★ Traditional. Begin at a varnished corner midway up the

left side of the *Cartwright Corner/Chocolate Flakes* gully. Start right of *Community Pillar* at a flat, vegetated area. The first pitch is not so nice, but the subsequent pitches make up for it. Gear: standard rack to a #6 Friend and brass nuts.

Pitch 1: 5.8 Climb the loose chimney to a ledge

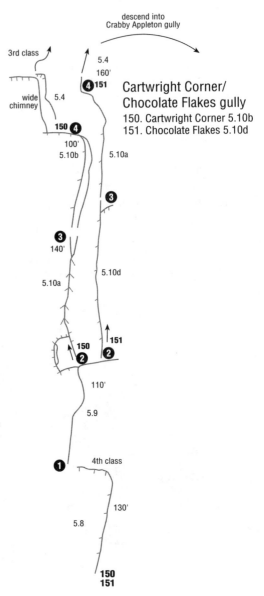

descend into
Crabby Appleton gully

3rd class

5.4
160'

151

wide chimney   5.4

**Cartwright Corner/
Chocolate Flakes gully**
150. Cartwright Corner 5.10b
151. Chocolate Flakes 5.10d

150   4

100'
5.10b   5.10a

3

3
140'

5.10d

5.10a

150   151
2   2

110'

5.9

4th class

5.8   130'

150
151

left of it, below another crack. 130 feet.

Pitch 2: 5.9 Move up the wide crack in a right-facing corner above the belay ledge. 110 feet.

Pitch 3: 5.10a Climb the left corner. It looks more difficult than it really is. Belay in an alcove. 140 feet.

Pitch 4: 5.10b Continue up the corner to a belay ledge. 100 feet.

Pitch 4 variation: 5.10d Top-rope the black, varnished face right of the corner using chips and pebbles.

Pitch 5: 5.4 Scramble to the summit. 160 feet.

Descend by hiking up the buttress to the top of the Crabby Appleton Area and taking that descent or the gully east of *Crabby Appleton*.

FA: Richard Harrison, Nick Nordblom, Paul Van Betten Wendell Broussard 1985

151. Chocolate Flakes 5.10d ★★★ Traditional. Begin as for *Cartwright Corner*, sharing the same first two pitches.

Pitches 1–2: Climb *Cartwright Corner*.

Pitch 3: 5.10d Climb the right, right-facing corner to a ledge and belay.

Pitch 4: 5.10a Continue to the top of the corner.

Pitch 5: 5.4 Scramble to the summit. 160 feet.

Descend by hiking up the buttress to the top of the Crabby Appleton Area and taking that descent down the ramp or descend the gully east of *Crabby Appleton*.

FA: Robert Findlay, Tom Ebanoff 1985

FFA: Paul Van Betten, Nick Nordblom 1985

152. Dukes of Hazard 5.9 ★★ Traditional. Climb the pillar 50 feet right of the *Cartwright Corner/Chocolate Flakes* gully. 100 feet.

FA: Randal Grandstaff, Shelby Shelton 1983

153. Five and Dime 5.10b ★★ Mixed, 4 bolts. Climb the sharp arête on the pillar, just right of *Dukes of Hazard*. Contrived and poorly bolted. 100 feet. Rappel off *Small Purchase*.

FA: Unknown

154. Small Purchase 5.10a ★★★★★ Traditional. Begin 15 feet right of *Five and Dime*, in an alcove below the right-facing corner. Take the corner to a fixed bolted anchor. Gear: standard rack, double

Steven Van Betten gets some purchase on Small Purchase *5.10a on the Community Pillar*

small Friends to #2. 100 feet. Rappel with a 60-meter rope.

FA: Joe Herbst 1970s

The Magic Triangle is a dark, triangular-shaped, pointed section of rock extending from the middle to the top of the wall between *Small Purchase* and *Edge of the Sun*.

155. Midnight Oil 5.11a ★★★ Traditional, 1 bolt. Begin directly below the Magic Triangle, right of

Small Purchase. Climb a corner and crack to a face with a thin seam splitting it. Finish on sloper mantels to a corner. Continue up, clipping a bolt, to fixed anchors. Scary. Gear: 2 ropes and doubles of everything to #4 Friend. Rappel.

FA: Richard Harrison, Paul Crawford, Randy Marsh 1983

156. Clone Babies 5.10d ★★ Traditional. Begin 50 yards right of *Midnight Oil.* Climb steep double cracks to the top of a pillar. Gear: brass wires and a standard rack to #3 Friend. 160 feet. Rappel using 2 ropes.

FA: Paul Crawford, Richard Harrison 1983

157. Magic Triangle 5.9+ ★★ Traditional. Begin in cracks on the left side of the Magic Triangle. Climb a right-angling ramplike feature up and right to the top of *Edge of the Sun.*

Pitch 1: 5.8 Climb a 3- to 4-inch crack up the lower left section of the Magic Triangle. 100 feet.

Pitch 2: 5.8 Continue up the crack system (still 3–4 inches). 100 feet.

Pitch 2 variation: 5.9, 2 bolts. Halfway up the crack, traverse out left onto the face. Face climbing and bolts lead to a belay ledge.

Pitch 3: 5.8 Traverse right, go down two steps and then up. Traverse the large ledge right to a crack just right of the center of the formation. 100 feet.

Pitch 4: 5.8 Climb up the crack and face to a ledge on the left. 120 feet.

Pitch 5: 5.8 Move up the crack and face to a large ledge. 120 feet.

Pitch 6: 5.9+ Traverse right 30 feet to a crack. Climb this up and then go left and up through a finger crack. A scary pitch. 165 feet.

Pitch 7: 5.5 A short section leads to the top. 40 feet.

To descend, from the summit go left to gain the top of the gully, just left of the Magic Triangle. Downclimbing and rappels lead to the base of the route (four 2-rope rappels).

FA: Joe Herbst, Randal Grandstaff 1977

"The Bottle" is a rock formation right of the Magic Triangle and left of *Edge of the Sun.* It looks like a bottle with a wide lower slab section that pinches off as it rises towards the top.

158. Bottle Bill 5.9 ★★ Traditional. This route climbs the crack system up the left side of the Bottle. Gear: long runners and Friends to #4.

Pitch 1: 5.9 Third-class behind a large detached block. Take a hand crack up to a face, then traverse left up a ramp to a niche.

Pitch 2: Climb out the left side, ignoring the off-width on the right. Climb right to reach a hole and belay.

Pitch 3: Move up to a roof. Climb left to a hanging belay.

Pitch 4: Pull the bulge and climb a right-facing corner to a big ledge.

Pitch 5: Climb overhangs to the top (or move off, traversing directly left).

Hike left and do three rappels and some third- and fourth-class climbing down a gully.

FA: Joe Herbst, Tom Kaufman 1977

159. Five Pack 5.10 ★★ Traditional. This route climbs the crack up the right side of the bottle formation.

Pitch 1: 5.7 Take the crack and chimney to a big ledge.

Pitch 2: 5.7 Take the face up using smaller cracks to a belay stance below a big roof.

Pitch 3: Climb the squeeze chimney around the roof.

Pitch 4: 5.10 Climb the crack to the base of another roof. Take the face around the right side of the roof and then head up to a crack between a roof and the main wall. Finish up the crack.

To descend, hike left and descend as for *Bottle Bill.*

FA: Joe Herbst, Tom Kaufman, Steve Allen, Scott Woodruff, Larry Hamilton 1977

160. Edge of the Sun 5.10d ★★★ Mixed. Begin just left of the arête at the entrance to the *Crabby Appleton* gully, right of *Five Pack.* Gear: to #3.5 Friend.

Pitch 1: 5.10a Climb the crack up the varnished wall to an odd face. Continue to a ledge on the left. 150 feet.

Pitch 2: 5.9+, 5 bolts. Move up and right off the ledge and climb the thin face left of the arête to a bolted belay under a roof. 80 feet.

Pitch 3: 5.10d, 4 bolts. Move left to a varnished face, clipping bolts to a bulge. Pull over the bulge and climb the vertical face, clipping bolts to the huge ledge at the top. Fixed anchor. 160 feet.

Rappel using 2 ropes.

FA: Dave Wonderly, Warren Egbert 1988

161. Lunar Escape 5.11a ★★★ Mixed. Begin 20 feet right of *Edge of the Sun*. Gear: standard rack to #2 Friend.

Pitch 1: 5.10a Climb the steep varnished face to a bolted anchor. Wires and small Friends. 80 feet.

Pitch 2: 5.10, 7 bolts, sport pitch. Traverse right. Move up the face to a bolted anchor.

Pitch 3: 5.11a Continue up to the anchors of *Edge of the Sun*, climbing a steep, bulging, varnished headwall.

Rappel *Edge of the Sun* using 2 ropes.

FA: Dave Wonderly, Warren Egbert 1988

▲ THE PINK CORNER
NE AM Sun Approach: 30 minutes

To reach the Pink Corner, take the trail out of the parking lot, heading into Pine Creek Canyon. Just after the foundation for an old homestead is a trail marker pointing down and left into a meadow, to the Pine Creek Loop and the Arnight Trail. Take the Arnight Trail into the meadow and across Pine Creek. After crossing the creek, continue on the trail until it splits. Take the Arnight Trail and the Oak Creek Trail, which head left, toward a low red band of rock. Look for a slight trail that heads up and right, below the right edge of the low red band. The trail is very faint and heads up the steep hill, along the left (east) side of a drainage. Upon approaching the low red band, cut right (west) across the drainage and continue uphill on the right side of the drainage. Head for a huge pink corner at the base of the escarpment, up and right of the red band. Routes are described from left to right.

162. Dog Police 5.10c ★★★★ Traditional. Climb the obvious straight-in crack 150 feet up the gully left of the pink arête, climbing the center of the east face on black, varnished rock. Move up to the white face to a ledge with a tree. Rappel using 2 ropes. A second pitch has been attempted by Paul Van Betten and Neil Cannon.

FA: Richard Harrison, Sal Mamusia, Paul Van Betten 1983

163. Without a Paddle 5.11d ★★★ Sport, 8 bolts. Climb the pink arête immediately left of the pink corner, to the bolted anchor under the roof.

FA: Mike Tupper 1988

164. Dependent Variable 5.12c ★★★ Mixed, 3 bolts. Climb the tips, lieback, pink corner 5 feet right of *Without a Paddle* to the anchor up and right on the right face. Loose rock getting to the first gear placement. Bolts are 1/4-inch and old star bolts (meaning they are sketchy!). A short second pitch leads to the anchor of *Without a Paddle*. Gear: to #1 Friend.

FA: Mike Tupper 1988

165. Cold Blue Steel 5.10b ★★★ Mixed, 5 bolts. Climb the varnished groove just right of *Dependent Variable*, sharing the same start. Loose rock getting to the first bolt. Be careful. Gear: bring supplemental gear to a #1.5 Friend.

FA: Greg Mayer 1988

166. Unknown 5.10b ★★★ Traditional. Climb the obvious black, varnished crack just right of *Cold Blue Steel* to the *Cold Blue Steel* anchors. Very loose crumbly rock to obtain the crack system. It would be five stars if it weren't for the dirt mound comprising the start. Gear: standard rack to #4 Friend. Rappel.

FA: Unknown

JUNIPER CANYON

Rose Tower ▲ Jack Rabbit Buttress ▲ Upper Jack Rabbit Buttress ▲ Brownstone Wall
Rainbow Wall ▲ Cloud Tower Area ▲ Rainbow Mountain/Ginger Buttress

To REACH JUNIPER CANYON from Las Vegas, take West Charleston Boulevard west, which turns into State Route 159. Drive over the 215 Beltway and zero your odometer. Turn right into the Red Rock Canyon National Conservation Area, 5.9 miles past the 215 (2 miles past Calico Basin Road). Enter the 13-mile Scenic Drive through the kiosk entrance booth.

Juniper Canyon is 10.5 miles from the entrance kiosk. Park in the Pine Creek Canyon parking lot.

Hike downhill on the well-beaten Pine Creek Trail. After about 10 minutes you will pass a junction with the signed Dale Trail on the right. Continue straight on the Pine Creek Trail as it meanders left. Shortly, at a large ponderosa pine tree, where the trail comes very close to Pine Creek, go left. Hike along the creek for 200 feet. Cross the creek, heading south until you reach a trail that meanders right (west) and then southwest, toward the rock. Hike up the hill and then take a left, heading south. Pass a large juniper tree on the right. Parallel the rock (heading slightly away from it) through a prickly section of cacti on a red dirt path. At a T where a wooden sign points left and right, take the trail left (west) for 15 minutes.

Roxanna Brock on the first free ascent of Emerald City *5.12d, Rainbow Wall.*

Photo courtesy of Roxanna Brock collection

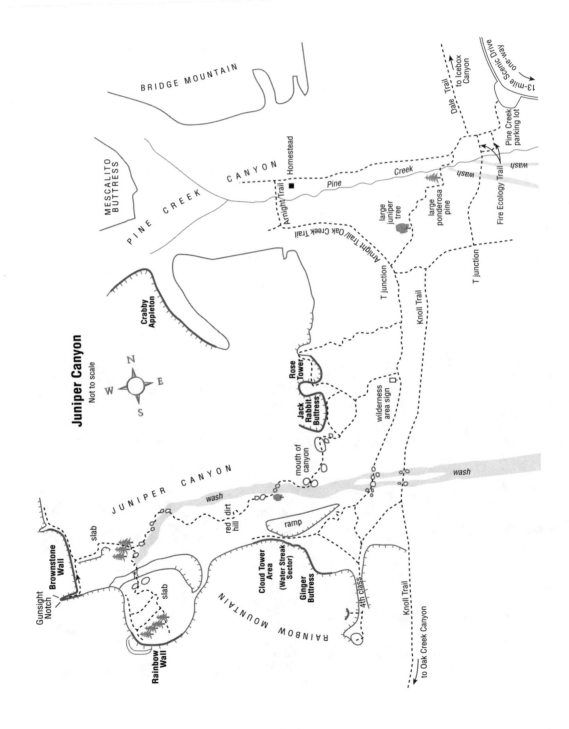

Juniper Canyon

Not to scale

▲ ROSE TOWER
SW PM Sun   Approach: 45 minutes

At a wilderness area signpost, take the trail going right, toward the rock. Follow a red dirt trail for 5 minutes and then take another red dirt trail cutting off right (northwest), toward the left side of Rose Tower. Hike up the gully left of Rose Tower, along the right edge. Pass under a low roof on the left corner of Rose Tower and scramble up the gully to a shady spot at a huge left-facing corner/chimney system. *Olive Oil* begins on the pocketed slab just left of the chimney. The first pitch ends in an alcove with a tree about 120 feet up. Routes are described from left to right.

Descent: Hike right, between the boulder and the left wall, reaching a sort-of drainage. Hike left up the drainage and then right to the top of the ridge. Traverse the ridge right and then slab down and left to a notch. Some fourth-class moves take you down to a notch. Take the trail east down the hill. It will eventually meet up with the approach trail.

1. One Armed Bandit 5.7 R ★★ Traditional. This climb is just left and up the gully from the classic *Olive Oil*. Gear: full rack including Friends to #6.

Pitch 1: 5.7 Climb the straight-in crack to the ledge on the right and set up a belay. 75 feet.

Pitch 2: 5.7 Head right, up the flakelike feature to its top. Angle left to a small ramp and back right to the top of the big left-facing corner and belay. 100 feet.

Pitch 3: 5.7 Follow the seam above the belay. Belay below the start of a chimney. 80 feet.

Pitch 4: 5.6 R Climb the loose, rotten chimney until it opens up. Continue up a left-facing crack to a second ledge and belay. 140 feet.

Pitch 5: 5.7 Climb up, following a crack and corner to its top. Belay on a large ledge. 110 feet.

Pitch 6: Fourth class. Scramble off the right side of the ledge to the top of the formation.
FA: Larry Hamilton, Tom Kaufman 1976

2. Olive Oil 5.7 ★★★★ Traditional. Begin on a pocketed slab left of a wide chimney. You can climb

this route with a shorter rope in more pitches. Gear: standard rack to a #4 Friend.

Pitch 1: 5.7 Climb the slab and then angle right to a thin crack at the top. Take the crack and flare to

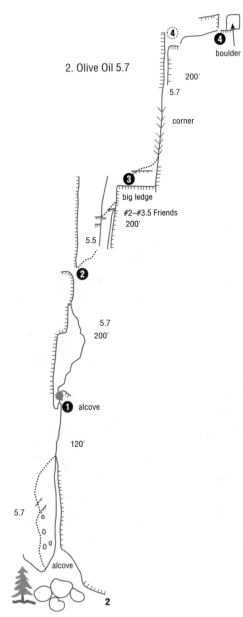

2. Olive Oil 5.7

a sandy alcove with a tree. 120 feet.

Pitch 2: 5.7 Take a right-angling crack out of the left side of the alcove. Take it and right, then up the wall. Angle left toward a right-facing corner at the top. Climb the right-facing corner to a rounded ledge. 200 feet.

Pitch 3: 5.5 Move right about 20 feet and take a crack through ledges, midway between right- and left-facing corners. Traverse right to the right-facing corner and take it up to a large ledge. Build a belay with #2 to #3.5 Friends. 200 feet.

Pitch 4: 5.7 Angle up and right on the featured, varnished face directly above the ledge. Obtain the left-facing, flared corner. Climb straight up the widening crack, pulling a few chimney squeezes. Continue up to a small ledge. Take a crack on the right, heading up and right to a large boulder and the top of the feature. 200 feet.

FA: *George and Joanne Urioste, John Williamson 1978*

▲ JACK RABBIT BUTTRESS
E AM Sun   Approach: 45 minutes

At a wilderness area signpost go right. About 150 yards before entering the mouth of Juniper Canyon start looking for a faint trail leading up and right to the base of Jack Rabbit Buttress. From the base of the main portion of the wall head left and around its corner. Pass a large, detached rock outcropping on the right and head to a north/south running gully. *Geronimo* climbs the first dogleg crack on the black, plated face on the left. Routes are described from left to right.

3. Geronimo 5.7 ★★★★ Traditional. This route starts around the corner left of the main Jack Rabbit face and *The Monday Funnies*. It gets better as you get higher. Facing east, it sees sun most of the day. Gear: an assortment, including micronuts, nuts, and Friends to #4.

Pitch 1: 5.6 Climb the dogleg crack just left of a white patch of rock at its base. Follow the crack, which is surrounded by black plates. Climb past a ledge and small bulge to a huge ledge. 160 feet.

Pitch 2: 5.6 Follow the crack feature off the left edge of the ledge. Continue up the crack and face to a bolted anchor on a ledge and belay. 180 feet.

Pitch 3: 5.7 Climb the black face, aiming for the

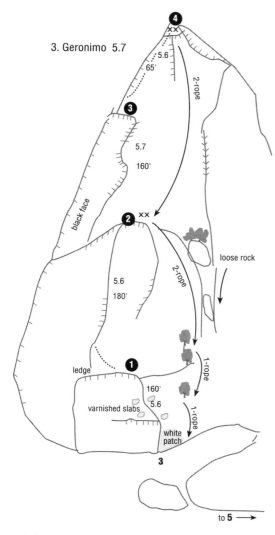

3. Geronimo 5.7

4. Juggernaut 5.10c/d ★★★ Traditional. This one-pitch route is on the main face of Jack Rabbit Buttress. The route begins 200 feet right of the left edge of the cliff base. Climb the good right-facing crack, starting on a section of pink rock. Follow the crack to a ledge, 15 feet up, with a large chockstone wedged into the crack. Continue climbing the crack to the fixed anchor, right of a big ledge. Gear: a set of micronuts and Friends to #2.5. 85 feet. Rappel. *FA: Paul Van Betten, Paul "Obie" Obanhein 1983*

5. The Monday Funnies 5.9 ★★★ Traditional. This route starts 200 feet right of the previous route. Climb the center of the east face of the rock formation, beginning in a large, obvious, cavelike feature. Some loose rock. Gear: wide selection, from micronuts to a # 5 Friend.

Pitch 1: 5.9 Start in the cave and chimney and climb up to a roof with a crack through its center. Climb the crack up and onto a ledge, below a short finger crack. Take the finger crack to another smaller roof, angling right, and tunnel behind a flake, which leads to a belay ledge. 90 feet.

Pitch 2: 5.8 From the ledge, follow the crack system to the right of the belay. Climb the crack to the next belay ledge.

Pitch 3: 5.7 Head for the two separate crack systems that run up and left across the wall. The left crack is filled with bushes. Work up, using the two cracks, leading to the top of the formation.

To descend, from the top of the formation, traverse and scramble the ridge back to the northwest. Eventually the formation will meet up with the *Olive Oil* gully on the right. Scramble down this gully back to the base of the wall. 1 hour. *FA: Mark Moore*

▲ UPPER JACK RABBIT BUTTRESS
SE AM Sun   Approach: 50 minutes

This is the next buttress past the Jack Rabbit Buttress to the southwest: it is just left of *Geronimo*. To approach, continue up the trail that leads into Juniper Canyon. Keep looking up and right for a large black boulder on the right. The routes start near this boulder and are described from left to right.

skyline on the left. This will lead to a small belay stance. 160 feet.

Pitch 4: 5.6 Head up and slightly right. Follow a low-angled face to the final belay and rappel anchor. 65 feet.

From the top of the formation, rappel with 2 ropes to the anchor above pitch 2. From there do another double-rope rappel to a tree. Two shorter, single-rope rappels reach the start and gully. *FA: Michelle and Bill Cramer 1992*

Descent: From the top, head directly west toward the base of Brownstone Wall. Once at the base of the wall, head left (south) and then east down Juniper Canyon.

6. Rose Hips 5.7 ★★★ Traditional. The large black boulder marks the start of this route.

Pitch 1: 5.7 Start at the base of a left-leaning chimney. Climb up and left of the chimney, for about 120 feet. Move into a crack that heads up and right. Set up a belay next to the crack at 200 feet.

Pitch 2: 5.7 Follow the crack, which leads to another chimney and roof. Turn the roof on the left side and finish up a left-facing corner. Belay in the crack over the roof. 110 feet.

Pitch 3: 5.6 Climb the left-facing crack until it slims to a shallow thin seam. Belay just before the crack peters out, making it impossible to get gear placements. 100 feet.

Pitch 4: 5.6 R Traverse right, across a run-out face for about 35 feet, until you reach a large corner/crack system. Follow the crack straight up. 185 feet.

Pitch 5: 5.4 Continue up the crack to a large belay ledge. 50 feet.

Pitch 6: 5.3 Follow the crack in the low-angled white face to the top of the formation.
FA: Chris DaBroski, John Hoffman 1999

7. Myster Z 5.7 ★★★ Traditional. Named in honor of a lost friend, Zach Martin. This route starts around the left corner of *Geronimo*, 100 yards north of where Juniper Canyon pinches off. Look for a tree/scrub oak in an alcove and start climbing.

Pitch 1: 5.6 Climb the dogleg crack just under the roof and chimney, and belay under the roof. 125 feet.

Pitch 2: 5.7 Climb over the roof and continue up the crack, moving right through the slot. Finish up the crack on the slabby face. 180 feet.

Pitch 3: Third class. Scramble up and left across the zebra-striped face to a bush at the base of a crack and belay. 190 feet.

Pitch 4: 5.6 Climb up the crack to a rock on a pedestal. 170 feet.

Pitch 5: 5.6 R Climb the run-out crack, stemming left around the bush, and move right to a crack leading through the roof. Set up the belay in a slot near a

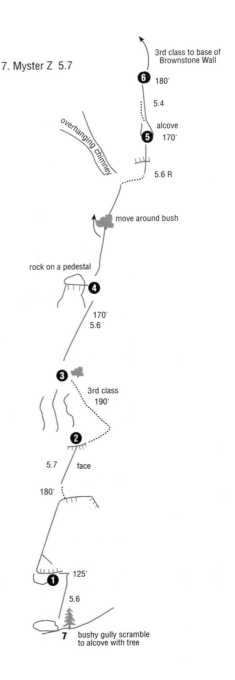

7. Myster Z 5.7

large rock. 170 feet.

Pitch 6: 5.4 Stem up a flaring crack leading to third-class climbing and the base of Brownstone Wall. 180 feet.

FA: Phil Broscovak, Jim Newberry 2002

▲ BROWNSTONE WALL
SE All-Day Sun   Approach: 2 hours

At a wilderness area signpost, take the trail going up and right, toward the cliff. Follow this trail as it parallels the rock, passing Rose Tower and Jack Rabbit Buttress. After hiking atop a very large boulder, descend its other side and go through bushes to reach two very large boulders, sitting side by side, blocking the trail and entrance to the wash. Climb over or crawl under the space between these boulders and then head right and up the wash for a short distance. When the terrain looks rough (bushes) go left, on the left side of the wash, well-marked with cairns. Stay left of the main wash but continue in the creek bed, moving through many boulders up and left. At a steep red dirt hill, climb out of the wash to a trail ascending it. At the top of the hill, continue up the canyon, hiking on the left side of the wash. After hiking through many boulders you will reach a spot under a large ponderosa pine where you can go slightly right under the pine or left, slabbing over a large boulder back into the wash. Go right, passing underneath the pines to the base of a large slab. Take the slab up and left, wandering along its left edge to its top, at the base of the Brownstone Wall. Routes are described from left to right.

Gunsight Notch descent: Hike to the top of Brownstone Wall and then hike south along the top of the wall to Gunsight Notch between Brownstone and Rainbow Walls. Do one rappel and then hike down the gully.

8. Peanut Brittle 5.6 ★★★ Traditional. Climb the varnished face left of *The Black Dagger*, starting at a pine tree.

Pitch 1: Third and easy fifth class. Take cracks to a recess and belay.

Pitch 2: 5.5 Climb out of the alcove and climb up for about 10 feet. Move right, around a corner. Take the crack that climbs through a varnished face to a stance. 150 feet.

Pitch 3: 5.5 Follow the crack farther, through a roof to a ledge and belay. 80 feet.

Pitch 4: 5.6 Pull a roof to an overhanging face to another roof. Surmount the second roof and belay on the ledge above. 150 feet.

Pitch 5: 5.5 Take a crack, continuing up through varnished faces to the summit of a pillar.

Pitches 6–7: Climb pitches 5 and 6 of *The Black Dagger*.

FA: Joanne and George Urioste 1978

9. The Black Dagger 5.8 ★★★★★ Traditional. Head up a right-facing corner, right of an overhang on white rock. This is the obvious splitter crack on the left side of the wall.

Pitch 1: 5.4 Climb the right-facing corner to a face to the top of a block below a white roof. 125 feet.

Pitch 2: 5.7 Climb through the roof using the crack on its left side. Move right on a varnished face to a right-facing corner. Take the corner up to a ledge below another large right-facing corner. 135 feet.

Pitch 3: 5.8 Climb the large right-facing corner. Belay below a chimney. 125 feet.

Pitch 4: Fourth class. Climb the chimney to a hole. Move left out the hole onto a large belay ledge on top of a pillar. 90 feet.

Pitch 5: 5.6 Move up a face to a right-facing corner. Move up and belay on the highest ledge, under a roof. 110 feet.

Pitch 6: 5.6 Climb the face to the roof. Pull the roof to a right-facing crack. Take the crack to a ledge. Scramble up cracks and slabs for 300 feet to the top of the Brownstone Wall.

FA: Joe Herbst, Rick Wheeler 1977

10. Cat Scratch Fever 5.8 ★★★ Traditional. Begin 100 feet right of *The Black Dagger*. This route follows crack systems to a roof. Pull the roof and take offset cracks up a pink and black wall through another roof to the top of the wall.

Pitch 1: 5.7 Take the crack and face to a bolted anchor underneath a roof. 150 feet.

Pitch 2: 5.8, 1 bolt. Move right to the right edge of the roof. Climb a crack to its end and then move left to obtain another crack. Follow the crack to a stance and belay. 150 feet.

Pitch 3: 5.6 Resume climbing the crack. 150 feet.

Pitch 4: Fourth class. Move right to another crack. Climb to a ledge underneath the second roof. 55 feet.

Pitch 5: 5.6 Pull the roof and take the crack to the top of the wall. 150 feet.

FA: Joanne and George Urioste, John Rosholt 1978

11. Me, Myself, and I 5.7 ★★ Traditional. Begin about 140 feet right of *Cat Scratch Fever*. Take the white face up to a main crack that splits the pink upper face. Gear: standard rack to #5 Friend.

Pitch 1: Easy fifth class. Start beneath the main crack system taking a gully-type formation up the white rock. Belay in a depression. 75 feet.

Pitch 2: 5.7 Take discontinuous cracks up to the pink-colored rock. Move left for 40 feet to the main crack system. 85 feet.

Pitch 3: 5.5 Climb the main crack system. 145 feet.

Pitch 4: 5.5 Continue up the main crack system. 165 feet.

Pitch 5: 5.7 Take a chimney to the top of the wall. 165 feet.

FA: Randal Grandstaff

12. Bad Guys Approaching 5.10c, A0 ★★ Traditional, 1/4-inch bolts. Climb the corner left of *Time's Up*. Gear: standard rack plus triples of Friends #3 and #4.

Pitch 1: 5.10a Climb the crack left of *Time's Up*.

Pitch 2: 5.10b/c, A0 Traverse right to a left-facing corner. Climb the corner to its top and continue up the face. Pendulum right, 15–20 feet to another crack. Move up the crack and then face-climb to the belay.

Pitch 3: 5.8 Continue up the face to a large belay ledge.

Pitch 4: 5.10c, 2 bolts. Traverse right and take a large left-facing corner to its top. Climb the off-width to 2 1/4-inch bolts.

Pitch 5: 5.10a Climb the face to the top of the

corner that ends at a belay station in poor rock. Very run-out. Fixed pins, dirty and scary. Best not to do this pitch.

Rappel.

FA: Paul Van Betten, Robert Findlay 1989

13. Time's Up 5.11d ★★★★ Mixed, 1/4-inch bolts. Climb the left side of the huge hourglass feature. Gear: standard rack to #4 Friend; you could lead this route on all traditional gear with big cams (Friends to #5 or #6).

Pitch 1: 5.9 Begin on the face below the left side of the large hourglass-shaped rock feature. Climb the face to the crack and the crack to a 2-bolt belay. 110 feet.

Pitch 2: 5.10a Move up the face and crack to a ledge out right and belay. 45 feet.

Pitch 3: 5.11d From the ledge, move left back into the crack. Take it as it widens into a chimney. Pull a roof at the top of the chimney, entering a thin stemming crack. Continue to two-bolt hanging belay. 110 feet.

Pitch 4: 5.10a Continue up the crack to a bolted anchor. 90 feet.

Pitch 5: 5.8 R Move up the crack and then take a loose face up and right to a big ledge at the top of the hourglass. 80 feet.

Rappel *The Nightcrawler* because the anchors are more safe.

FA: George and Joanne Urioste, Mike Ward, Bill Bradley 1984

FFA: Richard Harrison, Jay Smith

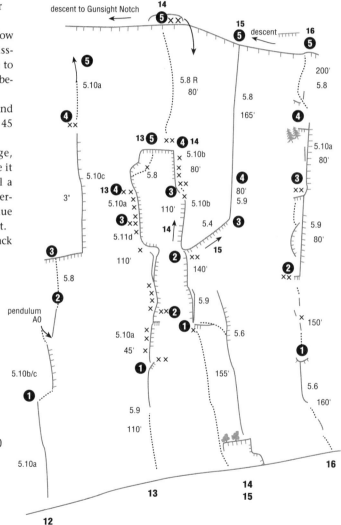

Brownstone Wall
12. Bad Guys Approaching 5.10c, A0
13. Time's Up 5.11d
14. The Nightcrawler 5.10b
15. Hourglass Diversion 5.9
16. High Anxiety 5.10a

14. The Nightcrawler 5.10b ★★★★★ Mixed. The route begins right of *Time's Up* and climbs the right side of the hourglass feature. Gear: standard rack to #3 Friend.

Pitch 1: 5.6 Begin on the face, down and right of the right side of the hourglass. Climb the face up and left to the crack. Take the crack up to the single-bolt belay. 155 feet.

Pitch 2: 5.9 Move up the wide crack to a chimney to a right-facing corner. Take it to where the angle decreases at a 2-bolt anchor. 140 feet.

Pitch 3: 5.10b, 6 bolts. Climb the orange right-facing corner as it thins. Move up the thin bolted face to a bolted anchor. 110 feet.

Pitch 4: 5.10b Move up the corner to the top of the hourglass feature and the bolted anchor. Rappel the route from here or climb pitch 5. 80 feet.

Pitch 5: 5.8 R Move up the thin face with little gear (brass wires) to the top of the cliff. 80 feet.

Rappel from fixed anchors or take the Gunsight Notch descent.

FA: George and Joanne Urioste 1978

15. Hourglass Diversion 5.9 ★★★ Traditional. Begin on *The Nightcrawler*, climbing pitches 1 and 2, and then traverse out right to a thin crack to the summit.

Pitches 1–2: Climb *The Nightcrawler* pitches 1 and 2.

Pitch 3: 5.4 From the top of pitch 2, traverse right on the right-angling ramp to the base of a thin, varnished crack.

Pitch 4: 5.9 Ascend the thin crack. 80 feet.

Pitch 5: 5.8 Continue climbing the crack to the top of the wall. 165 feet.

Rappel *The Nightcrawler* or take the Gunsight Notch descent.

FA: George and Joanne Urioste, John Rosholt 1978

16. High Anxiety 5.10a ★★★ Traditional. Climb the large, left-facing, varnished dihedral right of *The Nightcrawler* and left of the gap splitting the Brownstone Wall.

Pitch 1: 5.6 Begin on the white face, below and right of the big left-facing corner. Climb to a depression in the rock. 160 feet.

Pitch 2: 5.8, 1 bolt. Take discontinuous cracks and the face to the ledge and bolted anchor beneath the left-facing corner. 150 feet.

Pitch 3: 5.9 Take the flake left of the left-facing corner. Continue to a ledge and a bolted anchor. 80 feet.

Pitch 4: 5.10a Climb up the corner, as it widens to a chimney. Continue to a stance above trees. 80 feet.

Pitch 5: Take discontinuous, broken corner systems, ledges, and less-than-vertical faces to the top. 200 feet.

Rappel from the top of *The Nightcrawler* or take the Gunsight Notch descent.

FA: Joanne and George Urioste 1978

17. The Birthday Cake 5.6 ★★ Traditional. Begin on the far right of the right section of Brownstone Wall, above Jack Rabbit Buttress. Climb a low-angled, highly featured face, black and pink in color.

Pitch 1: 5.4 Climb the face to a stance.

Pitch 2: 5.4 Continue up the face to a bush-covered ledge.

Pitch 3: 5.6 Pull an overhang and continue up the face.

Pitches 4-6: Easy fourth and fifth class. Continue to the top of Juniper Peak.

Descend by hiking left (south) along the top of the Brownstone Wall. Descend by way of the first gully down to the base.

FA: Will Miller, George and Joanne Urioste 1978

▲ RAINBOW WALL
N AM Sun (in summer)   Approach: 2–4 hours

At a wilderness area signpost, take the trail going up and right, toward the cliff. Follow this trail as it parallels the rock, passing Rose Tower and Jack Rabbit Buttress. After hiking atop a very large boulder, descend its other side and go through bushes to reach two very large boulders, sitting side by side, blocking the trail and entrance to the wash. Climb over or crawl under the space between these boulders and then head right and up the wash for a short distance. When the terrain looks rough (bushes) go left, on the left side of the wash, well-marked with cairns. Stay left of the main wash but continue in the creek bed, moving

Brian O'Keefe ascending the Rainbow Wall approach slab using fixed ropes. Photo by Roxanna Brock

through many boulders up and left. At a steep red dirt hill, climb out of the wash to a trail ascending it. At the top of the hill, continue up the canyon, hiking on the left side of the wash. After hiking through many boulders you will reach a spot under a large ponderosa pine where you can go slightly right under the pine or left, slabbing over a large boulder back into the wash. Take a left, slabbing over a large boulder back into the wash (Brownstone Wall is to the right from under the large ponderosa). Take the wash up and left, reaching a big white slab. Go left up some bouldery sections. Do a couple of third- or fourth-class moves to the top of some boulders. Continue up and right through more boulders to reach the Rainbow Wall approach slab (with fixed ropes). After testing the ropes, hand-over-hand up the slab. Continue hiking up the slab, weaving back and forth across the center. Routes are described from left to right. Beware of the ring-tailed cats—they will not hurt you, but will steal the food right out of your hands!

Before Joe Herbst and Larry Hamilton did the first ascent of the *Herbst/Hamilton Route*, there were many attempts at climbing this wall. The burly approach, the remoteness, and the magnitude of the north-facing feature made for a daunting experience. After Herbst and Hamilton proved it could be done, there was an assault on the wall. *Battle Royal* was the second route done (still one of the most difficult) and the only one to be done in a single push. *Sergeant Slaughter* was next (another classic). The others followed. Later, after Leo Henson and Dan McQuade freed the *Herbst/Hamilton*, a storm of free climbers showed up, adding new routes, freeing aid lines, and even adding new aid lines. Several of the aid lines are still stout enough to have resisted free ascents. Few routes other than the *Herbst/Hamilton* get climbed on this wall. Beware of climbing here in the winter and spring when the rock can be wet or icy and easily fractures.

Alternate descent: Descend off south toward red, rounded features in the back of Oak Creek's north fork. Hike right (southwest) down the ridge above Oak Creek. Follow the hike-off per the top of *Levitation 29* in Oak Creek (Eagle Wall).

18. Sergeant Slaughter V, 5.12b or 5.10b, A2
★★★★ Traditional. Climb the crack system 30 feet

left of *The Big Payback* (the huge right-facing flare on the left side of the wall). Gear: doubles to #4 Friend, 1 each of #5 and #6; for aiding, bring 6 each of knifeblades, Lost Arrows, and angles (to 3/4-inch).

Pitch 1: 5.7 Climb the obvious straight-in crack on

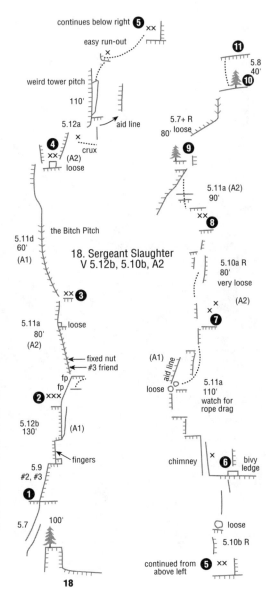

the far left of the wall. It looks somewhat dirty, but is good. Stop at a ledge. 100 feet.

Pitch 2: 5.12b or 5.9, A1 Continue up the crack, angling right. When it moves to the right take thin fingers up to a crack that widens to #6 Friend size. 130 feet.

Pitch 3: 5.11a or A2 Take the thin, loose crack up to enter a wide flare. Take it up, squeeze through its top, pulling a thin move to the anchors. 80 feet.

Pitch 4: 5.11d or A1 Take the squeeze flare up to a stance. Called the *Bitch Pitch* and you will find out why. 60 feet.

Pitch 5: 5.12a or A2, 2 bolts. Do a thin, technical move past a bolt up and right to a right-facing corner. Take the corner up and then traverse right on a thin face, past 1 bolt, up and right to fixed anchors. The aid variation traverses farther right to another right-facing crack, with run-out face climbing to the anchor. 110 feet.

Pitch 6: 5.10b R Loose and scary white-rock face climbing up and right to a huge bivy ledge. 80 feet.

Pitch 7: 5.11a or A1 Traverse left into the squeeze chimney. Take it up as it gets smaller. Pull out of it, onto a blocky ledge system. Climb thin seams up a right-facing corner and then move right to a ledge and belay. 110 feet.

Pitch 8: 5.10a R or A2, 2 bolts. Climb the loose, run-out face up to a ledge. The crux is off the belay. 80 feet.

Pitch 9: 5.11a or A2 Move up and left through ledge systems to a right-facing and leaning corner. Enter the corner and pull around the roof at the top to belay off a huge pine tree. 90 feet.

Pitch 10: 5.7+ R Move up a right-facing, right-angling corner to its top. Move slightly left and straight up on loose rock to a ledge and belay. 80 feet.

Pitch 11: 5.8 Take the face up to the top of the cliff. 40 feet.

Rappel the *Herbst/Hamilton*, with a 60-meter rope.
FA: Richard Harrison, Paul Van Betten 1984
FFA: Roxanna Brock, Brian McCray 1998

19. The Big Payback V, 5.10, A3 ★★★ Traditional/aid. This route climbs the huge right-facing flare up bright orange rock on the left side of the wall. This one is a serious undertaking. Gear:

doubles to #4 Friend, 1 each of #5 and #6; bring a good selection of pins including bird beaks and hooks; the crux pitches are entirely aid.

Pitch 1: 5.7 Climb the first pitch of *Sergeant Slaughter*. 100 feet.

Pitch 2: Third class. Traverse right to the thin crack below the wide flare. 40 feet.

Pitches 1–2 variation: 5.10 R Instead of doing the first two pitches, climb the unprotected face below the wide flare. 100 feet.

Pitch 3: A3 Take a thin crack up into the flare. 150 feet.

Pitch 4: A3 Continue up the wide flare. 100 feet.

Pitch 5: A3 Move up to the top of the roof and then belay. 150 feet.

Pitch 6: Traverse right to a crack and then take the crack up above the flare system. Scary. 100 feet.

Pitch 7: A3 Follow the crack system up, angling right to a big ledge (bivy ledge). 150 feet.

Pitch 8: A2 Move up and left on an unprotected face to another crack system. Take it up and angle right to a single-bolt belay station. 110 feet.

Pitch 9: 5.9, A2 Take the face up, angling right to a 2-bolt belay. 150 feet.

Pitch 10: 5.9, A1 Climb a crack up and right to a ledge. 150 feet.

Pitch 11: 5.9 Face-climb right and then move back left. 200 feet.

Rappel the *Herbst/Hamilton* with a 60-meter rope.
FA: Kevin Daniels, Tony Sartin, Dave Evans 1998

20. Emerald City V, 5.12d or 5.10c, A2 ★★★★ Traditional. Begin 100 yards right of *The Big Payback* on a slab right of the main crack system, near a large, dead tree stump. Gear: doubles to #5 Friend, 1 #6 Friend; for aiding, bring 4 knifeblades, 3 Lost Arrows, and 2 baby angles.

Pitch 1: 5.10b Take the slab up and left to a straight-in crack. Climb it to a fixed anchor. 100 feet.

Pitch 2: 5.12d or A1 Chalk up your sweaty palms, there are no holds on the stemming corner. Move up and right, climbing to a left-facing open book. Pull onto a ledge at a right-facing corner to a belay stance. 110 feet.

Pitch 3: 5.10a Step left to a crack system. Move up to another stance. 110 feet.

Pitch 4: 5.10c Move up and left, in a crack to a roof. Pull the roof and move up and right, past a large block to another stance. 150 feet.

Pitch 5: 5.12a or A1 Move up on a lichen-covered slab to a chimney. Squeeze up to a natural anchor. 120 feet.

Pitch 6: 5.10b R Move left around the chimney onto a face. Take the face up to a loose pillar. Climb the pillar to a left-facing crack. Hand-traverse left on a ledge with loose rock at the top of the crack. Pull up to the mega bivy ledge. Belay at a single-bolt belay. Scary and loose pitch. 130 feet.

Pitch 7 free line: 5.11b Take the crack, moving up and right from the ledge. Follow it up to a ledge with a natural anchor. 110 feet.

Pitch 7 aid line: A1 Take the crack straight above the belay ledge and anchor. 110 feet.

Pitch 8: 5.6 Traverse a ledge left to the top of the aid crack to below a right-facing arch. Free-climb only. 40 feet.

Pitch 9: 5.10c Take the right-facing arch up and right through loose rock. Then take a right-facing

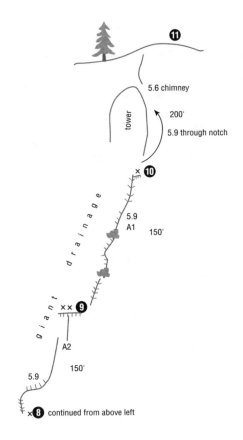

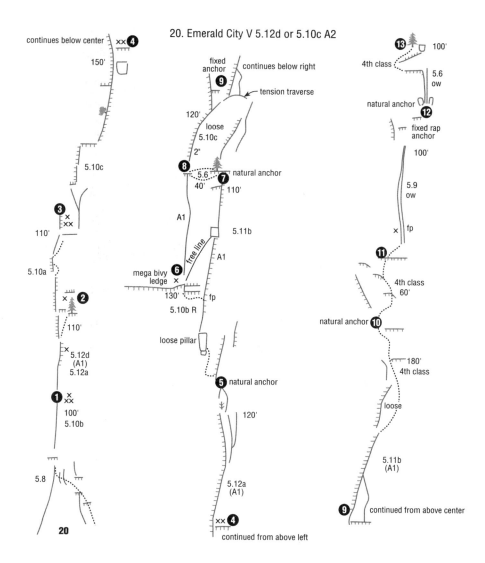

20. Emerald City V 5.12d or 5.10c A2

crack up to a fixed anchor, above a ledge. 120 feet.

Pitch 10: 5.11b or A1 Take the right-angling, right-facing crack up and right and then face-climb up and left on bulges to a ledge. Build a belay. 180 feet.

Pitch 11: Fourth-class up a wide groove to the base of a fat off-width. 60 feet.

Pitch 12: 5.9 Climb the off-width and belay on the big ledge above it. 100 feet.

Pitch 13: 5.6 Climb a short off-width and then

move up and right to a large pine tree. 100 feet.

Rappel the *Herbst/Hamilton* with a 60-meter rope.
FA: Randal Grandstaff, John Thacker 1983
FFA: Roxanna Brock, Brian McCray 1998

21. Crazy World V, 5.7, A4 ★ Traditional/aid. Follow a striking, thin line up the center of the wall, but not quite to the summit. Begin left of a large, black water streak. Gear: three sets of brass wires, two sets of Rocks, three sets of cams to #1 Friend, 2 #2 Friends, 1 each of #3, #4, and #5 Friends; also bring 7 short, thin knifeblades, 5 Lost Arrows, 15 RURPs, hooks including a Fish Hook, 4 3/8-inch bolt hangers, and copperheads (25 #1, 30 #2, 20 #3, 10 #4, and 25 3/8-inch extras).

Pitch 1: 5.7 Climb a fourth-class ramp to the top of a triangular nose. Take a groove up to a bolted belay.

Pitch 2: A3 Climb out of the groove and then move up the thin seam to a ledge right of a sharp, detached roof on the left.

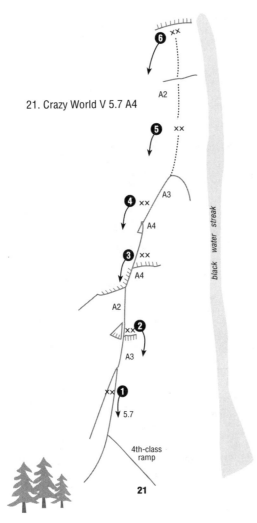

21. Crazy World V 5.7 A4

Pitch 3: A4 Continue up the seam to a right-facing corner. Pull a roof and then belay at the fixed anchor. One hook move.

Pitch 4: A4 Continue up the seam, alongside the detached block (A4) to a bolted anchor.

Pitch 5: A3 Take the seam up and right to a bashy ladder.

Pitch 6: A2 Finish up the bashy ladder, using some Friends in a horizontal crack. Finish at fixed anchors underneath a roof.

Rappel the route using 2 ropes
FA: Bart Groendycke, Todd Alston 1992

22. Battle Royale V, 5.9, A2 ★★ Traditional/aid. Begin in a crack left of a small pillar with a tree on it. Difficult for its grade. Loose rock and route finding. The first-ascent party bivied on the sloped ledge beneath the pitch 7 chimney in trash bags. Gear: many small Rocks, doubles to #4 Friend, 1 each of #5 and #6 Friends, #1 Lost Arrow, #1 and #2 knifeblade, 1 each of short-thick and long-thin Bugaboos, 1 bird beak.

Pitch 1: 5.7, A2 Climb the crack to a seam to a huge flake that you can see through. Above the flake, take a seam and then face-climb left to a belay below a left-facing crack.

Pitch 2: A2 Climb the left-facing crack to under a roof. Continue up another left-facing crack. Belay at a right-facing crack.

Pitch 3: A1 Take a seam right of the right-facing crack up to a left-facing crack. Take the left-facing crack past a large detached block to a chimney. Belay at a ledge with loose blocks above the chimney.

Pitch 4: A2 Climb a right-facing corner above ledge to a roof. Take the roof to a left-facing corner, up to a right-facing corner to ledge with a tree. Continue to the next ledge and belay.

Pitch 5: A2 Climb a right-facing corner on the left of the ledge through loose rock to the middle. Pendulum right to another right-facing corner. Climb up and pendulum again, right, to a left-facing corner. Take the left-facing corner up above a roof and belay.

Pitch 6: A2 Climb a loose right-facing corner to its top. Face-climb up and left to the base of a large chimney.

Pitch 7: 5.7 Chimney! Difficult squeeze to get in.

Think about the first ascensionists sleeping on the ledge below this chimney . . . not real cozy. 60 feet.

Pitch 8: 5.8 A1 Move up a left-facing crack and then enter another chimney. Belay at the top of the chimney. 80 feet.

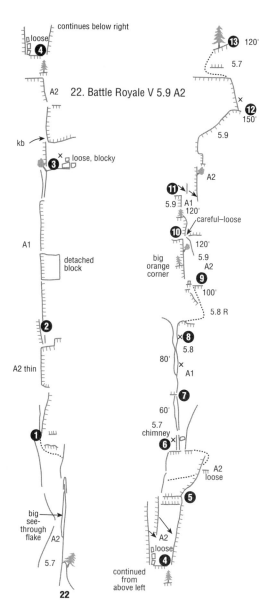

22. Battle Royale V 5.9 A2

Pitch 9: 5.8 R Move around the right side of the chimney and free-climb up a somewhat loose face to a ledge right of a huge right-facing crack with some loose blocks. 100 feet.

Pitch 10: 5.9, A2 Climb the huge right-facing crack through trees and loose blocks. 120 feet.

Pitch 11: 5.9, A1 Take a crack up and left to a pillar and stance. Sketchy, bad rock. 120 feet.

Pitch 12: A2 Pendulum right to right-facing crack. Continue up and then traverse right on bad, lichen-covered rock to a right-angling ramp. Take the ramp up to a 1-bolt belay stance. 150 feet.

Pitch 13: 5.7 Take a crack heading up and left to a ledge. Face-climb to a pine tree at the top. 120 feet.

Rappel the *Herbst/Hamilton* with a 60-meter rope.
FA: Richard Harrison, Nick Nordblom, Wendell Broussard 1983

23. Desert Solitaire V, 5.9 (5.11b), A3+ ★★★
Traditional/aid. Begin right of a narrow alcove under a roof. Nick Nordblom spent a winter contemplating, by ski lift, an ascent of what would become *Desert Solitaire*. When his partner became injured, Nordblom took the project on himself. His goal was to follow in the footsteps "of the masters" (Herbst and Hamilton). Upon completion of this route he rightly felt he was "in their shoes." Gear: doubles to #4 Friend, one set of brass wires, one set of micro Rocks, hooks including a bat hook, bird beaks, 6 rivet hangers, and 1 copperhead.

Pitch 1: 5.10d or 5.7, A1 Climb up and right on a slippery face to the top of the feature right of the alcove. Pull a roof and take discontinuous cracks to a sloping ledge with fixed anchors. 100 feet.

Pitch 2: 5.11b or A2 Climb up thin seams using microwires and brass nuts to a ledge with a pillar on it (and a nice crack exiting left). 120 feet.

Pitch 3: A3 Move up right to a wide crack. Continue to a left-facing, very thin corner. Climb the corner to a ledge with a big, very sharp cactus. Attempt to reach around the cactus to gain a crack. Climb right on some blocks and then left to a left-facing corner. Climb the corner and slabby bolted face to its left. 150 feet.

Pitch 4: A3 Take a bolted face up and right to the left edge of a right-facing corner. Move up and right

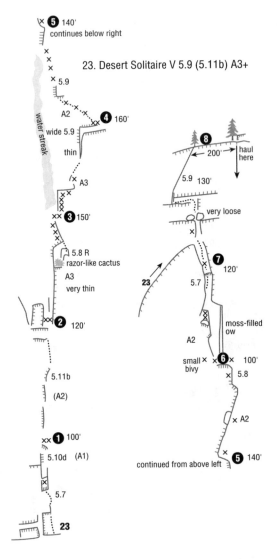

Pitch 6: A2 Move up the steep right-facing crack and then do an easy 5.8 belly flop onto a ledge up and left. 100 feet.

Pitch 7: 5.7, A2 From the left of the ledge, head up a dirty crack system, part of a large gully. Move up discontinuous cracks until you can traverse back right into the gully (above the mossy off-width). Climb the slippery slab and belay at a ledge. 120 feet.

Pitch 8: 5.9 Finish up the gully, clipping a bolt, to the top of a pillarlike feature. Clip another bolt and head up the face and crack through many loose boulders. Be *extremely* careful about what you touch. Loose rock will go straight down on top of your belayer (this is experience talking). Reach a ledge and traverse straight left 25 feet to the first crack system left of a low roof. Climb the crack up and right to a large pine tree. 130 feet. You will probably not put any gear in on this pitch because it will cause extreme rope drag. Haul off a small tree (backed up with Friends) about 200 feet up and right.

Rappel the *Herbst/Hamilton* with a 60-meter rope. FA: Nick Nordblom, rope solo 1989 (impressive!)

24. Rainbow Country V, 5.12d ★★★★ Mixed. Begin on the far-left side of the ledge at a right-facing corner. This is the direct and more difficult variation of the *Herbst/Hamilton*. Gear: brass wires, Rocks, 1 of everything to a #3.5 Friend.

Pitch 1: 5.11d, 6 bolts. Climb the right-facing crack and face up and right to the second-pitch anchors of the *Herbst/Hamilton*. 150 feet.

Pitches 3–6: Climb pitches 3–6 of the *Herbst/ Hamilton*.

Pitch 7: 5.11b Climb the face and squeeze chimney below a ledge and tree. Instead of obtaining the ledge (on the right) move up and left, climbing some ledge systems and discontinuous cracks. Obtain the right-facing crack. Move past the first set of anchors and belay at the second set. 100 feet.

Pitch 8: 5.11b Move up a thin face to a chimney. Pull out of the chimney and obtain a small roof. Pull the roof and climb to a ledge and anchor. 90 feet.

Pitch 9: 5.12d, 6 bolts. Pull the bulge onto the thin face and right-facing corner. Climb the face corner and arête to a stance above the roof. This is a sport pitch and you need only 1 small to medium

to the corner. A few hard aid moves take you to a widening crack. Step right to a ledge and build an anchor. 160 feet.

Pitch 5: 5.9, A2 Follow a line of rivets up and left on a thin slab to a small L-shaped crack. Move above the crack, taking bolts to a right-facing crack and belay. 140 feet.

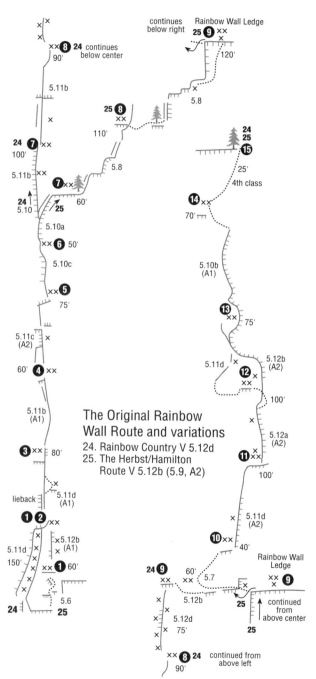

The Original Rainbow
Wall Route and variations
24. Rainbow Country V 5.12d
25. The Herbst/Hamilton
Route V 5.12b (5.9, A2)

sized nut. 75 feet.

Pitch 10: 5.12b Traverse slightly down and 40 feet right and then up and right to anchors at the base of the red dihedrals. 60 feet.

Pitches 11–15: Climb pitches 11–15 of the *Herbst/Hamilton*.

Rappel the *Herbst/Hamilton* with a 60-meter rope.

FA: Dan McQuade 1996

25. The Herbst/Hamilton Route (aka The Original Route) V, 5.12b or 5.9, A2

★★★★★ Mixed. This route is one of Red Rock's finest and the first one put up and freed on this wall. Striking crack systems and technical movement make for superb climbing. Gear: brass wires, Rocks, 1 of everything to a #3.5 Friend; for aiding bring 3 knifeblades, 3 Lost Arrows, and 2 baby angles.

Pitch 1: 5.6 Climb the low-angle slabs right of a crack to a ledge with old bolts on top of it. The ledge is just right of the main crack system splitting this wall. 60 feet.

Pitch 2: 5.12b or A1, 2 bolts. Climb left to the crack and take it up as it thins to a tiny seam. Do a big, thin edge move left and climb the thin, gray face to a small ledge and bolted anchor (or aid up the seam).

Pitches 1–2 variation: 5.11d, 6 bolts. Climb pitch 1 of *Rainbow Country*, instead of the first two pitches.

Pitch 3: 5.11d or A1 Move up a wide section of rock to a thin right-facing corner. Climb the corner and face. When a bolt appears out right of the corner, head that way *only* for free climbing: move onto the face right of the crack and take it up 15 feet; then traverse back left into the crack and up to a sloping ledge and anchors. The aid line goes straight up the crack. 80 feet.

Pitch 4: 5.11b or A1 Take the crack right of the ledge straight up to a small stance and anchors. 60 feet.

Pitch 5: 5.11c or A2 Move straight up a crack on very large, loose pillar. Move right

Dan McQuade and Leo Henson pull off the first free ascent of the Herbst/Hamilton Route *on the Rainbow Wall. Photo courtesy of Dan McQuade Collection*

to a thin seam and clip a bolt. Move up to ledge and continue up the crack to below a roof. Traverse right around the roof to a hanging belay. 75 feet.

Pitch 6: 5.10c Climb a right-facing crack up to bolted stance. 50 feet.

Pitch 7: 5.10a Move up a left-facing crack and thin slab to a wide chute. Climb up chute and move right to big ledge with a tree and belay. Good to run together with pitch 6. 60 feet.

Pitch 8: 5.8 Move right on the ledge to a big chimney. Climb the rock up the right side of the chimney. Move through another chimney, continuing up. Take a hand crack up, veering slightly right to a ledge and bolted belay. 110 feet.

Pitch 9: 5.8 Move down and right to a tree and a wide left-facing corner. Climb the corner and then move up and right on boulders and through the crack. Clip old bolts and traverse around right to a face. Take the face up to the "best bivy in Red Rock." Watch out for rope drag. 120 feet.

Pitch 10: 5.7 Traverse straight left on the ledge, clipping 1 bolt. And then move up and slightly right to a fixed anchor and small stance. 40 feet.

Pitch 11: 5.11d or A2 Climb the thin, left-facing corner. Dyno! It's good. 100 feet.

Pitch 12: 5.12a or A2 Continue up the thin, left-facing corner. Before reaching the roof traverse left and up to a ledge and fixed belay. 100 feet.

Pitch 13: 5.12b or A2, or 5.11d From the belay, traverse down and right and take the left-arching crack and roof up and left (5.12b or A2). Or, traverse down and left and then up to the top of the arch (5.11d). Finish the pitch in a pod. 75 feet.

Pitch 14: 5.10b or A1 Move out of the pod, over the roof. And take the left-facing crack to a good ledge and belay. 70 feet.

Pitch 15: Fourth class. Move up and right to a small pine tree. 25 feet.

Rappel with a 60-meter rope.

FA: Joe Herbst, Larry Hamilton 1973
FFA: Leo Henson 1994

26. Sauron's Eye V, 5.10d R, A4 ★★★ Traditional/aid. Climb the right-facing, left side of the immense red arch right of the *Herbst/Hamilton*. Climb through the middle of the roof and then up a blank face to a gully running up and right. The first ascensionist thought the arch looked like a big eye, thus the name. The feature is called Paiute Eye. Gear: three sets of Friends to #1, doubles of #2–#3, 1 each of #3.5–#6, many small to medium Rocks, a

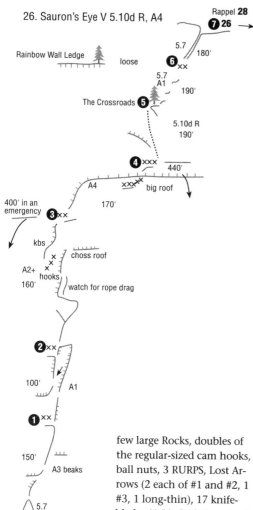

26. Sauron's Eye V 5.10d R, A4

Rappel **28**

7 **26** →

Rainbow Wall Ledge

5.7 180'

loose **6** xx

5.7 A1 190'

The Crossroads **5**

5.10d R 190'

4 xxx 440'

A4 xxx big roof

400' in an emergency **3** xx

kbs

A2+ hooks 160'

x chess roof

x x hooks

watch for rope drag

2 xx

100' A1

1 xx

150'

A3 beaks

5.7

26

few large Rocks, doubles of the regular-sized cam hooks, ball nuts, 3 RURPS, Lost Arrows (2 each of #1 and #2, 1 #3, 1 long-thin), 17 knifeblades (4 #1, 5 #2, 2 each of #3, #4, #5, #6).

This route was the unfortunate scene of an accident that almost took a well-known climber's life. With the help of a cell phone, a great partner, and an expert rescue crew, Warren Hollinger has recovered. That was his third climbing accident and he has not returned to the sport. Last we heard he was running marathons in Hawaii.

Pitch 1: 5.7, A3 Begin on top of a small pinnacle on the far-left side of the Paiute Eye (huge arch on the

wall). Climb discontinuous cracks up and right to a thin beak seam. 150 feet.

Pitch 2: A1 Climb a left-facing corner to a right-facing corner. Pendulum left to a right-facing crack. Belay at a fixed belay on a ledge. 100 feet.

Pitch 3: A2+, 3 bolts. Move up a seam to a right-facing corner under a roof. Hook-traverse left around the corner. Move up the bolted face to a right-facing knifeblade crack. 160 feet.

Pitch 4: A4, 5 bolts. Climb under, across, and over the center of the massive roof. Watch for the rope rubbing on the roof (for the second). It is best if the second aid-cleans the pitch. 170 feet.

Pitch 5: 5.10d R Climb the poorly protected face straight up to a ledge with a large pine, the Crossroads. Beware of the white soft rock. 190 feet.

Pitch 6: 5.7, A1 Climb discontinuous cracks and the loose groove up and right to a bolted belay. 190 feet.

Pitch 7: 5.7 Finish up the groove to a large ledge. 180 feet.

To descend, hike right across the top of the right side of the wall and rappel *Brown Recluse* using a 70-meter rope.

FA: Brian McCray 1999

27. The Kor Route IV ★ Traditional. Grade unknown. Begin where the rappel ends on *Brown Recluse*. Climb the center of the black, varnished face right of the Paiute Eye. The route climbs features up the lower portion of the *Brown Recluse* rappel and then heads up and left. Rappel *Brown Recluse*.

FA: Layton Kor, Allison Sheets

28. Brown Recluse V, 5.12a/b ★★ Mixed. Take the red rock ramp heading up and right to a red ledge 150 yards right of the right side of the Paiute Eye. Third-class up about 100 feet to a white rock ledge with a single-bolt anchor. Not the highest quality rock, but a fun adventure. Gear: one set of everything to #3 Friend.

Pitch 1: 5.10a, 9 bolts. Climb the face on the right of the ledge, just left of a right-facing corner to a belay ledge and fixed anchor. 120 feet.

Pitch 2: 5.11a, 4 bolts. Climb the face to a small roof. Pull the roof and move up to a seam and a fixed bolted anchor. 110 feet.

Pitch 3: 5.11c, 8 bolts. Climb the left-facing flake/corner (the brown dihedral) up and left to fixed anchors. 120 feet.

Pitch 4: 5.10b, 3 bolts. Move up the corner for a short distance and then step left onto the face. Follow bolts and inconspicuous gear up a thin seam and face, left to a ledge and bolted belay. Scary, loose pitch. 160 feet.

Pitch 5: 5.10c, 4 bolts. Take the crack up, angling slightly left to a bolted belay. Another scary, loose pitch. 120 feet.

Pitch 6: 5.11a, 5 bolts. Climb discontinuous seams up and slightly left to large ledges. Follow ledges up and right to the fixed bolted belay. 180 feet.

Pitch 7: 5.12a/b, 4 bolts. Climb ledges up and right to a thin, steep dihedral. Climb out dihedral using thin face holds. Move over a roof and then step right onto the face to reach the fixed bolted belay. 120 feet.

Pitch 8: 5.8, 3 bolts. Take the crack up and left to the fixed anchor. 100 feet.

Pitch 9: Fifth-class scrambling to summit. Traverse right and around ledges to reach a fixed anchor above the crack system. 75 feet.

Rappel with a 70-meter rope.
FA: Brian McCray, rope solo 1998
FFA: Brian McCray, Roxanna Brock 1998

29. Bird Hunter Buttress IV, 5.9

★★★ Mixed. An arrowhead found at the top of the first pitch is the reason for the name. Hike the high ledge at the base of *Brown Recluse* right to a large pine tree, at the rightmost part of the apron/ledge system. Just uphill and left of the pine you should be able to see a bolt. Take the easiest way up.

Pitch 1: 5.7, 3 bolts. Beginning at the base of the pine, climb up, veering left to the leftmost crack. Pull a bulge and continue up the face to a ledge. 130 feet.

Pitch 2: 5.7 Move left to obtain a crack. Follow it to a bolted belay. 50 feet.

Pitch 3: 5.7, 1 bolt. Continue up

the crack to another bolted belay. 115 feet.

Pitch 4: 5.8 Keep on, up the crack, up a chimney to a bolted belay beneath a tower feature leaning against the wall. 85 feet.

Pitch 5: 5.9, 5 bolts. Climb the steep face up and left to a bolted belay. 100 feet.

Pitch 6: 5.9, 3 bolts. Keep going up the face to another bolted belay and small stance. 75 feet.

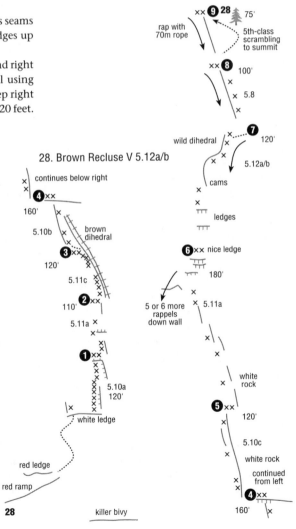

28. Brown Recluse V 5.12a/b

Pitch 7: 5.8, 1 bolt. Take the wide crack to the top of the tower.

Pitch 8: 5.9, 7 bolts. Climb up and right, along the face to a crack. Take the crack up to a ledge and belay. 120 feet.

Pitch 9: 5.8, 7 bolts. Move up the right-facing cor-

ner to a ledge below a pine tree. 125 feet.

Pitch 10: Fourth class. Take a broken ledge up and left to a pine tree. 50 feet.

Pitch 11: 5.7, 1 bolt. Climb the left-facing chimney to a bolted anchor where the chimney narrows. 95 feet.

Pitch 12: 5.8, 2 bolts. Head left onto a face to reach a crack. Climb the crack to a large ledge. 80 feet.

Pitch 13: 5.4, 1 bolt. Climb the face to blocky roofs with 1 bolt for the belay. 100 feet.

To descend, scramble left to reach a ledge. Then hike up to the top of *Brown Recluse* and rappel it using a 70-meter rope.

FA: George and Joanne Urioste 1982

30. Paiute Pillar IV, 5.9 ★★★ Traditional. Begin immediately right of the top of where you climbed, hand-over-hand, up the fixed ropes to reach the Rainbow Wall slabs. Traverse slabs right. Look for a dark red band, right of the top of the fixed ropes and a prominent splitter crack. Climb straight up the wall. See climbers topo for detail. Heady. You will be right of *Bird Hunter Buttress* and will cross it up high. Descend *Brown Recluse*.

FA: Vincent Poirier, Andrew Fulton 1998

▲ CLOUD TOWER AREA
NE AM Sun   Approach: 1 hour

At a wilderness area signpost, take the left-hand trail going straight. Go through the wash, hiking over boulders and looking for cairns. Hike out of the wash and back into another section of wash. Hike out, up and right, through some thick scrub oak. Reach a red dirt trail heading up and right. Follow it up a ramp to the Cloud Tower Area. Routes are described from left to right.

31. Tiger Crack 5.12b ★★★★★ Mixed. Begin left of *The Clod Tower*, on an easy crack that angles up to an overhanging tiger-striped wall. Be prepared to test your crack-climbing technique on every size. Gear: #Z3–#6 Friends and Rocks.

Pitch 1: 5.7 Climb the crack left of *The Clod Tower* to the base of an arching crack on an overhanging wall. 80 feet.

30. Paiute Pillar IV 5.9

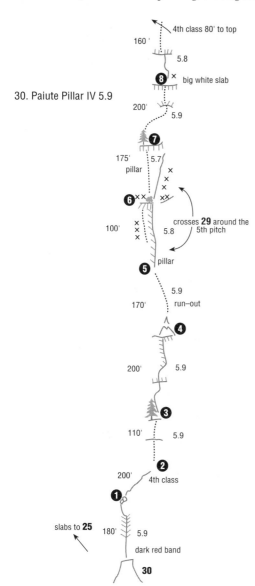

Rainbow Wall

Cloud Tower Area

Ginger Buttress Right

Water Streak
Sector
43–44

34

33

32

31

49

48

47

45

46

ramp

to Cloud
Tower

A bighorn swarm near Crimson Chrysalis. Photo by Roxanna Brock

Pitch 2: 5.12b, 2 bolts. Take the thin lieback flake to a thin finger crack. Continue up as the crack widens all the way to a #6 Friend. Undercling through the arch at the top. 80 feet.

Rappel from separate anchors or finish up *The Clod Tower* and rappel that route.

FA: Dan McQuade, Merlin Larsen 2001

32. The Clod Tower 5.10b/c ★★★★ Traditional.

On the left edge of the *Cloud Tower* formation is a small gully. To the left of that are two separate sets of vertical crack systems. Begin on an overhanging big brown wall with gold streaks. Climb the left crack, angling slightly right and finishing up a large flake, mushroom feature located just below the top of *Crimson Chrysalis*. "One of the best hand cracks in Red Rock," according to Dan McQuade.

Pitch 1: 5.10b/c From the large recess left of *Crimson Chrysalis* choose the leftmost of two cracks. Move up a steep hand crack in a varnished flare.

Pitch 2: 5.9 Continue as the crack narrows and the wall gets less steep.

Pitch 3: 5.9 Climb another, lighter-colored flare up. Move right to a prominent crack system.

Pitch 4: Follow the chimney and crack.

Pitch 5: Climb the chimney and crack.

Pitch 6: Climb the chimney and crack.

Pitch 7: Take a thin crack leading to a hand crack through a steep bulge.

Pitch 8: Scramble to the base of a wide gully and up to the base of the final pitch.

Pitch 9: Climb the right side of the gully to the summit.

The best and easiest way to descend is by rappeling *Crimson Chrysalis*. This requires serious roped scrambling up the gully to the west of the top of the route. This drainage will lead southwest to the top of the *Crimson Chrysalis* buttress. Rappel *Crimson Chrysalis* using 2 ropes. From the top of *Crimson Chrysalis*, it is also possible to descend the extension/descent as described for *Cloud Tower*.

FA: Mark Moore, Lars Holbeck 1977

At the top of the ramp, continue hiking west until you head back downhill, next to the cliff. Routes 34–37 begin here, after you hop down off a big boulder.

33. Hook, Climb and Whimper 5.10a R ★ Traditional.

Climb the face left of the start of *Crimson Chrysalis*, just before you head downhill at the top of the hike. Gear: standard rack to supplement the bolts, including micronuts and Friends to #2.5.

Pitch 1: 5.8 Start left of the obvious crack and start of *Crimson Chrysalis*. Climb the face to a high bolt,

Crimson Chrysalis
33. Hook, Climb, and Whimper 5.10a R
34. Crimson Chrysalis IV 5.8+

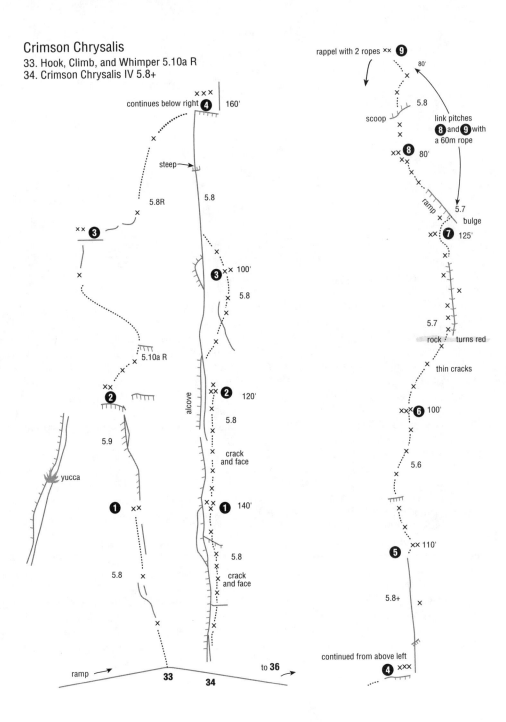

continues below right ❹ | 160'

steep →

5.8R

5.8

×× ❸

❸ ×× 100'

5.8

5.10a R

×× ❷   ❷ 120'

5.8

5.9

alcove

crack
and face

yucca

❶ ××   ❶ 140'

5.8

5.8
crack
and face

ramp →   to **36** →

33   **34**

rappel with 2 ropes ×× ❾

80'

5.8

scoop

link pitches
❽ and ❾ with
a 60m rope

×× ❽ 80'

5.7

ramp   bulge

×× ❼ 125'

5.7

rock   turns red

thin cracks

××× ❻ 100'

5.6

×× 110'

❺

5.8+

continued from above left

❹ ×××

heading for the right side of a small crack. Continue up the face to another bolt just down and left of the crack that leads to a 2-bolt belay.

Pitch 2: 5.9 From the belay, continue up the right-facing crack to a small belay ledge up and left of the top of the crack.

Pitch 3: 5.10a R From the belay, angle up and right, past 2 bolts to a small ledge/stance. Angle back left (run-out) to another bolt, and finish up the seam to a ledge and bolted anchor.

Pitch 4: 5.8 R Traverse right to a bolt. Continue up the run-out face to yet another bolt. From the last bolt traverse directly right to join the belay of pitch 4 of *Crimson Chrysalis*.

From this point, either continue up *Crimson Chrysalis* or rappel *Crimson Chrysalis* with 2 ropes.
FA: Bruce Lella, Mike Carr 1989

34. Crimson Chrysalis IV, 5.8+ ★★★★★ Traditional. Start at the right-facing corner with a crack in it.

Pitch 1: 5.8 Follow the crack up to the first bolted belay. 140 feet.

Pitch 2: 5.8 Continue climbing the main crack, and face to the right of it, to the next bolted belay. 120 feet.

Pitch 3: 5.8 From the belay, climb up the crack, angle right, and continue up the face to another bolted hanging belay. 100 feet.

Pitch 4: 5.8 From the belay, follow the main crack through a bulge. This will lead to the bolted anchor on a ledge. 160 feet.

Pitch 5: 5.8+ Continue following the crack past a small ledge feature and bolt. Follow the crack up to a small ledge and bolted belay. 110 feet.

Pitch 6: 5.6 Climb up to a bolt. Angle right to a couple more bolts on the face, and aim for the next bolted belay. 100 feet.

Pitch 7: 5.7 Work your way back and forth between thin cracks, clipping the bolts. Just past the third bolt, the rock turns red. Continue to the bolted belay. 125 feet.

Pitch 8: 5.7 Climb up and right over a steeper portion of rock to a ramp running up and left. Follow the ramp up until it ends, and finish up clipping the bolts in the black rock that lead left to the belay. 80 feet.

Pitch 9: 5.8 Climb up, passing 2 bolts that lead

Bobbi Bensman jams the last pitch of Cloud Tower 5.11d. Photo by Dan McQuade

to a little roof and scoop feature on the left. Pass this and continue up, clipping 2 more bolts, which bring you to the final belay and rappel anchors. 80 feet. The last two pitches can be linked together with a 60-meter rope.

Rappel using 2 ropes or do the extension/descent as described for *Cloud Tower*.
FA: George and Joanne Urioste 1979

35. Unknown 5.8+ ★★★ Mixed. 100 feet. Climb cracks and the face beginning right of *Crimson Chrysalis*. Rappel.
FA: Mr. and Mrs. Aaron Lennox
Topo of Cloud Tower

36. Cloud Tower IV, 5.11d (5.12d extension)

★★★★★ Traditional. Hike downhill 100 feet past *Crimson Chrysalis* to reach the obvious splitter crack start of *Cloud Tower*. Look for a tree growing out of the crack, 8 feet off the ground. Gear: small nuts, doubles of Friends to #1, a #2 Friend, doubles of Friends #2.5–#3.5, and 1 each #4 and #5 Friend.

Pitch 1: 5.8 Climb the chimney slot just below a tree. Continue up as the crack thins to a stance at another small tree. Some fixed slings. 150 feet.

Pitch 2: 5.8 Continue up the crack to a bushy ledge with loose rock. Take the fourth-class boulders up to another ledge, right of a small tree. 100 feet.

Pitch 3: 5.7 Move up and left, past the tree to a vertical hand crack. Take the crack up to a ledge. Continue up the crack a bit as it thins. Cut left across a face and up to a large, long ledge and bolted anchor (original anchor was 5 feet higher, but this is a better stance). 100 feet.

Pitch 4: 5.11d, 1 bolt. Climb up thin cracks right of a right-facing dihedral to a face with a bolt. Take the thin finger crack up the dihedral, angling slightly right to some good ledges at the top. Belay in a small alcove beneath a roof. 100 feet.

Pitch 5: 5.10a Climb to roof and then move right, around it, to a 3-inch crack. Follow the crack up as it widens. Traverse left into the off-width. Head left onto the face and to a stance and crack for gear anchors. 140 feet.

Pitch 6: 5.6 Move right, back into the crack, and chimney up. Chimney through the slot between the wall and a pillar. Step down and belay on a good ledge. 50 feet.

Pitch 6 variation: 5.10a R Climb the face right of the pillar up to the top of the pillar and build an anchor in the crack to the right.

It is possible to link pitches 5 and 6 with a 60-meter rope and good communication.

Pitch 7: 5.11d Hand- and fist-jam up the steep crack. Pull a tiny roof at the top. 160 feet.

36. Cloud Tower IV, 5.11d (5.12d extension)

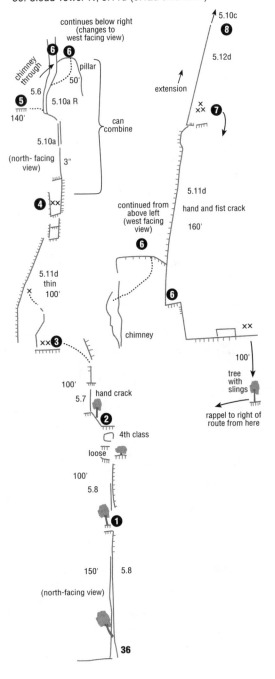

Rappel pitch 7 160 feet to fixed bolted anchors on the far-right of a sloping ledge. Do a single-rope rappel to a large tree (100 feet). Rappel toward the front of the buttress (north face) using trees to reach the top of the second pitch. Rappel over the first two pitches. Difficult rope pull from the ground.

FA: Paul Van Betten, Richard Harrison, Nick Nordblom 1983 (pitches 1–7)

Cloud Tower extension 5.12d:

Pitch 8: 5.12d Climb the thin lieback seam, clipping bolts. Do a short boulder problem on a face and continue up a sandy crack with loose rock. Pull over a big capped boulder. Take it to a ledge system, continuing to a boulder below an obvious clean crack. Bolted anchor.

Pitch 9: 5.10c Climb the hand crack above the boulder as it widens to an off-width and squeeze chimney. Well protected. Look for good huecoed holds on the face (50 feet). Continue up to the little notch below *Crimson Chrysalis*. Sit there and belay. 120 feet. Avoid keeping a big Friend in the top of the off-width, because the rope tends to wiggle it out as you top-out the slab above. From here you can hike a short distance to the top of *Crimson Chrysalis* and rappel it or continue on.

FA: Merlin Larsen, Dan McQuade 2003 (pitches 8 and 9)

Pitch 10: From the top of *Crimson Chrysalis*, fourth-class right to the next north-facing buttress.

Pitch 11: 5.8 Ascend the chimney in the recess of the buttress to a big chockstone. Belay in a box corner on top of the chockstone to avoid rope drag. 40 feet.

Pitch 12: 5.10a Climb the left side of the corner in an obvious clean, hand-sized crack (the other crack is

continues below right

wide). Continue up the corner, past looser rock (5.7/ 5.8) to the top of formation.

At the top, descend down and right (west) in a drainage. Look for rappel stations with old slings. It is possible to avoid the rappels with technical downclimbing, but it is best to do this only in daylight. This takes you to the bottom of the drainage and a 200-foot rappel (2 ropes) to the base of the wall, west of the start to *Cloud Tower*. To avoid the 200-foot rappel, head west, up and over the ridge and descend the Rainbow Wall drainage. These are good descents off *Crimson Chrysalis* because they avoid rappeling over other climbing parties and getting ropes stuck.

▲ RAINBOW MOUNTAIN/GINGER BUTTRESS
E AM Sun   Approach: 1 hour

At a wilderness area signpost, take the left-hand trail going straight. Go through the wash, hiking over boulders and looking for cairns. Hike out of the wash and back into another section of wash. Hike out, up and right, through some thick scrub oak. After exiting the wash, look for a trail that heads south toward the gully left (east) of *Ginger Cracks*. Fourth-class scramble up this gully to reach the following routes. Climb left out of this wash/gully onto a ledge with trees, grass, and bushes. Routes are described from left to right.

37. Fist or Flips 5.10 ★★★★ Traditional. This one-pitch killer crack ascends a short pillar left of *Power Failure*. Rappel from slings on top.
FA: Paul Van Betten, Mike Ward early 1980s

38. Power Failure 5.10c ★★★★ Mixed. This route begins at the top of the ledge in the wash. Begin below the smiley-face dish above a water-streaked slab on the east face of Rainbow Mountain.

Pitch 1: 5.9, 2 bolts. Climb a huecoed face with a bolt to a ledge. Move up and right to a tree and then take a crack, angling up and right. Traverse right on the face, clipping a bolt to a small stance and a 2-bolt belay anchor. 130 feet.

Pitch 2: 5.10c, 5 bolts. Take a crack up and slightly right. After a left-facing crack, move back up and left.

Rainbow Mountain
38. Power Failure 5.10c
39. Somewhere Over the Rainbow IV 5.11c

descent

39

38

Ginger Buttress Right

40

42

Water
Streak
Sector

43, 44

41

45

46

47

48 49

to 34

ramp

Finish up a crack and ramp to a bolted stance on a bulge, left of a left-facing corner. 160 feet.

Pitch 3: 5.9+ Move back right to the left-facing corner and take it to the smiley-face ledge. Belay on the smooth, water-polished ledge at a two bolt belay. 160 feet.

Rappel using 2 ropes or continue on *Somewhere Over the Rainbow.*

FA: Bill Hotz, Joanne Urioste, George Urioste, Teresa Krolak, Sam Pratt, Gary Fike 1998

39. Somewhere Over the Rainbow IV, 5.11c

★★★★ Traditional. Begin on *Power Failure.* After pitch 3 scramble and climb up and right 300 feet to a large ledge (some easy fifth class and loose rock). Traverse the ledge left about 500 feet, under a roof to the far-left edge and a black, varnished wall with a tiny seam ascending it. The last three pitches are not recommended. Gear: doubles of #1.5, #3, and #3.5 Friends; also bring #00, #0, #4, #4.5, and #5 Friends.

Pitch 1: 5.11a Climb the tiny varnished seam to an ear flake. Follow the nice crack to the Pod and belay at the bolted anchor. 140 feet.

Pitch 2: 5.7 Chimney out of the Pod to a right-facing crack. Take a seam and face up and left, through ledges to a stance and fixed anchor. Beware of the rope getting stuck in the crack. 100 feet.

Pitch 3: 5.11b Take the face up and left to a very thin, varnished crack. Ascend the crack to a right-facing crack and off-width. Climb the easy off-width to a stance to its right. 130 feet.

Pitch 4: 5.8 R Move left into the off-width and then exit left onto a featured face. Take the face up to a crack, angling slightly right. Move up to a ledge. Take the gearless face up to a hole (#4 Friend) and continue up the face with some cracks and seams to a ledge and stance. 120 feet. (Alternate belay: Continue past the ledge up and right to a good stance below a right-facing crack. No fixed anchor. From here you can combine pitches 5 and 6.)

Pitch 5: 5.10c Climb the right-facing crack to a chockstone. Move right and continue as it steepens (great hand jamming) to a hanging bolted belay. 110 feet.

Pitch 6: 5.11d Climb the chossy wide crack up to a

Geoff Conely on Unimpeachable Groping *5.10d, Rainbow Mountain.* Photo by Mike Clifford

left-facing, steepening hand crack. Take it up until it ends and then pull a roof to the next anchor. 50 feet.

Pitch 7: 5.9 Continue up the crack, pulling onto a sloping ledge. Traverse the ledge right to a left-facing crack pulling, onto another sloping ledge to anchors. 120 feet.

Pitch 8: 5.10c Take the crack above and slightly to the left of the belay to a small ledge and loose boulders. Climb up and left through "the bush"—full-on bushwhacking—to a stance in a chimney. 150 feet.

Pitch 9: 5.8 Climb out of the chimney right and then move up and left through thick bushes, moss, and grass-covered ledges through another right-facing chimney. Pull out of the chimney left and head up and left to a left-facing crack. Belay just out of the crack at a stack of dead trees. 130 feet.

Pitch 10: 5.8 Move right across a thin ledge to a good ledge right of a large chimney. Climb up to a ledge and then take the off-width up and right. Reach a tree and then a large crack. Take the crack above the ledge up to a ledge with big boulders, the top. Sign the register. 150 feet.

Rappel using two ropes. The second rappel ends midway on pitch 8. Rappel to the top of pitch 7 and continue rappeling the entire route.
FA: Roxanna Brock, Gary Fike 2001

40. Unimpeachable Groping IV, 5.10d ★★★★

Mixed. This route starts down and right of a large water streak (*Power Failure*) at the only pine tree at the base of the wall. It climbs the face and finishes at the same point on the formation as *Ginger Cracks*. Gear: carry plenty of quick draws (16) and a selection of midsized Rocks and Friends to #2.

Pitch 1: 5.10b Start by climbing up the tree until you can reach the first bolt. Clip the bolt and then face-climb up to a right-facing corner. Pass the corner and several bolts that lead to a bolted anchor on the face. 135 feet.

Pitch 2: 5.10c Continue up, following bolts that lead to another bolted anchor. 150 feet.

Pitch 3: 5.10b Climb the crack system that leads to a large ledge. 50 feet.

Pitch 4: 5.10d Follow the line of bolts to a corner on the right of a large recess. Take this to another bolted anchor. 125 feet.

Pitch 5: 5.10d Continue working your way up the short bolted face to another bolted anchor. 85 feet.

Pitch 6: 5.10c Face-climb up, staying left of the right edge of the wall and arête to a bolted anchor. 80 feet.

Pitch 7: 5.10b Continue up the face, working your way right to the top of the formation. 160 feet.

Rappel the route using 2 ropes.
FA: Michael Clifford, George Urioste 1999

41. Ginger Cracks IV, 5.9 ★★★★ Traditional.

Climb just right of the center of the *Ginger Crack* buttress's north face. Start down and right, around the corner from a large black water streak and right of the a large off-width chimney system that runs up and right on the wall. Follow a series of vertical cracks up the wall.

Pitch 1: 5.7 Climb the 6-inch, flaring, leftmost of two cracks to a large ledge. Move right to the right crack and then back left and up the side of an alcove. Belay at the top of a flake. 140 feet.

Pitch 2: 5.8 Step right and down around the flake and enter a vertical crack that opens to a chimney. Follow this through a roof and up to a ledge at the base of a right-facing corner. 145 feet.

Pitch 3: 5.7 Climb the right-facing corner to where the crack ends. 85 feet.

Pitch 4: 5.9 Traverse up and right to obtain the rightmost crack. Take it up, past 1 bolt and then back left to a belay. 150 feet.

Pitch 5: 5.8 Continue straight up the crack. Traverse a face left before reaching a large ledge. 155 feet.

Pitch 6: Fourth class. Climb a corner to another ledge and then scramble up the crack left of a bushy crack. Take a face to another large ledge, at a left-facing corner. 140 feet.

Pitch 7: 5.6 Take the left-facing corner up to a ledge. Traverse the ledge right to a larger left-facing corner. Finish atop a ledge. 110 feet.

Scramble up and left to a notch. One rappel to the south takes you down into the smiley-face ledge at the top of *Power Failure*. Third-class scramble down to the low, right (north) side of the dish and find the fixed anchors at the top of *Power Failure*. Rappel *Power Failure* with 2 ropes (three rappels).
FA: Mark Moore, Lars Holbeck 1977

42. Cayenne Corners 5.10d ★★★ Traditional. This

route is 200 feet right of *Ginger Cracks*. Start in a large recess located at the beginning of the ramp leading up to the Cloud Tower Area. Begin down and left of the Water Streak Sector, in the first left-facing corner

left of the base. The corner is dark brown and the
face to the right is white. Gear: a set of Rocks and a
double set of Friends to #4, and 1 #5; also carry several longer slings for the roof pitches.

Pitch 1: 5.9 Start up a left-facing crack. Toward the
top, angle right to a bolt, just left of another crack,
and continue to a bolted belay on a ledge. 165 feet.

Pitch 2: 5.10d Step right into a vertical crack and
follow it up a left-facing hand crack to a roof. Traverse
right, hand jamming the crack and following it as it
narrows to fingertips. Finish on a ledge. 185 feet.

Pitch 3: 5.9 Step left into the second crack feature.
Halfway up, step back right into the
main crack and climb to a bolted belay ledge—off right. 110 feet.

Pitch 4: 5.10c Take the crack to an
off-hands crack and small roof. Head
right and then straight up to just under a roof and bolted belay. 140 feet.

Pitch 5: 5.9 Angle left to a bolt.
Climb over the left edge of the roof
and follow cracks to the final belay
anchor. 90 feet.

Rappel the route using 2 ropes.
*FA: Jimmy Pinjuv, Andrew Fulton,
Steve Porcella, Gary Sutherland 2000*

WATER STREAK SECTOR

This little portion of cliff is up and
right of *Ginger Cracks*, tucked away in
a large opening at the bottom of the
ramp that leads to the Cloud Tower
Area. The main portion of the wall
has big black water streaks running
down the face. From the bottom of
the ramp, head straight south. This
leads into a gully and the wall is easily seen up on the right.

43. Chimney 5.8 ★★★ Traditional.
Climb the left edge and right-facing
corner of the Water Streak Sector.
Gear: larger gear for the second
pitch, up to a #3.5 Friend.

Pitch 1: 5.8 Climb the ramp and

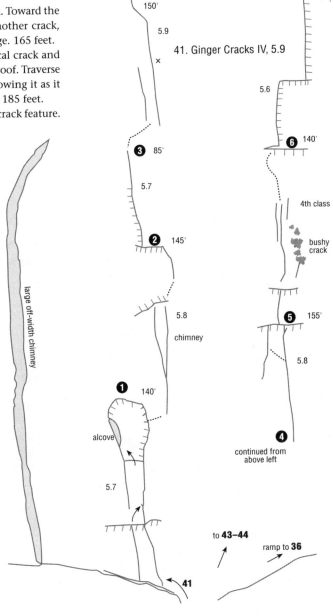

corner, which leads up and left to a ledge at the base of a right-facing corner. 70 feet.

Pitch 2: Head left into the large right-facing corner and follow it to a ledge at the top. 160 feet.

Traverse right to the anchor of *After Hours* and rappel with 2 ropes (175 feet). From the ledge toward the bottom there is another anchor. A short 70-foot rappel reaches the ground.

FA: Gary Sutherland, Jimmy Pinjuv 1997

44. After Hours 5.10b R/X ★ Traditional. This route climbs up and right of the two large water streaks on the wall, just right of the previous route and a left-facing corner. Off the ledge, atop pitch 1, the gear is very thin—be careful!

Pitch 1: 5.6 Work your way up the face to a bolted anchor near a bushy ledge. 70 feet.

Pitch 2: 5.10b R/X Climb the thin, poorly protected face just right of the rightmost water streak. The higher you get the easier the climbing. 175 feet.

Rappel the route using 2 ropes. From the ledge toward the bottom there is another anchor. A short 70-foot rappel reaches the ground

FA: Gary Sutherland, Jimmy Pinjuv 1997

The following two routes are located on the face down and right of the Water Streak Sector.

45. Sweet Honey Pumpkin Love 5.10c ★★★ Traditional. This route starts off the left side of a bushy ledge at the bottom of this wall. Gear: a set of micronuts, Rocks, and Friends to #5 or larger for the pitch 2 off-width.

Pitch 1: 5.9 R From the ledge, traverse left across the run-out face to a left-facing crack. Follow the crack up and then step right to belay next to a bush atop a ledge. 110 feet.

Pitch 2: 5.10c Head left into a varnished slot with a hand crack. Lieback up the crack until it opens to a nasty off-width, Bombay chimney. Climb the chimney to its top and angle left to a belay stance above it. 85 feet.

Pitch 3: 5.9 Take a hand crack to its top at the base of a tree. 140 feet.

Walk and scramble off the back and left of the for-

mation, leading to the top of the Water Streaks Sector. Do one double-rope rappel using the anchor atop *After Hours*. This will lead to another anchor and a short 70-foot rappel to the ground. (Same rappel as *Chimney* and *After Hours*.)

FA: Jimmy Pinjuv, Gary Sutherland 1997

46. It's a Boy! It's a Girl! 5.10c ★★★ Traditional. Now-deceased Jules George named this route after the "feeling of being born" while climbing the cracks. This route begins down and right of the bushy ledge mentioned at the start of the previous route, in the center of the large black face. Gear: standard rack up to #3 Friend.

Pitch 1: 5.8 Climb the center of the large black face to a belay ledge. 165 feet.

Pitch 2: 5.10c Head slightly left and then back right to enter a right-facing corner system that separates, forming two cracks. Belay just below a steep chimney at the base of the V slot at a bolted anchor. 160 feet.

Pitch 3: 5.10b Work your way up the wide V slot, staying left at the top, to a bolted anchor. 160 feet.

Rappel the route using 2 ropes.

FA: George Urioste, Mike Clifford, Jules George, Bill Hotz 1999

47. The Pachyderm 5.9 ★★★ Traditional. Begin a quarter of the way up the ramp leading to the Cloud Tower Area. Climb two corner systems that are right of *It's a Boy! It's a Girl!* Start in the right-facing chimney corner system with white rock on the left and a black smooth face on the right.

Pitch 1: 5.8 Climb the right-facing corner to a small recess at the top of the corner system. 130 feet.

Pitch 2: 5.9 Head up and slightly right, following cracks and passing bolts to a small belay ledge. 100 feet.

Pitch 3: 5.6 Traverse right, aiming for a chimney up and to the right. Follow the chimney to the first ledge and belay. 150 feet.

Pitch 4: 5.7 Continue up the chimney to another belay ledge. 160 feet.

Pitch 5: 5.6 Climb a short pitch to the top of the tiny formation. 50 feet.

From the top of the formation, do four rappels down and into the gully on the back (west) side of the wall. Follow the gully down, back to the base of the wall.

FA: George and Joanne Urioste 1980

The next two routes are located left of the *Cloud Tower* buttress.

48. Test Tube 5.9 ★★★ Traditional. Continue up the ramp toward the Cloud Tower Area. A large gully system is on the left side of the *Cloud Tower* buttress. This route climbs up the second gully to the left of the left edge of the buttress. Gear: a hefty rack including doubles of #1–#3 Friends; bring extra webbing to leave on rappel anchors.

Pitch 1: 5.9 Climb a dihedral for 130 feet. The dihedral ends at the start of a large chimney. Belay here. 140 feet.

Pitch 2: 5.7 Squirm up the chimney. Belay at a good stance about 80 feet up.

Pitch 3: 5.7 Continue up the chimney to its end and the top of the formation. 80 feet.

To descend, from the top of the formation look for a tree to the right (west; at the top of *Spare Rib*). This is the start of four half-rope rappels that lead into the gully right of the route's start.

FA: George and Joanne Urioste 1980

49. Spare Rib 5.8 ★★★ Mixed, 1/4-inch bolts. Traditional. Begin 35 feet right of *Test Tube*, just left of the left edge of the *Cloud Tower* buttress. *Spare Rib* climbs a lichen-covered wall.

Pitch 1: 5.8 Climb a thin seam/crack that is split by black rock on the left. Follow it up past an old bolt to a small bolted belay. 80 feet.

Pitch 2: 5.8 Move left into a vertical crack. Climb it, passing 4 bolts to another bolted belay on a tiny ledge. 80 feet.

Pitch 3: 5.8 Head up a bolted face, supplementing with gear where needed, to another bolted belay. 85 feet.

Pitch 4: 5.6 Continue up the face, passing 1 bolt, to a ledge with a tree. Belay off the tree. 90 feet.

Rappel from the tree (same descent as *Test Tube*).

FA: George and Joanne Urioste 1980

OAK CREEK CANYON

Solar Slab Area ▲ Black Arch Wall ▲ Eagle Wall ▲ Painted Bowl ▲ Celebration Wall
The Fork ▲ Blood Wall ▲ The Triad ▲ Afterburner Cliff

To REACH OAK CREEK CANYON from Las Vegas, take West Charleston Boulevard westward, which turns into State Route 159. Drive over the 215 Beltway and set your odometer at zero. Turn right into the Red Rock Canyon National Conservation Area, 5.9 miles past the 215 Beltway (2 miles past Calico Basin Road). Enter the 13-mile Scenic Drive through the kiosk entrance booth.

Oak Creek Canyon is 12.1 miles from the entrance kiosk. Just after mile marker 12, cross a large wash and turn right on the dirt road. Drive 0.8 mile to a large, fenced lot.

Take the trail out of the parking area, heading southwest toward the canyon. After 15 minutes, you will pass a trail on the left, which is the highway access to Oak Creek. Here the trail you are following makes a right curve and starts paralleling the wash. After 1 mile of hiking from the parking area, you will reach a signed junction with the Knoll Trail. Continue straight. You will pass a sign on your hike up, noting that the canyons of Red Rock are designated wilderness areas.

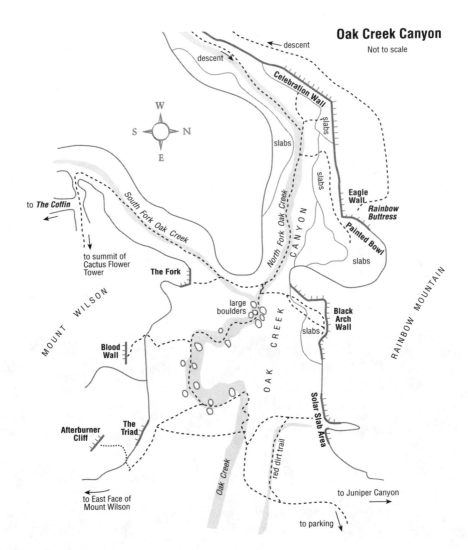

▲ SOLAR SLAB AREA
S All-Day Sun Approach: 45 minutes

To reach the Solar Slab Area, pass the junction with the Knoll Trail and continue on the main trail as it goes around a small bend and down a short hill. A red dirt trail will cut off to the right, heading up and right beneath the right-hand wall. Routes are on lower and upper tiers, divided by the huge Solar Slab Ledge. Routes are described from left to right.

LOWER TIER

1. Beulah's Book 5.9– ★★★★ Traditional. *Beulah's Book* climbs the huge, right-facing corner on the left edge of a huge, black, varnished face. Begin in the corner that has a huge detached block lodged above an oak tree growing out the base. Gear: standard rack to #5 Friend.

Pitch 1: 5.6, 1 bolt. Climb a right-facing corner past

the block. Move left onto the face and then up and right into a chimney. Take the chimney to a recess that forms a ledge and belay. 160 feet.

Pitch 2: 5.9-, 1 bolt. Continue up the corner to a roof, passing a bolt. Head left to a bolted belay on a ledge. 160 feet.

Pitch 2 variation: 5.8 Follow a line of bolts on the face left.

Pitch 3: 5.5 Climb the run-out face up and right to left-leaning cracks and belay. 150 feet.

Pitch 4: 5.3 Climb up and right to a large ledge, littered with big boulders. 60 feet.

Pitch 5: Third class. Move up and slightly right to the Solar Slab Ledge. 150 feet.

To descend, traverse the ledge right and rappel *Solar Slab Gully* using 1 rope.
FA: Randal Grandstaff, Dave Anderson 1979

2. Johnny Vegas 5.9 or 5.7 ★★★ Traditional. This route climbs up 40 feet right of *Beulah's Book* and 25 feet left of the *Solar Slab Gully*. Locate a large white pillar next to a shallow scooped-out corner. Scramble 25 feet up, onto the top of the pillar, to start the route. Gear: standard rack and Friends to #4.

Pitch 1: 5.7 Climb a hand and finger crack for 55 feet. Move up and left across the varnished face. This leads to the base of an obvious right-facing corner and bolted belay. 150 feet.

Pitch 2: 5.7 Climb up a dihedral for 25 feet and then move up and right to another crack. Follow this crack until it ends. From there, traverse left across a featured face to the bolted belay in an alcove. 130 feet.

Pitch 3: 5.9 Lieback up the pink-colored, right-facing dihedral, move right to a bolt, and continue up the crack. Once you turn the corner, cut back up left on a steep face until you reach lower-angled rock. Move up and left to a bolted belay on low-angled rock. 180 feet.

Pitch 3 variation: 5.7 Move right on the ledge, avoiding the right-facing corner, to an arête. Climb plates up and then move left to join with the pitch. 180 feet.

Pitch 4: 5.4 Climb slabs to the Solar Slab Ledge beneath *Solar Slab*. 150 feet.

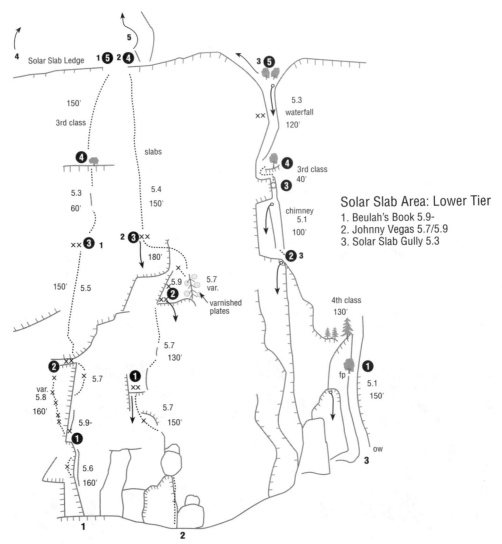

Solar Slab Ledge

150'
3rd class

slabs

5.3
60'

5.4
150'

5.3
waterfall
120'

3rd class
40'

chimney
5.1
100'

Solar Slab Area: Lower Tier
1. Beulah's Book 5.9-
2. Johnny Vegas 5.7/5.9
3. Solar Slab Gully 5.3

180'

150' | 5.5

5.9 | 5.7 var.

varnished plates

5.7
130'

4th class
130'

var.
5.8
160'

5.7
130'

5.7
150'

5.9-

fp

5.1
150'

5.6
160'

ow

Rappel straight down the face with 2 ropes.
FA: Harrison Shull, Tom Cecil, Dave Cox, Todd Hewitt 1994

3. Solar Slab Gully 5.3 ★★★ Begin 25 feet right of *Johnny Vegas* at the gully right of the large, black, varnished face. Take the second gully/crack system right of the black face, and eventually climb into the first gully.

Pitch 1: 5.1 Climb a varnished off-width to a be-

lay ledge with a tree and fixed pin. 150 feet.

Pitch 2: Fourth class. Scramble left, up a bushy gully. Then take ledges past an oak tree with rappel slings to a niche beneath a dark water-polished chimney. 130 feet.

Pitch 2 variation: Head out left onto the face, climbing the face straight up, and rejoin the route at the pitch 3 belay.

Pitch 3: 5.1 Climb the black chimney, past a threaded rappel, past a chockstone with rappel slings, to a belay ledge up and left. 100 feet.

Pitch 4: Third class. Take the right-facing crack/
chimney to a ledge with a tree. 40 feet.

Pitch 5: 5.3 Climb the slippery waterfall groove,
passing a bolt and piton belay. Continue, scrambling
up and left, exiting onto Solar Slab Ledge. 120 feet.

Rappel the route using 1 rope (seven rappels) or 2
ropes (four rappels).

FA: Unknown 1970s

UPPER TIER

The following routes begin on the huge ledge above
the previous three routes. Use any of the first three
routes to access the base of these upper tier routes.

4. Going Nuts IV, 5.6 ★ Traditional. This route
climbs loose, rotten rock above *Beulah's Book*. Start
under a large arch.

Pitch 1: 5.6 Climb up a crack using the large face
holds. Belay on a ledge using a series of jugs. 150 feet.

Pitch 2: 5.5 From the belay, head up and left toward the left edge of the top of the arch. Just past the
arch, angle back right on the loose, rotten, run-out
face. Finish on the ledge just left of the top of pitch 2
of *Solar Slab*. 160 feet.

To descend, from the ledge walk right to join *Solar Slab* atop the second pitch. Rappel *Solar Slab* and
then rappel *Solar Slab Gully* with 1 rope or 2.

FA: Unknown

5. Solar Slab IV, 5.6 ★★★★★ Traditional. This
route begins about 100 feet left of the top of *Solar
Slab Gully*. Gear: standard rack to #3 Friend.

Pitch 1: 5.6 Take the varnished face, left of the large
left-facing corner, up and right to a crack. Take the
crack to a large ledge with a bush. 165 feet.

Pitch 2: 5.5 Take the left-leaning ramp up and left
to a right-facing corner. Follow it up to a large ledge
with a dead tree. 150 feet.

Pitch 3: 5.6 Step right to obtain a crack, and climb
it to a ledge. Traverse right again to a right-facing corner. Climb to a belay ledge beneath a left-facing corner. 160 feet.

Pitch 4: 5.6 Move right to the left-facing corner and
flake. Climb up to a roof. Traverse down and right to
a belay ledge. 150 feet.

Pitch 5: 5.5 Take the hand crack above the belay
to a stance and belay. 140 feet. (Pitches 5 and 6 can
be combined using a 60-meter rope.)

Pitch 6: 5.4 Continue up the crack, which becomes a right-facing corner that forms the right side

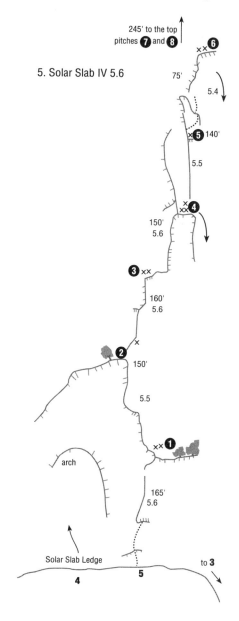

5. Solar Slab IV 5.6

of a pillar. Climb the face up and right to a left an-gling crack. Take the crack to its end and traverse right to a right-facing corner. Move up to a huge ledge. 75 feet. Rappel from here using 2 ropes or con-tinue third and fourth class 245 feet to the top of the low-angle feature.

Pitch 7: Fourth class. Scramble up a slab to the base of a right-facing, left-leaning corner. 140 feet.

Pitch 8: 5.5 Climb the corner to the top of the fea-ture. 105 feet.

To descend, traverse right across the top to the second gully right (east), the gully right of *The Friar*. Scramble fourth and easy fifth class down the gully. There are two single-rope rappels required during the gully descent.

FA: Joe Herbst, Tom Kaufman, Larry Hamilton 1975

6. Sunflower IV, 5.9 ★★★ Traditional. Begin 10 feet right of the top of *Solar Slab Gully*.

Pitch 1: 5.6 Climb a vertical crack ending on a big ledge, right of some bushes. Natural belay. 165 feet.

Pitch 2: 5.8 Continue up a crack, using some fin-ger locks, to a large ledge with one bolt and fixed nut anchor. 100 feet.

Pitch 3: 5.8, 1 bolt. Continue up the jam crack to its end. Angle left past 1 bolt (new 3/8-inch), to a hang-ing bolted belay. The anchor has three bolts: new 3/8-inch, old 1/4-inch, and old 3/8-inch. 165 feet.

Pitch 4: 5.9, 5 bolts. Move up the exposed face, clipping 5 bolts (the second is 1/4-inch) to another crack. Continue up the crack to a small ledge and belay. Aim for the large left-facing corner. 165 feet.

Pitch 5: 5.7 Climb up the crack and left-facing cor-ner past a small roof to the top. Belay in a small alcove.

Pitch 6: 5.6 Continue up the corner.

Pitch 7: 5.6 Finish up the corner.

Pitch 8: Easy fifth class up slabs.

To descend, traverse right across the top to the second gully right (east), the gully right of *The Friar*. Scramble fourth and easy fifth class down the gully. There are two single-rope rappels required during the gully descent.

FA: Jon Martinet, Randal Grandstaff 1979

7. Sundog IV, 5.9 ★★★ Mixed. After reaching the Solar Slab Ledge on one of the first three routes

walk right and up to a point 50 feet left of a gully on the upper right edge of the Solar Slab Wall. Fol-low discontinuous cracks and corners up and right of *Sunflower*.

Pitch 1: 5.7, 1 bolt. Climb the face left of two shallow, left-facing corners. Tricky gear placements. Finish on a ledge below a big, left-facing corner. 80 feet.

Pitch 2: 5.7 Climb the left-facing corner to a bolted anchor on a ledge. 100 feet.

Pitch 3: 5.8, 4 bolts. Ascend the face, passing two bulges to cracks and a face. Continue to a stance with a bolted anchor. 165 feet.

Pitch 4: 5.9, 8 bolts. Take the face through a steep section to a slab and then a tiny crack. Fixed anchors in a scoop. 155 feet.

Pitch 5: 5.8 Take the right-facing, right-leaning corner to a steep, 1-foot-wide crack. Finish on a ledge with fixed anchors. 165 feet.

Pitch 5 variation: Take the right-facing, right-leaning corner to its top. Traverse up and right to reach a poorly protected face on the left. Climb it to the belay ledge. 170 feet.

Rappel the route using 2 ropes. One 50-meter rope gets you to the ground from the top of pitch 2.

FA: Ed Prochaska, Joanne Urioste 1997

SOLAR SLAB RIGHT

Reach the following routes by hiking up a tree-filled gully down and slightly right of the *Solar Slab Gully*.

8. Horndog 5.8+ ★★ Traditional. This route climbs up right of *Solar Slab Gully*, to the top of a ledge right of the Solar Slab Ledge. A variation climbs to the top of the Solar Slab Wall by linking with *Sundog*. The combination is called *Horndogger Select*. Gear: two sets of Rocks, a set of Friends to #4, doubles of #2 and #3 Friends for the belays.

Pitch 1: 5.8+ Climb the crack to before it merges with an overhang. Exit right to a crack and horns, which lead to a short white headwall. Climb the headwall and move right to belay in the first dark re-cess reached. 150 feet.

Pitch 2: 5.8 Continue up the line of huecos until you reach an overhanging bulge, at about 85 feet. Move left and follow a left-leaning crack. Continue up to the first large ledge and belay. 160 feet.

Pitch 3: Fourth class. Scramble left over the top of a gully/chimney to belay at the base of the right-angling fist crack. 140 feet.

Pitch 3 variation: 5.7 Climb the fist crack to ledges below the Solar Slab Wall.

Pitch 4: Third class. Move out right around a ledge and then back left to the anchors.

Rappel the route using 2 ropes or link with *Sundog* for *Horndogger Select*.
FA: Unknown

Variation, *Horndogger Select* IV, 5.8+:

Pitch 5: 5.6 R Climb the short cliff between large ledges, or third-class right to a gully to gain the upper ledges.

Pitch 6: Climb up discontinuous cracks for 60 feet. Climb a dark left-facing corner to a single-bolt belay at its top. 175 feet.

Pitch 7: 5.8+ Climb up and right past 2 bolts. Continue heading slightly right to reach a crack. Follow this to a belay in an area of dark-colored jugs. 150 feet.

Pitch 8: 5.7+ Climb past an overhang and delicate horns to a narrow ledge. Follow the ledge left, moving up to place gear and back down to proceed. Continue until you reach a vertical crack. Belay in the crack. 150 feet.

Pitch 9: 5.4 Move up the crack and corner. 155 feet.

Pitch 10: 5.4 Finish up the crack and face to the top. 165 feet.

Descend the same as *Sundog*.
FA: David Pollari, Shawn Pereto 1993

9. The Friar 5.9+ ★★★ Traditional. Begin 100 feet right of *Horndogger Select*, beneath a varnished right-facing corner in some trees and bushes. *The Friar is topped with an obvious large*

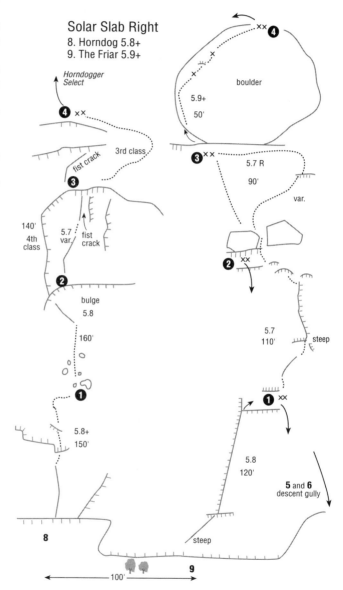

Solar Slab Right
8. Horndog 5.8+
9. The Friar 5.9+

boulder. Gear: standard rack to a #3 Friend.

Pitch 1: 5.8 Do one difficult boulder move off the ground to a ledge (easiest below and left of the right-facing corner). Head up the perfect, black, varnished dihedral. At the top, step right onto a large ledge. Traverse right to the bolted anchors. 120 feet.

Pitch 2: 5.7 Climb a crack angling up and right to a roof and left-facing crack. Continue up the crack, traversing left to a small foot ledge and a 2-bolt anchor (beneath a very large ledge). Some loose rock. 110 feet.

Pitch 3: 5.7 R Climb straight up from the belay to the topmost ledge. Move up a face to the bolted anchor under a roof.

Pitch 3 variation: Feels safer. Traverse right to a ledge below the right side of the roof (boulder). Delicate face climbing takes you up under the roof. Traverse back left, under the roof, to the anchor.

The last 30 feet of both pitch 3 variations are unprotected on somewhat loose rock. 90 feet.

Pitch 4: 5.9+ Move straight up and slightly left onto a huge ledge. Walk to the backside (north) of the boulder. Climb the northwest arête and then take the face past 2 bolts, moving up and right to the summit anchors. 50 feet.

Rappel the backside of the boulder, and then rappel the route in three rappels using 2 ropes.
FA: Joe Herbst, Tom Kaufman, Steve Allen 1977

BYRD PINNACLE

Byrd Pinnacle is the prominent black, angular slab resting against the face 200 feet right of *The Friar* and right of the *Solar Slab/Sunflower* descent gully.

10. WHOOSH 5.8 ★★★ Traditional. Climb the off-width and chimney left of Byrd Pinnacle. Descent unknown.
FA: Joe Herbst, Matt McMackin

11. Byrd Pinnacle: Left 5.8 ★★★ Traditional. Climb the hand crack right of *Whoosh* and left of Byrd Pinnacle. At the top, merge with *The A Crack*. Descend the gully to the right (east).
FA: Joe Herbst, John Byrd, Matt McMackin, Nanouk Borche 1973

12. Xyphoid Fever 5.10 ★★ Traditional. Climb the

center of Byrd Pinnacle. Pull the crack through the roof and merge with *The A Crack* to the top. Gear: standard rack to #5 Friend. Descend the gully to the right (east).
FA: Joe Herbst 1977

13. The A Crack 5.9+ ★★★ Traditional. Climb the right side of Byrd Pinnacle. Gear: standard rack to #6 Friend including some small nuts for the second pitch.

Pitch 1: 5.9 Start just left of *Red Zinger*. Climb the wide flake heading left; follow it to its end. Continue up the slab to the bolted anchor on the same ledge system as the first pitch to *Red Zinger*.

Pitch 2: 5.9+ Follow a thin seam until it opens up. Continue up the crack to the bolted belay and rappel.
FA: Joe Herbst, John Byrd 1973

14. Red Zinger 5.10d ★★★★★ Traditional. This west-facing, left-facing finger crack dihedral has Indian Creek (Utah) written all over it. Most climb only the first pitch; others link the two pitches, making for an enlivening adventure!

Pitch 1: 5.10d Climb the crack to a large ledge. 90 feet.

Pitch 2: 5.10d Continue up the corner and traverse left under the roof to a fixed anchor.

Rappel. 50 feet.
FA: Joe Herbst 1970s

The following routes begin on the far right, east-facing wall. Descents unknown.

15. Tickled Pink 5.11 ★★ Traditional. Begin 300 feet left of *La Muerte* on a brown varnished face with bushy ledges. Climb the 2-inch, left-angling crack on the left side of the face.
FA: Joe Herbst

16. Wise Guys' Off Size 5.10d ★★ Traditional. Begin the same as *Tickled Pink*, but climb the off-width on the right side of the face. Two pitches. Gear: to a #5 Friend.
FA: Mark Moore, Joe Herbst 1973

17. La Muerte 5.10 ★★★ Traditional. This route

climbs the east-facing wall seen when hiking into Oak Creek Canyon. Climb the 300-foot white face with a big black splotch on it. The route ascends an off-width up the center of the varnished splotch. Three pitches.

FA: Joe Herbst, Mark Moore 1973

▲ BLACK ARCH WALL
S All-Day Sun   Approach: 90 minutes

Follow the trail to where it goes downhill and parallels the Solar Slab Area on the right, and the wash on the left. When you reach a point where you are directly beneath the route *Johnny Vegas*, take the trail downhill and into the wash. Hike through the wash for approximately 45 minutes to where you have to scramble up many large boulders to continue (just before you reach the split of the north and south forks). At this point there will be an enormous black arching roof on the right side of the wash, with a big, rounded, lighter-colored slab at its base. Approach the routes from the slab on the far-left (west) end of the wall, just below the left edge of the black arch. Bushwhack up and right to the top of the slab. Routes are described from left to right.

For the following routes, hike straight up to the base of the wall, on the left edge of the black arch, where a low roof slants down and left.

18. Black Betty 5.10 ★★★ Mixed. Begin at the base of the far-left end of the black arch. Climb up to the left edge of a low roof, clipping 1 bolt below it. Move up and left. Take a finger crack to the top of a small pillar and belay. Rappel.
FA: Tom Cecil 1995

19. Black Widow 5.11 ★★★ Mixed. Begin 30 feet

right of *Black Betty*, on the right side of the low roof.

Pitch 1: Take double cracks up and left past 6 bolts through the roof to under the black arch. Belay under the roof.

Pitch 2: Climb over the massive roof of the arch. Take cracks up and left to the top of the cliff.

Rappel.

FA: Tom Cecil 1995

Head straight up and right—mostly third-class scrambling with some fourth- and fifth-class moves to reach the following routes.

20. There and Back Again 5.8 ★★ Traditional. Begin about 150 yards right of *Black Widow*, on the big detached block slab with varnished splotches called Knobissimo Slab. Climb the center of the slab to a ledge and then take cracks up to a left-facing dihedral. Then move up and left across a varnished face to the top.

Pitch 1: 5.5 Climb the center of Knobissimo Slab to the ledge at its top. 170 feet.

Pitch 2: 5.7 Take the face, cracks, and corner to the top of a tower. 160 feet.

Pitch 3: 5.8 Face-climb up and left, then move back right to a corner. Take it to a belay ledge at its top. 120 feet.

Pitch 4: 5.8 A short steep face is located on the left. Take the thin crack, heading up to a dihedral. Climb the dihedral. When you reach loose blocks, exit left to a ledge and belay. 80 feet.

Pitch 5: 5.8 Pull through a steep corner, exiting left to easier climbing. 80 feet.

Pitch 6: Fourth class. Scramble up and left to the Painted Bowl.

To descend, look for the spot with bushes and a pine tree in the Painted Bowl. A smaller pine with slings is located just below the larger one. Rappel from there with 2 ropes to the lowest of several scrub-oak-bush-filled ledges. Rappel with 2 ropes again to a ledge 30 feet above the ground. Rappel with 1 rope to mother earth.

FA: Jim Boone, Ellen Dempsey 1980

21. Tuscarora 5.12b ★★★ Mixed. Begin 50 feet right of *There and Back Again* and 100 feet left of

Black Orpheus, directly below a low roof and just above the Knobissimo Slab. *Tuscarora* climbs midway up a pillar to the left of the start of *Black Orpheus* (*Black Orpheus* tops out on this pillar feature). Gear: to a #4 Friend.

Pitch 1: Climb a pink slab to straight up underneath the left side of the left roof feature. 165 feet.

Pitch 2: Climb the crack up and left of the roof.

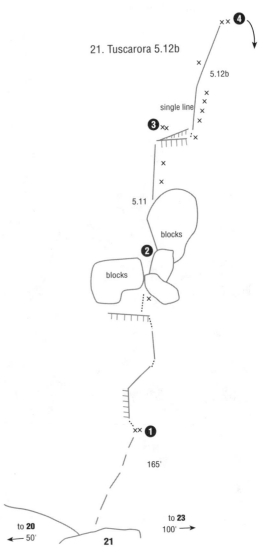

Continue up under a huge, overhanging block. Climb to the top of the block, from the right side and belay.

Pitch 3: 5.11 Continue up and right to the left side of a downward sloping ramp.

Pitch 4: 5.12b Take the finger crack up and right as it gets wider and wider.

Rappel with 2 ropes.

FA: Tom Cecil, Tony Barnes, John "The Gambler" Rosholt 1995

An unknown George and Joanne Urioste route climbs between *Tuscarora* and *The Bandit*.

22. The Bandit 5.11b R ★★ Traditional. *The Bandit* climbs the prominent left-facing crack right of *Tuscarora*, between *Tuscarora* and *Black Orpheus*.

Pitch 1: Climb the 5.10 lieback arch that moves into a short 5.11a dihedral.

Pitch 2: 5.11b R Traverse left, under a big arch/roof a full rope length to some old Urioste anchors.

Rappel with 2 ropes.

FA: Russ Ricketts, Adam Wilbur 2001

23. Black Orpheus IV, 5.9+ ★★★★ Traditional. This is the first crack right of the recessed slab comprising the middle of the wall. Climb the left-facing corner, moving up and left into a red, right-facing wall at the top. Finish above and right of the Painted Bowl. Joanne and George Urioste named this route after a 1959 Portuguese film, based on the Greek legend of Orpheus, about a mythical minstrel who fell in love with a country girl named Eurydice.

Pitch 1: 5.7 Climb a left-facing crack past a 2-bolt belay (the original anchors) on the left face. Continue to a notch and belay. 110 feet.

Pitch 2: 5.9, 1 bolt. Step left to a left-angling crack and move up, passing 1 bolt. Step back right, climbing a left-facing corner to another ledge and belay. 140 feet.

Pitch 3: 5.7 Move up and left on left-angling, broken ledges. Take cracks up past a large detached block. Continue through a varnished section to a stance below a white lower-angled section of rock. 110 feet.

Pitch 4: 5.6 R Move up the white face to a ledge beneath a ramp that heads up and left. Take a left-facing crack to a ledge. 190 feet.

Pitch 5: 5.2 R Take the ramp up and left to a ledge. 140 feet.

Pitch 6: 5.6 Continue left and up, across a slab to another ledge. Belay under a low overhang on the far left edge of the ledge system. 160 feet.

Pitch 7: 5.0 Traverse 20 feet to the base of a right-facing dihedral. 60 feet.

Pitch 8: 5.9 Climb the dihedral and chimney above. Move right and belay on a ledge (needs big Friends). 150 feet.

Pitch 9: 5.9+ Move up ledges to reach the short, thin, steep crack with 2 bolts. From a right-facing corner, climb parallel cracks on the right wall. 110 feet.

Pitch 10: 5.6 Climb the finger crack, angling right to a bolt and a couple ledges to a fixed belay. 120 feet.

Pitch 11: 5.5, 4 bolts. Climb the large right-facing corner, passing a bolt. At the top traverse right to a stance and fixed anchor. The fourth bolt, while original, is very far left and nearly always skipped to reduce rope drag (or because it's not spotted). 120 feet.

Pitch 12: Third class. Climb to a ledge where you begin the descent.

There are three *Black Orpheus* descent options, each of which can take 3 hours if you make no mistakes:

Single-rope descent: Move left (west) along summit slabs to a ramp heading down. At the base of the ramp, do an 80-foot rappel to a large ledge. Walk right for 140 feet to the end of the ledge and rappel another 80 feet. This leads through a chimney to a vegetated ledge. Scramble down and left on ledges to another 80-foot rappel. This takes you to the Painted Bowl. Hike down and right (toward *Levitation 29*, to the slabs leading down into the wash). Hike 150 yards down the wash to the fork and turn left. The Black Arch Wall will be on your left.

Double-rope descent: This is the easiest and quickest way down. From the top of Black Orpheus scramble up the third-class slabs to a large ledge that runs left (west). Walk across this ledge until you can see a flake next to the ledge, where the ledge system begins to descend. Hike down, behind this flake, to a ledge and bolted anchor, located at the far side of the ledge. Do a 165-foot rappel to a midway rappel station. Do a 170-foot rappel leading to some third-class slabs. Head west down the slabs until you reach a bushy ledge that angles down and left. Scramble down this (second and third class), aiming for the main wash and doing one more section of third class to reach the wash. Hike down the wash left, turning left at the fork to reach the Black Arch Wall on the left.

Walk-off descent: This option often has ice in the winter months. Hike right and descend the next gully right (east), the gully left of the Solar Slab Area. *FA: Joanne and George Urioste 1979*

24. Bossa Nova 5.11 ★★★ Traditional. This route was named after a style of samba-type of music called "new groove," which became popular after the Portuguese film *Black Orpheus* was released. Begin 30 feet right of *Black Orpheus*. Start on a big flake wedged behind a left-facing crack.

Pitch 1: 5.11 Climb the flake to a dihedral/chimney. Move left into the obvious dihedral with a finger

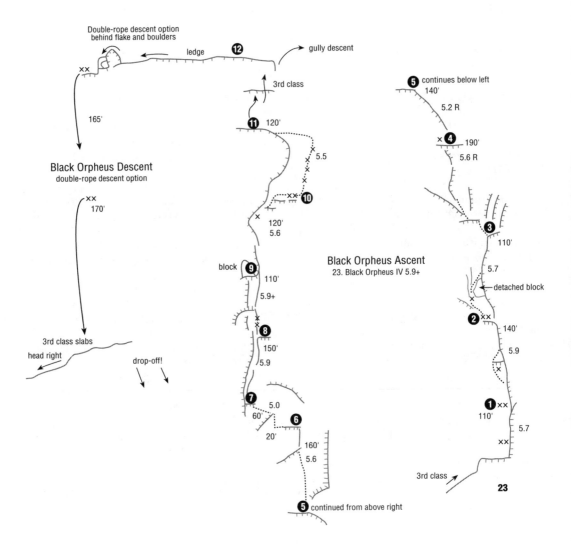

crack. Follow this up to the bolted anchor on a sloping ledge. 150 feet.

Pitch 2: Walk right on the ledge, around a fin, and pull onto a sloping shelf. Move up a right-facing flake. Mantel on the thin holds, continuing up the overhanging face to a group of large stacked boulders, which make up a right-facing corner. 100 feet.

Pitch 3: 5.9 Move up and right about 15 feet and then back left through the overhang with a good nut placement. Continue up the painted section of *Black Orpheus*, to the top of the fifth pitch.

Descend the same as *Black Orpheus*.
FA: Merlin Larsen, Jim Munson 1996

▲ EAGLE WALL
S All-Day Sun   Approach: 2 hours

Follow the trail to where it goes downhill and parallels the Solar Slab Area on the right, and the wash on the left. When you reach a point where you are directly beneath the route *Johnny Vegas*, take the trail downhill and into the wash. Hike through the wash for approximately 45 minutes to where you have to scramble up many large boulders to continue (just before you reach the split of the north and south forks). At this point there will be an enormous black arching roof on the right side of the wash, the Black Arch Wall. From the Black Arch Wall, hike up Oak Creek Canyon until it splits into the north and south forks. Take the right (north) fork to where hiking in the wash gets increasingly difficult and there is a large growth of bushes. Continue up the right side of the wash to reach the far-left edge of a 400-foot slab/ledge system, heading up and right. Follow the slab to the right edge of the Eagle Wall and the left edge of the Painted Bowl. The Eagle Wall is on the left and named for the eagle-in-flight feature in the center of the wall. Routes are described from left to right.

North Fork Canyon descent: Hike the ridgeline left (west) toward the limestone cliffs high above the

sandstone, to the back of the canyon. Upon reaching a bright red band of rock heading down into the wash, at the back of the canyon, hike down along the right (west) edge of the rock. Continue down to the wash and then take the wash back to the base of the wall or route. A long, vigorous hike with fourth- and fifth-class scrambling. To the car: 3–5 hours.

25. Dances with Beagles 5.11 ★★★ Mixed. Begin left of a varnished pillar and 20 feet right of the right edge of a huge arch. Take a flare up to a crack. Move up and right to a small ledge. Gear: standard rack to #1.5 Friend and 18 quickdraws.

Pitch 1: 5.8, 2 bolts. Take a corner to a straight-in crack on a steep, varnished face. Move up and right to a blocky ledge with a fixed anchor. 150 feet.

Pitch 2: 5.11, 2 bolts. Move up and right from the belay to a reach crack that leans left. Take the crack up to under a roof. Pull the roof and belay at the fixed anchor above it. 130 feet.

Pitch 3: 5.11, 17 bolts. Steep climbing up the face. 160 feet.

Rappel with 2 ropes.

FA: Jeff Rhoades, Todd Swain 1993

26. Eagle Dance IV, 5.10c, A0 ★★★★ Mixed. While installing this route the first ascensionists dropped a piton. In those days their budget was tight, so they were careful not to lose gear. While aggressively hunting for their piton, they noticed a large eagle flying high above the cliff and they stopped to watch it. "The bird was huge and high, like an airplane," reminisces Joanne Urioste. "We said to the magic eagle, 'please let us find our piton.' And when we looked down, there it was, so we named the route Eagle Dance." There is also an image of an eagle in flight in the center of the wall; it's headed westward and the top of pitch four is just below its head. This route is about 250 feet right of *Dances with Beagles*, 50 feet right of a very large, black, varnished pillar leaning against the rock. The third pitch intersects the neck of the

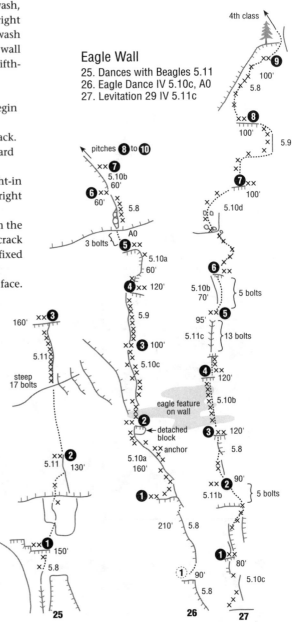

Eagle Wall
25. Dances with Beagles 5.11
26. Eagle Dance IV 5.10c, A0
27. Levitation 29 IV 5.11c

eagle feature on the wall. Gear: standard rack to #2.5 Friend and an aider.

Pitch 1: 5.8 Climb the corner system to a left-angling crack. Where the crack ends take a ramp angling up and right to a 2-bolt belay. 210 feet.

Pitch 2: 5.10a, 10 bolts. Head right past 2 bolts to obtain a seam that climbs up and left. Follow the seam past 8 bolts and a bolted anchor to an anchor atop a huge detached block. 160 feet.

Pitch 3: 5.10c, 13 bolts. Move up past bolts to a fixed belay at a black band. 100 feet.

Pitch 4: 5.9, 9 bolts. Follow the face up to a downward-sloping belay ledge. 120 feet.

Pitch 5: 5.10a, 3 bolts. Move right to a short left-facing corner, and continue up a right-facing corner to the belay ledge. 60 feet.

Pitch 6: 5.8, A0, 8 bolts. Take a thin crack to a steep bulge. Clip bolts, then take a thin crack up and left to a bolted belay. 60 feet. Rappel the route from here or continue climbing.

Pitch 7: 5.10b Climb this short pitch to a bolt ladder. 60 feet.

Pitch 8: 5.10c, 7 bolts. Pass the belay and continue in a groove past 7 more bolts up a left-facing corner. Belay on a ledge. 60 feet.

Pitch 9: 5.9, 4 bolts. Climb a left-facing corner up and left to a large ledge. 130 feet.

Pitch 10: Fourth and fifth class. Continue up the corner to the top.

Take the North Fork Canyon descent.
FA: George and Joanne Urioste 1980

27. Levitation 29 IV, 5.11c ★★★★★ Mixed. This is definitely one of the classics—featured in the book *Fifty Favorite Climbs*. Begin 150 feet right of *Eagle Dance*, on varnished cracks extending 150 feet up to a large roof. Gear: standard rack to a #3 Friend.

Pitch 1: 5.10c, 4 bolts. Climb discontinuous crack systems past bolts to a sloping ledge beneath a left-facing corner. Fixed anchor. 80 feet.

Pitch 2: 5.11b, 8 bolts. Move onto the face right. Head up and right to under a small roof. Clip a bolt, then traverse left and pull over the roof. Move left to a bolted belay. 90 feet.

Pitch 3: 5.8, 2 bolts. Climb the crack above the belay for 75 feet and then traverse right and up to a bolted belay. 120 feet.

Pitch 4: 5.10b, 7 bolts. Take the bolted face and crack to a fixed anchor below a steeper wall. 120 feet.

Pitch 5: 5.11c, 13 bolts. Pull the bulge in the crack above the belay and obtain a thin, technical dihedral. Continue to a bolted anchor. 95 feet.

Pitch 6: 5.10b, 5 bolts. Take seams up the face and left to a bolted anchor. 70 feet. Rappel from here with a 70-meter rope or continue climbing.

Pitch 7: 5.10d, 13 bolts. Heads up on this one. Climb up and left to a scoop. Move through the middle of the scoop on loose flakes and huecos. Head out the top right side to a ledge and bolted anchor. 100 feet.

Pitch 8: 5.9, 7 bolts. Face-climb up about 20 feet and right 20 feet to reach a crack. Move up the crack and then traverse left to a sloping ledge with a bolted anchor. 100 feet.

Pitch 9: 5.8, 7 bolts. Move up and left to a right-facing dihedral to a bolted anchor on a face beneath a large ledge and tree. 100 feet.

Pitch 10: Fourth class. Scramble up and right to a drainage that takes you to the summit and a large tree. Take the North Fork Canyon descent. 20 feet.
FA: George and Joanne Urioste, Bill Bradley 1981
FFA: Lynn Hill, John Long, Joanne Urioste 1981

▲ PAINTED BOWL
S All-Day Sun   Approach: 2.5 hours

Approach as for Eagle Wall. The Painted Bowl begins at the very top right edge of Eagle Wall. Hike up and right of the Eagle wall. Named because there is a natural bowl-like feature beneath the towering walls and the rock is very colorful. Routes are described from left to right.

North Fork Canyon descent: Hike the ridgeline left (west) toward the limestone cliffs high above the sandstone, to the back of the canyon. Upon reaching a bright red band of rock heading down into the wash, at the back of the canyon, hike down along the right (west) edge of the rock. Continue down to the wash and then take the wash back to the base of the wall or route. A long, vigorous hike with fourth- and fifth-class scrambling. To the car: 3–5 hours.

28. Mountain Beast IV, 5.11a ★★★★ Traditional. This route branches off *The Ringtail* to the left midway up the fourth pitch. The first ascent is an interesting story. Years after the first ascent of *The Ringtail*, Joanne Urioste began putting up this route with Mike Moreo. When Moreo decided not to continue, Joanne hauled all her gear and supplies to the top of the cliff (a *very long* haul!) and fixed ropes. George Urioste offered to help with the bolting. With this first ascent Joanne proved herself to be a true Mountain Beast (her daughter, Susi, named the route). Gear: standard rack.

Pitches 1–3: Climb *The Ringtail*.

Pitch 4: 5.8 Climb steep cracks on the wall left of the belay, past a single bolt to a fixed belay ledge near the nose. 80 feet.

Pitch 5: 5.10b, 8 bolts. Move right and then head up the face, passing bolts to a fixed belay beneath a left-facing corner. 145 feet.

Pitch 6: 5.10a, 4 bolts. Climb the corner to a ledge. Move up to a thin varnished crack. Continue up to a bolted belay on a small ledge with a pine tree. 150 feet.

Pitch 7: 5.7 Move right again to reach a corner system leading to a big ledge with a large pine tree. 150 feet.

Pitch 8: 5.5 Angle up and left past several bolts to a bolted anchor. 165 feet.

Take the North Fork Canyon descent.

FA: Joanne and George Urioste, Mike Moreo 1997

29. The Ringtail IV, 5.11a ★★★ Traditional. This route is about 100 yards up and right of *Levitation 29*, at the far right edge of Eagle Wall. Climb the left side of the black tower. Gear: standard rack.

Pitch 1: 5.9 Climb the thin left-angling crack. Toward the top, head right along a face to a roof. Climb under the roof, exiting out the left edge. Follow this up to the bolted belay under another roof. 115 feet.

Pitch 2: 5.11a, 6 bolts. Step right from the belay and climb up the face passing 3 bolts. Just past the fourth bolt, traverse left, clipping 2 more bolts (crux). This will lead to a bolted belay at a left-facing corner. 60 feet.

Pitch 3: 5.10b, 2 bolts. Climb up the fragile face passing 2 bolts, which leads to a right-facing corner. Follow the corner up to the bolted belay. 110 feet.

Pitch 4: 5.9 Continue stemming up the main corner system. The crack will lead to another bolted belay. 90 feet.

Pitch 5: Continue up, following the corner and chimney that lead to a final belay ledge with fixed gear. 70 feet.

Descend with four 2-rope rappels, or take *Rainbow Buttress* to the top and take the North Fork Canyon descent.

FA: George and Joanne Urioste 1981

30. Rainbow Buttress IV, 5.8 ★★★ Traditional.

Begin right of *The Ringtail*, on the right side of the black tower and left of an arch feature. Climb the tower using the cracks that ascend its right edge. Continue up and right using crack systems to the summit. Gear: standard rack plus doubles of #3.5 and #4 Friends.

Pitch 1: 5.4 Climb a left-angling crack to its end. Traverse right across a face to a ledge and belay. 80 feet.

Pitch 2: 5.8 Pull past a capped left-facing corner and take the face to a big ledge. Move up the left-facing corner above the ledge to another ledge and belay. 100 feet.

Pitch 3: 5.7 Take the off-width up to a right-facing corner to a chimney. Face-climb right to an alcove and then up to a right-facing corner. Finish on a belay ledge below a bush. 110 feet.

Pitch 4: 5.5 Take the double crack system to the top of the black tower and belay. Some chimney climbing. 100 feet.

Pitch 5: 5.6 From the top of the tower, step right, into a crack. Traverse a face 15 feet to reach a right-facing corner. For 40 feet ascend the corner and then traverse across the face. Belay at the base of a left-facing corner, above a large pedestal. 110 feet.

Pitch 6: 5.6 Climb the left-facing corner to its end

(fist, chimney, and more!). Continue to a ledge and belay. 150 feet.

Pitch 7: 5.5 Continue upward progress through a loose chimney. Upon reaching a downward-sloping ledge, move down and left to belay at a large pine tree. 100 feet.

Pitch 8: 5.5 X Climb a face left of a left-facing corner and tree. Move up and left to reach a ledge. Then head right to a ledge 40 feet short of the summit. 135 feet.

Pitch 9: Fourth class. Scramble to the summit on a rotten pink face with some cracks. 40 feet.

Take the North Fork Canyon descent.

FA: Joe Herbst, Joe Frani 1975

31. Kaleidoscope Cracks IV, 5.8 ★★★ Traditional.

Begin as for *Rainbow Buttress*, and then climb the rightmost of the crack systems right of *Rainbow Buttress*'s pitch 2. Gear: standard rack to #5 Friend.

Pitches 1–2: Climb *Rainbow Buttress*.

Pitch 3: Third class. Walk right on a big ledge to a pine tree and belay. 150 feet.

Pitch 4: 5.7 Climb the face above the tree to a bolt. Move up and left to a bulge. Pull it and head right to a belay ledge. 80 feet.

Pitch 5: 5.8 Take a black, varnished, right-facing corner to where it forks. Head left to a short varnished wall above a ledge. Climb the wall and belay on another ledge. 90 feet.

Pitch 6: 5.7 Climb a face, moving right and around to a bolt. Continue up and right to crack systems that lead to a big chimney. 70 feet.

Pitch 7: 5.8 Pull the bulge in the chimney. Take the cracks up the left side to a ledge with a tree. 90 feet.

Pitch 8: 5.5 Climb the vertical crack off the ledge for 45 feet. Traverse right to a chimney and belay. 80 feet.

Pitch 9: 5.7 Ascend the chimney and belay on a ledge. 100 feet.

Pitch 10: 5.5 Climb the chimney, using discontinuous cracks. 80 feet.

Pitch 11: 5.5 Continue up the chimney to a large ledge. 80 feet.

Pitch 12: Fourth class. Scramble to the summit on

a rotten pink face with some cracks (same last pitch as *Rainbow Buttress*). 40 feet.

Take the North Fork Canyon descent.

FA: George and Joanne Urioste 1977

32. Strawberry Sweat IV, 5.9 ★★★ Traditional. *Strawberry Sweat* is located at the left side of the upper level of the Painted Bowl. Begin 500 feet right of *Kaleidoscope Cracks* at a crack in pink rock. Gear: standard rack to #5 Friend.

Pitch 1: Fourth class. Begin in a chimney right of the crack. Move up to a ledge on the left. 60 feet.

Pitch 2: 5.3 Climb the crack off the ledge to above a tree. 80 feet.

Pitch 3: 5.9, 4 bolts. Continue up the crack and then traverse left to another crack. Climb it to a stance and belay. 150 feet.

Pitch 4: 5.7 Resume climbing the crack. 80 feet.

Pitch 5: 5.7 Continue up the crack. 80 feet.

Pitch 6: 5.7 Continue up the crack, staying on the buttress nose. Belay at a fixed piton and bolt. 120 feet.

Pitch 7: 5.7 Head straight up, passing a bolt to a large pine tree. 80 feet.

Pitch 8: Third class. Scramble to the summit.

Take the North Fork Canyon descent.

FA: George and Joanne Urioste 1980

33. Chicken Lips IV, 5.10a ★★★ Traditional. This is located in the middle of the upper level of the Painted Bowl. Link *Black Orpheus* with this route for seventeen pitches of fun (climb *Black Orpheus*, descend to the Painted Bowl, and hike to the base of *Chicken Lips*).

Pitch 1: 5.10a, 7 bolts. Take a thin crack up a water-polished face. Belay on a ledge beneath a large right-facing corner. 100 feet.

Pitch 2: 5.10a Climb the right-facing corner, heading right when it pinches off to above a large pine tree. Then head back left to a ledge and belay beneath the right-facing corner. 110 feet.

Pitch 3: 5.8, 3 bolts. Take the corner up 60 feet, to just before the crack pinches off. Traverse left onto a nose. Climb the nose, past bolts, to a bolted belay on a ledge. 130 feet.

Pitch 4: 5.10a, 7 bolts. Climb the face left of the

nose to a large ledge with a big pine tree. 150 feet.

Pitch 5: 5.9, 4 bolts. Lieback up a right-facing dihedral to a belay ledge. 120 feet.

Pitch 6: 5.8, 1 bolt. Climb a chimney, pulling a roof to a deep alcove and belay. 130 feet.

Pitch 7: 5.6 Take the chimney to the top. 120 feet.

Take the North Fork Canyon descent.

FA: George and Joanne Urioste 1980

▲ CELEBRATION WALL
S All-Day Sun   Approach: 3 hours

Follow the trail to where it goes downhill and parallels the Solar Slab Area on the right, and the wash on the left. When you reach a point where you are directly beneath the route *Johnny Vegas*, take the trail downhill and into the wash. Hike up Oak Creek Canyon until it splits into the north and south forks, just past Black Arch Wall. Take the right (north) fork. Pass the section where the wash is choked off by polished slabs, boulders, and bushes. Head slightly left and then avoid the slippery slabs where possible by exiting into boulders and bushes on either side of the wash. When you reach a piece of rock with two large cracks angling up and slightly left (the Ski Tracks), celebrate—you have finally reached Celebration Wall! Routes are described from left to right.

North Fork Canyon descent: Hike the ridgeline left (west) toward the limestone cliffs high above the sandstone, to the back of the canyon. Upon reaching a bright red band of rock heading down into the wash, at the back of the canyon, hike down along the right (west) edge of the rock. Continue down to the wash and then take the wash back to the base of the wall or route. A long, vigorous hike with fourth- and fifth-class scrambling. To the car: 3–5 hours.

34. Coltrane IV, 5.9 ★★ Mixed. Left of a 250-foot slab, left of the Ski Tracks, are several overhangs, broken in two places. Start beneath the leftmost break. Reach the base by way of a third-class traverse to the right from a usually dry waterfall.

Pitch 1: 5.9, 6 bolts. Take a steep face up to easier ground. Move left and then up and right to a ledge below a right-facing corner. 145 feet.

Pitch 2: 5.7, 4 bolts. Head straight up the face to a fixed belay. 165 feet.

Pitch 3: 5.8, 3 bolts. Climb straight up 80 feet and then traverse right to the fixed belay. 165 feet.

Pitch 4: 5.8, 4 bolts. Climb out right to a white pedestal. From its summit, downclimb the right side 20 feet and then climb 20 feet to the right. Move directly up to a ledge and a fixed belay. 165 feet.

Pitch 5: Fourth class. Climb to a large ledge above.

Pitch 6: Fourth class. Traverse straight left on the ledge.

Take the North Fork Canyon descent.

FA: George and Joanne Urioste 1979

35. The Easter Egg 5.6 ★

Traditional. Climb up and right to the top of a large white ramp that leads to a pillar, just right of some roof/arch systems and left of a large right-facing dihedral. Begin on top of

the pillar about 100 feet above the wash. This route has a lot of loose rock. Gear: standard rack to #3.5 Friend.

Pitch 1: 5.6 Climb cracks up black rock to about midway. Angle right and then cut back left and up, following cracks to the huge right-angling ramp, and belay. 120 feet.

Pitch 2: 5.6 Take the ramp up and right to its top. 40 feet.

Descend by heading down the large ramp to rappel anchors, left of a large black block.

Rappel with 2 ropes to the base.

FA: George and Joanne Urioste 1979

36. Underhanging Overhang IV, 5.6+ ★★★

Traditional. There are two huge, black, vertical water streaks on the right side of the wall. This route climbs left of the water streaks, the left Ski Track, the leftmost of two huge cracks climbing up the wall and veering left.

Pitch 1: Begin on very polished, black patina. End at the top of the face where the crack begins to diagonal left, on a low-angle ledge. 80 feet.

Pitch 2: Take the crack, moving up and left under a roof to the left side of the roof. 120 feet.

Pitch 3: Continue following the crack to a big ledge.

Pitch 4: Step right into a left-facing corner, the farthest one left. Take the crack up to a small belay stance.

Pitch 5: Continue up the crack, pull a roof, and belay on a sloping ledge below a steeper wall.

Pitch 6: Move up the steep, varnished face and then traverse left to a crack in white rock. Climb up to a ledge and belay.

Pitch 7: Exit the right side of the ledge, pulling an overhang. Climb through the notch in the roof. Belay on the ledge above.

Pitch 8: 5.6+ Take a crack through the black varnish. When the angle lessens, step right to a belay ledge. 185 feet.

Pitch 9: 5.3 Climb up the face to the summit pine trees. 80 feet.

Take the North Fork Canyon descent.

FA: Joe Frani, Margo Youngi 1975

37. Catwalk IV, 5.6+ ★★★ Traditional. This route begins 100 feet to the right of *Underhanging Overhang* and climbs the right Ski Track. Finish on last two pitches of *Underhanging Overhang*.

Pitch 1: Fourth and fifth class. From a bushy ledge, scramble up and right on slabs to the base of the right Ski Track crack, below a double set of roofs (on the left side of a small arch). 150 feet.

Pitch 2: 5.6 From a belay ledge with bushes, follow cracks up through two roofs. Continue up a crack to an alcove and belay at the base of a right-facing corner.

Pitch 3: 5.6 Take the right-facing corner up to another right-facing corner below some scrub oak. Belay below a tower where the black water streak begins. 150 feet.

Pitch 4: 5.5 Climb to the top of the pillar, scram-

bling up the face left to a large ledge.

Pitch 5: 5.5 Climb the right-facing corner. 110 feet.

Pitch 6: 5.5 Continue up the corner to a ledge below a brown face with a chimney on the left.

Pitch 7: 5.6 Climb the right-facing chimney on black patina to a ledge up and left (the top of three ledges). 100 feet.

Pitches 8–9: Finish on pitches 8 and 9 of *Underhanging Overhang*.

Take the North Fork Canyon descent.

FA: Margo Young, Joe Frani 1975

SOUTH FORK CANYON

There is a worthwhile route in the back of Oak Creek Canyon's south fork. Follow the trail to where it goes downhill and parallels the Solar Slab Area on the right, and the wash on the left. When you reach a point where you are directly beneath the route *Johnny Vegas*, take the trail downhill and into the wash. Hike up Oak Creek Canyon until it splits into the north and south forks, just past Black Arch Wall. Take the left (south) fork. Hike up the wash until you reach a large slab on the left leading up to another drainage. Head east, up the slab, to reach a fixed rope on a large pine. Ascend this and go left and up more slabs until you reach two small boulders. Follow cairns up a long scrub-oak gully to a notch. Continue to the notch and a short wall on the left side. Climb this to more slabs. Move right along the rim of the canyon until you can cross to the south side. From this point you have a direct view of *The Coffin*. Hike south, up slabs and a gully to the base.

38. The Coffin IV, 5.5, A2 ★★ Traditional/aid.

Pitch 1: 5.5, A1 Climb a dirty slab and corner that lead to a crack. Climb the crack, passing a pod. Continue up a wide crack to a tree belay. 120 feet.

Pitch 2: A1 Climb a crack to a fork. Head right into a wide section and finish on a small ledge system. 100 feet.

Pitch 3: A1 Move up the steep crack past pods into the Coffin and belay. 110 feet.

Pitch 4: A1 Stem up and out of the Coffin to really good rock. Follow a crack up to a small recess and belay. 120 feet.

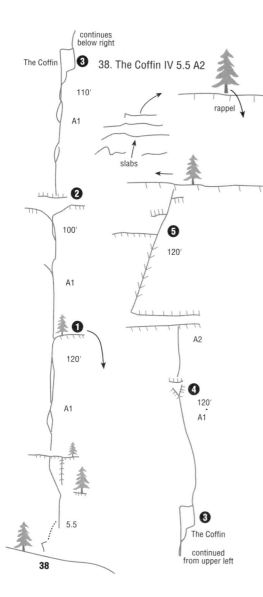

continues
below right

The Coffin ❸ 38. The Coffin IV 5.5 A2

110'

rappel

A1

slabs

❷

100'

❺

120'

A1

❶

120'

A2

A1

❹

120'
A1

A1

❸

The Coffin

5.5

continued
from upper left

38

right to a tree and rappel. At the bottom of the rappel, thread 2 70-meter ropes and rappel down to the Coffin. Rappel again off fixed nuts to the top of pitch 1, and from there rappel to the base.

FA: Brian Bowman, Dave Melchoir

▲ THE FORK
NW PM Sun   Approach: 1.75 hours

Follow the trail to where it goes downhill and parallels the Solar Slab Area on the right, and the wash on the left. When you reach a point where you are directly beneath the route *Johnny Vegas*, take the trail downhill and into the wash. Hike up Oak Creek Canyon until it splits into the north and south forks. This wall is on the left at the fork. It has two, large, left-facing dihedrals to the right of the routes and is located directly across from the Painted Bowl. The routes begin about 200 feet above the wash. Scramble up slabs to get there. Routes are described from left to right.

39. TC Arête 5.11 ★★★ Mixed. Climb up the "outrageous" arête left of the left-facing dihedrals. Start up using bolts for protection and then use "way thin free pro!" Gear: small.

Pitch 1: Climb the red, right-facing corner to a ledge and fixed anchor.

Pitch 2: Continue up the open-book seam to under a roof and a fixed belay.

Rappel.

FA: Tom Cecil

40. Oakey Dokey 5.10 ★★ Traditional. Begin 30 feet right of the previous route, beneath a roof in the center of the wall, left of the leftmost huge dihedral. Gear: standard rack to #4 Friend and brass wires.

Pitch 1: 5.9 Go up and right to a ledge with a bush. Continue up and right to the base of a left-facing corner, on the left side of a roof. Take the corner up and right. Go right under an eyebrow roof and up to belay on the right side of a small ledge. 150 feet.

Pitch 2: 5.10 Move up and right to a ledge at the base of an "inverted staircase flake," underneath

Pitch 5: A2 Climb the crack to a weird ledge system. Traverse left to a corner. Follow the corner up to a large ledge. 120 feet.

To descend, from the top of the pitch 5 walk left until you can climb an easy slab to the top. Walk back

THE FORK

descent

39 40

and left of the roof formed by the left-facing dihedral. 100 feet.

Pitch 3: 5.9 Climb the face left of the flake. Move up into the left-facing dihedral.

Pitch 4: Take the big left-facing dihedral to the top of the cliff.

Descend by traversing the huge summit slab down and right in the south fork of Oak Creek Canyon.
FA: Bob Harrington, Alan Bartlett, Bill St. Jean 1978

▲ BLOOD WALL
NE AM Sun   Approach: 1 hour

The Blood Wall is a dark blood-red rock formation 100 yards above the wash in the center of the wall across from the Solar Slab Area. The wall begins out of a bowl-like formation and there is a large pine tree at the top center of the wall. Follow the trail to where it goes downhill and parallels the Solar Slab Area on the right,

and the wash on the left. When you reach a point where you are directly beneath the route *Johnny Vegas*, take the trail downhill and into the wash. Pass the trail that heads out of the wash to the Triad (where a red-rock formation blocks the wash) and continue up the wash 300 feet to a low-angled slab. Third-class scramble up and left on slabs toward the base in the bowl.

41. Crack McMuffin 5.7+ ★★★ Traditional. Begin on the left side of the varnished wall and take the crack that extends up and right to the pine tree at the top, center of the wall.

Pitch 1: 5.7 Climb up and right to a pine tree on a ledge. Continue up for another 80 feet as the crack steepens. 100 feet.

Pitch 2: 5.7+ Take the crack up and right. 120 feet.

Pitch 3: 5.6 Continue to the pine tree at the top of the feature. 80 feet.

Descend by walking left (east). Do two single-rope

rappels to reach a gully. Take the gully down and around to the front of the wall. You can also do a 150-foot rappel to the base of the third-class approach slabs.
FA: Stephanie Petrilak, Mike Gilbert, Joanne Urioste 1979

▲ THE TRIAD
NE AM Sun   Approach: 45 minutes

Follow the trail to where it goes downhill and parallels the Solar Slab Area on the right, and the wash on the left. When you reach a point where you are directly beneath the route *Johnny Vegas*, take the trail downhill and into the wash. Continue in the main wash until you reach a red rock formation blocking it, with a large pine tree on the left. Hike up the hill left for 5 minutes to the wall. On the left is a north-facing wall, with a large right-facing corner that shields the left-side face with three obvious vertical cracks. Routes are described from left to right.

Descent: Walk off right, down a bushy hill that takes you to a point about 100 yards right of the cliff.

42. Beauty 5.9 ★★★ Traditional. Gear: to #5 Friend.
Pitch 1: Climb the off-width crack on the far left to a single-bolt belay station. 100 feet.
Pitch 2: Continue up the chimney to the top of the cliff. 100 feet.
FA: Joe Herbst, John Byrd

43. Truth 5.6 ★★★ Traditional. Climb the middle of the three cracks, a chimney. Run-out. Gear: big Friends to #6. 150 feet.
FA: Joe Herbst

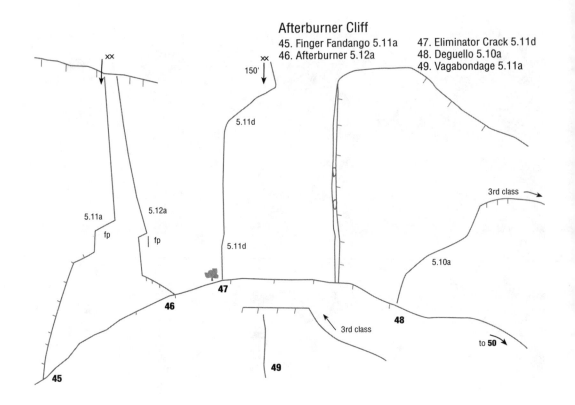

Afterburner Cliff
45. Finger Fandango 5.11a
46. Afterburner 5.12a
47. Eliminator Crack 5.11d
48. Deguello 5.10a
49. Vagabondage 5.11a

44. Wisdom 5.7 ★★★ Traditional. Climb the rightmost of the three cracks, a loose chimney. Fixed anchors. 100 feet. Rappel.
FA: Joe Herbst

▲ AFTERBURNER CLIFF
NE AM Sun   Approach: 1.25 hours

This cliff is located far up and left of the Triad. From the Triad, hike up and left alongside the base of Mount Wilson's northeast side. Scary third- and fourth-class scrambling takes you 200 yards up to a white and black 150-foot wall. Routes are described from left to right.

45. Finger Fandango 5.11a ★★★ Traditional. Climb a right-facing corner to a fixed pin and then climb the finger crack to its top. Rappel using 2 ropes.
FA: Paul Van Betten, Jay Smith, Paul Obenheim 1984

46. Afterburner 5.12a ★★★★ Traditional. Climb the finger crack with a fixed pin located 30 feet right of the previous route. Rappel.
FA: Paul Van Betten, Sal Mamusia 1984

47. Eliminator Crack 5.11d ★★★★★ Traditional.

Begin 30 feet right of *Afterburner* at a *pure* finger crack! Lovely. Move up and right 150 feet to find the fixed anchor. Rappel using 2 ropes.
FA: Paul Van Betten, Randy Marsh 1984

48. Deguello 5.10a ★★★ Traditional. Climb the crack, angling up and right to a ramp. Exit up and right off the ramp.
FA: Sal Mamusia, Danny Meyers, Paul Van Betten, Brad Stewart 1984

49. Vagabondage 5.11a ★★★ Traditional. This route is on the tier directly below and slightly right of the classic *Eliminator Crack*. Climb a thin finger crack, which opens to hand crack toward the top. 80 feet.
FA: Mike Ward, Danny Meyers

50. '34 Ford with Flames 5.10d ★★ Traditional. Begin down and right of the previous routes on light-brown rock. Climb a right-angling crack. Gear: standard rack including brass wires.
FA: Mike Ward, Bob Yoho 1985

Somewhere on this side of Oak Creek is an old Warren Harding route, but we could not get the information on it.

MOUNT WILSON

MOUNT WILSON NORTH
Willy's Couloir ▲ Horseshoe Wall ▲ Aeolian Wall ▲ Ramen Pride Area ▲ Cactus Flower Tower

MOUNT WILSON SOUTH

MOUNT WILSON sits between Oak Creek and First Creek Canyons. The routes described here are on the east and the south faces of the peak and are reached from different parking areas, the old Oak Creek Campground parking area and the First Creek Canyon parking area. In this chapter, we put hiking descent information before approaches because the descents are the same for all routes that climb to the summit. Both descents require fifth-class scrambling. The Oak Creek Canyon descent requires a rappel, and some climbers may prefer to rappel portions of the First Creek Canyon descent.

Oak Creek Canyon south fork descent: From the summit of Mount Wilson, hike west toward the back of Oak Creek Canyon. Take the third gully system that heads down and right (north) on slick, water-polished rock, into the south fork of Oak Creek. Continue down for 15 minutes. Upon reaching an impasse, rappel from a small tree (single rope) and continue down the wash. At a large red rock section of the wash (just below and west of the Triad in Oak Creek Canyon) move up and slightly right, paralleling the wash. Hike behind Wilson's Pimple (a tiny mountain below and northeast of Mount Wilson) and back to the parking area at the old Oak Creek Campground. 4 hours.

First Creek Canyon descent: From the summit of Mount Wilson, hike down slabs southwest toward the back of First Creek Canyon. At the base of the southwest-angling slabs, hike left (southeast), scrambling down third- and fourth-class slabs. Bushwhack down into the wash. Take the wash to the First Creek Canyon Trail (paralleling the wash), which leads to the First Creek Canyon parking area. 4 hours.

MOUNT WILSON NORTH

From Las Vegas, take West Charleston Boulevard west, which turns into State Route 159. Drive over the 215 Beltway and zero your odometer. Drive 9 miles and park at the turnout for the old Oak Creek Campground (3.8 miles past the Red Rock Canyon 13-mile Scenic Drive entrance). Park so you leave enough room for other vehicles.

Hike around the gate and onto an old road. Pass a sign to Oak Creek Canyon (2.5 miles), hike across a roadbed, and continue on the road for about 2 miles. The road travels toward Mount Wilson, northwest, and then moves around the backside of Wilson's Pimple (a tiny mountain below and on the northeast side of Mount Wilson).

When the old road curves behind Wilson's Pimple, cut left (no distinct trail) up a hill. Take a rib up to the right side of a low pink band of rock with a dark red band above it. Traverse the pink band left (south) for about 50 yards to a rocky breakdown. Move up the breakdown until you reach the top of the dark red band of rock. Just above the band, heading northwest, is the Resolution Arête Gully (aka White Rot Gully).

▲ WILLY'S COULOIR
E/W AM/PM Sun   Approach: 1.5 hours

Sketchy approach: From the top of the dark red band of rock, traverse a catwalk left along the top of the band for 100 feet to a rappel station and the base of a rock gully. Do some easy fifth-class scrambling and hand-over-hand up ropes to a tree ledge. Move left up the gully system, angling left behind a huge ear of rock. Hike up and left to the farthest

Larry Hamilton on the summit of Mount Wilson after the first ascent of the Aeolian Wall 1975.

337

Photo courtesy of the Larry Hamilton Collection

point behind the ear, to black, varnished walls.

Less sketchy approach: Head up and right, up the Aeolian Wall approach, the Resolution Arête Gully. At the top of the gully, cut up and left to reach the top of a low formation. Hike left and down to the space between the ear and the main wall.

Routes are described from left to right.

The following three routes are located on the black, varnished face on the left (east) as you walk into Willy's Couloir.

1. Otters are People Too 5.8 ★★ Traditional.
Climb a right-leaning crack above a short rock pillar.

Pitch 1: 5.8 Climb the right-leaning crack and ramp through a short wide section to a small ledge and belay.

Pitch 2: 5.7 Continue up the crack to a huge ledge.

To descend, traverse the ledge right to the fixed anchors of *Slick Willy*. Rappel using 2 ropes (two rappels).
FA: John Rosholt, Josh Cross 1996

2. Slick Willy 5.11a, A0 ★★ Traditional. Begin
right of the previous route, below a bolt ladder. Gear: standard rack plus 3 each of #1.5 and #2 Friends.

Pitch 1: 5.11a, A0, 4 bolts. Aid up the short bolt ladder to obtain a right-facing, right-leaning crack. Take the crack up to a ledge, two-thirds of the way up and belay.

Pitch 2: 5.11a Continue up the crack to the huge ledge. 100 feet.

Rappel from the fixed anchors using 2 ropes (two rappels).
FA: John Rosholt 1996

3. Free Willy 5.11d ★★ Traditional. Begin 20 feet
up the hill and right of *Slick Willy* atop several boulders. The meat of this route climbs a $1\frac{1}{4}$- to $1\frac{1}{2}$-inch crack. Gear: standard rack to #2.5 Friend with doubles of #1.5–#2.5 Friends.

Pitch 1: 5.10d Climb the straight-up finger crack above the boulders. Move up and right to reach a ledge below a right-facing flake and belay.

Pitch 2: 5.11d Follow a flake around right and then back left to a bolted anchor on a sloping ledge.

Pitch 3: 5.11a Climb the right-facing corner up to a ledge. Traverse the ledge left and take the face up and left to the top of *Slick Willy*.

Rappel from the fixed anchors with 2 ropes (2 rappels).

FA: *John Rosholt, Josh Cross, Jack Herrick 1996*

The following three routes climb the right (west) side of Willy's Couloir or Mount Wilson's east face.

4. Dogma V, 5.11c ★★★★ Traditional. Begin near the farthest point up the couloir, at a wide chimney. It is quicker to simul-climb pitches 6–8 and 15–17. Gear: one set of everything to #4 Friend (including #Z3 Friend or #00 TCU), and 15 quickdraws.

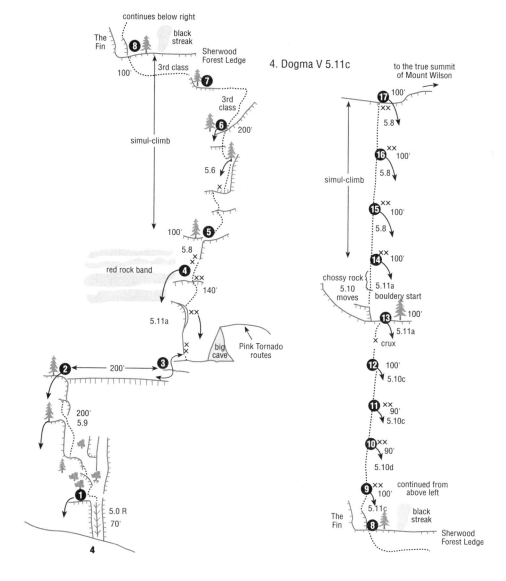

4. Dogma V 5.11c

Pitch 1: 5.0 R Climb the corner in the center of the chimney. Belay on the ledge left at the top. 70 feet.

Pitch 2: 5.9 Do not continue up the good-looking chimney. Instead, head left, scrambling through shrubs and ledges to a right-facing corner. Climb the face to its right to a ledge with a tree (the rappel). Continue up, past a ledge to a larger ledge and tree. 200 feet.

Pitch 3: Traverse right on the ledge and then work up to the base of a thin seam left of a cave. The cave is formed by a large section of rock (marking the top of the Pink Tornado routes). 200 feet.

Pitch 4: 5.11a Climb the face to a thin seam. Move up to a right-facing chimney and ear, passing rappel anchors on the right to obtain the ledge atop the ear. Step slightly right onto a thin, slopey face. Take the face up to a ledge and anchors beneath a runoff trough. 140 feet.

Pitch 5: 5.8 Pull over a small lip, clip a couple bolts, and head up the trough. Belay at a pine tree on a ledge, left of the drainage. 100 feet.

Pitch 6: 5.6 Face-climb up the slippery drainage to under a roof, clip a bolt, and pull the roof. Move up the face to another big tree (above the rappel tree). 200 feet.

Pitch 7: Third class. Take a ramp up and right and then hike back left to a good ledge and tree.

Pitch 8: Third class. Traverse the slab up and left to the leftmost edge of the Sherwood Forest Ledge, just right of The Fin, a huge right-facing corner. 100 feet.

Pitch 9: 5.11c Get ready to climb the Horseshoe Wall. Begin on a right-facing flake right of The Fin. Climb it to the featured, varnished face. Take the face up and right, clipping bolts to a bolted belay. 100 feet.

Pitch 10: 5.10d Continue straight up the face. Weird climbing. Bolts and gear. 90 feet.

Pitch 11: 5.10c Continue up the face. Bolted pitch. No gear. 90 feet.

Pitch 12: 5.10c Continue up the face and crack. 100 feet.

Pitch 13: 5.11a Move up to a bolt. Head right and then up the face slightly right to a large ledge and pine tree. 100 feet.

Pitch 14: 5.11a Careful on this bouldery start. Traverse the ledge left to a short right-facing corner.

Take it up to a ledge. Continue up the face to a bolted anchor. 100 feet.

Pitches 15–16: 5.8 Climb two 100-foot pitches up the face.

Pitch 17: 5.8 Continue up the face. Finish on bolts just below the top of the cliff. 100 feet.

Rappel the route with a 60-meter rope (watch the end of your rope: some rappels are close to the full rope length). Or hike to the top of Mount Wilson and descend via the south fork of Oak Creek Canyon or via First Creek Canyon.
FA: Mike Lewis, Brian McCray 1999

5. Pink Tornado Left 5.9 ★★★ Traditional. A smooth white slab leans against the wall at the entrance to Willy's Couloir. This route begins in the chimney that ascends the left side of the slab and climbs a formation called the Pink Tornado (a slabby formation that is slender at its base). Gear: standard rack.

Pitch 1: 5.7 Climb the smooth chimney to a ledge.

Pitch 2: 5.9 Take the wide crack and chimney up the left side of the Pink Tornado to a bolted anchor above and left of the crack.

Pitch 2 variation: 5.9, 2 bolts. Take the face directly above the ledge to the fixed anchors.

Pitch 3: 5.7 Climb the face to belay at the top of a right-arching crack.

Pitch 4: 5.5 Continue up the face to the top of a huge, dark red formation that leans against the wall. Connect with *Pink Tornado Right.*

Pitch 5: 5.7 Angle up and right, off the right side of the large ledge.

Pitch 6: 5.7 Continue up to Sherwood Forest Ledge. Rappel *Dogma,* with a 60-meter rope.
FA: Don Giesek, Geoffrey Conley 1975

6. Pink Tornado Right 5.10 ★★★ Traditional. Just before entering Willy's Couloir, turn right, before where a smooth white slab leans against the wall at the couloir entrance. Begin in one of the double cracks right of this slab and climb past the right side of the Pink Tornado (a slabby formation that is slender at its base). Gear: standard rack.

Pitch 1: 5.8 Climb the rightmost of the double

cracks to the right side of the Pink Tornado feature.

Pitch 1 variation: 5.9 Climb the leftmost of the double cracks.

Pitch 2: 5.10 Climb the off-width on the right side of the Pink Tornado.

Pitch 3: 5.7 Climb the face and belay.

Pitch 4: 5.7 Continue up the face to the top of the huge, dark red formation that leans against the wall.

Pitches 5–6: Climb pitches 5 and 6 of *Pink Tornado Left*.

Rappel *Dogma* with a 60-meter rope.

FA: Don Giesek, Geoffrey Conley 1975

▲ HORSESHOE WALL
E AM Sun   Approach: 1.5 hours

This wall sits atop Sherwood Forest Ledge. (The Sherwood Forest Club is a nonlanded nudist club affiliated with the American Association for Nude Recreation. We think somebody got naked up there, hence the name of the ledge.) This wall is bordered on the left by The Fin, a large right-facing corner/fin feature, and on the right by *Resolution Arête*. Reach the wall by climbing one of routes 4–6. Or, from the top of the Resolution Arête Gully, continue up and left across a third-class hillside, eventually gaining the gully left of *Resolution Arête*. Third-, fourth-, and fifth-class up the gully. At the top, exit left and climb to the enormous Sherwood Forest Ledge system. Routes are described from left to right.

7. Scotty IV, 5.10a ★★ Traditional. Begin 100 feet left of the leftmost pine tree growing on the right side of the ledge. Take a right-angling crack to a left-facing corner. Continue up the left-facing corner to the base of an overhanging bulge, The Mushroom. Climb the left side of The Mushroom. Rappel *Dogma*, with a 60-meter rope. Or from the Mount Wilson summit, descend via Oak Creek Canyon's south fork or via First Creek Canyon.

FA: Scott Gilbert, Geoffrey Gilbert 1978

8. Gwondonna Land Boogie IV, 5.9 ★★★ Traditional. Begin 200 feet right of *Scotty*. *Gwondonna Land Boogie* crosses *Scotty* midway up the wall, then

climbs to *Scotty*'s left side and a large flake. It then follows the flake to the summit. Gear: standard rack and brass wires.

Pitch 1: 5.9 Run-out at the start. Take a thin corner up and left. Undercling out a roof and then head up and right. Move right to the second crack system and take it to where it unites with a corner at a roof. Pull the roof and belay.

Pitch 2: 5.8 Climb a left-leaning crack to a right-leaning crack.

Pitch 3: 5.8 Continue up to a ledge. 75 feet.

Pitch 4: 5.9 Climb the thin corner above the ledge to a roof. Pull the roof on the left side.

Pitch 5: 5.8 Take steep cracks to a ledge, taking you to the left of *Scotty*.

Pitch 6: 5.7 Move up and left to a ledge with many trees. Belay at the first tree.

Pitch 7: Third class. Traverse the ledge left to a large chimney.

Pitch 8: 5.9 Ascend the chimney, through two roofs to a ledge atop a pillar. Run-out.

Pitches 9–10: 5.9 Move up a corner. Belay and then continue to the top of the corner.

Rappel *Dogma*, with a 60-meter rope. Or from the Mount Wilson summit, descend via Oak Creek Canyon's south fork or via First Creek Canyon.

FA: Geoffrey Conley, Phil Broscovak 1981

▲ AEOLIAN WALL
E AM Sun   Approach: 1.5 hours

This wall is the distinctive diamond-shaped wall right of *Resolution Arête*, and bounded on the right by Wind God Tower. To get there, follow the main Mount Wilson North directions and continue up the breakdown/gully, heading up and right. At the top of the gully, cut up and left to reach the top of a low formation. At the intersection with the lower left (south) fork of the gully, head left and down for 30 feet. Then head back up (west) for about 25 minutes to a ledge system. Routes are described from left to right.

9. Sentimental Journey IV, 5.9 ★★★ As traditional as it gets. This was the first route up Mount Wilson's east face and the first big route in Red

Rock. It was later named by Red Rock climbing historian, Larry DeAngelo. The first ascensionists said if he climbed it, he could name it. From the top of the Resolution Arête Gully, continue up and left across a third-class hillside, eventually gaining the gully left of *Resolution Arête*. Third-, fourth-, and fifth-class up the gully. At the top, exit left and climb to the enormous Sherwood Forest Ledge system. *Sentimental Journey* climbs the central crack system up the right-hand headwall (left of *Resolution Arête*) for several hundred feet. Easier rock leads to the summit.

Descend *Dogma,* the south Fork of Oak Creek Canyon or First Creek Canyon.

FA: John Williamson, Keith Hogan 1970 (via Willy's Couloir to Sherwood Forest Ledge); Joe Herbst 1971 (the second ascent, solo, the day before his wedding, via Resolution Arête Gully to Sherwood Forest Ledge)

10. Resolution Arête V, 5.11b or 5.9, A0 ★★★
Traditional. Take the ledge system left to a ponde-

rosa pine. Begin 40 feet left of the pine. Gear: standard rack to #5 Friend and doubles of #1.0–1.5 Friends, and plenty of slings.

Pitch 1: 5.9 Traverse left of the pine tree for 40 feet on a thin face to a right-facing corner. Climb to a belay with 1 bad bolt. 100 feet.

Pitch 2: 5.8 Continue up the crack to the top of a red pillar formation. 150 feet.

Pitch 3: 5.9 Take the face up and right of the pillar up to a right-facing corner. Difficult gear placements. Move up to belay near the base of a chimney. 155 feet.

Pitch 4: 5.8 Climb the chimney. Continue up to the highest ledge in the white rock, above the red band. 150 feet.

Pitch 5: 5.8 Face-climb for 50 feet and then head up and right to the lower of two large pine trees. 160 feet.

Pitch 6: Third and fourth class. Take loose rock up and right to a notch and then go left, through the notch (created by the triangular feature leaning against the Aeolian Wall). Continue for about 80 feet to a

right-facing corner with some loose
blocks in it. 180 feet.

Pitch 7: 5.9+ Climb the loose corner
as it turns into a nice stemming corner.
Belay in a recess. 140 feet.

Pitch 8: 5.9 Take the face and crack
upward to a belay stance 20 feet below a
roof. 100 feet.

Pitch 9: 5.11b or 5.9, A0 Climb and
pull the roof using fixed gear and the finger crack. Pull over onto a face and continue up to a belay stance. Fixed gear. 100
feet.

Pitch 10: 5.10d Climb a corner with
difficult gear to start. Bust left to finish on
a large, sloping ledge with 1 bolt. 90 feet.
It is possible to rappel 100 feet from here
and bivy, protected from weather, on the
Sherwood Forest Ledge.

Pitch 11: 5.8 Move up the sloping
ledge to its end. Take a left-facing dihedral to just below a notch. 150 feet.

Pitch 12: 5.8 Take a short face to a
ledge with a large block and a crack
emerging from its left edge. 150 feet.

Pitch 13: 5.9+ Called "the tricky hand
traverse," this section takes the left-
diagonaling crack up and left to a belay
at the base of a chimney. 100 feet.

Pitch 14: 5.7 Climb the chimney and
then face-climb up and right to the right
edge of a ledge, right of a large pillar. 160 feet.

Pitch 15: Fourth class. Go into a hole on the right
side of the pillar and belay at the base of a chimney.
80 feet.

Pitch 16: 5.9 Climb the chimney, moving left as it
gets more difficult. Take the face up and left to a huge
ledge with a tree. Some rope drag. 150 feet.

Pitch 17: Walk left on the huge ledge, The Catwalk.
120 feet.

Pitch 18: 5.8 Climb the left portion of the huge
chimney at the end of The Catwalk to a belay below
a white rotten roof. 120 feet.

Pitch 19: 5.7 Carefully pull the roof, on loose rock.
Climb to a sloping ledge with a big pine. 80 feet.

Pitch 20: Fourth class. Scramble up and left. 160 feet.

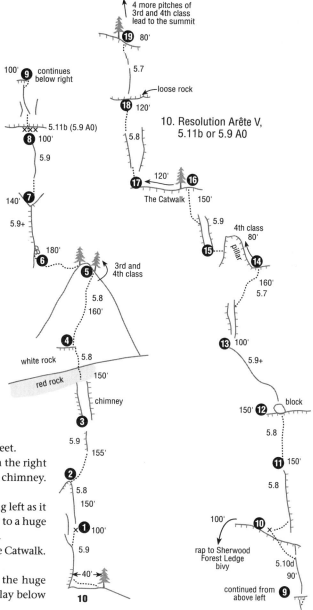

10. Resolution Arête V,
5.11b or 5.9 A0

Pitch 21: Third and fourth class. Climb up and right. 150 feet.

Pitch 22: Fourth class. Move straight up broken sections of rock. 150 feet.

Pitch 23: Third and fourth class. Continue to the summit.

To descend, hike to the top of the formation and head left to the *Dogma* anchors and rappel with a 60-meter rope. Or, hike down the back via either the south fork of Oak Creek Canyon or First Creek Canyon.
FA: Phil Broscovak, Geoffrey Conley 1981
FFA: Paul Van Betten, Richard Harrison 1984

11. Inti Watana IV, 5.10c ★★★★ Mixed. Appropriately named, this route always catches the first morning sun: *Inti Watana* means "the hitching post of the sun" in Quechua, the ancient language of the Incas. The Incas believed that if you did not tie the sun down every evening it would not come up in the morning. To reach the base, take the ledge system left. One hundred feet before reaching a ponderosa pine (the start of *Resolution Arête*), take a gully up and right to a large chockstone. Pass through a hole on its left. Begin uphill and left of the 200-foot formation leaning against the main Aeolian Wall. The route climbs to the top of a pillar left of the Aeolian Wall proper.

Pitch 1: 5.9+, 7 bolts. Climb a face to a recess and bolted belay. 90 feet.

Pitch 2: 5.10c, 8 bolts. Continue up the steepening face to a bolted belay stance (#1 Friend for the crux). 100 feet.

Pitch 3: 5.8 Take the face up and right and then back left to the bolted belay. 130 feet.

Pitch 4: 5.9, 3 bolts. Climb the face and small cracks (#00–#1 Friends) to a belay alcove. 140 feet.

Pitch 5: 5.7 Move right to reach a hand crack, taking it to a ledge. Step right again to another crack and climb it to a bolted belay. 130 feet.

Pitch 6: 5.9, 9 bolts. Take the face up and right to a large ledge. 130 feet.

Pitch 7: 5.9 Move right to a small crack, leading to an S-shaped crack, over a roof. Continue to a hanging bolted belay. 165 feet.

Pitch 8: 5.9+, 6 bolts. Take the face to a recessed ledge, "The Snoring Prosthadontist Ledge" (named for

Steve Rhodes). 130 feet.

Pitch 9: 5.9, 5 bolts. Climb over a large roof. 50 feet.

Pitch 10: 5.9, 12 bolts. Step left and climb the face to a hanging belay. 110 feet.

Pitch 11: 5.9, 6 bolts. Continue up the face to a bolted stance. 60 feet.

Pitch 12: 5.10b, 6 bolts. Move up the face, stepping

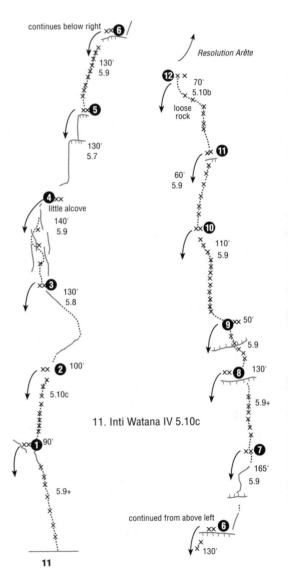

11. Inti Watana IV 5.10c

left over loose rock to a bolted anchor. 70 feet.

Rappel using 2 50-meter ropes (combining pitches 9 and 10, 11 and 12) or continue up *Resolution Arête* to the summit.

FA: Michael Clifford, George Urioste, Sam Pratt, Rick Nolting, Bill Holtz, Steve Rhodes 1997

AEOLIAN WALL LEFT

Follow the main approach for the Aeolian Wall. Upon reaching the top of the gully and continuing to the ledge system, head up and right to reach the base of a huge formation that leans against the center of the Aeolian Wall. Climb cracks up the center of this buttress (5.7) to reach a large pine and the start of these routes.

12. The Aeolian Wall Original Route V, 5.9, A3+ ★★★★

Traditional/aid. An aeolian harp emits melodious sounds as wind blows across its strings. In the center of the Aeolian Wall are two large, left leaning gashes. The left gash and left-facing corner beneath it comprise this route. The approach

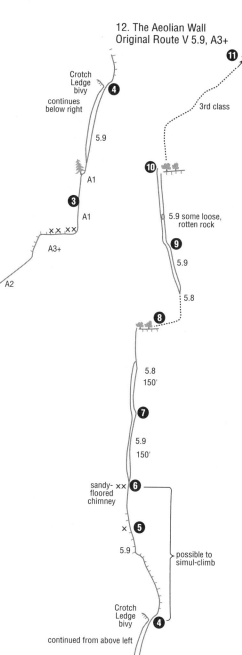

12. The Aeolian Wall
Original Route V 5.9, A3+

pitches involve a 5.9+, which climbs to third and fourth class up to a ledge beneath the start of the route. Gear: 2 baby angles, 3 angles, 6 Lost Arrows, 4 knifeblades, 2 Bugaboos, Rocks, brass wires, and Friends to #4.

Pitch 1: 5.8 Move up and left on the face to reach a right-angling ramp. Take the face and crack up and right to a ledge.

Pitch 2: A3, 1 bolt. Take a left-facing corner, past 1 bolt to a crack angling up and right. Belay at a small stance.

Pitch 3: A3+, 4 bolts. Continue up and right to under a roof. Pull the roof and belay.

Pitch 4: 5.9, A1 Continue up the mossy crack, passing a tree and entering a chimney. Belay on the ledge up and left, after the chimney (the Crotch Ledge, an okay bivy).

Pitch 5: 5.9, 1 bolt. Climb the crack up and slightly left to a left-facing corner. Move up, as it turns to a right-facing corner, and belay.

Pitch 6: Continue up the corner and crack to a bolted belay in a sandy cave at the base of a chimney. A better bivy than Crotch Ledge.

Pitch 7: 5.9 Climb the chimney to a belay halfway up. 150 feet.

Pitch 8: 5.8 Finish up the chimney and take the crack out of it to a large ledge. 150 feet.

Pitch 9: 5.9 Face-climb directly right and then straight up to a chimney. Enter the chimney and climb it partway up.

Pitch 10: 5.9 Finish up the chimney to the belay ledge on the top right. Some loose rock.

Pitch 11: Third class. Scramble up slabs to the summit.

Hike to the top of the formation and head left to the *Dogma* anchors and rappel with a 60-meter rope. Or, hike down the back via the south fork of Oak Creek Canyon.

FA: Joe Herbst, Larry Hamilton 1975

13. Woodrow V, 5.10b R ★ Traditional. In the center of Aeolian Wall are two, large, left-leaning gashes. This route climbs the right gash (or groove) that goes all the way to the top of the cliff, linking with the top of *The Aeolian Wall Original Route* at the top. This is an extremely serious route for those who know

how to move on loose rock and are comfortable climbing long pitches with little protection. The wall itself takes hours to approach and it requires a lot of easy fifth class to get up to the main face. The first-ascent party put up the route with 3 or 4 bolts and 1 rope. They climbed it on-sight, in one day, with no recon. The route turned out to be very exciting and bold under those circumstances. They had no way of bailing off the route because they had only one rope. The second-ascent party had an enormous epic on this climb, some suffering from hypothermia. Richard Harrison led them up the wall and to safety in cold, rain, and snow—an example of Harrison's notorious "cool" under pressure. Gear: to #4 Friend.

Pitch 1: 5.10a (5.10d by modern standards), 2 bolts. Climb the scantily protected face, left of a black water streak, to the base of the right gash mentioned in *The Aeolian Wall Original Route* description. Belay at a bolted anchor. Very run-out.

Pitch 2: 5.10a (5.10b/c by modern standards), 1 bolt. Finish up the face. Unprotected. Wendell Broussard says, "You might as well not have a rope." Pitches 4 and 5 of *The Woman of Mountain Dreams*, are so near to the first two pitches of *Woodrow* that you might be coerced into climbing them instead.

Pitches 3–4: 5.8 Climb up the gash in a chimney and then up a hand crack to a large ledge. Black, varnished rock.

Pitch 5: 5.9 Climb the face off the ledge that opens up right in front of you. Little gear.

Pitch 6: 5.10a Traverse up and left to meet the top of pitch 8 of *The Aeolian Wall Original Route*.

Pitches 7–9: Finish on *The Aeolian Wall Original Route*, pitches 9–11.

Hike to the top of the formation and head left to the *Dogma* anchors and rappel with a 60-meter rope. Or, hike down the back via the south fork of Oak Creek Canyon.

FA: Richard Harrison, John Long 1981

AEOLIAN WALL RIGHT

Follow the main approach for the Aeolian Wall. Upon reaching the top of the gully and continuing to the ledge system, descend slightly to reach another gully that heads westward. Hike up this second gully for 110 feet, scrambling up red rock. Cut left to a large pine.

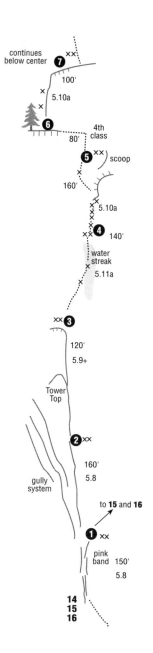

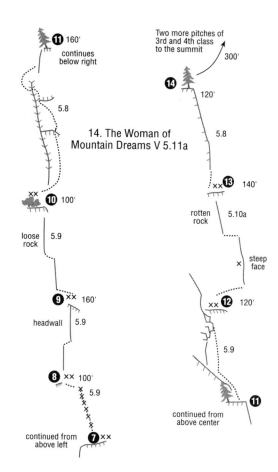

Wind God Tower forms the right boundary of Aeolian Wall. It is a tower at the base and just right of the center of Aeolian Wall, beneath the water streaks to the right of the start of *Woodrow*. In the middle of this tower, at its base, are cracks up the face. The following three routes share the first pitch and are otherwise described left to right.

14. The Woman of Mountain Dreams V, 5.11a

★★★ Traditional. This route follows a line up the center of Aeolian Wall. This route is dedicated to Lorraine Putnam, an aspiring writer who was killed in an auto accident prior to this route's completion. This route was named after one of her short stories.

Pitch 1: 5.8 Climb up and left through off-widths and grooves to a bolted anchor above a pink band. Stay out of the mossy corners. 150 feet.

Pitch 2: 5.8 Keep left, remaining in a crack system formed by a 500-foot pillar, to a bolted anchor. 160 feet.

Pitch 3: 5.9+ Stay in the crack, which leads to the highest ledge above the tower and a bolted anchor. 120 feet.

Pitch 4: 5.11a, 2 bolts. Situated just right of *Woodrow*. Take the slab/face up to the rightmost water streak. Belay at a hanging bolted anchor. 140 feet.

Pitch 5: 5.10a, 6 bolts. Follow 5 bolts to an arching, right-facing dihedral. Move left, up a face, past 1 bolt to a bolted anchor in a scoop. 160 feet.

Pitch 6: Fourth class. Take the face up 25 feet and traverse left to a large ledge. 80 feet.

Pitch 7: 5.10a, 2 bolts. From a tree on the ledge, climb the rightmost crack to a sloping ledge with bolted anchor. 100 feet.

Pitch 8: 5.9, 6 bolts. Take the face and thin cracks up for 75 feet and then traverse left to a stance with a bolted anchor. 100 feet.

Pitch 9: 5.9 Take a crack up for 15 feet and then move right for 5 feet to reach a steep headwall with a crack. Take it up to another sloping ledge and bolted anchor. 160 feet.

Pitch 10: 5.9 Move left to obtain a crack, climbing it to its end. Go left again to another chossy crack, which leads to a bushy, bolted belay ledge. 100 feet.

Pitch 11: 5.8 Head right, around a corner to a face. Continue up the face, passing a ledge. When below a roof, move left onto the left face (little protection). Take it up to where you can move back right into a crack system. Take it to a pine tree and belay. 160 feet.

Pitch 12: 5.9 Take a ramp up and left for 50 feet. Move up the face from there to reach blocky corners that lead to a big ledge with bolted anchors. 120 feet.

Pitch 13: 5.10a, 1 bolt. Traverse right (scary) to a thin crack. Move up the crack and overhanging face. When the gear thins out, move left to another crack up bad rock. Continue to a ledge and bolted anchor. 140 feet.

Pitch 14: 5.8 Take a chossy corner to a pine tree. 120 feet.

Pitch 15: Third and fourth class. Do not be fooled by the apparent simplicity of these last two pitches. Some tricky moves. Head right, around a corner, and then up and right to a gully with some awkward positions. 155 feet.

Pitch 16: Third and fourth class. Move up to a flat section. Scramble to the summit. 150 feet.

Hike to the top of the formation and head left to the *Dogma* anchors and rappel with a 60-meter rope. Or, hike down the back via the south fork of Oak Creek Canyon.

FA: Aitor Uson, Joanne Urioste 1998

15. Pagan Sacrifice V, 5.11c or 5.10, A2 ★★

Mixed. This route follows *The Gift of the Wind Gods* for five pitches and then takes a vertical crack right of Wind God Tower's center. Gear: standard rack to #2 Friend, doubles of #4.

Pitches 1–5: Climb pitches 1–5 of *The Gift of the Wind Gods*.

Pitch 6: 5.11c or A2, 2 bolts. Climb out the left side of a maroon spot. Traverse right on a face to a bolted anchor.

Pitch 7: 5.9+ R Take a crack. Then head left clipping 2 bolts, and then move back right to a stance.

Pitch 8: 5.8 Take straight-up cracks and then move right to cracks that lead to a ledge. 190 feet.

Pitch 9: 5.4 Move right on the ledge and begin climbing above a tree, veering right. Loose rock to the summit.

Hike to the top of the formation and head left to the *Dogma* anchors and rappel with a 60-meter rope. Or, hike down the back via the south fork of Oak Creek Canyon.

FA: Robert Warren, Steve Johnson 1997

16. The Gift of the Wind Gods V, 5.10d ★★★★

Mixed. This route climbs five pitches to a maroon spot, moves right and up to the right side of Wind God Tower, and then finishes up to the top of the Aeolian Wall. In the early spring of 1996 Urioste was doing a run at the base of Mount Wilson. "It was one of those days when a north wind blows through the desert, creating a clearness that makes all images more intense." Urioste glanced up at the Aeolian wall, "and a crack system jumped out at me," she

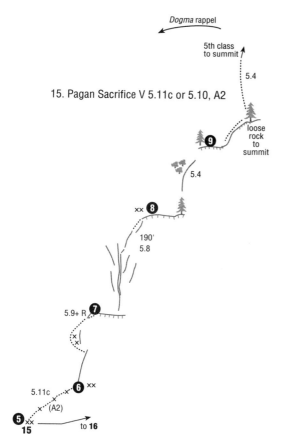

Dogma rappel

5th class
to summit

5.4

15. Pagan Sacrifice V 5.11c or 5.10, A2

loose
rock
to
summit

9

5.4

xx **8**

190'
5.8

5.9+ R **7**

5.11c **6** xx

(A2)

5 xx
15   to **16**

feet and then move right 15 feet to a slender crack. Take the crack to a stance below a large bush. 130 feet.

Pitch 3: 5.8 Climb the crack, stepping right midway up to another crack. Move up to a bolted anchor. 160 feet.

Pitch 4: 5.10d, 5 bolts. Move left into a thin crack and take it up through a steep section to a bolted stance. 150 feet.

Pitch 5: 5.8 Continue up the crack to a bolted belay (this was the high point for parties prior to the FA). 95 feet.

Pitch 6: 5.9+, 4 bolts. Move up the crack, and then head up and right on the face to a bolted stance. 85 feet.

Pitch 7: 5.10c, 11 bolts. Traverse right on slopey feet (there is one sucker bolt up 15 feet). Move up and right following the line of bolts. Continue across the overhanging face to a notch at the base of a large right-facing dihedral (the right edge of Wind God Tower). 160 feet.

Pitch 8: 5.9 Climb the wide crack and a roof to a bolted stance. 100 feet.

Pitch 9: 5.7 Take the corner and crack system up to a small pine. 150 feet.

Pitch 10: Easy fifth class. Scramble to the top of the wall. 60 feet.

Hike to the top of the formation and head left to the *Dogma* anchors and rappel with a 60-meter rope. Or, hike down the back via the south fork of Oak Creek Canyon.

FA: Patrick Putnam, Michael Clifford, Joanne Urioste 1996

▲ RAMEN PRIDE AREA
NE AM Sun   Approach: 1.5 hours

Follow the main Mount Wilson North directions but continue on the road behind Wilson's Pimple until you are on the right (north) edge of the east face of Mount Wilson. Take the main gully up and left (southwest) toward a huge pillar (Cactus Flower Tower). This involves funky, but easy, fifth-class moves. Routes are described from left to right.

17. The League of Notions 5.9 ★★ Traditional. From the top of the gully, walk left 150 yards. This route begins on the leftmost corner on the wall.

exclaims. "It filled my consciousness, affecting me deeply. I felt compelled to climb it, even though I'd not climbed in 10 years, while raising my children. I arranged to do *Epinephrine* with Mike Clifford so I could get back into climbing and I ended up feeling well enough to swing leads. I advanced to leading 5.10 fairly quickly and then recruited Clifford to see if the Aeolian Wall route would go. It did, and it was a very spiritual experience." Gear: standard rack to #2 Friend, doubles of #4.

Pitch 1: 5.8 Climb up and left through off-widths and grooves to a bolted anchor above a pink band. Stay out of the mossy corners. 150 feet.

Pitch 2: 5.10a, 3 bolts. Take the face right for 20

Gear: standard rack to #4.

Pitch 1: Climb a right-facing corner.

Pitch 2: On small holds, move down and right to a chimney. Climb it until it pinches off. Belay below the constriction.

Pitch 3: Continue up the chimney as it pinches off to a flake. Take the flake to rappel anchors.

Rappel the route with 2 ropes.

FA: Mark Moore, Randal Grandstaff 1976

18. Homunculus 5.9 ★★★ Traditional. Begin 80 feet right of the previous route, at a left-facing corner and slot capped by an improbable roof.

Pitch 1: Start right of the slot in the left-facing corner and finish on the right side of a ledge.

Pitch 2: Traverse to the left side of the ledge and climb out the face left to a horn. Move up and right to a crack, climbing up and into a slot.

Pitch 3: Chimney up.

Pitch 4: Continue up the chimney to the steep corner of the chimney's left side.

Pitch 5: Finger to fist up to a bolted anchor beneath the roof.

Rappel the route using 2 ropes.

FA: Mark Moore, David Anderson 1977

RAMEN PRIDE CLIFF

The Ramen Pride Cliff sits at the base of the Cactus Flower Tower. It is a black wall that sits at the top of the hike-up gully, just left of a gully leading to the base of the Cactus Flower Tower. Routes are described from left to right.

Descent: Rappel using 1 rope.

19. Ramen Pride 5.11 ★★★ Traditional. Begin on a right-angling crack and climb to a right-facing corner. Finish up under a roof at a bolted anchor. Gear: standard rack to #3 Friend.

FA: Paul Van Betten, Sal Mamusia 1983

20. Zippy 5.8 ★★ Traditional. Begin 10 feet right of the previous route on another right-angling, broken crack up to a right-facing overhang in black rock. Take it up to a bolted anchor just left of a left-facing dihedral.

FA: Paul Van Betten, Sal Mamusia 1983

21. Stemtation 5.9+ ★ Traditional. Climb the left-facing dihedral 20 feet right of the previous route. Rappel from a tree on top.

FA: Paul Van Betten, Sal Mamusia 1983

▲ CACTUS FLOWER TOWER
E AM Sun   Approach: 2.5–3 hours

Follow the directions to the Ramen Pride Area. Ascend the gully and ledge systems right of Ramen Pride Cliff. High in the gully, climb a mossy slab to an alcove ledge with a right-facing corner/chimney. The right side of this corner is heavily huecoed and is the beginning of the first pitch.

22. Cinnamon Hedgehog IV, 5.10a R ★★ Traditional. Climb the cracks and face up the center of the northeast face of Cactus Flower Tower. This is a serious route. It took the first-ascent party three tries to find the base of the route they wanted to do. Gear: a 60-meter rope; standard rack and doubles of small- and medium-sized Friends.

Pitch 1: 5.7 Climb the "holier than thou" dihedral into the "moss-some" corner above it to a ledge. 100 feet. Rappel off the left edge of the ledge and hike/scramble around the northeast ridge of the feature until you are below the northeast face of the Cactus Flower Tower.

Pitch 2: 5.9 R, 2 bolts. Begin on white rock, climbing up and right past 2 bolts. Move slightly left to a crack. 200 feet.

Pitch 3: 5.8, 2 bolts. Take the crack to its end. Continue up and right on the face, past 2 bolts to a left-leaning crack. Take the crack to an anchor. 200 feet.

Pitch 4: Continue up the crack and chimney about 50 feet. Exit right onto a slab and take seams and cracks out of the red and into the white rock. Belay off an anchor in white rock. 200 feet.

Pitch 5: 5.10a R, 1 bolt. A tricky pitch with good gear. Climb a steep face, veering slightly left to a good ledge. Need #00, #0, and #3.5 Friends for the anchor. 150 feet.

Pitch 6: 5.3 Continue up a low-angle boulder to a gully. Cross the gully and take a slab to a catwalk ledge (three feet wide and varnished) 60 feet. Walk the ledge right (north), making a small jump over a gully to a pine tree.

Pitch 7: 5.6 Head up a large ramp, angling right for 30 feet to a crack. Continue up, tunneling through a chimney and popping out on the summit.

Descend by walking west down the ridge. Stay high for 15 or so minutes, downclimbing third- to easy fifth-class gullies, corners, and chimneys. Continue down and left into the red-colored rock, staying high and trending west. Near the end of the ridge, in a red gully corner, is a small tree with slings (on the left). A 60-foot rappel leads to a 5- to 10-minute bushwhack through manzanita and scrub oak. Staying high and left is easiest. Before the south fork of Oak Creek Canyon, reach a huge pine tree. Rappel or downclimb (easy fifth class) and enter the south fork. Hike out Oak Creek Canyon. 2 hours.

FA: Andrew Fulton and friend

MOUNT WILSON SOUTH

From Las Vegas, take West Charleston Boulevard west, which turns into State Route 159. Drive over the 215 Beltway and zero your odometer. Drive 9.6 miles past the 215 (4.4 miles past the Red Rock Canyon 13-mile Scenic Drive entrance), and park at the First Creek Canyon trailhead. Park so you leave enough room for other vehicles.

▲ MOUNT WILSON SOUTH
SE AM Sun   Approach: 2–3 hours

Take the trail out of the parking area, heading southwest into First Creek Canyon. Hike the trail to where it goes down, next to and parallel to the creek. Cross the creek and take a faint trail up and right to the top of the hillside.

23. Dirtbagger's Compensation 5.10a ★★★ Traditional. This route climbs a red spire on the southeast corner of Mount Wilson, characterized by several water troughs running down its face. Hike along the top of the hillside, heading west. Hike up and right before a low red band. Go up a steep gully to a black, varnished, southeast-facing wall. There is a huge pine tree on the right at the base of the wall,

at the top of the gully. Gear: standard rack to #4 Friend.

Pitch 1: 5.8 Begin below a small pillar, left of the large pine tree. Climb a crack to a chimney beginning where the pillar separates from the rock.

Pitch 2: 5.10a Climb a right-facing corner.

Pitch 3: Third class. Move up to a ledge.

Pitch 4: 5.8 Move up a right-facing corner to a crack. Belay on a ledge.

Pitch 5: Second class. Traverse the ledge right, to the center of the large pillar formation and beneath protection bolts and a varnished face.

Pitch 6: 5.8 Take the face up and then veer right to a crack. Belay on a ledge under a roof.

Pitch 7: 5.8 Take the face up and left to water grooves. Move up grooves to horns and belay. 150 feet.

Pitch 8: 5.6 R Continue up and then right to a ledge below the top. 140 feet.

Pitch 9: Fourth class. Move up and right to the summit.

Rappel using 2 ropes (bring extra webbing to secure anchors).

FA: Shawn Pereto, Dave Polari 1993

24. Equalizer Arête IV, 5.9 R/X ★★ Traditional. This route climbs the southeast face of Blue Diamond Ridge, which comprises the left side of Mount Wilson's main east face. From the First Creek Canyon parking area, take a dirt road that parallels the First Creek Trail through desert and nearly to the approach gully. Ascend the second gully to the right (north). Take it up, curving right. Traverse right to get onto the ridge. This is one of the most serious approaches in Red Rock and was the second grade V established in Red Rock in a day. There is a lot of serious climbing. Bailing off this route would be very involved and require 2 60-meter ropes. Gear: standard rack and a 60-meter rope.

Pitch 1: 5.9 Climb the obvious crack to a ledge.

Pitch 2: 5.8 Climb the face through loose rock to a belay below parallel cracks.

Pitch 3: 5.9 Take parallel cracks to a ledge with a tree.

Pitch 4: 5.8 Move up and right, across a face and over an overhang, to a left-facing corner. Belay on a ledge.

Pitch 5: 5.9 R Continue up a face, pulling a roof (loose rock) to a sloping belay ledge.

Pitch 6: 5.8 Climb a trough to a giant boulder. Simul-climb a face up a distinctive saddle (about halfway up the route), passing large ponderosa pines. Belay atop blocks.

Pitch 7: 5.9 Pull a roof to the right and take a crack to a tree and belay.

Pitch 8: 5.7 Take a crack straight up to a ledge.

Pitch 9: 5.9 R/X Climb the exposed and poorly protected Equalizer Arête. Equalize a #1 and #1.5 Friend about halfway up (your only pro) and run it out to the belay.

Pitch 10: 5.7 Climb across the face, left to a tree and belay.

Pitch 11: 5.9 R/X Move left, across the face to a crack. Clip the fixed stopper in the crack and tip-toe around a loose block. Continue up and left to a tree.

Pitch 11 variation: 5.7 Face-climb right to a chimney. Take the chimney to the top. Beware of large loose blocks.

To descend, hike to the top of the formation and head right to the *Dogma* anchors and rappel or take the First Creek Canyon descent.

FA: Paul Van Betten, Andrew Fulton 1997

25. Son of Wilson IV, 5.10a ★★★ Traditional. This route is on the left side of the basin that is below and left of *Lady Wilson's Cleavage.* From the left edge of Mount Wilson's east face, hike up the narrow gully to the right of the second low red band. Hike through a thin corridor, up a gully to a basin or cirque area. This section of rock feature is brown at the bottom, then pink to a thin red strip in the middle to whiter rock on top. This route climbs the off-width on the left side.

Pitch 1: Climb the off-width/chimney with a crack arching up and left into it.

Pitch 2: 5.10a Continue up the off-width to a chockstone and belay.

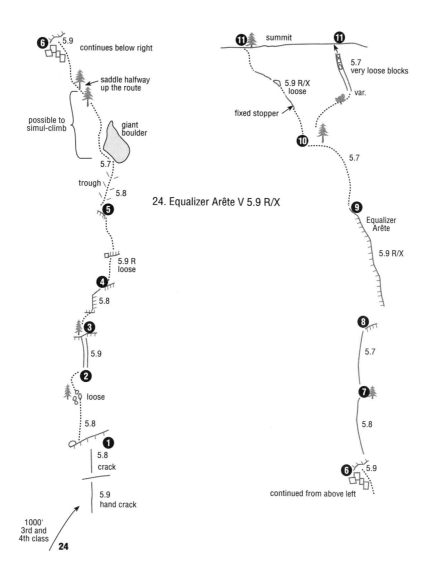

24. Equalizer Arête V 5.9 R/X

Pitch 3: 5.9 Take the off-width/chimney to where it pinches down to a squeeze chimney. Belay above that.

Pitch 4: 5.8 Charge up the chimney as it becomes a Bombay chimney. Belay above it.

Pitch 5: Take the crack up to the second of two ledges.

Pitch 6: 5.9 Climb the right-facing corner.

Pitch 7: Continue up the crack.

To descend, hike to the top of the formation and head right to the *Dogma* anchors, rappeling with a 60-meter rope. Or, descend via First Creek Canyon.
FA: Pat Brennan, Steve Untch 1990

26. Lady Wilson's Cleavage IV, 5.9+ ★★★ Traditional. Only do this one if you like big 'ole crack. It requires 1500 feet of fourth- and fifth-class scrambling to reach the big ledge with the huge ponderosa pine at the base. Watch out for loose rock at the top.

Gear: standard rack to #5 Friend.

Pitch 1: 5.8 Climb the hand, fist and off-width crack using the face on either side to a good ledge. 120 feet.

Pitch 2: 5.7 Continue up the crack to a dirty recess. 80 feet.

Pitch 3: 5.7 Continue up the crack to a wide section and belay in some trees below a roof (where a horizontal crack passes through this section of wall). 140 feet.

Pitch 4: 5.8 Continue up the crack, pulling a roof. Move up a left-facing crack system to ledges with trees. 150 feet.

Pitch 5: 5.8 Squirm up a chimney. 165 feet.

Pitch 6: 5.7 Move a bit right to a gully. Take the left side of the gully to a belay under a tree at a large varnished chimney.

Pitch 7: 5.9 Chimney up.

Pitch 8: 5.6 Move up a gully to the base of another chimney.

Pitch 9: 5.6 Climb the chimney to a loose, dirty ledge with a tree (loose rock, careful of your belayer). Start on the wall left of the chimney and move up it, finishing on a crack that takes you to the top of the wall.

To descend, hike to the top of the formation and head right to the *Dogma* anchors and rappel with a 60-meter rope. Or, descend via First Creek Canyon.

FA: Joe Herbst, George and Joanne Urioste 1977

FIRST CREEK CANYON

Indecision Peak ▲ Lotta Balls Wall ▲ Alcohol Wall ▲ Romper Room
First Creek Slabs ▲ Slippery Peak Apron

FROM LAS VEGAS, take West Charleston Boulevard west, which turns into State Route 159. Drive over the 215 Beltway and zero your odometer. Drive 9.6 miles past the 215 (4.4 miles past the Red Rock Canyon 13-mile Scenic Drive entrance), and park at the First Creek Canyon trailhead. Park so you leave enough room for other vehicles.

Take the trail out of the parking area, heading southwest into the canyon. Drop down into a sandy basin with many trees and bushes, parallel and near to the wash. Continue alongside the wash until just before reaching a low band of red rock on the left-hand side. Hike up over a hill to reach a higher trail paralleling the cliff. You will pass a sign on the hike up, noting that the canyons of Red Rock are designated wilderness areas.

▲ INDECISION PEAK
N AM Sun   Approach: 45 minutes

Hike the higher trail until you are just past the low red band. Hike up and left over the top of the red band

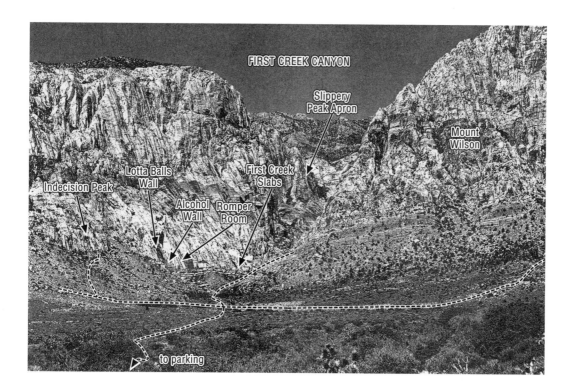

FIRST CREEK CANYON

Slippery Peak Apron

Mount Wilson

Lotta Balls Wall

First Creek Slabs

Indecision Peak

Alcohol Wall   Romper Room

to parking

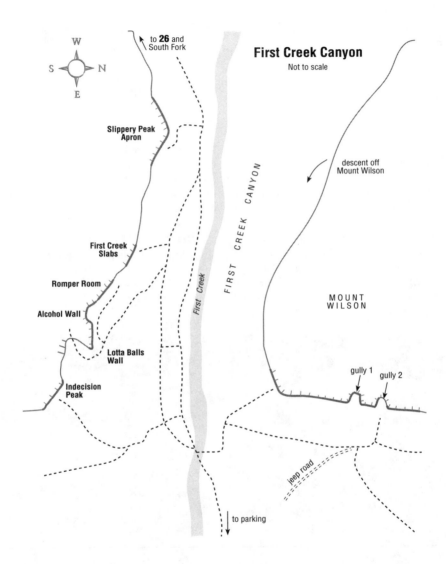

to a lone feature that looks like a left-facing open book. Two cracks ascend its light tan face. The right crack is part of a large left-facing dihedral. Routes are described from left to right.

Descent: Walk off right and scramble down the gully right of the feature.

1. Lucky Nuts 5.10b ★★ Traditional. Beginning on a detached triangular-shaped flake at the base, climb the left crack, a flare. Gear: standard rack to #4 Friend. *FA: Randal Grandstaff, Dave Anderson 1977*

2. Mudterm 5.9 ★★ Traditional. Ascend the right crack, beginning where several chockstones are wedged in the base. Gear: a #4 Friend. *FA: Joe Herbst 1976*

▲ LOTTA BALLS WALL
NE AM Sun Approach: 40 Minutes

Once on the higher trail, hike along the cliff until you are directly below a large black wall, somewhat recessed and polished in its center. Take a faint trail that meanders up and left to the base. The left side of this wall is the Lotta Balls Wall. Routes are described from left to right.

Descent: Scramble fourth and fifth class down the gully directly east (left) of Lotta Balls Wall. This requires two (obvious) rappels.

The following route is on the level above and left of Lotta Balls Wall. Reach the base by ascending one of the Lotta Balls Wall routes or by climbing the descent gully.

3. Kick in the Balls 5.8 ★★ Traditional. Start 100 feet above and left of the descent gully, on dark

brown rock with bright green and yellow lichen. A perfect crack splits the wall's center. Gear: cams to a #6 Friend.

Pitch 1: 5.8 Begin on the finger crack that splits the center of the wall. Climb up, as it widens, to fixed anchors on the left.

Pitch 2: 5.8 Continue up the large crack to a detached block in the center of the crack. Continue to the top of the feature, using off-width and chimney techniques.
FA: Josh Thompson, Brian Kosta 1996

The following routes are on the main Lotta Balls Wall.

4. Power to Spare 5.8 ★★★ Mixed. Begin on the left edge of the main Lotta Balls Wall and climb the huge fin that forms the left side of the wall. Begin just right of a large boulder. Gear: Rocks and Friends to #0.

Pitch 1: 5.8, 6 bolts. Climb a varnished section of

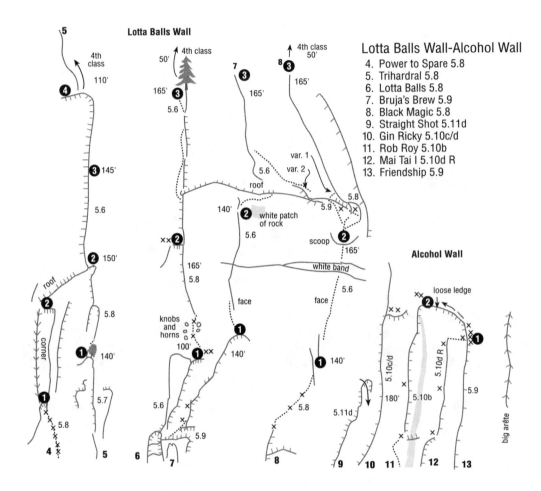

Lotta Balls Wall

Lotta Balls Wall-Alcohol Wall

4. Power to Spare 5.8
5. Trihardral 5.8
6. Lotta Balls 5.8
7. Bruja's Brew 5.9
8. Black Magic 5.8
9. Straight Shot 5.11d
10. Gin Ricky 5.10c/d
11. Rob Roy 5.10b
12. Mai Tai I 5.10d R
13. Friendship 5.9

Alcohol Wall

the low-angled face, then move up and left to an open-book, thin corner. Climb to fixed anchors on the left wall.

Pitch 2: Continue up the perfect corner to anchors below the roof, on the left edge.

Rappel using 2 ropes.

FA: Matt and Mark Hermann, Derek Willmott, Mandy Kellner 1995

5. Trihardral 5.8 ★★★ Traditional. Climb the enormous right-facing corner created by the fin on the left side of the wall.

Pitch 1: 5.7 Begin 15 feet right of the previous route at a vertical crack. Climb it up to the start of the corner and a ledge. Belay. 140 feet.

Pitch 2: 5.8 Continue up the corner to a ledge and belay. Beware of loose blocks. 150 feet.

Pitch 3: 5.6 Continue up the corner and crack. 145 feet.

Pitch 4: Fourth class. Step left at the top of the corner and take the white face to the top of the cliff. 110 feet.

FA: Joe and Betsy Herbst, George and Joanne Urioste, Randal Grandstaff 1976

LOTTA BALLS WALL

to ③

descent
gully

⑤ ⑥ ⑦ ⑧

④

④

Alcohol
Wall

⑤

⑥ ⑦

⑧

6. Lotta Balls 5.8 ★★★★ Traditional. Begin 30 feet right of *Trihardral*, just right of a blocky pillar leaning against the wall and left of a roof and left-facing corner.

Pitch 1: 5.6 Climb the crack up and left to a left-facing corner. Then take a whitish flake, angling up and right to its top and a bolted belay. 100 feet.

Pitch 2: 5.8, 2 bolts. Climb the black, varnished face up and left to a right-facing corner. Climb onto the top of a white pillar, part of the corner, and belay. 165 feet.

Pitch 3: 5.6 Continue up the right-facing corner and then step left at the roof, heading up and left to the top of the cliff. 165 feet.

Pitch 4: Fourth class. Scramble 50 feet to the top of the formation.

FA: Betsy and Joe Herbst, Randal Grandstaff, Tom Kaufman 1977

7. Bruja's Brew 5.9 ★★★★ Traditional. Start on top of a large white boulder beneath a large, overhanging flake, 8 feet right of *Lotta Balls*.

Pitch 1: 5.9 Take the right-facing flake to its top. Continue up the black, varnished face to the left side of a small roof. Climb the left-facing corner above the roof to a stance atop a tiny pillar (formed by the left-facing section of rock above the roof). Belay at fixed anchors. 140 feet.

Pitch 2: 5.6 Move up the black, varnished face, angling slightly left. Take the line of weakness to a thin flaring crack below a roof. 140 feet.

Pitch 3: 5.6 Climb to the roof and pull the right side using the crack. Take the crack to the top of the feature. 165 feet.

FA: Todd Swain, Debbie Brenchley 1991

8. Black Magic 5.8 ★★★★ Traditional. Begin left of a sloping left-facing corner, 10 feet right of *Bruja's Brew*.

Pitch 1: 5.8, 3 bolts. Take the crack that ascends left of a roof, up over the roof and into a corner. When the crack ends, step right, taking the varnished face up and right to a headwall with a series of very short vertical cracks. Belay there. 140 feet.

Pitch 2: 5.6 Continue up the face, moving straight

up the varnish through the white band of rock to a belay stance in a scoop (created by varnished edges). 165 feet.

Pitch 3: 5.8, 1 bolt. Move up to the roof, tending right toward the nose. Move up and clip a bolt and then move back left over the top of the roof to the main crack. Take the crack to the top. 165 feet.

Pitch 3 variation 1: 5.9, 1 bolt. Climb up and to the roof, pull the roof in a crack and move into the prominent crack above. Take the crack to the summit. 165 feet.

Pitch 3 variation 2: 5.6, 1 bolt. Climb up to the roof, and then head directly left on a ramp angling up and over the roof, clipping 1 bolt. Finish on *Bruja's Brew*. 165 feet.

Pitch 4: Fourth class. Scramble 50 feet to the top of the cliff.

FA: George and Joanne Urioste 1978

▲ ALCOHOL WALL (AKA MYSTERIOUS AMPHITHEATER)
NE AM Sun   Approach: 40 minutes

Once on the higher trail that parallels the wash, hike along the cliff until you are directly below a large black wall, somewhat recessed and polished in its center. Take a faint trail that meanders up and left to the base. The left side of this wall is Lotta Balls Wall. The recessed, polished wall is Alcohol Wall. It begins at a large right-facing dihedral on the left side of the wall. Gear: bring brass wires. Routes are described from left to right.

Descent: Rappel using 2 ropes.

9. Straight Shot 5.11d ★★★ Traditional. This route climbs the short right-facing corner 10 feet left of the main corner on the far left of this wall. Climb the steep corner to a flake. Rappel off fixed wires.

FA: Paul Van Betten, Nick Nordblom 1983

10. Gin Ricky 5.10c/d ★★★★ Traditional. Climb the huge right-facing corner making up the left edge of this wall. End at fixed anchors above a ledge that angles up from the right. The anchor is 180 feet off the ground—watch rope ends when

ALCOHOL WALL

Lotta Balls
Wall

Romper
Room

rappeling. Gear: standard rack to #3 Friend.
FA: Nick Nordblom, Randal Marsh 1983

11. Rob Roy 5.10b ★★★★ Mixed, 3 bolts. Climb the crack that begins left of a low roof. Go straight up into a small left-facing corner, left of a black water streak. Take it to the top, where there is a ledge system and fixed anchors. Gear: small Friends.
FA: Richard Harrison, Paul Crawford, Paul Van Betten, Paul Obenheim 1983

12. Mai Tai I, 5.10d R ★★★★ Mixed, 3 bolts. This is the next left-facing corner system on the wall, 10 feet right of *Rob Roy*. Follow the corner up. Halfway up, head slightly right to another, smaller left-facing corner. After the third bolt, climb right and then left to the anchor of *Rob Roy*. Gear: small Friends.
FA: Richard Harrison, Paul Crawford, Paul Van Betten, Paul Obenheim 1983

13. Friendship 5.9 ★★★ Mixed. The next left-facing corner, and the largest of the three on this wall, is 12 feet right of *Mai Tai*. Climb a crack to over a roof and then to an alcove. Two pitches. The second pitch finishes on *Rob Roy*. Gear: standard rack to #5 Friend.
FA: Joe Herbst 1978

▲ ROMPER ROOM
NE AM Sun   Approach: 45 Minutes

Once on the higher trail that parallels the wash, hike along the cliff until you are directly below a large black wall, somewhat recessed and polished in its center. Take a faint trail that meanders up and left to the base. The left side of this wall is Lotta Balls Wall. Romper Room is the white wall right of the recessed middle (Alcohol Wall). Routes are described from left to right.

14. Guise and Gals 5.4 ★★★ Traditional. Begin 20 feet right of a large left-facing corner (*Friendship*) on the right edge of the Alcohol Wall, at the next crack system behind a large boulder. Climb the corner to the tiny white pillar. Left of the crack are fixed anchors. Rappel using 1 rope.
FA: Kimi Harrison, Leslie Appling 1992

15. Girls and Buoys 5.5 ★★★ Traditional. Begin just right of the previous route, right of a large boulder, in a water runnel. Move up and left. Take cracks to fixed anchors on the middle pillar feature. Gear: standard rack to #3 Friend. Rappel.
FA: Kimi Harrison, Leslie Appling 1992

16. Kindergarten Cop 5.7+ ★★★ Mixed, 4 bolts. Begin 20 feet right of the previous route, on the right edge of a triangular-shaped roof, above a boulder. Climb up the right edge of the roof and onto a varnished face. Continue up and right, up the center of a white face to a fixed anchor. Gear: standard rack to #4 Friend. Rappel using 2 ropes.
FA: Todd and Donette Swain 1994

17. Magic Mirror 5.5 ★★ Traditional. Begin 10 feet right of *Kindergarten Cop*, climbing a large left-facing corner. When the corner starts to steepen at a bulge on the left, head right to the shared fixed anchors with *Kindergarten Cop*. Rappel using 2 ropes.
FA: Todd and Donette Swain 1994

18. Buzz, Buzz 5.4 ★★★ Traditional. Begin 12 feet right of *Magic Mirror*. Climb a crack to up underneath a roof. Gear: standard rack to #3 Friend. Rappel.
FA: Leslie Appling, Kimi Harrison 1992

The following three routes climb a black, varnished face that is capped by a small roof, right of routes 14–18.

19. Doobie Dance 5.7 ★★ Traditional. Climb the crack 8 feet right of the face's left edge. Follow the crack to a fixed anchor just below the roof. Rappel.
FA: Unknown 1970s

20. Romper Room 5.7+ ★★ Traditional. Climb three separate crack and flake systems up the center of the varnished face to three-quarters of the way up. Then take the middle crack up to another flake system. Step left and up to the fixed anchor below the roof. Gear: standard rack to #3.5 Friend. Rappel.
FA: Unknown 1970s

21. Algae on Parade 5.7 ★★ Traditional. Climb

the left-facing corner system making up the right side of the varnished wall. Gear: to #4 Friend.

Pitch 1: 5.7 Climb up and step left before the first bunch of bushes. Pull a tiny roof and continue up the black face to the ledge left of the next large bush.

Pitch 2: Head up and right to the main crack system. Follow it up the wall. Enter a left-facing corner and belay.

Pitch 3: Follow the crack system to the top.

Descend by hiking up and left to Lotta Balls Wall. Descend the Lotta Balls Wall descent gully.

FA: John Martinet, Jeff Gordon 1978

▲ FIRST CREEK SLABS
NE AM Sun   Approach: 50 minutes

First Creek Slabs are around the corner and 100 feet right of *Algae on Parade*. Reach the area via the higher trail that parallels the wash. Hike it for 200 feet beyond the turnoff for Lotta Balls Wall. Then head up the hill (south) to the base of the wall until you reach the large white pillar that leans against the wall.

22. Rising Moons 5.5 ★★★ Traditional. Look for a large white pillar leaning against the wall with a varnished off-width chimney at the base.

Pitch 1: Take the right-slanting, varnished chimney up and right to a big ledge. Move up to the base of the right-facing corner created where the pillar meets the wall. 150 feet.

Pitch 2: Move left into a right-facing corner. Belay near the top of the pillar at bolted anchors. 140 feet.

Pitch 3: Take the widening crack off the top of the pillar, moving up and right to a huge ledge. 90 feet.

Rappel using 2 ropes, off a tree on the top ledge to fixed anchors at the top of pitch 2. Rappel to the top of pitch 1, then walk off right or left.

FA: Jono McKinney 1990

▲ SLIPPERY PEAK APRON
NNE AM Sun   Approach: 1 hour

Hike along the cliff passing a large black wall, the Lotta Balls Wall, and continue past the First Creek Slabs to the base of a huge dark red slab. This is Slippery Peak Apron. Slippery Peak is the pointed peak above the slab. Routes are described from left to right.

23. The Red and the Black 5.7 ★★★ Traditional. Climb crack systems and the face up the center of Slippery Peak Apron.

Pitch 1: 5.7, 1 bolt. Climb a right-facing, upside-down staircase corner up to a left-facing corner. Before a roof, move out of the corner right to a right-facing corner. Climb it to a large ledge and belay. 135 feet.

Pitch 1 variation: 5.8, 1 bolt. After the staircase corner, move right to under a roof. Pull the roof and take the right-facing corner to the belay ledge. 135 feet.

Pitch 2: 5.6 Take the face up and right to another ledge. Continue up to a crack. Follow the crack up. Face-climb up and left to a left-facing corner. Belay under a roof. 130 feet.

Pitch 3: 5.5 R Take the face, pulling some roofs to the top of the cliff. 180 feet.

Rappel *Real Domestic Chickens* or *Advance Romance*.

FA: John Martinet, Jeff and Scott Gordon 1978

24. Real Domestic Chickens 5.10 ★★★ Mixed. Begin right of the previous route, up the middle of Slippery Peak Apron. Gear: to #1 Friend.

Pitch 1: 5.10, 6 bolts. Climb to a fixed anchor. 140 feet.

Pitch 2: 5.9, 4 bolts. Continue up to the fixed anchor. 145 feet.

Rappel using 2 ropes.

FA: Rick Dennison, Mark Fredrick, Dan Cox 1994

25. Advance Romance 5.6 ★★★ Traditional. This route ascends the left-facing corner on the far-right side of Slippery Peak Apron. Three pitches. Rappel the route using 2 ropes.

FA: John Martinet, Scott Gordon 1978

The following route is located up the left (south) fork of First Creek Canyon, past Slippery Peak Apron.

26. Stout Hearted Men IV, 5.9 ★★ Traditional. Hike up First Creek Canyon until just past Slippery Peak Apron. At this point, head up the left (south)

FIRST CREEK SLABS

22

fork for a short distance to where the dramatic Raven Buttress is directly in front of you. Scramble up to a ledge with a few large pine trees. Easy climbing leads to a belay ledge below a right-facing dihedral. Climb up the dihedral, soon passing a 5.9 roof. Continue up the obvious crack system for a few pitches to a good ledge on the top of a tower. Straightforward climbing leads up and left, across the headwall to a crack. This crack leads back right through a break in the over-hangs. A short fourth-class pitch takes you to the large Crow's Nest ledge. The upper buttress involves several hundred feet of third-class climbing. To descend, from the top of the buttress scramble up and east to the summit of Indecision Peak. Take a tricky descent east into the desert. Alternatively, follow the large ledge system down and west from the Crow's Nest into the approach canyon. Gear: standard rack.

FA: Larry DeAngelo, Bill Thiry 2003

BLACK VELVET CANYON

BLACK VELVET CANYON NORTH
The Monument ▲ Sandstone Mountain ▲ Burlap Buttress North ▲ Burlap Buttress South

WHISKEY PEAK
The Schwa Area ▲ Rad Cliffs/Whiskey Peak Gully ▲ Whiskey Peak East ▲ Frogland Area
Ixtlan Wall ▲ Wholesome Fullback Area ▲ Whiskey Peak West

BLACK VELVET PEAK
Black Velvet Wall ▲ The Black Tower ▲ Black Velvet Peak West ▲ Western Spaces Wall

FROM LAS VEGAS, take West Charleston Boulevard west, which turns into State Route 159. Continue on SR 159 until it ends at SR 160. The Blue Diamond Travel Center is on the south side of SR 160 at the intersection. Turn right (west) on SR 160, drive 4.8 miles, and make a right turn onto a dirt road. Cross the cattle guard and pass a big parking lot on the left (for mountain bikers) and continue on. After 1.5 miles, the road curves left, but continue straight. Drive through a couple low washes and then curve left (west) towards the canyon. The road ends at the trailhead.

Hike the old roadbed out of the west end of the parking lot until it makes a hairpin turn to the left. Leave the road for a trail that heads slightly right and down, into Black Velvet Canyon. You will pass a sign on your hike up, noting that the canyons of Red Rock are designated wilderness areas.

side of the trail, up against the trail. Take a faint trail going right (north). Hike until it moves down into a large wash. Scramble through large boulders to get across the wash (heading up the wash, west, a bit for easier access). Move up and right toward the bushy, boulder-filled gully coming down through the break in a low pink band of rock. This gully, the largest on the north section of cliff, passes an enormous boulder down and left of the low pink band. Continue up directly to the base of the huge roof (the *Desert Crack* roof). Routes are described from left to right.

Descent: For routes that reach the top of the formation, descend the backside, heading west. Take the gully system that runs south, reaching the ground next to *Desert Gold*.

The following routes begin far up the gully left of the obvious *Desert Crack* roof.

BLACK VELVET CANYON NORTH

▲ THE MONUMENT
S All-Day Sun   Approach: 1 hour

Hike the trail into Black Velvet Canyon for 5 minutes to where there is a grouping of five yuccas on the left

1. Unremembered 5.10d/11a ★★★ Climb the hand crack that arches up and right. This is an easier version of *Eliminator Crack*, in Oak Creek Canyon. Gear: to #3 Friend. Rappel.
FA: Nick Nordblom, Wendell Broussard mid 1980s

2. Unremembered 5.10b ★★ Traditional. Begin just right of the previous route. Gear: small gear and brass nuts. Rappel.
FA: Mike Ward, Wendell Broussard

Donny Burroughs sends the second pitch of Ixtlan 5.11c, Black Velvet Canyon. Photo by Dan McQuade

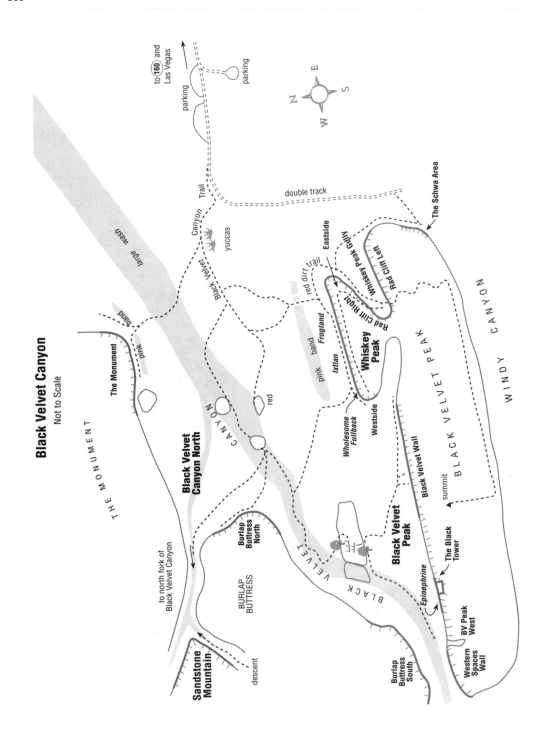

Black Velvet Canyon

Not to Scale

to 160 and Las Vegas

parking

parking

parking

double track

The Schwa Area

Canyon Trail

yuccas

red dirt trail

Eastside

Whiskey Peak Gully

Rad Cliff Left

large wash

Black Velvet

Rad Cliff Right

Frogland

pink band

Ixtlan

Whiskey Peak

pink band

Westside

Wholesome Fullback

THE MONUMENT

The Monument

red

CANYON

Black Velvet Canyon North

BLACK VELVET PEAK

N E

S

W

WINDY CANYON

summit

Black Velvet Wall

to north fork of Black Velvet Canyon

Burlap Buttress North

BURLAP BUTTRESS

BLACK VELVET CANYON

Black Velvet Peak

Epinephrine

The Black Tower

BV Peak West

Sandstone Mountain

descent

Burlap Buttress South

Western Spaces Wall

3. Scumby 5.8 ★★ This is the approach pitch to *Desert Crack*, *Desert Reality*, and *Desert Gold*. Climb the crack left of the chossy, left-facing corner beneath the massive *Desert Gold* roof. When the crack thins, traverse right into the left-facing corner, up to a sloping ledge and bolted anchors. Gear: Friends to #3. Rappel with one rope.
FA: Mike Ward, Paul Van Betten 1987

4. Violent Stems 5.12a ★★ Traditional. Climb the chossy-looking, left-facing dihedral just right of *Scumby*. Gear: brass wires, Rocks, and Friends to #3. Rappel with one rope.
FA: Paul Van Betten 1987

5. Clipper 5.11a ★★ Mixed, 1 bolt. Start around the corner from *Violent Stems*. Climb the thin right-facing corner 5 feet right of *Violent Stems* to the bolted anchors of *Scumby*. Gear: brass wires, Rocks, and Friends to #1. Rappel with one rope.
FA: Paul Van Betten, Mike Ward 1987

6. Desert Gold 5.13a ★★★★★ Traditional. This route links *Scumby* with *Desert Crack* into the most perfect crack climb in the Red Rock, offering every size from fingers to off-width. Gear: cams to #4 Friend.

Pitch 1: Climb *Scumby* or one of routes 3–5 to reach the sloping ledge and bolted anchors below the roof crack. 90 feet.

Pitch 2: **Desert Crack: 5.12d**, 1 bolt. Clip a bolt above the anchor and then climb around the corner, left and up 10 feet. Traverse back right into a perfect finger crack. Take it as it widens to the roof and belay on gear and a bolt on the right face. 60 feet.
FA: Paul Van Betten, Sal Mamusia 1987

Pitch 3: **Desert Reality: 5.11c** Traditional. Climb out the enormous roof crack, as it widens. Dyno for the finishing jug and worm up to a fixed thread anchor. 50 feet.
FA: Paul Van Betten, Richard Harrison 1984
It is preferable to clean the route by downclimbing, or rappel from the top anchor with 2 ropes.
FA (all pitches): Stefan Glowacz 1987

7. Seduction Line 5.11 ★★ Traditional. Begin 200 yards right of *Desert Gold*. Climb a petite right-facing corner to fixed anchors. 80 feet.
FA: Unknown 1988

8. Hand Bone 5.10b ★★★ Traditional. Begin 75 yards right of *Seduction Line*. This is a short but great hand crack. Rappel from the fixed anchor.
FA: Unknown 1988

9. Chinese Handcuffs 5.11d ★★★★★ Traditional. Begin 200 yards right of *Hand Bone*. Climb the straight-in finger crack in white rock. Rappel from the fixed anchor.
FA: Mike Tupper 1988

10. Lizard Locks 5.11 ★★ Traditional. Begin 50 feet right of *Chinese Handcuffs* at a left-facing corner. Gear: standard rack to #2 Friend. Rappel from the fixed anchor.
FA: Unknown 1988

11. All the Right Moves 5.10 ★★ Traditional. Begin just right of *Lizard Locks* and climb to the shared anchor with *Lizard Locks*. Gear: small and brass wires.
FA: Unknown 1988

12. The Down Staircase 5.8 ★ Traditional. Climb the first major crack system right of a large, white rock scar. Begin below a low roof. Gear: standard rack to #4 Friend.
Pitch 1: Climb the left-facing corner/slot to a bushy ledge. 130 feet.
Pitch 2: Continue past the ledge to a widening crack system to another bushy ledge. 160 feet.
Pitch 3: From the ledge, head left up discontinuous crack and chimney systems. 130 feet.
Pitch 4: Third class. Scramble up the ridge to the top. 200 feet.
FA: Randal Grandstaff, Mark Moore 1975

13. Slotsafun 5.9 ★ Traditional. Begin 40 feet right of the previous route. Gear: standard rack to #4 Friend.
Pitch 1: Climb the large, wide, left-facing corner

Bob Conz going for the gold on Clipper *5.11a under* Desert Gold, The Monument. Photo by Roxanna Brock

to a roof three-quarters of the way up. 150 feet.
Pitch 2: Move behind the roof, in a chimney, and then climb up onto a white face. Angle right to a bushy ledge.
Pitch 3: Third class. Scramble up the ridge to the top. 200 feet.
FA: Mark Moore 1975

14. The Blue Diamond Sanction 5.8+ ★★★ Traditional. Climb the corner right of the large, white rock scar, at a gully. Move up, angling left. Finish up

a wide/off-width section. Climb to the same ledge where the previous route finishes. Gear: standard rack to #4 Friend. Rappel using 2 ropes.
FA: Mark Moore 1977

15. Cornucopia 5.10a ★★★ Traditional. Begin in the next crack system right of *The Blue Diamond Sanction*. Begin on top of a scree ledge system with a large bush on top. Gear: standard rack to #5 Friend.

Pitch 1: 5.8 Climb the left-facing corner. Traverse right and enter a crack that makes up a huge flake system. Enter a chimney and belay on the ledge beneath roofs. 80 feet.

Pitch 2: 5.10a Take a crack up a steep face to a very large horn. Continue up and then step left to a ledge. 100 feet.

Pitch 3: 5.7 Pull a roof and climb to a chimney. Belay right of the top, as the chimney closes down. 80 feet.

Pitch 4: 5.7 Steep climbing leads to a big ledge. 150 feet.

Pitch 5: Fourth class. Scramble up and left on the ledge to where it is possible to look down on *The Blue Diamond Sanction* route and gully.

Pitch 6: 5.10a Climb a varnished, steep, blank face up to a corner/crack system. Continue past a large scrub oak and make easy moves to obtain a large tree on a ledge. 150 feet.

Pitch 7: Third class. Scramble to the top of the feature. 300 feet.
FA: Mark Moore 1976

▲ SANDSTONE MOUNTAIN
E AM Sun   Approach: 1 hour

Hike the trail into Black Velvet Canyon for 10 minutes to where it cuts down (right) into the wash (15 feet past where a trail heads left and up toward a pink band and Whiskey Peak). Take the right-hand trail down and then head left (west) up the large wash. Continue up the wash, scrambling over boulders until the low pink band on the left side of the wash breaks down. Hike through boulders, head up and right to the right (north) fork of Black Velvet Canyon. Continue until you are west of Burlap Buttress. There the wash forks again.

16. Mogave Buttress V, 5.9 ★★ Traditional. This route climbs the prominent feature that divides the wash at the end of Black Velvet Canyon's north fork. A very committing climb of 2000 feet leads to the summit of Sandstone Mountain. Gear: standard rack and a 60-meter rope. To descend, head west from the summit and descend a gully, heading down and south (the gully is on the left as you climb the route).
FA: Andrew Fulton, Steve Enger

▲ BURLAP BUTTRESS NORTH
NE AM Sun   Approach: 1 hour

Hike the trail into Black Velvet Canyon for 10 minutes to where it cuts down (right) into the wash (15 feet past where a trail heads left and up toward a pink band and Whiskey Peak). Take the right-hand trail down and then head left (west) up the large wash. Continue up the wash, scrambling over boulders until the low pink band on the left breaks down. Hike through boulders. Head up and right, reaching a rib leading to the center of the east side of Burlap Buttress. Traverse right to reach the routes, described from left to right.

Descent: Head north, walking on ledge systems and scrambling to the backside of the formation. Take the gully on the right (north) side of the peak. Make sure you stay on the left side of the gully (you cannot get down if you go right). Upon reaching the ground, hike right (south) to the start of the route.

17. The Teabob 5.8 ★★ Traditional. Begin on the right side of the white, triangular-shaped slab. Take the crack that makes up the right edge, climbing to midway up the slab. Climb a shallow right-facing corner off the slab and onto the smooth, black, varnished wall above it. Follow the corner to the right edge of the face. Step left to a right-facing corner. Take the corner and face up to the top of the wall. Third-class scramble to the summit of the formation. Gear: standard rack to #3.5 Friend.
FA: Mark Moore 1975

18. Ripcord 5.8+ ★★ Traditional. Begin 25 feet right of *The Teabob*, in the crack left of a low rectangular-shaped roof. Climb the wide corner up and

left. Step right into a wider section. As it thins, continue up and right to a bushy ledge. Third-class scramble to the top of the formation. Gear: standard rack to #4 Friend.
FA: Mark Moore 1975

19. Arrow Place 5.9 ★★ Traditional. Begin 12 feet right of *Ripcord*. Gear: standard rack to #4 Friend.

Pitch 1: 5.9 Climb the left-facing flake/crack system up and left. Step left to a ledge and belay from bolts. 80 feet.

Pitch 2: 5.9 Move right and take a crack up the black, varnished face, right of a white face. Move left to the bolted belay. 80 feet.

Pitch 3: 5.7 Move right to a chimney/crack system and then back left to a tree. Rappel the route with a 60-meter rope.

Variation finish: 5.6 Continue to the top of the formation (2 pitches).
FA: Dick Tonkin, George Urioste, Mike Ward 1979

20. Wishbone 5.8 ★★ Traditional. Begin 40 feet right of *Arrow Place*, left of the largest white boulder at the base of the wall. Climb the crack that starts out thin and widens as you ascend it to the wishbone split. This is at the top of a white feature to the right. Take the crack heading up and right, finishing on a hand crack to a bolted anchor. Rappel using 2 ropes.
FA: Randal Grandstaff, Mark Moore 1975

▲ BURLAP BUTTRESS SOUTH
S AM Sun   Approach: 45 minutes

Hike the trail into Black Velvet Canyon for 10 minutes to where it cuts down (right) into the wash (15 feet past where a trail heads left and up toward a pink band and Whiskey Peak). Take the right-hand trail down and then head left (west) up the large wash. Continue up the wash, scrambling over boulders until the wash pinches off and is impassible. Head up

and right, up a ramp, to just left of the big broken arch. Routes are described from left to right. The following routes begin on the far left of this wall.

21. C-Monster 5.9 ★★ Mixed. Begin 300 feet left of *Kidney Pie*, the large right-facing flake on the left side of this wall. Scramble onto a ledge 50 feet up. Climb a right-facing corner beneath an arching roof (*not* the big arch on the wall). Climb to beneath the roof and break off left to a left-facing corner. Climb to a ledge at the top of the wall. Gear: doubles of #00 and #0 Friends, singles to #2.5 Friend, and brass wires. Rappel or take the face above the ledge to the top of the cliff and hike off left.
FA: Ryan Wolf, Andrew Fulton, Steve Enger 1999

22. Kidney Pie 5.8 ★★ Traditional. Climb the right-facing flake on the far-left side of the wall, left of the big arch. Hike off to the left.
FA: Mark Moore 1975

23. The Corn Flake 5.9 ★★ Traditional. Climb the left-facing flake located 10 feet right of the previous route. Continue past the overhang above. Hike off to the left.
FA: Cal Folsom, Lars Holbeck 1975

24. Moving over Stone 5.11c ★★ Traditional. This route is on the face right of the previous route. Gear: brass wires and Friends to #2.5.
    Pitch 1: 5.9+ Ascend the face to bolted anchors. 75 feet.
    Pitch 2: 5.11c Continue up the face to bolted anchors above a ledge on a steep face. 75 feet.
    Rappel.
FA: Randal Grandstaff, Randy Marsh 1991

25. Children of the Sun 5.10b ★★ Mixed. Begin 5 feet left of the left edge of the arch. Loose.
    Pitch 1: 5.8+ Move up and left to underneath a roof. Pull the right side of the roof and continue up and right

to a bolted anchor below a roof, left of a ledge.

Pitch 2: 5.10b Traverse straight right, up onto the ledge. Take a crack that splits the face through a roof and up the wall to a belay on a large ledge left of a left-facing corner.

Pitch 2 variation: 5.10 From the anchors, head straight up, pulling the roof. Continue past bolts up and right to another roof. Connect with pitch 2 here.

Pitch 3: 5.7 Take a face up to a ramp that angles up and right. Belay on a ledge at the top of the ramp.

Pitch 4: 5.9 Take a left-facing corner halfway up and then traverse left, out onto a face. Finish on a large ledge.

Rappel anchors are left of the top-out. Three 2-rope rappels lead to the ground.
FA: Tom Cecil, Tony Barnes 1994

26. Unknown 5.11d ★★★ Traditional. A huge left-facing corner makes up the right side of the arch. Climb this corner to a roof. Traverse under the roof left and pull out the left side to climb thin, somewhat crumbly cracks up and right to a fixed anchor. Gear: small wires and Friends to #3. Rappel using 2 ropes.
FA: Unknown

27. K-Day 5.12 ★★★ Mixed, 4 bolts. Begin above boulders right of the huge arch. Climb the varnished face left of a curving crack on the right. Finish up a left-facing corner to bolted anchors. 150 feet. Rappel using 2 ropes.
FA: Paul Van Betten, Jay Smith 1990

WHISKEY PEAK

Whiskey Peak is the satellite peak to Black Velvet Peak. To reach it, hike the Black Velvet Canyon Trail for 10 minutes to a trail that heads up and left toward the left edge of a prominent low pink band under Whiskey Peak. (This trail is 15 feet before the spot where the main trail cuts down into the large wash. Do not head right into the wash.) Upon reaching the pink band, scramble over the boulders to get to its top and to the red dirt trail that skirts the base of Whiskey Peak.

Whiskey Peak Gully descent: Hike the top of Whiskey Peak left (east) to a ridge that heads south, toward the start of the gully. Upon reaching a saddle, head left (east), down the gully. Stay on the high left (north) side of the gully, hiking down white slabs of rock. Upon entering the gully, do some third- and fourth-class scrambling, following a trail that meanders through the left side and center of the gully. At the mouth, traverse left to reach a trail that heads down. Cut left onto the red dirt trail that takes you around to the north side of Whiskey Peak (this is the red dirt trail that skirts the base of the peak west). 30–45 minutes.

▲ THE SCHWA AREA
SE AM Sun   Approach: 45 minutes

Upon reaching the red dirt trail that skirts the base of Whiskey Peak, hike up and left (southeast) to the Whiskey Peak Gully (the descent route from the peak). Hike past the gully, continuing left (southeast) for another 500 feet to a smooth black wall. Routes are described from left to right.

Alternate approach: From the parking area, hike the old roadbed westward until it makes a hairpin turn to the left. Here is where you head slightly right to reach Black Velvet Canyon. However, you can continue on the road south toward Mud Spring (see the Windy Peak chapter) or Windy Canyon until you come to an obvious path that heads up the hillside.

28. Longriders 5.12a ★★★ Traditional. Climb the black, varnished dihedral at the mouth of the canyon between Black Velvet and Windy Canyons. The route is on the right side. Years ago a *Climbing* magazine cover photo showed this pitch. Descent unknown.
FA: Paul Van Betten, Jay Smith 1981

29. Unknown ★★★ Traditional. Climb the tips crack that Paul Crawford gave up on. Descent unknown.
FA: Paul Van Betten 1981

30. The Schwa 5.10d ★★★★ Traditional. Climb a finger crack to rattly hands, to hands, to fist crack. Partway up, pop left and shake out on the big diving-board feature. This is in the same crack category as

The Fox (Calico Basin) and *Left Out* (Willow Springs). Descent unknown.
FA: Joe Herbst 1977

31. Apostrophe 5.9+ ★★★ Traditional. Climb the corner system 20 feet right of the previous route. Descent unknown.
FA: Joe Herbst 1977

32. High Plains Drifter 5.10d ★★★ Mixed. This climbs a scalloped-looking, smooth black face and is near a giant blocky ceiling. Descent unknown.
FA: Paul Crawford, Jay Smith 1981

▲ RAD CLIFFS/WHISKEY PEAK GULLY
Approach: 40 minutes

The Rad Cliffs are the cliff bands located on either side of the Whiskey Peak Gully (the descent gully from the peak) on the south side of Whiskey Peak. Upon reaching the red dirt trail that skirts the base of Whiskey Peak, hike up and left (southeast) to the Whiskey Peak Gully.

The routes here are all traditional in nature. Most of the names were given by Larry DeAngelo, local climber and author, and inspired by his daughter who is an extreme Harry Potter fan. The formation is named after Daniel Radcliffe, the actor who plays Harry Potter in the movies. It is divided into left and right sections and the routes are described from left to right.

RAD CLIFF LEFT
NE AM Sun

The cliffs on the left side of the Whiskey Peak Gully.

33. First Year 5.0 ★★ Traditional. At the far-left end of the Rad Cliff is a buttress (Phoenix Buttress) with a prominent jam crack. Below and slightly left of this is a smaller, low-angle buttress that ends on a ledge at the base of the main buttress. On its left side is an easy knobby chimney leading to a ledge.
FA: Unknown

34. Hufflepuff 5.5 ★★ Traditional. Climb the pleasant right-facing dihedral up the center of the lower buttress.
FA: Unknown

35. Second Year 5.3 ★★ Traditional. Begin on the right side of the lower buttress. Climb the face and a few thin cracks to the main ledge.
FA: Unknown

36. Ravenclaw 5.5 ★★ Traditional. From the main ledge, go up and left in a third-class gully to a point where it steepens. Follow a crack on the right past a knobby overhang. Continue up easier rock to the top of the buttress. Descend by scrambling down and left to a clean smooth gully. Go down this and turn left at its base. Take a talus tunnel to the gully where you started.
FA: Unknown

37. Fright of the Phoenix 5.7 ★★★ Traditional. From the main ledge, climb the upper buttress (Phoenix Buttress), starting in a crack on the right edge. Long pitch. This is a reasonably adventurous face climb with no bolts. Gear: bring plenty of small Rocks and runners, and some small Friends. Either continue to the top of the buttress and scramble down the *Ravenclaw* descent, or traverse right for an airy fourth-class pitch to the top of *The Dementor* and rappel from the tree with 2 ropes.
FA: Larry DeAngelo, Jason Fico

38. Azkaban Jam 5.9 ★★★ Traditional. This prominent jam crack is on the right side of Phoenix Buttress. Be careful of the loose block 30 feet up. Gear: Friends to #4. From the belay at the top of the crack, traverse right on an airy fourth-class catwalk and continue to the rappel tree at the top of *The Dementor*.
FA: Unknown

39. Rita Skeeter 5.9 ★★ Traditional. Face-climb the right-angling arête just right of *Azkaban*. Protection is tricky. A little scary.
FA: Xavier Wasiak, Larry DeAngelo

40. Moaning Myrtle 5.9+ ★ Traditional. Myrtle is probably moaning because she is less than 6 foot 4 inches and this route becomes dramatically harder without a very long reach. Climb easy rock up the broken dihedral to the right of *Azkaban*. When the

dihedral becomes blank and overhanging, make a long stretch left to gain the arête. Continue up the squeeze chimney to the top. On the first ascent, a little creative lasso work provided extra (welcome) protection at the crux. Gear: a few finger-sized Friends are handy. Rappel *The Dementor*.
FA: Larry DeAngelo

41. The Dementor 5.10 ★★ Traditional. This route makes a direct ascent of an ominous A-shaped cave that is left of *The Basilisk Fang*. Somewhat scary. Start in the brushy gully beneath the cave. Climb a 50-foot, fourth-class pitch to a small ledge. The second pitch starts with a 5.8 crack up the right side of the cave. Climb to a point where you can chimney between converging walls. Chimney out and down until you can swing out around the lip and into the daylight. To minimize rope drag, it is best to set up a hanging belay immediately above the cave exit. A short moderate pitch leads past some loose rock to the rappel tree. Gear: several hand-sized Friends and a few small ones, a #5 Friend, and some finger-sized passive gear.
FA: Larry DeAngelo, Paul Crosby

42. The Basilisk Fang 5.6 ★ Traditional. About 50 yards right of the Phoenix Buttress is a curving rib called the Basilisk Fang. Face climbing leads straight to the top. Protection is limited, but adequate. The top of this route is immediately adjacent to *The Dementor*, which you can rappel.
FA: Jason Fico, Larry DeAngelo

43. The Chamber of Secrets 5.7 ★★★ Traditional. On the right side of *The Basilisk Fang* is an easy gully. Climb this to an interesting vertical tunnel. Chimney up, then follow the clean, smooth hand and fist crack in the right-facing dihedral. Rappel *The Dementor*.
FA: Larry DeAngelo, Jason Fico

The next two routes are best climbed after doing *Frogland* or another route that takes the Whiskey Peak Gully descent. They are located 200 feet below the top of the gully. From the previous routes, continue hiking up the Whiskey Peak Gully to where it begins to narrow. Move left (south) toward two large, white boulders at the middle base of the east-facing wall. Look for a striking low-angle corner. Despite their names, these are not beginner routes.

44. Back to Basics 5.7 ★★ Traditional. Begin beneath a right-facing corner, left of a larger right-facing corner capped by a roof, on the far left. Bouldery start. Take a flake system up and left to the top of a pillar to a bolted anchor. Rappel with a 60-meter rope.
FA: Wendell Broussard, Ed Prochaska 1992

45. First Grader 5.6 ★ Traditional. Begin 12 feet right at a finger crack that climbs to a run-out face. Limited protection. Finish at the bolted anchor under the roof. Rappel with a 60-meter rope.
FA: Wendell Broussard, Ed Prochaska 1992

RAD CLIFF RIGHT
SW/E AM Sun
The cliffs on the right side of the Whiskey Peak Gully.

46. The Slytherin Slab 5.5 ★ Traditional. Begin about 50 yards left of *The Cadillac Crack* and immediately left of a large dirty chimney. Start right of the rounded prow of the buttress, then go straight up the crest, finishing in a hand crack after about 180 feet. Protection is somewhat intricate. To descend, go right past a few bushes and down a bushy crack (fourth class). Rappel *The Cadillac Crack*.
FA: Larry DeAngelo, Mark Rosenthal

47. The Cadillac Crack 5.9 ★★★★ Traditional. At the very base of the Whiskey Peak Gully, on the south side, is a clean off-width crack in a right-facing dihedral. Climb the off-width (5.9) to an alcove, then chimney and jam a hand crack (5.8) to a large ledge. Gear: to #5 Friend. Rappel with 2 ropes.
FA: It is likely that this route was done in 1975 by Joe Herbst and Randal Grandstaff. Larry DeAngelo came across a "scouting" photo of it while looking at Grandstaff's slides for his book Red Rock Odyssey. *According to DeAngelo, "it is inconceivable that Randal could have shown the photo to Joe without them immediately going out to climb it." DeAngelo's name for*

the route connects it with Grandstaff's Chrysler Crack (in Sandstone Quarry)—"but this is a nicer ride!" DeAngelo says.

48. Dark Arts 5.9 ★★★ Traditional. About 30 feet right of *The Cadillac Crack* is a white pedestal leaning against the darkly varnished face. From the top of the pedestal, face-climb up and left to a narrow ledge. Follow this left for about 20 feet until you can climb easy rock that leads to a small left-facing dihedral above. Climb the dihedral, and then join *The Cadillac Crack* for the final chimney and jam. A variation, going up and right from the middle of the traverse, has also been done. Gear: 2–3 Friends in the thin-hand to hand range, and a small TCU. Rappel with 2 ropes.
FA: Larry DeAngelo, George Urioste

49. Diagon Alley 5.7 ★ Traditional. Immediately right of *Dark Arts* is a right-slanting crack. Follow this to a good ledge. You can probably rappel from the uninspiring tree here, or fourth-class up a short distance and rappel *The Cadillac Crack* with 2 ropes.
FA: Unknown

▲ WHISKEY PEAK EAST
NE AM Sun Approach: 30 minutes

Upon reaching the red dirt trail that skirts the base of Whiskey Peak, hike up the hill 50 feet toward an S-shaped crack. Routes are described from left to right.

50. Schaeffer's Delight 5.8 ★★★★ Mixed, 7 bolts. Begin 60 feet left of the hike up, 10 feet left of the S crack comprising *Lazy Buttress*, at an overhanging bulge. Pull the bulge, move left and head up the

black, varnished face to a tree. Mike Petrilak put up this route after shattering his hip in a climbing fall in the Tetons. Rappel using 1 rope.

FA: Mike Petrilak, Mike Ward, George Urioste 1984

51. Lazy Buttress 5.6 ★★★ Traditional. Climb the S-shaped crack 50 feet left of the hike up and about 200 feet left of *Frogland*. Begin in a left-facing corner and move up as it turns into a right-facing corner. Veer left and then summit the peak.

Pitch 1: Climb up the S crack, staying left on the face. Continue up to a tree and anchor on a prominent ledge, up and left of the crack.

Pitch 2: Step right, around the pinnacle/tower feature, into the crack. Climb the low-angle face on the right, passing a tree in the crack. Continue up the low-angle face to a large belay ledge. Rappel from here or continue climbing.

Pitch 3: Head up and left to the left edge of the roof. Pull the roof onto the black face angling up and left to a big ledge (Lovers Ledge).

Pitch 4: Ascend the headwall above via a crack.

Descend left (east) to reach the Whiskey Peak Gully descent.

FA: Mac McMackin, Nanouk Borche, Joe and Betsy Herbst 1973

52. Crown Royal 5.8 ★★★ Traditional. Begin 100 feet right of *Lazy Buttress*. Start in a corner with a crack in the middle of it. The left face is black and the right face is white (with some black varnish).

Pitch 1: Climb a right-facing crack. Continue until you reach another crack out right; step right and climb that crack. Step back left to a ledge and belay.

Pitch 2: Climb the crack that makes up the edge of a flake system to its top. Traverse left to a left-facing crack/corner system, below a bush. Step left around the bush. Finish up the crack/corner system to a belay below a roof.

Pitch 3: Climb straight up the crack to a bushy ledge and belay.

Pitch 4: Follow crack systems to another ledge and belay.

Pitch 5: Take a crack and the face to the top of the cliff.

Descend via the Whiskey Peak Gully descent.

FA: Unknown 1980s

▲ FROGLAND AREA
NE AM Sun   Approach: 30 minutes

Hike the Black Velvet Canyon Trail for 10 minutes to a trail that heads up and left toward the left edge of a prominent low pink band under Whiskey Peak. (This trail is 15 feet before the spot where the main trail cuts down into the large wash. Do not head right into the wash.) Upon reaching the pink band, scramble over the boulders to get to its top and to the red dirt trail that skirts the base of Whiskey Peak. Head right (west) on the red dirt trail. Continue 50 feet to where several medium-sized trees grow up on the right side of the trail. Take a trail left here, heading toward the cliff. Upon reaching the cliff, traverse the base (of the cliff) on a thin trail for about 150 feet. At the first opportunity to move up to a ledge system 6 feet up, take it. The following start off the right side of this ledge, to the right of a huge, white, featureless slab. Routes are described from left to right.

53. Unknown 5.7 ★★ Traditional. Begin 20 feet left of *Frogland*, on the middle-left portion of the ledge. Climb the crack, angling up and right to fixed anchors below the first-pitch ledge of *Frogland*. Rappel using 2 ropes or finish on *Frogland*.

FA: Unknown

54. Raindance 5.10d R ★★ Mixed. Begin 10 feet left of the thin white pillar, marking the start of *Frogland*. Climb a black, varnished face to a bolt, below a crack. Climb the flakey crack, clipping 3 more bolts. Traverse left, head up the crack, and then move back right. Finish up the crack, clipping bolts to the top of *Frogland*'s first pitch. Gear: standard rack to #2.5 Friend. Rappel from the top of *Frogland*'s first pitch using 2 ropes or continue up *Frogland*.

FA: Dave Wonderly, Don Wilson 1990

55. Frogland 5.8 ★★★★★ Traditional. Begin on a finger crack, off the far-right edge of the ledge. Climb up to the crack right of a white pillar. Climb to the top of the pillar and take the crack to the top of the cliff. This description recounts the route most

FROGLAND AREA

White Slab

FA

53

54

55

56

white
pillar

to 57

parties climb. The first-ascent party did a slightly different variation, which is indicated on the Frogland Area overlay photo. Gear: standard rack to #3.5 Friend.

Pitch 1: 5.7 Climb the finger crack left of a low roof, between two trees, to a ledge. Climb the crack up the right edge of a white pillar. From the top of the pillar, continue up the left-facing crack to a tree on a ledge. Move up the left-facing corner to a large, bush-filled ledge. 130 feet.

Pitch 2: 5.6 Take the crack that heads right off the top of the ledge and then takes a sharp left after 8 feet. Continue up the crack, pulling onto some ledge systems. At print time, a 2-bolt belay was located on the

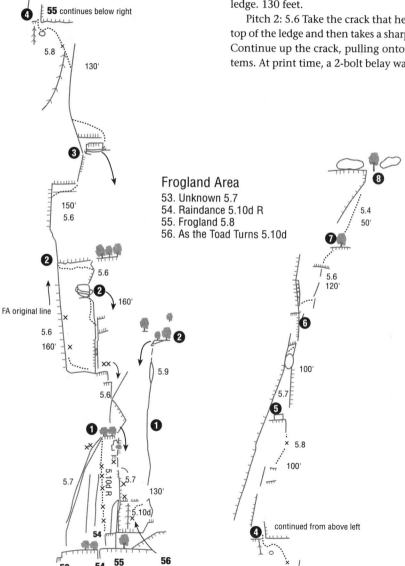

Frogland Area
53. Unknown 5.7
54. Raindance 5.10d R
55. Frogland 5.8
56. As the Toad Turns 5.10d

largest ledge (65 feet). From the left edge of the large block ledge where the bolted anchors are located, climb the off-width/chimney to underneath a second roof. From there (where the crack is about 3.5 inches wide), step left onto the steep face. Take the face to a ledge with a large slung boulder and belay. 160 feet.

FA pitch 2: The pitch was originally done by traversing straight left on the large block ledge to the corner left of the bolted anchors above the first pitch. That corner was followed to underneath the roof to where pitch 3 traverses left under the roof. 160 feet.

Pitch 3: 5.6 Climb the steep short crack above the boulder at the belay. Traverse left underneath a roof, on a handrail, to a corner. Take the right-facing corner up to below another roof. Traverse right 5 feet on good footing. Pull a steep move on the right side of the overhang to reach a left-facing crack. Continue to a tiny recessed stance under a roof and between two cracks. 150 feet.

Pitch 4: 5.8 Move up and right atop the belay block. Face-traverse left, over the belay, to a crack. Take the crack up until you can step left to the arête, clipping a bolt. Move up and left underneath a roof. Traverse under the roof, using hidden pockets, to a crack. Take the crack (right of an arête) to the ledge above and left of the roof. Belay (bigger Friends and small Rocks). 130 feet.

Pitch 5: 5.8 Take the right-facing corner up to a thin, white face. Clip a bolt on the face and take a crack above the face to a ledge on the left below an overhang. 100 feet.

Pitch 6: 5.7 Stem between two corners up to under a large boulder wedged in the crack. Tunnel under the boulder and up to underneath the right edge of a roof. Step out right onto the face and continue up a right-facing crack. Belay in an alcove/groove above the roof. Place gear to avoid getting the rope stuck in the crack at the roof. Large Friends and small Rocks for the belay. 100 feet.

Pitch 7: 5.6 Move up the crack to a point where there are loose blocks. Step right to thin crack systems up the face, moving up and right to under a small roof. Pull the roof and head up and right to a large ledge. 120 feet.

Pitch 8: 5.4 Climb the featured face right of the crack system. 50 feet.

Leah Hemberry styling up Frogland *5.8*

Descend via the Whiskey Peak Gully descent.
FA: Mike Gilbert, Joanne and George Urioste 1978

56. As the Toad Turns 5.10d ★★ Traditional. Start on *Frogland*. Gear: standard rack to #3 Friend.

Pitch 1: 5.10d Move right under a small roof, clipping a bolt. Pull the roof and continue up discontinuous cracks and flakes on a varnished face to a small stance. 130 feet.

Pitch 2: 5.9 Continue to the top of the pillar. Rappel into *Frogland.*

FA: Nick Nordblom, Jenni Stone, Jay Smith 1989

57. Romance is a Heart Breakin' Affair 5.10a ★★

Traditional. Begin on a small buttress one gully right of *Frogland.* Climb a broken buttress to reach a hole, up high, that can be crawled into. End on bushy ledge. 150 feet. Gear: standard rack to #3 Friend. Make one rappel, using 2 ropes.

FA: Nick Nordblom, Richard Harrison, Brad Ball 1989

▲ IXTLAN WALL
N No Sun   Approach: 40 minutes

Hike the Black Velvet Canyon Trail for 10 minutes to a trail that heads up and left toward the left edge of a prominent low pink band under Whiskey Peak. (This trail is 15 feet before the spot where the main trail cuts down into the large wash. Do not head right into the wash.) Upon reaching the pink band, scramble over the boulders to get to its top and to the red dirt trail that skirts the base of Whiskey Peak. Head right (west) on the red dirt trail. Continue 50 feet to where several medium-sized trees grow up on the right side of the trail. Take a trail left here, heading toward the cliff. Upon reaching the cliff, traverse the base (of the cliff) on a thin trail for about 300 feet (150 feet right of the Frogland Area).

58. Kenny Laguna 5.10d ★★★

Traditional. Start atop a ledge system, at the largest low roof (25 feet off the ground), 30 feet right of a large boulder at the base. Gear: doubles of standard rack to #3 Friend, brass wires.

Pitch 1: 5.10d Climb a small dihedral. Follow a crack out the right side of the roof. Climb up and left, through a corner to a belay ledge. 80 feet.

Pitch 2: 5.10d Follow a huge right-facing corner up to a roof and flake system. Pull the roof and take the crack to where it ends at a fixed anchor.

Rappel using 2 ropes.

FA: Richard Harrison, Paul Crawford, Paul Van Betten, Sal Mamusia, Chick Corea 1983

59. Perplexity 5.10d ★

Mixed, 5 bolts. Begin 20 feet right of *Kenny Laguna,* just right of the right edge of the low roof section. Climb the black, varnished face, angling up and left past 2 bolts to a small ledge (left of the first-pitch anchor on *The Misunderstanding*). Continue up and left and then follow the crack moving up and right, connecting with the second-pitch anchors of *The Misunderstanding.* Gear: standard rack to #3 Friend and doubles of #00–#0.5 Friends. Rappel using 1 rope, two rappels.

FA: Todd and Donette Swain 1994

60. The Misunderstanding 5.9 ★★★

Traditional. Begin the same as the previous route, but climb the crack up the center of a recess in the cliff line. It is easy to link the two pitches. Gear: to #3.5 Friend, doubles of #3.5.

Pitch 1: 5.9 Head straight up the crack, moving left around a roof. Climb to bolted anchors on the ledge left. 70 feet.

Pitch 2: 5.9 Move right into the crack and climb to anchors up and left, above the roof. 70 feet.

Rappel using 1 rope, two rappels.

FA: Dave Anderson, Randal Grandstaff 1975

61. Miss Conception 5.10 ★

Mixed. Begin 5 feet right of the previous route, off the top of a ledge, right of the white left-facing corner. Gear: standard rack including 2 #3 Friends and many quickdraws.

Pitch 1: 5.9, 2 bolts. Climb a left-facing varnished corner up to a stance below a roof. Move up and right, clipping 2 bolts in the white rock. Head to the fixed anchor up and right. 60 feet.

Pitch 2: 5.10 Continue straight up the black, varnished face until just right of a right-facing corner. 100 feet.

Rappel using 2 ropes.

FA: Todd and Donette Swain 1995

62. Return to Forever 5.10d ★★★

Traditional. Begin 10 feet right of *Miss Conception,* at a mass of blocks atop a white ledge system. Gear: several #3 and #4 Friends.

Pitch 1: 5.10d Climb the off-width crack to a ledge with a fixed anchor in the crack. 60 feet.

IXTLAN WALL

Pitch 2: 5.10d Continue up the crack until it reaches the pitch 2 anchor of *Miss Conception*. 110 feet. Rappel from here or continue up.

Pitch 3: 5.8 Continue up the crack. Needs better anchor.

Rappel the route using 2 ropes.

FA: Richard Harrison, Paul Crawford, Paul Van Betten, Sal Mamusia, Stanley Clarke 1983

63. Mazatlan 5.10d ★★★★ Begin 15 feet right of *Return to Forever*, in a thin right-facing corner. Climb the corner and then move onto the face left to clip the anchors before reaching the roof. Rappel using 2 ropes. Or climb (fifth class) to the top of the cliff and descend via the Whiskey Peak Gully descent.

FA: Dave Anderson, Randal Grandstaff 1978

64. Ixtlan 5.11c ★★★★ Mixed. In the book *Journey to Ixtlan*, Carlos Castaneda describes arduous trials and tests of the body and will that Don Juan, his mentor, uses to prepare him to see things as they "really are" instead of by conventional standards like sight and language. You will find this route "without routines, free, fluid," like Castaneda's encounter. Begin 5 feet right of *Mazatlan*, in a thin right-facing corner. Gear: medium Rocks and Friends to #5.

Pitch 1: 5.11c, sport, 7 bolts. Climb the right-facing thin corner. Traverse right and up to fixed bolt anchors and a hanging belay. 60 feet.

Ixtlan Wall

58. Kenny Laguna 5.10d
59. Perplexity 5.10d
60. The Misunderstanding 5.9
61. Miss Conception 5.10
62. Return to Forever 5.10d
63. Mazatlan 5.10d
64. Ixtlan 5.11c

65. Matzoland 5.12a
66. Cabo San Looseness 5.10 R
67. Sand Felipe 5.9+
68. Sandblast 5.10a R
69. Triassic Sands 5.10c
70. Cole Essence 5.11c
71. Archeopteryx 5.11a R

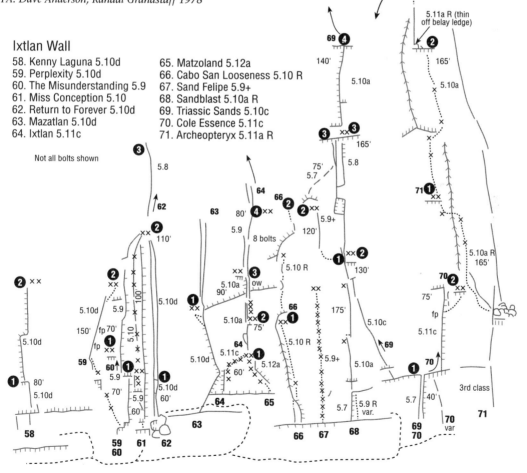

Pitch 2: 5.10a Climb up the rattly, loose flakes and blocks to fixed bolt anchors. Scary. Back up the anchor with #3.5–#4 Friend, since the bolts are in somewhat suspect rock. 75 feet.

Pitch 3: 5.10a, 4 bolts. Climb the off-width using the original bolts for pro (1/4- and 3/8-inch) or use Friends to #5. Continue to a right-facing corner and roof. Pull the roof and move up the crack to fixed bolt anchors. The bolts on this pitch were placed aiding with a very large homemade wooden cam. 90 feet. Most people do three single-rope rappels from here (move the knot over the edge just below the pitch 3 anchors when rappeling, to prevent stuck ropes). Or continue up.

The upper pitches have entirely original bolts.

Pitch 4: 5.9, 8 bolts. Climb past original 1/4-inch bolts through a squeeze chimney to a fixed anchor. 80 feet.

Pitch 5: 5.8 Climb the chimney to its top. Exit onto the face and a fixed belay. 80 feet.

Pitch 6: Easy fifth class, 2 bolts. Traverse right 30 feet to a large ledge.

Pitch 7: 5.9+, 2 bolts. Follow the crack that leads to the left side of the base of a towerlike feature. Belay on a blocky ledge. 100 feet.

Pitch 8: 5.10a, 3 bolts. Move right to a corner and take it to its top. 150 feet. Fourth-class scramble up 200 feet to the top of the cliff.

Descend via the Whiskey Peak Gully descent.

FA: "Spiderman" Dan Goodwin, Joanne Urioste, George Urioste 1981

65. Matzoland 5.12a ★★★ Sport, 6 bolts. Begin 20 feet right of the previous route, at a steep left-facing corner and face. Climb directly to the first-pitch anchors of *Ixtlan*. Rappel with 1 rope.

FA: Dan McQuade 1997

66. Cabo San Looseness 5.10 R ★ Mixed. Begin around right of *Matzoland* on the arête between the orange Ixtlan Wall, on the left, and the black, varnished Triassic Sands Wall, on the right.

Pitch 1: Climb alongside the arête up to anchors 10 feet below a roof.

Pitch 2: Continue up a thin seam to a roof. Climb the right-facing corner to its top. Follow thin crack

systems up and slightly left, staying right of the next roof. Move up to the anchor.

FA: Unknown 1980s

67. Sand Felipe 5.9+ ★★★★ Sport, 16 bolts. Begin 5 feet right of the arête at a line of bolts up a varnished face. Rappel using 2 ropes.

FA: N. Modelo, T. Cate 1994

68. Sandblast 5.10a R ★★★★ Traditional. Begin 10 feet right of the previous route, at a left-facing corner with a chimney crack. Gear: standard rack to #3 Friend.

Pitch 1: 5.10a Climb the chimney to a ledge. Take a thin crack straight up. 175 feet.

Pitch 1 variation: 5.9 R At the start, climb an arête that makes up the right side of the chimney. Continue up the vertical crack after reaching the ledge.

FA: Joe Herbst, Larry Hamilton 1972
FFA: Paul Van Betten, Nick Nordblom 1987

Pitch 2: 5.9+ Climb a thin vertical crack. Take it up to below an arching roof and belay (possibly fixed anchors added after first ascent). 120 feet.

Pitch 3: 5.7 Climb a discontinuous crack system that gets wide toward the top. Finish on the left edge of the ledge where pitch 3 of *Triassic Sands* tops out. 75 feet. Traverse right and rappel *Triassic Sands* with 2 ropes.

FA: Paul Van Betten, Nick Nordblom 1987

69. Triassic Sands 5.10c ★★★★★ Traditional. Begin 10 feet down and right of the previous route, at a left-facing flake and chimney. Gear: standard rack to #3 Friend, doubles of #2–#3.

Pitch 1: 5.7 Climb the black, varnished, wide crack/corner and chimney to a ledge and belay off a large wedged block. 40 feet.

Pitch 2: 5.10c Traverse the ledge left 5 feet to a steep, orange finger-to-hand crack. Take the crack up through a small roof as it widens to fist size and continues to a bolted anchor. 130 feet. It is easy to combine the first two pitches.

Pitch 3: 5.8 Continue up the crack to a downward-sloping ledge and fixed anchor. 165 feet. Rappel from here or continue.

Pitch 4: 5.10a, 1 bolt. Climb the right-facing corner up and left of the belay to a small ledge. Classic pitch! 140 feet. You can also rappel from here using 2 ropes, or continue.

Pitches 5–6: Fourth and easy fifth class. Take broken corners to the top of the feature.

Descend via the Whiskey Peak Gully descent.

FA: Joe Herbst, Larry Hamilton 1972
FFA: Augie Klien, Tom Kaufman, Randal Grandstaff, Chris Robbins, Joe Herbst 1979

70. Cole Essence 5.11c ★★★ Begin on *Triassic Sands*. Climb the blank-looking corner above and right of the first pitch topped by a roof. Gear: to #1 Friend and brass wires, doubles of the small stuff.

Pitch 1: 5.7 Climb the chimney to a ledge and belay off a large block (same as *Triassic Sands*). Or climb a broken crack system 15 feet right of *Triassic Sands*. 40 feet.

Pitch 2: 5.11c Take the striking left-facing dihedral to a single piton. Traverse right to fixed anchors below the roof. 75 feet. Rappel or continue up *Archaeopteryx*.

FA: Charles Cole, Randal Grandstaff 1990

71. Archaeopteryx 5.11a R ★★ Mixed, 1/4-inch bolts. Begin 10 feet right of *Triassic Sands* in a crack on the left side of a gully. Gear: brass wires and Friends to #2.

Pitch 1: 5.10a R, 3 bolts. Third-class up and right at the base of a gully. At a bush climb a crack up and left, coming near the *Cole Essence* anchors. Continue up the face, right of the prominent arête. Cross left over the arête to belay at a bolted anchor on a ledge. 165 feet.

Pitch 2: 5.10a, 4 bolts. Move up, climbing the face left of the arête. Clip a bolt under the roof and traverse right of the arête, onto a face. Follow the face up past 2 more bolts to a ledge and belay. 165 feet.

Pitch 3: 5.11a R Follow a thin crack off belay (be careful: if you fall here you could hit the ledge!). Finish up the crack and take a face to a ledge and belay. 120 feet.

Traverse left to a fixed anchor and rappel into *Triassic Sands* using 2 ropes.

FA: Nick Nordblom, Lynn Robison 1988

▲ WHOLESOME FULLBACK AREA
N No Sun   Approach: 40 minutes

Hike the Black Velvet Canyon Trail for 10 minutes to a trail that heads up and left toward the left edge of a prominent low pink band under Whiskey Peak. (This trail is 15 feet before the spot where the main trail cuts down into the large wash. Do not head right into the wash.) Upon reaching the pink band, scramble over the boulders to get to its top and to the red dirt trail that skirts the base of Whiskey Peak. Head right (west) on the red dirt trail. Continue 50 feet to where several medium-sized trees grow up on the right side of the trail. Take the trail left here, heading toward the cliff. Upon reaching the cliff, traverse the base on a thin trail for about 500 feet (200 feet right of Ixtlan Wall).

Alternate approach: Hike the Black Velvet Canyon trail for 10 minutes to a trail that cuts down into the wash (15 feet past where a trail cuts up toward the pink band and Whiskey Peak). Take the trail down and head left (west) up the wash. Where the low pink band breaks down, a trail intersects the wash on the left. Take this trail straight up to the base of the Wholesome Fullback Area (with a large pillarlike feature).

Routes are described from left to right.

72. Wholesome Fullback 5.10a R ★★★★ Traditional. Maybe this should be named *Wholesome Sandbag*? This route climbs the crack on the left side of the pillar feature. Begin 10 feet right of a right-facing corner, right of a pine tree that is on top of some blocks. Gear: to #3.5 Friend.

Pitch 1: 5.10a R Take the thin crack up. After heading right to the left-facing corner that makes up the left side of the pillar, build a belay on a sloping ledge. 150 feet.

Pitch 2: 5.8 Continue up the left-facing corner as it widens. Chimney through to the top of the feature and then downclimb to the right side of the pillar and fixed anchors above a ledge. 80 feet.

Rappel *Our Father* using 2 ropes.

FA: Cal Folsom, Lars Holbeck 1975

Amber variation: 5.10a R ★★ Traditional. Begin on *Wholesome Fullback*. Where the crack jogs right into the wide left-facing corner, continue straight up the

WHOLESOME FULLBACK AREA

Amber var. 72

Whiskey Peak
West

72

73

74

75

76

to 77–78

wall. Jog left to a left-facing flake and take it to its top. Traverse right to the top of *Wholesome Fullback*.

Rappel *Our Father* using 2 ropes.
FA: Nick Nordblom, Teresa Krolak 1998

73. Unknown 5.10d ★★★ Traditional. Climb between *Wholesome Fullback* and *Delicate Sound of Thunder*. Two pitches. The second pitch is 5.9 and finishes just left of an arête at a large ledge at the top of the pillar. Gear: standard rack and brass wires. Heads up: This route could have an "R" rating. Rappel *Our Father* using 2 ropes.
FA: Jay Smith, Paul Crawford early 1980s

74. The Delicate Sound of Thunder 5.11c ★★★★ Mixed. Begin 20 feet right of *Wholesome Fullback* on the black, varnished front face of the pillar. Gear: brass wires, Rocks, and Friends to #2.5.

Pitch 1: 5.11c, 4 bolts. Climb thin edges and a crack past small gear and bolts. Move right after the fourth bolt, and then move up to the right edge of a roof and left-facing corner. Continue up to belay in a large alcove. Tricky gear placements at anchor. 100 feet.

Pitch 2: 5.11a, 5 bolts. Run-out. Take a crack up and right to the varnished arête. Climb the face left of the arête to the top of the pillar (the arête makes up the right-facing corner of *Our Father*). Finish at *Our Father* anchors. 140 feet.

Rappel *Our Father* using 2 ropes.
FA: Dave Wonderly, Marge Floyd, Dave Evans 1988

75. Our Father 5.10d ★★★★ Traditional. Begin 5 feet right of the previous route at a right-leaning, left-facing corner. Gear: small Rocks and Friends to #3.5, doubles of #2–#3.5.

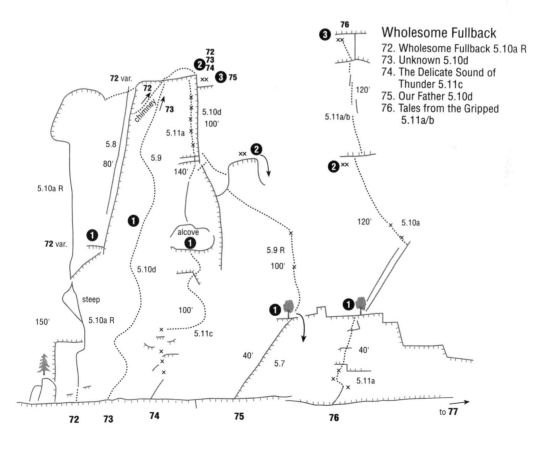

Wholesome Fullback

72. Wholesome Fullback 5.10a R
73. Unknown 5.10d
74. The Delicate Sound of Thunder 5.11c
75. Our Father 5.10d
76. Tales from the Gripped 5.11a/b

Pitch 1: 5.7 Take the corner up to a tree and belay on a ledge. 40 feet.

Pitch 2: 5.9 R, 2 bolts. Step off the right side of the ledge and go up the varnished face, clipping bolts. After the second bolt move back left into the right-facing corner. Take it up, making a jog right to bolted anchors atop a small pinnacle. 100 feet.

Pitch 3: 5.10d Traverse left into the huge right-facing corner. Take it up to the bolted anchors even with the top of the pillar. 100 feet.

Rappel using 1 60-meter rope or 2 shorter ropes. *FA: Rick Wheeler, Joe Herbst, Randal Grandstaff, Vern Clevenger 1977*

76. Tales from the Gripped 5.11a/b ★★★ Mixed. Climb the face 15 feet right of *Our Father*, below right-slanting parallel cracks above a ledge.

Pitch 1: 5.11a Climb a right-angling crack up to a face to underneath a roof. Pull the roof on the right and take the face up and right to a ledge with a tree and belay. 40 feet.

Pitch 2: 5.10a Climb the rightmost of the parallel cracks to its end. Move up and left out of the crack, clipping bolts. Continue up and left to a fixed anchor beneath a roof. 120 feet.

Pitch 3: 5.11a/b Go up and left in the black face, through seams and past bolts to the base of a corner that is below a huge roof near the top of the cliff. 120 feet.

FA: Todd Swain, Elaine Mathews 1990

▲ WHISKEY PEAK WEST
W PM Sun (summer only)   Approach: 40 minutes

Hike the Black Velvet Canyon trail for 10 minutes to where it cuts down into the wash (15 feet past where a trail cuts up toward the pink band and Whiskey Peak). Take the trail down and head left (west) up the wash. Where the low pink band breaks down, a trail intersects the wash on the left. Take this trail straight up to the base of the Wholesome Fullback Wall (with a large pillarlike feature). Pass this wall and head around right to the gully that leads to Whiskey Peak's west face. Both routes begin left of the most notable feature on the wall, a left-angling, black, varnished corner topped by a roof. Routes are described from left to right.

77. Closed on Monday 5.9+ ★★★ Traditional. Begin 50 feet left of *Only the Good Die Young*. Climb a thin crack and corner. Gear: large selection of brass wires and small Rocks. Rappel from *old* fixed anchor. *FA: Joe Herbst, Stephanie Petrilak 1978*

78. Only the Good Die Young 5.11b/c ★★★ Mixed. Climb the left-facing corner right of the previous route and left of the large corner topped by a roof. Gear: standard rack and brass wires.

Pitch 1: 5.10b Start off a large block at the base. Clip a bolt and then take the corner up, exiting right at the top to a bolted belay. Small gear. 60 feet.

Pitch 2: 5.11a, 5 bolts. Head right, moving up and over a roof. Take cracks up to a bolted belay right of another roof. 70 feet.

Pitch 3: 5.10a, 4 bolts. Climb the left face of the corner system to a bolted belay under a roof. 60 feet.

Pitch 4: 5.11b/c, 8 bolts. Take the crack up for 10 feet, then traverse right 15 feet to under a roof. Most people avoid clipping the fifth bolt on this pitch, an original Urioste 3/8-inch bolt. It is best left unclipped to reduce rope drag (or use a long sling). Pull the roof and then climb the varnished face to a crack. Crack-climb to the summit. 160 feet.

Descend by scrambling right, into the gully between this wall and the Black Velvet Wall. Some fifth class.
FA: Mike Ward, George and Joanne Urioste, Bob Findlay, Bill Bradley 1985

BLACK VELVET PEAK

▲ BLACK VELVET WALL
N No Sun (AM in summer)   Approach: 1 hour

The Black Velvet Wall is an enormous black, smooth, patinaed wall. It has the greatest concentration of classic multipitch routes in all of Red Rock. To get there, hike the canyon trail for 10 minutes to where it cuts down (right) into the wash (15 feet past where the trail cuts up and left toward the pink band and Whiskey Peak). Take the trail right and head left (west) up the wash. Continue up the wash, scrambling over boulders until the wash pinches off and is impassable. Take a faint trail, heading left into some trees and bushes to the base of a short wall. Scramble up and right on the wall at a low ledge that allows you to continue up and right. A crack climbs the last 10 feet (5.0). At the top of the short wall you will be at the far right base of the Black Velvet Wall. Hike up the ramp left to reach the following routes. The farthest routes are located far up and left of the climb up, just before entering the gully. Routes are described from left to right.

Black Velvet Wall descent: Depending on where you top-out, hike either left or right to reach the summit of the Black Velvet Wall. From there, take the ridge that heads south to another ridge that runs east-west. Follow the east-west ridge, heading east (left) almost as far as you can hike before heading

downhill. Scramble down the left (north) side of the ridge to reach the notch at the top of the Whiskey Peak Gully descent. Upon reaching a saddle head right (east), down Whiskey Peak Gully. Stay on the high left (north) side of the gully, hiking down white slabs of rock. Upon entering the gully do some third- and fourth-class scrambling, following a trail that meanders through the left side and center of the gully. At the mouth, traverse left to reach a trail that heads down. Cut left onto the red dirt trail that takes you around to the north side of Whiskey Peak. (This is the red dirt trail that skirts the base of the peak west.) Before reaching a grouping of trees on the right, head down and right (on the southeast side of the low pink band). This takes you to the main canyon trail. Go right (east) on the trail to obtain the parking lot. 1.5 hours.

79. Spark Plug 5.10a ★★★ Traditional. Old-school rating. *Spark Plug* is the first line right of a prominent right-facing corner. Continue straight up in

black, varnished rock. Begin 40 yards left of *Refried Brains*, on the left side of a big slab. Climb the thin left-angling corner/crack, moving up to bolted anchors under the roof/dihedral where *Cutting Edge* steps right. 150 feet. Gear: standard rack to #2.5 Friend, triples of #3 and #4, and brass wires. Rappel using 2 ropes.

FA: Paul Van Betten, Sal Mamusia 1983

80. Cutting Edge 5.11b/c ★★★★ Mixed. Begin on *Spark Plug* and step right to a very thin right-angling dike. Heel hooks and friction technique will get you through this one with a good pump. Climb past bolts to a bolted anchor. 130 feet. Gear: brass wires and Friends to #1. Rappel using 1 rope.

FA: Danny Meyers 1987

81. Smooth as Silk 5.11a R ★★★ Traditional. Start at the left edge of a huge, bulbous, pillar-type feature, 50 feet right of the previous route. Take the leftmost right-angling crack that heads up to the left edge of the pillar feature. Gear: brass wires and Friends to #3.5.

Pitch 1: 5.11a R Take the right-angling crack up and right to a face. Take the face to a bolted anchor in a recess. 140 feet.

Pitch 2: 5.10a Take the splitter wavy crack up varnished black rock to anchors. 150 feet.

Rappel using 2 ropes.

FA: Jay Smith, Paul Crawford, Randal Grandstaff, Dave Diegleman 1981

82. Refried Brains IV, 5.9 ★★★ Traditional. Begin 20 feet left of a large boulder that leans against the wall, at a crack that angles up and right.

Pitch 1: 5.9 Follow the crack past a bolt, angling right. Move back left and then straight up the wall on steeper ground. Climb a thin left-facing corner past a bolt. Continue to a ledge with a bolted anchor. 125 feet.

Pitch 2: 5.8 Move left to the crack system and take it and the face right of a right-facing corner and roof (a steeper section of rock). Follow it up to the top of a pillar with a large tree and belay. 150 feet.

Pitch 3: 5.9 Traverse right to reach a crack. Take it up as it opens in a few spots to a small stance. 130 feet.

Pitch 4: 5.9 Step left and climb to the top of the left edge of the white, phallic tower feature. Enter a crack that heads left to a ledge and fixed belay. 170 feet.

Pitch 5: 5.9, 4 bolts. Climb the face left of the arête and large right-facing corner to a bolted belay. 70 feet. From here it is best to rappel the route, but you can also continue to the top of the buttress.

Pitch 6: 5.8 Take steep cracks to a hanging belay. Poor anchor. 150 feet.

Pitch 7: 5.7, 1 bolt. Move up and left to a varnished corner. Climb the corner, then move left to a ledge with a bolted anchor. 75 feet.

Pitch 8: 5.8, 2 bolts. Take a thin crack on overhanging rock to a ledge with a bolted anchor. 120 feet.

Pitch 9: 5.7 Take a corner to a tree-filled ledge. 100 feet. Scramble up and right (fourth class) for 1000 feet to the summit.

Descend via the Black Velvet Wall descent.

FA: Joanne and George Urioste, Stephanie Petrilak 1979

83. The Flesh IV, 5.10d ★★★ Mixed, 5 bolts. Start on *Refried Brains*. Cut right on the first pitch to obtain a huge corner. Follow this corner system to a large roof at the top. Turn the roof using a hand crack. Follow this to the top. Seven pitches. Third class to the top of the formation and take the Black Velvet Wall descent.

FA: Richard Harrison, Jay Smith 1984

84. American Ghostdance 5.12a ★★ Mixed. Begin at a tree on a ledge, 3 feet right of the previous route. Begin directly above the tree. Gear: standard rack to #2.5 Friend.

Pitch 1: 5.12a, 8 bolts. Climb up to a bolt and move right along pockets. Move back left to another bolt and then straight up to bolted anchors. 130 feet.

Pitch 2: 5.10, 4 bolts. Climb straight up to a roof and pull around the left side. Continue up to a crack system, left of some bushes. Take the crack to a ledge at the base of a right-facing corner. 170 feet.

Pitch 3: 5.10, 6 bolts. From the right edge of the ledge, head straight up to a light black water streak, which emerges from a thin right-facing corner above. Climb to a bolted belay. 130 feet.

Pitch 4: 5.9, 3 bolts. Continue up the face, angling

Black Velvet Wall, Left (East) Side
82. Refried Brains IV 5.9
83. The Flesh IV 5.10d
84. American Ghost-
    dance 5.12a

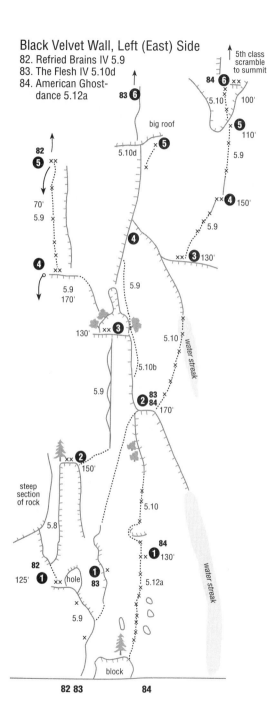

82 83   84

right to a crack and belay. 150 feet.

Pitch 5: 5.9, 2 bolts. Continue up the crack system and then step left onto the face. Move up and left to a right-facing corner. Single-bolt belay. 110 feet.

Pitch 6: 5.10, 3 bolts. Step around the left side of the corner. Climb up and left to a bolted belay on a ledge, right of a right-facing corner. 100 feet.

Pitch 7: Fifth-class scrambling for 1000 feet leads to the summit.

Descend via the Black Velvet Wall descent.
FA: Jordy Morgan, Kevin Fosburg 1988

85. Sandstone Samurai 5.11a R/X ★ Mixed. Begin right of the two big water streaks that run down the center of the wall. This route climbs to a left-facing corner with a water streak down its left side. This route was put up in a sort of rebellion against bolts, in response to the first ascent of *Prince of Darkness*. Gear: standard rack with brass wires and Friends to #2.

Pitch 1: 5.10d R, 4 bolts. Start 10 feet right of the rightmost water streak and 40 feet right of *American Ghostdance*. Climb white low-angle rock to the black face right of a swoosh that goes up and left. Move up hueco features and vertical seams to a bolted anchor. 140 feet.

Pitch 2: 5.10b R/X, 1 bolt. Climb up the wall using short seams to access the second bolted anchor. This is a serious pitch with marginal gear. 130 feet.

Pitch 3: 5.10a R Head slightly left to a vertical seam. When it ends, continue up to a larger crack system, moving straight up the wall. The crack ends and then begins again. The bolted anchor is just left of where it begins again. 145 feet.

Pitch 4: 5.10a R Climb up and left to a tiny left-angling crack until it ends at a fixed anchor. 150 feet.

Pitch 5: 5.10d R, 5 bolts, 1 pin. Head up and left across the black water streak to the bolted anchor, right of a right-facing corner. 150 feet.

Rappel the route using 2 ropes.
FA: Paul Van Betten, Nick Nordblom 1988

86. Rock Warrior 5.10b R ★★★★ Mixed. Begin the same as *Sandstone Samurai*, between a low roof and short pillar of rock. Like *Sandstone Samurai*, this

Black Velvet Wall

85. Sandstone Samurai 5.11a R/X
86. Rock Warrior 5.10b R
87. Prince of Darkness 5.10c
88. Yellow Brick Road 5.10d
89. Dream of Wild Turkeys 5.10a
90. The Gobbler 5.10b
91. 18-Year Mcallan 5.11d
92. Fiddler on the Roof 5.10d
93. Johnny Come Lately 5.10d
94. Overhanging Hangover 5.10 b/c
95. Early Times 5.10b/c
96. Sour Mash 5.10a

Not all bolts are shown

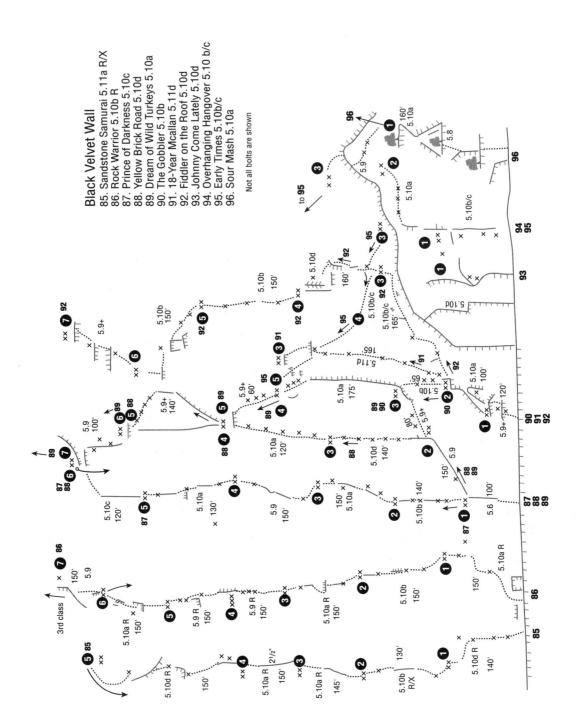

route was put up in a sort of rebellion against bolts, this one in response to the first ascent of *Dream of Wild Turkeys*.

Pitch 1: 5.10a R, 2 bolts. Climb up and right on the white, slabby rock leading up and right to the comfort of the first bolt. Climb the face, veering right to the bolted anchors. 150 feet.

Pitch 2: 5.10b, 3 bolts. Take the face up and left to a bolt. Move straight up the face to a left-facing corner. Take the arête of the corner up to a seam. The seam ends at the fixed anchor. 150 feet.

Pitch 3: 5.10a R, 2 bolts. Move up and left through the face and discontinuous cracks to a roof. Pull the roof, heading right to a seam. Continue to fixed anchors. 150 feet.

Pitch 4: 5.9 R, 3 bolts. Continue up the crack and face to another bolted belay left of a left-facing corner. 150 feet.

Pitch 5: 5.9 R, 3 bolts. Move up the left-facing corner, then take the face up past the right side of a roof to bolted anchors above. 150 feet.

Pitch 6: 5.10a R, 1 bolt. Take the face up to a roof. Pull the roof and then climb right, up discontinuous cracks to another fixed anchor. 150 feet. Rappel from here using 2 ropes or continue up.

Pitch 7: 5.9 Scramble to lower-angled rock. One quarter-inch bolt and one fixed nut make up the anchor. 150 feet.

Pitch 8: Third-class scramble for 1000 feet to the top of the wall.

Take the Black Velvet Wall descent.

FA: Richard Harrison, Jay Smith, Nick Nordblom 1983

87. Prince of Darkness 5.10c ★★★ Mixed (not a sport route). This is one of the most popular routes in Red Rock. Many holds have broken since the first ascent. Begin 30 feet right of *Rock Warrior* at a crack that heads up vertically to a right-slanting crack. Climb straight up the varnished face. Gear: Rocks with #1–#3 Friends, 15 quickdraws.

Pitch 1: 5.6 Climb a low-angled face to a vertical crack. Take the crack to a bolted belay, left of a long right-angling crack. (Pitch 1 of *Dream of Wild Turkeys*.) 100 feet.

Pitch 2: 5.10b, 14 bolts. Continue up the varnished face to a bolted hanging belay. 140 feet.

Pitch 3: 5.10a, 15 bolts. Climb up and right on the face, using discontinuous cracks to another bolted hanging belay. 150 feet.

Pitch 4: 5.9, 12 bolts. Move left 8 feet and then take the face and broken crack up, veering right, to a bolted anchor. 150 feet.

Pitch 5: 5.10a, 7 bolts. Climb up and left through two crack systems to a bolted hanging belay. Original bolts at anchor. 130 feet.

Pitch 6: 5.10c, 11 bolts. Take a finger crack up the face. Step right to reach anchors on *Dream of Wild Turkeys*. 120 feet.

Rappel *Dream of Wild Turkeys* using 2 ropes.

FA: George Urioste, Mike Ward, Joanne Urioste, Bill Bradley 1985

88. Yellow Brick Road 5.10d ★★★ Mixed. This route is a variation of *Dream of Wild Turkeys*, and takes a line up and left after pitch 2, connecting back in at the top of pitch 4 (pitch 5 of *Dream of Wild Turkeys*). Gear: standard rack to #3 Friend.

Pitch 1: 5.6 Climb a low-angled face to a vertical crack. Take the crack to a bolted belay, left of a long right-angling crack. 100 feet.

Pitch 2: 5.9, 2 bolts. Head right up the right-angling crack to a bolted belay. 150 feet.

Pitch 3: 5.10d, 7 bolts. Continue up the crack and then take the bolted face straight up to a bolted anchor. 140 feet.

Pitch 4: 5.10a Continue up the face to a belay ledge (top of *Dream of Wild Turkeys* pitch 5). 120 feet.

Finish on *Dream of Wild Turkeys*.

Rappel *Dream of Wild Turkeys* using 2 ropes.

FA: George Urioste, Mike Ward, Joanne Urioste, Bill Bradley 1985

89. Dream of Wild Turkeys 5.10a ★★★★★
Mixed. One of the first routes on the wall and an all-time classic! Joanne and George Urioste considered themselves among the turkeys of the climbing world. They did not identify with the elite group, but kept to themselves and "bumbled around on their own." Says Joanne Urioste, "We didn't advertise what we were doing and we didn't feel particularly competent since we always seemed to be having epics. A top local climber told me that he'd ascended the center of the Velvet Wall, but when we started up

the route there were rappel slings two pitches up and then there were no more signs of an ascent. We realized it had not been climbed and it became our 'dream' to complete it. I was thrilled and got a certain adrenaline rush out of doing a route that one of the better-known local climbers had bailed on. At that time *Dream of White Horses* was a route in the UK that symbolized the standards of the bold, elite in-crowd. By naming our route *Dream of Wild Turkeys*, we were poking a bit of fun at the attitude of exclusion that the in-crowd can sometimes exhibit." Gear: standard rack to #3 Friend and many quickdraws.

Pitch 1: 5.6 Climb a low-angled face to a vertical crack. Take the crack to a bolted belay, left of a long right-angling crack. 100 feet.

Pitch 2: 5.9, 2 bolts. Head right up the right-angling crack to a bolted belay. 150 feet.

Pitch 3: 5.9+, 6 bolts. Continue up the crack and then traverse out right, taking a line of bolts to the base of a very large left-facing corner. Belay at fixed anchors. Be careful of ropes getting stuck in the crack beneath these anchors. 80 feet.

Pitch 4: 5.10a, 3 bolts. Climb the crack to its top. Traverse left and up to a bolted anchor. 175 feet.

Pitch 5: 5.9+, 6 bolts. Climb up and left to a small ledge and bolted belay below a thin crack that splits a water streak. 60 feet.

Pitch 6: 5.9+, 10 bolts. Take a ramp, moving up and right to a vertical crack. Climb the crack to its end and take the face up and left to a sloping ledge atop a thin vertical crack. 140 feet.

Pitch 7: 5.9, 5 bolts. Climb straight up the vertical crack to a bolted belay ledge. 100 feet. Rappel from here using 2 ropes or continue up.

Pitch 8: Fourth class. Take ramps up to a large ledge beneath a steep wall. 90 feet.

Pitch 9: 5.9, 7 bolts. Ascend the steep wall using thin cracks to a bolted stance. 140 feet.

Pitch 10: 5.9, 4 bolts. Take the face and crack left of the most obvious crack. 150 feet.

Pitch 11: 5.7, 1 bolt. Take the face and crack up to a large bushy ledge called Turkeyland (an excellent bivy). 160 feet.

Rappel from here with 2 ropes or continue to the top of the wall.

Pitch 12: Fourth-class for 1000 feet to the summit of the wall. Likely has original bolts, but can probably be backed up with natural gear. Take the Black Velvet Wall descent.
FA: George and Joanne Urioste 1980

90. The Gobbler 5.10b ★★★★ Mixed. An alternative start to *Dream of Wild Turkeys*. This route begins between *Dream of Wild Turkeys* and the left edge of the huge arch on the right of the wall. Gear: standard rack to #3 Friend.

Pitch 1: 5.9+, 7 bolts. Take the face up and then traverse right on a thin ledge to under a left-leaning roof/corner. Climb up under the corner, left, to a recessed ledge and bolted anchor. Watch out for rope drag. 120 feet.

Pitch 2: 5.10a, 1 bolt. Climb a low-angled crack/ramp up and right to a bolt. Traverse the face left to reach a wide crack. Take the crack and chimney up to a ledge and bolted belay. 100 feet.

Pitch 3: 5.10b, 7 bolts. Take the steep face up to the base of a left-facing corner/flake (pitch 3 of *Dream of Wild Turkeys*). 65 feet. Finish on *Dream of Wild Turkeys* or rappel using 2 ropes.
FA: George and Joanne Urioste, Bill Bradley, Mike Ward 1980

91. 18-Year Mcallen 5.11d ★★★★ Mixed, 10 bolts. Begin the same as *The Gobbler*, doing the first 2 pitches. Gear: to #1.5 Friend, brass wires, and 15 quickdraws.

Pitch 1: 5.9+, 7 bolts. Take the face up and then traverse right on a thin ledge to under a left-leaning roof/corner. Climb up under the corner, left, to a recessed ledge and bolted anchor. Watch out for rope drag. 120 feet.

Pitch 2: 5.10a, 1 bolt. Climb a low-angled crack/ramp up and right to a bolt. Traverse the face left to reach a wide crack. Take the crack and chimney up to a ledge and bolted belay. 100 feet.

Pitch 3: 5.11d Head slightly right and straight up the varnished face using discontinuous seams and edges. Traverse left from the last bolt on a thin slippery face to the anchors. 165 feet.

Rappel using 2 ropes.
FA: Pier and Randy Marsh 1994

92. Fiddler on the Roof 5.10d ★★★★★ Traditional. Begin the same as the previous two routes, climbing the first two shared pitches. Gear: standard rack to #3 Friend and brass wires.

Pitch 1: 5.9+, 7 bolts. Take the face up and then traverse right on a thin ledge to under a left-leaning roof/corner. Climb up under the corner, left, to a recessed ledge and bolted anchor. Watch out for rope drag. 120 feet.

Pitch 2: 5.10a, 1 bolt. Climb a low-angled crack/ramp up and right to a bolt. Traverse the face left to reach a wide crack. Take the crack and chimney up to a ledge and bolted belay. 100 feet.

Pitch 3: 5.10b/c, 2 bolts. Traverse right. At a right-facing corner clip a bolt, step down, and then move up. Continue right on small edges and thin seams to a fixed anchor at the center of and above the roof. Inconspicuous gear. Prusiks are handy if you fall off. Watch the rope over the sharp roof edge if someone does fall. 165 feet.

Pitch 4: 5.10d, 2 bolts. A classic pitch! Climb straight up the varnished face using thin seams to a right-facing corner. Traverse up and left and pull around an arête after clipping a bolt. Take a seam up to a bolted anchor. 160 feet.

Pitch 5: 5.10b, 6 bolts. Climb the varnished face to a bolted anchor. 150 feet.

Pitch 6: 5.10b, 3 bolts. Take the face up and left to a ledge. Clip a bolt and then move left, then up to a belay. 150 feet.

Pitch 7: 5.9+ Pull thin moves up a smooth face to belay anchors on a ledge.

Rappel *Dream of Wild Turkeys*.

FA: Dave Wonderly, Warren Egbert, Jennifer Richards 1990

Begin the following routes under the big arch, right of the large right-facing dihedral

93. Johnny Come Lately 5.10d ★★ Sport. 9 bolts. Begin below the right facing dihedral, climb alongside it to the bolted anchors. 170 feet.

Pitch 2: 5.10a Mixed. 7 bolts. Climb into the second pitch of *Overhanging Hangover*. 160 feet. Rappel using 2 ropes.

FA: Unknown 1980s

94. Overhanging Hangover 5.10b/c ★★ Mixed. Begin 20 feet right of the previous route.

Pitch 1: 5.10b/c, 7 bolts. Climb up to anchors up and right of *Johnny Come Lately* anchors, below an obvious crack system.180 feet.

Pitch 2: 5.10a, 6 bolts. Climb up the crack to the roof. Traverse right under the roof to anchors at its right edge. 150 feet.

Pitch 3: 5.9 Traditional. Scramble up and right in a crack system to bolted anchors, then pull over the overhang, left to another set of anchors and belay. 50 feet. Rappel using 2 ropes.

FA: George and Joanne Urioste, Spiderman Dan Goodwin 1981

95. Early Times 5.10b/c ★★ Traditional. Climb *Overhanging Hangover* and then continue climbing up and left to the top of pitch 4 of *Dream of Wild Turkeys*.

Pitches 1–3: Climb pitches 1–3 of *Overhanging Hangover*.

Pitches 4–5: 5.10b/c Climb up and left along the run-out face to the pitch 4 anchors of *Dream of Wild Turkeys*. Either continue up *Dream of Wild Turkeys* or rappel using 2 ropes.

FA: Bob Findlay 1980s

Sour Mash/Early Times Connector: 5.9 ★★ Mixed, 2 bolts. This pitch climbs between the top of pitch 1 of *Sour Mash* and connects with the top of pitch 2 of *Early Times*.

FA: George and Joanne Urioste (connector)

96. Sour Mash 5.10a ★★★★★ Mixed. Begin right of *Johnny Come Lately* beneath a triangular-shaped formation above a ledge, below the right portion of the massive arching roof. Very nice "natural passage."

Pitch 1: 5.10a, 4 bolts. Climb the face right of a right-facing crack to a ledge with a tree. Exit the ledge, ascending a right-facing corner. Traverse right to a straight-in crack, reaching a ledge making up the base of the dark triangle. Take the left-facing crack moving up and left (the right side of the triangle) off the right edge of the ledge. Exit left onto the face, following bolts. Climb a right-angling ramp up and right to a ledge and belay. 160 feet.

Pitch 2: 5.8, 7 bolts. Traverse right, around an arête,

96. Sour Mash 5.10a

Not all bolts are shown

past a bolt, and up to a roof. Pull the roof to reach another, smaller roof. Pull the second roof, clip a bolt, and take a right-slanting crack up, passing a bolted anchor. Step right onto a face and then up a crack that makes a hard right into a left-facing corner. Climb the corner and move left to a ledge and up a face, right of a right-facing corner. Finish on a ledge with a bolted belay. 160 feet.

Pitch 3: 5.7 Take the crack above the ledge up and then angle left to a hanging bolted belay. 70 feet.

Pitch 4: 5.9 Continue up the crack to a bolted belay. 130 feet.

Pitch 5: 5.10a, 9 bolts. Climb the bolted, thin crack to a right-facing corner. Follow the crack up and angle right beneath a white roof. Belay on a ledge up and right. 100 feet.

Pitch 6: 5.9+, 6 bolts. Move up and left, over the white roof to a thin crack that heads up and right. Traverse left up a thin face and some ripples to a left-facing corner. Step right, around the corner to a fixed anchor below a bush-filled crack up and right. 75 feet.

Rappel into *Fiddler on the Roof*, using 2 ropes.

FA: George and Joanne Urioste 1980

▲ THE BLACK TOWER
N No Sun (AM in summer)   Approach: 1 hour

The Black Tower is an enormous 800-foot varnished pillar up against the right edge of Black Velvet Wall. To get there, approach as you would for Black Velvet Wall until the wash pinches off and is impassible. Take a faint trail that heads left into some trees and bushes to the base of a short wall. Scramble up and right on the wall at a low ledge that allows you to continue up and right. A crack climbs the last 10 feet (5.0). At the top of the short wall you will be at the far-right base of Black Velvet Wall. Hike down and right, back into the wash. Routes are described from left to right.

Black Velvet Wall descent: Hike left or right to reach the summit of the Black Velvet Wall. From there, take the ridge that heads south to another ridge that runs east-west. Follow the east-west ridge, heading east (left) almost as far as you can hike before heading downhill. Scramble down the left (north) side of the ridge to reach the notch at the top of the Whiskey Peak Gully descent. Upon reaching a saddle head

THE BLACK TOWER

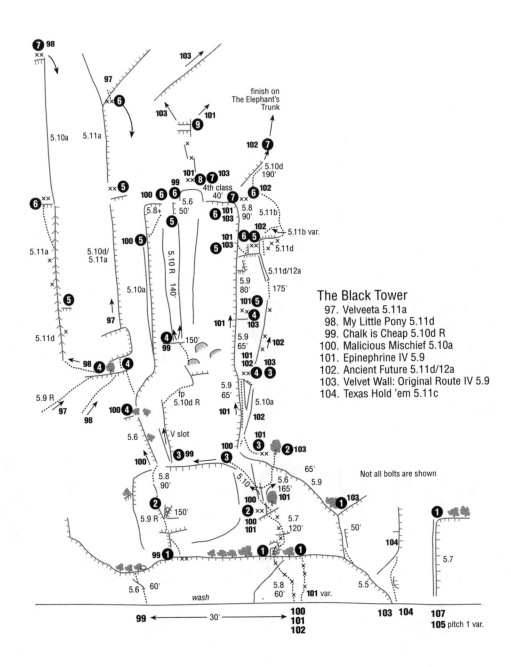

The Black Tower

97. Velveeta 5.11a
98. My Little Pony 5.11d
99. Chalk is Cheap 5.10d R
100. Malicious Mischief 5.10a
101. Epinephrine IV 5.9
102. Ancient Future 5.11d/12a
103. Velvet Wall: Original Route IV 5.9
104. Texas Hold 'em 5.11c

Not all bolts are shown

right (east), down Whiskey Peak Gully. Stay on the high left (north) side of the gully, hiking down white slabs of rock. Upon entering the gully do some third- and fourth-class scrambling, following a trail that meanders through the left side and center of the gully. At the mouth, traverse left to reach a trail that heads down. Cut left onto the red dirt trail that takes you around to the north side of Whiskey Peak (this is the red dirt trail that skirts the base of the peak west). Before reaching a grouping of trees on the right, head down and right (on the southeast side of the low pink band). This takes you to the main canyon trail. Go right (east) on the trail to obtain the parking lot. 1.5 hours.

97. Velveeta 5.11a ★★ Traditional. For this route, do not hike down into the wash. Begin on Black Velvet Wall, on *Sour Mash*. Then traverse up and right to the left-facing corner, left of the Black Tower. (You can also start on *My Little Pony*.)

Pitches 1–3: Climb pitches 1–3 of *Sour Mash*.

Pitch 4: 5.9 R Face-climb up and right to the base of the rightmost of two obvious parallel crack systems ascending the wall left of the Black Tower.

Pitch 5: 5.10d/11a Though the rock appears suspect in spots, the gear is bomber. Climb the dead-vertical corner to a bulge with a ledge. Use flakes out left when it is more convenient than climbing the corner.

Pitch 6: 5.11a Continue up to the left-facing corner. Rappel *Epinephrine* with 2 ropes.

FA: Richard Harrison, Wendell Broussard 1990

98. My Little Pony 5.11d ★★ Traditional. For this route, do not hike down into the wash. Start down and right of *Sour Mash*, on a low-angled prow.

Pitch 1: 5.6 Scramble up the prow to a face, continuing to the top of a left-angling ramp. Belay at a tree.

Pitch 2: 5.10a, 1 bolt. Step right off the ramp onto a face. Angle up and right to under a small overhang. Continue to a bushy ledge.

Pitch 3: 5.10, 1 bolt. Step off the right side of the ledge and take the face up and right to another ledge.

Pitch 4: 5.8 Climb a right-facing corner to its end. Top out on a face. Head up and right to a large ledge

with trees, below the rightmost of two obvious parallel crack systems.

Pitch 5: 5.11d, 1 bolt. Climb up the face above the middle of the ledge to an arête. Take the arête to a ledge.

Pitch 6: 5.11a, 3 bolts. Continue up the arête to a crack, then step left onto the face and take it to a ledge with bolted anchors.

Pitch 7: 5.10a Climb straight up the crack to a ledge.

Rappel using 2 ropes.

FA: Paul Van Betten, Richard Harrison, Shelby Shelton 1990

99. Chalk is Cheap 5.10d R ★★ Traditional. Start beneath the left-angling ramp, 30 left of *Epinephrine*.

Pitch 1: 5.6 Scramble up and left, up a face to the base of a left-angling ramp. Belay at a tree. 60 feet.

Pitch 2: 5.9 R Take the face up and slightly left to a right-facing corner. Go up and left, over the left side of the roof and belay in a slot among blocks. 150 feet.

Pitch 3: 5.8 Take the crack above the belay to a face and broken corner, heading up and left. Step right to belay atop a pillar, beneath a V slot in varnished rock. 90 feet.

Pitch 4: 5.10d R Follow the crack up the left side of the V slot, then move right to underneath a roof. Pull the roof by way of a crack out the left side. Move up to a stance atop big, varnished plates. Move up and left to the base of the center vertical seam and belay. 150 feet.

Pitch 5: 5.10 R Take the middle or leftmost vertical seam to the base of a left-facing corner. 140 feet.

Pitch 6: 5.6 Take the left-facing corner to the top of the Black Tower. 50 feet. Rappel *Epinephrine* using 2 ropes.

FA: Mike Ward, Mike Clifford, Eric Sutton 1989

100. Malicious Mischief 5.10a ★★★ Traditional. Begin on *Epinephrine*, and climb the first two and three-quarter pitches. Then cut left to end up on the left side of the Black Tower.

Pitches 1–2: Climb pitches 1 and 2 of *Epinephrine*.

Pitch 3: 5.6 Climb above the anchor and step right onto the face. Move up a crack with a tree in it, through a steep section and into a chimney. Ascend the chimney to where it opens up and then step right onto the face. Take the face up to just below the right-facing edge of the Black Tower and traverse left to a belay ledge.

Pitch 4: Easier climbing up and left leads to a sloping ledge beneath a large chimney.

Pitch 5: 5.10a Climb up and then move right into the left-facing corner, off-width crack. Climb it to where it tightens down, providing a belay.

Pitch 6: 5.8+ Face-climb out of the chimney and up to the top of the Black Tower.

Rappel *Epinephrine* using 2 ropes.
FA: Joe Herbst, Stephanie Petrilak, Mike Gilbert 1978

101. Epinephrine IV, 5.9 ★★★★★ Traditional. The classic of the area! Climb the chimneys that comprise the right side of the Black Tower and then head up and right, taking a corner and face system to the top of the wall. This is a big wall. Gear: standard rack to #4 Friend.

Pitch 1: 5.8, 4 bolts. Begin at the plumb line of the right edge of the Black Tower, at a water-polished pocketed face. The start is 15 feet right of a right-angling crack and groove, on a steep wall beneath 1 bolt. Climb the gray face up and left to a large bush-filled ledge. Belay below a small roof and next to a flake. 60 feet.

Pitch 1 variation: 3 bolts. A line of 1/4-inch bolts is located 8 feet right of the main pitch 1 start. Climb the face up pockets to the ledge above. Not recommended due to the quality of the bolts and hangers.

Pitch 2: 5.7, 3 bolts. Climb the flake to a left-facing corner, beneath a roof. Traverse onto the face right. Climb up to under a roof. Pull the roof and take the low-angled face up and left to a corner. Climb up the corner to a small stance and bolted belay. 120 feet.

Pitch 3: 5.6 Climb above the anchor and step right onto the face. Move up a crack with a tree in it, through a steep section and into a chimney. Ascend the chimney to where it opens up and then step right onto the face. Take the face up 50 feet to a ledge, right of the right-facing edge of the Black Tower and above a tree. Bolted anchors. 165 feet.

Pitch 4: 5.9 Move up and left, staying right of the main chimney, climbing through a hand crack, flakes, and ledges. Traverse left into the chimney (where the

chimney on the right widens). Squeeze up to where it widens to 4 inches in the back. Step right onto a ledge and bolted anchor. 65 feet.

Pitch 5: 5.9 Move left, back into the chimney. Take it up as it steepens and becomes smaller and more slippery. When you cannot take any-more, step right onto a ledge with a bolted belay. 65 feet.

Pitch 6: 5.9, 1 bolt. Move right

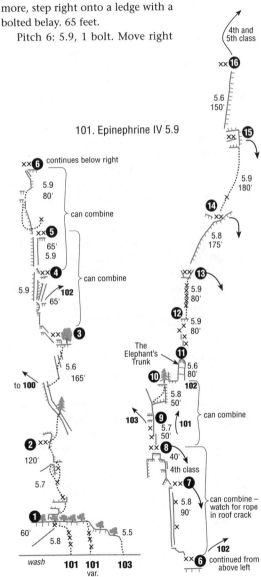

101. Epinephrine IV 5.9

along the ledge and then chimney up (wide) to a bolt. Continue up the wall and then step across to the outside wall. Pull a bulge and move up the face that connects with the top of the chimney. Pull onto a ledge and then take a left-facing corner up to a large ledge and bolted anchor. 80 feet. (It is also possible to stay in the crack and climb this section to the fixed anchors.)

Pitch 7: 5.8, 2 bolts. Move left up some small edges into the final chimney. Scoot up the chimney to where it pinches off. Step left onto a ledge and then move up and right to the bolted hanging belay. 90 feet. Rappel from here using a 60-meter rope or continue to the top!

Pitch 8: Fourth class. Scramble up and left to the top of the Black Tower—big bivy ledge or hang out. When Wendell Broussard, Lynn Hill, and John Long did this route they cooked steaks on this ledge. 40 feet. Rappel using a 60-meter rope or continue.

Pitch 9: 5.7, 2 bolts. Take the varnished face up and left to a downward-sloping ledge in a corner below a roof. 50 feet.

Pitch 10: 5.8 Ascend the corner to where it is broken and blocky. Traverse right across a featured face to a small stance in a corner above a bush, and below a ledge. 50 feet.

Pitch 11: 5.6 Take the ledge right to the base of the Elephant's Trunk. Climb the center of the Trunk, which leans against the wall, to its top and bolted anchors. 80 feet.

Pitch 12: 5.9, 2 bolts. Climb the crack and face to bolted anchors. 80 feet.

Pitch 13: 5.9, 5 bolts. Continue up the face to a bolted anchor in a recess. 80 feet. Rappel using 2 60-meter ropes or continue.

Pitch 14: 5.8 Take a left-facing corner/flake up to a bolted anchor on a sloping ledge. 175 feet.

Pitch 15: 5.9 Climb right up the face, clipping a bolt to underneath the roof. Pull the roof on the right and move up to a left-facing corner. Belay off bolted anchors under a roof. 180 feet.

Pitch 16: 5.6 Pull over the left side of the roof, taking a left-facing corner up to an arête. Finish on smooth gray face. 150 feet.

Pitch 17: Fourth- and fifth-class up and left of the final anchors. Move up ramps and across faces to reach

Hidetaka Suzuki squeezes up the Epinephrine 5.9 *chimneys.* Photo by Dan McQuade

a long ledge underneath some large pines. Traverse the ledge all the way right. Scramble up, right of the pines, and head to the summit of the peak.

Descend via the Black Velvet Wall descent.

FA: George and Joanne Urioste, Joe Herbst 1978

102. Ancient Future 5.11d/5.12a ★★★★ Mixed. Begin on *Epinephrine*, and get a mix of chimney climbing and thin, technical fun, all in one route.

Pitches 1–3 : Climb the first three pitches of *Epinephrine*.

Pitch 4: 5.10a, 1 bolt. Head left from the anchor, staying right of the main chimney. Climb through a hand crack, flakes, and ledges. Go right where the chimney on the right widens (at the point where *Epinephrine* traverses left into the main chimney). Follow the flared chimney past 1 bolt to the bolted anchor of pitch 4 of *Epinephrine*, on a small ledge. 100 feet. You can also just climb *Epinephrine* pitch 4 (5.9).

Pitch 5: 5.11d/5.12a, 3 bolts. Climb the thin flake parallel to the *Epinephrine* chimney system to a thin face. Take the face to a wider crack ending on a ledge at the pitch 6 bolted anchors of *Epinephrine*. 175 feet.

Pitch 6: 5.11b or d, 3 bolts. 5.11d Climb up, passing 3 bolts on a thin face at an undercut dihedral.

5.11b variation: Aid up, preclipping the 3 bolts. Come back to the ledge and throw to big holds (long move) over the roof at the pitch 5 anchors. Continue up to bolted anchors. 100 feet.

Pitch 7: 5.10d Continue climbing to the top of the Elephant's Trunk, the pitch 10 bolted anchor of *Epinephrine*. 190 feet.

You can rappel *Epinephrine* from here using 2 ropes. Be careful when pulling the ropes on the first rappel, they sometimes get stuck. Or continue up *Epinephrine* and descend via the Black Velvet Wall descent.
FA: Dan McQuade 1997

103. Velvet Wall: Original Route IV, 5.9 ★★ Traditional. This route begins 50 feet right of *Epinephrine*, at a left-angling ledge system. Link up with *Epinephrine* at the pitch 3 anchors and climb to the top of pitch 9, then cut off left to the base of the huge right-angling ramp that heads to the top of the cliff. Gear: standard rack to #4 Friend.

Pitch 1: 5.5 Climb the ledges up and left to the far right edge of the bushy ledge atop *Epinephrine*'s pitch 1. Continue up, following a line of bushes to a big, flat, bushy ledge. 50 feet.

Pitch 2: 5.6 Take a right-facing flake and crack up and left to a tree and the bolted anchors atop *Epinephrine* pitch 3. 65 feet.

Connect with *Epinephrine* pitch 4.

Pitches 3–7: Climb pitches 4–8 of *Epinephrine*.

Pitch 8: 5.8, 2 bolts. Take the varnished face up and left to a downward-sloping ledge in a corner below a roof. Ascend the corner to where it is broken and blocky. Traverse right across a featured face to a small stance in a corner above a bush, and below a large ledge. 150 feet.

Pitch 9: Climb up and left, through broken rock and cracks to a large bowl-like feature.

Pitch 10: Fourth class. Take the ramp system up and right for 1500 feet to the top of the wall.

Descend from the top by way of the Black Velvet Wall descent.
FA: Tom Kaufman, Joe Herbst 1973

104. Texas Hold 'em 5.11c ★★★ Mixed. Begin just right of the previous route beneath a left-facing corner. Gear: standard rack with doubles of Friends to #4.

Pitch 1: 5.9 Take discontinuous ledge systems up and right to a left-facing corner. Move up the corner until you reach a bush. Move left to a bushy ledge with a bolted anchor. 160 feet.

Pitch 2: 5.9 Move up to a bush, and then angle right to another bush and into a left-facing corner. Climb it and then head directly right, past a bolt to a bolted anchor. 160 feet.

Pitch 3: 5.6 Move right (skipping the line of bolts above the anchor) along the ledge to a left-facing corner. Climb it to a large ledge. Traverse right on the ledge to another left-facing corner (top of *Yellow Rose of Texas* pitch 4). 130 feet.

Pitch 4: 5.8 Climb the corner. Pass a bolted belay after 80 feet and continue up left-angling crack systems to another bolted anchor. 160 feet.

Pitch 5: 5.10d, 3 bolts. The Panhandle Crack. Jam a crack beginning at 4 inches that thins to 2.5 inches. Move up through a roof and then belay on a big ledge with bolted anchors, the left edge of the Texas Tower. 165 feet.

Pitch 6: 5.9 Climb pitch 2 of *Texas Tower Connection*. Climb the leftmost, thin, left-angling crack, with minimal gear, to a bolted stance. 100 feet.

Pitch 7: 5.11c, 6 bolts. Move directly up a thin crack, passing a bolt, and head into a right-angling thin crack. Pass 2 bolts to the end of the crack and

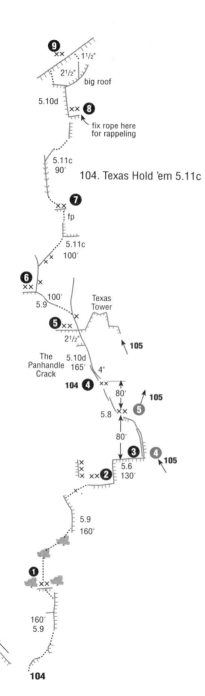

104. Texas Hold 'em 5.11c

then climb a thin face to the left side of a roof. Take a left-facing corner up to a thin crack and finish on a ledge with bolted anchors. 100 feet.

Pitch 8: 5.11c, 3 bolts. Step left into a corner. Continue past the corner, taking a face right to a left-facing corner. Climb the corner to a bolted anchor in a recess. 90 feet.

Pitch 9: 5.10d Climb a right-facing corner above the belay to where it bends to the right, forming a roof with a crack out the center. Climb out the roof crack (2 1/2 to 1 1/2 inches) or traverse underneath the roof on a ledge. Finish on a face up to a right-angling ledge.

Rappel using 2 ropes, or finish on *Lone Star* beginning on the ramp of pitch 13. **Important!:** If rappeling, be sure to tie the end of one of the ropes off to the anchor below the last pitch or you will not be able to get back into the belay.
FA: John Rosholt, Bob Conz 1997

105. Yellow Rose of Texas 5.11a ★★★ Mixed. To the right of the Black Tower is a flake shaped like the state of Texas. This is the Texas Tower. This route climbs the right side of the tower. Gear: standard rack to #5 Friend.

Pitch 1: 5.10a, 1 bolt. A big pool is located 35 feet up and right of *Epinephrine* (most of the time it does not hold water). Climb directly out of this pool in a crack, clipping 1 bolt on the way to a large ledge system. 90 feet.

Pitch 1 variation: 5.7 Climb the left-facing corner/chimney on the far left of this wall.

Pitch 2: 5.8, 2 bolts. Head directly up, in a thin varnished crack. 85 feet.

Pitch 3: Fourth class. Climb left. Belay at a gully, below the rightmost of two cracks. 130 feet.

Pitch 4: 5.8 Take the crack above the belay to a ledge and bolted belay. 90 feet.

Pitch 5: 5.8 Climb a wide crack up and left to another ledge. 60 feet.

Pitch 6: 5.11a, 4 bolts. Move right to obtain a face. Climb the face past bolts to a crack. Take the crack left to a ledge with bolted anchors. 80 feet.

Pitch 7: 5.9 Pull the off-width to another ledge. 50 feet.

Pitch 8: 5.9 Take the right-facing corner to the top of the Texas Tower and the bolted anchor. 50 feet.

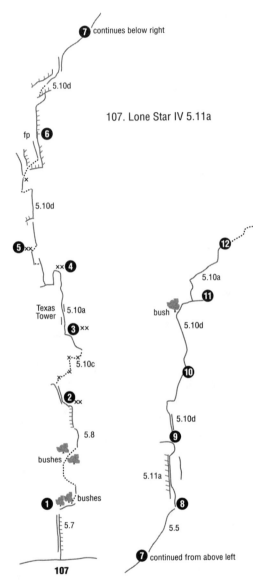

7 continues below right

5.10d

107. Lone Star IV 5.11a

fp 6

5.10d

5 xx

xx 4

Texas
Tower 5.10a

3 xx

x–·x
5.10c

2 xx

5.8

bushes

1 bushes

5.7

107

15

5.3

14

5.9+

13

12

5.10a

11

bush

5.10d

10

5.10d

9

5.11a

8

5.5

7 continued from above left

Rappel the route using 2 ropes, downclimbing the fourth-class pitch 3.
FA: Joe Herbst, George Urioste, Joanne Urioste 1978

106. The Texas Tower Connection 5.10b ★★★
Traditional. This route climbs between the Texas

Tower and the Elephant's Trunk (pitch 10 of *Epinephrine*). Climb the *Yellow Rose of Texas* to the top of the Texas Tower. Gear: standard rack to #5 Friend.

Pitch 1: 5.8 Rappel off the top of the Texas Tower to a flat ledge, 20 feet down. (Reclimb this side of the tower.)

Pitch 2: 5.10a Climb the leftmost, thin, left-angling crack, with minimal gear, to a bolted stance. 100 feet.

Pitch 3: 5.10b, 2 bolts. Climb down and left 10 feet, then climb upward for 15 feet. Traverse directly left, past bolts to an anchor. This is not the safest pitch for the second. 40 feet.

Pitch 4: 5.9, 7 bolts. Take the corner straight above the anchor, stepping right at the top to a bolted anchor. 80 feet.

Pitch 5: Continue up and left to the Elephant's Trunk, pitch 10 on *Epinephrine*.

Rappel *Epinephrine* from the top of the Elephant's Trunk or finish up *Epinephrine*.
FA: George Urioste, Joe Herbst, Joanne Urioste 1980

107. Lone Star IV, 5.11a ★★★ Traditional. This route is somewhat of a mountaineering route. Paul Crawford describes it as the Red Rock version of the West Face of El Capitan, at an easier grade. "One of the finer achievements on the wall. A perfect all-day affair!" Begin at a wide left-facing corner (the pitch 1 variation of *Yellow Rose of Texas*), left of a large pool. Bring a standard rack with doubles of Friends to #4.

Descend by way of the Black Velvet Wall descent.
FA: Richard Harrison, Paul Crawford, Paul Van Betten, Paul Obenheim 1984

▲ BLACK VELVET PEAK WEST
N No Sun   Approach: 1.5 hours

Start the approach as for the Black Velvet Wall. From the far-right base of the Black Velvet Wall, hike down and right, into the wash as you would to approach the Black Tower. Stay in the wash, hiking up it 150 yards to a small canyon that forks left. Fifth-class up a white slab and water runnel for about 60 feet (there have been ropes hanging there in the past, but they are not reliable—we know from experience!). At the top of the water runnel, step left and climb a third-class chimney. A long and very difficult approach.

108. Great Expectations IV, 5.10a ★★ Mixed.

This route climbs a tower to a face to a right-facing corner. Gear: double set of Rocks and Friends to #3.

Pitch 1: 5.7, 3 bolts. Traverse right out of the chimney/gully to a bolt. Move straight up to a flake that leads to a bolted anchor. 125 feet.

Pitch 2: Fourth class. Take the flake farther up to a bolted anchor atop the white tower. 40 feet.

Pitch 3: 5.8, 8 bolts. Climb left for 20 feet, passing a bolt, and then move up the face to a bolted anchor. 130 feet.

Pitch 4: 5.8, 5 bolts. Continue up the face to a bolted belay. 140 feet.

Pitch 5: 5.9, 6 bolts. Move left to obtain a crack. Follow it to its end and then move up the steep face to a bolted anchor. 110 feet.

Pitch 6: 5.8, 2 bolts. Climb right, reaching a depression. Take cracks and a chimney to a bolted anchor in a recess. 130 feet.

Pitch 7: 5.10a Exit left out of the recess to a right-facing corner. Climb to a 3-bolt anchor. 110 feet.

Pitch 7 variation: 5.9, 7 bolts. Exit right out of the cave and take the face up, right of the right-facing corner to the 3-bolt anchor. 110 feet.

Rappel the route using 2 ropes.

FA: George and Joanne Urioste, Mike Ward, Bill Bradley 1985

▲ WESTERN SPACES WALL
N No Sun   Approach: 1.5 hours

Follow the directions to Black Velvet Wall. From the far-right base of Black Velvet Wall, hike down and right, into the wash as you would to approach the Black Tower. Continue up, deeper west into Black Velvet Canyon, up the south fork of the wash. Hike 15 minutes past *Epinephrine* (approximately 150 yards)

to where a small canyon forks left. Just after that the wash opens up and an enormous slab is located on the left side of the wash. A prominent crack ascends the middle of the slab (the start of *Sick for Toys*). Routes are described from left to right.

Option 1, rappel descent: From the top of the routes, walk south and then west toward the lowest

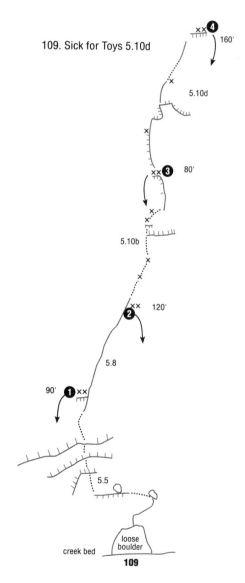

109. Sick for Toys 5.10d

109

portion of the western edge of the top of the Western Spaces Wall. Rappel down the large gully/chimney, then do a short walk to the top of the big water streaks. Two consecutive 165-foot rappels take you to the base of the wall.

Option 2, walk-off descent: From the top of the routes, walk south and then go west toward the lowest portion of the western edge of the top of the Western Spaces Wall. Rappel down the large gully/chimney, then do a short walk to the top of the big water streaks. Pass the rappel descent and continue west and down the first major gully you come to. This will lead you down into the southern fork of the Black Velvet Canyon. Hike the wash east, out of the canyon.

109. Sick for Toys 5.10d ★★★★★ Traditional. A well-protected route, "you can pop off at any time and not get hurt." This route starts out of the wash just right of the approach to *Great Expectations* and left of a large boulder in the wash. To the left of the large boulder is a big slab. The route climbs the left side of the slab, through a couple of low roofs. Wendell Broussard calls this the best slab he has ever climbed, including those in Yosemite, Joshua Tree, and so on. Gear: standard rack to #2.5 Friend and brass wires.

Pitch 1: 5.5 Heads-up off the deck. Climb up the boulder (what feels like a 5.9 boulder problem). At the top, head right and then back left, toward the base of a couple roofs. Climb up three series of roofs to a

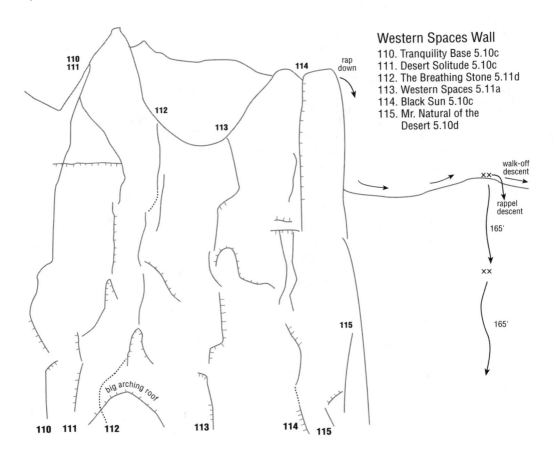

Western Spaces Wall
110. Tranquility Base 5.10c
111. Desert Solitude 5.10c
112. The Breathing Stone 5.11d
113. Western Spaces 5.11a
114. Black Sun 5.10c
115. Mr. Natural of the
       Desert 5.10d

bolted belay ledge. 90 feet.

Pitch 2: 5.8 Follow the main crack, leading up and right to another bolted anchor. 120 feet.

FA: Unknown (pitches 1 and 2)

Pitch 3: 5.10b, 4 bolts. Climb the face, clipping bolts. At the roof, climb out the left side up onto a ledge. Continue up the face, heading right after clipping 2 more bolts to a right-facing corner. Follow this to the bolted anchor. 80 feet.

Pitch 4: 5.10d, 2 bolts. Climb the right-facing crack to a bolt, and continue up to a roof. Climb over the roof on the left side. Clip a bolt and angle right to a ledge and bolted anchor. 160 feet.

Rappel using 2 ropes.

FA: Brad Stewart, Danny Meyers 1988 (pitches 3 and 4)

Moderate canyoneering up several slots (each with rappel anchors) takes you farther upcanyon to the following routes.

110. Tranquility Base 5.10c ★★★ Traditional. This route begins right of the previous route and starts off the big chockstone that marks the last section of canyoneering.

Pitch 1: 5.10c, 3 bolts. Climb a thin face to a bolt, then move left toward a ledge. Continue past the ledge, clipping bolts to a roof. Climb around the left side of the roof. Continue to a bolted anchor.

Pitch 2: 5.7 Head up and right across the face to a right-facing corner and crack. Follow the crack to its end.

Pitch 3: 5.10c, 3 bolts. Step right off the belay ledge and climb up, clipping a couple bolts, to reach a small ledge. Climb past the ledge, past a bolt, to a crack. Belay just below the point where the crack splits.

Pitch 4: 5.10c Climb up, veering right, to the base of an arête. Climb the left side of the arête, passing several bolts. Belay in a small alcove.

Pitch 5: 5.10a Follow a crack that heads left, leading to a large ledge. This belay ledge is shared with *Desert Solitude* pitch 6.

Pitch 6: 5.9 From the left side of the ledge, climb up the face a short distance and enter a crack. Follow the crack up until it joins another crack on the right and belay.

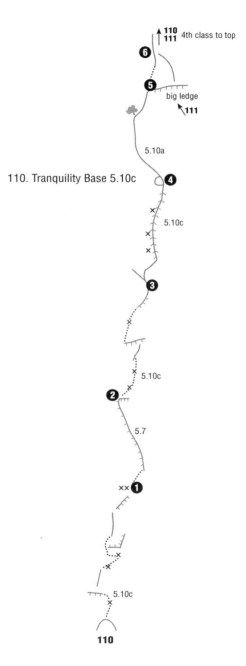

110
111 4th class to top

big ledge
111

5.10a

110. Tranquility Base 5.10c

5.10c

5.10c

5.7

5.10c

110

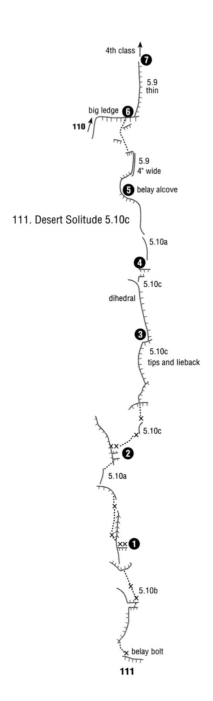

4th class

7

5.9
thin

big ledge **6**

110

5.9
4" wide

5 belay alcove

111. Desert Solitude 5.10c

5.10a

4

5.10c

dihedral

3

5.10c
tips and lieback

5.10c

2

5.10a

1

5.10b

belay bolt

111

Pitch 7: Fourth class. Follow the main crack system to the top.
FA: Dave Wonderly, Warren Egbert 1989

111. Desert Solitude 5.10c ★★★ Traditional. This route climbs the section of rock that is down and left of the large arching roof above *The Breathing Stone* start. The fourth pitch climbs a large, obvious, left-facing dihedral. Gear: standard rack, doubles of Friends to #4.

Pitch 1: 5.10b, 2 bolts. Begin off a ledge that has 1 bolt for the belay. Climb up the face to a right-facing corner. Climb the corner until reaching a break. Move through the break and head right up the face, clipping bolts. Reach a roof and then climb left to a crack. Follow it to a ledge and bolted anchor.

Pitch 2: 510a, 2 bolts. Step left off the ledge, moving around an arête. Climb the face and left edge of the arête through a few bolts. Above the arête, head right to another bolted anchor, right of a right-facing corner.

Pitch 3: 5.10c, 2 bolts. Head right across the face, clipping a couple bolts to reach a small ledge. Continue up the main crack system, which becomes so thin you are forced to lieback up it. Belay at the base of a left-facing dihedral.

Pitch 4: 5.10c Climb a dihedral until it ends. Step right to a short crack, capped by a tiny roof. Head right to the belay ledge.

Pitch 5: 5.10a Follow the crack up and left to a ledge and alcove.

Pitch 6: 5.9 Move up and right, traversing under a roof to the right. Finish up in a 4-inch crack that leads to a tiny ledge. Pass the ledge and some others, aiming for the large belay ledge shared with *Tranquility Base* pitch 5.

Pitch 7: 5.9 Climb the rightmost crack until it rejoins the crack system on the left (*Tranquility Base*) and belay.

Pitch 8: Fourth class. Scramble up the main gully to the top of the wall.
FA: Dave Wonderly, Warren Egbert 1989

112. The Breathing Stone 5.11d ★★★ Mixed. This route starts on the face directly below a large

112. The Breathing Stone 5.11d

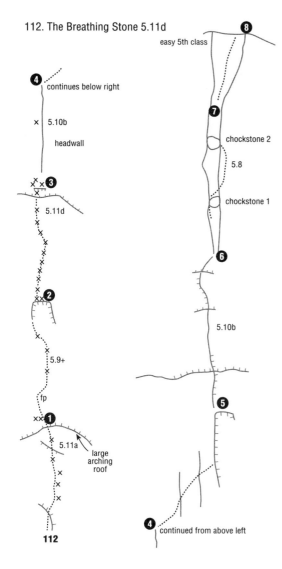

easy 5th class

continues below right

× 5.10b

headwall

chockstone 2

5.8

chockstone 1

5.11d

5.10b

5.9+

fp

5.11a

large
arching
roof

4 continued from above left

112

arching roof. Gear: standard rack with doubles of #0.5–#1.5 Friends.

Pitch 1: 5.11a Start directly below the large arching roof at a left-facing corner. Climb the face passing several bolts, which lead to left of the center of the big roof.

Pull the roof to a bolted belay just above it.

Pitch 2: 5.9+, 3 bolts, 1 pin. Head up to a fixed pin. Step right and up, passing 3 bolts to the left edge of a large pillar. Belay atop the pillar at a bolted anchor.

Pitch 3: 5.11d Follow the line of bolts up to a small roof. A small nut and Friend can be used below the roof. Pull the roof to a bolt, which leads to a small bolted belay ledge.

Pitch 4: 5.10b Climb the crack in the headwall, passing a bolt on the left. Belay at the top of the crack.

Pitch 5: Head right, across the face, passing a couple thin crack systems. Continue right until you reach a left-facing corner. Follow the corner up to the first ledge you come to, down and right of a large roof system.

Pitch 6: 5.10b Climb the crack that goes to the first of two roofs. Pull the roof, following the crack system to the second roof. Pull the second roof and climb to the base of a wide chimney/gully system and belay.

Pitch 7: 5.8 Climb the wide chimney/gully system to a large chockstone and head right onto a face. Follow the face up until even with a second chockstone. At this point, reenter the gully and continue up until you can build an anchor.

Pitch 8: Fifth class. Continue scrambling up the gully system to the top of the wall.

FA: Dave Wonderly, Dave Evans, Jennifer Richards 1989

113. Western Spaces 5.11a ★★★ Traditional. This route starts on a ledge system to the right of the previous route and the large arching roof. The route begins off a ledge that is approached from the right. Gear: standard rack with doubles of #0.5–#1.5 Friends.

Pitch 1: 5.10a, 1 bolt. Start on the left end of the ledge and climb up a right-facing corner until it ends. Continue up the face to a small ledge on the left. Step right, moving up to a bolt and continue to a bolted belay ledge.

Pitch 2: 5.10c, 1 bolt. Head up and right toward a bolt, and then veer right to a left-facing crack. Climb the crack to its top and then move left to a tiny right-facing crack. There is a bolted anchor just up and left of the crack.

Pitch 3: 5.9 Climb up and right on the face to the

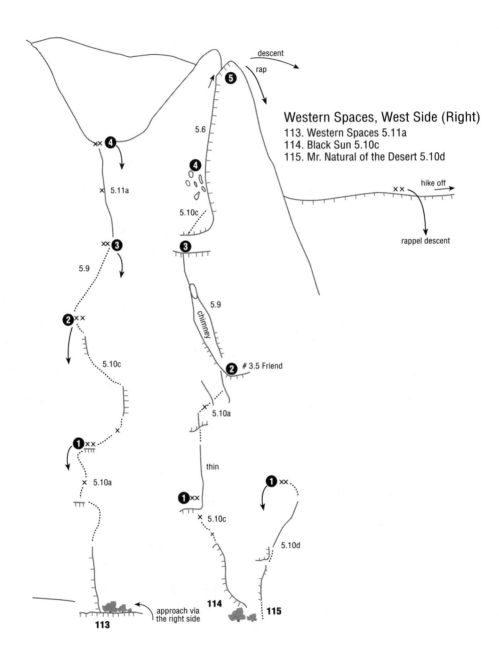

descent

rap

Western Spaces, West Side (Right)
113. Western Spaces 5.11a
114. Black Sun 5.10c
115. Mr. Natural of the Desert 5.10d

hike off

rappel descent

5.6

❺

❹

5.10c

5.11a

❸

5.9

❷

5.10c

5.9

chimney

❸

❷ # 3.5 Friend

5.10a

thin

❶

5.10a

❶ 5.10c

❶

5.10d

114

115

approach via
the right side

113

base of a crack and a bolted anchor.

Pitch 4: 5.11a, 1 bolt. Follow a thin seam up, passing a bolt on the left. Finish the crack at a bolted anchor.

Rappel using 2 ropes.

FA: Don Wilson, Dave Wonderly, Warren Egbert 1989

114. Black Sun 5.10c ★★★ Traditional. This route climbs the right side of Western Spaces Wall and tops out on a pillar formation easily seen from the wash. Gear: a double set of Rocks, doubles of #0–#1 Friends, and singles to #4 Friend.

Pitch 1: 5.10c Start next to a couple bushes at the base. Climb a right-facing corner until it ends. Continue up the face, passing a couple bolts that lead to a bolted belay ledge.

Pitch 2: 5.10a, 1 bolt. Climb the thin crack on the right (brass wires). When the crack ends, follow the face up and over a roof. Step right and clip a bolt, continue right to a belay ledge (needs a #3.5 Friend).

Pitch 3: 5.9 Step left and climb a chimney to a boulder at its top. Finish up the crack to the left of the boulder, ending at a belay ledge beneath a roof.

Pitch 4: 5.10c Climb up and over a roof, heading slightly right. Stay in the large, left-facing corner. Move past several holes. Belay just past this "sea of holes."

Pitch 5: 5.6 Follow the left-facing corner to the top of the wall.

FA: Dave Wonderly, Warren Egbert 1989

115. Mr. Natural of the Desert 5.10d ★★★★★ Traditional. This one-pitch route climbs just right of the previous route and left of the right edge of the Western Spaces Wall. Climb a right-facing corner until it ends. Head up and right to a perfect finger and hand crack, which leads to a bolted anchor. Gear: standard rack to #3 Friend. Rappel using 2 ropes.

FA: Warren Egbert, Dave Wonderly 1989

WINDY PEAK

Windy Peak South Face ▲ Windy Peak East Face ▲ Mud Springs Canyon

FROM LAS VEGAS, take West Charleston Boulevard west, which turns into State Route 159. Continue on SR 159 until it ends (at a T) at SR 160. The Blue Diamond Travel Center is on the south side of SR 160 at the intersection. Turn right (west) on SR 160 and drive 5.8 miles. Turn right onto a dirt road, just before a paved pull-out on the right. Cross a cattle guard and zero the odometer. Drive 0.3 mile and take a right out of the wash, on a road that parallels the cliffs. At 0.4 mile take the left-hand fork, heading toward the cliffs. At 0.7 mile the road splits. Take the right fork and drive 0.8 mile to another fork (1.5 miles from SR 160). Take the left fork and park.

▲ WINDY PEAK SOUTH FACE
S All-Day Sun Approach: 2 hours

From the parking area, hike west, down into a wash and back out. Veer right (north) toward a canyon at the base of Windy Peak's south side. Upon reaching a gully that heads up and right to a cavernous crack, go left up a grassy scree ridge to the top of the rock feature south of Windy Peak. At the summit of this outcropping, a huge rock platform called the Football Field, head right (north) to a white slab skirt along the base of the south-facing wall. It is easiest to ascend (third class) from a point two-thirds of the way (west) up the skirt. Hike left to the base of the first route. Routes are described from left to right.

Windy Peak descent: From the top of Windy Peak, hike left (west) to the second finger gully that heads off the peak. Take the gully down to a bushy gully running south. Follow the gully all the way down to the second point at which you can traverse left (east). Head down the Windy Peak skirt to the base of the routes. 45 minutes (2.5 hours to the car).

1. Jubilant Song 5.7 ★★★★★ Traditional. Old-school rating, more like 5.9. Climb the crack systems that lead up to under the two consecutive large arches on the feature. Traverse under the top arch and head to the summit. Gear: standard rack to #4 Friend.

Pitch 1: 5.7 Climb the leftmost of parallel cracks beneath the huge arches up high, beginning left of the lower arch. Finish on a ledge with a tree. 150 feet.

Pitch 2: 5.7 Continue up the widening crack. Belay on a ledge where a large flake is wedged in the crack. 150 feet.

Pitch 3: 5.5 Follow ledge systems up and right to a ledge below a large flake wedged into the huge right-facing corner. 90 feet.

Pitch 4: 5.5 Move up, right of the huge right-facing corner. Pass a cactus on a crumbly ledge and belay on a ledge right of the huge right-facing corner, 35 feet below the roof. 100 feet.

Pitch 5: 5.6 Take the huge corner up to the roof and then traverse right to where the roof ends and belay on a small ledge. 120 feet.

Pitch 6: 5.5 Continue to the right, taking the face right of a left-facing corner (right edge of the arch) up to a huge ledge. Scramble up and left into a right-facing corner to a tree. 60 feet.

Pitch 6 variation: 5.8 Go directly up from the belay, pulling an overhang. Continue up and right to the huge ledge to the same belay as for the main pitch 6.

Pitch 7: 5.7 Take the wide crack up to a tree. Traverse right around the tree and take a slippery water runnel up to a sloping ledge and belay. 130 feet.

Pitch 8: 5.7 Take the water runnel up and then traverse left to a huge right-facing corner. Climb the corner to the summit. 120 feet.

Pitch 8 variation: 5.5 Head left, ascending a

Evan Firstman triumphant on the crux pitch of Jubilant Song 5.7, Windy Peak.

Photo by Roxanna Brock

WINDY PEAK AND SOUTHERN OUTCROPS

Not to scale

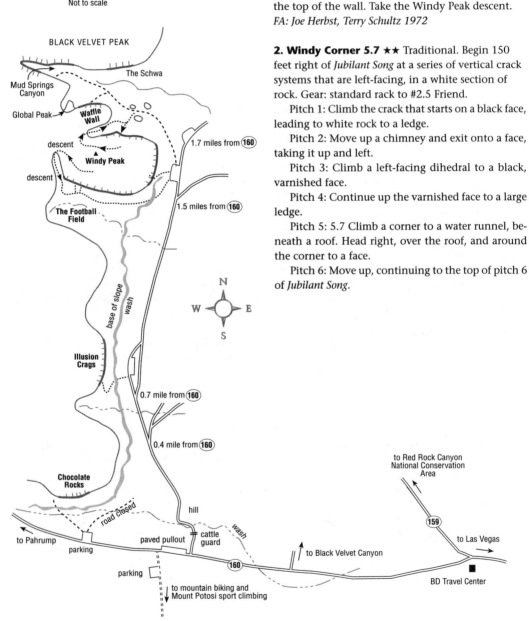

varnished pillar and left-facing crack to the summit. 100 feet.

Scramble for 300 feet, angling left (northwest) to the top of the wall. Take the Windy Peak descent.
FA: Joe Herbst, Terry Schultz 1972

2. Windy Corner 5.7 ★★ Traditional. Begin 150 feet right of *Jubilant Song* at a series of vertical crack systems that are left-facing, in a white section of rock. Gear: standard rack to #2.5 Friend.

Pitch 1: Climb the crack that starts on a black face, leading to white rock to a ledge.

Pitch 2: Move up a chimney and exit onto a face, taking it up and left.

Pitch 3: Climb a left-facing dihedral to a black, varnished face.

Pitch 4: Continue up the varnished face to a large ledge.

Pitch 5: 5.7 Climb a corner to a water runnel, beneath a roof. Head right, over the roof, and around the corner to a face.

Pitch 6: Move up, continuing to the top of pitch 6 of *Jubilant Song.*

Pitches 7–8: Climb pitches 7–8 of *Jubilant Song*.

Scramble for 300 feet, angling left (northwest) to the top of the wall. Take the Windy Peak descent.

FA: George and Joanne Urioste 1977

3. Hot Fudge Thursday 5.8 ★★★★ Mixed. Begin about 150 feet right of *Windy Corner*. Start off the bushy ledge system off the ground, accessed from the left side. Climb off the right edge of the ledge, left of a pine tree.

Pitch 1: 5.6 Climb a crack system, moving right and up to a bolted belay. 160 feet.

Pitch 2: 5.9 Continue up a face, staying left of the series of small roofs to another bolted belay. 160 feet.

Pitch 3: 5.8 Climb up, then step left to a vertical crack system that turns into a left-facing corner and leads to a belay. 165 feet.

Pitch 4: 5.6 Climb the black section of rock, passing through steeper bulges to a ledge and belay. 160 feet.

Pitch 5: 5.9 Climb a face to a crack that leads to a ledge. Belay at a bolted anchor beneath roofs. 155 feet.

Pitch 6: 5.9 Head left, clipping a bolt, to another ledge beneath a notch, which leads to the summit. 40 feet.

Pitch 7: Fourth class. Scramble through the notch to the top of the cliff. 165 feet. Take the Windy Peak descent.

FA: George and Joanne Urioste 1977

4. Slabotomy 5.9 ★★ Traditional. Ascend the run-out slab to the left of *Ain't No Saint* to the pitch 1 anchors of *Ain't No Saint*. Finish at the top of pitch 1 of *Ain't No Saint*. Rappel using 2 ropes.

FA: Danny Rider, Luis Saca 1997

5. Ain't No Saint 5.10 ★ Traditional. Begin in a small gully left of a corner shaped like a backwards L.

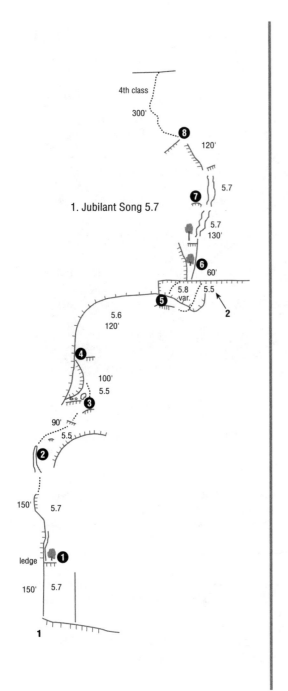

1. Jubilant Song 5.7

4th class

300'

8

120'

5.7

7

5.7
130'

6 60'

5.8
var.   5.5

5

2

5.6
120'

4

100'
5.5

3

90'

5.5

2

150'   5.7

ledge   **1**

150'   5.7

1

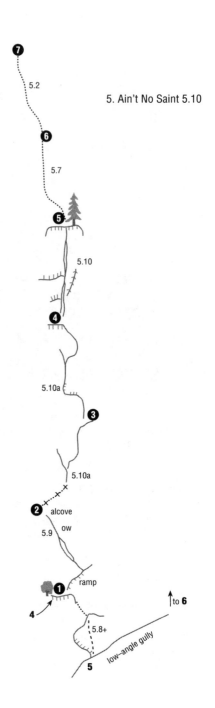

5. Ain't No Saint 5.10

7

5.2

6

5.7

5

5.10

4

5.10a

3

5.10a

2   alcove

ow

5.9

1   ramp

4   ↑to **6**

5.8+

low–angle gully

5

Pitch 1: 5.8+ Climb a corner and face. Head up and left to a ledge and belay.

Pitch 2: 5.9 Take a ramp right, heading for a off-width crack. Climb the off-width and crack to the top and belay in a sloping alcove.

Pitch 3: 5.10a Head right, following bolts to a crack. Follow the crack to below a roof.

Pitch 4: 5.10a Pull the roof and take a crack system up and right to a ledge below other roofs.

Pitch 5: 5.10 Climb a very thin crack through roofs. Move right and take the face up to a ledge and pine tree.

Same top-out as *Saint Stephen*.

Pitch 6: 5.7 Move up and left to slabs.

Pitch 7: 5.2 Climb slabs to the summit.

Take the Windy Peak descent.

FA: Danny Rider, Luis Saca 1997

6. Saint Stephen 5.8+ ★★ Traditional. Begin on the right edge of the wall above the white slabs, 200 feet above the top of the white ramp, the lower of two ramps. This route is located to the left of a pillar that leans against the far-right side of the south face.

Pitch 1: Take thin, side-by-side, vertical cracks up a varnished slab. Take corners above the slab to a ledge on the left.

Pitch 2: Step left into a corner, large and slippery.

Pitch 3: Step left again, out of the corner system, onto a steep face. Take the crack, which widens as it traverses up and left.

Pitch 4: Continue up and left.

Pitch 5: Climb up and left to a tree on a large ledge (top of *Ain't No Saint* pitch 5).

Same finish as *Ain't No Saint*.

Pitch 6: 5.7 Move up and left to slabs.

Pitch 7: 5.2 Climb slabs to the summit.

Take the Windy Peak descent.

FA: Joe Herbst, Larry Hamilton 1974

7. Joanne of Arch 5.9 ★★★ Traditional. Traverse right to the east portion of Windy Peak's south face. Climb a third-class ramp that angles up and left from the east side. Above this ramp is a varnished, black face with an arching, left-facing dihedral ascending it.

Pitch 1: 5.7 From the top of the third-class ramp, take a crack that ascends to directly below the apex of the arch. Traverse right, at the top, to a ledge. 100 feet.

Pitch 2: 5.9 Climb cracks up to the left-facing dihedral. Move up the dihedral and belay from a single bolt at its top. 80 feet.

Pitch 3: 5.8 Take a face up and left. Pull the roof at the peak of the arch and belay. Rappel.

FA: George and Joanne Urioste 1977

▲ WINDY PEAK EAST FACE
SE AM Sun   Approach: 40 minutes

Windy Peak's east face is directly in front of the parking area. Hike into the wash and back uphill to the base of the routes. Routes begin just to the right of a low pink band and are described from left to right.

Descent: Descend the gully south of the east face, rappeling with a single rope where needed.

8. The Free Crack 5.7 ★★ Traditional. Start just right of the left edge of the crag and just right of a roof. Climb the leftmost of two corners up to a ledge. Continue up the corner, using cracks in black rock and moving left. Then move right and straight up the wall.

FA: Joe Herbst 1973

9. The Aid Crack 5.10 ★★ Traditional. Begin just right of the previous route. Take thin cracks up and right to a blocky ledge system. Rappel.

FA: Joe Herbst 1973

10. Jackass Flats 5.5 ★★ Traditional. This three-pitch route climbs the huge S-shaped crack 80 feet right of the previous route. This is the prominent feature on the wall. Start up on the blocky ledge system. Take the crack up and left to the left edge of the roof. 300 feet.

FA: Joe Herbst, Matt McMackin 1973

11. Action by Knight 5.10 ★★ Traditional. Begin 70 feet to the right of *Jackass Flats* at a large, broken, boulder field gully and a right-facing corner.

Pitch 1: 5.6 Scramble up and enter a crack that

leads to a ledge beneath a right-facing corner. 80 feet.

Pitch 2: Climb the corner to the top of a block, which leads to below the middle of a roof.

Pitch 3: 5.10, 2 bolts. Take a ramp left, then move up the face to a crack, continuing to just below the roof. Move left to the left side of the roof. 100 feet.

Pitch 3 variation, *Mother of Knight*: 5.8 Continue straight up the right-facing corner, ascending the right side of the roof. 100 feet.

FA: Betsy and Joe Herbst 1974

12. Diet Delight 5.8+ ★★★ Traditional. Start down and 150 feet right, around the corner from *Action by Knight* on the black, varnished section of cliff that faces directly east.

Pitch 1: 5.8+ Begin on the top of a 25-foot, bush-covered slab. At the top, head directly right. Move to a vertical crack system and belay. 100 feet.

Pitch 2: 5.8 Continue up the left-facing corner sys-

tems to down and left of bushy ledges. Take a right-facing corner to a ledge. 165 feet.

Pitch 3: 5.7 Climb a right-facing corner to a ramp that heads up and right. At the top of the ramp, take a left-facing corner to a ledge. Scramble to the top from there.

Pitch 3 variation: 5.9- Climb up and slightly left, following the hand crack. Continue to the top of the cliff.

FA: George and Joanne Urioste 1977

13. The Black and White Crack 5.3 ★★ Traditional. Begin 200 feet right of the previous route, on the right edge of the crag. Climb the large left-facing corner system where the rock on the left is black and the rock on the right is white. Scramble up the bushy gully system to the base of a corner. Climb the corner for two pitches. Careful of loose rock on the right at the top. Walk off right, down a gully.

FA: George and Joanne Urioste 1977

▲ MUD SPRINGS CANYON
NE AM Sun   Approach: 2–3 hours

From the first Windy Peak parking area, drive north 0.2 mile (to 1.7 miles from SR 160). Park on the left. From the parking area, angle right (northwest) and down, veering to the backside (north side) of Windy Peak. Routes are described from left to right.

WINDY PEAK NORTH FACE

14. Midsummer Night Scheme 5.7 ★★ Traditional. Head up a drainage left (southwest) to the base of Windy Peak's north face. Hike the bushy gully for 0.25 mile to the base of a wide crack system. Scramble third class to the base of a wide crack. Climb the crack as it becomes more difficult and then finish on fourth- and fifth-class terrain. Walk off. Head west from the top and go down the only major gully right of the start of the route. 2 hours.
FA: Joe Herbst, Mark Moore 1973

WAFFLE WALL

Waffle Wall is located on the next peak formation northwest of Windy Peak. From where you cut off the trail to obtain Windy Peak's north face, continue up the canyon to the second gully on the left. Hike up the gully to a crack on the north side.

15. Los Frijoles Humanos 5.8 ★★ Traditional. Begin in a crack left of a gap.

Pitch 1: 5.6 Climb the white-colored slab that makes up the bottom right portion of the wall. 100 feet.

Pitch 2: 5.8, 2 bolts. Move up and left for about 30 feet and then climb straight up. Pass through swells on varnished rock to a thin crack. Take the crack to where you can traverse left to a bolted belay in a

hollowed-out feature. 165 feet.

Pitch 3: 5.7 Climb up to a roof and then traverse left to where you can pull over it. Continue up the face and cracks to a bolted anchor. 165 feet.

Pitch 4: 5.6 Climb straight up the wall to a block at the top. 120 feet.

Rappel using 2 ropes.

FA: George and Joanne Urioste 1979

GLOBAL PEAK

The following two routes climb Global Peak, the second peak northwest of Windy Peak. From the parking area, hike up the canyon to the third gully on the left. Hike up the gully to the base of a large wall on the north side. Walk up the north fork of Mud Springs Canyon to where you are just east of waterfalls. Scramble northeast, up slopes and ramps to the west end of the north branch.

16. Chuckawalla 21 5.9 ★★★ Mixed. Four-star, 3-hour hike. Begin 50 feet left of a large rib and crack system on a featureless wall.

Pitch 1: 5.9, 2 bolts. Take a ramp up and left to a right-facing dihedral. Climb it and then move up to a bolted anchor. 150 feet.

Pitch 2: 5.9, 10 bolts. Climb the bolted face to a bolted anchor, beneath a right-facing corner. 160 feet.

Pitch 3: 5.6 Climb the corner and then step left to a left-facing corner. Take the corner up to a bolted belay just right of a roof. 130 feet.

Pitch 4: 5.8 Take crack systems up to a bolted anchor. 160 feet.

Pitch 5: 5.5 Move up a right-facing dihedral and then ascend a crack right of it to a ledge. 150 feet.

Pitch 6: 5.4 Easy climbing to the summit. 120 feet.

Rappel using 2 55-meter or longer ropes.

FA: George Urioste, Joe Herbst, Joanne Urioste 1978

17. The Sidewinder 5.7 ★★ Traditional. Begin 40 feet right of *Chuckawalla 21* at a rib with a crack to its right. The route climbs a right-angling crack system.

Pitch 1: 5.7 Take a face up, crossing two ledges to a left-facing corner. Top it out and take cracks to a large ledge. 150 feet.

Pitch 2: 5.5 Take crack systems up and right to the

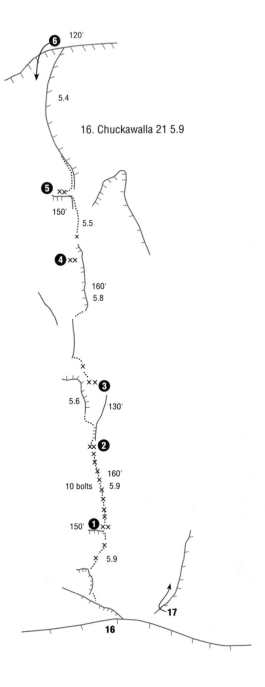

16. Chuckawalla 21 5.9

right edge of a roof. Move left and take loose slabs to a fixed anchor.

Pitch 3: Fourth class. Lieback up the crack to a ramp. Follow the ramp up to below a roof.

Pitch 4: 5.6 Ascend to under the roof and then pull its left side. Follow a face up to a stance.

Pitch 5: 5.6 Take a ramp to a large ledge.

Pitches 6–7: 5.5 Take cracks and the face to the top.

Rappel *Chuckawalla 21* using 2 55-meter or longer ropes.

FA: George and Joanne Urioste 1978

MAIN MUD SPRINGS CANYON

From the parking area, continue up the canyon to the main Mud Springs Canyon. There will be a point that requires some scrambling around some water and falls. Stay to the north to work around them. This will lead to the north branch of the Mud Springs Canyon.

18. Ronestone Cowboy 5.10 ★★ Traditional. A prominent zigzag crack ascends up and left on this south-facing wall.

Pitch 1: Climb a corner.

Pitch 2: Climb the zigzag crack.

Pitch 3: Ascend a chimney.

Pitch 4: Finish in the gully. Descent unknown.

FA: David Anderson 1976

19. Mito 5.8 ★★★ Traditional. Begin around the corner about 200 feet right of *Ronestone Cowboy*. Parallel cracks ascend the left edge of the east face of this varnished cliff. Climb the rightmost of the two cracks. Gear: standard rack to #5 Friend.

Pitch 1: 5.8 Begin in broken rock beneath the crack system. Climb to a large ledge. Continue up in an S-shaped crack to another, smaller ledge.

Pitch 2: Continue up the crack to where it peters out and starts veering right. Step left, moving up to a large crack. Climb up to a ledge. 150 feet.

Pitch 3: Finish up the crack to the summit.

Descend by hiking north to a gully. Hike down the gully, heading east back toward the lush desert floor.

FA: Tom Kaufman, Joe Herbst 1973

THE SOUTHERN OUTCROPS

Illusion Crags ▲ Chocolate Rocks

ILLUSION CRAGS and Chocolate Rocks make up the Southern Outcrops. From Las Vegas, take West Charleston Boulevard west, which turns into State Route 159. Continue on SR 159 until it ends at SR 160. The Blue Diamond Travel Center is on the south side of SR 160 at the intersection. See Windy Peak and Southern Outcrops map on page 416.

▲ ILLUSION CRAGS
E AM Sun   Approach: 25 minutes

At the SR 159 intersection with SR 160, turn right (west) on SR 160 and drive 5.8 miles. Turn right onto a dirt road, just before a paved pull-out on the right. Cross a cattle guard and zero the odometer. Drive 0.3 mile and turn right out of the wash, on a road that parallels the cliffs. At 0.4 mile fork left, heading toward the cliff. At 0.7 mile the road forks. Take the left fork and park.

From the parking area, hike down into a wash and back out. Hike directly west to the black, varnished rock outcropping. You will pass a sign on your hike up, noting that the canyons of Red Rock are designated wilderness areas. The routes begin on the far-left side of the cliff, up from the gully/drainage bordering the left edge. Routes are described from left to right.

1. French Bulges 5.7 ★★ Traditional. Scramble up to a pine tree. Climb the right-facing corner system to a bulge on the right. Pull the bulge to a bushy ledge. Gear: standard rack to #3 Friend. Walk off right (between this wall and *Chameleon Pinnacle*).
FA: Nanouk Borche, Joe Herbst 1973

2. Arm Forces 5.9 ★★★★ Traditional. Begin 15 feet right of *French Bulges* at a large, white, right-facing corner with a yucca and a couple bushes at its base. Climb the corner, staying in the leftmost crack. Follow it up to a roof, continue up to another roof, move up to a ledge, and then pull a final roof. Gear: standard rack to #3 Friend. Walk off right.
FA: Joe Herbst, Nanouk Borche 1973

3. Mirage 5.7 ★★ Traditional. Climb the crack in the white rock to a small roof. Follow the crack up to a larger roof. Top-out in the crack system. Gear: standard rack to #4 Friend. Walk off right.
FA: Betsy and Joe Herbst, Joanne Urioste 1976

4. Morph Out! 5.7 ★ Traditional. Begin the same as *Chameleon Pinnacle*, 100 feet right of the previous routes. Start in an alcove, then climb up a left-facing corner to a large block atop a pillar. Climb up the left side of this block. Continue up the face left of the Chameleon Pinnacle formation. Walk off left.
FA: Todd and Donette Swain 1994

5. Chameleon Pinnacle 5.4 ★★ Traditional. Start the same as the previous route in an alcove at the base of the pinnacle. Climb right out of the alcove to a low-angled face. Take the face up through blocky sections to the pinnacle summit. Walk off left.
FA: Bill Lowman, Betsy and Joe Herbst, Matt McMackin, Nanouk Borche, Howard Booth 1973

6. Changelings 5.6 ★ Traditional. Begin 20 feet right of the previous route, at the right arête system. Take the blunt/blocky arête up, finishing on

the face right of the previous route. Rappel from a natural thread with 1 rope.
FA: Donette and Todd Swain 1994

7. Lady in Question 5.11 ★★★ Traditional. Start about 100 feet right of the previous route. Start behind a bush in a big corner system. Climb to the right side of the left arch. Take this straight up to a ledge. Step left, taking a thin vertical seam to a sloping ledge. Continue to a left-facing corner to the top.
FA: Joe Herbst 1978

8. Hanging Tough 5.8 ★★★ Traditional. Begin on *Lady in Question*, climbing to the ledge. Instead of stepping left, continue up a crack system that develops into a larger left-facing corner to the top of the cliff.
FA: Joe and Betsy Herbst 1973

9. Sweet Little Whore 5.9 ★★★ Traditional. Begin down, right, and around the corner 25 feet from the previous two routes. Start behind a tree at the base. Climb to underneath a roof. Enter a crack system that angles up and left to a ledge. Leave the ledge and climb straight up the face. Difficult start. Rappel *False Perception*.
FA: Joe Herbst, Tom Kaufman 1973

10. Skinny Mini 5.9 ★★★ Traditional. Begin just right of the previous route. Climb straight up the nose of the feature. Difficult start. Rappel *False Perception*.
FA: Joe Herbst 1973

11. False Perception 5.10d ★★★★ Mixed. Begin just right of the previous route. Climb the brown patinaed face to a bulge. Pull the bulge and take the thin seam to the bolted anchors. Gear: Rocks and Friends to #1. There might be 1 bolt drilled in hollow rock on the route. Rappel using 2 ropes.
FA: Todd and Donette Swain 1993

12. Spell Me 5.11 ★★ TR. Hike around the corner down and right from routes 9–11, to a shorter face. Climb the crack that angles up and left in the black

rock to a small ledge. Step left on the ledge. Take a thin seam up, passing bolts to a horizontal. Step back right. Finish on top of a block. Possible, but dangerous lead with brass wires and a standard rack to #2.5 (3 bolts). Rappel from slings around a block using 2 ropes.
FA: Todd Swain, Bobby Knight 1993

13. Petit Deceit 5.8 ★ Traditional. Begin the same as the previous route, staying left of the bushes. Climb up a left-facing corner. Move right onto a black patinaed face. Follow it to the big ledge atop a stack of blocks. Rappel from *Spell Me* anchors using 2 ropes.
FA: Todd Swain, Bobby Knight 1993

14. Sensual 5.7 ★★★ Traditional. Climb the black corner. Descent unknown.
FA: John Long, Joe Herbst, Richard Harrison 1973

15. Sensible 5.7 ★★★ Traditional. Climb the crack system right of *Sensual*.
FA: Stephanie Petrilak, Betsy Herbst, Joe Herbst 1973

▲ CHOCOLATE ROCKS
S All-Day Sun   Approach: 15 minutes

At the SR 159 intersection with SR 160, turn right (west) on SR 160 and drive 6.8 miles. Turn right onto a dirt road that is blocked by a locked fence. This turn is located just past where the road changes from one lane to two. Park here and leave room for other vehicles.

From the parking area, cross the fence and head down (north) into a wash. Cross the wash and hike up and left toward a dark outcropping above a short white band. You will pass a sign on your hike up, noting that the canyons of Red Rock are designated wilderness areas. Approach from the right side of the white band. Scramble up the right side of a small red band, up and left to the base of the following routes. Routes are described from left to right.

Descent: Single-rope rappel down *Minute Maid*.

16. Combination Corner 5.8 ★★★ Traditional. Begin at the cracks below and left of a white face, above the black rock. Climb the left crack to a hori-

zontal. Stay left to the top. Gear: standard rack to #5 Friend. Rappel *Minute Maid.*
FA: Mark Moore, Joe Herbst 1973

17. Spinach 5.10b/c ★★★ Traditional. The next crack right of the previous route is the first crack left of an arête. Take the crack to a horizontal. Finish up the off-width, left of the white face. Gear: standard rack to #5 Friend. Rappel *Minute Maid.*
FA: Joe Herbst 1973

18. Shortcake 5.6 ★★★ Traditional. Start around the corner right of the previous routes on a low-angle, black, varnished face. Climb straight up the face to a fixed anchor. Rappel.
FA: Joe Herbst 1972

19. Minute Maid 5.6 ★★★ Traditional. Climb the crack just right of the face of *Shortcake*, behind a

pillarlike feature, to fixed anchors. Rappel.
FA: Joe Herbst 1972

20. The Gallows 5.10b ★★★ Traditional. Begin 10 feet right of *Minute Maid.* Take an arête up and right to a big block that rests on the wall at the top. Follow the block up and right to a ledge with a tree. Short route. Rappel.
FA: John Long, Joe Herbst, Richard Harrison 1973

21. Zacker Cracker 5.8+ ★★★ Traditional. Climb up the left side of the fin, right of *The Gallows.*
FA: Joe Herbst 1972

22. Potso's Pudding 5.6 ★★ Traditional. Take a crack up the right side of the fin, finishing at the top of *Zacker Cracker.* Gear: medium-sized Rocks and Friends.
FA: Betsy and Joe Herbst 1972

23. Mc-Crack-En 5.7 ★★★ Traditional. This route climbs a large flake at the next corner right of two faces, right of the previous route. Climb the flake up the corner to a roof. Traverse left and follow the crack up and around right to the top of the feature.
FA: Matt McMackin, Nanouk Borche, Richard Harrison, John Long 1973

24. Peanut Butter and Jam 5.9+ ★★★★★ Traditional. Climb the next crack to the right of the previous route. Start on top of a block, climbing a chossy-looking, block-filled Bombay chimney. Follow the crack system to the top. Some of the best pure crack climbing around.
FA: Joe Herbst, David Hop 1973

25. The Little Engine that Could 5.6 ★★ Traditional. Climb the wide chimney that has a large white chockstone wedged in its top. Begin just right of a flake system. Gear: cams to #5 Friend.
FA: Howard Booth, David Hop, Joe Herbst 1973

APPENDIX A
FRIEND SIZES IN INCHES

#Z1	0.22–0.31	#1.25	0.83–1.30
#Z2	0.28–0.39	#1.5	0.90–1.40
#Z3	0.33–0.48	#1.75	0.98–1.61
#Z4	0.41–0.63	#2	1.14–1.73
#Z5	0.51–0.75	#2.5	1.30–2.16
#Z6	0.67–0.94	#3	1.70–2.60
#00	0.40–0.63	#3.5	2.00–3.23
#0	0.51–0.75	#4	2.52–3.94
#0.5	0.67–0.94	#5	3.31–5.43
#1	0.75–1.14	#6	4.64–7.64

APPENDIX B
BOLTING IN RED ROCK

Thanks to the American Safe Climbing Association (ASCA; *www.safeclimbing.org*), many Red Rock routes have been rebolted. Unfortunately, the local BLM office requires that the bolts be replaced by hand—but the ASCA is still doing it! Kudos. Please support the ASCA and the climbers who participate.

Thanks to: Greg Barnes, Jason Addy, Dave Anderson, Rachel Arst, Jed Botsford, Gary Fike, Lawrence Garcia, Emily Hazelton, Jack Hoeflich, Barry Hutten, Jesse Jackson, Sam Johnson, Bryan Law, Mark Limage, Mike and Mark from Canada, Maggie Merchant, Rick Poedtke, Paul Rasmussen, Matthew Schutz, Justin Shields, Laura Snider, George Urioste, Chris Van Leuven, René Vitins, Mike White, Karin Wuhrmann.

ROUTE	NOTES	DATE
Arrow Place	Replaced all anchor bolts.	11/02
Black Orpheus	Replaced all bolts, (15) except the last bolt on the last pitch. While original, it is very far left and almost always skipped to reduce rope drag (or because it's not spotted).	03/02
Bodiddly	Replaced third bolt, which was a ⅜-inch buttonhead with an old Leeper hanger.	03/02
Chicken Eruptus	Replaced both protection bolts.	03/02
Chuckawalla	(aka Chuckawalla 21)Replaced all bolts.	11/02
Cold September Corner	One bolt at anchor replaced, rap rings installed.	03/04

ROUTE	NOTES	DATE
Dark Shadows	Replaced 5 bolts: first-pitch protection bolts, 1 bolt at pitch 3 belay, 1 bolt at original pitch 4 belay, and the protection bolt on pitch 5.	10/01
Doobie Dance	Replaced anchor.	03/02
Dream of Wild Turkeys	Replaced 39 bolts: all bolts to pitch 11 except one each at pitch 10 and 11 belays, and the old pitch 4 belay (usually skipped), which has 1⅜-inch, 1¼ inch original bolts. Pitch 10 and 11 belays now have 1⅜-inch, 1½-inch, and 1 double-clip point. Original Urioste ¼-inch hangers were left at the request of George Urioste. Update 04/04: second protection bolt on pitch 2 replaced.	03/01 04/04
Eagle Dance	Replaced 72 bolts: all bolts replaced except the 4 bolts on the last pitch (130-foot 5.9 crack), and the fourth bolt on the short 5.10 pitch above the bolt ladder. This latter bolt was the only original Urioste protection bolt on the entire route that was ⅜-inch, located next to a 1½-inch crack.	03/02
Early Times	Replaced 18 bolts. All bolts except the fourth and tenth on pitch 1, and pitch 2 anchor (usually skipped).	04/01
Epinephrine	Replaced 6 bolts: all protection bolts on pitches 1 and 2. All bolts to the top of the tower are bomber (thanks to Dan McQuade!). Most bolts above the tower are a mix of rusty ⅜-inch with bad SMC hangers and ¼-inch bolts. There is a good ½-inch bolt at each belay except the very last, which is an old ⅜-inch and an old ¼-inch (easily backed up with a #3 Friend). Back up the protection bolts where possible, and use Screamers.	11/01
Fiddler on the Roof	Replaced 3 bolts: 1 at each of the first three anchors above the roof.	10/01
Forget Me Knot	Replaced 2 bolts.	11/02
Friendship Route	Replaced 3 bolts.	03/02
Frogland	Replaced 7 bolts.	11/02
Great Red Book	Replaced all 5 bolts.	11/02
Head Case	Replaced 4 hangers.	11/02
Ixtlan	Replaced 9 bolts: 7 bolts on pitch 1, and 1 bolt each at pitch 2 and 3 belays. Old SMC hangers on ⅜-inch bolts replaced at belays 2 and 3 with camouflaged ring hangers.	03/01
Just in Case	Replaced 1 hanger.	11/02
Kemosabe	Replaced the bolt.	03/02
La Cierta Edad	First three pitches replaced: 5 protection bolts and 6 anchor bolts.	03/04
Levitation 29	All bolts replaced.	NA
Lotta Balls	Crux protection bolt replaced, and 1 bolt at the first-pitch belay anchor replaced.	03/02
Mai Tai (I) First Creek	Replaced all 3 bolts.	03/02

ROUTE	NOTES	DATE
No Laughing Matter/Serious Business	Replaced anchor.	11/02
Only the Good Die Young	Replaced 23 bolts: all bolts on route except last protection bolt on 5.11 traverse on pitch 4—an original Urioste ⅜-inch bolt, best left unclipped to minimize rope drag.	10/01
Out of Control	Replaced anchor.	11/02
Overhanging Hangover	Replaced 2 bolts on first pitch.	03/04
Prince of Darkness	Replaced 57 bolts: all remaining ¼-inch protection bolts, and 1 at pitch 5 anchor. Two original bolts were left at pitch 5 anchor at the request of George Urioste.	03/01
Ringtail	Replaced all 16 bolts.	11/02
Risky Business	Replaced 3 bolts: pitch 1 anchor and first protection bolt on pitch 2.	10/01
Rob Roy	Replaced all 5 bolts: 3 protection, and 2 at anchor.	03/02
Rock Warrior	Replaced 27 bolts: all bolts to the top of pitch 6 replaced.	03/01
Sandstone Samurai	Replaced first bolt.	03/01
Schaeffer's Delight	Replaced all 7 protection bolts.	03/01
Slabba Dabba Do	Replaced 3 bolts.	11/01
Sour Mash	Replaced 26 bolts: all remaining bad bolts replaced.	10/01
Sour Mash to Early Times Connector	Replaced 2 protection bolts on this Urioste 5.9 connector pitch.	10/01
Spark Plug	Replaced anchor.	03/04
The Next Century	Replaced 2 bolts at pitch 1 belay, and 6 hangers on pitch 2.	11/02
Triassic Sands	Replaced 2 bolts. Old anchor bolt replaced at pitch 2 anchor (this bolt was in a flare above current anchor, and was eliminated, and a good bolt was placed next to 2 OK modern bolts at the current anchor); and 4 protection bolts next to a loose flake on pitch 3 were replaced with 1 good bolt at the original second bolt. These bolts may or may not have been original, and since there is no solid pro due to the flake and since there are some loose/suspect holds, consensus was that 1 should be replaced even though the climbing is easy.	11/01
Yellow Brick Road	Replaced 13 bolts: all remaining ¼-inch bolts replaced.	03/01
Y2K	Replaced 2 hangers.	11/02

APPENDIX C

CONSERVATION AND CLIMBING ORGANIZATIONS

LAS VEGAS CLIMBER'S LIAISON COUNCIL (LVCLC)

The rock climbing surrounding Las Vegas is a precious commodity. The Las Vegas Climber's Liaison Council was created to enable the climbing community to deal effectively with land managers and with one another. Their mission: The Las Vegas Climber's Liaison Council is dedicated to ensuring climbing access, encouraging stewardship of the environment, and cultivating a sense of community in a world-class climbing destination. The LVCLC holds a variety of events each year, including crag cleanups. Their website provides up-to-date information on the latest Las Vegas climbing news regarding access, trail closures, campground changes, and more. Membership in the LVCLC is free, though optional donations will earn you a place in one of their supporter categories. The LVCLC extends an invitation to climbers from around the globe: join us in protecting Red Rock. *www.LVCLC.org*

FRIENDS OF RED ROCK CANYON

Friends of Red Rock Canyon supports the Bureau of Land Management in the protection and enrichment of Red Rock Canyon National Conservation Area. The group addresses urban encroachment, loss of native species habitat, as well as overuse, transportation, and parking within the conservation area. PO Box 97; Blue Diamond, NV 89004; (702) 515-5360; *www.friendsof redrockcanyon.org*

RED ROCK CANYON INTERPRETIVE ASSOCIATION

Red Rock Canyon Interpretive Association is a not-for-profit association whose goal is to enhance the recreational, educational, and interpretive programs of the Bureau of Land Management and other governmental agencies. The association encourages an awareness of the natural history, cultural history, and sciences of southern Nevada and Red Rock. (702) 515-5367; *www.redrockcanyonlv.org*

LEAVE NO TRACE

Leave No Trace Center for Outdoor Ethics is a national nonprofit that promotes responsible outdoor recreation through education, research, and partnerships. Leave No Trace builds awareness, appreciation, and respect for our wildlands. *www.LNT.org*

AMERICAN SAFE CLIMBING ASSOCIATION (ASCA)

The American Safe Climbing Association replaces deteriorating anchors on classic climbs in the United States and educates climbers and the public about climbing safety. See Appendix B for the good work they have done in Red Rock. *www.safeclimbing.org*

THE ACCESS FUND

The Access Fund is a national nonprofit dedicated to keeping climbing areas open and to conserving the climbing environment. PO Box 17010, Boulder CO 80308; (303) 545-6772; *www.accessfund.org*

APPENDIX D
SUPPLIES, LODGING, FOOD, AND RESOURCES

CLIMBING SHOPS
Desert Rock Sports
8221 W Charleston Blvd, Suite 106
(702) 254-1143
http://desertrocksportslv.com
Galyans Sporting Goods
1308 W Sunset Rd
Henderson NV
(702) 855-5000
Sport Chalet
8825 W Charleston Blvd
(702) 255-7570
Sport Chalet
701 Marks St
Henderson, NV
(702) 451-1211
Sport Chalet
7230 Arroyo Crossing Parkway
(702) 263-6756
www.sportchalet.com
Recreational Equipment Incorporated (REI)
2220 Village Walk Dr
Henderson NV
(702) 896-7111

CLIMBING GYMS
Red Rock Climbing Center
8201 W Charleston Blvd, Ste B
(702) 254-5604
www.redrockclimbingcenter.com
Nevada Climbing Center
3065 E Patrick Ln, #4
(702) 898-8192

GUIDE SERVICES AND CLIMBING SCHOOLS
American Alpine Institute
(360) 671-1505; *www.aai.cc/*
Jackson Hole Mountain Guides
8221 W Charleston Blvd, Ste 106
(702) 254-0885; *www.jhmg.com*
Mountain Skills
(702) 325-1616
www.climbingschoolusa.com
National Outdoor Leadership School (NOLS)
(307) 332-5300
(800) 710-6657; *www.nols.edu*
Sky's the Limit
(800) 733-7597

LODGING, CAMPING, SHOWERS

HOTELS/MOTELS
Bonnie Springs Motel
Hwy 159 (south of the Scenic Drive); 1 Bonnie Springs Rd.
(702) 875-4400
www.bonniesprings.com/motel.html
JW Marriott Las Vegas
221 S Rampart Blvd
(702) 869-7777
www.marriott.com
Sin City Youth Hostel
1208 Las Vegas Blvd S
(702) 868-0222
www.sincityhostel.com
Suncoast Hotel and Casino
9090 Alta Dr
(702) 636-7111 or (877) 677-7111; *www.suncoastcasino.com*

Holiday Inn Express at the Lakes
8669 W Sahara Ave
(702) 256-3766
www.hiexpress.com

CASINO HOTELS
Bellagio
3600 Las Vegas Blvd S
(702) 693-7111
Circus Circus
2880 Las Vegas Blvd S
(702) 734-0410
www.circuscircus.com
MGM Grand
3799 Las Vegas Blvd S
(702) 891-7777
www.mgmgrand.com
Rio
3700 W Flamingo Rd
(866) 746-7671
www.riolasvegas.com
Palms
4321 W Flamingo Rd
(702) 942-7777; *www.palms.com*
Stratosphere
2000 Las Vegas Blvd S
(702) 380-7777
www.stratospherehotel.com

CAMPING
Red Rock Canyon Campground
(702) 515-5371
Call to reserve a group campsite. Individual campsites are assigned on a first-come, first-served basis. Open Labor Day through Memorial Day.

SHOWERS
Red Rock Climbing Center
8201 W Charleston Blvd
Home of the $4 shower!
Sin City Youth Hostel
1208 Las Vegas Blvd S

BUFFETS
Rio
Carnival World Buffet
3700 W Flamingo Rd
Paris
Le Village Buffet
3655 Las Vegas Blvd S
Bellagio
The Buffet at Bellagio
3600 Las Vegas Blvd S

GRUB
Bagel Café
301 North Buffalo Drive
Chicago Brewing Company
2201 S Fort Apache Rd
BJ's Restaurant & Brewery
10840 W Charleston Blvd
Rocco's New York Italian Deli
1181 S Buffalo

Rocco's NY Pizzeria
10860 W Charleston Blvd (in
strip mall behind Olive Garden)
Baja Fresh
8780 W Charleston Blvd, Ste 100
Tropical Smoothie Café
10260 W Charleston
Frank & Finas
5550 W Charleston Blvd
Souper Salad
2051 N Rainbow
Thai Garden
8826 S. Eastern Ave

GROCERIES
Trader Joe's
7575 W Washington Ave
Whole Foods
8855 W Charleston Blvd
Wild Oats Community Market
7250 W Lake Mead Blvd

HANGOUTS
Borders Books
10950 W Charleston Blvd/215
Beltway

Barnes & Noble Books
8915 W Charleston Blvd
Starbucks
Nearly every corner on
Charleston Blvd

INTERNET
Sahara West Library
9600 W Sahara Ave
(702) 507-3630
Hours Mon–Thu 9:00 A.M.–9:00
P.M., Fri–Sun 10:00 A.M.–6:00 P.M.
Tropical Smoothie Café
10260 W Charleston Blvd

MOVIE THEATERS
Regal Cinema Act Three
9400 W Sahara Ave
Century 16 Suncoast
9090 Alta Dr

WEBSITES
www.lasvegas.com
www.lvclc.org

APPENDIX E
CONTACT INFORMATION

Red Rock Canyon National Conservation Area
Visitors Center: (702) 515-5350
Extended access permits: (702) 515-5050
Climbing rangers: (702) 515-5138 or 515-5042

Bureau of Land Management
Las Vegas Field Office
HCR 33 Box 5500
Las Vegas, NV 89124
(702) 515-5000

EMERGENCY SERVICES
911
Las Vegas Fire Department: (702) 383-2888
UMC Medical Center: (702) 383-2000

GLOSSARY

Aid climbing (n) Direct use of fixed or climber-placed protection used for upward advancement on route when climbing, using gear for upward progress.

Back in the day Back when climbers were bolder, when traditional climbing was more the norm, when climbing first began, when climbing first began at a particular area.

Beta (n) Information about a route or the sequence of moves on a route.

Biner (n) Abbreviation for carabiner, a short loop of metal with a gate on it; used to attach things together.

Bivy (n, v) Camping spot, to sleep out.

Bombay chimney (n) A chimney with a large flare at the bottom, creating an alcove feature. A chimney crack that is wider at the bottom and that narrows as it progresses up the wall.

Chossy (adj) Dirty, loose, crumbly rock.

Committing (adj) A route, move, or sequence that requires you to totally go for it.

Continuous (adj) Nonstopping, a section or route that does not let up for the entire length.

Crimper (n) Small edge hold that requires a tight grip with the hands to hold onto it.

Crux (n), Cruxy (adj) The hardest section or move of a climb.

Dihedral (n) A corner or crack formed when two walls come together at a right angle, forming a corner, much like an open book; often conducive to stemming techniques. See also *open book*.

Edge (n, v) A small, horizontal hold; to stand on hold with the corner of a shoe, thus maximizing the pressure applied to a small area of rubber.

Elvis leg (n) The uncontrollable shaking of a leg during a climb, often due to a combination of nerves and over-contraction of muscles. Also called "sewing-machine leg."

FA (n) Abbreviation for "first ascent." Often seen in guidebooks to list the people responsible for the route, the first to climb it.

FFA (n) Abbreviation for "first free ascent," the first ascent that did not use aid-climbing techniques.

Finger crack (n) A crack climbed by using fingertips, entire fingers, and/or finger jamming; called a "tips crack" if use of fingertips is primary.

Fist crack (n) A crack climbed by placing fists inside it (fist jamming).

Flash (v) To climb a route on the first attempt without falling. You may have beta or previous viewing of others climbing the route.

Free climbing (n) Use of only natural rock features to make upward progress on a route; gear used only for protection in the event of a fall.

Free solo (v) Free climbing without any protection or a rope.

Hand crack (n) A crack climbed by hand cupping or hand jamming.

Heady (adj) Describes a route that requires you to keep your cool; generally means run-out, difficult routefinding, and/or poor rock quality.

Hueco(s) (n) Large hole or pocket in the rock.

Off-width (ow) (n) A wide crack requiring arm barring and/or hand and feet stacking to ascend.

On-sight (v) To climb a route on the first try without falling, without any beta, practice, or viewing.

Open book (n) A corner or dihedral appearing as a book does when it is opened.

Pink point (v) An outdated term that means to redpoint with preplaced protection. Only used by people who enjoy keeping track of such silly things more then they enjoy climbing.

Pro (n) Short for protection (i.e., gear).

Protection (n) Any gear (such as a cam, nut, and so on) used to protect the lead climber in case of a fall.

Pumped (adj) When the forearms fill with lactic

acid and blood, causing the hands to open up.

Rap-bolt (v) To place bolts on a route on rappel.

Redpoint (v) To lead a route using information obtained from climbing it, but climbing it without falling or hanging on the rope.

Rope solo (v) To climb without a partner, but using a rope and gear to protect against a fall.

Routefinding (n) Locating the correct path of travel up a route.

Run-out (adj) Long distance between bolts or gear or placements.

Sandbag (v), sandbagged (adj) To give incorrect, bad, or not all the information about a route.

Second (n) The second person ascending the route (generally a multipitch route), in which this second climber top-ropes behind the "first" or lead climber.

Send (v) To redpoint a route, as in "she sent the route."

Sewing machine leg (n) See *Elvis leg*.

Simul-climb (v) The act of two or three people simultaneously climbing on the same rope, secured by protection, but not belaying in the traditional sense. Sometimes called a "running belay."

Sketchy (adj) Not secure.

Slabby (adj) Low-angle rock with no holds.

Splitter (n) A crack that separates a portion of the rock or cliff face, usually vertical in nature. A perfect, flawless crack.

Sport climbing (n) Free climbing that focuses on extreme gymnastic difficulty; climbing that uses preplaced protection bolts.

Sporty (adj) Said of a route that has a long distance between bolts or gear placements.

Stick-clip (v), stick clip (n) To clip a piece of gear above you to create a top-rope situation; also, a pole used to get the rope above you to create a top-roped portion of the route.

Straight-in (adj) Describes a parallel crack.

Top out (v) To make it to the top or summit of a route or formation.

Trad (adj) Short for "traditional," the original type of climbing in which you place protection in natural features while ascending the rock.

Traditional climbing (n) See *trad*.

Whipper (n) A long fall.

REFERENCES

Barnes, Greg. *Red Rocks Climbing SuperTopo*, 1st ed. Mill Valley, CA: SuperTopo, 2004.

Brock, Roxanna. *Las Vegas Limestone*. Las Vegas: Flying Carpet Publishing, 2000.

DeAngelo, Larry, and Bill Thiry. *Red Rock Odyssey, Classic Traditional Climbs*. Las Vegas: Verex Press, 2004.

Faulk, Randy. *A Climbers Guide to the Red Rocks of Nevada*. Las Vegas: R.T. Publications, 1992.

Jensen, Rob. *Red Rocks Bouldering*. Las Vegas: self-published, 2002.

McMillen, Jared. *Las Vegas Bouldering*. Las Vegas: TYB Photography, 2002.

———. *Red Rock Sport Climbing Guide*. Las Vegas: TYB Photography, 2003.

Swain, Todd. *Rock Climbing Red Rocks*. 3rd ed. Helena, MT: The Globe Pequot Press, 2000.

Urioste, Joanne. *Red Rock Canyon, the Red Book Supplement*. Las Vegas: Joanne Urioste, 1984.

———. *The Red Rocks of Southern Nevada* (The Red Book). Las Vegas: Joanne Urioste, 1984.

INDEX OF ROUTES

ABOUT THE AUTHORS

Author Roxanna Brock

Roxanna Brock retired from a career in chemical engineering at IBM in 1993, with the goal of focusing exclusively on rock climbing. Traveling the world to pursue her passion, Roxanna has climbed 5.13c sport routes, 5.13a traditional climbs, and A3+ aid routes. She has freed many aid lines in Red Rock (up to 5.12d) and has put up new free and aid lines in the United States as well as in Pakistan and Kyrgyzstan. Roxanna wrote and self-published the *Las Vegas Limestone* and *Best Sport Climbs of the New River Gorge* rock-climbing guidebooks. She also wrote the *CERCA Country Guide to Mountain Biking (2005)*, a guide to mountain-biking destinations within a 400-mile radius of Las Vegas, with stories and full-color scenic photography. Sharing her infatuation with the outdoors, Roxanna pursues a career in freelance writing, documenting her adventures and the resulting physical and personal achievements. Her works have appeared in the *Las Vegas Review Journal, She Sends Magazine, American Alpine Journal, Rock and Ice* magazine, *Gripped Magazine, Climbing* magazine, *Las Vegas Magazine*, and more. Roxanna's postcards of lovely Red Rock Canyon are available at the RRCNCA Visitors Center.

Author Jared McMillen

Jared McMillen was born and raised in Minnesota, far from any rock climbing or even the thought of it. Shortly after high school, during a visit to Boulder, Colorado, Jared watched climbers in Eldorado Canyon scaling rock faces with grace and ease. Shortly afterward, he signed up with the Boulder Rock School and subsequently committed himself to climbing as a lifestyle and profession. He has climbed at world-class crags in the United States and in Europe, redpointing routes to 5.14b and on-sighting routes to 5.13a. He is the author of *Red Rock Sport Climbing Guide* and has contributed to the *Las Vegas Review Journal, CERCA* magazine, *Rock and Ice* magazine, *Las Vegas Magazine*, and more. He works as a freelance photographer, documenting the world's best adventures in *Climbing* and *Gripped* magazines. Jared now lives in Las Vegas and is grateful to have Red Rock Canyon in his backyard.

ABOUT THE UIAA

UIAA

The UIAA is the international federation for climbing and mountaineering and is recognised by and works closely with the Olympic Movement, United Nations, and World Conservation Union. The UIAA promotes access for the freedom to enjoy mountaineering in a responsible way with minimum impact on the environment. Through a network of experts in 98 member associations in 68 different countries, the UIAA helps to protect mountain areas and climbing sites and encourages development for local communities. The UIAA has a Summit Charter and a dossier of proposals to promote cooperation and peace, protection of the environment, and sporting excellence. For further information visit *www.uiaa.ch*.

The UIAA encourages the inclusion of information in guidebooks that helps visitors from overseas to understand the most important information about local access, grades, and emergency procedures. The UIAA also encourages climbers and mountaineers to share knowledge and views on issues such as safety, ethics, and good practice in mountain sports. The UIAA is not responsible for, and accepts no liability for, the technical content or accuracy of the information in this guidebook. Climbing, hill walking, and mountaineering are activities with a danger of personal injury and death. Participants should be aware of, understand and accept these risks, and be responsible for their own actions and involvement.

INTERNATIONAL GRADE COMPARISON CHART

UIAA	USA	GB	F	D	AUS
V-	5.5	4a	5a	V	13
V	5.6		5b		
		4b		VI	14
V+	5.7		5c		
VI-	5.8	4c		VIIa	15
VI	5.9	5a	6a	VIIb	
VI+	5.10a		6a+	VIIc	16
VII-	5.10b	5b	6b	VIIIa	17
VII	5.10c		6b+	VIIIb	18
VII+	5.10d	5c	6c	VIIIc	19
VIII-	5.11a		6c+	IXa	20
	5.11b	6a			21
VIII	5.11c		7a	IXb	22
	5.11d				23
VIII+	5.12a	6b	7a+	IXc	24
IX-	5.12b		7b	Xa	25
	5.12c	6c	7b+		26
IX	5.12d	7a	7c	Xb	27
IX+	5.13a		7c+	Xc	28
X-	5.13b		8a	XIa	29
	5.13c	7b	8a+		30
X	5.13d		8b	XIb	31
X+	5.14a		8b+		32
XI-	5.14b		8c		33
	5.14c		8c+		34
XI	5.14d		9a		

ABOUT THE MOUNTAINEERS

THE MOUNTAINEERS, founded in 1906, is a nonprofit outdoor activity and conservation club, whose mission is "to explore, study, preserve, and enjoy the natural beauty of the outdoors . . . . " Based in Seattle, Washington, the club is now one of the largest such organizations in the United States, with seven branches throughout Washington State.

The Mountaineers sponsors both classes and year-round outdoor activities in the Pacific Northwest, which include hiking, mountain climbing, ski-touring, snowshoeing, bicycling, camping, kayaking, nature study, sailing, and adventure travel. The club's conservation division supports environmental causes through educational activities, sponsoring legislation, and presenting informational programs.

All club activities are led by skilled, experienced instructors, who are dedicated to promoting safe and responsible enjoyment and preservation of the outdoors.

If you would like to participate in these organized outdoor activities or the club's programs, consider a membership in The Mountaineers. For information and an application, write or call The Mountaineers, Club Headquarters, 7700 Sand Point Way NE, Seattle, WA 98115; 206-521-6001. You can also visit the club's website at *www.mountaineers.org* or contact The Mountaineers via email at *clubmail@mountaineers.org*.

The Mountaineers Books, an active, nonprofit publishing program of the club, produces guidebooks, instructional texts, historical works, natural history guides, and works on environmental conservation. All books produced by The Mountaineers Books fulfill the club's mission.

Send or call for our catalog of more than 500 outdoor titles:

The Mountaineers Books
1001 SW Klickitat Way, Suite 201
Seattle, WA 98134
800-553-4453
mbooks@mountaineersbooks.org
www.mountaineersbooks.org

The Mountaineers Books is proud to be a corporate sponsor of The Leave No Trace Center for Outdoor Ethics, whose mission is to promote and inspire responsible outdoor recreation through education, research, and partnerships. The Leave No Trace program is focused specifically on human-powered (nonmotorized) recreation.

Leave No Trace strives to educate visitors about the nature of their recreational impacts, as well as offer techniques to prevent and minimize such impacts. Leave No Trace is best understood as an educational and ethical program, not as a set of rules and regulations.

For more information, visit *www.LNT.org*, or call 800-332-4100.

OTHER TITLES YOU MIGHT ENJOY FROM THE MOUNTAINEERS BOOKS

Climbing: Training for Peak Performance, *Clyde Soles*

Rock Climbing: Mastering Basic Skills, *Craig Luebben*

**Mountaineering: The Freedom of the Hills,
7th Edition,** *The Mountaineers*

Ice & Mixed Climbing: Modern Technique, *Will Gadd*

Big Wall Climbing, *Jared Ogden*

OTHER TITLES IN THE *A CLIMBING GUIDE* SERIES

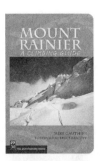

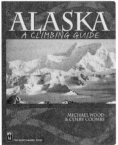

Mount Rainier: A Climbing Guide,
   Mike Gauthier

Washington Ice: A Climbing Guide,
   Jason D. Martin & Alex Krawarik

Alaska: A Climbing Guide, *Mike Wood &
   Colby Coombs*

Bugaboo Rock: A Climbing Guide,
   Randall Green & Joe Bensen

Idaho: A Climbing Guide, *Tom Lopez*

Available at fine bookstores and outdoor stores,
by phone at 800-553-4453 or on the Web at
www.mountaineersbooks.org

THE MOUNTAINEERS BOOKS